# INTRODUCTION TO
# PROGRAMMING
# WITH

## COMPREHENSIVE VERSION

## Y. Daniel Liang

*Armstrong Atlantic State University*

PEARSON

Prentice
Hall

Upper Saddle River, NJ 07458

**Library of Congress Cataloging-in-Publication Data on File**

Vice President and Editorial Director, ECS: *Marcia J. Horton*
Executive Editor: *Tracy Dunkelberger*
Assistant Editor: *Carole Snyder*
Editorial Assistant: *Christianna Lee*
Executive Managing Editor: *Vince O'Brien*
Managing Editor: *Camille Trentacoste*
Production Editor: *Rose Kernan*
Director of Creative Services: *Paul Belfanti*
Creative Director: *Juan Lopez*
Cover Designer: *Heather Scott*
Managing Editor, AV Management and Production: *Patricia Burns*
Art Editor: *Xiaohong Zhu*
Director, Image Resource Center: *Melinda Reo*
Manager, Rights and Permissions: *Zina Arabia*
Manager, Visual Research: *Beth Brenzel*
Manager, Cover Visual Research and Permissions: *Karen Sanatar*
Manufacturing Manager, ESM: *Alexis Heydt-Long*
Manufacturing Buyer: *Lisa McDowell*
Executive Marketing Manager: *Robin O'Brien*
Marketing Assistant: *Mack Patterson*
Photo Credits:
Cover: Two-headed serpent pectoral, 1400-1520 AD, Aztec. Bridgeman Art Library.
Part Opener: The Goddess Chalchihuitlicue, found in the Valley of Mexico, 1300-1500 AD (stone), Aztec / Musée de l'Homme, Paris, France / Bridgeman Art Library.
Chapter Opener: Mayan God Shel, Mexico. Photographer: Philip Coblentz. Courtesy Brand X Pictures.

© 2007 Pearson Education, Inc.
Pearson Prentice Hall
Pearson Education, Inc.
Upper Saddle River, NJ 07458

The author and publisher of this book have used their best efforts in preparing this book. These efforts include the development, research, and testing of the theories and programs to determine their effectiveness. The author and publisher make no warranty of any kind, expressed or implied, with regard to these programs or the documentation contained in this book. The author and publisher shall not be liable in any event for incidental or consequential damages in connection with, or arising out of, the furnishing, performance, or use of these programs.

Printed in the United States of America

10 9 8 7 6 5 4 3 2 1

**ISBN: 0-13-225445-x**

Pearson Education Ltd., *London*
Pearson Education Australia Pty. Ltd., *Sydney*
Pearson Education Singapore, Pte. Ltd.
Pearson Education North Asia Ltd., *Hong Kong*
Pearson Education Canada, Inc., *Toronto*

Pearson Educación de Mexico, S.A. de C.V.
Pearson Education—Japan, *Tokyo*
Pearson Education Malaysia, Pte. Ltd.
Pearson Education, Inc., *Upper Saddle River, New Jersey*

*To Samantha, Michael, and Michelle*

# PREFACE

After ten years of Java momentum, C++ remains a popular programming language widely used in the industry and taught in academia. Java is ideal for developing GUI, Internet and cross-platform applications, whereas C++ excels in system programming such as operating systems and compilers. Java and C++ will co-exist and compliment each other.

There are many C++ texts. What distinguishes this book from others are the fundamentals-first approach and the writing style. The *fundamentals-first approach* introduces fundamental programming concepts on control statements, loops, functions, and arrays before introducing object-oriented programming. The writing style of this book can be summarized in two words: *clear* and *concise*. The concepts are *clearly* explained using simple, short, and stimulating examples. The explanations are *concisely* presented with many figures and tables.

fundamentals-first

clear

concise

## Versions

The book is available in two versions:

■ The Brief Version (Chapters 1–14).

■ The Comprehensive Version (Chapters 1–20).

The following diagram summarizes the contents in the comprehensive version:

---

**Introduction to Programming with C++, Comprehensive Version**

Part 1 Fundamentals of Programming
   Chapter 1 Introduction to Computers, Programs, and C++
   Chapter 2 Primitive Data Types and Operations
   Chapter 3 Selection Statements
   Chapter 4 Loops
   Chapter 5 Functions
   Chapter 6 Arrays
   Chapter 7 Pointers and C-Strings
   Chapter 8 Recursion

Part 2 Object-Oriented Programming
   Chapter 9 Objects and Classes
   Chapter 10 More on Objects and Classes
   Chapter 11 Inheritance and Polymorphism

Chapter 12 File Input and Output
Chapter 13 Operator Overloading
Chapter 14 Exception Handling

Part 3 Data Structures
   Chapter 15 Templates
   Chapter 16 Linked Lists, Stacks, and Queues
   Chapter 17 Trees, Heaps, and Priority Queues
   Chapter 18 Algorithm Efficiency and Sorting
   Chapter 19 STL Containers
   Chapter 20 STL Algorithms

Appendixes

---

The *Brief Version* introduces fundamentals of programming, problem-solving, and object-oriented programming. This version is suitable for a course on introduction to problem solving and object-oriented programming.

brief version

The *Comprehensive Version* contains all the chapters in the brief version. Additionally, it covers data structures and advanced C++ programming.

comprehensive version

## Teaching Strategies

There are several strategies in teaching C++. This book adopts the *fundamentals-first* strategy, proceeding at a steady pace through all the necessary and important basic concepts, then moving to object-oriented programming, and then to the use of the object-oriented approach to build interesting applications with exception handling, I/O, and data structures.

fundamentals-first

fundamental programming
techniques

From my own experience, confirmed by the experiences of many colleagues, we have found that learning basic logic and *fundamental programming techniques* like loops and stepwise refinement is essential for new programmers to succeed. Students who cannot write code in procedural programming are not able to learn object-oriented programming. A good introduction on primitive data types, control statements, functions, and arrays prepares students to learn object-oriented programming.

using OOP effectively

The fundamentals-first approach reinforces object-oriented programming (OOP) by first presenting the procedural solutions and then demonstrating how they can be improved using the object-oriented approach. Students can learn when and how to apply OOP effectively.

object-early failed?
object-right
problem solving

At every SIGCSE (Computer Science Education) conference prior to 2005, the object-early approach was trumpeted and the voice for the fundamentals-first approach was muted. This has been changed when some former proponents of object-early began to air their frustrations and declared that object-early failed. This book is fundamentals-first and *object-right*. OOP is introduced just right in time after fundamental programming techniques are covered.

Programming isn't just syntax, classes, or objects. It is really *problem solving*. Loops, functions, and arrays are fundamental techniques for problem solving. From fundamental programming techniques to object-oriented programming, there are many layers of abstraction. Classes are simply a layer of abstraction. Applying the concept of abstraction in the design and implementation of software projects is the key to developing software. The overriding objective of this book, therefore, is to teach students to use many layers of abstraction in solving problems and to see problems in small detail and in large scale. The examples and exercises throughout this book center on problem solving and foster the concept of developing reusable components and using them to create practical projects.

## Learning Strategies

A programming course is quite different from other courses. In a programming course, you learn from examples, from practice, and from mistakes. You need to devote a lot of time to writing programs, testing them, and fixing errors.

practice

For first-time programmers, learning C++ is like learning any high-level programming language. The fundamental point in learning programming is to develop the critical skills of formulating programmatic solutions for real problems and translating them into programs using selection statements, loops, and functions.

programmatic solution

object-oriented programming

Once you acquire the basic skills of writing programs using loops, functions, and arrays, you can begin to learn object-oriented programming. You will learn how to develop object-oriented software using class encapsulation and class inheritance.

## Pedagogical Features

teaching by example
learning by doing

The philosophy of the Liang Series is *teaching by example and learning by doing*. Basic features are explained by example so that you can learn by doing. This book uses the following elements to get the most from the material:

- **Objectives** list what students should have learned from the chapter. This will help them to determine whether they have met the objectives after completing the chapter.

- **Introduction** opens the discussion with a brief overview of what to expect from the chapter.

- **Examples**, carefully chosen and presented in an easy-to-follow style, teach programming concepts. This book uses many small, simple, and stimulating examples to demonstrate important ideas.

- **Chapter Summary** reviews the important subjects that students should understand and remember. It helps them to reinforce the key concepts they have learned in the chapter.

■ **Optional Sections** cover nonessential but valuable features. Instructors may choose to include or skip an optional section or to cover it later. The section headers of optional sections are marked by 🔀 .

■ **Review Questions** are grouped by sections to help students track their progress and evaluate their learning.

■ **Programming Exercises** are grouped by sections to provide students with opportunities to apply on their own the new skills they have learned. The level of difficulty is rated easy (no asterisk), moderate (*), hard (**), or challenging (***). The trick of learning programming is practice, practice, and practice. To that end, this book provides a great many exercises.

■ **Interactive Self-Test** lets students test their knowledge interactively online. The Self-Test is accessible from the Companion Website. It provides more than one thousand multiple-choice questions organized by sections in each chapter. The Instructor Resource Website contains the quiz generator with additional multiple-choice questions.

■ **Notes**, **Tips**, and **Cautions** are inserted throughout the text to offer valuable advice and insight on important aspects of program development.

 **Note**
Provides additional information on the subject and reinforces important concepts.

 **Tip**
Teaches good programming style and practice.

 **Caution**
Helps students steer away from the pitfalls of programming errors.

# Chapter Dependency

The following diagram shows the chapter dependency. Note that Chapter 8, "Recursion," Chapter 12, "File Input and Output," and Chapter 13, "Operator Overloading," can be covered in flexible orders.

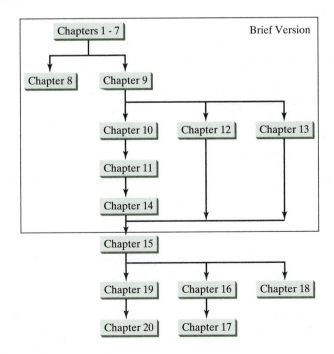

# C++ Development Tools

You can use a text editor, such as the Windows Notepad or WordPad, to create C++ programs, and you can compile and run the programs from the command window. You also can use a C++ development tool, such as Visual C++, Dev-C++, and C++Builder. These tools support an integrated development environment (IDE) for rapidly developing C++ programs. Editing, compiling, building, executing, and debugging programs are integrated in one graphical user interface. Using these tools effectively will greatly increase your programming productivity. How to create, compile, and run programs using Visual C++ and Dev-C++ is introduced in Chapter 1. Detailed tutorials on Visual C++ and C++Builder are in the supplements on the Companion Website.

The programs in this book have been tested on Visual C++, C++Builder, and the GNU C++ compiler.

# Companion Website

The companion Website at www.prenhall.com/liang or www.cs.armstrong.edu/liang/cpp contains the following resources:

- Answers to review questions

- Solutions to even-numbered programming exercises

- Source code for the examples in the book

- Interactive Self-Test (organized by sections for each chapter)

- Supplements

- Resource links

- Errata

# Supplements

The text covers the essential subjects. The supplements extend the text to introduce additional topics that might be of interest to readers. The following supplements are available from the Companion Website.

| Supplements for Introduction to Programming with C++ | |
| --- | --- |
| **Part I General Supplements**<br>A Glossary<br>B Installing and Configuring C++ Compiler<br>C Compiling and Running C++ from the<br>    Command Window<br>D C++ Coding Style Guidelines<br><br>**Part II IDE Supplements**<br>A Visual C++ 2005 Tutorial<br>B Learning C++ Effectively with Visual C++<br>C Dev-C++ Tutorial<br>D C++Builder Tutorial<br>E Learning C++ Effectively with C++Builder | **Part III Preprocessor**<br>A Preprocessor Directives<br><br>**Part IV Advanced C++ Topics**<br>A Multiple Inheritance<br>B Namespaces<br>C Operator Keywords<br><br>**Part V Legacy Topics**<br>A Redirecting Input/Output<br>B Using Command-Line Argument<br>C C goto Statements<br>D C printf Statements |

# Instructor Resource Website

The Instructor Resource Website accessible from www.prenhall.com/liang contains the following resources:

- Microsoft PowerPoint slides with interactive buttons to view full-color, syntax-highlighted source code and to run programs without leaving the slides.

- Sample exams. In general, each exam has four parts:

  1. Multiple-choice questions or short-answer questions (most of these are different from the questions in the self-test on the Companion Website)

  2. Correct programming errors

  3. Trace programs

  4. Write programs

- Solutions to all the exercises. Students will have access to the solutions of even-numbered exercises in the book's Companion Website.

- Web-based quiz generator. (Instructors can choose chapters to generate quizzes from a large database of more than 2000 questions.)

- Online quiz. (Students can take the online quiz for each chapter, and a quiz report will be sent to the instructor.)

Some readers have requested the materials from the Instructor Resource Website. Please understand that these are for instructors only. Such requests will not be answered.

# Acknowledgments

I would like to thank Ray Greenlaw and my colleagues at Armstrong Atlantic State University for enabling me to teach what I write and for supporting me in writing what I teach. I thank the students in my C++ class for proofreading the draft.

This book was greatly enhanced thanks to the following reviewers:

| | |
|---|---|
| Dan Lipsa | Armstrong Atlantic State University |
| Hui Liu | Missouri State University |
| Ronald Marsh | University of North Dakota |
| Charles Nelson | Rock Valley College |
| Martha Sanchez | University of Texas at Dallas |
| Kate Stewart | Tallahassee Community College |
| Margaret Tseng | Montgomery College |
| Barbara Tulley | Elizabethtown College |

It is a great pleasure, honor, and privilege to work with Prentice Hall. I would like to thank Marcia Horton, Tracy Dunkelberger, Robin O'Brien, Christianna Lee, Carole Snyder, Mack Patterson, Vince O'Brien, Camille Trentacoste, Xiaohong Zhu, Rose Kernan and their colleagues for organizing, producing, and promoting this project, as well as Shelly Gerger-Knechtl for copy editing and Scott Disanno for proofreading.

As always, I am indebted to my wife, Samantha, for her love, support, and encouragement.

**Y. Daniel Liang**
liang@armstrong.edu
www.cs.armstrong.edu/liang/cpp

# BRIEF CONTENTS

# CONTENTS

# PART 1

# FUNDAMENTALS OF PROGRAMMING

The first part of the book is a stepping stone that will prepare you to embark on the journey of learning C++. You will begin to know C++ and will develop fundamental programming skills. Specifically, you will learn how to write simple C++ programs with primitive data types, control statements, functions, arrays, pointers, and recursion.

## Chapter 1
Introduction to Computers, Programs, and C++

## Chapter 2
Primitive Data Types and Operations

## Chapter 3
Selection Statements

## Chapter 4
Loops

## Chapter 5
Functions

## Chapter 6
Arrays

## Chapter 7
Pointers and C-Strings

## Chapter 8
Recursion

## Prerequisites for Part 1

This book does not require any prior programming experience, nor any mathematics, other than elementary high school algebra and basic computer skills such as using Windows, Internet Explorer, and Microsoft Word.

basic computer skills

You may cover the concept and simple examples of recursive programming in §§8.1–8.3 in Chapter 8, "Recursion," after Chapter 5, "Functions."

recursion

You may cover Chapter 18, "Algorithm Efficiency and Sorting," after Chapter 6, "Arrays." Two simple sorting algorithms are introduced in Chapter 6. Chapter 18 introduces several advanced sorting algorithms.

sorting algorithms

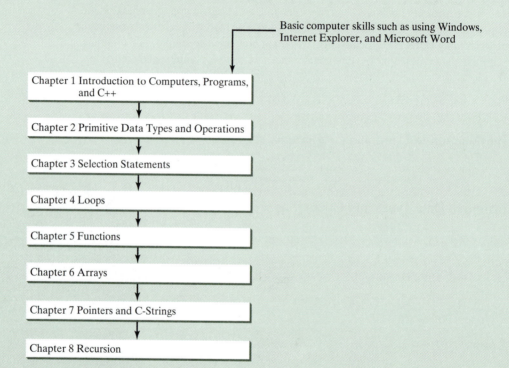

Basic computer skills such as using Windows, Internet Explorer, and Microsoft Word

# CHAPTER 1

# INTRODUCTION TO COMPUTERS, PROGRAMS, AND C++

## Objectives

- To review computer basics, programs, and operating systems (§§1.2–1.4).

- (Optional) To represent numbers in binary, decimal, and hexadecimal (§1.5).

- To know the history of C++ (§1.6).

- To write a simple C++ program (§1.7).

- To understand the C++ program development cycle (§1.8).

- (Optional) To develop C++ using Visual C++ (§1.9).

- (Optional) To develop C++ using Dev-C++ (§1.10).

- (Optional) To develop C++ using command line tools on Windows (§1.11).

- (Optional) To develop C++ using command line tools on Unix (§1.12).

## 1.1 Introduction

You use word processors to write documents, Web browsers to explore the Internet, and email programs to send email over the Internet. Word processors, browsers, and email programs are all examples of software that runs on computers. Software is developed using programming languages. C++ is a popular and powerful programming language. Most application software such as word processors, browsers, and email programs are developed using C++. This book will introduce you to developing programs using C++.

You are about to begin an exciting journey, learning a powerful programming language. Before the journey, it is helpful to review computer basics, programs, and operating systems, and to become familiar with number systems. You may skip the review in §§1.2–1.4 if you are familiar with such terms as CPU, memory, disks, operating systems, and programming languages. You may also skip §1.5 and use it as reference when you have questions regarding binary and hexadecimal numbers.

## 1.2 What Is a Computer?

hardware<br>software

A computer is an electronic device that stores and processes data. A computer includes both *hardware* and *software*. In general, hardware is the physical aspect of the computer that can be seen, and software is the invisible instructions that control the hardware and make it perform specific tasks. Computer programming consists of writing instructions for computers to perform. You can learn a programming language without knowing computer hardware, but you will be better able to understand the effect of the instructions in the program if you do. This section gives a brief introduction to computer hardware components and their functionality.

A computer consists of the following major hardware components, as shown in Figure 1.1.

- Central Processing Unit (CPU)

- Memory (main memory)

- Storage Devices (disks, CDs, tapes)

- Input and Output Devices (monitors, keyboards, mice, printers)

- Communication Devices (modems and network interface cards (NICs))

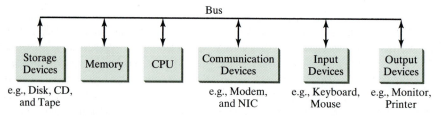

**FIGURE 1.1** A computer consists of CPU, memory, hard disk, floppy disk, monitor, printer, and communication devices.

The components are connected through a subsystem called a *bus* that transfers data between the components.

### 1.2.1 Central Processing Unit

CPU

The *central processing unit* (*CPU*) is the brain of a computer. It retrieves instructions from memory and executes them. The CPU usually has two components: a *control unit* and an *arithmetic/logic unit*. The control unit controls and coordinates the actions of the other components. The arithmetic and logic unit performs numeric operations (addition, subtraction, multiplication, division) and logical operations (comparisons).

Today's CPU is built on a small silicon semiconductor chip with millions of transistors. The *speed* of the CPU is mainly determined by clock speed. Every computer has an internal clock. The faster the clock speed, the more instructions are executed in a given period of time. The clock emits electronic pulses at a constant rate, and these are used to control and synchronize the pace of operations. The unit of measurement is called a *hertz* (Hz), with 1 hertz equaling 1 pulse per second. The clock speed of computers is usually measured in *megahertz* (MHz) (1 MHz is 1 million Hz). The speed of the CPU has been improved continuously. If you buy a PC now, you can get an Intel Pentium 4 Processor at 3 *gigahertz* (GHz) (1 GHz is 1000 MHz).

*speed*

*hertz*

*megahertz*

*gigahertz*

### 1.2.2  Memory

Computers use zeros and ones because digital devices have two stable states, referred to as *zero* and *one* by convention. Data of various kinds, such as numbers, characters, and strings, are encoded as a series of *bits* (*binary digits*: zeros and ones). *Memory* stores data and program instructions for the CPU to execute. A memory unit is an ordered sequence of *bytes*, each holding eight bits, as shown in Figure 1.2.

*bit*

*byte*

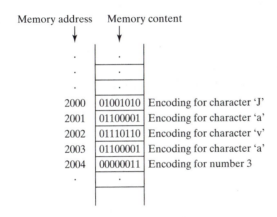

**FIGURE 1.2**   Memory stores data and program instructions.

The programmer needs not to be concerned about the encoding and decoding of data, which is performed automatically by the system based on the encoding scheme. The encoding scheme varies. For example, character 'J' is represented by 01001010 in one byte in the popular ASCII encoding. A small number such as 3 can be stored in a single byte. If a computer needs to store a large number that cannot fit into a single byte, it uses several adjacent bytes. No two data items can share or split the same byte. A byte is the minimum storage unit.

A program and its data must be brought to memory before they can be executed. A memory byte is never empty, but its initial content may be meaningless to your program. The current content of a memory byte is lost whenever new information is placed in it.

Every byte has a unique address. The address is used to locate the byte for storing and retrieving data. Since the bytes can be accessed in any order, the memory is also referred to as *RAM* (random-access memory). Today's personal computers usually have at least 128 megabytes of RAM. A *megabyte* (abbreviated MB) is about 1 million bytes. For a precise definition of megabyte, please see http://en.wikipedia.org/wiki/Megabyte. Like the CPU, memory is built on silicon semiconductor chips containing thousands of transistors embedded on their surface. Compared to the CPU chips, memory chips are less complicated, slower, and less expensive.

*RAM*

*megabyte*

*megabyte URL*

### 1.2.3   Storage Devices

Memory is volatile, because information is lost when the power is turned off. Programs and data are permanently stored on storage devices and are moved to memory when the computer actually uses them. The reason for this is that memory is much faster than storage devices. There are four main types of storage devices:

- Disk drives (hard disks and floppy disks)
- CD drives (CD-R, CD-RW, and DVD)
- Tape drives
- USB flash drives

drive

*Drives* are devices for operating a medium, such as disks, CDs, and tapes.

#### Disks

hard disk

floppy disk

There are two kinds of disks: *hard disks* and *floppy disks.* Personal computers usually have a 3.5-inch floppy disk drive and a hard drive. A floppy disk has a fixed capacity of about 1.44 MB. Hard disk capacities vary. The capacity of the hard disks of the latest PCs is in the range of 30 gigabytes to 160 gigabytes. Hard disks provide much faster performance and larger capacity than floppy disks. Both disk drives are often encased inside the computer. A floppy disk is removable. A hard disk is mounted inside the case of the computer. Removable hard disks are also available. Floppy disks will eventually be replaced by CD-RW and flash drives.

#### CDs and DVDs

CD-R

CD-RW

CD stands for compact disc. There are two types of CD drives: CD-R and CD-RW. A *CD-R* is for read-only permanent storage, and the user cannot modify its contents once they are recorded. A *CD-RW* can be used like a floppy disk, and thus can be read and rewritten. A single CD can hold up to 700 MB. Most software is distributed through CD-ROMs. Most new PCs are equipped with a CD-RW drive that can work with both CD-R and CD-RW.

DVD stands for digital versatile disc. DVDs and CDs look alike. You can store data using a CD or DVD. A DVD can hold more information than a CD. A standard DVD storage is 4.7 GB in capacity.

#### Tapes

*Tapes* are mainly used for backup of data and programs. Unlike disks and CDs, tapes store information sequentially. The computer must retrieve information in the order it was stored. Tapes are very slow. It would take one to two hours to back up a 1-gigabyte hard disk.

#### USB Flash Drives

*USB flash drives* are popular new devices for storing and transporting data. They are small—about the size of a pack of gum. They act like a portable hard disk that can be plugged into the USB port of your computer. USB flash drives are currently available with up to 2 GB storage capacity.

### 1.2.4   Input and Output Devices

Input and output devices let the user communicate with the computer. The common input devices are *keyboards* and *mice.* The common output devices are *monitors* and *printers.*

#### The Keyboard

A computer *keyboard* resembles a typewriter keyboard except that it has extra keys for certain special functions.

function key

*Function keys* are located at the top of the keyboard with prefix F. Their use depends on the software.

modifier key

A *modifier key* is a special key (e.g., Shift, Alt, Ctrl) that modifies the normal action of another key when the two are pressed in combination.

The *numeric keypad,* located on the right-hand corner of the keyboard, is a separate set of number keys for quick input of numbers.

numeric keypad

*Arrow keys,* located between the main keypad and the numeric keypad, are used to move the cursor up, down, left, and right.

arrow key

The *Insert, delete, page up,* and *page down keys,* located above the arrow keys, are used in word processing for performing insert, delete, page up, and page down.

### The Mouse

A *mouse* is a pointing device. It is used to move an electronic pointer called a cursor around the screen or to click on an object on the screen to trigger it to respond.

### The Monitor

The *monitor* displays information (text and graphics). The resolution and dot pitch determine the quality of the display.

The *resolution* specifies the number of pixels per square inch. Pixels (short for "picture elements") are tiny dots that form an image on the screen. A common resolution for a 17-inch screen, for example, is 1024 pixels wide and 768 pixels high. The resolution can be set manually. The higher the resolution, the sharper and clearer the image is.

screen resolution

The *dot pitch* is the amount of space between pixels. Typically, it has a range from 0.21 to 0.81 millimeters. The smaller the dot pitch, the better the display.

dot pitch

## 1.2.5 Communication Devices

Computers can be networked through communication devices. The commonly used communication devices are the dialup modem, DSL, cable modem, and network interface card. A dialup *modem* uses a phone line and can transfer data at a speed up to 56,000 bps (bits per second). A *DSL* (digital subscriber line) also uses a phone line and can transfer data at a speed twenty times faster than a dialup modem. A cable modem uses the TV cable line maintained by the cable company. A cable modem is as fast as DSL. A *network interface card* (*NIC*) is a device that connects a computer to a *local area network* (*LAN*). The LAN commonly is used in business, universities, and government organizations. A typical NIC called *10BaseT* can transfer data at 10 *mbps* (*million bits per second*).

modem

DSL

NIC

LAN

mbps

## 1.3 Programs

Computer *programs,* known as *software,* are instructions to the computer. You tell a computer what to do through programs. Without programs, a computer is an empty machine. Computers do not understand human languages, so you need to use computer languages to communicate with them.

software

The language a computer speaks is the computer's native language or machine language. The *machine language* is a set of primitive instructions built into every computer. Machine languages are different for different types of computers. The instructions are in the form of binary code, so you have to enter binary codes for various instructions. Programming using a native machine language is a tedious process. Moreover, the programs are highly difficult to read and modify. For example, to add two numbers, you might have to write an instruction in binary like this:

machine language

```
1101101010011010
```

*Assembly language* is a low-level programming language in which a mnemonic is used to represent each of the machine language instructions. For example, to add two numbers, you might write an instruction in assembly code like this:

assembly language

```
ADDF3 R1, R2, R3
```

assembler

Assembly languages were developed to make programming easy. Since the computer cannot understand assembly language, however, a program called *assembler* is used to convert assembly language programs into machine code, as shown in Figure 1.3.

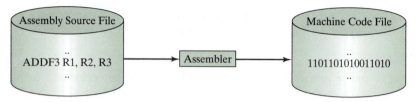

**FIGURE I.3**   Assembler translates assembly language instructions to machine code.

Since assembly language is machine-dependent, an assembly program can only be executed on a particular machine. Assembly programs are written in terms of machine instructions with easy-to-remember mnemonic names. The high-level languages were developed in order to overcome the platform-specific problem and make programming easier.

high-level language

The *high-level languages* are English-like and easy to learn and program. Here, for example, is a high-level language statement that computes the area of a circle with radius 5:

```
area = 5 * 5 * 3.1415;
```

There are over one hundred high-level languages. The popular languages are:

■ COBOL (COmmon Business Oriented Language)

■ FORTRAN (FORmula TRANslation)

■ BASIC (Beginner All-purpose Symbolic Instructional Code)

■ Pascal (named for Blaise Pascal)

■ Ada (named for Ada Lovelace)

■ Visual Basic (Basic-like visual language developed by Microsoft)

■ Delphi (Pascal-like visual language developed by Borland)

■ C (whose developer designed B first)

■ C++ (an object-oriented language, based on C)

■ Java

■ C# (a Java-like language developed by Microsoft)

Each of these languages was designed for a specific purpose. COBOL was designed for business applications and is used primarily for business data processing. FORTRAN was designed for mathematical computations and is used mainly for numeric computations. BASIC, as its name suggests, was designed to be learned and used easily. Ada was developed for the Department of Defense and is mainly used in defense projects. Visual Basic and Delphi are used in developing graphical user interfaces and in rapid application development. C combines the power of an assembly language with the ease of use and portability of a high-level language. C++ is popular for system software projects like writing compilers and operating systems. The Microsoft Windows operating system was coded using C++. Java, developed by Sun Microsystems, is widely used for developing Internet applications. C# (pronounced C sharp) is a new language developed by Microsoft for developing applications based on Microsoft .NET platform.

source program
compiler

A program written in a high-level language is called a *source program*. Since a computer cannot understand a source program, a program called a *compiler* is used to translate the source program into a machine-language program. The machine-language program is often then linked with other supporting library code to form an executable file. The executable file can be executed on the machine, as shown in Figure 1.4. On Windows, executable files have extension .exe.

**FIGURE 1.4**    A source program is compiled into a machine-language file, which is then linked with the system library to form an executable file.

# 1.4  Operating Systems

The *operating system* (*OS*) is the most important program that runs on a computer to manage and control its activities. You are probably using Windows (98, NT, 2000, XP, or ME), Mac OS, or Linux. Windows is currently the most popular PC operating system. Application programs, such as a Web browser or a word processor, cannot run without an operating system. The interrelationship of hardware, operating system, application software, and the user is shown in Figure 1.5.

OS

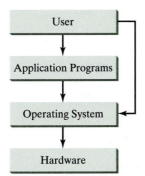

**FIGURE 1.5**    The operating system is the software that controls and manages the system.

The major tasks of the operating systems are:

■ Controlling and monitoring system activities

■ Allocating and assigning system resources

■ Scheduling operations

## 1.4.1    Controlling and Monitoring System Activities

Operating systems are responsible for security, ensuring that unauthorized users do not access the system. Operating systems perform basic tasks, such as recognizing input from the keyboard, sending output to the monitor, keeping track of files and directories on the disk, and controlling peripheral devices, such as disk drives and printers. Operating systems also make sure that different programs and users running at the same time do not interfere with each other.

## 1.4.2    Allocating and Assigning System Resources

The OS is responsible for determining what computer resources (CPU, memory, disks, input and output devices) a program needs and for allocating and assigning them to run the program.

### 1.4.3   Scheduling Operations

The OS is responsible for scheduling programs to use the system resources efficiently. Many of today's operating systems support such techniques as *multiprogramming, multithreading,* or *multiprocessing* to increase system performance.

multiprogramming

*Multiprogramming* allows multiple programs to run simultaneously by sharing the CPU. The CPU is much faster than the other components. As a result, it is idle most of the time; for example, while waiting for data to be transferred from the disk or from other sources. A multiprogramming OS takes advantage of this by allowing multiple programs to use the CPU when it would otherwise be idle. For example, you may use a word processor to edit a file while the Web browser is downloading a file at the same time.

multithreading

*Multithreading* allows concurrency within a program, so that its subunits can run at the same time. For example, a word-processing program allows users to simultaneously edit text and save it to a file. In this example, editing and saving are two tasks within the same application. These two tasks may run on separate threads concurrently.

multiprocessing

*Multiprocessing,* or parallel processing, uses two or more processors together to perform a task. It is like a surgical operation where several doctors work together on one patient.

##  1.5  (Optional) Number Systems

 **Note**
You can skip this section and use it as reference when you have questions regarding binary and hexadecimal numbers.

binary number

Computers use *binary numbers* internally because storage devices like memory and disk are made to store 0s and 1s. A number or a character inside a computer is stored as a sequence of 0s and 1s. Each 0 or 1 is called a *bit*. The binary number system has two digits, 0 and 1.

decimal number

Since we use *decimal numbers* in our daily life, binary numbers are not intuitive. When you write a number like 20 in a program, it is assumed to be a decimal number. Internally, computer software is used to convert decimal numbers into binary numbers, and vice versa.

Most of time, you write programs using decimal number systems. However, if you write programs to deal with a system like an operating system, you need to use binary numbers to reach down to the "machine-level." Binary numbers tend to be very long and cumbersome.

hexadecimal number

*Hexadecimal numbers* are often used to abbreviate binary numbers, with each hexadecimal digit representing exactly four binary digits. The hexadecimal number system has sixteen digits: 0, 1, 2, 3, 4, 5, 6, 7, 8, 9, A, B, C, D, E, and F. The letters A, B, C, D, E, and F correspond to the decimal numbers 10, 11, 12, 13, 14, and 15.

The digits in the decimal number system are 0, 1, 2, 3, 4, 5, 6, 7, 8, and 9. A decimal number is represented using a sequence of one or more of these digits. The value that each digit in the sequence represents depends on its position. A position in a sequence has a value that is an integral power of 10. For example, the digits 7, 4, 2, and 3 in decimal number 7423 represent 7000, 400, 20, and 3, respectively, as shown below:

$$\boxed{7 \mid 4 \mid 2 \mid 3} = 7 \times 10^3 + 4 \times 10^2 + 2 \times 10^1 + 3 \times 10^0$$
$$10^3 \; 10^2 \; 10^1 \; 10^0 \quad = 7000 + 400 + 20 + 3 = 7423$$

base
radix

The decimal number system has ten digits, and the position values are integral powers of 10. We say that 10 is the *base* or *radix* of the decimal number system. Similarly, the base of the binary number system is 2 since the binary number system has two digits and the base of the hex number system is 16 since the hex number system has sixteen digits.

### 1.5.1 Conversions between Binary Numbers and Decimal Numbers

Given a binary number $b_n b_{n-1} b_{n-2} \ldots b_2 b_1 b_0$, the equivalent decimal value is

*binary to decimal*

$$b_n \times 2^n + b_{n-1} \times 2^{n-1} + b_{n-2} \times 2^{n-2} + \ldots + b_2 \times 2^2 + b_1 \times 2^1 + b_0 \times 2^0$$

The following are examples of converting binary numbers to decimals:

| Binary | Conversion Formula | Decimal |
|---|---|---|
| 10 | $1 \times 2^1 + 0 \times 2^0$ | 2 |
| 1000 | $1 \times 2^3 + 0 \times 2^2 + 0 \times 2^1 + 0 \times 2^0$ | 8 |
| 10101011 | $1 \times 2^7 + 0 \times 2^6 + 1 \times 2^5 + 0 \times 2^4 +$ $1 \times 2^3 + 0 \times 2^2 + 1 \times 2^1 + 1 \times 2^0$ | 171 |

To convert a decimal number $d$ to a binary number is to find the bits $b_n, b_{n-1}, b_{n-2}, \ldots, b_2,$ $b_1,$ and $b_0$ such that

*decimal to binary*

$$d = b_n \times 2^n + b_{n-1} \times 2^{n-1} + b_{n-2} \times 2^{n-2} + \ldots + b_2 \times 2^2 + b_1 \times 2^1 + b_0 \times 2^0$$

These bits can be found by successively dividing $d$ by 2 until the quotient is 0. The remainders are $b_0, b_1, b_2, \ldots, b_{n-2}, b_{n-1},$ and $b_n$.

For example, the decimal number 123 is 1111011 in binary. The conversion is done as follows:

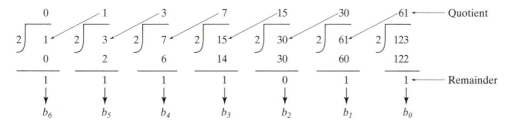

**Tip**
The Windows Calculator, as shown in Figure 1.6, is a useful tool for performing number conversions. To run it, choose *Programs, Accessories,* and *Calculator* from the Start button.

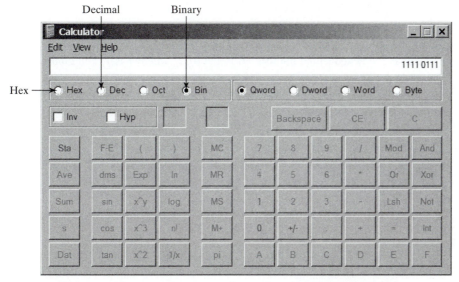

**FIGURE 1.6** You can perform number conversions using the Windows Calculator.

### 1.5.2 Conversions between Hexadecimal Numbers and Decimal Numbers

hex to decimal

Given a hexadecimal number $h_n h_{n-1} h_{n-2} \ldots h_2 h_1 h_0$, the equivalent decimal value is

$$h_n \times 16^n + h_{n-1} \times 16^{n-1} + h_{n-2} \times 16^{n-2} + \ldots + h_2 \times 16^2 + h_1 \times 16^1 + h_0 \times 16^0$$

The following are examples of converting hexadecimal numbers to decimals:

| Hexadecimal | Conversion Formula | Decimal |
|---|---|---|
| 7F | $7 \times 16^1 + 15 \times 16^0$ | 127 |
| FFFF | $15 \times 16^3 + 15 \times 16^2 + 15 \times 16^1 + 15 \times 16^0$ | 65535 |
| 431 | $4 \times 16^2 + 3 \times 16^1 + 1 \times 16^0$ | 1073 |

decimal to hex

To convert a decimal number $d$ to a hexadecimal number is to find the hexadecimal digits $h_n, h_{n-1}, h_{n-2}, \ldots, h_2, h_1$, and $h_0$ such that

$$d = h_n \times 16^n + h_{n-1} \times 16^{n-1} + h_{n-2} \times 16^{n-2} + \ldots$$
$$+ h_2 \times 16^2 + h_1 \times 16^1 + h_0 \times 16^0$$

These numbers can be found by successively dividing $d$ by 16 until the quotient is 0. The remainders are $h_0, h_1, h_2, \ldots, h_{n-2}, h_{n-1}$, and $h_n$.

For example, the decimal number 123 is 7B in hexadecimal. The conversion is done as follows:

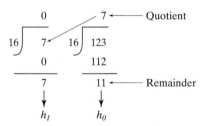

### 1.5.3 Conversions between Binary Numbers and Hexadecimal Numbers

hex to binary

To convert a hexadecimal number to a binary number, simply convert each digit in the hexadecimal number into a four-digit binary number using Table 1.1.

For example, the hexadecimal number 7B is 1111011, where 7 is 111 in binary, and B is 1011 in binary.

binary to hex

To convert a binary number to a hexadecimal, convert every four binary digits from right to left in the binary number into a hexadecimal number.

For example, the binary number 1110001101 is 38D, since 1101 is D, 1000 is 8, and 11 is 3, as shown below.

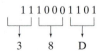

**Note**

Octal numbers are also useful. The octal number system has eight digits, 0 to 7. A decimal number 8 is represented as 10 in the octal system.

**TABLE 1.1** Converting Hexadecimal to Binary

| Hexadecimal | Binary | Decimal |
|:---:|:---:|:---:|
| 0 | 0 | 0 |
| 1 | 1 | 1 |
| 2 | 10 | 2 |
| 3 | 11 | 3 |
| 4 | 100 | 4 |
| 5 | 101 | 5 |
| 6 | 110 | 6 |
| 7 | 111 | 7 |
| 8 | 1000 | 8 |
| 9 | 1001 | 9 |
| A | 1010 | 10 |
| B | 1011 | 11 |
| C | 1100 | 12 |
| D | 1101 | 13 |
| E | 1110 | 14 |
| F | 1111 | 15 |

# 1.6 History of C++

C, C++, Java, and C# are very similar and related. C++ evolved from C. Java was modeled after C++. C# is a subset of C++ with some features similar to Java. If you know one of these languages, it is easy to learn the others.

C evolved from the B language and the B language evolved from the BCPL language. *BCPL* was developed by Martin Richards in the mid-1960s for writing operating systems and compilers. Ken Thompson incorporated many features from BCPL in his *B language* and used it to create early versions of the UNIX operating system at Bell Laboratories in 1970 on a DEC PDP-7 computer. Both BCPL and B were typeless, i.e., every data item occupies a fixed-length "word" or "cell" in memory. How a data item is treated, for example, as a number or a string, is the responsibility of the programmer. Dennis Ritchie extended the B language by adding types and other features in 1971 to develop the UNIX operating system on a DEC PDP-11 computer. Today, *C* is portable and hardware independent. C is widely used for developing operating systems.

*C++* is an extension of C, developed by Bjarne Stroustrup at Bell Labs during 1983–1985. C++ added a number of features that improved the C language. Most importantly, it added the support of using classes for object-oriented programming. Object-oriented programming can make programs easy to develop and easy to maintain. C++ could be considered a superset of C. The features of C are supported by C++. C programs can be compiled using C++ compilers. After learning C++, you will be able to read and understand C programs as well.

An international standard for C++ was created by the American National Standards Institute (ANSI) in 1998. The *ANSI standard* is an attempt to ensure that C++ is portable, i.e., your programs compiled using one vendor's compiler can be compiled without errors from any other vendors on any platform. Since the standard has been around for a while, all the major vendors now support the ANSI standard. Nevertheless, the C++ compiler vendors may add proprietary features into the compiler. So, it is possible that your program may compile fine by one compiler, but have to modify the code in order to be compiled by a different compiler.

BCPL

B

C

C++

ANSI standard

## 1.7 A Simple C++ Program

Let us begin with a simple C++ program that displays the message "Welcome to C++!" on the console. The program is shown in Listing 1.1.

### LISTING 1.1    Welcome.cpp

include library

main function

comment
output

successful return

```
1 #include <iostream>
2
3 int main()
4 {
5   // Display Welcome to C++ to the console
6   std::cout << "Welcome to C++!" << std::endl;
7
8   return 0;
9 }
```

```
Welcome to C++!
```

line number

directive

header file

main function

console output
stream insertion operator

std

successful exit
comment

line comment
paragraph comment

The *line numbers* are not part of the program, but are displayed for reference purposes. So, don't type line numbers in your program.

Line 1 is a compiler *directive* that tells the compiler to include the `iostream` library in this program, which is needed to support console input and output. The library like `iostream` is called a *header file* in C++, because it is usually included at the header of a program.

Every C++ program is executed from a main function. A function is a construct that contains statements. The *main function* defined in lines 3–9 contains two statements. The statements are enclosed in a block that starts with a left brace, {, (line 4) and ends with a right brace, } (line 9). Every statement in the block must end with a semicolon (;) known as the statement terminator.

The statement in line 6 displays a message to the console. `std::cout` stands for console output. The `<<` operator, referred to as the *stream insertion operator,* sends a string to the console. A string must be enclosed in quotation marks. The statement in line 6 first outputs the string "welcome to C++!" to the console, and then outputs `std::endl`. Note that `endl` stands for *end line*. Sending `std::endl` to the console outputs a new line and flushes the output buffer to ensure that the output is displayed immediately.

What is `std`? `std` stands for standard name space. `std::` is placed in front of `cout` and `endl` to denote that `cout` and `endl` are in the standard name space.

The statement in line 8

```
return 0;
```

is placed at the end of every main function to exit the program. The value `0` indicates that the program has terminated successfully.

Line 5 is a *comment* that documents what the program is and how the program is constructed. Comments help programmers to communicate and understand the program. Comments are not programming statements and thus are ignored by the compiler. In C++, comments are preceded by two slashes (//) on a line, called a *line comment,* or enclosed between /* and */ on one or several lines, called a *paragraph comment.* When the compiler sees //, it ignores all text after // on the same line. When it sees /*, it scans for the next */ and ignores any text between /* and */.

Here are examples of the two types of comments:

```
// This application program prints Welcome to C++!
/* This application program prints Welcome to C++! */
/* This application program
   prints Welcome to C++! */
```

*Keywords*, or *reserved words*, are words that have a specific meaning to the compiler and cannot be used for other purposes in the program. There are two keywords: **int** and **return** in this program.

**Note**

You are probably wondering about such points as why the main function is declared this way and why `std::cout << "Welcome to C++!" << std::endl` is used to display a message to the console. Your questions cannot be fully answered yet. For the time being, you will just have to accept that this is how things are done. You will find the answers in the coming chapters.

**Note**

Like any other programming language, C++ has its own syntax, and you need to write code that obeys the *syntax rules*. The C++ compiler will report syntax errors if your program violates the syntax rules. Pay close attention to the punctuation. The redirection symbol `<<` is two succesive `<`'s. There are two consecutive colons (`:`) between **std** and **cout**. Every statement in the function ends with a semicolon (`;`).

syntax rules

**Caution**

C++ source programs are *case-sensitive*. It would be wrong, for example, to replace `main` in the program with `Main`.

case-sensitive

The program in Listing 1.1 displays one message. Once you understand the program, it is easy to extend it to display more messages. For example, you can rewrite the program to display three messages, as shown in Listing 1.2.

**LISTING 1.2** `Welcome1.cpp`

```
1 #include <iostream>
2 int main()
3 {
4   std::cout << "Welcome to C++!" << std::endl;
5   std::cout << "Welcome to C++.NET!" << std::endl;
6   std::cout << "Welcome to C++ Compiler!" << std::endl;
7
8   return 0;
9 }
```

include library
main function

output

successful return

```
Welcome to C++!
Welcome to C++.NET!
Welcome to C++ Compiler!
```

# 1.8 C++ Program Development Cycle

You have to create your program and compile it before it can be executed. This process is repetitive, as shown in Figure 1.7. If your program has compilation errors, you have to fix them by modifying the program, and then recompile it. If your program has runtime errors or does not produce the correct result, you have to modify the program, recompile it, and execute it again.

**Note**

A C++ *source file* typically ends with the extension .cpp. Some compilers may accept other file name extensions (e.g., .c, .cp, or .c), but you should stick with the .cpp extension to be compliant with all ANSI C++ compilers.

.cpp source file

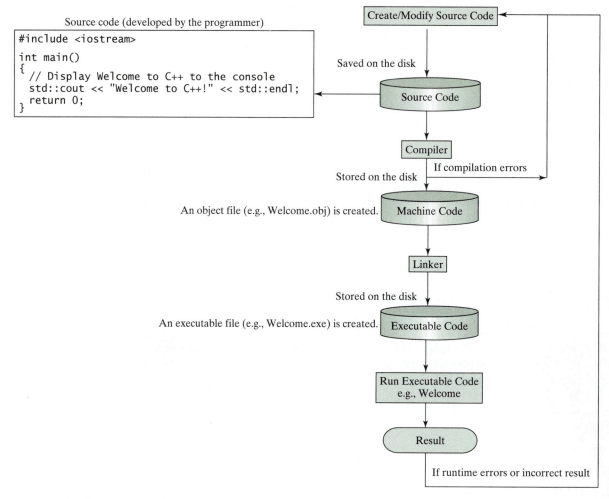

Source code (developed by the programmer)

```
#include <iostream>

int main()
{
 // Display Welcome to C++ to the console
 std::cout << "Welcome to C++!" << std::endl;
 return 0;
}
```

**FIGURE 1.7** The C++ programming-development process consists of creating/modifying source code, compiling, linking, and executing programs.

compiler command

> ### Note
>
> The C++ *compiler command* performs three tasks in sequence: *preprocessing, compiling,* and *linking*. The compiler first processes the directives. The directives start with the # sign. For example, the **include** statement in line 1 of Listing 1.1 is a directive to tell the compiler to include a library. The compiler then translates the source code into a machine code file called object file, and finally, it links the object file with supporting library files to form an executable file. On Windows, the object file is stored on disk with an .obj extension and the executable files are stored with an .exe extension. On UNIX, the object file has an **.o** extension and the executable files do not have file extensions.

IDE

You can develop a C++ program from a command line or from an IDE. An IDE is a software that provides an *integrated development environment* (*IDE*) for rapidly developing C++ programs. Editing, compiling, building, debugging, and online help are integrated in one graphical user interface. Just enter source code in one window or open an existing file in a window, then click a button, menu item, or function key to compile and run the program. Examples of popular IDEs are Microsoft Visual C++, Borland C++Builder, and Dev-C++.

The following sections introduce how to develop a C++ program from Visual C++ and Dev-C++. The use of C++Builder is provided in the supplements on the Companion Website.

## 1.9 Developing C++ Programs Using Visual C++

Visual C++ is a component of Microsoft Visual Studio .NET for developing C++ programs. A free version named *Visual C++ 2005 Express Edition* is included in the book's Companion CD-ROM. This section introduces how to create a project, create a program, compile, and run the program.

### 1.9.1 Getting Started with Visual C++

Visual C++ is easy to install. If you need help on installation, please refer to Visual *C++ Tutorial* in the supplements.

Suppose you have installed Visual C++ 2005 Express Edition. You can launch VC++ from the Windows Start button by choosing *All Programs, Visual C++ 2005 Express Edition, Microsoft Visual C++ 2005 Express Edition.* The Visual C++ 2005 Express Edition user interface appears, as shown in Figure 1.8.

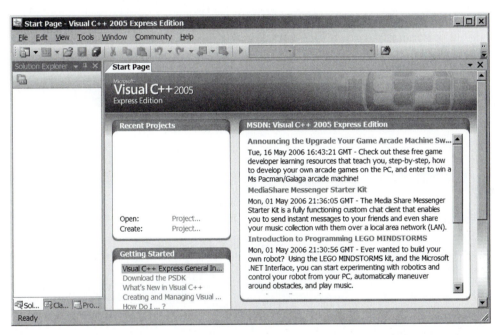

**FIGURE 1.8** The VC++ user interface is a single window that performs editing, compiling, debugging, and running programs.

### 1.9.2 Creating a Project

To create C++ programs in Visual C++, you have to first create a project. A project is like a holder that ties all the files together. Here are the steps to create a project:

1. Choose *File, New, Project* to display the New Project window, as shown in Figure 1.9.

2. Choose *Win32* in the project types column and *Win32 Console Application* in the Templates column. Type `bookexample` in the Name field and `c:\smith` in the Location field. Click *OK* to display the Win32 Application Wizard window, as shown in Figure 1.10.

3. Click *Next* to display the application settings window, as shown in Figure 1.11.

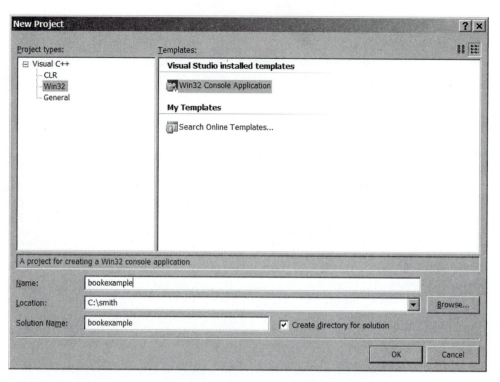

**FIGURE 1.9** You need to create a project before creating programs.

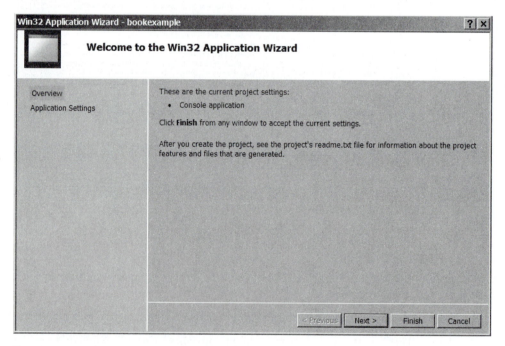

**FIGURE 1.10** Win32 Application Wizard creates a project for Win32 applications.

4. Select *Console application* in the Application type section and check *Empty project* in the Additional options section. Click *Finish* to create a project. You will see the project named **bookexample** in the solution explorer, as shown in Figure 1.12.

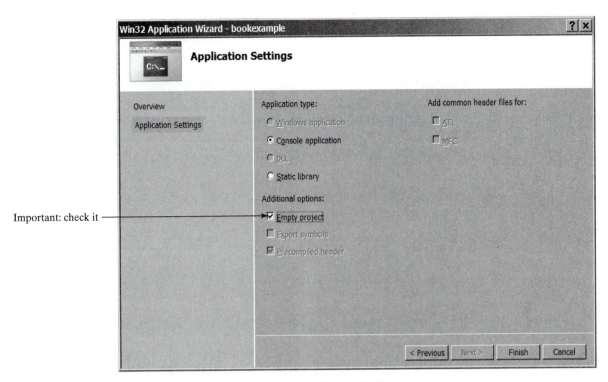

Important: check it —

**FIGURE 1.11**    Win32 Application Settings window lets you set the application type.

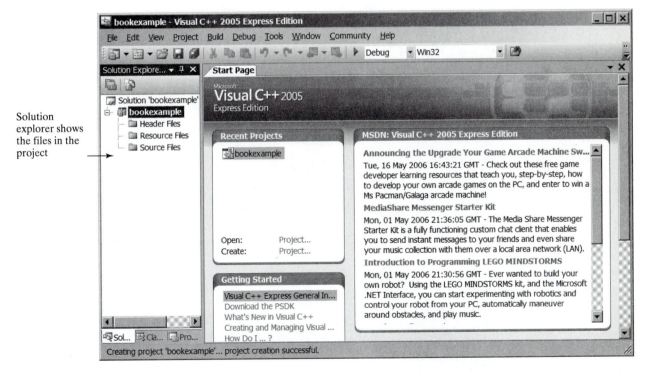

Solution
explorer shows
the files in the
project

**FIGURE 1.12**    A project is created for C++ console applications.

## 1.9.3   Creating a C++ Program

After you created a project, you can create programs in the project. Here are the steps to create a C++ program for Listing 1.1:

1. Choose *Add, Add New Item* from the context menu of the bookexample project (see Figure 1.13) to display the Add New Item window, as shown in Figure 1.14.

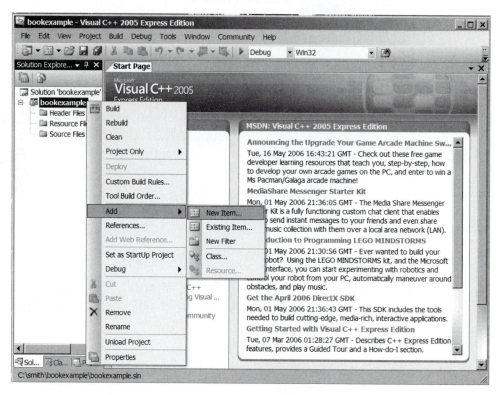

**FIGURE 1.13** You can open the Add New Item window from the project's context menu.

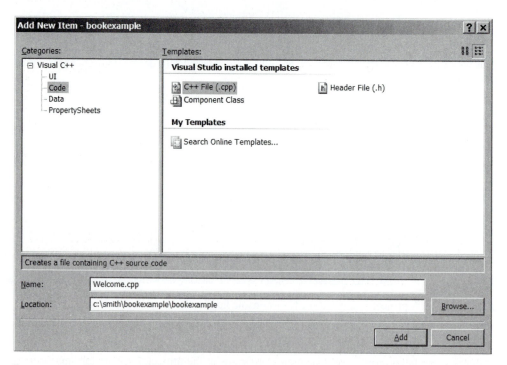

**FIGURE 1.14** You can specify the file type, name, and location to create a file.

2. Choose Code in the Categories column and C++ File (.cpp) in the Templates column. Enter `Welcome` in the Name field and `c:\smith\bookexample\bookexample` in the Location field. Click *Add* to create the file, as shown in Figure 1.15.

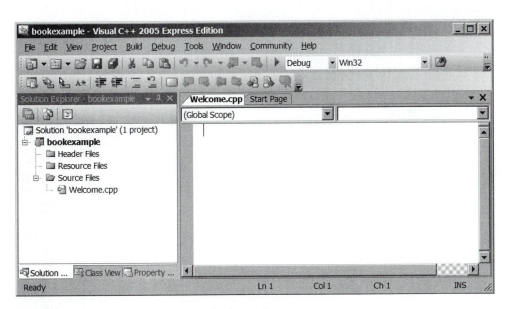

**FIGURE 1.15**   Welcome.cpp is created in the project.

3. Enter the code for Welcome.cpp exactly from Listing 1.1, as shown in Figure 1.16.

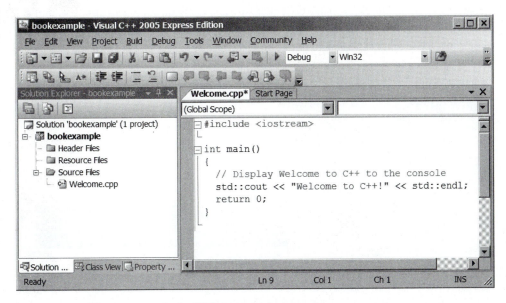

**FIGURE 1.16**   The source code for Welcome.cpp is entered.

## 1.9.4   Compiling a C++ Program

After you created a program, you can compile it. You may compile it by choosing *Build, Compile,* or press Ctrl+F7, or choose *Compile* in the context menu for Welcome.cpp, as shown in Figure 1.17.

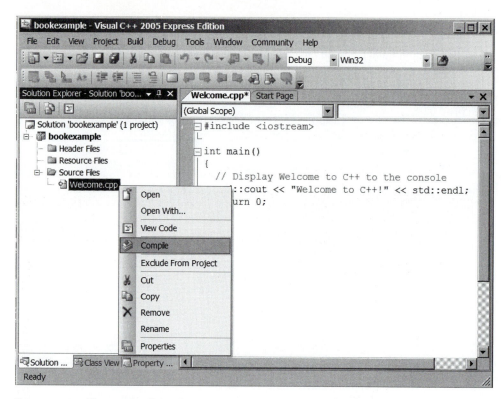

**FIGURE 1.17** Choose the Compile command to compile the program.

## 1.9.5 Running a C++ Program

To run the program, choose *Debug, Start Without Debugging,* or press Ctrl+F5. You will see a dialog box, as shown in Figure 1.18(a). Click *Yes* to continue. You will see the output is displayed in a DOS window, as shown in Figure 1.18(b).

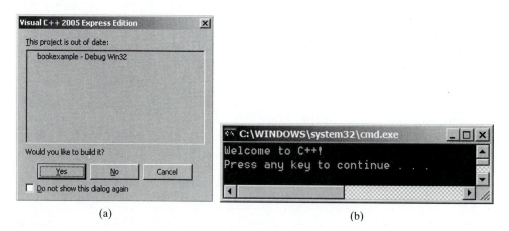

(a)                                                                 (b)

**FIGURE 1.18** The output is displayed in a DOS window.

**Note**

compile and run

The Run command invokes the Compile command if the program is not compiled or was modified after the last compilation.

**Note**

Each project can have only one file that contains a main function. If you need to create another       one main function
file with a main function, you have two options:

- Remove the current file that contains a main function from the project by choosing *Remove* from the context menu of the program, as shown in Figure 1.19. (Note that you can add an existing file to the project by choosing *File, Add Existing Item.*)

- Create a new project for the new program.

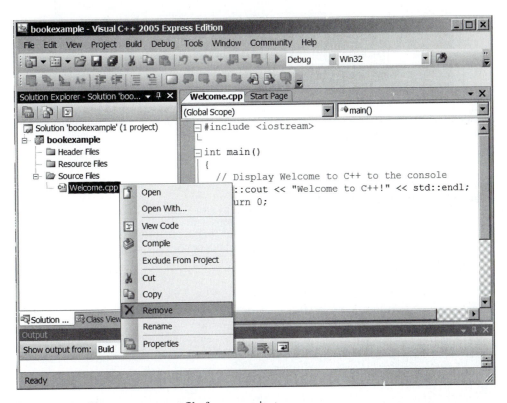

**FIGURE 1.19**   You can remove a file from a project.

## 1.10 Developing C++ Programs Using Dev-C++

Dev-C++ is a free C++ IDE, which can be downloaded from http://www.bloodshed.net/dev/devcpp.html. Visual C++ is much more powerful than Dev-C++. But Dev-C++ is simpler and easier than Visual C++ for new IDE users.

### 1.10.1   Getting Started with Dev-C++

Dev-C++ is easy to install. If you need help on installation, please refer to *Dev-C++ Tutorial* in the supplements.

Suppose you have installed Dev-C++. You can launch Dev-C++ from Windows Start button by choosing *All Programs, Bloodshed Dev-C++, Dev-C++*. The Dev-C++ user interface appears, as shown in Figure 1.20.

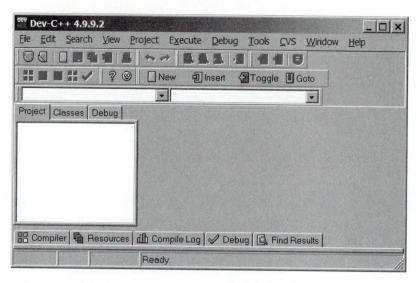

**FIGURE 1.20** The Dev-C++ user interface is a single window that performs functions for editing, compiling, debugging, and running programs.

### 1.10.2 Creating a Program

To create a C++ program in Dev-C++, follow the steps here:

1. Choose *File, New, Source File,* an untitled file appears in the content pane, as shown in Figure 1.21.

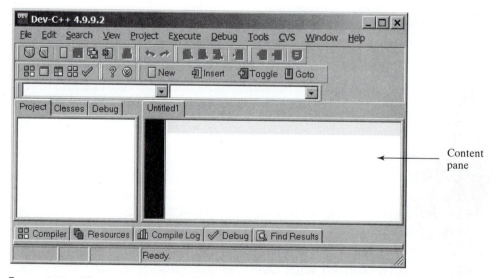

**FIGURE 1.21** The contents of the file are displayed in the content pane.

2. Type in the code exactly from Listing 1.1 in the content pane, as shown in Figure 1.22.

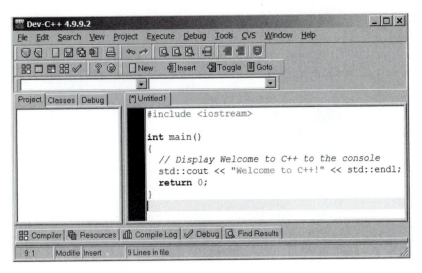

**FIGURE 1.22**    The code is entered in the content pane.

3. Choose *File, Save* to display the Save File dialog box, as shown in Figure 1.23. Enter `Welcome.cpp` in the File name field and click *Save* to save the file into `Welcome.cpp`. (Note: you may change the directory in the Save in field to save the file in any directory.)

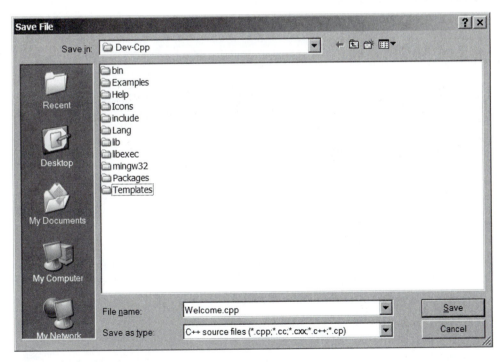

**FIGURE 1.23**    You may save the file in any directory.

4. After you save the file, you will see the Welcome.cpp tab appear in the content pane, as shown in Figure 1.24.

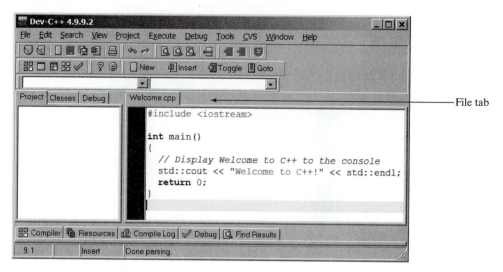

**FIGURE 1.24** The Welcome.cpp tab appears in the content pane.

### 1.10.3 Compiling a C++ Program

After you created a program, you can compile it. You may compile it by choosing *Execute, Compile,* or press Ctrl+F9, or choose the *Compile* toolbar button ( ), as shown in Figure 1.25. The compile status is displayed in a dialog box, as shown in Figure 1.26. You may close this dialog box now.

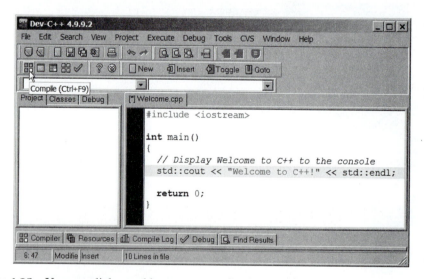

**FIGURE 1.25** You can click a tool button to compile the program.

### 1.10.4 Running a C++ Program

To run the program, choose *Execute, Run,* or press F9, or click the *Run* toolbar button ( ). A Windows command window is displayed, but quickly disappeared. You almost cannot see the command window. To see this window, you have to add the following statement before the **return** statement, as shown in Figure 1.27:

```
system("PAUSE");
```

This statement pauses the execution and prompts the user to enter any key to continue.

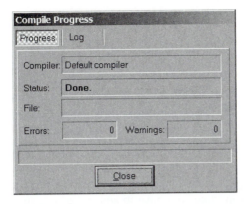

**FIGURE 1.26**   The compilation status is displayed.

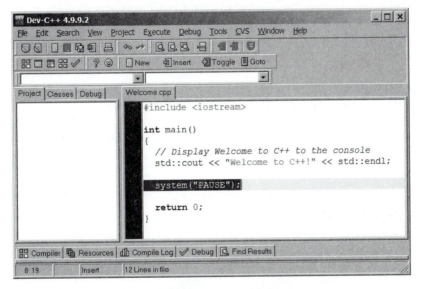

**FIGURE 1.27**   The statement `system("PAUSE")` is added.

Recompile and run the program. You will see the command window displayed, as shown in Figure 1.28.

**FIGURE 1.28**   The command window displays the console output.

**Tip**
You may compile and run the program using one command by choosing *Execute, Compile &* *Run*, or pressing F9, or clicking the Compile & Run toolbar button ( ⊞ ).

compile and run

**Note**
If you have *multiple programs* in the content pane, choose the one you want to run from the file tab and use the Compile & Run command to run the selected program.

multiple programs

# 1.11 Developing C++ Programs from Command Line on Windows

 **Note**

DOS commands

To develop programs from Window's command line, you need to know how to use *DOS commands.* Please see Supplement I.C, "Compiling and Running C++ from the Command Window" on how to use basic DOS commands. All the supplements are accessible from the Companion Website.

compilers

When you install Dev-C++ in the previous section, a popular *compiler,* known as the GNU C++ compiler, is automatically installed in `c:\dev-cpp\bin\g++.exe`. GNU is an organization devoted to develop open source software (see www.gnu.org). To use the compiler directly from the command line, you have to add `c:\dev-cpp\bin` into PATH environment variable. Here are the steps to add the new paths in Windows 2000 and Windows XP:

1. Choose Systems from the Window's Control Panel to display the Systems Properties dialog, as shown in Figure 1.29(a).

2. Choose the *Advanced* tab and click *Environment Variables* to display the Environment Variables dialog as shown in Figure 1.29(b).

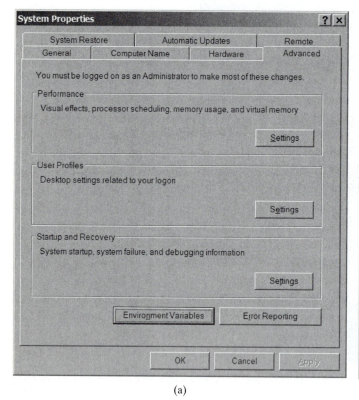

(a)

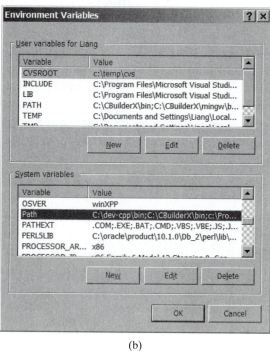

(b)

**FIGURE 1.29** You need to add compilers in the environment path.

3. Choose *Path* in the System variable section and click *Edit* to add the paths.

text editor

You can use any *text editor* to create and edit a C++ source code file. Figure 1.30 shows how to use the NotePad to create and edit the source code file.

g++ compiler

To compile Welcome.cpp using the GNU C++ compiler, type the command **g++ Welcome.cpp -o Welcome**, as shown in Figure 1.31. If there are no syntax errors, an executable file named Welcome.exe is created. You can run it by typing **Welcome**.

**FIGURE 1.30** You can create a C++ source file using Windows NotePad.

GNU C++
compiler →

Run →

**FIGURE 1.31** You can compile using the GNU C++ compiler.

## 1.12 Developing C++ Programs on UNIX

 **Note**

To develop programs on UNIX, you need to know how to use *UNIX commands*. Please see Supplement I.D, "Compiling and Running C++ from UNIX" on how to use basic UNIX commands.

UNIX commands

By default, a GNU C++ *compiler* is automatically installed on UNIX. You can use the **vi** or **emacs** editor to create a C++ source code file. Figure 1.32(a) shows how to use the **vi** editor to create and edit the source code file named Welcome.cpp (using the command `vi Welcome.cpp`).

compilers

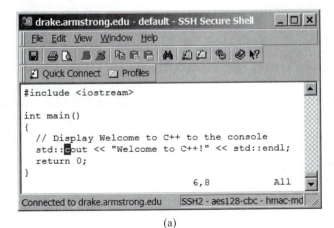

(a)

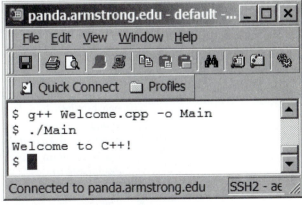

(b)

**FIGURE 1.32** (a) You can create a C++ source file using the vi editor. (b) You can compile a C++ source file using the GNU compiler.

To compile Welcome.cpp using the *GNU compiler,* type the command `g++ Welcome.cpp -o Main`, as shown in Figure 1.32(b). If there are no syntax errors, an executable file named `Main` is created. You can run it by typing `./Main`, as shown in Figure 1.32(b).

## KEY TERMS

| | |
|---|---|
| assembly language    7 | keyword (or reserved word)    15 |
| binary numbers    10 | machine language    7 |
| bit    5 | main function    14 |
| block    14 | memory    5 |
| byte    5 | modem    7 |
| Dev-C++    23 | network interface card (NIC)    7 |
| cable modem    7 | operating system (OS)    9 |
| central processing unit (CPU)    4 | pixel    7 |
| comment    14 | resolution    7 |
| compiler    8 | software    4 |
| dot pitch    7 | source code    16 |
| DSL (digital subscriber line)    7 | source file    16 |
| **g++** command    28, 30 | storage devices    6 |
| hardware    4 | statement    14 |
| hexadecimal numbers    10 | statement terminator    14 |
| high-level programming language    8 | stream insertion operator    14 |
| Integrated Development Environment (IDE)    16 | Visual C++    17 |

## CHAPTER SUMMARY

■ A computer is an electronic device that stores and processes data. A computer includes both *hardware* and *software.* In general, hardware is the physical aspect of the computer that can be seen, and software is the set of invisible instructions that control the hardware and make it perform tasks.

■ Computer *programs,* known as *software,* are instructions to the computer. You tell a computer what to do through programs. Computer programming consists of writing instructions for computers to perform.

■ The *machine language* is a set of primitive instructions built into every computer. *Assembly language* is a low-level programming language in which a mnemonic is used to represent each of the machine-language instructions.

■ *High-level languages* are English-like and easy to learn and program. There are over one hundred high-level languages. A program written in a high-level language is called a *source program.* Since a computer cannot understand a source program, a program called a *compiler* is used to translate the source program into a machine language program, which is then linked with other supporting library code to form an executable file.

■ The *operating system* (*OS*) is a program that manages and controls a computer's activities. Application programs, such as Web browsers and word processors, cannot run without an operating system.

- C++ is an extension of C, developed by Bjarne Stroustrup at Bell Labs during 1983–1985. C++ added a number of features that improved the C language. Most importantly, it added the support of using classes for object-oriented programming.

- C++ source files end with the .cpp extension. You can develop C++ applications from the command line or using an IDE such as Visual C++ and Dev-C++.

- Every C++ program is executed from a main function. A function is a construct that contains statements.

## REVIEW QUESTIONS

 **Note**
Answers to review questions are on the Companion Website at www.cs.armstrong.edu/liang/cpp.

### Sections 1.2–1.4

**1.1**    Define hardware and software.

**1.2**    Define machine language, assembly language, and high-level programming language.

**1.3**    What is an operating system?

### Section 1.5 Number Systems

**1.4**    Convert the following decimal numbers into hexadecimal and binary numbers:

> 100;  4340;  2000

**1.5**    Convert the following binary numbers into hexadecimal numbers and decimal numbers:

> 1000011001;  100000000;  100111

**1.6**    Convert the following hexdecimal numbers into binary and decimal numbers:

> FEFA9;  93;  2000

### Sections 1.6–1.12

**1.7**    Describe the history of C++. Can C++ run on any machine? What is needed to compile and run C++ programs?

**1.8**    What are the input and output of a C++ compiler?

**1.9**    List some C++ development tools. Are tools like Visual C++ and Dev-C++ different languages from C++, or are they dialects or extensions of C++?

**1.10**    What is the relationship between C, C++, Java, and C#?

**1.11**    Explain the C++ keywords. List some C++ keywords you learned in this chapter.

**1.12**    Is C++ case-sensitive? What is the case for C++ keywords?

**1.13**    What is the C++ source filename extension, and what is the C++ executable filename extension on Windows?

**1.14**    What is a comment? What is the syntax for a comment in C++? Is the comment ignored by the compiler?

**1.15**    What is the statement to display a string on the console?

**1.16** Identify and fix the errors in the following code:

```
1 include <iostream>
2
3 int main
4 {
5   // Display Welcome to C++ to the console
6   std::cout << "Welcome to C++!" << std::endl;
7   return 0;
8 }
```

**1.17** What is the command to compile a C++ program using the GNU compiler? What is the command to run a C++ application on Windows and on UNIX?

## PROGRAMMING EXERCISES

**1.1** (*Creating, compiling, and running a C++ program*) Create a source file containing a C++ program. Perform the following steps to compile the program and run it:

1. Create a file named **Welcome.cpp** for Listing 1.1. You can use an IDE or any editor that will save your file in text format.
2. Compile the source file.
3. Run the program.
4. Replace "Welcome to C++" with "My first program" in the program; save, compile, and run the program. You will see the message "My first program" displayed.
5. Replace **main** with **Main**, and recompile the source code. The compiler returns an error message because the C++ program is case-sensitive.
6. Change it back, and compile the program again.

# CHAPTER 2

# PRIMITIVE DATA TYPES AND OPERATIONS

## Objectives

- To write C++ programs to perform simple calculations (§2.2).

- To read input from the keyboard using the **cin** object (§2.3).

- To simplify programming by omitting the **std::** prefix (§2.4).

- To use identifiers to name elements in the program (§2.5).

- To use variables to store data (§§2.6–2.7).

- To program with assignment statements and assignment expressions (§2.7).

- To use constants to store permanent data (§2.8).

- To declare variables using numeric data types (§2.9).

- To use operators to write numeric expressions (§2.9).

- To convert numbers to a different type using casting (§2.10).

- To represent character using the **char** type (§2.11).

- To become familiar with C++ documentation, programming style, and naming conventions (§2.13).

- To distinguish syntax errors, runtime errors, and logic errors (§2.14).

- To debug logic errors (§2.15).

## 2.1 Introduction

In the preceding chapter, you learned how to create, compile, and run a C++ program. In this chapter, you will be introduced to C++ primitive data types and related subjects, such as variables, constants, data types, operators, and expressions. You will learn how to write programs using primitive data types, input and output, and simple calculations.

## 2.2 Writing Simple Programs

To begin, let's look at a simple program that computes the area of a circle. The program reads in the radius of a circle and displays its area. The program will use variables to store the radius and the area and will use an expression to compute the area.

*algorithm*

Writing this program involves designing algorithms and data structures, as well as translating algorithms into programming codes. An *algorithm* describes how a problem is solved in terms of the actions to be executed, and it specifies the order in which the actions should be executed. Algorithms can help the programmer plan a program before writing it in a programming language. The algorithm for this program can be described as follows:

1. Read in the radius.

2. Compute the area using the following formula:

$$area = radius \times radius \times \pi$$

3. Display the area.

Many of the problems you will meet when taking an introductory course in programming using this text can be described with simple, straightforward algorithms. As your education progresses, and you take courses on data structures or on algorithm design and analysis, you will encounter complex problems that require sophisticated solutions. You will need to design accurate, efficient algorithms with appropriate data structures in order to solve such problems.

Data structures involve data representation and manipulation. C++ provides data types for representing integers, floating-point numbers (i.e., numbers with a decimal point), characters, and Boolean types. These types are known as *primitive data types,* or *fundamental types.* C++ also supports array and some advanced data structures, such as strings and vectors.

*primitive data types*

To novice programmers, coding is a daunting task. When you *code,* you translate an algorithm into a programming language understood by the computer. You already know that every C++ program begins its execution from the main function. The outline of the main function would look like this:

```cpp
int main()
{
  // Step 1: Read in radius

  // Step 2: Compute area

  // Step 3: Display the area
}
```

The program needs to read the radius entered by the user from the keyboard. This raises two important issues:

- Reading the radius.
- Storing the radius in the program.

*variable*

Let's address the second issue first. In order to store the radius, the program needs to declare a symbol called a *variable* that will represent the radius. Variables are used to store data and computational results in the program.

*descriptive names*

Rather than using **x** and **y**, choose *descriptive names*: in this case, **radius** for radius, and **area** for area. Specify their data types to let the compiler know what **radius** and **area** are, indicating whether they are integer, floating-point number, or something else. Declare **radius** and **area** as double-precision floating-point numbers. The program can be expanded as follows:

```
int main()
{
  double radius;
  double area;
  // Step 1: Read in radius

  // Step 2: Compute area

  // Step 3: Display the area
}
```

The program declares **radius** and **area** as variables. The reserved word **double** indicates that **radius** and **area** are double-precision floating-point values stored in the computer.

The first step is to read in **radius**. You will learn how to read a number from the keyboard later. For the time being, let us assign a fixed number to **radius** in the program.

The second step is to compute **area** by assigning the expression **radius * radius * 3.14159** to **area**.

In the final step, print **area** on the console by directing it to the **std::cout** object.

The complete program is shown in Listing 2.1.

## LISTING 2.1    ComputeArea.ccp

```
1 #include <iostream>
2
3 int main()
4 {                                                    memory
5   double radius;                       radius  [ ? ]
6   double area;                         area    [ ? ]
7
8   // Step 1: Read in radius
9   radius = 20;                         radius [20]
10
11  // Step 2: Compute area
12  area = radius * radius * 3.14159;    area   [1256.636]
13
14  // Step 3: Display the area
15  std::cout << "The area is ";
16  std::cout << area << std::endl;
17
18  return 0;
19 }
```

```
The area is 1256.62
```

Variables such as **radius** and **area** correspond to memory locations. Every variable has a name, a type, a size, and a value. Line 5 *declares* that **radius** can store a **double** value. The value is not defined until you *assign a value*. Line 9 assigns **20** into **radius**. Similarly, line 6 declares variable **area**, and line 12 assigns a value into **area**. If you comment line 9, the program would compile and run, but the result is unpredictable, because radius may be assigned any value.

*declaring variable*
*assign value*

Line 15 sends a string "The area is " to the console. Line 16 sends the value in variable **area** to the console. Note that there are no quotation marks around **area**. If quotation marks were placed around **area**, it would send the string literal "area" to the console.

incremental development
and testing

**Tip**

This example consists of three steps. It is a good approach to develop and test these steps incrementally by adding one step at a time. You should apply this approach to all the programs, although the problem solving steps are not explicitly stated in many programs in this book.

concatenating output

**Tip**

You can combine multiple outputs in one statement. For example, the following one statement performs the same function as lines 15–16:

```
std::cout << "The area is " << area << std::endl;
```

When executing this statement, the string "The area is" is sent to the output object first, then the value of variable **area**, and finally **std::endl** outputs a new line.

## 2.3 Reading Input from the Keyboard

In Listing 2.1, the radius is fixed in the source code. To use a different radius, you have to modify the source code and recompile it. Obviously, it is not convenient. You can use the **std::cin** object to read input from the keyboard, as shown in Listing 2.2.

### LISTING 2.2 ComputeArea1.ccp

```
1 #include <iostream>
2
3 int main()
4 {
5     // Step 1: Read in radius
6     double radius;
7     std::cout << "Enter a radius: ";
8     std::cin >> radius;
9
10    // Step 2: Compute area
11    double area = radius * radius * 3.14159;
12
13    // Step 3: Display the area
14    std::cout << "The area is " << area << std::endl;
15
16    return 0;
15 }
```

input

```
Enter a radius: 2 ⏎Enter
The area is 12.5664
```

prompt

Line 7 displays a string "Enter a radius: " to the console. This is known as a *prompt*, because it directs the user to enter an input. Your program should always tell the user what to enter when expecting input from the keyboard.

**std::cin**
stream extraction operator

Line 8 uses the **std::cin** object to read a value from the keyboard. Note that **cin** stands for console input. The **>>** symbol, referred to as the *stream extraction operator*, assigns an input to a variable. As shown in the sample output, the program displays the prompting message "Enter a radius: ", the user then enters number 2, which is assigned to variable **radius**. The **cin** object causes a program to wait until data is typed at the keyboard and the Enter key is pressed. C++ automatically converts the data read from the keyboard to the data type of the variable.

Note that the **>>** symbol is the opposite of the **<<** symbol. The **>>** indicates that the data flows from **cin** to a variable. The **<<** symbol shows that data flows from a variable or a string to **cout**.

multiple input

You can use one statement to read multiple values. For example, the following statement reads three values into variable **x1**, **x2**, and **x3**:

```
std::cin >> x1 >> x2 >> x3;
```

You need to enter three numbers separated by spaces and presses the Enter key to end the input. For example, if you enter

```
10 20 30
```

then press the Enter key, x1, x2, and x3 become 10, 20, and 30, respectively.

## 2.4 Omitting the `std::` Prefix

You have noticed that `std::cout`, `std::endl`, and `std::cin` all start with `std::`. So what is `std`? `std` means the standard namespace. C++ divides the world into "namespaces" to resolve potential naming conflicts. `std::cout` means that `cout` belongs to the standard namespace. It is tedious to type `std::` repeatedly. There are two solutions to eliminate the `std::` prefix.

The first solution is to add the statement:

first solution

```
using namespace std;
```

This tells the compiler that any object without an explicit qualifier belongs to the standard namespace. Listing 2.3 uses this statement to rewrite Listing 2.2. The `std::` prefix for `cout`, `cin`, and `endl` are omitted.

**LISTING 2.3  ComputeArea2.ccp**

```
 1 #include <iostream>
 2 using namespace std;                                    standard namespace
 3
 4 int main()
 5 {
 6   // Step 1: Read in radius
 7   double radius;
 8   cout << "Enter a radius: ";
 9   cin >> radius;
10
11   // Step 2: Compute area
12   double area = radius * radius * 3.14159;
13
14   // Step 3: Display the area
15   cout << "The area is " << area << endl;
16
17   return 0;
18 }
```

The second solution is to add the statements:

second solution

```
using std::cout;
using std::cin;
using std::endl;
```

So the compiler knows that `cout`, `cin`, and `endl` are in the standard namespace before they are referenced. Listing 2.4 uses these statements to rewrite Listing 2.2.

**LISTING 2.4  ComputeArea3.ccp**

```
 1 #include <iostream>
 2 using std::cout;                                         standard namespace
 3 using std::cin;
 4 using std::endl;
 5
 6 int main()
 7 {
 8   // Step 1: Read in radius
 9   double radius;
```

```
10    cout << "Enter a radius: ";
11    cin >> radius;
12
13    // Step 2: Compute area
14    double area = radius * radius * 3.14159;
15
16    // Step 3: Display the area
17    cout << "The area is " << area << endl;
18
19    return 0;
18  }
```

## 2.5 Identifiers

identifier

Just as every entity in the real world has a name, so you need to choose names for the things you will refer to in your programs. Programming languages use special symbols called *identifiers* to name such programming entities as variables, constants, and functions. Here are the rules for naming identifiers:

- An identifier is a sequence of characters that consists of letters, digits, and underscores (_).

- An identifier must start with a letter or an underscore. It cannot start with a digit.

- An identifier cannot be a reserved word. (See Appendix A, "C++ Keywords," for a list of reserved words.)

- An identifier can be of any length, but your C++ compiler may impose some restriction. Use identifiers of 31 characters or fewer to ensure portability.

For example, **area** and **radius** are legal identifiers, whereas **2A** and **d+4** are illegal identifiers because they do not follow the rules. The compiler detects illegal identifiers and reports syntax errors.

**Note**

case-sensitive

Since C++ is *case-sensitive*, X and x are different identifiers.

**Tip**

descriptive names

Identifiers are used for naming variables and functions and other things in a program. Descriptive identifiers make programs easy to read. Besides choosing *descriptive names* for identifiers, there are naming conventions for different kinds of identifiers. Naming conventions are summarized in §2.13, "Programming Style and Documentation."

**Caution**

the _ character

Do not name identifiers that begin with underscores to avoid confusions, because C++ compilers may use names like that internally.

## 2.6 Variables

Variables are used to store data in a program. In the program in Listing 2.4, **radius** and **area** are variables of double-precision, floating-point type. You can assign any numerical value to **radius** and **area**, and the values of **radius** and **area** can be reassigned. For example, you can write the code shown below to compute the area for different radii:

```
// Compute the first area
radius = 1.0;
area = radius * radius * 3.14159;
std::cout << area;
```

```
// Compute the second area
radius = 2.0;
area = radius * radius * 3.14159;
std::cout << area;
```

### 2.6.1  Declaring Variables

Variables are for representing data of a certain type. To use a variable, you declare it by telling the compiler the name of the variable as well as what type of data it represents. This is called a *variable declaration*. Declaring a variable tells the compiler to allocate appropriate memory space for the variable based on its data type. Here is the syntax for declaring a variable:

```
datatype variableName;
```

Here are some examples of variable declarations:                                          declaring variable

```
int x;                 // Declare x to be an integer variable;
double radius;         // Declare radius to be a double variable;
double interestRate;   // Declare interestRate to be a double variable;
char a;                // Declare a to be a character variable;
```

The examples use the data types **int**, **double**, and **char**. Later in this chapter you will learn more about data types.

If variables are of the same type, they can be declared together, as follows:

```
datatype variable1, variable2, …, variablen;
```

The variables are separated by commas. For example,

```
int i, j, k; // Declare i, j, and k as int variables
```

 **Note**

By convention, variable names are in lowercase. If a name consists of several words, concatenate    naming variables
all of them and capitalize the first letter of each word except the first. Examples of variables are
**radius** and **interestRate**.

## 2.7 Assignment Statements and Assignment Expressions

After a variable is declared, you can assign a value to it by using an *assignment statement*. In    assignment statement
C++, the equal sign (=) is used as the *assignment operator*. The syntax for assignment state-    assignment operator
ments is as follows:

```
variable = expression;
```

An *expression* represents a computation involving values, variables, and operators that    expression
together evaluates to a value. For example, consider the following code:

```
int x = 1;               // Assign 1 to variable x;
double radius = 1.0;     // Assign 1.0 to variable radius;
x = 5 * (3 / 2) + 3 * 2; // Assign the value of the expression to x;
x = y + 1;               // Assign the addition of y and 1 to x;
area = radius * radius * 3.14159; // Compute area
```

A variable can appear in both sides of the assignment operator. For example,

```
x = x + 1;
```

In this assignment statement, the result of `x + 1` is assigned to `x`. If `x` is `1` before the statement is executed, then it becomes `2` after the statement is executed.

To assign a value to a variable, the variable name must be on the left of the assignment operator. Thus, `1 = x` would be wrong.

In C++, an assignment statement also can be treated as an expression that evaluates to the value being assigned to the variable on the left-hand side of the assignment operator. For this reason, an assignment statement is also known as an *assignment expression*. For example, the following statement is correct:

assignment expression

```
cout << (x = 1);
```

which is equivalent to

```
x = 1;
cout << x;
```

The following statement is also correct:

```
i = j = k = 1;
```

which is equivalent to

```
k = 1;
j = k;
i = j;
```

 **Note**

In an assignment statement, the data type of the variable on the left must be compatible with the data type of the value on the right. For example, `int x = 1.0` would be illegal because the data type of `x` is `int`. You cannot assign a **double** value (`1.0`) to an `int` variable without using type casting. Type casting is introduced in §2.8, "Numeric Type Conversions."

 **Note**

In C++, any expression can be used as a statement. So the following statement is correct, but does not make any practical sense:

```
2 / 3; // A syntactic correct statement
```

The GNU compiler (gcc) warns about this kind of statement if you compile with the option `-Wall` (enable all warnings). It reports "statement has no effect."

## 2.7.1   Declaring and Initializing Variables in One Step

Variables often have initial values. You can declare a variable and initialize it in one step. Consider, for instance, the following code:

```
int x = 1;
```

This is equivalent to the next two statements:

```
int x;
x = 1;
```

You can also use a shorthand form to declare and initialize variables of the same type together. For example,

```
int i = 1, j = 2;
```

**Tip**

A variable must be declared before it can be assigned a value. A variable declared in a function must be assigned a value. Otherwise, the value is unpredictable. Whenever possible, declare a variable and assign its initial value in one step. This will make the program easy to read and avoid programming errors.

**Note**

C++ allows an alternative syntax for declaring and initializing variables, as shown in the following example:

```cpp
int i(1), j(2);
```

which is equivalent to

```cpp
int i = 1, j = 2;
```

## 2.8 Named Constants

The value of a variable may change during the execution of the program, but a *constant* represents permanent data that never changes. In our **ComputeArea** program, $\pi$ is a constant. If you use it frequently, you don't want to keep typing 3.14159; instead, you can name a constant for $\pi$. Here is the syntax for declaring a constant:

constant

```cpp
const datatype CONSTANTNAME = VALUE;
```

A constant must be declared and initialized in the same statement. The word **const** is a C++ keyword which means that the constant cannot be changed. For example, you may define $\pi$ as a constant and rewrite the program in Listing 2.4 as in Listing 2.5.

**LISTING 2.5** ComputeArea4.ccp

```cpp
 1 #include <iostream>
 2 using namespace std;
 3
 4 int main()
 5 {
 6     const double PI = 3.14159;                        constant PI
 7
 8     // Step 1: Read in radius
 9     double radius = 20;
10
11     // Step 2: Compute area
12     double area = radius * radius * PI;
13
14     // Step 3: Display the area
15     cout << "The area is ";
16     cout << area << std::endl;
17
18     return 0;
19 }
```

**Caution**

By convention, constants are named in uppercase: **PI**, not **pi** or **Pi**.

naming constants

**Note**

There are three benefits of using constants: (1) you don't have to repeatedly type the same value; (2) the value can be changed in a single location, if necessary; (3) descriptive constant names make the program easy to read.

benefits of constants

## 2.9 Numeric Data Types and Operations

Every data type has a range of values. The compiler allocates memory space to store each variable or constant according to its data type. C++ provides primitive data types for numeric values, characters, and Boolean values. This section introduces numeric data types. Table 2.1 lists the numeric data types with their typical ranges and storage sizes.

**TABLE 2.1**    Numeric Data Types

| Name | Synonymy | Range | Storage Size |
|---|---|---|---|
| short | short int | $-2^{15}$ ($-32,768$) to $2^{15} - 1$ (32,767) | 16-bit signed |
| unsigned short | unsigned short int | 0 to $2^{16} - 1$ (65535) | 16-bit unsigned |
| int | | $-2^{31}$ ($-2147483648$) to $2^{31} - 1$ (2147483647) | 32-bit signed |
| unsigned int | unsigned | 0 to $2^{32} - 1$ (4294967295) | 32-bit unsigned |
| long | long int | $-2^{31}$ ($-2147483648$) to $2^{31} - 1$ (2147483647) | 32-bit signed |
| unsigned long | unsigned long int | 0 to $2^{32} - 1$ (4294967295) | 32-bit unsigned |
| float | | Negative range:<br>    $-3.4028235E+38$   to $-1.4E-45$<br><br>Positive range:<br>    1.4E$-$45 to 3.4028235E$+$38 | 32-bit IEEE 754 |
| double | | Negative range:<br>    $-1.7976931348623157E+308$ to $-4.9E-324$<br><br>Positive range:<br>    4.9E$-$324 to 1.7976931348623157E$+$308 | 64-bit IEEE 754 |
| long double | | Negative range:<br>    $-1.18E+4932$ to 3.37E$-$4932<br><br>Positive range:<br>    3.37E$-$4932 to 1.18E$+$4932<br><br>Significant decimal digits: 19 | 80-bit |

signed vs. unsigned

C++ uses three types for integers: **short**, **int**, and **long**. Each integer type comes in two flavors: *signed* and *unsigned*. Half the numbers represented by a signed short is negative and the other half is positive. All the numbers represented by an unsigned short are non-negative. Because you have the same storage size for both, the largest number you can store in an unsigned integer is twice as big as the largest positive number you can store in a signed integer. If you know the value stored in a variable is always non-negative, declare it as unsigned.

size may vary

The size of the data types may vary depending on the compiler and computer you are using. Typically, **int** and **long** have the same size. On some systems, **long** requires 8 bytes.

**Tip**

You can use the **sizeof** function to find the size of a type. For example, the following statement displays the size of **int**, **long**, and **double** on your machine:

**sizeof** function

```
cout << sizeof(int) << " " << sizeof(long) << " " << sizeof(double);
```

**Note**

short int is synonymous to short. unsigned short int is synonymous to unsigned short. unsigned int is synonymous to unsigned. long int is synonymous to long. unsigned long int is synonymous to unsigned long. For example,

```
short int i = 2;
```

is the same as

```
short i = 2;
```

synonymous types

C++ uses three types for *floating-point* numbers: float, double, and long double. The double type is usually twice as big as float. So, the double is known as double precision, while float is single precision. The long double is even bigger than double. For most applications, using the double type is desirable.

floating-point

## 2.9.1 Numeric Literals

A *literal* is a constant value that appears directly in a program. For example, 34, 1000000, and 5.0 are literals in the following statements:

literal

```
int i = 34;
long k = 1000000;
double d = 5.0;
```

An *integer literal* is stored in memory as an int type value. On a system that uses 4 bytes to represent an int value, value is between $-2^{31}$ (−2147483648) and $2^{31}-1$ (2147483647). The literal 2147483648 is too long as an int literal. To denote an integer literal of the long type, append the letter L or l to it (e.g., 2147483648L). L is preferred because l (lowercase L) can easily be confused with 1 (the digit one). Since 2147483648 exceeds the range for the int values, it must be denoted as 2147483648L.

integer literal

long literal

**Note**

By default, an integer literal is a decimal number. To denote an octal integer literal, use a leading *0* (zero), and to denote a hexadecimal integer literal, use a leading *0x* or *0X* (zero x). For example, the following code displays the decimal value 65535 for hexadecimal number FFFF and decimal value 8 for octal number 10:

octal and hex literals

```
cout << 0xFFFF << " " << 010;
```

Hexadecimal numbers, binary numbers, and octal numbers were introduced in §1.5, "Number Systems."

*Floating-point literals* are written with a decimal point. 2.0 is a floating-point number, but 2 is an integer. By default, a floating-point literal is treated as a double type value. For example, 5.0 is considered a double value, not a float value. You can make a number a float by appending the letter f or F. For example, you can use 100.2f or 100.2F to denote a float literal.

floating-point literals

Floating-point literals can also be specified in *scientific notation*; for example, 1.23456e+2, the same as 1.23456e2, is equivalent to $1.23456 \times 10^2 = 123.456$, and 1.23456e-2 is equivalent to $1.23456 \times 10^{-2} = 0.0123456$. E (or e) represents an exponent and can be either in lowercase or uppercase.

scientific notation

**Note**

The float and double types are used to represent numbers with a decimal point. Why are they called *floating-point numbers*? These numbers are stored into scientific notation. When a number such as 50.534e+1 is converted into scientific notation such as 5.0534, its decimal point is moved (i.e., floated) to a new position.

why called floating-point?

### 2.9.2  Numeric Operators

operators +, -, *, /, %

The operators for numeric data types include the standard arithmetic operators: addition (+), subtraction (-), multiplication (*), division (/), and modulus (%), as shown in Table 2.2.

**TABLE 2.2**  Numeric Operators

| Operator | Name | Example | Result |
|---|---|---|---|
| + | Addition | 34 + 1 | 35 |
| − | Subtraction | 34.0 − 0.1 | 33.9 |
| * | Multiplication | 300 * 30 | 9000 |
| / | Division | 1.0 / 2.0 | 0.5 |
| % | Modulus | 20 % 3 | 2 |

integer division

The result of *integer division* is an integer. The fractional part is truncated. For example, 5 / 2 yields 2, not 2.5, and −5 / 2 yields −2, not −2.5.

integer modulus

The modulus (%) operator yields the remainder after division. The left-hand operand is the dividend and the right-hand operand is the divisor. Therefore, 7 % 3 yields 1, 12 % 4 yields 0, 26 % 8 yields 2, and 20 % 13 yields 7.

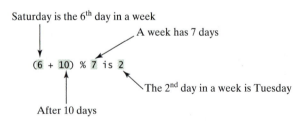

The % operator is often used for positive integers but can also be used with negative integers. The remainder is negative only if the dividend is negative. For example, −7 % 3 yields −1, −12 % 4 yields 0, −26 % −8 yields −2, and 20 % −13 yields 7. In C++, the % operator is for integers only.

Modulus is very useful in programming. For example, an even number % 2 is always 0, and an odd number % 2 is always 1. So you can use this property to determine whether a number is even or odd. Suppose today is Saturday and you and your friends are going to meet in 10 days. What day is in 10 days? You can find that day is Tuesday using the following expression:

Saturday is the 6th day in a week

A week has 7 days

(6 + 10) % 7 is 2

The 2nd day in a week is Tuesday

After 10 days

Listing 2.6 gives a program that obtains minutes and remaining seconds from an amount of time in seconds. For example, 500 seconds contains 8 minutes and 20 seconds.

### LISTING 2.6  DisplayTime.cpp

```cpp
1 #include <iostream>
2 using namespace std;
3
```

```
 4 int main()
 5 {
 6   int seconds = 500;
 7   int minutes = seconds / 60;
 8   int remainingSeconds = seconds % 60;
 9   cout << seconds << " seconds is " << minutes <<
10      " minutes and " << remainingSeconds << " seconds " << endl;
11
12   return 0;
13 }
```

```
500 seconds is 8 minutes and 20 seconds
```

Line 7 obtains the minutes using **seconds / 60**. Line 8 (**seconds % 60**) obtains the remaining seconds after taking away minutes.

The + and – operators can be both unary and binary. A *unary* operator has only one operand; a *binary* operator has two operands. For example, the – operator in –5 can be considered a *unary operator* to negate number 5, whereas the – operator in 4 – 5 is a *binary operator* for subtracting 5 from 4.

unary operator

binary operator

**Note**

C++ allows you to assign an integer value to a floating-point variable and a floating-point value to an integer variable vice versa. When assigning a floating-point value to an integer variable, the fraction part of the floating-point value is truncated (*not rounded*). For example, see the following code:

floating-point to integer

```
int i = 34.7;    // i becomes 34
float f = i;     // f is now 34
float g = 34.3;  // g becomes 34.3
long j = g;      // j is now 34
```

**Caution**

When a variable is assigned a value that is too large to be stored, it causes *overflow*. For example, executing the following statement causes *overflow*, because the largest value that can be stored in a variable of the **short** type is **32767**. **32768** is too large.

overflow

```
short value = 32767 + 1;
```

When a variable is assigned a value that is too small to be stored, it causes *underflow*. For example, executing the following statement causes *underflow*, because the smallest value that can be stored in a variable of the **short** type is −32768.−32769 is too small.

underflow

```
short value = -32769;
```

C++ does not report warnings or errors on overflow and underflow. So be careful when working with numbers close to the maximum or minimum range of a given type.

## 2.9.3 Arithmetic Expressions

Writing numeric expressions in C++ involves a straightforward translation of an arithmetic expression using C++ operators. For example, the arithmetic expression

$$\frac{3 + 4x}{5} - \frac{10(y - 5)(a + b + c)}{x} + 9\left(\frac{4}{x} + \frac{9 + x}{y}\right)$$

can be translated into a C++ expression as:

```
(3 + 4 * x) / 5 - 10 * (y - 5) * (a + b + c) / x +
9 * (4 / x + (9 + x) / y)
```

The numeric operators in a C++ expression are applied the same way as in an arithmetic expression. Operators contained within pairs of parentheses are evaluated first. Parentheses can be nested, in which case the expression in the inner parentheses is evaluated first. Multiplication, division, and modulus operators are applied next. If an expression contains several multiplication, division, and modulus operators, they are applied from left to right. Addition and subtraction operators are applied last. If an expression contains several addition and subtraction operators, they are applied from left to right.

Listing 2.7 gives a program that converts a Fahrenheit degree to Celsius using the formula $celsius = \left(\frac{5}{9}\right)(fahrenheit - 32)$.

### LISTING 2.7 FahrenheitToCelsius.cpp

```
 1 #include <iostream>
 2 using namespace std;
 3
 4 int main()
 5 {
 6   // Enter a degree in Fahrenheit
 7   double fahrenheit;
 8   cout << "Enter a degree in Fahrenheit: ";
 9   cin >> fahrenheit;
10
11   // Obtain a celsius degree
12   double celsius = (5.0 / 9) * (fahrenheit - 32);
13
14   // Display result
15   cout << "Fahrenheit " << fahrenheit << " is " <<
16       celsius << " in Celsius" << endl;
17
18   return 0;
19 }
```

input fahrenheit

compute celsius

display result

```
Enter a degree in Fahrenheit: 100  ⏎Enter
Fahrenheit 100 is 37.7778 in Celsius
```

integer vs. decimal division

Be careful when applying division. Division of two integers yields an integer in C++. $\frac{5}{9}$ is translated to `5.0 / 9` instead of `5 / 9` in line 12, because `5 / 9` yields `0` in C++.

### 2.9.4 Shorthand Operators

Very often the current value of a variable is used, modified, and then reassigned back to the same variable. For example, the following statement adds the current value of i with value 8 and assigns the result back to i:

```
i = i + 8;
```

shorthand operator

C++ allows you to combine assignment and addition operators using a *shorthand operator*. For example, the preceding statement can be written as:

```
i += 8;
```

The `+=` is called the *addition assignment operator*. Other shorthand operators are shown in Table 2.3.

There are two more shorthand operators for incrementing and decrementing a variable by 1. This is handy because that's often how much the value needs to be changed. These two operators are `++` and `--`. They can be used in prefix or suffix notation, as shown in Table 2.4.

++ and --

**TABLE 2.3**    Shorthand Operators

| Operator | Name | Example | Equivalent |
|----------|------|---------|------------|
| += | Addition assignment | i += 8 | i = i + 8 |
| -= | Subtraction assignment | i -= 8 | i = i - 8 |
| *= | Multiplication assignment | i *= 8 | i = i * 8 |
| /= | Division assignment | i /= 8 | i = i / 8 |
| %= | Modulus assignment | i %= 8 | i = i % 8 |

**TABLE 2.4**    Increment and Decrement Operators

| Operator | Name | Description |
|----------|------|-------------|
| ++var | Preincrement | The expression (++*var*) increments *var* by *1* and evaluates to the *new* value in *var* *after* the increment. |
| var++ | Postincrement | The expression (*var*++) evaluates to the *original* value in *var* and increments *var* by *1*. |
| --var | Predecrement | The expression (--*var*) decrements *var* by *1* and evaluates to the *new* value in *var* *after* the decrement. |
| var-- | Postdecrement | The expression (*var*--) evaluates to the *original* value in *var* and decrements *var* by *1*. |

If the operator is *before* (prefixed to) the variable, the variable is incremented or decremented by 1, then the *new* value of the variable is returned. If the operator is *after* (suffixed to) the variable, the original *old* value of the variable is returned, then the variable is incremented or decremented by 1. Therefore, the prefixes ++x and --x are referred to, respectively, as the *preincrement operator* and the *predecrement operator*; and the suffixes x++ and x-- are referred to, respectively, as the *postincrement operator* and the *postdecrement operator*. The prefix form of ++ (or --) and the suffix form of ++ (or --) are the same if they are used in isolation, but they cause different effects when used in an expression. The following code illustrates this:

preincrement, predecrement
postincrement, postdecrement

```
int i = 10;                    Same effect as   int newNum = 10 * i;
int newNum = 10 * i++;         ──────────────►   i = i + 1;
```

In this case, i is incremented by 1, then the *old* value of i is returned and used in the multiplication. So newNum becomes 100. If i++ is replaced by ++i as follows,

```
int i = 10;                    Same effect as   i = i + 1;
int newNum = 10 * (++i);       ──────────────►   int newNum = 10 * i;
```

i is incremented by 1, and the new value of i is returned and used in the multiplication. Thus newNum becomes 110.

Here is another example:

```
double x = 1.0;
double y = 5.0;
double z = x-- + (++y);
```

After all three lines are executed, y becomes 6.0, z becomes 7.0, and x becomes 0.0.

The increment operator ++ and the decrement operator — can be applied to all integer and floating-point types. These operators are often used in loop statements. A *loop statement* is a structure that controls how many times an operation or a sequence of operations is performed in succession. This structure, and the subject of loop statements, is introduced in Chapter 4, "Loops."

### Caution

operand evaluation order

For most binary operators, C++ does not specify the *operand evaluation order*. Normally, you assume that the left operand is evaluated before the right operand. This is not guaranteed in C++. For example, suppose **i** is **1**, the expression

```
++i + i
```

evaluates to **4** (2 + 2) if the left operand (**++i**) is evaluated first and evaluates to **3** (2 + 1) if the right operand (**i**) is evaluated first.

Since C++ cannot guarantee the operand evaluation order, you should not write the code that depends on the operand evaluation order.

### Note

Like the assignment operator (=), the operators (+=, -=, *=, /=, %=, ++, and --) can be used to form an assignment statement as well as an expression. For example, in the following code, **x += 2** is a statement in the first line and is an expression in the second line:

```
x += 2; // Statement
cout << (x += 2); // Expression
```

expression statement

If a statement is used as an expression, it is called an *expression statement*.

### Caution

There are no spaces in the shorthand operators. For example, **+ =** should be **+=**.

## 2.10 Numeric Type Conversions

Sometimes it is necessary to mix numeric values of different types in a computation. Consider the following statements:

```
byte i = 100;
long k = i * 3 + 4;
double d = i * 3.1 + k / 2;
```

Are these statements correct? C++ allows binary operations on values of different types. When performing a binary operation involving two operands of different types, C++ automatically converts the operand based on the following rules:

converting operands

1. If one of the operands is **long double**, the other is converted into **long double**.

2. Otherwise, if one of the operands is **double**, the other is converted into **double**.

3. Otherwise, if one of the operands is **float**, the other is converted into **float**.

4. Otherwise, if one of the operands is **unsigned long**, the other is converted into **unsigned long**.

5. Otherwise, if one of the operands is **long**, the other is converted into **long**.

6. Otherwise, if one of the operands is **unsigned int**, the other is converted into **unsigned int**.

7. Otherwise, both operands are converted into **int**.

For example, the result of `1 / 2` is `0`, because both operands are `int` values. The result of `1.0 / 2` is `0.5`, since 1.0 is `double` and 2 is converted to 2.0.

C++ also allows you to manually convert a value from one type to another using a casting operator. The syntax is

> type casting

```
static_cast<type>(value)
```

where `value` is a variable, a literal, or an expression and `type` is the type you wish to convert the `value` to. For example, the following statement

```
cout << static_cast<double>(1) / 2;
```

displays `0.5`, because `1` is converted to `1.0` first, then `1.0` is divided by `2`. However, the statement

```
cout << 1 / 2;
```

displays `0`.

**Note**

It is worth mentioning that static casting can also be done using the `(type)` syntax, i.e., giving the target type in parentheses, followed by a variable, a literal, or an expression. For example,

```
int i = (int)5.4;
```

This is the same as

```
int i = static_cast<int>(5.4);
```

This is called the *C-style cast*. It has been replaced by the C++ `static_cast` operator.

> C-Style cast

Casting a variable of a type with a small range to a variable of a type with a larger range is known as *widening a type*. Casting a variable of a type with a large range to a variable of a type with a smaller range is known as *narrowing a type*. Narrowing a type, such as assigning a `double` value to an `int` variable, may cause *loss of precision*. Lost information might lead to inaccurate results.

> widening a type
> narrowing a type
> loss of precision

**Note**

Casting does not change the variable being cast. For example, `d` is not changed after casting in the following code:

```
double d = 4.5;
int i = static_cast<int>(d); // d is not changed
```

**Note**

The GNU C++ compiler will give a warning when you narrow a type unless you use `static_cast` to make the conversion explicit.

> compiler warning

Listing 2.8 gives a program that displays the sales tax with two digits after the decimal point.

**LISTING 2.8**  `SalesTax.cpp`

```
1 #include <iostream>
2 using namespace std;
3
4 int main()
5 {
```

```
6    // Enter purchase amount
7    double purchaseAmount;
8    cout << "Enter purchase amount: ";
9    cin >> purchaseAmount;
10
11   double tax = purchaseAmount * 0.06;
12   cout << "Sales tax is " << static_cast<int>(tax * 100) / 100.0;
13
14   return 0;
15 }
```

```
Enter purchase amount: 197.55  ⏎Enter
Sales tax is 11.85
```

*formatting numbers*

Variable **purchaseAmount** stores the purchase amount entered by the user (lines 7–9). Suppose the user entered 197.55. The sales tax is 6% of the purchase, so the **tax** is evaluated as 11.853 (line 11). The statement in line 12 displays the tax 11.85 with two digits after the decimal point. Note that **static_cast<int>(tax * 100)** is 1185, so **static_cast<int> (tax * 100) / 100.0** is 11.85.

## 2.11 Character Data Type and Operations

**char** type

The character data type, **char**, is used to represent a single character. A character literal is enclosed in single quotation marks. Consider the following code:

```
char letter = 'A';
char numChar = '4';
```

The first statement assigns character **A** to the **char** variable **letter**. The second statement assigns the digit character **4** to the **char** variable **numChar**.

**char** literal

### Caution

A string literal must be enclosed in quotation marks. A character literal is a single character enclosed in single quotation marks. So **"A"** is a string, and **'A'** is a character.

*character encoding*

Computers use binary numbers internally. A character is stored as a sequence of 0s and 1s in a computer. To convert a character to its binary representation is called *encoding*. There are different ways to encode a character. How characters are encoded is defined by an *encoding scheme*.

*ASCII*

Most computers use *ASCII (American Standard Code for Information Interchange)*, a 7-bit encoding scheme for representing all uppercase and lowercase letters, digits, punctuation marks, and control characters. See Appendix B, "The ASCII Character Set," for a list of ASCII characters and their decimal and hexadecimal codes. On most systems, the size of the **char** type is 1 byte.

**char** increment and decrement

### Note

The increment and decrement operators can also be used on **char** variables to get the next or preceding character. For example, the following statements display character **b**:

```
char ch = 'a';
cout << ++ch;
```

*read character*

### Note

To read a character from the keyboard, use

```
cout << "Enter a character: ";
char ch;
cin >> ch;
```

## 2.11.1   Escape Sequences for Special Characters

C++ allows you to use escape sequences to represent special characters, as shown in Table 2.5. An escape sequence begins with the backslash character (\) followed by a character that has a special meaning to the compiler.

**TABLE 2.5**   Character Escape Sequences

| Character Escape Sequence | Name | ASCII Code |
|---|---|---|
| \b | Backspace | 8 |
| \t | Tab | 9 |
| \n | Linefeed | 10 |
| \f | Formfeed | 12 |
| \r | Carriage return | 13 |
| \\ | Backslash | 92 |
| \' | Single quote | 39 |
| \" | Double quote | 34 |

Suppose you want to print the quoted message shown below:

```
He said "C++ is powerful"
```

Here is how to write the statement:

```
cout << "He said \"C++ is powerful\"";
```

> **Note**
>
> The characters ' ', '\t', '\f', '\r', and '\n' are known as the *whitespace* characters:                    whitespace

> **Note**
>
> The following two statements both display a string and move the cursor to the next line.
>
> ```
> cout << "Welcome to C++\n";
> cout << "Welcome to C++" << endl;
> ```
>
> \n vs. endl
>
> However, using **endl** ensures that the output is displayed immediately on all platforms.

## 2.11.2   Casting between **char** and Numeric Types

A **char** can be cast into any numeric type, and vice versa. When an integer is cast into a **char**, only its lower 8 bits of data are used (assume that your system stores a char in 8 bits); the other part is ignored. For example, see the following code:

```
char c = 0XFF41; // The lower 8 bits hex code 41 is assigned to c
cout << c;       // c is character A
```

When a floating-point value is cast into a **char**, the floating-point value is first cast into an **int**, which is then cast into a **char**.

```
char c = 65.25; // Decimal 65 is assigned to t
cout << c;      // c is character A
```

When a **char** is cast into a numeric type, the character's ASCII is cast into the specified numeric type. For example, see the following code:

```
int i = 'A';  // The ASCII code of character A is assigned to i
cout << i;    // i is 65
```

numeric operators on
characters

 **Note**

The **char** type is treated as if it is an integer of the byte size. All *numeric operators* can be applied to **char** operands. A **char** operand is automatically cast into a number if the other operand is a number or a character. For example, the following statements

```
int i = '2' + '3'; // (int)'2' is 50 and (int)'3' is 51
cout << "i is " << i << endl; // i is decimal 101

int j = 2 + 'a'; // (int)'a' is 97
cout << "j is " << j << endl;
cout << j << " is the ASCII code for character " <<
  static_cast<char>(j) << endl;
```

display

```
i is 101
j is 99
99 is the ASCII code for character c
```

**Note**

It is worthwhile to note that the ASCII for lowercase letters are consecutive integers starting from the code for **'a'**, then for **'b'**, **'c'**, ..., and **'z'**. The same is true for the uppercase letters. Furthermore, the ASCII code for **'a'** is greater than the code for **'A'**. So **'a'** – **'A'** is the same as **'b'** – **'B'**. For a lowercase letter *ch*, its corresponding uppercase letter is **static_cast<char>('A' + (ch – 'a'))**.

## 2.12 Case Studies

In the preceding sections, you learned about variables, constants, primitive data types, operators, and expressions. You are now ready to use them to write interesting programs. This section presents three examples: computing loan payments, breaking a sum of money down into smaller units, and displaying the current time.

### 2.12.1 Example: Computing Loan Payments

This example shows you how to write a program that computes loan payments. The loan can be a car loan, a student loan, or a home mortgage loan. The program lets the user enter the interest rate, number of years, and loan amount and then computes the monthly payment and the total payment. It concludes by displaying the monthly and total payments.

The formula to compute the monthly payment is as follows:

$$\frac{loanAmount \times monthlyInterestRate}{1 - \dfrac{1}{(1 + monthlyInterestRate)^{numberOfYears \times 12}}}$$

You don't have to know how this formula is derived. Nonetheless, given the monthly interest rate, number of years, and loan amount, you can use it to compute the monthly payment.

Here are the steps in developing the program:

1. Prompt the user to enter the annual interest rate, number of years, and loan amount.

2. Obtain the monthly interest rate from the annual interest rate.

3. Compute the monthly payment using the preceding formula.

4. Compute the total payment, which is the monthly payment multiplied by 12 and multiplied by the number of years.

5. Display the monthly payment and total payment.

In the formula, you have to compute $(1 + monthlyInterestRate)^{numberOfYears \times 12}$. C++ contains the **pow(a, b)** function in the **cmath** library, which can be used to compute $a^b$. For example,

**pow(a, b)** function

```
cout << pow(2.0, 3)
```

displays 8. Note that the first parameter in **pow(a, b)** must be a decimal value.

Listing 2.9 gives the complete program.

## LISTING 2.9 ComputeLoan.cpp

```
 1 #include <iostream>
 2 #include <cmath>
 3 using namespace std;
 4
 5 int main()
 6 {
 7   // Enter yearly interest rate
 8   cout << "Enter yearly interest rate, for example 8.25: ";
 9   double annualInterestRate;
10   cin >> annualInterestRate;
11
12   // Obtain monthly interest rate
13   double monthlyInterestRate = annualInterestRate / 1200;
14
15   // Enter number of years
16   cout << "Enter number of years as an integer, for example 5: ";
17   int numberOfYears;
18   cin >> numberOfYears;
19
20   // Enter loan amount
21   cout << "Enter loan amount, for example 120000.95: ";
22   double loanAmount;
23   cin >> loanAmount;
24
25   // Calculate payment
26   double monthlyPayment = loanAmount * monthlyInterestRate / (1
27     - 1 / pow(1 + monthlyInterestRate, numberOfYears * 12));
28   double totalPayment = monthlyPayment * numberOfYears * 12;
29
30   // Format to keep two digits after the decimal point
31   monthlyPayment = static_cast<int>(monthlyPayment * 100) / 100.0;
32   totalPayment = static_cast<int>(totalPayment * 100) / 100.0;
33
34   // Display results
35   cout << "The monthly payment is " << monthlyPayment <<
36     "\nThe total payment is " << totalPayment << endl;
37
38   return 0;
39 }
```

include **cmath** library

enter interest rate

monthlyPayment

totalPayment

display result

```
Enter yearly interest rate, for example 8.25: 6.25 ↵Enter
Enter number of years as an integer, for example 5: 15 ↵Enter
Enter loan amount, for example 120000.95: 60000 ↵Enter
The monthly payment is 514.45
The total payment is 92601.7
```

To use the **pow(a, b)** function, you have to include **cmath** in the program (line 2) in the same way you include the **iostream** library (line 1).

The program prompts the user to enter **annualInterestRate**, **numberOfYears**, and **loanAmount** in lines 7–23. If you entered an input other than a numeric value, a runtime error would occur. In Chapter 14, "Exception Handling," you will learn how to handle the exception so that the program can continue to run.

Each new variable in a function must be declared once and only once. Choose the most appropriate data type for the variable. For example, **numberOfYears** is better declared as **int** (line 17), although it could be declared as **long**, **float**, or **double**. Note that **unsigned short** might be the most appropriate for **numberOfYears**. For simplicity, however, the examples in this book will use **int** for integer and **double** for floating-point values.

The formula for computing the monthly payment is translated into C++ code in lines 26–27.

formatting numbers

The statements in lines 31–32 are for formatting the number to keep two digits after the decimal point. For example, if **monthlyPayment** is **2076.0252175**, **static_cast<int>(monthlyPayment * 100)** is **207602**. Therefore, **static_cast<int>(monthlyPayment * 100) / 100.0** yields **2076.02**.

## 2.12.2   Example: Counting Monetary Units

This section presents a program that classifies a given amount of money into smaller monetary units. The program lets the user enter an amount as a **double** value representing a total in dollars and cents, and outputs a report listing the monetary equivalent in dollars, quarters, dimes, nickels, and pennies, as shown in the sample output.

Your program should report the maximum number of dollars, then the maximum number of quarters, and so on, in this order.

Here are the steps in developing the program:

1. Prompt the user to enter the amount as a decimal number such as **11.56**.

2. Convert the amount (e.g., **11.56**) into cents (**1156**).

3. Divide the cents by **100** to find the number of dollars. Obtain the remaining cents using the cents remainder **100**.

4. Divide the remaining cents by **25** to find the number of quarters. Obtain the remaining cents using the remaining cents remainder **25**.

5. Divide the remaining cents by **10** to find the number of dimes. Obtain the remaining cents using the remaining cents remainder **10**.

6. Divide the remaining cents by **5** to find the number of nickels. Obtain the remaining cents using the remaining cents remainder **5**.

7. The remaining cents are the pennies.

8. Display the result.

The complete program is given in Listing 2.10.

### LISTING 2.10   ComputeChange.cpp

```
1 #include <iostream>
2 using namespace std;
3
4 int main()
5 {
6    // Receive the amount
7    cout << "Enter an amount in double, for example 11.56: ";
```

```
 8   double amount;
 9   cin >> amount;
10
11   int remainingAmount = static_cast<int>(amount * 100);
12
13   // Find the number of one dollars
14   int numberOfOneDollars = remainingAmount / 100;          dollars
15   remainingAmount = remainingAmount % 100;
16
17   // Find the number of quarters in the remaining amount
18   int numberOfQuarters = remainingAmount / 25;             quarters
19   remainingAmount = remainingAmount % 25;
20
21   // Find the number of dimes in the remaining amount
22   int numberOfDimes = remainingAmount / 10;                dimes
23   remainingAmount = remainingAmount % 10;
24
25   // Find the number of nickels in the remaining amount
26   int numberOfNickels = remainingAmount / 5;               nickels
27   remainingAmount = remainingAmount % 5;
28
29   // Find the number of pennies in the remaining amount
30   int numberOfPennies = remainingAmount;                   pennies
31
32   // Display results
33   cout << "Your amount " << amount << " consists of \n" <<  display result
34     "\t" << numberOfOneDollars << " dollars\n" <<
35     "\t" << numberOfQuarters << " quarters\n" <<
36     "\t" << numberOfDimes << " dimes\n" <<
37     "\t" << numberOfNickels << " nickels\n" <<
38     "\t" << numberOfPennies << " pennies";
39
40   return 0;
41 }
```

```
Enter an amount in double, for example 11.56: 11.56  [↵ Enter]
Your amount 11.56 consists of
   11 dollars
   2 quarters
   0 dimes
   1 nickels
   1 pennies
```

The variable **amount** stores the amount entered from the keyboard (lines 7–9). This variable should not be changed because the amount has to be used at the end of the program to display the results. The program introduces the variable remainingAmount (line 11) to store the changing remainingAmount.

The variable **amount** is a **double** decimal representing dollars and cents. It is converted to an **int** variable remainingAmount, which represents all the cents. For instance, if **amount** is **11.56**, then the initial remainingAmount is **1156**. The division operator yields the integer part of the division. So **1156 / 100** is **11**. The remainder operator obtains the remainder of the division. So **1156 % 100** is **56**.

The program extracts the maximum number of singles from the total amount and obtains the remaining amount in the variable remainingAmount (lines 14–15). It then extracts the maximum number of quarters from remainingAmount and obtains a new

**remainingAmount** (lines 18–19). Continuing the same process, the program finds the maximum number of dimes, nickels, and pennies in the remaining amount.

One serious problem with this example is the possible *loss of precision* when casting a **double** amount to an **int remainingAmount**. This could lead to an inaccurate result. If you try to enter the amount **10.03, 10.03 * 100**, it becomes **1002.9999999999999**. You will find that the program displays **10** dollars and **2** pennies. To fix the problem, enter the amount as an as integer value representing cents (see Exercise 2.9).

As shown in the sample output, **0** dimes, **1** nickels, and **1** pennies are displayed in the result. It would be better not to display **0** dimes, and to display **1** nickel and **1** penny using the singular forms of the words. You will learn how to use selection statements to modify this program in the next chapter (see Exercise 3.4).

### 2.12.3 Example: Displaying the Current Time

This section presents a program that displays the current time in GMT (Greenwich Mean Time) in the format hour:minute:second, such as 13:19:8.

The **time(0)** function, in the **ctime** header file, returns the current time in seconds elapsed since the time 00:00:00 on January 1, 1970 GMT, as shown in Figure 2.1. This time is known as the *UNIX epoch* because 1970 was the year when the UNIX operating system was formally introduced.

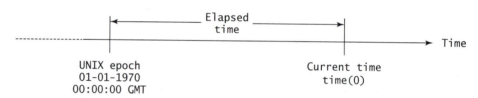

**FIGURE 2.1**  The **time(0)** returns the number of seconds since the UNIX epoch.

You can use this function to obtain the current time, and then compute the current second, minute, and hour as follows.

1. Obtain the total seconds since midnight, Jan 1, 1970 in **totalSeconds** by invoking **time(0)** (e.g., 1103203148 seconds).

2. Compute the current second from **totalSeconds % 60** (e.g., 1103203148 seconds % 60 = 8, which is the current second).

3. Obtain the total minutes **totalMinutes** by dividing **totalSeconds** by 60 (e.g., 1103203148 seconds / 60 = 18386719 minutes).

4. Compute the current minute from **totalMinutes % 60** (e.g., 18386719 minutes % 60 = 19, which is the current minute).

5. Obtain the total hours **totalHours** by dividing **totalMinutes** by 60 (e.g., 18386719 minutes / 60 = 306445 hours).

6. Compute the current hour from **totalHours % 24** (e.g., 306445 hours % 24 = 19, which is the current hour).

Listing 2.11 shows the complete program followed by a sample run.

### LISTING 2.11  ShowCurrentTime.cpp

```
1 #include <iostream>
2 #include <ctime>
3 using namespace std;
4
```

```
5  int main()
6  {
7    // Obtain the total seconds since the midnight, Jan 1, 1970
8    int totalSeconds = time(0);

10   // Compute the current second in the minute in the hour
11   int currentSecond = totalSeconds % 60;

13   // Obtain the total minutes
14   int totalMinutes = totalSeconds / 60;

16   // Compute the current minute in the hour
17   int currentMinute = totalMinutes % 60;

19   // Obtain the total hours
20   long totalHours = totalMinutes / 60;

22   // Compute the current hour
23   int currentHour = (int)(totalHours % 24);

25   // Display results
26   cout << "Current time is " << currentHour << ":"
27     << currentMinute << ":" << currentSecond << " GMT" << endl;

29   return 0;
30 }
```

totalSeconds

currentSecond

totalMinutes

currentMinute

totalHours

currentHour

preparing output

```
Current time is 13:19:8 GMT
```

When **time(0)** (line 8) is invoked, it returns the difference, measured in seconds, between the current GMT and midnight, January 1, 1970 GMT.

# 2.13 Programming Style and Documentation

*Programming style* deals with what programs look like. A program can compile and run properly even if written on only one line, but writing it all on one line would be bad programming style because it would be hard to read. *Documentation* is the body of explanatory remarks and comments pertaining to a program. Programming style and documentation are as important as coding. Good programming style and appropriate documentation reduce the chance of errors and make programs easy to read. So far you have learned some good programming styles. This section summarizes them and gives several guidelines. More detailed guidelines on programming style and documentation can be found in Supplement E, "C++ Coding Style Guidelines," on the Companion Website.

programming style

## 2.13.1 Appropriate Comments and Comment Styles

Include a summary at the beginning of the program to explain what the program does, its key features, its supporting data structures, and any unique techniques it uses. In a long program, you also should include comments that introduce each major step and explain anything that is difficult to read. It is important to make comments concise so that they do not crowd the program or make it difficult to read.

## 2.13.2 Naming Variables and Constants

Make sure that you choose descriptive names with straightforward meanings for the variables, constants, and functions in your program. Names are case-sensitive. Follow the conventions adopted in this book for naming variables and constants.

Avoid using abbreviation for identifiers. Using complete words is more descriptive. For example, **numberOfStudents** is better than **numStuds**, **numOfStuds**, or **numOfStudents**.

### 2.13.3 Proper Indentation and Spacing

indent code

A consistent indentation style makes programs clear and easy to read. *Indentation* is used to illustrate the structural relationships between a program's components or statements. C++ compiler can read the program even if all of the statements are in a straight line, but it is easier to read and maintain code that is aligned properly. Indent each subcomponent or statement *two* spaces more than the structure within which it is nested.

A single space should be added on both sides of a binary operator, as shown in the following statement:

```
int i = 3+4 * 4;     ◄────── Bad style

int i = 3 + 4 * 4;   ◄────── Good style
```

A single space line should be used to separate segments of the code to make the program easier to read.

## 2.14 Programming Errors

Programming errors are unavoidable, even for experienced programmers. Errors can be categorized into three types: syntax errors, runtime errors, and logic errors.

### 2.14.1 Syntax Errors

syntax error

Errors that occur during compilation are called *syntax errors* or *compilation errors*. Syntax errors result from errors in code construction, such as mistyping a keyword, omitting some necessary punctuation, or using an opening brace without a corresponding closing brace. These errors are usually easy to detect, because the compiler tells you where they are and what caused them. For example, compiling the following program results in a syntax error, as shown in Figure 2.2.

syntax error

```cpp
// ShowSyntaxErrors.cpp: The program contains syntax errors
#include <iostream>
using namespace std;

int main()
{
  i = 30;
  cout << i + 4;

  return 0;
}
```

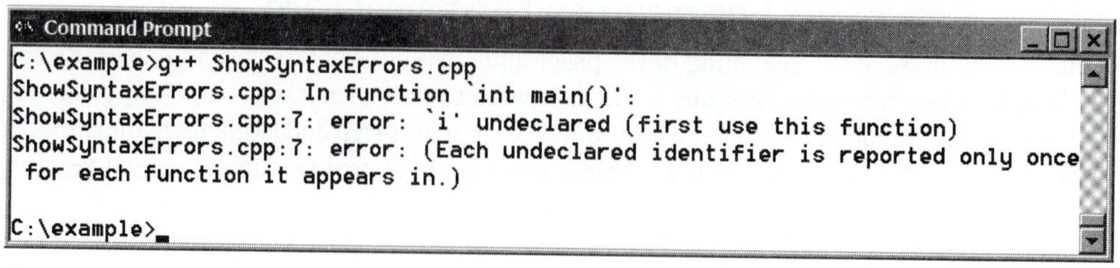

```
Command Prompt                                                    _ □ ×
C:\example>g++ ShowSyntaxErrors.cpp
ShowSyntaxErrors.cpp: In function `int main()':
ShowSyntaxErrors.cpp:7: error: `i' undeclared (first use this function)
ShowSyntaxErrors.cpp:7: error: (Each undeclared identifier is reported only once
 for each function it appears in.)

C:\example>_
```

**FIGURE 2.2** The compiler reports syntax errors.

Three lines of errors are reported. All are the result of not declaring variable **i**. Since a single error will often display many lines of compilation errors, it is a good practice to start debugging from the top line and work downward. Fixing errors that occur earlier in the program may also fix additional errors that occur later.

### 2.14.2   Runtime Errors

*Runtime errors* are errors that cause a program to terminate abnormally. Runtime errors occur while an application is running if the environment detects an operation that is impossible to carry out. Input errors are typical runtime errors.

An *input error* occurs when the user enters an unexpected input value that the program cannot handle. For instance, if the program expects to read in a number, but instead the user enters a string, this causes data-type errors to occur in the program. To prevent input errors, the program should prompt the user to enter the correct type of values. It may display a message like "Please enter an integer" before reading an integer from the keyboard.

*runtime errors*

### 2.14.3   Logic Errors

*Logic errors* occur when a program does not perform the way it was intended to. Errors of this kind occur for many different reasons. For example, suppose you wrote the following program to add **number1** to **number2**.

```cpp
// ShowLogicErrors.cpp: The program contains a logic error
#include <iostream>
using namespace std;

int main()
{
  int number1 = 3;
  int number2 = 3;
  number2 += number1 + number2;
  cout << "number2 is " << number2 << endl;

  return 0;
}
```

The program does not have syntax errors or runtime errors, but it does not print the correct result for **number2**. See if you can find the error.

## 2.15  Debugging

In general, syntax errors are easy to find and easy to correct because the compiler gives indications as to where the errors came from and why they are there. Runtime errors are not difficult to find either, since the operating system displays them on the console when the program aborts. Finding logic errors, on the other hand, can be very challenging.

Logic errors are called *bugs*. The process of finding and correcting errors is called *debugging*. A common approach to debugging is to use a combination of methods to narrow down to the part of the program where the bug is located. You can *hand-trace* the program (i.e., catch errors by reading the program), or you can insert print statements in order to show the values of the variables or the execution flow of the program. This approach might work for a short, simple program. But for a large, complex program, the most effective approach for debugging is to use a debugger utility.

*bugs*
*debugging*
*hand-traces*

The C++ IDE tools, such as Visual C++ and C++Builder, include integrated debuggers. The debugger utilities let you follow the execution of a program. They vary from one system to another, but they all support most of the following helpful features:

- **Executing a single statement at a time:** The debugger allows you to execute one statement at a time so that you can see the effect of each statement.

- **Tracing into or stepping over a function:** If a function is being executed, you can ask the debugger to enter the function and execute one statement at a time in the function, or you can ask it to step over the entire function. You should step over the entire function if you know that the function works. For example, always step over system-supplied functions, such as `pow(a, b)`.

- **Setting breakpoints:** You can also set a breakpoint at a specific statement. Your program pauses when it reaches a breakpoint and displays the line with the breakpoint. You can set as many breakpoints as you want. Breakpoints are particularly useful when you know where your programming error starts. You can set a breakpoint at that line and have the program execute until it reaches the breakpoint.

- **Displaying variables:** The debugger lets you select several variables and display their values. As you trace through a program, the content of a variable is continuously updated.

- **Displaying call stacks:** The debugger lets you trace all of the function calls and lists all pending functions. This feature is helpful when you need to see a large picture of the program-execution flow.

- **Modifying variables:** Some debuggers enable you to modify the value of a variable when debugging. This is convenient when you want to test a program with different samples but do not want to leave the debugger.

debugging in IDE

 **Tip**

If you use Microsoft Visual C++, please refer to Supplement II.B, "*Learning C++ Effectively with Microsoft Visual C++*," on the Companion Website. The supplement shows you how to use a debugger to trace programs and how debugging can help learning C++ effectively.

## KEY TERMS

## CHAPTER SUMMARY

■ C++ provides integer types (`short`, `int`, `long`, `unsigned short`, `unsigned int`, and `unsigned long`) that represent signed and unsigned integers of various sizes, and floating-point types (`float`, `double`, and `long double`) that represent floating-point numbers of various precisions. Character type (`char`) represents a single character. These are called primitive data types. When a variable is declared, it is assigned memory space. The actual sizes of these types are dependent on the compiler.

■ C++ provides operators that perform numeric operations: + (addition), − (subtraction), * (multiplication), / (division), and % (modulus). Integer division (/) yields an integer result. The modulus operator (%) yields the remainder of the division.

■ The increment operator (++) and the decrement operator (−−) increment or decrement a variable by 1. If the operator is prefixed to the variable, the variable is first incremented or decremented by 1, then used in the expression. If the operator is a suffix to the variable, the variable is incremented or decremented by 1, but then the original old value is used in the expression.

■ All the numeric operators can be applied to characters. When an operand is a character, the character's code value is used in the operation.

■ You can use casting to convert a value of one type into another type. Casting a variable of a type with a small range to a variable of a type with a larger range is known as *widening a type*. Casting a variable of a type with a large range to a variable of a type with a smaller range is known as *narrowing a type*. Narrowing a type may lose precision.

■ Programming errors can be categorized into three types: syntax errors, runtime errors, and logic errors. Errors that occur during compilation are called *syntax errors* or *compilation errors*. *Runtime errors* are errors that cause a program to terminate abnormally. *Logic errors* occur when a program does not perform the way it was intended to.

## REVIEW QUESTIONS

### Sections 2.2–2.8

**2.1** Which of the following identifiers are valid?

`x`, `X`, `a++`, `--a`, `4#R`, `$4`, `#44`, `apps`

**2.2** Which of the following are C++ keywords?

`main`, `include`, `int`, `x`, `y`, `radius`

**2.3** Translate the following pseudocode into C++ code:

■ Step 1: Declare a `double` variable named `miles` with initial value `100`;
■ Step 2: Declare a `double` constant named `MILE_TO_KILOMETER` with value `1.609`;
■ Step 3: Declare a `double` variable named `kilometer`, multiply `miles` and `MILE_TO_KILOMETER` and assign the result to `kilometer`.
■ Step 4: Display `kilometer` to the console.

**2.4** What are the benefits of using constants? Declare an `int` constant `SIZE` with value `20`.

### Section 2.9 Numeric Data Types and Operations

**2.5** Assume that `int a = 1` and `double d = 1.0`, and that each expression is independent. What are the results of the following expressions?

```
a = 46 / 9;
a = 46 % 9 + 4 * 4 - 2;
a = 45 + 43 % 5 * (23 * 3 % 2);
a %= 3 / a + 3;
d = 4 + d * d + 4;
d += 1.5 * 3 + (++a);
d -= 1.5 * 3 + a++;
```

**2.6** Show the result of the following expressions:

```
56 % 6
78 % -4
-34 % 5
-34 % -5
5 % 1
1 % 5
```

**2.7** Find the size of **short**, **int**, **long**, **float**, and **double** on your machine.

**2.8** What is the result of `25 / 4`? How would you rewrite the expression if you wished the result to be a floating-point number?

**2.9** Are the following statements correct? If so, show the output.

```
cout << "the output for 25 / 4 is " << 25 / 4 << endl;
cout << "the output for 25 / 4.0 is " << 25 / 4.0 << endl;
```

**2.10** How would you write the following arithmetic expression in C++?

$$\frac{4}{3(r + 34)} - 9(a + bc) + \frac{3 + d(2 + a)}{a + bd}$$

**2.11** Which of these statements are true?

A. Any expression can be used as a statement in C++.
B. The expression `x++` can be used as a statement.
C. The statement `x = x + 5` is also an expression.
D. The statement `x = y = x = 0` is illegal.

**2.12** Which of the following are correct literals for floating-point numbers?

`12.3`, `12.3e+2`, `23.4e-2`, `-334.4`, `20`, `39F`, `40D`

**2.13** Identify and fix the errors in the following code:

```
1 #include <iostream>
2 using namespace std;
3
4 int Main()
5 {
6     int i = k + 1;
7     cout << i++ << << endl;
8
9     int i = 1;
10    cout << i++ << << endl;
```

```
11
12   return 0;
13 }
```

## Section 2.10 Numeric Type Conversions

**2.14**   Can different types of numeric values be used together in a computation?

**2.15**   What does an explicit conversion from a **double** to an **int** do with the fractional part of the *double* value? Does casting change the variable being cast?

**2.16**   Show the following output:

```
double f = 12.5F;
int i = f;
cout << "f is " << f << endl;
cout << "i is " << i << endl;
```

## Section 2.11 Character Data Type and Operations

**2.17**   Use print statements to find out the ASCII code for '1', 'A', 'B', 'a', 'b'. Use print statements to find out the character for the decimal code 40, 59, 79, 85, 90. Use print statements to find out the character for the hexadecimal code *40, 5A, 71, 72, 7A*.

**2.18**   Which of the following are correct literals for characters?

```
'1', '\t', '&', '\b', '\n'
```

**2.19**   How do you display characters \ and "?

**2.20**   Evaluate the following:

```
int i = '1';
int j = '1' + '2';
int k = 'a';
char c = 90;
```

**2.21**   Can the following conversions involving casting be allowed? If so, find the converted result.

```
char c = 'A';
int i = c;

float f = 1000.34f;
int i = f;

double d = 1000.34;
int i = d;
int i = 97;
char c = i;
```

**2.22**   How do you obtain the current minute?

## Sections 2.13–2.15

**2.23**   How do you denote a comment line and a comment paragraph?

**2.24**   What are the naming conventions for constants and variables? Which of the following items can be a constant or a variable according to the naming conventions?

```
MAX_VALUE, Test, read, readInt
```

**2.25** Reformat the following program according to the programming style and documentation guidelines:

```cpp
#include <iostream>
using namespace std;

int main()
{
 cout << "2 % 3 = "<<2%3;
    return 0;
}
```

**2.26** Describe syntax errors, runtime errors, and logic errors.

## PROGRAMMING EXERCISES

### Note

Solutions to even-numbered exercises are on the Companion Website at www.cs.armstrong.edu/liang/cpp. Solutions to all exercises are on the Instructor Resource Website at www.prenhall.com/liang. The *level of difficulty* is rated easy (no star), moderate ($^*$), hard ($^{**}$), or challenging ($^{***}$).

### Debugging Tip

The compiler usually gives a reason for a syntax error. If you don't know how to correct it, compare your program closely with similar examples in the text character by character.

level of difficulty

learn from examples

### Sections 2.2–2.10

**2.1** (*Converting Celsius to Fahrenheit*) Write a program that reads a Celsius degree in double and converts it to Fahrenheit and displays the result. The formula for the conversion is as follows:

```
fahrenheit = (9 / 5) * celsius + 32
```

### Hint

In C++, **9 / 5** is **1**, so you need to write **9.0 / 5** in the program to obtain the correct result.

**2.2** (*Computing the volume of a cylinder*) Write a program that reads in the radius and length of a cylinder and computes volume using the following formulas:

```
area = radius * radius * π
volume = area * length
```

**2.3** (*Converting feet into meters*) Write a program that reads a number in feet, converts it to meters, and displays the result. One foot is **0.305** meters.

**2.4** (*Converting pounds into kilograms*) Write a program that converts pounds into kilograms. The program prompts the user to enter a number in pounds, converts it to kilograms, and displays the result. One pound is **0.454** kilograms.

**2.5**$^*$ (*Financial application: calculating tips*) Write a program that reads the subtotal and the gratuity rate, and computes the gratuity and total. For example, if the user enters **10** for subtotal and **15** percent for gratuity rate, the program displays **$1.5** as gratuity and **$11.5** as total.

**2.6**$^{**}$ (*Summing the digits in an integer*) Write a program that reads an integer between **0** and **1000** and adds all the digits in the integer. For example, if an integer is **932**, the sum of all its digits is **14**.

**Hint**
Use the % operator to extract digits, and use the / operator to remove the extracted digit. For instance, `932 % 10 = 2` and `932 / 10 = 93`.

## Section 2.11 Character Data Type and Operations

**2.7**\* (*Converting an uppercase letter to lowercase*) Write a program that converts an uppercase letter to a lowercase letter.

**Hint**
In the ASCII table (see Appendix B), uppercase letters appear before lowercase letters. The offset between any uppercase letter and its corresponding lowercase letter is the same. So you can find a lowercase letter from its corresponding uppercase letter, as follows:

```
int offset = 'a' - 'A';
char lowercase = uppercase + offset;
```

**2.8**\* (*Finding the character of an ASCII code*) Write a program that receives an ASCII code (an integer between 0 and 128) and displays its character. For example, if the user enters 97, the program displays character a.

## Section 2.12

**2.9**\* (*Financial application: monetary units*) Rewrite Listing 2.10, ComputeChange.cpp, to fix the possible loss of accuracy when converting a **double** value to an **int** value. Enter the input as an integer whose last two digits represent the cents. For example, the input 1156 represents 11 dollars and 56 cents.

**2.10**\* (*Financial application: calculating interests*) If you know the balance and annual percentage interest rate, you can compute the interest on the next monthly payment using the following formula:

```
interest = balance × (annualInterestRate / 1200)
```

Write a program that reads the balance and annual percentage interest rate and displays the interest for the next month.

**2.11**\* (*Financial application: calculating the future investment value*) Write a program that reads in investment amount, annual interest rate, and number of years, and displays the future investment value using the following formula:

```
accumulatedValue =
    investmentAmount x (1 + monthlyInterestRate)^{numberOfYears*12}
```

For example, if you entered amount 1000, annual interest rate 3.25%, and number of years 1, the future investment value is 1032.98.

**Hint**
Use the `pow(a, b)` function to compute a raised to the power of b.

**2.12**\*\* (*Financial application: compound value*) Suppose you save $100 *each* month into a savings account with the annual interest rate 5%. So, the monthly interest rate is 0.05 / 12 = 0.00417. After the first month, the value in the account becomes

```
100 * (1 + 0.00417) = 100.417
```

After the second month, the value in the account becomes,

    (100 + 100.417) * (1 + 0.00417) = 201.252

After the third month, the value in the account becomes,

    (100 + 201.252) * (1 + 0.00417) = 302.507

and so on.

Write a program to display the account value after the sixth month. (In Exercise 4.30, you will use a loop to simplify the code and display the account value for any month).

## CHAPTER 3

# SELECTION STATEMENTS

## Objectives

- To declare **bool** type and write Boolean expressions using comparison operators (§3.2).

- To implement selection control using simple **if** statements (§§3.3-3.4).

- To combine conditions using logical operators (**&&**, **||**, and **!**) (§3.5).

- To implement selection control using **if ... else** statements (§3.6).

- To implement selection control using nested **if** statements (§§3.7-3.9).

- To implement selection control using **switch** statements (§3.10).

- To write expressions using the conditional operator (§3.11).

- To display formatted output using the stream manipulators (§3.12).

- To know the rules governing operator precedence and operator associativity (§3.13).

- To declare an enumerated type for an ordered list of values (§3.14).

## 3.1 Introduction

In Chapter 2, "Primitive Data Types and Operations," if you assigned a negative value for **radius** in Listing 2.1, ComputeArea.cpp, the program would print an invalid result. If the radius is negative, you don't want the program to compute the area. Like all high-level programming languages, C++ provides selection statements that let you choose actions with two or more alternative courses. You can use selection statements in the following *pseudocode* (i.e., natural language mixed with programming code) to rewrite Listing 2.1:

```
if the radius is negative
    the program displays a message indicating a wrong input;
else
    the program computes the area and displays the result;
```

Selection statements use conditions. Conditions are Boolean expressions. This chapter first introduces Boolean types, values, operators, and expressions.

## 3.2 The **bool** Data Type

Often in a program you need to compare two values, such as whether **i** is greater than **j**. C++ provides six *relational operators* (also known as *comparison operators*) in Table 3.1 that can be used to compare two values.

**TABLE 3.1** Relational Operators

| Operator | Name | Example | Result |
|----------|------|---------|--------|
| < | Less than | 1 < 2 | true |
| <= | Less than or equal to | 1 <= 2 | true |
| > | Greater than | 1 > 2 | false |
| >= | Greater than or equal to | 1 >= 2 | false |
| == | Equal to | 1 == 2 | false |
| != | Not equal to | 1 != 2 | true |

**Note**

You can also *compare characters*. Comparing characters is the same as comparing the ASCII codes of the characters. For example, **'a'** is larger than **'A'** because the ASCII code of **'a'** is larger than the ASCII code of **'A'**.

**Caution**

The equality comparison operator is two equal signs (==), not a single equal sign (=). The latter symbol is for assignment.

The result of the comparison is a Boolean value: **true** or **false**. A variable that holds a Boolean value is known as a *Boolean variable*. The **bool** data type is used to declare Boolean variables. For example, the following statement assigns **true** to the variable **lightsOn**:

```
bool lightsOn = true;
```

Internally, C++ uses **1** to represent **true** and **0** for **false**. If you display a bool value to the console, **1** is printed if the value is **true** and **0** if the value is **false**.

For example,

```
cout << (1 < 2);
```

displays **1**, because **1 < 2** is **true**.

*(margin notes)* why selection? pseudocode • comparison operators • compare characters • == vs. = • Boolean variable

```
cout << (1 > 2);
```

displays 0, because 1 > 2 is **false**.

**Note**

In C++, you can assign a numeric value to a **bool** variable. Any nonzero value evaluates **true**
and zero value evaluates **false**. For example, after the following assignment statements, **b1** and
**b3** become **true**, and **b2** becomes **false**:

bool and numbers

```
bool b1 = -1.5; // b1 is true
bool b2 = 0; // b2 is false
bool b3 = 1.5; // b1 is true
```

## 3.3 **if** Statements

The programs that you have written so far execute in sequence. Often, however, you are faced
with situations in which you must provide alternative paths. C++ provides the **if** statements,
which can be used to control the execution path.

A simple **if** statement executes an action if and only if the condition is **true**. The syntax
for a simple **if** statement is shown below:

**if** statement

```
if (booleanExpression)
{
  statement(s);
}
```

The execution flow chart is shown in Figure 3.1(a).

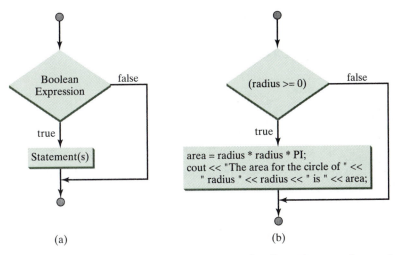

(a)　　　　(b)

**FIGURE 3.1**　An **if** statement executes statements if the **booleanExpression** evaluates to
**true**.

If the **booleanExpression** evaluates to **true**, the statements in the block are executed.
As an example, see the following code:

```
if (radius >= 0)
{
  area = radius * radius * PI;
  cout << "The area for the circle of " <<
    " radius " << radius << " is " << area;
}
```

The flow chart of the preceding statement is shown in Figure 3.1(b). If the value of **radius** is greater than or equal to **0**, then the **area** is computed and the result is displayed; otherwise, the two statements in the block will not be executed.

 **Note**

The **booleanExpression** is enclosed in parentheses. Thus, for example, the outer parentheses in the following **if** statements are required.

Outer parentheses required

Braces can be omitted if the block contains a single statement

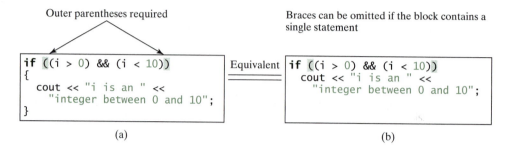

```
if ((i > 0) && (i < 10))
{
  cout << "i is an " <<
    "integer between 0 and 10";
}
```

(a)

Equivalent

```
if ((i > 0) && (i < 10))
  cout << "i is an " <<
    "integer between 0 and 10";
```

(b)

The braces can be omitted if they enclose a single statement.

 **Caution**

Forgetting the braces when they are needed for grouping multiple statements is a common programming error. If you modify the code by adding new statements in an **if** statement without braces, you will have to insert the braces if they are not already in place.

Listing 3.1 gives a program that checks whether a number is even or odd. The program prompts the user to enter an integer (line 9) and displays "number is even" if it is even (lines 11–12) and "number is odd" if it is odd (lines 14–15).

**LISTING 3.1** TestBoolean.cpp

```
1  #include <iostream>
2  using namespace std;
3
4  int main()
5  {
6    // Prompt the user to enter an integer
7    int number;
8    cout << "Enter an integer: ";
9    cin >> number;
10
11   if (number % 2 == 0)
12     cout << number << " is even.";
13
14   if (number % 2 != 0)
15     cout << number << " is odd.";
16
17   return 0;
18 }
```

enter input

check even

check odd

```
Enter an integer: 4  ↵Enter
4 is even.
```

```
Enter an integer: 5  ↵Enter
5 is odd.
```

**Caution**

Adding a semicolon at the end of an **if** clause, as shown in (a) in the following code, is a common mistake:

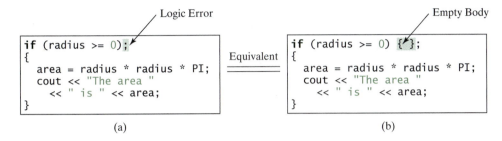

Logic Error    Empty Body

```
if (radius >= 0);
{
  area = radius * radius * PI;
  cout << "The area "
    << " is " << area;
}
```
(a)

Equivalent
═══════

```
if (radius >= 0) {};
{
  area = radius * radius * PI;
  cout << "The area "
    << " is " << area;
}
```
(b)

This mistake is hard to find, because it is neither a compilation error nor a runtime error; it is a logic error. The code in (a) is equivalent to (b) with an empty body.

## 3.4 Example: Guessing Birth Dates

This section uses the **if** statements to write an interesting game program. The program can find your birth date. The program prompts you to answer whether your birth date is in the following five sets of numbers:

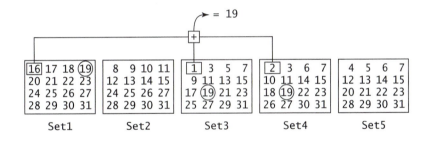

= 19

| Set1 | Set2 | Set3 | Set4 | Set5 |

Your birth date is the sum of the first numbers in the sets where your birth date appears. For example, if your birth date is **19**, it appears in Set1, Set3, and Set4. The first numbers in these three sets are **16**, **1**, and **2**. Their summation is **19**.

Listing 3.2 gives a program that prompts the user to answer whether the date is in Set1 (lines 10–16), in Set2 (lines 22–28), in Set3 (lines 34–40), in Set4 (lines 46–52), and in Set5 (lines 58–64). The program adds the first number in the set to **date** (lines 19, 31, 43, 55, 67) if the number is in the set.

### LISTING 3.2  GuessBirthDate.cpp

```
1 #include <iostream>
2 using namespace std;
3
4 char main()
5 {
6   int date = 0; // Date to be determined
7   char answer;
8
9   // Prompt the user for Set1
10   cout << "Is your birth date in Set1?" << endl;
11   cout << "16 17 18 19\n" <<
12          "20 21 22 23\n" <<
```

date to be determined

```
13              "24 25 26 27\n" <<
14              "28 29 30 31" << endl;
15      cout << "Enter N for No and Y for Yes: ";
16      cin >> answer;
17
```

in Set1?
```
18      if (answer == 'Y')
19        date += 16;
20
21      // Prompt the user for Set2
22      cout << "\nIs your birth date in Set2?" << endl;
23      cout << " 8  9 10 11\n" <<
24              "12 13 14 15\n" <<
25              "24 25 26 27\n" <<
26              "28 29 30 31"   << endl;
27      cout << "Enter N for No and Y for Yes: ";
28      cin >> answer;
29
```

in Set2?
```
30      if (answer == 'Y')
31        date += 8;
32
33      // Prompt the user for Set3
34      cout << "\nIs your birth date in Set3?" << endl;
35      cout << " 1  3  5  7\n" <<
36              " 9 11 13 15\n" <<
37              "17 19 21 23\n" <<
38              "25 27 29 31" << endl;
39      cout << "Enter N for No and Y for Yes: ";
40      cin >> answer;
41
```

in Set3?
```
42      if (answer == 'Y')
43        date += 1;
44
45      // Prompt the user for Set4
46      cout << "\nIs your birth date in Set4?" << endl;
47      cout << " 2  3  6  7\n" <<
48              "10 11 14 15\n" <<
49              "18 19 22 23\n" <<
50              "26 27 30 31" << endl;
51      cout << "Enter N for No and Y for Yes: ";
52      cin >> answer;
53
```

in Set4?
```
54      if (answer == 'Y')
55        date += 2;
56
57      // Prompt the user for Set5
58      cout << "\nIs your birth date in Set5?" << endl;
59      cout << " 4  5  6  7\n" <<
60              "12 13 14 15\n" <<
61              "20 21 22 23\n" <<
62              "28 29 30 31" << endl;
63      cout << "Enter N for No and Y for Yes: ";
64      cin >> answer;
65
```

in Set5?
```
66      if (answer == 'Y')
67        date += 4;
68
69      cout << "Your birth date is " << date << endl;
70
71      return 0;
72 }
```

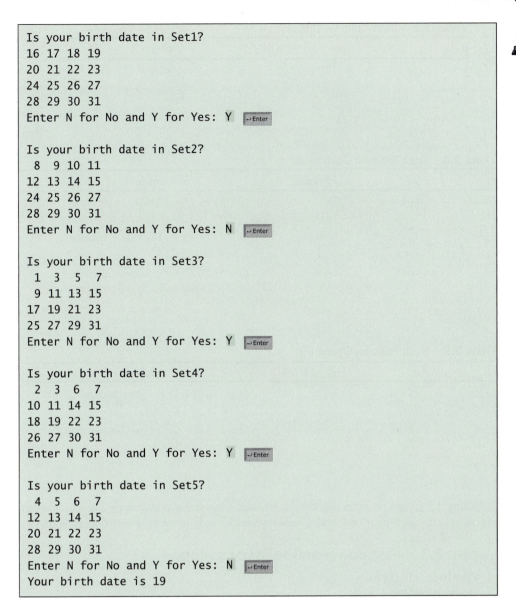

```
Is your birth date in Set1?
16 17 18 19
20 21 22 23
24 25 26 27
28 29 30 31
Enter N for No and Y for Yes: Y  ⏎Enter

Is your birth date in Set2?
 8  9 10 11
12 13 14 15
24 25 26 27
28 29 30 31
Enter N for No and Y for Yes: N  ⏎Enter

Is your birth date in Set3?
 1  3  5  7
 9 11 13 15
17 19 21 23
25 27 29 31
Enter N for No and Y for Yes: Y  ⏎Enter

Is your birth date in Set4?
 2  3  6  7
10 11 14 15
18 19 22 23
26 27 30 31
Enter N for No and Y for Yes: Y  ⏎Enter

Is your birth date in Set5?
 4  5  6  7
12 13 14 15
20 21 22 23
28 29 30 31
Enter N for No and Y for Yes: N  ⏎Enter
Your birth date is 19
```

## 3.5 Logical Operators

Sometimes, the execution path is determined by a combination of several conditions. You can use logical operators to combine these conditions. *Logical operators*, also known as *Boolean operators*, operate on Boolean values to create a new Boolean value. Table 3.2 contains a list of Boolean operators. Table 3.3 defines the not ( ! ) operator. The not ( ! ) operator negates **true** to **false** and **false** to **true**. Table 3.4 defines the and (**&&**) operator. The and (**&&**) of two Boolean operands is **true** if and only if both operands are **true**. Table 3.5 defines the **or** (|) operator. The **or** (|) of two Boolean operands is **true** if at least one of the operands is **true**.

**TABLE 3.2** Boolean Operators

| Operator | Name | Description |
|----------|------|-------------|
| ! | not | logical negation |
| && | and | logical conjunction |
| \|\| | or | logical disjunction |

**TABLE 3.3** Truth Table for Operator !

| p | !p | Example |
|---|---|---|
| true | false | !(1 > 2) is true, because (1 > 2) is false. |
| false | true | !(1 > 0) is false, because (1 > 0) is true. |

**TABLE 3.4** Truth Table for Operator &&

| p1 | p2 | p1 && p2 | Example |
|---|---|---|---|
| false | false | false | (2 > 3) && (5 > 5) is false, because |
| false | true | false | either (2 > 3) or (5 > 5) is false. |
| true | false | false | (3 > 2) && (5 > 5) is false, because |
| | | | (5 > 5) is false. |
| true | true | true | (3 > 2) && (5 >= 5) is true, because |
| | | | (3 > 2) and (5 >= 5) are both true. |

**TABLE 3.5** Truth Table for Operator ||

| p1 | p2 | p1 || p2 | Example |
|---|---|---|---|
| false | false | false | (2 > 3) || (5 > 5) is false, because (2 > 3) |
| false | true | true | and (5 > 5) are both false. |
| true | false | true | (3 > 2) || (5 > 5) is true, because (3 > 2) |
| true | true | true | is true. |

Listing 3.3 gives a program that checks whether a number is divisible by 2 and 3, whether a number is divisible by 2 or 3, and whether a number is divisible by 2 or 3 but not both.

**LISTING 3.3** TestBooleanOperators.cpp

```
1  #include <iostream>
2  using namespace std;
3
4  int main()
5  {
6    int number;
7    cout << "Enter an integer: ";
8    cin >> number;
9
10   if (number % 2 == 0 && number % 3 == 0)
11     cout << number << " is divisible by 2 and 3." << endl;
12
13   if (number % 2 == 0 || number % 3 == 0)
14     cout << number << " is divisible by 2 or 3." << endl;
15
16   if ((number % 2 == 0 || number % 3 == 0) &&
17       !(number % 2 == 0 && number % 3 == 0))
18     cout << number << " divisible by 2 or 3, but not both." << endl;
19
20   return 0;
21 }
```

enter input

&&

||

```
Enter an integer: 4  ↵Enter
4 is divisible by 2 or 3.4
divisible by 2 or 3, but not both.
```

```
Enter an integer: 18  ↵Enter
18 is divisible by 2 and 3.
18 is divisible by 2 or 3.
```

**(number % 2 == 0 && number % 3 == 0)** (line 10) checks whether the number is divisible by 2 and 3. **(number % 2 == 0 || number % 3 == 0)** (line 13) checks whether the number is divisible by 2 or 3. So, lines 16–17

```
((number % 2 == 0 || number % 3 == 0) &&
  !(number % 2 == 0 && number % 3 == 0))
```

check whether the number is divisible by **2** or **3**, but not both.

### Note

*De Morgan's law*, named after Indian-born British mathematician and logician Augustus De Morgan (1806–1871), can be used to simplify Boolean expressions. The law states

De Morgan's law

```
!(condition1 && condition2) is same as !condition1 || !condition2
!(condition1 || condition2) is same as !condition1 && !condition2
```

So, line 17 in the preceding example,

```
!(number % 2 == 0 && number % 3 == 0)
```

can be simplified using an equivalent expression

```
(number % 2 != 0 || number % 3 != 0)
```

As another example,

```
!(n == 2 || n == 3)
```

is better written as

```
n != 2 && n != 3
```

If one of the operands of an **&&** operator is **false**, the expression is **false**; if one of the operands of an **||** operator is **true**, the expression is **true**. C++ uses these properties to improve the performance of these operators.

When evaluating **p1 && p2**, C++ first evaluates **p1** and then evaluates **p2** if **p1** is **true**; if **p1** is **false**, it does not evaluate **p2**. When evaluating **p1 || p2**, C++ first evaluates **p1** and then evaluates **p2** if **p1** is **false**; if **p1** is **true**, it does not evaluate **p2**. Therefore, **&&** is referred to as the *conditional* or *short-circuit AND* operator, and **||** is referred to as the *conditional* or *short-circuit OR* operator.

short-circuit operator

### Caution

In mathematics, you can write the condition

```
x < y < z
```

x < y < z?

But, in C++ you have to write

```
(x < y) && (y < z)
```

If you write **(x < y < z)** in C++, C++ first evaluates **(x < y)** to a Boolean value and then this Boolean value is compared with **z**, which would lead to a logic error.

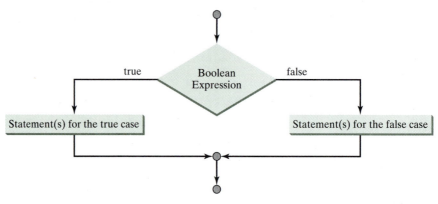

**Note**

C++ also supports the bitwise **&** and **|** operators. See Appendix D, "Bit Manipulations," for details.

## 3.6 `if . . . else` Statements

A simple **if** statement takes an action if the specified condition is **true**. If the condition is **false**, nothing is done. But what if you want to take alternative actions when the condition is **false**? You can use an **if . . . else** statement. The actions that an **if . . . else** statement specifies differ based on whether the condition is **true** or **false**.

Here is the syntax for this type of statement:

```
if (booleanExpression)
{
  statement(s)-for-the-true-case;
}
else
{
  statement(s)-for-the-false-case;
}
```

The flow chart of the statement is shown in Figure 3.2.

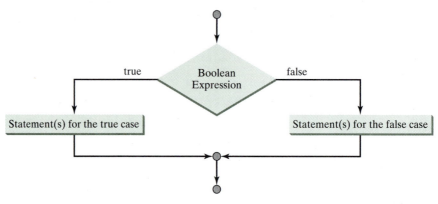

**FIGURE 3.2** An `if . . . else` statement executes statements for the **true** case if the **booleanExpression** evaluates to **true**; otherwise, statements for the **false** case are exe-

If the **booleanExpression** evaluates to **true**, the **statement(s)** for the true case is executed; otherwise, the **statement(s)** for the false case is executed. For example, consider the following code:

```
if (radius >= 0)
{
  area = radius * radius * PI;
  cout << "The area for the circle of radius " <<
    radius << " is " << area;
}
else
{
  cout << "Negative radius";
}
```

If **radius >= 0** is **true**, **area** is computed and displayed; if it is **false**, the message **"Negative radius"** is printed.

As usual, the braces can be omitted if there is only one statement within them. The braces enclosing the `cout << "Negative radius"` statement can therefore be omitted in the preceding example.

Using the `if ... else` statement, you can rewrite the code for determining whether a number is even or odd in Listing 3.1, as follows:

```
if (number % 2 == 0)
  cout << number << " is even.";
else
  cout << number << " is odd.";
```

This is more efficient because whether `number % 2` is `0` is tested only once.

Listing 3.4 presents a program that lets the user enter a year and checks whether it is a leap year.

A year is a *leap year* if it is divisible by `4` but not by `100` or if it is divisible by `400`. So you can use the following Boolean expression to check whether a year is a leap year:

leap year

```
(year % 4 == 0 && year % 100 != 0) || (year % 400 == 0)
```

## LISTING 3.4  LeapYear.cpp

```
1 #include <iostream>
2 using namespace std;
3
4 int main()
5 {
6   cout << "Enter a year: ";
7   int year;
8   cin >> year;
9
10  // Check if the year is a leap year
11  bool isLeapYear =                                    leap year?
12    (year % 4 == 0 && year % 100 != 0) || (year % 400 == 0);
13
14  // Display the result
15  if (isLeapYear)                                      if statement
16    cout << year << " is a leap year.";
17  else
18    cout << year << " is not a leap year.";
19
20  return 0;
21 }
```

```
Enter a year: 2008  ⏎Enter
2008 is a leap year.
```

```
Enter a year: 2002  ⏎Enter
2002 is not a leap year.
```

## 3.7 Nested **if** Statements

The statement in an `if` or `if ... else` statement can be any legal C++ statement, including another `if` or `if ... else` statement. The inner `if` statement is said to be *nested* inside the outer `if` statement. The inner `if` statement can contain another `if` statement; in fact, there is no limit to the depth of the nesting. For example, the following is a *nested* `if` statement:

nested `if` statement

```
if (i > k)
{
  if (j > k)
    cout << "i and j are greater than k";
}
else
  cout << "i is less than or equal to k";
```

The `if (j > k)` statement is nested inside the `if (i > k)` statement.

The nested `if` statement can be used to implement multiple alternatives. The statement given in Figure 3.3(a), for instance, assigns a letter grade to the variable **grade** according to the score, with multiple alternatives.

```
if (score >= 90.0)
   grade = 'A';
else
  if (score >= 80.0)
    grade = 'B';
  else
    if (score >= 70.0)
      grade = 'C';
    else
      if (score >= 60.0)
        grade = 'D';
      else
        grade = 'F';
```
(a)

Equivalent
═══════
This is better

```
if (score >= 90.0)
   grade = 'A';
else if (score >= 80.0)
   grade = 'B';
else if (score >= 70.0)
   grade = 'C';
else if (score >= 60.0)
   grade = 'D';
else
   grade = 'F';
```
(b)

**FIGURE 3.3** A preferred format for multiple alternative `if` statements is shown in (b).

The execution of this `if` statement proceeds as follows. The first condition **(score >= 90.0)** is tested. If it is **true**, the grade becomes **'A'**. If it is **false**, the second condition **(score >= 80.0)** is tested. If the second condition is **true**, the grade becomes **'B'**. If that condition is **false**, the third condition and the rest of the conditions (if necessary) continue to be tested until a condition is met or all of the conditions prove to be **false**. If all of the conditions are **false**, the grade becomes **'F'**. Note that a condition is tested only when all of the conditions that come before it are **false**.

The `if` statement in Figure 3.3(a) is equivalent to the `if` statement in Figure 3.3(b). In fact, Figure 3.3(b) is the preferred writing style for multiple alternative `if` statements. This style avoids deep indentation and makes the program easy to read.

 **Note**

matching **else** with **if**

The **else** clause matches the most recent unmatched `if` clause in the same block. For example, the following statement in (a) is equivalent to the statement in (b):

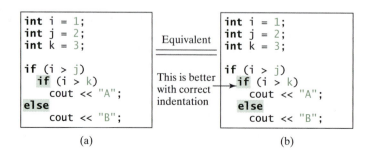

```
int i = 1;
int j = 2;
int k = 3;

if (i > j)
  if (i > k)
    cout << "A";
else
    cout << "B";
```
(a)

Equivalent
═══════
This is better
with correct
indentation

```
int i = 1;
int j = 2;
int k = 3;

if (i > j)
  if (i > k)
    cout << "A";
  else
    cout << "B";
```
(b)

The compiler ignores indentation. Nothing is printed from the statement in (a) and (b). To force the **else** clause to match the first **if** clause, you must add a pair of braces:

```
int i = 1; int j = 2; int k = 3;
if (i > j)
{
  if (i > k)
    cout << "A";
}
else
  cout << "B";
```

This statement prints **B**.

### Tip

Often new programmers write the code that assigns a test condition to a **bool** variable like the code in (a):

assign **bool** variable

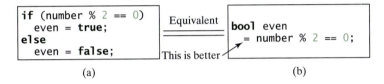

```
if (number % 2 == 0)
    even = true;
else
    even = false;
```
(a)

Equivalent
_____
This is better

```
bool even
    = number % 2 == 0;
```
(b)

The code can be simplified by assigning the test value directly to the variable, as shown in (b).

### Caution

To test whether a **bool** variable is **true** or **false** in a test condition, it is redundant to use the equality comparison operator like the code in (a):

test **bool** value

```
if (even == true)
    cout << "It is even.";
```
(a)

Equivalent
_____
This is better

```
if (even)
    cout << "It is even.";
```
(b)

Instead, it is better to use the **bool** variable directly, as shown in (b). Another good reason to use the **bool** variable directly is to avoid errors that are difficult to detect. Using the = operator instead of the == operator to compare equality of two items in a test condition is a common error. It could lead to the following erroneous statement:

```
if (even = true)
    cout << "It is even.";
```

This statement does not have syntax errors. It assigns **true** to **even** so that **even** is always **true**.

### Tip

If you use Visual C++, please refer to Supplement II.B, "*Learning C++ Effectively with Visual C++*" on the Companion Website. This supplement shows you how to use a debugger to trace a simple if–else statement.

debugging in IDE

## 3.8 Example: Computing Taxes

This section uses nested **if** statements to write a program to compute personal income taxes. The United States federal personal income tax is calculated based on filing status and taxable income. There are four filing statuses: single filers, married filing jointly, married filing separately, and head of household. The tax rates for 2002 are shown in Table 3.6. If you are, say, single with a taxable income of $10,000, the first $6,000 is taxed at 10% and the other $4,000 is taxed at 15%. So your tax is $1,200.

**TABLE 3.6** 2002 U.S. Federal Personal Tax Rates

| Tax Rate | Single Filers | Married Filing Jointly or Qualifying Widow/Widower | Married Filing Separately | Head of Household |
|---|---|---|---|---|
| 10% | Up to $6,000 | Up to $12,000 | Up to $6,000 | Up to $10,000 |
| 15% | $6,001–$27,950 | $12,001–$46,700 | $6,001–$23,350 | $10,001–$37,450 |
| 27% | $27,951–$67,700 | $46,701–$112,850 | $23,351–$56,425 | $37,451–$96,700 |
| 30% | $67,701–$141,250 | $112,851–$171,950 | $56,426–$85,975 | $96,701–$156,600 |
| 35% | $141,251–$307,050 | $171,951–$307,050 | $85,976–$153,525 | $156,601–$307,050 |
| 38.6% | $307,051 or more | $307,051 or more | $153,526 or more | $307,051 or more |

Your program should prompt the user to enter the filing status and taxable income and computes the tax for the year 2002. Enter 0 for single filers, 1 for married filing jointly, 2 for married filing separately, and 3 for head of household.

Your program computes the tax for the taxable income based on the filing status. The filing status can be determined using `if` statements outlined as follows:

```
if (status == 0)
{
  // Compute tax for single filers
}
else if (status == 1)
{
  // Compute tax for married file jointly
}
else if (status == 2)
{
  // Compute tax for married file separately
}
else if (status == 3)
{
  // Compute tax for head of household
}
else
{
  // Display wrong status
}
```

For each filing status, there are six tax rates. Each rate is applied to a certain amount of taxable income. For example, of a taxable income of $400,000 for single filers, $6,000 is taxed at 10%, (27950 − 6000) at 15%, (67700 − 27950) at 27%, (141250 − 67700) at 35%, and (400000 − 307050) at 38.6%.

Listing 3.5 gives the solution to compute taxes for single filers. The complete solution is left as an exercise.

**LISTING 3.5** ComputeTaxWithSelectionStatement.cpp

```
1 #include <iostream>
2 using namespace std;
3
4 int main()
5 {
6   // Prompt the user to enter filing status
7   cout << "Enter the filing status\n"
8        << "(0-single filer, 1-married jointly,\n"
```

```
 9         << "2-married separately, 3-head of household): ";
10    int status;
11    cin >> status;                                                enter status
12
13    // Prompt the user to enter taxable income
14    cout << "Enter the taxable income: ";
15    double income;
16    cin >> income;                                                enter income
17
18    // Compute tax
19    double tax = 0;                                               compute tax
20
21    if (status == 0)
22    {
23      // Compute tax for single filers
24      if (income <= 6000)
25        tax = income * 0.10;
26      else if (income <= 27950)
27        tax = 6000 * 0.10 + (income - 6000) * 0.15;
28      else if (income <= 67700)
29        tax = 6000 * 0.10 + (27950 - 6000) * 0.15 +
30          (income - 27950) * 0.27;
31      else if (income <= 141250)
32        tax = 6000 * 0.10 + (27950 - 6000) * 0.15 +
33          (67700 - 27950) * 0.27 + (income - 67700) * 0.30;
34      else if (income <= 307050)
35        tax = 6000 * 0.10 + (27950 - 6000) * 0.15 +
36          (67700 - 27950) * 0.27 + (141250 - 67700) * 0.30 +
37          (income - 141250) * 0.35;
38      else
39        tax = 6000 * 0.10 + (27950 - 6000) * 0.15 +
40          (67700 - 27950) * 0.27 + (141250 - 67700) * 0.30 +
41          (307050 - 141250) * 0.35 + (income - 307050) * 0.386;
42    }
43    else if (status == 1)
44    {
45      // Compute tax for married file jointly
46      // Left as exercise
47    }
48    else if (status == 2)
49    {
50      // Compute tax for married separately
51      // Left as exercise
52    }
53    else if (status == 3)
54    {
55      // Compute tax for head of household
56      // Left as exercise
57    }
58    else
59    {
60      cout << "Error: invalid status";
61      return 0;
62    }
63
64    // Display the result
65    cout << "Tax is " << static_cast<int>(tax * 100) / 100.0 << endl;    display tax
66
67    return 0;
68 }
```

```
Enter the filing status
(0-single filer, 1-married jointly,
2-married separately, 3-head of household): 0  ⏎Enter
Enter the taxable income: 400000  ⏎Enter
Tax is 130599
```

The program receives the filing status and taxable income. The multiple alternative **if** statements (lines 21, 43, 48, 53, 58) check the filing status and compute the tax based on the filing status.

## 3.9 Example: A Math Learning Tool

This example creates a program for a first grader to practice subtractions. The program randomly generates two single-digit integers **number1** and **number2** with **number1 > number2** and displays a question such as "What is 9−2?" to the student, as shown in the sample output. After the student types the answer, the program displays a message to indicate whether the answer is correct.

**rand** function

To generate a random number, use the **rand()** function in the **cstdlib** header file. This function returns a random positive integer. In fact, the numbers produced by **rand()** are pseudorandom, i.e., it produces the same sequence of numbers every time it is executed on the same system. For example, executing these three statements will get the same numbers 130, 10982, and 1090 every time on my machine.

```
cout << rand() << endl;
cout << rand() << endl;
cout << rand() << endl;
```

**srand** function

Why? The reason is that the algorithm used by the **rand()** function uses a value called the *seed* to control how to generate the numbers. By default the seed value is **1**. If you change the seed to a different value, the sequence of random numbers will be different. To change the seed, use the **srand(seed)** function in the **cstdlib** header file. To ensure that the seed value is different each time you run the program, use **time(0)**. As discussed in §2.12.3, "Example: Displaying the Current Time," invoking **time(0)** returns the current time in seconds elapsed since the time 00:00:00 on January 1, 1970 GMT. So, the following code will display a random integer every second you run it on any machine:

```
srand(time(0));
cout << rand() << endl;
```

To obtain a random integer between **0** and **9**, use

```
rand() % 10
```

The program may work as follows:

- **Step 1:** Generate two single-digit integers into **number1** and **number2**.

- **Step 2:** If **number1 < number2**, swap **number1** with **number2**.

- **Step 3:** Prompt the student to answer "what is number1−number2?"

- **Step 4:** Check the student's answer and display whether the answer is correct.

The complete program is shown in Listing 3.6.

**LISTING 3.6** SubtractionTutor.cpp

```
 1 #include <iostream>
 2 #include <ctime> // For time function
 3 #include <cstdlib> // For rand and srand functions
 4 using namespace std;
 5
 6 int main()
 7 {
 8   // 1. Generate two random single-digit integers
 9   srand(time(0));
10   int number1 = rand() % 10;
11   int number2 = rand() % 10;
12
13   // 2. If number1 < number2, swap number1 with number2
14   if (number1 < number2)
15   {
16     int temp = number1;
17     number1 = number2;
18     number2 = temp;
19   }
20
21   // 3. Prompt the student to answer "what is number1 - number2?"
22   cout << "What is " << number1 << " - " << number2 << "? ";
23   int answer;
24   cin >> answer;
25
26   // 4. Grade the answer and display the result
27   if (number1 - number2 == answer)
28     cout << "You are correct!";
29   else
30     cout << "Your answer is wrong.\n" << number1 << " - " << number2
31       << " should be " << (number1 - number2) << endl;
32
33   return 0;
34 }
```

include **ctime**
include **cstdlib**

set a seed
random number1
random number2

swap numbers

enter answer

display result

```
What is 5 - 2? 3  ⏎Enter
You are correct!
```

```
What is 4 - 2? 1  ⏎Enter
Your answer is wrong.
4 - 2 should be 2
```

To swap two variables **number1** and **number2**, a temporary variable **temp** (line 16) is used to first hold the value in **number1**. The value in **number2** is assigned to **number1** (line 17) and the value in **temp** is assigned to **number2** (line 18).

## 3.10 **switch** Statements

The **if** statement in Listing 3.5 makes selections based on a single **true** or **false** condition. There are four cases for computing taxes, which depend on the value of **status**. To fully account for all the cases, nested **if** statements were used. Overuse of nested **if** statements makes a program difficult to read. C++ provides a **switch** statement to handle multiple conditions efficiently. You could write the following **switch** statement to replace the nested **if** statement in Listing 3.5:

```
switch (status)
{
  case 0:   compute taxes for single filers;
            break;
  case 1:   compute taxes for married file jointly;
            break;
  case 2:   compute taxes for married file separately;
            break;
  case 3:   compute taxes for head of household;
            break;
  default:  cout << "Errors: invalid status" << endl;
}
```

The flow chart of the preceding `switch` statement is shown in Figure 3.4.

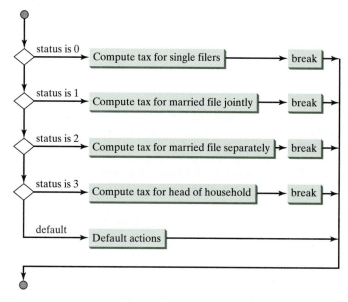

**FIGURE 3.4** The `switch` statement checks all cases and executes the statements in the matched case.

This statement checks to see whether the status matches the value 0, 1, 2, or 3, in that order. If matched, the corresponding tax is computed; if not matched, a message is displayed. Here is the full syntax for the `switch` statement:

`switch` statement

```
switch (switch-expression)
{
  case value1:  statement(s)1;
                break;
  case value2:  statement(s)2;
                break;
  ...
  case valueN:  statement(s)N;
                break;
  default:      statement(s)-for-default;
}
```

The `switch` statement observes the following rules:

■ The **switch-expression** must yield an integral value, and must always be enclosed in parentheses.

- The `value1`, ..., and `valueN` are integral constant expressions, meaning that they cannot contain variables in the expression, such as 1 + x.

- When the value in a `case` statement matches the value of the `switch-expression`, the statements *starting from this case* are executed until either a `break` statement or the end of the switch statement is reached.

- The keyword `break` is optional. The `break` statement immediately ends the `switch` statement.

- The `default` case, which is optional, can be used to perform actions when none of the specified cases matches the `switch-expression`.

- The `case` statements are checked in sequential order, but the order of the cases (including the default case) does not matter. However, it is good programming style to follow the logical sequence of the cases and place the default case at the end.

### Note

In C++, a `char` or `bool` value is treated as an integral. So, this type of value can be used in a switch statement as a switch expression or case value.

integral value

### Caution

Do not forget to use a `break` statement when one is needed. Once a case is matched, the statements starting from the matched case are executed until a `break` statement or the end of the `switch` statement is reached. This phenomenon is referred to as the *fall-through behavior*. For example, the following code prints character **a** three times if ch is `'a'`:

without **break**

fall-through behavior

```
switch (ch) {
  case 'a' : cout << ch;
  case 'b' : cout << ch;
  case 'c' : cout << ch;
}
```

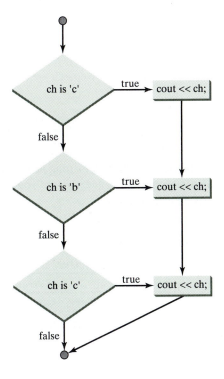

### Tip

To avoid programming errors and improve code maintainability, it is a good idea to put a comment in a case clause if `break` is purposely omitted.

## 3.11 Conditional Expressions

You might want to assign a value to a variable that is restricted by certain conditions. For example, the following statement assigns **1** to **y** if **x** is greater than **0**, and **−1** to **y** if **x** is less than or equal to **0**:

```
if (x > 0)
  y = 1;
else
  y = -1;
```

Alternatively, as in this example, you can use a conditional expression to achieve the same result:

```
y = (x > 0) ? 1 : -1;
```

Conditional expressions are in a completely different style, with no explicit **if** in the statement. The syntax is shown next:

```
booleanExpression ? expression1 : expression2;
```

conditional expression

The result of this *conditional expression* is **expression1** if **booleanExpression** is **true**; otherwise the result is **expression2**.

Suppose you want to assign the larger number between variable **num1** and **num2** to **max**. You can simply write a statement using the conditional expression:

```
max = (num1 > num2) ? num1 : num2;
```

For another example, the following statement displays the message "num is even" if **num** is even, and otherwise displays "num is odd:"

```
cout << ((num % 2 == 0) ? "num is even" : "num is odd");
```

 **Note**

The symbols **?** and **:** appear together in a conditional expression. They form a conditional operator. This operator is called a *ternary operator* because it uses three operands. It is the only ternary operator in C++.

## 3.12 Formatting Output

You already know how to display console output using the **std::cout** object. C++ provides additional functions for formatting how a value is printed. These functions are called *stream manipulators* and are included in the **iomanip** header file. Table 3.7 summarizes several useful stream manipulators.

stream manipulator

**TABLE 3.7** Frequently Used Stream Manipulator

| Operator | Description |
|---|---|
| setw(width) | Specifies the width of a print field |
| setprecision(n) | Sets the precision of a floating-point number |
| fixed | Displays floating-point numbers in fixed-point notation |
| showpoint | Causes a floating-point number to be displayed with a decimal point with trailing zeros even if it has no fractional part |
| left | Justifies the output to the left |
| right | Justifies the output to the right |

By default, **cout** uses just the number of the positions needed for an output. You can use **setw(width)** to specify the minimum number of positions for an output. For example, the statements

setw(width) manipulator

```cpp
cout << setw(8) << "C++" << setw(6) << 101 << endl;
cout << setw(8) << "Java" << setw(6) << 101 << endl;
cout << setw(8) << "HTML" << setw(6) << 101 << endl;
```

display

| 8 characters | 6 characters |
|---|---|
| C++ | 101 |
| Java | 101 |
| HTML | 101 |

In line 1, **set(8)** specifies that "C++" is printed in eight position. So, there are five spaces before C++. **set(6)** specifies that 101 is printed in six position. So, there are three spaces before 101.

You can specify the total number of digits printed for a floating-point number using the **setprecision(n)** manipulator, where **n** is the total number of digits that appear before and after the decimal point. If a number to be displayed has more digits than the specified precision, the number will be rounded. For example, the statement

setprecision(n) manipulator

```cpp
double number = 12.34567;
cout << setw(10) << setprecision(5) << number;
cout << setw(10) << setprecision(4) << number;
cout << setw(10) << setprecision(3) << number;
cout << setw(10) << setprecision(8) << number;
```

displays

| 10 characters | 10 characters | 10 characters | 10 characters |
|---|---|---|---|
| 12.346 | 12.35 | 12.3 | 12.34567 |

The first value is displayed with the precision **5**. So, **12.34567** is rounded to **12.346**. The second value is displayed with the precision **4**. So, **12.34567** is rounded to **12.35**. The second value is displayed with the precision **3**. So, **12.34567** is rounded to **12.3**. The precision for the last value is set to **8**, which is more than the number of the digits in **12.3457**. In this case, the precision manipulator has no effect.

**Note**

Unlike the **setw** manipulator, the **setprecision** manipulator remains in effect until it is changed to a new precision. So,

```cpp
double number = 12.34567;
cout << setw(10) << setprecision(3) << number;
cout << setw(10) << number;
cout << setw(10) << number;
```

displays

| 10 characters | 10 characters | 10 characters |
|---|---|---|
| 12.3 | 12.3 | 12.3 |

The precision is set to **3** for the first value, and it remains effective for the subsequent two values, because it has not been changed.

`fixed` manipulator

Sometimes, the computer automatically displays a large floating-point number in scientific notation. For example, on my Windows machine, the statement

```
cout << 232123434.357;
```

displays

```
      10
   characters
┌─────────────┬──────────────────────────────────────────────┐
│ 2.32123e+08 │                                              │
└─────────────┴──────────────────────────────────────────────┘
```

You can use the `fixed` manipulator to force the number to be displayed in non-scientific notation with a fixed number of digits after the decimal point. For example, the statement

```
cout << fixed << 232123434.357;
```

displays

```
      10
   characters
┌──────────────────┬─────────────────────────────────────────┐
│ 232123434.357000 │                                         │
└──────────────────┴─────────────────────────────────────────┘
```

By default, the fixed number of digits after the decimal point is 6. You can change it using the `fixed` manipulator along with the `setprecision` manipulator. When the `setprecision` manipulator is used after the `fixed` manipulator, the `setprecision` manipulator specifies the number of digits after the decimal point. For example, the following statements

```
double monthlyPayment = 345.4567;
double totalPayment = 78676.887234;
cout << fixed << setprecision(2);
cout << setw(10) << monthlyPayment << endl;
cout << setw(10) << totalPayment << endl;
```

display

```
      10
   characters
┌─────────────┬──────────────────────────────────────────────┐
│      345.46 │                                              │
│    78676.89 │                                              │
└─────────────┴──────────────────────────────────────────────┘
```

The `setprecision(2)` manipulator after `fixed` manipulator specifies that the precision after the decimal point is 2. So, `monthlyPayment` is displayed as `345.46` and `totalPayment` is displayed as `78676.90`. Once the `fixed` manipulator is used, it is applied to all subsequent floating-point numbers to be displayed.

By default, floating-point numbers that do not have a fractional part are not displayed with a decimal point. You can use the `fixed` manipulator to force the floating-point numbers to be displayed with a decimal point and a fixed number of digits after the decimal point. Alternatively, you can use the `showpoint` manipulator together with the `setprecision` manipulator.

`showpoint` manipulator

For example, the following statements

```
cout << setprecision(6);
cout << 1.23 << endl;
cout << showpoint << 1.23 << endl;
cout << showpoint << 123.0 << endl;
```

display

| 10 characters |
|---|

```
1.23
1.23000
123.000
```

The `setprecision(6)` function sets the precision to `6`. So, the first number `1.23` is displayed as `1.23`. Because the `showpoint` manipulator forces the floating-point number to be displayed with a decimal point and trailing zeros if necessary to fill in the positions, the second number `1.23` is displayed as `1.23000` with a trailing zero, and the third number `123.0` is displayed as `123.000` with a decimal point and trailing zero.

You can use the `left` manipulator to left-justify the output and use the `right` manipulator to right-justify the output. On most systems, the default justification is right. For example,

**left** manipulator
**right** manipulator

```
cout << right;
cout << setw(8) << 1.23 << endl;
cout << setw(8) << 351.34 << endl;
```

display

| 8 characters |
|---|

```
    1.23
351.34
```

```
cout << left;
cout << setw(8) << 1.23 << endl;
cout << setw(8) << 351.34 << endl;
```

display

| 8 characters |
|---|

```
1.23
351.34
```

## 3.13 Operator Precedence and Associativity

Operator precedence and associativity determine the order in which operators are evaluated. Suppose that you have this expression:

```
3 + 4 * 4 > 5 * (4 + 3) - 1
```

What is its value? How does the compiler know the execution order of the operators? The expression in the parentheses is evaluated first. (Parentheses can be nested, in which case the expression in the inner parentheses is executed first.) When evaluating an expression without parentheses, the operators are applied according to the *precedence* rule and the associativity rule. The precedence rule defines precedence for operators, as shown in Table 3.8, which contains the operators you have learned so far. Operators are listed in decreasing order of precedence from top to bottom. Operators with the same precedence appear in the same group. (See Appendix C, "Operator Precedence Chart," for a complete list of C++ operators and their precedence.)

precedence

**TABLE 3.8** Operator Precedence Chart

| Precedence | Operator |
|---|---|
| | **var++** and **var−−** (postfix), **static_cast<type>()** (cast) |
| | +, − (Unary plus and minus), **++var** and **−−var** (prefix) |
| | **!** (Not) |
| | *, /, % (Multiplication, division, and modulus) |
| | +, − (Binary addition and subtraction) |
| | <, <=, >, >= (Comparison) |
| | ==, != (Equality) |
| | **&&** (AND) |
| | **||** (OR) |
| | =, +=, −=, *=, /=, %= (Assignment operator) |

associativity

If operators with the same precedence are next to each other, their *associativity* determines the order of evaluation. All binary operators except assignment operators are *left-associative*. For example, since + and − are of the same precedence and are left-associative, the expression

$$a - b + c - d \quad \overset{equivalent}{=\!=\!=\!=} \quad ((a - b) + c) - d$$

Assignment operators are *right-associative*. Therefore, the expression

$$a = b += c = 5 \quad \overset{equivalent}{=\!=\!=\!=} \quad a = (b += (c = 5))$$

Suppose **a**, **b**, and **c** are **1** before the assignment; after the whole expression is evaluated, **a** becomes **6**, **b** becomes **6**, and **c** becomes **5**. Note that left associativity for the assignment operator would not make sense.

Applying the operator precedence and associativity rule, the expression **3 + 4 * 4 > 5 * (4 + 3) − 1** is evaluated as follows:

```
3 + 4 * 4 > 5 * (4 + 3) − 1
                                   ──── (1) inside parentheses first
3 + 4 * 4 > 5 * 7 − 1
                                   ──── (2) multiplication
3 + 16 > 5 * 7 − 1
                                   ──── (3) multiplication
3 + 16 > 35 − 1
                                   ──── (4) addition
19 > 35 − 1
                                   ──── (5) subtraction
19 > 34
                                   ──── (6) greater than
false
```

**Tip**

You can use parentheses to force an evaluation order as well as to make a program easy to read. Use of redundant parentheses does not slow down the execution of the expression.

# 3.14 Enumerated Types

You have used numeric type, **char** type, and **bool** type to declare variables. C++ enables you to declare your own type, known as *enumerated type*, using the **enum** keyword. For example,

```
enum Day {MONDAY, TUESDAY, WEDNESDAY, THURSDAY, FRIDAY};
```

declares an enumerated type named **Day** with possible values **MONDAY**, **TUESDAY**, **WEDNESDAY**, **THURSDAY**, and **FRIDAY** in this order.

*define enumerated type*

An enumerated type defines a list of enumerated values. Each value is an identifier, not a string. The identifiers are known to the program once they are declared in the type.

By convention, an enumerated type is named with the first letter of each word capitalized and a value of an enumerated type is named like a constant with all uppercase letters.

*naming convention*

Once a type is defined, you can declare a variable of that type:

```
Day day;
```

The variable **day** can hold one of the values defined in the enumerated type. For example, the following statement assigns enumerated value **MONDAY** to variable **day**:

```
day = MONDAY;
```

As with any other type, you can declare and initialize a variable in one statement:

```
Day day = MONDAY;
```

Furthermore, C++ allows you to declare an enumerated type and variable in one statement. For example,

```
enum Day {MONDAY, TUESDAY, WEDNESDAY, THURSDAY, FRIDAY} day = MONDAY;
```

 **Caution**

An enumerated value can not be redeclared. For example, the following code would cause a syntax error:

*declare only once*

```
enum Day {MONDAY, TUESDAY, WEDNESDAY, THURSDAY, FRIDAY};
const int MONDAY = 0; // Error: MONDAY already declared.
```

An enumerated variable holds a value. Often your program needs to perform a specific action depending on the value. For example, if the value is **MONDAY**, play soccer; if the value is **TUESDAY**, take piano lesson, and so on. You can use an **if** statement or a **switch** statement to test the value in the variable, as shown in (a) and (b).

```
if (day == MONDAY)
{
    // process Monday
}
else if (day == TUESDAY)
{
    // process Tuesday
}
else
    ...
```

Equivalent

```
switch (day)
{
    case MONDAY:
        // process Monday
        break;
    case TUESDAY:
        // process Tuesday
        break;
    ...
}
```

(a)                                        (b)

integers

Enumerated values are stored as *integers* in memory. By default, the values correspond to 0, 1, 2, ..., in the order of their appearance in the list. So, MONDAY, TUESDAY, WEDNESDAY, THURSDAY, and FRIDAY correspond to the integer values 0, 1, 2, 3, and 4. You can explicitly assign an enumerated value with any integer value. For example,

```
enum Color {RED = 20, GREEN = 30, BLUE = 40};
```

RED has an integer value 20, GREEN 30, and BLUE 40.

If you assign integer values for some values in the enumerated type declaration, the other values will receive default values. For example,

```
enum City {PARIS, LONDON, DALLAS = 30, HOUSTON};
```

PARIS will be assigned 0, LONDON 1, DALLAS 30, and HOUSTON 31.

You can assign an enumerated value to an integer variable. For example,

```
int i = PARIS;
```

This assigns 0 to i.

comparing values

Enumerated values can be compared on their assigned integer values using the six comparison operators. For example, (PARIS < LONDON) yields true.

Listing 3.7 gives an example of using enumerated types.

## LISTING 3.7 TestEnumeratedType.cpp

```
 1 #include <iostream>
 2 using namespace std;
 3
 4 int main()
 5 {
 6   enum Day {MONDAY = 1, TUESDAY, WEDNESDAY, THURSDAY, FRIDAY} day;
 7
 8   cout << "Enter a day (1 for Monday, 2 for Tuesday, etc): ";
 9   int dayNumber;
10   cin >> dayNumber;
11
12   switch (dayNumber) {
13     case MONDAY:
14       cout << "Play soccer" << endl;
15       break;
16     case TUESDAY:
17       cout << "Piano lesson" << endl;
18       break;
19     case WEDNESDAY:
20       cout << "Math team" << endl;
21       break;
22     default:
23       cout << "Go home" << endl;
24   }
25
26   return 0;
27 }
```

declare enumerated type (line 6)

enter an integer (line 10)

check values (line 12)

```
Enter a day (1 for Monday, 2 for Tuesday, etc): 1 ↵Enter
Play soccer
```

```
Enter a day (1 for Monday, 2 for Tuesday, etc): 4  ⏎Enter
Go home
```

Line 6 declares an enumerated type **Day** and declares a variable named **day** in one statement. Line 10 reads an **int** value from the keyboard. The **switch** statement in lines 12–24 checks whether day is MONDAY, TUESDAY, WEDNESDAY, or others to display a message accordingly.

## KEY TERMS

| | |
|---|---|
| Boolean expression    68 | fall-through behavior    85 |
| Boolean value    68 | if statement    69 |
| **bool** type    68 | operator associativity    89 |
| **break** statement    84 | operator precedence    89 |
| conditional operator    86 | short-circuit operator    75 |
| enumerated type    91 | switch statement    83 |

## CHAPTER SUMMARY

■  The relational operators (`<`, `<=`, `==`, `!=`, `>`, `>=`) work with numbers and characters and yield a Boolean value. The Boolean operators **&&**, **||**, and **!** operate with Boolean values and variables.

■  When evaluating **p1 && p2**, C++ first evaluates **p1** and then evaluates **p2** if **p1** is **true**; if **p1** is **false**, it does not evaluate **p2**. When evaluating **p1 || p2**, C++ first evaluates **p1** and then evaluates **p2** if **p1** is **false**; if **p1** is **true**, it does not evaluate **p2**.

■  Selection statements are used for building selection steps into programs. There are several types of selection statements: **if** statements, **if . . . else** statements, nested **if** statements, **switch** statements, and conditional expressions.

■  The various **if** statements all make control decisions based on a Boolean expression. Based on the **true** or **false** evaluation of that expression, these statements take one of two possible courses.

■  The **switch** statement makes control decisions based on a switch expression of type **char**, **byte**, **short**, or **int**.

■  The keyword **break** is optional in a switch statement, but it normally is used at the end of each case in order to terminate the remainder of the **switch** statement. If the **break** statement is not present, the next **case** statement will be executed.

■  The operators in arithmetic expressions are evaluated in the order determined by the rules of parentheses, operator precedence, and associativity.

■  Parentheses can be used to force the order of evaluation to occur in any sequence. Operators with higher precedence are evaluated earlier. The associativity of the operators determines the order of evaluation for operators of the same precedence.

■  All binary operators except assignment operators are left-associative, and assignment operators are right-associative.

## REVIEW QUESTIONS

### Section 3.2 The **bool** Data Type

**3.1**     List six comparison operators.

**3.2**     Assume that x is 1, show the result of the following Boolean expressions:

```
(x > 0)
(x < 0)
(x != 0)
(x >= 0)
(x != 1)
```

### Section 3.3 **if** Statements

**3.3**     What is wrong in the following code?

```
if radius >= 0
{
  area = radius * radius * PI;
  cout << "The area for the circle of " <<
    " radius " << radius << " is " << area;
}
```

### Section 3.5 Logical Operators

**3.4**     Assume that x is 1, show the result of the following Boolean expressions:

```
(true) && (3 > 4)
!(x > 0) && (x > 0)
(x > 0) || (x < 0)
(x != 0) || (x == 0)
(x >= 0) || (x < 0)
(x != 1) == !(x == 1)
```

**3.5**     Write a Boolean expression that evaluates to **true** if a number stored in variable num is between 1 and 100.

**3.6**     Write a Boolean expression that evaluates to **true** if a number stored in variable num is between 1 and 100 or the number is negative.

**3.7**     Assume that x and y are **int** type. Which of the following are correct expressions?

```
x > y > 0
x = y && y
x /= y
x or y
x and y
(x != 0) || (x = 0)
```

**3.8**     Can the following conversions involving casting be allowed? If so, find the converted result.

```
bool b = true;
int i = b;

i = 1;
b = i;
```

**3.9**     Suppose that x is 1. What is x after the evaluation of the following expression?

```
(x > 1) && (x++ > 1)
```

**3.10**    Show the output of the following program:

```cpp
#include <iostream>
using namespace std;

int main()
{
  char x = 'a';
  char y = 'c';

  cout << ++x << endl;
  cout << y++ << endl;
  cout << (x > y) << endl;
  cout << (x - y) << endl;

  return 0;
}
```

## Section 3.7 Nested **if** Statements

**3.11**    Suppose x = 3 and y = 2, show the output, if any, of the following code. What is the output if x = 3 and y = 4? What is the output if x = 2 and y = 2? Draw a flowchart of the following code:

```cpp
if (x > 2)
{
  if (y > 2)
  {
    int z = x + y;
    cout << "z is " << z << endl;
  }
}
else
  cout << "x is " << x << endl;
```

**3.12**    Which of the following statements are equivalent? Which ones are correctly indented?

| | | | |
|---|---|---|---|
| ```if (i > 0) if``` <br> ```(j > 0)``` <br> ```x = 0; else``` <br> ```if (k > 0) y = 0;``` <br> ```else z = 0;``` | ```if (i > 0) {``` <br> ```  if (j > 0)``` <br> ```    x = 0;``` <br> ```  else if (k > 0)``` <br> ```    y = 0;``` <br> ```}``` <br> ```else``` <br> ```  z = 0;``` | ```if (i > 0)``` <br> ```  if (j > 0)``` <br> ```    x = 0;``` <br> ```  else if (k > 0)``` <br> ```    y = 0;``` <br> ```  else``` <br> ```    z = 0;``` | ```if (i > 0)``` <br> ```  if (j > 0)``` <br> ```    x = 0;``` <br> ```  else if (k > 0)``` <br> ```    y = 0;``` <br> ```else``` <br> ```  z = 0;``` |
| (a) | (b) | (c) | (d) |

**3.13**    Suppose x = 2 and y = 3, show the output, if any, of the following code. What is the output if x = 3 and y = 2? What is the output if x = 3 and y = 3? (Hint: please indent the statement correctly first.)

```cpp
if (x > 2)
  if (y > 2)
  {
    int z = x + y;
    cout << "z is " << z << endl;
  }
```

```
   else
      cout << "x is " << x << endl;
```

**3.14** Are the following two statements equivalent?

```
if (income <= 10000)
   tax = income * 0.1;
else if (income <= 20000)
   tax = 1000 +
      (income - 10000) * 0.15;
```

```
if (income <= 10000)
   tax = income * 0.1;
else if (income > 10000 &&
         income <= 20000)
   tax = 1000 +
      (income - 10000) * 0.15;
```

**3.15** Which of the following is a possible output from invoking **rand()**?

323.4, 5, 34, 1, 0.5, 0.234

**3.16** How do you generate a random integer $i$ such that $0 \le i < 20$?
How do you generate a random integer $i$ such that $10 \le i < 20$?
How do you generate a random integer $i$ such that $10 \le i \le 50$?

### Section 3.10 **switch** Statements

**3.17** What data types are required for a **switch** variable? If the keyword **break** is not used after a case is processed, what is the next statement to be executed? Can you convert a **switch** statement to an equivalent **if** statement, or vice versa? What are the advantages of using a **switch** statement?

**3.18** What is **y** after the following **switch** statement is executed?

```
x = 3; y = 3;
switch (x + 3)
{
   case 6:  y = 1;
   default: y += 1;
}
```

**3.19** Use a **switch** statement to rewrite the following **if** statement and draw the flow-chart for the **switch** statement:

```
if (a == 1)
   x += 5;
else if (a == 2)
   x += 10;
else if (a == 3)
   x += 16;
else if (a == 4)
   x += 34;
```

### Section 3.11 Conditional Expressions

**3.20** Rewrite the following **if** statement using the conditional operator:

```
if (count % 10 == 0)
   cout << count << "\n";
else
   cout << count << " ";
```

### Section 3.12 Formatting Output

**3.21** To use stream manipulators, which header file must be included?

**3.22** Show the output of the following statements:

```
cout << setw(10) << "C++" << setw(6) << 101 << endl;
cout << setw(8) << "Java" << setw(5) << 101 << endl;
cout << setw(6) << "HTML" << setw(4) << 101 << endl;
```

**3.23**   Show the output of the following statements:

```
double number = 93123.1234567;
cout << setw(10) << setprecision(5) << number;
cout << setw(10) << setprecision(4) << number;
cout << setw(10) << setprecision(3) << number;
cout << setw(10) << setprecision(8) << number;
```

**3.24**   Show the output of the following statements:

```
double x = 1345.4567;
double y = 866.887234;
cout << fixed << setprecision(2);
cout << setw(8) << monthlyPayment << endl;
cout << setw(8) << totalPayment << endl;
```

**3.25**   Show the output of the following statements:

```
cout << right;
cout << setw(6) << 21.23 << endl;
cout << setw(6) << 51.34 << endl;
```

**3.26**   Show the output of the following statements:

```
cout << left;
cout << setw(6) << 21.23 << endl;
cout << setw(6) << 51.34 << endl;
```

## Section 3.13 Operator Precedence and Associativity

**3.27**   List the precedence order of the Boolean operators. Evaluate the following expressions:

```
true || true && false
true && true || false
```

**3.28**   Show and explain the output of the following code:

```
a. int i = 0;
   i = i + (i = 1);
   cout << i << endl;
```

```
b. int i = 0;
   i = (i = 1) + i;
   cout << i << endl;
```

**3.29**   Assume that `int a = 1` and `double d = 1.0`, and that each expression is independent. What are the results of the following expressions?

```
a = (a = 3) + a;
a = a + (a = 3);
a += a + (a = 3);
a = 5 + 5 * 2 % a--;
a = 4 + 1 + 4 * 5 % (++a + 1);
d += 1.5 * 3 + (++d);
d -= 1.5 * 3 + d++;
```

## PROGRAMMING EXERCISES

**Pedagogical Note**

think before coding

For each exercise, students should carefully analyze the problem requirements and design strategies for solving the problem before coding.

**Pedagogical Note**

document analysis and design

Instructors may ask students to *document analysis and design* for selected exercises. Students should use their own words to analyze the problem including the input, output, and what needs to be computed and describe how to solve the problem using pseudo code.

**Debugging Tip**

learn from mistakes

Before you ask for help, read and explain the program to yourself, and trace it using several representative input by hand or using an IDE debugger. You learn how to program from debugging your own mistakes.

### Sections 3.2–3.3

**3.1** (*Validating triangles*) Write a program that reads three edges for a triangle and determines whether the input is valid. The input is valid if the sum of any two edges is greater than the third edge. Here are the sample runs of this program:

```
Enter three edges: 1 2 1 ⏎Enter
Can edges 1, 2, and 1 form a triangle? false
```

```
Enter three edges: 2 2 1 ⏎Enter
Can edges 2, 2, and 1 form a triangle? true
```

**3.2** (*Checking whether a number is even*) Write a program that reads an integer and checks whether it is even. For example, if your input is **25**, the output should be:

```
Enter an integer: 25 ⏎Enter
Is 25 an even number? false
```

```
Enter an integer: 2000 ⏎Enter
Is 2000 an even number? true
```

**3.3** (*Using the **&&** and **||** operators*) Write a program that prompts the user to enter an integer and determines whether it is divisible by **5** and **6**, whether it is divisible by **5** or **6**, and whether it is divisible by **5** or **6**, but not both. Here is a sample runs of this program:

```
Enter an integer: 10 ⏎Enter
Is 10 divisible by 5 and 6? false
Is 10 divisible by 5 or 6? true
Is 10 divisible by 5 or 6, but not both? true
```

### Sections 3.4–3.9

**3.4**   (*Financial application: monetary units*) Modify Listing 2.10, ComputeChange.cpp, to display the non-zero denominations only, using singular words for single units like 1 dollar and 1 penny, and plural words for more than one unit like 2 dollars and 3 pennies. (Use **23.67** to test your program.)

**3.5**\*   (*Sorting three integers*) Write a program that sorts three integers. The integers are entered from the console and stored in variables **num1**, **num2**, and **num3**, respectively. The program sorts the numbers so that $num1 \leq num2 \leq num3$.

**3.6**   (*Computing the perimeter of a triangle*) Write a program that reads three edges for a triangle and computes the perimeter if the input is valid. Otherwise, display that the input is invalid. The input is valid if the sum of any two edges is greater than the third edge (also see Exercise 3.1).

**3.7**   (*Financial application: computing taxes*) Listing 3.5 gives the source code to compute taxes for single filers. Complete Listing 3.5 to give the complete source code.

**3.8**   (*Finding the number of days in a month*) Write a program that prompts the user to enter the month and year and displays the number of days in the month. For example, if the user entered month 2 and year 2000, the program should display that February 2000 has 29 days. If the user entered month 3 and year 2005, the program should display that March 2005 has 31 days.

**3.9**\*   (*Game: addition tutor*) Listing 3.6, SubtractionTutor.cpp, randomly generates a subtraction question. Revise the program to randomly generate an addition question with two integers less than **100**.

**3.10**\*   (*Game: addition for three numbers*) Listing 3.6, SubtractionTutor.cpp, randomly generates a subtraction question. Revise the program to randomly generate an addition question with three integers less than **100**.

# CHAPTER 4

# LOOPS

## Objectives

- To use `while`, `do-while`, and `for` loops to execute statements repeatedly (§§4.2–4.4).

- To understand the flow of control in loops (§§4.2–4.4).

- To use Boolean expressions to control loops (§§4.2–4.4).

- To know the similarities and differences of three types of loops (§4.5).

- To write nested loops (§§4.6–4.7).

- (Optional) To implement program control with `break` and `continue` (§§4.8–4.9).

- (Optional) To read and write data from/to a file (§4.10).

## 4.1 Introduction

Suppose that you need to print a string (e.g., `"Welcome to C++!"`) a hundred times. It would be tedious to have to write the following statement a hundred times:

```
cout << "Welcome to C++!\n";
```

why loop?

C++ provides a powerful control structure called a *loop,* which controls how many times an operation or a sequence of operations is performed in succession. Using a loop statement, you simply tell the computer to print a string a hundred times without having to code the print statement a hundred times.

Loops are structures that control repeated executions of a block of statements. The concept of looping is fundamental to programming. C++ provides three types of loop statements: `while` loops, `do-while` loops, and `for` loops.

## 4.2 The `while` Loop

**while** loop

The syntax for the `while` loop is as follows:

```
while (loop-continuation-condition)
{
  // Loop body
  Statement(s);
}
```

loop body
iteration

The `while` loop flow chart is shown in Figure 4.1(a). The part of the loop that contains the statements to be repeated is called the *loop body.* A one-time execution of a loop body is referred to as an *iteration of the loop.* Each loop contains a `loop-continuation-condition`, a Boolean expression that controls the execution of the body. It is always evaluated before the loop body is executed. If its evaluation is true, the loop body is executed; if its evaluation is false, the entire loop terminates and the program control turns to the statement that follows the `while` loop. For example, the following `while` loop prints `Welcome to C++!` a hundred times.

```
int count = 0;
while (count < 100)
{
  cout << "Welcome to C++!\n";
  count++;
}
```

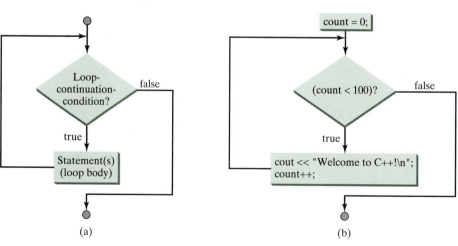

(a)                                                   (b)

**FIGURE 4.1**    The `while` loop repeatedly executes the statements in the loop body when the `loop-continuation-condition` evaluates to `true`.

The flow chart of the preceding statement is shown in Figure 4.1(b). The variable **count** is initially **0**. The loop checks whether **(count < 100)** is **true**. If so, it executes the loop body to print the message **Welcome to C++!** and increments count by **1**. It repeatedly executes the loop body until **(count < 100)** becomes **false**. When **(count < 100)** is **false** (i.e., when count reaches **100**), the loop terminates and the next statement after the loop statement is executed.

**Note**

The **loop-continuation-condition** must always appear inside the parentheses. The braces enclosing the loop body can be omitted only if the loop body contains one or no statement.

**Caution**

Make sure that the **loop-continuation-condition** eventually becomes **false** so that the program will terminate. A common programming error involves *infinite loops*. That is, the program cannot terminate because of a mistake in the **loop-continuation-condition**. For instance, if you forgot to increase **count** (i.e., **count++**) in the code, the program would not stop. To terminate the program, close the command window if you run from Visual C++.

infinite loop

**Tip**

If you use Visual C++, please refer to Supplement II B, "*Learning C++ Effectively with Visual C++*" on the Companion Website. This supplement shows you how to use a debugger to trace a simple loop statement.

debugging in IDE

## 4.2.1 Example: An Improved Math Learning Tool

The math subtraction tutor program in Listing 3.6, SubtractionTutor.cpp, generates just one question for each run. You can use a loop to generate questions repeatedly. Listing 4.1 gives a program that generates ten questions and reports the number of the correct answers after a student answers all ten questions. The program also displays the time spent on the test, as shown in sample output.

**LISTING 4.1   SubtractionTutorLoop.cpp**

```
 1 #include <iostream>
 2 #include <ctime> // for time function
 3 #include <cmath> // for the srand and rand functions
 4 using namespace std;
 5
 6 int main()
 7 {
 8   int correctCount = 0; // Count the number of correct answers
 9   int count = 0; // Count the number of questions
10   long startTime = time(0);
11
12   while (count < 10)
13   {
14     // 1. Generate two random single-digit integers
15     srand(time(0));
16     int number1 = rand() % 10;
17     int number2 = rand() % 10;
18
19     // 2. If number1 < number2, swap number1 with number2
20     if (number1 < number2)
21     {
22       int temp = number1;
23       number1 = number2;
24       number2 = temp;
25     }
26
```

correct count
total count
get start time

loop

display a question

grade an answer

increase correct count

increase control variable

get end time
test time

display result

```
27      // 3. Prompt the student to answer "what is number1 - number2?"
28      cout << "What is " << number1 << " - " << number2 << "? ";
29      int answer;
30      cin >> answer;
31
32      // 4. Grade the answer and display the result
33      if (number1 - number2 == answer) {
34        cout << "You are correct!\n";
35        correctCount++;
36      }
37      else
38        cout << "Your answer is wrong.\n" << number1 << " - " <<
39          number2 << " should be " << (number1 - number2) << endl;
40
41      // Increase the count
42      count++;
43    }
44
45    long endTime = time(0);
46    long testTime = endTime - startTime;
47
48    cout << "Correct count is " << correctCount << "\nTest time is "
49        << testTime << " seconds\n";
50
51    return 0;
52  }
```

```
What is 1 - 1? 0 ⏎Enter
You are correct!

What is 7 - 2? 5 ⏎Enter
You are correct!

What is 9 - 3? 4 ⏎Enter
Your answer is wrong.
9 - 3 should be 6

What is 6 - 6? 0 ⏎Enter
You are correct!

What is 9 - 6? 2 ⏎Enter
Your answer is wrong.
9 - 6 should be 3

What is 9 - 7? 2 ⏎Enter
You are correct!

What is 0 - 0? 1 ⏎Enter
Your answer is wrong.
0 - 0 should be 0

What is 6 - 5? 1 ⏎Enter
You are correct!
```

```
What is 5 - 4? 1 ⏎Enter
You are correct!

What is 0 - 0? 0 ⏎Enter
You are correct!

Correct count is 7
Test time is 58 seconds
```

The program uses the control variable `count` to control the execution of the loop. `count` is initially `0` (line 9) and is increased by `1` in each iteration (line 42). A subtraction question is displayed and processed in each iteration. The program obtains the time before the test starts in line 10, the time after the test ends in line 45, and computes the test time in line 46.

## 4.2.2  Controlling a Loop with User Confirmation

The preceding example executes the loop ten times. Suppose you want the user to decide whether to take another question, you can let the uses control the loop with a user *confirmation*. The template of the program can be coded as follows:

confirmation

```cpp
char continueLoop = 'Y';
while (continueLoop == 'Y')
{
  // Execute body once

  // Prompt the user for confirmation
  cout << "Enter Y to continue and N to quit: ";
  cin >> continueLoop;
}
```

You can rewrite Listing 4.1 with user confirmation to let the user decide whether to continue the next question.

## 4.2.3  Controlling a Loop with a Sentinel Value

Another common technique for controlling a loop is to designate a special value when reading and processing a set of values. This special input value, known as a *sentinel value,* signifies the end of the loop.

sentinel value

Listing 4.2 writes a program that reads and calculates the sum of an unspecified number of integers. The input `0` signifies the end of the input. Do you need to declare a new variable for each input value? No. Just use one variable named `data` (line 8) to store the input value and use a variable named `sum` (line 12) to store the total. Whenever a value is read, assign it to `data` (lines 9, 20) and added to `sum` (line 15) if it is not zero.

### LISTING 4.2  `SentinelValue.cpp`

```cpp
1  #include <iostream>
2  using namespace std;
3
4  int main()
5  {
6    cout << "Enter an int value (the program exits" <<
7      " if the input is 0): ";
8    int data;
9    cin >> data;
10
```

input data

loop

output result

```
11    // Keep reading data until the input is 0
12    int sum = 0;
13    while (data != 0)
14    {
15      sum += data;
16
17      // Read the next data
18      cout << "Enter an int value (the program exits" <<
19        " if the input is 0): ";
20      cin >> data;
21    }
22
23    cout << "The sum is " << sum << endl;
24
25    return 0;
26 }
```

```
Enter an int value (the program exits if the input is 0): 2 ⏎Enter
Enter an int value (the program exits if the input is 0): 3 ⏎Enter
Enter an int value (the program exits if the input is 0): 4 ⏎Enter
Enter an int value (the program exits if the input is 0): 0 ⏎Enter
The sum is 9
```

If data is not **0**, it is added to the sum (line 15) and the next items of input data are read (lines 18–20). If data is **0**, the loop body is no longer executed and the **while** loop terminates. The input value **0** is the sentinel value for this loop. Note that if the first input read is **0**, the loop body never executes, and the resulting sum is **0**.

numeric error

### Caution

Don't use floating-point values for equality checking in a loop control. Since floating-point values are approximations for some values, using them could result in imprecise counter values and inaccurate results. This example uses **int** value for **data**. If a floating-point type value is used for **data**, **(data != 0)** may be **true** even though **data** is exactly **0**. For example,

```
double data = pow(sqrt(2.0), 2) - 2;
if (data == 0)
  cout << "data is zero";
else
  cout << "data is not zero";
```

Like **pow**, **sqrt** is a function in the **cmath** header file for computing the square root of a number. The variable **data** in the above code should be zero, but it is not, because of rounding-off errors.

## 4.3 The **do-while** Loop

do-while loop

The **do-while** loop is a variation of the **while** loop. Its syntax is given below:

```
do
{
  // Loop body;
  Statement(s);
} while (loop-continuation-condition);
```

Its execution flow chart is shown in Figure 4.2.

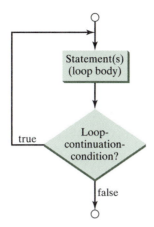

**FIGURE 4.2**  The **do-while** loop executes the loop body first and then checks the **loop-continuation-condition** to determine whether to continue or terminate the loop.

The loop body is executed first. Then the **loop-continuation-condition** is evaluated. If the evaluation is **true**, the loop body is executed again; if it is **false**, the **do-while** loop terminates. The major difference between a **while** loop and a **do-while** loop is the order in which the **loop-continuation-condition** is evaluated and the loop body executed. The **while** loop and the **do-while** loop have equal expressive power. Sometimes one is a more convenient choice than the other. For example, you can rewrite the **while** loop in Listing 4.2 using a **do-while** loop, as shown in Listing 4.3.

**LISTING 4.3**  TestDoWhile.cpp

```
1 #include <iostream>
2 using namespace std;
3
4 int main()
5 {
6    // Keep reading data until the input is 0
7    int sum = 0;
8    int data = 0;
9
10   do                                                    loop
11   {
12      sum += data;
13
14      // Read the next data
15      cout << "Enter an int value (the program exits" <<
16        " if the input is 0): ";
17      cin >> data;                                       input
18   }
19   while (data != 0);
20
21   cout << "The sum is " << sum << endl;
22
23   return 0;
24 }
```

What would happen if **sum** and **data** are not initialized to **0**? Would it cause a syntax error? No. It would cause a logic error, because **sum** and **data** could be initialized to any value.

**Tip**

Use the `do-while` loop if you have statements inside the loop that must be executed at least once, as in the case of the `do-while` loop in the preceding **TestDoWhile** program. These statements must appear before the loop as well as inside the loop if you use a `while` loop.

## 4.4 The `for` Loop

Often you write a loop in the following common form:

```
i = initialValue;  // Initialize loop control variable
while (i < endValue)
{
  // Loop body
  ...
  i++; // Adjust loop control variable
}
```

A `for` loop can be used to simplify the above loop:

```
for (i = initialValue; i < endValue; i++)
{
  // Loop body
  ...
}
```

**for** loop

In general, the syntax of a `for` loop is as shown below:

```
for (initial-action; loop-continuation-condition;
     action-after-each-iteration)
{
  // Loop body;
  Statement(s);
}
```

The flow chart of the `for` loop is shown in Figure 4.3(a).

The `for` loop statement starts with the keyword `for`, followed by a pair of parentheses enclosing initial-action, loop-continuation-condition, and action-after-each-iteration, and followed by the loop body enclosed inside braces. `initial-action`, `loop-continuation-condition`, and `action-after-each-iteration` are separated by semicolons.

control variable

A `for` loop generally uses a variable to control how many times the loop body is executed and when the loop terminates. This variable is referred to as a *control variable*. The initial-action often initializes a control variable, the action-after-each-iteration usually increments or decrements the control variable, and the loop-continuation-condition tests whether the control variable has reached a termination value. For example, the following `for` loop prints `Welcome to C++!` a hundred times:

```
int i;
for (i = 0; i < 100; i++)
{
  cout << "Welcome to C++!\n";
}
```

The flow chart of the statement is shown in Figure 4.3(b). The `for` loop initializes `i` to `0`, then repeatedly executes the statement to display a message and evaluates `i++` while `i` is less than `100`.

The initial-action, `i = 0`, initializes the control variable, `i`. The `loop-continuation-condition`, `i < 100`, is a Boolean expression. The expression is evaluated at the beginning

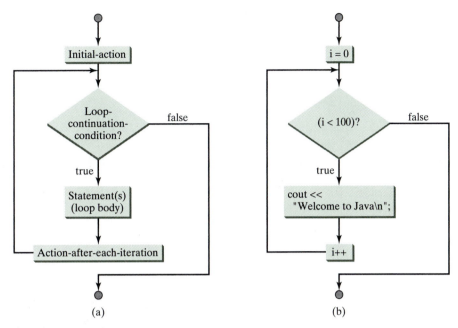

**FIGURE 4.3**    A **for** loop performs an initial action once, then repeatedly executes the statements in the loop body, and performs an action after an iteration when the **loop-continuation-condition** evaluates to **true**.

of each iteration. If this condition is **true**, execute the loop body. If it is **false**, the loop terminates and the program control turns to the line following the loop.

The **action-after-each-iteration**, **i++**, is a statement that adjusts the control variable. This statement is executed after each iteration. It increments the control variable. Eventually, the value of the control variable should force the **loop-continuation-condition** to become **false**. Otherwise the loop is infinite.

```cpp
for (int i = 0; i < 100; i++)
{
  cout << "Welcome to C++!\n";
}
```

If there is only one statement in the loop body, as in this example, the braces can be omitted.

Listing 4.4 presents an example that sums a series that starts with 0.01 and ends with 1.0. The numbers in the series will increment by 0.01, as follows: 0.01 + 0.02 + 0.03 and so on.

**LISTING 4.4    TestSum.cpp**

```cpp
1 #include <iostream>
2 using namespace std;
3
4 int main()
5 {
6   // Initialize sum
7   double sum = 0;
8
9   // Add 0.01, 0.02, ..., 0.99, 1 to sum
10  for (double i = 0.01f; i <= 1.0f; i = i + 0.01f)          loop
11    sum += i;
12
13  // Display result
```

```
14    cout << "The sum is " << sum;
15
16    return 0;
17 }
```

The sum is 50.5

The **for** loop (lines 10–11) repeatedly adds the control variable **i** to the sum. This variable, which begins with **0.01**, is incremented by **0.01** after each iteration. The loop terminates when **i** exceeds **1.0**.

The **for** loop initial action can be any statement, but it often is used to initialize a control variable. From this example, you can see that a control variable can be a **double** type. In fact, it can be any data type.

If you replace line 10 by

```
for (double i = 0.01; i <= 1.0; i = i + 0.01)
```

you will be stunned to see that sum is **49.5**. For a discussion of this error, please see www.cs.armstrong.edu/liang/cpp/note.pdf.

**Tip**

The control variable must be declared inside the control structure of the loop or before the loop. If the loop control variable is used only in the loop, and not elsewhere, it is good programming practice to declare it in the **initial-action** of the **for** loop. If the variable is declared inside the loop control structure, it cannot be referenced outside the loop. For example, you cannot reference **i** outside the **for** loop in the preceding code, because it is declared inside the **for** loop.

**Note**

The **initial-action** in a **for** loop can be a list of zero or more comma-separated variable declaration statements or assignment expressions. For example,

```
for (int i = 0, j = 0; (i + j < 10); i++, j++)
{
    // Do something
}
```

The **action-after-each-iteration** in a **for** loop can be a list of zero or more comma-separated statements. For example,

```
for (int i = 1; i < 100; cout << i, i++);
```

This example is correct, but it is not a good example, because it makes the code difficult to read. Normally, you declare and initialize a control variable as initial action and increment or decrement the control variable as an action after each iteration.

**Note**

If the **loop-continuation-condition** in a **for** loop is omitted, it is implicitly **true**. Thus the statement given below in (a), which is an infinite loop, is correct. Nevertheless, it is better to use the equivalent loop in (b) to avoid confusion:

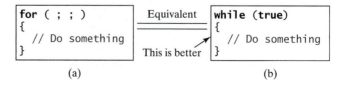

```
for ( ; ; )
{
    // Do something
}
```
(a)

Equivalent

This is better

```
while (true)
{
    // Do something
}
```
(b)

## 4.5 Which Loop to Use?

The `while` loop and `for` loop are called *pre-test loops* because the continuation condition is checked before the loop body is executed. The `do-while` loop is called *post-test loop* because the condition is checked after the loop body is executed. The three forms of loop statements, `while`, `do-while`, and `for`, are expressively equivalent; that is, you can write a loop in any of these three forms. For example, a `while` loop in (a) in the following figure can always be converted into the `for` loop in (b):

pre-test loop
post-test loop

```
while (loop-continuation-condition)
{
    // Loop body
}
```

Equivalent

```
for ( ; loop-continuation-condition; )
{
    // Loop body
}
```

(a)                                   (b)

A `for` loop in (a) in the next figure generally can be converted into the `while` loop in (b) except in certain special cases (see Review Question 4.12 for such a case):

```
for (initial-action;
     loop-continuation-condition;
     action-after-each-iteration)
{
    // Loop body;
}
```

Equivalent

```
initial-action;
while (loop-continuation-condition)
{
    // Loop body;
    action-after-each-iteration;
}
```

(a)                                   (b)

Use the loop statement that is most intuitive to you. In general, a `for` loop may be used if the number of repetitions is known, as, for example, when you need to print a message a hundred times. A `while` loop may be used if the number of repetitions is not known, as in the case of reading the numbers until the input is `0`. A `do-while` loop can be used to replace a `while` loop if the loop body has to be executed before the continuation condition is tested.

### Caution

Adding a semicolon at the end of the `for` clause before the loop body is a common mistake, as shown below. In (a), the semicolon signifies the end of the loop prematurely. The loop body is actually empty, as shown in (b). (a) and (b) are equivalent.

Error

```
for (int i = 0; i < 10; i++);
{
    cout << "i is " << i << endl;
}
```

(a)

Empty Body

```
for (int i = 0; i < 10; i++) { };
{
    cout << "i is " << i << endl;
}
```

(b)

Similarly, the loop in (c) is also wrong. (c) is equivalent to (d).

Error

```
int i = 0;
while (i < 10);
{
    cout << "i is " << i << endl;
    i++;
}
```

(c)

Empty Body

```
int i = 0;
while (i < 10) { };
{
    cout << "i is " << i << endl;
    i++;
}
```

(d)

In the case of the **do-while** loop, the semicolon is needed to end the loop.

```
int i = 0;
do
{
  cout << "i is " << i << endl;
  i++;
} while (i < 10); ◄─────── Correct
```

## 4.6 Nested Loops

Nested loops consist of an outer loop and one or more inner loops. Each time the outer loop is repeated, the inner loops are reentered and started anew.

Listing 4.5 presents a program that uses nested **for** loops to print a multiplication table.

LISTING 4.5 MultiplicationTable.cpp

```
 1 #include <iostream>
 2 #include <iomanip>
 3 using namespace std;
 4
 5 int main()
 6 {
 7   cout << "          Multiplication Table\n";
 8   cout << "------------------------------------\n";
 9
10   // Display the number title
11   cout << "   | ";
12   for (int j = 1; j <= 9; j++)
13     cout << setw(3) << j;
14
15   cout << "\n";
16
17   // Print table body
18   for (int i = 1; i <= 9; i++)
19   {
20     cout << i << " | ";
21     for (int j = 1; j <= 9; j++)
22     {
23       // Display the product and align properly
24       cout << setw(3) << i * j;
25     }
26     cout << "\n";
27   }
28
29   return 0;
30 }
```

table title — (line 7)

table body — (line 18)

nested loop — (line 21)

```
      Multiplication Table
------------------------------------
   | 1   2   3   4   5   6   7   8   9
 1 | 1   2   3   4   5   6   7   8   9
 2 | 2   4   6   8  10  12  14  16  18
 3 | 3   6   9  12  15  18  21  24  27
 4 | 4   8  12  16  20  24  28  32  36
 5 | 5  10  15  20  25  30  35  40  45
 6 | 6  12  18  24  30  36  42  48  54
 7 | 7  14  21  28  35  42  49  56  63
 8 | 8  16  24  32  40  48  56  64  72
 9 | 9  18  27  36  45  54  63  72  81
```

The program displays a title (line 7) on the first line and dashes (–) (line 8) on the second line. The first **for** loop (lines 12–13) displays the numbers 1 through 9 on the third line.

The next loop (lines 18–27) is a nested **for** loop with the control variable i in the outer loop and j in the inner loop. For each i, the product i * j is displayed on a line in the inner loop, with j being 1, 2, 3, ..., 9. The **setw(3)** manipulator (line 24) specifies the width for each number to be displayed.

## 4.7 Case Studies

Control statements are fundamental in programming. The ability to write control statements is essential in learning programming. *If you can write programs using loops, you know how to program!* For this reason, this section presents three additional examples of how to solve problems using loops.

### 4.7.1 Example: Finding the Greatest Common Divisor

This section presents a program that prompts the user to enter two positive integers and finds their greatest common divisor.

The greatest common divisor (*gcd*) of two integers 4 and 2 is 2. the greatest common divisor of two integers 16 and 24 is 8. How do you find the greatest common divisor? Let the two input integers be n1 and n2. You know that number 1 is a common divisor, but it may not be the greatest common divisor. So you can check whether k (for k = 2, 3, 4, and so on) is a common divisor for n1 and n2, until k is greater than n1 or n2. Store the common divisor in a variable named gcd. Initially, gcd is 1. Whenever a new common divisor is found, it becomes the new gcd. When you have checked all the possible common divisors from 2 up to n1 or n2, the value in variable gcd is the greatest common divisor. The idea can be translated into the following loop:

gcd

```
int gcd = 1;
int k = 1;

while (k <= n1 && k <= n2)
{
  if (n1 % k == 0 && n2 % k == 0)
    gcd = k;
  k++;
}
// After the loop, gcd is the greatest common divisor for n1 and n2
```

The complete program is given in Listing 4.6.

**LISTING 4.6** GreatestCommonDivisor.cpp

```
 1 #include <iostream>
 2 using namespace std;
 3
 4 int main()
 5 {
 6   // Prompt the user to enter two integers
 7   cout << "Enter first integer: ";
 8   int n1;
 9   cin >> n1;
10
11   cout << "Enter second integer: ";
12   int n2;
13   cin >> n2;
14
```

input

input

gcd

```
15    int gcd = 1;
16    int k = 1;
17    while (k <= n1 && k <= n2)
18    {
19      if (n1 % k == 0 && n2 % k == 0)
20        gcd = k;
21      k++;
22    }
23
24    cout << "The greatest common divisor for " << n1 << " and "
25         << n2 << " is " << gcd;
26
27    return 0;
28 }
```

output

```
Enter first integer: 125 ↵Enter
Enter second integer: 2525 ↵Enter
The greatest common divisor for 125 and 2525 is 25
```

think before you type

How did you write this program? Did you immediately begin to write the code? No. It is important to *think before you type*. Thinking enables you to generate a logical solution for the problem without concern about how to write the code. Once you have a logical solution, type the code to translate the solution into a program. The translation is not unique. For example, you could use a **for** loop to rewrite the code as follows:

```
for (int k = 1; k <= n1 && k <= n2; k++)
{
  if (n1 % k == 0 && n2 % k == 0)
    gcd = k;
}
```

multiple solutions

A problem often has *multiple solutions.* The gcd problem can be solved in many ways. Exercise 4.15 suggests another solution. A more efficient solution is to use the classic Euclidean algorithm. See http://www.cut-the-knot.org/blue/Euclid.shtml for more information.

You might think that a divisor for a number **n1** cannot be greater than **n1 / 2**. So you would attempt to improve the program using the following loop:

```
for (int k = 1; k <= n1 / 2 && k <= n2 / 2; k++)
{
  if (n1 % k == 0 && n2 % k == 0)
    gcd = k;
}
```

erroneous solutions

This revision is wrong. Can you find the reason? See Review Question 4.9 for the answer.

### 4.7.2   Example: Finding the Sales Amount

You have just started a sales job in a department store. Your pay consists of a base salary and a commission. The base salary is $5,000. The scheme shown below is used to determine the commission rate.

| Sales Amount | Commission Rate |
|---|---|
| $0.01–$5,000 | 8 percent |
| $5,000.01–$10,000 | 10 percent |
| $10,000.01 and above | 12 percent |

Your goal is to earn $30,000 a year. This section writes a program that finds out the minimum amount of sales you have to generate in order to make $30,000.

Since your base salary is $5,000, you have to make $25,000 in commissions to earn $30,000 a year. What is the sales amount for a $25,000 commission? If you know the sales amount, the commission can be computed as follows:

```
if (salesAmount >= 10000.01)
  commission =
    5000 * 0.08 + 5000 * 0.1 + (salesAmount - 10000) * 0.12;
else if (salesAmount >= 5000.01)
  commission = 5000 * 0.08 + (salesAmount - 5000) * 0.10;
else
  commission = salesAmount * 0.08;
```

This suggests that you can try to find the **salesAmount** to match a given commission through incremental approximation. For **salesAmount** of $0.01 (1 cent), find commission. If commission is less than $25,000, increment **salesAmount** by 0.01 and find commission again. If the commission is still less than $25,000, repeat the process until the commission is greater than or equal to $25,000. This is a tedious job for humans, but it is exactly what a computer is good for. You can write a loop and let a computer execute it painlessly. The idea can be translated into the following loop:

```
Set COMMISSION_SOUGHT as a constant;
Set INITIAL_SALES_AMOUNT as a constant;
do
{
  Increase salesAmount by 1 cent;
  Compute the commission from the current salesAmount;
} while (commission < COMMISSION_SOUGHT);
```

The complete program is given in Listing 4.7.

## LISTING 4.7  FindSalesAmount.cpp

```
 1 #include <iostream>
 2 #include <iomanip>
 3 using namespace std;
 4
 5 int main()
 6 {
 7   // The commission sought
 8   const double COMMISSION_SOUGHT = 25000;          constants
 9   const double INITIAL_SALES_AMOUNT = 0.01;
10   double commission = 0;
11   double salesAmount = INITIAL_SALES_AMOUNT;
12
13   do                                               loop
14   {
15     // Increase salesAmount by 1 cent
16     salesAmount += 0.01;
17
18     // Compute the commission from the current salesAmount;
19     if (salesAmount >= 10000.01)
20       commission =
21         5000 * 0.08 + 5000 * 0.1 + (salesAmount - 10000) * 0.12;
22     else if (salesAmount >= 5000.01)
23       commission = 5000 * 0.08 + (salesAmount - 5000) * 0.10;
24     else
25       commission = salesAmount * 0.08;
26   }
```

```
27     while (commission < COMMISSION_SOUGHT);
28
29     // Display the sales amount
30     cout << "The sales amount $" << fixed << setprecision(2) <<
31       (salesAmount * 100) / 100.0 <<
32       "\nis needed to make a commission of $" << COMMISSION_SOUGHT;
33
34     return 0;
35 }
```

fixed precision

```
The sales amount $210833.34
is needed to make a commission of $25000.00
```

The do-while loop (lines 13–27) is used to repeatedly compute commission for an incremental salesAmount. The loop terminates when commission is greater than or equal to a constant COMMISSION_SOUGHT.

In Exercise 4.17, you will rewrite this program to let the user enter COMMISSION_SOUGHT dynamically.

You can improve the performance of this program by estimating a higher INITIAL_SALES_AMOUNT (e.g., 25000).

What is wrong if saleAmount is incremented after the commission is computed as follows?

```
do
{
  // Compute the commission from the current salesAmount;
  if (salesAmount >= 10000.01)
    commission =
      5000 * 0.08 + 5000 * 0.1 + (salesAmount - 10000) * 0.12;
  else if (salesAmount >= 5000.01)
    commission = 5000 * 0.08 + (salesAmount - 5000) * 0.10;
  else
    commission = salesAmount * 0.08;

  // Increase salesAmount by 1 cent
  salesAmount += 0.01;
} while (commission < COMMISSION_SOUGHT);
```

off-by-one error

The change is erroneous because salesAmount is 1 cent more than is needed for the commission when the loop ends. This is a common error in loops, known as the *off-by-one error*.

**Tip**

This example uses constants COMMISSION_SOUGHT and INITIAL_SALES_AMOUNT. Using *constants* makes programs easy to read and maintain.

constants

### 4.7.3 Example: Displaying a Pyramid of Numbers

This section presents a program that prompts the user to enter an integer from 1 to 15 and displays a pyramid. If the input integer is 12, for example, the output is shown as follows:

```
Enter the number of lines: 12 ⏎Enter
                              1
                           2  1  2
                        3  2  1  2  3
                     4  3  2  1  2  3  4
                  5  4  3  2  1  2  3  4  5
               6  5  4  3  2  1  2  3  4  5  6
            7  6  5  4  3  2  1  2  3  4  5  6  7
         8  7  6  5  4  3  2  1  2  3  4  5  6  7  8
      9  8  7  6  5  4  3  2  1  2  3  4  5  6  7  8  9
  10  9  8  7  6  5  4  3  2  1  2  3  4  5  6  7  8  9 10
11 10  9  8  7  6  5  4  3  2  1  2  3  4  5  6  7  8  9 10 11
12 11 10  9  8  7  6  5  4  3  2  1  2  3  4  5  6  7  8  9 10 11 12
```

Your program receives the input for an integer (numberOfLines) that represents the total number of lines. It displays all the lines one by one. Each line has three parts. The first part comprises the spaces before the numbers; the second part, the leading numbers, such as 3 2 1 in line 3; and the last part, the ending numbers, such as 2 3 in line 3.

Each number occupies three spaces. Display an empty space before a double-digit number, and display two empty spaces before a single-digit number.

You can use an outer loop to control the lines. At the nth row, there are (numberOfLines − n) * 3 leading spaces, the leading numbers are n, n − 1, ..., 1, and the ending numbers are 2, ..., n. You can use three separate inner loops to print each part.

Here is the algorithm for the problem:

```
Input numberOfLines;

for (int row = 1; row <= numberOfLines; row++)
{
  Print (numberOfLines - row) * 3 leading spaces;
  Print leading numbers row, row - 1, ..., 1;
  Print ending numbers 2, 3, ..., row - 1, row;
  Start a new line;
}
```

The complete program is given in Listing 4.8.

## LISTING 4.8  PrintPyramid.cpp

```
1 #include <iostream>
2 using namespace std;
3
4 int main()
5 {
6   // Prompt the user to enter the number of lines
7   cout << "Enter the number of lines: ";
8   int numberOfLines;
9   cin >> numberOfLines;                                    input line number
10
11  if (numberOfLines < 1 || numberOfLines > 15)             check input
12  {
13    cout << "You must enter a number from 1 to 15";
14    return 0;
15  }
```

```
16
17    // Print lines
18    for (int row = 1; row <= numberOfLines; row++)
19    {
20      // Print NUMBER_OF_LINES - row) leading spaces
21      for (int column = 1; column <= numberOfLines - row; column++)
22        cout << "  ";
23
24      // Print leading numbers row, row - 1, ..., 1
25      for (int num = row; num >= 1; num--)
26        cout << ((num >= 10) ? " " : "  ") << num;
27
28      // Print ending numbers 2, 3, ..., row - 1, row
29      for (int num = 2; num <= row; num++)
30        cout << ((num >= 10) ? " " : "  ") << num;
31
32      // Start a new line
33      cout << endl;
34    }
35
36    return 0;
37 }
```

print lines (line 18)

print spaces (line 21)

print leading numbers (line 25)

print ending numbers (line 29)

a new line (line 33)

The conditional expression (num >= 10) ? " " : "  " in lines 26 and 30 displays a single empty space before the number if the number is greater than or equal to 10, and otherwise displays with two empty spaces before the number. Instead of using the conditional expression, you may replace it with the format function setw(3) to simplify the program.

Printing patterns like this one and the ones in Exercises 4.18 and 4.19 are good exercise for practicing loop control statements. The key is to understand the pattern and to describe it using loop control variables.

## 4.8 (Optional) Keywords **break** and **continue**

Two keywords, break and continue, can be used in loop statements to provide the loop with additional control.

break

- **break** immediately ends the innermost loop that contains it. In other words, break breaks out of a loop.

continue

- **continue** only ends the current iteration. Program control goes to the end of the loop body. In other words, continue breaks out of an iteration.

You have already used the keyword **break** in a **switch** statement. You can also use break and continue in a loop. Normally, these two keywords are used with an if statement. Listings 4.8 and 4.9 present two programs to demonstrate the effect of the break and continue keywords in a loop.

The program in Listing 4.9 adds the integers from 1 to 20 in this order to sum until sum is greater than or equal to 100. Without the if statement (line 13), this program would calculate the sum of the numbers from 1 to 20.

### LISTING 4.9 TestBreak.cpp

```
1 #include <iostream>
2 using namespace std;
3
4 int main()
5 {
6   int sum = 0;
7   int number = 0;
8
```

```
 9    while (number < 20)
10    {
11      number++;
12      sum += number;
13      if (sum >= 100) break;
14    }
15
16    cout << "The number is " << number << endl;
17    cout << "The sum is " << sum << endl;
18
19    return 0;
20  }
```

break

```
The number is 14
The sum is 105
```

The program in Listing 4.10 adds all the integers from 1 to 20 except 10 and 11 to sum. With the **if** statement in the program (line 12), the **continue** statement is executed when number becomes 10 or 11. The **continue** statement ends the current iteration so that the rest of the statement in the loop body is not executed; therefore, number is not added to sum when it is 10 or 11.

## LISTING 4.10 TestContinue.cpp

```
 1  #include <iostream>
 2  using namespace std;
 3
 4  int main()
 5  {
 6    int sum = 0;
 7    int number = 0;
 8
 9    while (number < 20)
10    {
11      number++;
12      if (number == 10 || number == 11) continue;
13      sum += number;
14    }
15
16    cout << "The sum is " << sum;
17
18    return 0;
19  }
```

continue

```
The sum is 189
```

**Note**
The **continue** statement is always inside a loop. In the **while** and **do-while** loops, the **loop-continuation-condition** is evaluated immediately after the **continue** statement. In the **for** loop, the **action-after-each-iteration** is performed, then the **loop-continuation-condition** is evaluated, immediately after the **continue** statement.

**Tip**
You can always write a program without using **break** or **continue** in a loop. See Review Question 4.13. In general, it is appropriate to use **break** and **continue** if their use simplifies coding and makes programs easier to read.

**Note**

The C language has a `goto` statement. You can also use it in C++. However, using it will make your program vulnerable to errors. The `break` and `continue` statements are different from the `goto` statement. The `goto` statement can transfer the control anywhere in the program indiscriminately, but the `break` and `continue` statement operate only in a `loop` or a `switch` statement.

## 4.9 Example: Displaying Prime Numbers

This section presents a program that displays the first fifty prime numbers in five lines, each of which contains ten numbers. An integer greater than 1 is *prime* if its only positive divisor is 1 or itself. For example, 2, 3, 5, and 7 are prime numbers, but 4, 6, 8, and 9 are not.

The problem can be broken into the following tasks:

- Determine whether a given number is prime.

- For number = 2, 3, 4, 5, 6, . . ., test whether the number is prime.

- Count the prime numbers.

- Print each prime number, and print ten numbers per line.

Obviously, you need to write a loop and repeatedly test whether a new number is prime. If the number is prime, increase the count by 1. The count is 0 initially. When it reaches 50, the loop terminates.

Here is the algorithm for the problem:

```
Set the number of prime numbers to be printed as
  a constant NUMBER_OF_PRIMES;
Use count to track the number of prime numbers and
  set an initial count to 0;
Set an initial number to 2;

while (count < NUMBER_OF_PRIMES)
{
  Test if number is prime;
  if (number is prime)
  {
    Print the prime number and increase the count;
  }

  Increment number by 1;
}
```

To test whether a number is prime, check whether the number is divisible by 2, 3, 4, up to number/2. If a divisor is found, the number is not a prime. The algorithm can be described as follows:

```
Use a boolean variable isPrime to denote whether
  the number is prime; Set isPrime to true initially;

for (int divisor = 2; divisor <= number / 2; divisor++)
{
  if (number % divisor == 0)
  {
    Set isPrime to false
    Exit the loop;
  }
}
```

The complete program is given in Listing 4.11.

LISTING 4.11   PrimeNumber.cpp

```cpp
 1 #include <iostream>
 2 #include <iomanip>
 3 using namespace std;
 4
 5 int main()
 6 {
 7   const int NUMBER_OF_PRIMES = 50; // Number of primes to display
 8   const int NUMBER_OF_PRIMES_PER_LINE = 10; // Display 10 per line
 9   int count = 0; // Count the number of prime numbers
10   int number = 2; // A number to be tested for primeness
11
12   cout << "The first 50 prime numbers are \n";
13
14   // Repeatedly find prime numbers
15   while (count < NUMBER_OF_PRIMES)
16   {
17     // Assume the number is prime
18     bool isPrime = true; // Is the current number prime?
19
20     // Test if number is prime
21     for (int divisor = 2; divisor <= number / 2; divisor++)
22     {
23       if (number % divisor == 0)
24       {
25         // If true, the number is not prime
26         isPrime = false; // Set isPrime to false
27         break; // Exit the for loop
28       }
29     }
30
31     // Print the prime number and increase the count
32     if (isPrime)
33     {
34       count++; // Increase the count
35
36       if (count % NUMBER_OF_PRIMES_PER_LINE == 0)
37       {
38         // Print the number and advance to the new line
39         cout << setw(4) << number << endl;
40       }
41       else
42         cout << setw(4) << number << " ";
43     }
44
45     // Check if the next number is prime
46     number++;
47   }
48
49   return 0;
50 }
```

count prime numbers

check primeness

exit loop

print if prime

```
The first 50 prime numbers are
    2    3    5    7   11   13   17   19   23   29
   31   37   41   43   47   53   59   61   67   71
   73   79   83   89   97  101  103  107  109  113
  127  131  137  139  149  151  157  163  167  173
  179  181  191  193  197  199  211  223  227  229
```

subproblem

This is a complex example for novice programmers. The key to developing a programmatic solution to this problem, and to many other problems, is to break it into *subproblems* and develop solutions for each of them in turn. Do not attempt to develop a complete solution in the first trial. Instead, begin by writing the code to determine whether a given number is prime, then expand the program to test whether other numbers are prime in a loop.

To determine whether a number is prime, check whether it is divisible by a number between **2** and **number/2** inclusive. If so, it is not a prime number; otherwise, it is a prime number. For a prime number, display it. If the count is divisible by **10**, advance to a new line. The program ends when the count reaches **50**. There is a $100,000 award waiting for the first individual or group who discovers a prime number with at least 10,000,000 decimal digits. See http://www.eff.org/awards/coop.php.

### Note

The program uses the **break** statement in line 26 to exit the **for** loop as soon as the number is found to be a nonprime. You can rewrite the loop (lines 21–29) without using the **break** statement, as follows:

```
for (int divisor = 2; divisor <= number / 2 && isPrime;
    divisor++)
{
  // If true, the number is not prime
  if (number % divisor == 0)
  {
   // Set isPrime to false, if the number is not prime
   isPrime = false;
  }
}
```

However, using the **break** statement makes the program simpler and easier to read in this case.

 ## 4.10 (Optional) Simple File Input and Output

You used the **cin** to read input from the keyboard and the **cout** to write output to the console. You can also read and write data from/to a file. This section introduces simple file input and output. Detailed coverage of file input and output will be presented in Chapter 12.

### 4.10.1   Writing to a File

To write data to a file, first create an object of the **ofstream** type:

```
ofstream output;
```

To specify a file, invoke the **open** function from **output** as follows:

```
output.open("numbers.txt");
```

This statement creates a file named **numbers.txt**. If this file already exists, the contents are destroyed and a new file is created. Later you will learn classes and objects. The variable **output** actually references an object of the **ofstream** class. Invoking the **open** function is to associate a file with the stream.

### Note

More details on objects will be introduced in Chapter 9, "Objects and Classes." For the time being, you will just have to accept that this is how to perform simple file input and output in C++.

To write data, use the stream insertion operator (`<<`) in the same way that you send data to the `cout` object. For example,

```
output << 95 << " " << 56 << " " << 34 << endl;
```

This statement writes numbers **95**, **56**, and **34** to the file. Numbers are separated by spaces, as shown in Figure 4.4.

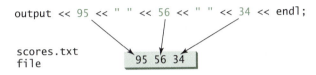

```
scores.txt
file
```

**FIGURE 4.4**   The output stream sends data to the file.

After you have done with the file, invoke the `close` function from `output` as follows:

```
output.close();
```

Listing 4.12 gives the complete program for writing data to a file.

**LISTING 4.12**   `SimpleFileOutput.cpp`

```cpp
 1 #include <iostream>
 2 #include <fstream>
 3 using namespace std;
 4
 5 int main()
 6 {
 7   ofstream output;
 8
 9   // Create a file
10   output.open("numbers.txt");
11
12   // Write numbers
13   output << 95 << " " << 56 << " " << 34;
14
15   // Close file
16   output.close();
17
18   cout << "Done" << endl;
19
20   return 0;
21 }
```

include **fstream** header

declare output

open file

output to file

close file

Since `ofstream` is defined in the `fstream` header file, line 2 includes this header file.

including **<fstream>** header

## 4.10.2   Reading from a File

To read data from a file, first declare a variable of the `ifstream` type:

```
ifstream input;
```

To specify a file, invoke the `open` function from `input` as follows:

```
input.open("numbers.txt");
```

This statement opens a file named `numbers.txt` for input.

To read data, use the stream extraction operator (`>>`) in the same way that you read data from the `cin` object. For example,

```
input >> score1;
input >> score2;
input >> score3;
```

These statements read three numbers from the file into variables score1, score2, and score3, as shown in Figure 4.5.

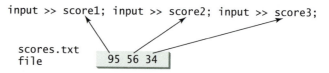

```
input >> score1; input >> score2; input >> score3;

scores.txt
file          95 56 34
```

**FIGURE 4.5** The input stream reads data from the file.

After you have done with the file, invoke the close function from input as follows:

input.close();

Listing 4.13 gives the complete program for writing data to a file.

## LISTING 4.13 SimpleFileInput.cpp

include **fstream** header

declare output

open file

input from file

close file

```cpp
 1  #include <iostream>
 2  #include <fstream>
 3  using namespace std;
 4
 5  int main()
 6  {
 7    ifstream input;
 8
 9    // Open a file
10    input.open("numbers.txt");
11
12    int score1, score2, score3;
13
14    // Read data
15    input >> score1;
16    input >> score2;
17    input >> score3;
18
19    cout << "Total score is " << score1 + score2 + score3 << endl;
20
21    // Close file
22    input.close();
23
24    cout << "Done" << endl;
25
26    return 0;
27  }
```

```
Total score is 185
Done
```

including **<fstream>** header

Since ifstream is defined in the **fstream** header file, line 2 includes this header file.

### 4.10.3 Testing End of a File

eof function

Listing 4.13 reads three numbers from the data file. If you don't know how many numbers are in the file and want to read them all, how do you know the end of file? You can invoke the eof() function on the input object to detect it. Listing 4.14 revises Listing 4.13 to read all lines from the file numbers.txt.

**LISTING 4.14**   `TestEndOfFile.cpp`

```
1  #include <iostream>
2  #include <fstream>                                              include fstream header
3  using namespace std;
4
5  int main()
6  {
7    ifstream input;                                               declare object
8
9    // Open a file
10   input.open("numbers.txt");                                   open file
11
12   int score;
13   int total = 0;
14
15   // Read data
16   while (!input.eof()) // Continue to read if not end of file   end of file?
17   {
18     input >> score;                                            input from file
19     cout << score << endl;
20     total += score;
21   }
22
23   cout << "Total score is " << total << endl;
24
25   // Close file
26   input.close();                                               close file
27
28   cout << "Done" << endl;
29
30   return 0;
31 }
```

```
95
56
34
Total score is 185
Done
```

The program reads data in a loop (lines 16–21). Each iteration of the loop reads one number. The loop terminates when the input reaches the end of file.

When there is nothing more to read, `eof()` returns `true`. How does the program know there is nothing to read? This information is obtained from the operating system. When the program reads the last item **34**, it attempts to read beyond **4** and detected the *end of file*.

To read data correctly, you need to know exactly how data is stored. For example, the program in Listing 4.14 would not work if the score is a `double` value with a decimal point.

end of file?

read right data

## KEY TERMS

## CHAPTER SUMMARY

- Program control specifies the order in which statements are executed in a program. There are three types of control statements: sequence, selection, and repetition. The preceding chapters introduced sequence and selection statements. This chapter introduced the repetition statements.

- There are three types of repetition statements: the `while` loop, the `do-while` loop, and the `for` loop. In designing loops, you need to consider both the loop control structure and the loop body.

- The `while` loop checks the `loop-continuation-condition` first. If the condition is `true`, the loop body is executed; if it is `false`, the loop terminates. The `do-while` loop is similar to the `while` loop, except that the `do-while` loop executes the loop body first and then checks the `loop-continuation-condition` to decide whether to continue or to terminate.

- Since the `while` loop and the `do-while` loop contain the `loop-continuation-condition`, which is dependent on the loop body, the number of repetitions is determined by the loop body. The `while` loop and the `do-while` loop often are used when the number of repetitions is unspecified.

- The `for` loop generally is used to execute a loop body a predictable number of times; this number is not determined by the loop body. The loop control has three parts. The first part is an initial action that often initializes a control variable. The second part, the `loop-continuation-condition`, determines whether the loop body is to be executed. The third part is executed after each iteration and is often used to adjust the control variable. Usually, the loop control variables are initialized and changed in the control structure.

- Two keywords, `break` and `continue`, can be used in a loop. The `break` keyword immediately ends the innermost loop, which contains the break. The `continue` keyword only ends the current iteration.

## REVIEW QUESTIONS

### Sections 4.2–4.7

4.1    How many times is the following loop body repeated? What is the printout of the loop?

```
int i = 1;
while (i > 10)
    if ((i++) % 2 == 0)
        cout << i << endl;
```

(a)

```
int i = 1;
while (i < 10)
    if ((i++) % 2 == 0)
        cout << i << endl;
```

(b)

4.2    What are the differences between a `while` loop and a `do-while` loop?

4.3    Do the following two loops result in the same value in `sum`?

```
for (int i = 0; i < 10; ++i)
{
    sum += i;
}
```

(a)

```
for (int i = 0; i < 10; i++)
{
    sum += i;
}
```

(b)

**4.4**  What are the three parts of a **for** loop control? Write a **for** loop that prints the numbers from **1** to **100**.

**4.5**  What does the following statement do?

```
for ( ; ; )
{
   do something;
}
```

**4.6**  If a variable is declared in the **for** loop control, can it be used after the loop exits?

**4.7**  Can you convert a **for** loop to a **while** loop? List the advantages of using **for** loops.

**4.8**  Convert the following **for** loop statement to a **while** loop and to a **do-while** loop:

```
long sum = 0;
for (int i = 0; i <= 1000; i++)
   sum = sum + i;
```

**4.9**  Will the program work if **n1** and **n2** are replaced by **n1 / 2** and **n2 / 2** in line 17 in Listing 4.6?

## Section 4.8 Keywords **break** and **continue**

**4.10**  What is the keyword **break** for? What is the keyword **continue** for? Will the following program terminate? If so, give the output.

```
int balance = 1000;              int balance = 1000;
while (true)                     while (true)
{                               {
   if (balance < 9)                 if (balance < 9)
      break;                           continue;
   balance = balance - 9;          balance = balance - 9;
}                               }

cout << "Balance is " <<        cout << "Balance is "
   balance << endl;                 << balance << endl;
```

              (a)                               (b)

**4.11**  Can you always convert a **while** loop into a **for** loop? Convert the following **while** loop into a **for** loop:

```
int i = 1;
int sum = 0;
while (sum < 10000)
{
   sum = sum + i;
   i++;
}
```

**4.12**  The **for** loop on the left is converted into the **while** loop on the right. What is wrong? Correct it.

```
for (int i = 0; i < 4; i++)          int i = 0;
{                   Converted        while (i < 4)
   if (i % 3 == 0) continue;   ──►   {
   sum += i;        Wrong               if (i % 3 == 0) continue;
}                   conversion         sum += i;
                                       i++;
                                    }
```

**4.13** Rewrite the programs `TestBreak` and `TestContinue` in Listings 4.9 and 4.10 without using `break` and `continue` statements.

## Comprehensive

**4.14** Identify and fix the syntax errors in (a) and logic errors in (b).

```
for (int i = 0; i < 10; i++);
  sum += i;

if (i < j);
  cout << i
else
  cout << j;

while (j < 10);
{
  j++;
};

do
{
  j++;
} while (j < 10)
```

(a)

```
int total = 0, num = 0;

do
{
  // Read the next data
  cout << "Enter an int value, " <<
    "\nexit if the input is 0: ";
  int num;
  cin >> num;

  total += num;
} while (num != 0);

cout << "Total is " << total << endl;
```

(b)

**4.15** Show the output of the following programs:

```
for (int i = 1; i < 5; i++)
{
  int j = 0;
  while (j < i)
  {
    cout << j << " ";
    j++;
  }
}
```

(a)

```
int i = 0;
while (i < 5)
{
  for (int j = i; j > 1; j--)
    cout << j << " ";
  cout << "****" << endl;
  i++;
}
```

(b)

```
int i = 5;
while (i >= 1)
{
  int num = 1;
  for (int j = 1; j <= i; j++)
  {
    cout << num << "xxx";
    num *= 2;
  }

  cout << endl;
  i--;
}
```

(c)

```
int i = 1;
do
{
  int num = 1;
  for (int j = 1; j <= i; j++)
  {
    cout << num << "G";
    num += 2;
  }

  cout << endl;
  i++;
} while (i <= 5);
```

(d)

**4.16** Reformat the following programs according to the programming style and documentation guidelines proposed in §2.14:

```
#include <iostream>
using namespace std;
int main()
{
  int i = 0;
  if (i>0)
  i++;
  else
  i--;

  char grade;

  if (i >= 90)
    grade = 'A';
  else
    if (i >= 80)
      grade = 'B';
}
```
(a)

```
#include <iostream>
using namespace std;
int main() {
for (int i = 0; i<10; i++)
  if (i>0)
    i++;
  else
    i--;
}
```
(b)

**4.17**   Count the number of iterations in the following loops.

```
int count = 0;
while (count < n)
{
  count++;
}
```
(a)

```
for (int count = 0;
   count < n; count++)
{
}
```
(b)

```
int count = 5;
while (count < n)
{
  count++;
}
```
(c)

```
int count = 5;
while (count < n)
{
  count = count + 3;
}
```
(d)

# PROGRAMMING EXERCISES

**Pedagogical Note**

A problem often can be solved in many different ways. Students are encouraged to explore various solutions.

explore solutions

### Sections 4.2–4.6

**4.1**   (*Repeating additions*) Listing 4.1, SubtractionTutorLoop.cpp, generates ten random subtraction questions. Revise the program to generate ten random addition questions for two integers between 1 and 15. Display the correct count and test time.

**4.2**\*   (*Counting positive and negative numbers and computing the average of numbers*) Write a program that reads an unspecified number of integers, determines how many positive and negative values have been read, and computes the total and average of the input values (not counting zeros). Your program ends with the input 0. Display the average as a floating-point number. (For example, if you entered 1, 2, and 0, the average should be 1.5.)

**4.3** (*Conversion from kilograms to pounds*) Write a program that displays the following table (note that **1** kilogram is **2.2** pounds):

```
Kilograms      Pounds

1              2.2
3              6.6
...
197            433.4
199            437.8
```

**4.4** (*Conversion from miles to kilometers*) Write a program that displays the following table (note that **1** mile is **1.609** kilometers):

```
Miles      Kilometers

1          1.609
2          3.218
...
9          14.481
10         16.09
```

**4.5*** (*Conversion from kilograms to pounds*) Write a program that displays the following two tables side-by-side (note that **1** kilogram is **2.2** pounds):

```
Kilograms      Pounds  |  Pounds      Kilograms

1              2.2     |  20          9.09
3              6.6     |  25          11.36
...
197            433.4   |  510         231.82
199            437.8   |  515         234.09
```

**4.6*** (*Conversion from miles to kilometers*) Write a program that displays the following two tables side-by-side (note that **1** mile is **1.609** kilometers):

```
Miles      Kilometers  |  Kilometers      Miles

1          1.609       |  20              12.430
2          3.218       |  25              15.538
...
9          14.481      |  60              37.290
10         16.09       |  65              40.398
```

**4.7*** (*Financial application: computing future tuition*) Suppose that the tuition for a university is **$10,000** this year and tuition increases **5%** every year. Write a program that uses a loop to compute the tuition in ten years. Write another program that computes the total cost of four years worth of tuition starting ten years from now.

**4.8** (*Finding the highest score*) Write a program that prompts the user to enter the number of students, each student's score, and finally displays the highest score.

**4.9*** (*Finding the two highest scores*) Write a program that prompts the user to enter the number of students, each student's score, and finally displays the highest score and the second-highest score.

**4.10** (*Finding numbers divisible by 5 and 6*) Write a program that displays all the numbers from **100** to **1000**, ten numbers per line, which are divisible by **5** and **6**.

**4.11** (*Finding numbers divisible by 5 or 6, but not both*) Write a program that displays all the numbers from **100** to **200**, ten numbers per line, that are divisible by **5** or **6**, but not both.

**4.12** (*Finding the smallest $n$ such that $n^2 > 12000$*) Use a `while` loop to find the smallest integer $n$ such that $n^2$ is greater than **12,000**.

**4.13** (*Finding the largest $n$ such that $n^3 < 12000$*) Use a `while` loop to find the largest integer $n$ such that $n^3$ is less than 12,000.

**4.14**[*] (*Displaying the ACSII character table*) Write a program that prints the characters in the ASCII character table from `'!'` to `'~'`. Print ten characters per line.

## Section 4.7 Case Studies

**4.15**[*] (*Computing the greatest common divisor*) Another solution for Listing 4.6 to find the greatest common divisor of two integers **n1** and **n2** is as follows: First find **d** to be the minimum of **n1** and **n2**, then check whether **d, d-1, d-2, ..., 2**, or **1** is a divisor for both **n1** and **n2** in this order. The first such common divisor is the greatest common divisor for **n1** and **n2**.

**4.16**[**] (*Finding the factors of an integer*) Write a program that reads an integer and displays all its smallest factors. For example, if the input integer is **120**, the output should be as follows: **2, 2, 2, 3, 5**.

**4.17**[*] (*Financial application: finding the sales amount*) Rewrite Listing 4.7, FindSalesAmount.cpp, as follows:

■ Use a **for** loop instead of a **do-while** loop.

■ Let the user enter **COMMISSION_SOUGHT** instead of fixing it as a constant.

**4.18**[*] (*Printing four patterns using loops*) Use nested loops that print the following patterns in four separate programs:

```
Pattern I        Pattern II        Pattern III        Pattern IV

1                1 2 3 4 5 6                  1       1 2 3 4 5 6
1 2              1 2 3 4 5                  2 1         1 2 3 4 5
1 2 3            1 2 3 4                  3 2 1           1 2 3 4
1 2 3 4          1 2 3                  4 3 2 1             1 2 3
1 2 3 4 5        1 2                  5 4 3 2 1               1 2
1 2 3 4 5 6      1                  6 5 4 3 2 1                 1
```

**4.19**[**] (*Printing numbers in a pyramid pattern*) Write a nested **for** loop that prints the following output:

```
                        1
                    1   2   1
                1   2   4   2   1
            1   2   4   8   4   2   1
        1   2   4   8  16   8   4   2   1
    1   2   4   8  16  32  16   8   4   2   1
  1   2   4   8  16  32  64  32  16   8   4   2   1
1   2   4   8  16  32  64 128  64  32  16   8   4   2   1
```

**Hint**

Here is the pseudocode solution:

```
for the row from 0 to 7
{
  Pad leading blanks in a row using a loop like this:
  for the column from 1 to 7-row
    cout << "   ";

  Print left half of the row for numbers 1, 2, 4, up to
    2^row using a look like this:
  for the column from 0 to row
    cout << "   " << pow(2, column);

  Print the right half of the row for numbers
    2^row-1, 2^row-2, ..., 1 using a loop like this:
  for (int column = row - 1; column >= 0; col--)
    cout << "   " << pow(2, column);
```

```
   Start a new line
   cout << endl;
}
```

You need to figure out how many spaces to print before the number. This is dependent on the number. If a number is a single digit, print four spaces. If a number has two digits, print three spaces. If a number has three digits, print two spaces.

The pow() function was introduced in Listing 2.9, ComputeLoan.cpp, Can you write this program without using it?

**4.20*** (*Printing prime numbers between 2 and 1000*) Modify Listing 4.12 to print all the prime numbers between 2 and 1000, inclusively. Display eight prime numbers per line.

## Comprehensive

**4.21*** (*Financial application: comparing loans with various interest rates*) Write a program that lets the user enter the loan amount and loan period in number of years and displays the monthly and total payments for each interest rate starting from 5% to 8%, with an increment of 1/8. If you enter the loan amount 10,000 for five years, it will display a table as follows:

```
Loan Amount: 10000
Number of Years: 5
Interest Rate      Monthly Payment      Total Payment

5%                 188.71               11322.74
5.125%             189.28               11357.13
5.25%              189.85               11391.59
...
7.85%              202.16               12129.97
8.0%               202.76               12165.83
```

**4.22*** (*Financial application: loan amortization schedule*) The monthly payment for a given loan pays the principal and the interest. The monthly interest is computed by multiplying the monthly interest rate and the balance (the remaining principal). The principal paid for the month is therefore the monthly payment minus the monthly interest. Write a program that lets the user enter the loan amount, number of years, and interest rate, then displays the amortization schedule for the loan. If you enter the loan amount 10,000 for one year with an interest rate of 7%, it will display a table as follows:

```
Loan Amount: 10000
Number of Years: 1
Annual Interest Rate: 7%

Monthly Payment: 865.26
Total Payment: 10383.21

Payment#     Interest     Principal     Balance

1            58.33        806.93        9193.07
2            53.62        811.64        8381.43
...
11           10.0         855.26        860.27
12            5.01        860.25          0.01
```

### Note

The balance after the last payment may not be zero. If so, the last payment should be the normal monthly payment plus the final balance.

**Hint**

Write a loop to print the table. Since monthly payment is the same for each month, it should be computed before the loop. The balance is initially the loan amount. For each iteration in the loop, compute the interest and principal, and update the balance. The loop may look like this:

```
for (i = 1; i <= numberOfYears * 12; i++)
{
  interest = monthlyInterestRate * balance;
  principal = monthlyPayment - interest;
  balance = balance - principal;
  cout << i << "\t\t" << interest
    << "\t\t" << principal << "\t\t" << balance << endl;
}
```

**4.23**[*] (*Demonstrating cancellation errors*) A cancellation error occurs when you are manipulating a very large number with a very small number. The large number may cancel out the smaller number. For example, the result of **100000000.0** + **0.000000001** is equal to **100000000.0**. To avoid cancellation errors and obtain more accurate results, carefully select the order of computation. For example, in computing the following series, you will obtain more accurate results by computing from right to left rather than from left to right:

$$1 + \frac{1}{2} + \frac{1}{3} + \cdots + \frac{1}{n}$$

Write a program that compares the results of the summation of the preceding series, computing from left to right and from right to left with **n** = **50000**.

**4.24**[*] (*Summing a series*) Write a program to sum the following series:

$$\frac{1}{3} + \frac{3}{5} + \frac{5}{7} + \frac{7}{9} + \frac{9}{11} + \frac{11}{13} + \cdots + \frac{95}{97} + \frac{97}{99}$$

**4.25**[**] (*Computing* $\pi$) You can approximate $\pi$ by using the following series:

$$\pi = 4\left(1 - \frac{1}{3} + \frac{1}{5} - \frac{1}{7} + \frac{1}{9} - \frac{1}{11} + \frac{1}{13} - \cdots - \frac{1}{2i - 1} + \frac{1}{2i + 1}\right)$$

Write a program that displays the $\pi$ value for **i** = **10000, 20000,** ..., and **100000**.

**4.26**[**] (*Computing* e) You can approximate e by using the following series:

$$e = 1 + \frac{1}{1!} + \frac{1}{2!} + \frac{1}{3!} + \frac{1}{4!} + \cdots + \frac{1}{i!}$$

Write a program that displays the **e** value for **i** = **10000, 20000,** ..., and **100000**. (*Hint:* Since $i! = i \times (i - 1) \times \cdots \times 2 \times 1$, $\frac{1}{i!}$ is $\frac{1}{i(i - 1)!}$. Initialize **e** and **item** to be **1** and keep adding a new **item** to **e**. The new item is the previous item divided by **i** for **i** = 2, 3, 4, ....)

**4.27** (*Displaying leap years*) Write a program that displays all the leap years, ten years per line, in the twenty-first century (from 2001 to 2100).

**4.28**[**] (*Displaying first days of each month*) Write a program that prompts the user to enter the year and first day of the year, and displays the first day of each month in the year on the console. For example, if the user entered year 2005, and 6 for Saturday, January 1, 2005, your program should display the following output:

January 1, 2005 is Saturday

. . .

December 1, 2005 is Thursday

**4.29**\*\* (*Displaying calendars*) Write a program that prompts the user to enter the year and first day of the year, and displays the calendar table for the year on the console. For example, if the user entered year 2005, and 6 for Saturday, January 1, 2005, your program should display the calendar for each month in the year, as follows:

**January 2005**

| Sun | Mon | Tue | Wed | Thu | Fri | Sat |
| --- | --- | --- | --- | --- | --- | --- |
|     |     |     |     |     |     | 1   |
| 2   | 3   | 4   | 5   | 6   | 7   | 8   |
| 9   | 10  | 11  | 12  | 13  | 14  | 15  |
| 16  | 17  | 18  | 19  | 20  | 21  | 22  |
| 23  | 24  | 25  | 26  | 27  | 28  | 29  |
| 30  | 31  |     |     |     |     |     |

. . .

**December 2005**

| Sun | Mon | Tue | Wed | Thu | Fri | Sat |
| --- | --- | --- | --- | --- | --- | --- |
|     |     |     |     | 1   | 2   | 3   |
| 4   | 5   | 6   | 7   | 8   | 9   | 10  |
| 11  | 12  | 13  | 14  | 15  | 16  | 17  |
| 18  | 19  | 20  | 21  | 22  | 23  | 24  |
| 25  | 26  | 27  | 28  | 29  | 30  | 31  |

**4.30**\* (*Financial application: compound value*) Suppose you save **$100** *each* month into a savings account with the annual interest rate **5%**. So, the monthly interest rate is **0.05/12 = 0.00417**. After the first month, the value in the account becomes

    100 * (1 + 0.00417) = 100.417

After the second month, the value in the account becomes,

    (100 + 100.417) * (1 + 0.00417) = 201.252

After the third month, the value in the account becomes,

    (100 + 201.252) * (1 + 0.00417) = 302.507

and so on.

Write a program that prompts the user to enter an amount (e.g., **100**), the annual interest rate (e.g., **5**), and the number of months (e.g., **6**), and display the amount in the savings account after the given month.

## CHAPTER 5

# FUNCTIONS

## Objectives

- To create functions, invoke functions, and pass arguments to a function (§§5.2–5.4).

- To understand the differences between pass-by-value and pass-by-reference (§§5.5–5.6).

- To use function overloading and understand ambiguous overloading (§5.7).

- To use function prototypes for declaring function headers (§5.8).

- To know how to use default arguments (§5.9).

- To create header files for reusing functions (§5.11).

- To determine the scope of local and global variables (§5.13).

- To develop applications using the C++ mathematical functions (§5.14).

- To design and implement functions using stepwise refinement (§5.15).

- (Optional) To improve runtime efficiency using inline functions (§5.16).

## 5.1 Introduction

In the preceding chapters, you learned about such functions as `pow(a, b)`, `rand()`, `srand(seed)`, and `main()`. A function is a collection of statements that are grouped together to perform an operation. When you call the `pow(a, b)` function, for example, the system actually executes several statements in order to return the result.

This chapter introduces several topics that involve, or are related to, functions. You will learn how to create your own functions with or without return values, invoke a function with or without parameters, overload functions using the same names, and apply function abstraction in the program design.

## 5.2 Creating a Function

In general, a function has the following syntax:

```
returnValueType functionName(list of parameters)
{
  // Function body;
}
```

Let's take a look at a function created to find which of two integers is bigger. This function, named `max`, has two `int` parameters, `num1` and `num2`, the larger of which is returned by the function. Figure 5.1 illustrates the components of this function.

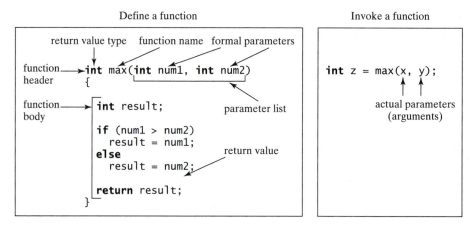

**FIGURE 5.1**   A function declaration consists of a function header and a function body.

function header

The *function header* specifies the *return value type*, *function name*, and *parameters* of the function.

A function may return a value. The `returnValueType` is the data type of the value the function returns. Some functions perform desired operations without returning a value. In this case, the `returnValueType` is the keyword `void`. For example, the `returnValueType` in the `srand` function is `void`. The function that returns a value is called a *value-returning function* and the function that does not return a value is called a *void function*.

value-returning function
void function

parameter
argument
parameter list
function signature

The variables defined in the function header are known as *formal parameters* or simply *parameters*. A parameter is like a placeholder. When a function is invoked, you pass a value to the parameter. This value is referred to as an *actual parameter or argument*. The *parameter list* refers to the type, order, and number of the parameters of a function. The function name and the parameter list together constitute the *function signature*. Parameters are optional; that is, a function may contain no parameters.

The function body contains a collection of statements that define what the function does. The function body of the **max** function uses an **if** statement to determine which number is larger and return the value of that number. A return statement using the keyword **return** is *required* for a value-returning function to return a result. The function terminates when a return statement is executed.

**Caution**

You need to declare a separate data type for each parameter. For instance, `int num1, num2` should be replaced by `int num1, int num2`.

## 5.3 Calling a Function

In creating a function, you give a definition of what the function is to do. To use a function, you have to *call* or *invoke* it. There are two ways to call a function; the choice is based on whether the function returns a value or not.

If the function returns a value, a call to the function is usually treated as a value. For example,

```
int larger = max(3, 4);
```

calls `max(3, 4)` and assigns the result of the function to the variable `larger`. Another example of a call that is treated as a value is

```
cout << max(3, 4);
```

which prints the return value of the function call `max(3, 4)`.

**Note**

A value-returning function also can be invoked as a statement in C++. In this case, the caller simply ignores the return value. This is rare, but permissible if the caller is not interested in the return value.

When a program calls a function, program control is transferred to the called function. A called function returns control to the caller when its return statement is executed or when its function-ending closing brace is reached.

Listing 5.1 shows a complete program that is used to test the **max** function.

### LISTING 5.1  TestMax.cpp

```
 1 #include <iostream>
 2 using namespace std;
 3
 4 // Return the max between two numbers
 5 int max(int num1, int num2) {              declare max function
 6   int result;
 7
 8   if (num1 > num2)
 9     result = num1;
10   else
11     result = num2;
12
13   return result;
14 }
15
16 int main()                                 main function
17 {
```

```
18    int i = 5;
19    int j = 2;
20    int k = max(i, j);
21    cout << "The maximum between " << i <<
22      " and " << j << " is " << k;
23
24    return 0;
25 }
```

```
The maximum between 5 and 2 is 5
```

This program contains the **max** function and the **main** function. The **main** function is just like any other function except that it is invoked by the operating system to execute the program.

A function must be declared before it is invoked. Since the **max** function is invoked by the **main** function, it must be declared before the **main** function.

When the **max** function is invoked (line 20), variable **i**'s value **5** is passed to **num1**, and variable **j**'s value **2** is passed to **num2** in the **max** function. The flow of control transfers to the **max** function. The **max** function is executed. When the **return** statement in the **max** function is executed, the **max** function returns the control to its caller (in this case the caller is the **main** function). This process is illustrated in Figure 5.2.

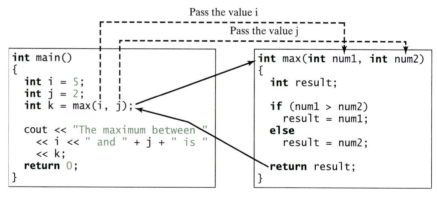

**FIGURE 5.2**  When the **max** function is invoked, the flow of control transfers to the **max** function. Once the **max** function is finished, it returns the control back to the caller.

### 5.3.1  Call Stacks

Each time a function is invoked, the system stores its arguments and variables in an area of memory, known as a *stack,* which stores elements in last-in first-out fashion. When a function calls another function, the caller's stack space is kept intact, and new space is created to handle the new function call. When a function finishes its work and returns to its caller, its associated space is released.

Understanding call stacks helps comprehend how functions are invoked. The variables defined in the **main** function are **i**, **j**, and **k**. The variables defined in the **max** function are **num1**, **num2**, and **result**. The variables **num1** and **num2** are defined in the function signature and are parameters of the function. Their values are passed through function invocation. Figure 5.3 illustrates the variables in the stack.

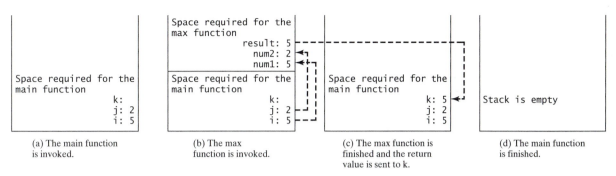

(a) The main function is invoked.

(b) The max function is invoked.

(c) The max function is finished and the return value is sent to k.

(d) The main function is finished.

**FIGURE 5.3**   When the `max` function is invoked, the flow of control transfers to the `max` function. Once the `max` function is finished, it returns the control back to the caller.

**Tip**

If you use Visual C++, please refer to Supplement II.B, "*Learning C++ Effectively with Visual C++*" on the Companion Website. This supplement shows you how to use a debugger to trace function invocations.

debugging in IDE

## 5.4  void Functions

The preceding section gives an example of a value-returning function. This section shows how to declare and invoke a void function. Listing 5.2 gives a program that declares a function named **printGrade** and invokes it to print the grade for a given score.

### LISTING 5.2   TestVoidFunction.cpp

```cpp
 1 #include <iostream>
 2 using namespace std;
 3
 4 // Print grade for the score
 5 void printGrade(double score)            printGrade function
 6 {
 7   if (score >= 90.0)
 8     cout << 'A';
 9   else if (score >= 80.0)
10     cout << 'B';
11   else if (score >= 70.0)
12     cout << 'C';
13   else if (score >= 60.0)
14     cout << 'D';
15   else
16     cout << 'F';
17 }
18
19 int main()                               main function
20 {
21   cout << "Enter a score: ";
22   double score;
23   cin >> score;
24
25   cout << "The grade is ";
26
27   printGrade(score);                     invoke printGrade
28
29   return 0;
30 }
```

```
Enter a score: 78.5  ↵Enter
The grade is C
```

The **printGrade** function is a **void** function. It does not return any value. A call to a **void** function must be a statement. So, it is invoked as a statement in line 26 in the main function. This statement is like any C++ statement terminated with a semicolon.

invoke **void** function

**Note**

return in **void** function

A **return** statement is not needed for a **void** function, but it can be used for terminating the function and returning to the function's caller. The syntax is simply

```
return;
```

This is rare, but sometimes useful for circumventing the normal flow of control in a void function. For example, the following code has a return statement to terminate the function when the score is invalid:

```
// Print grade for the score
void printGrade(double score)
{
  if (score < 0 || score > 100) {
    cout << "Invalid score";
    return;
  }

  if (score >= 90.0)
    cout << 'A';
  else if (score >= 80.0)
    cout << 'B';
  else if (score >= 70.0)
    cout << 'C';
  else if (score >= 60.0)
    cout << 'D';
  else
    cout << 'F';
}
```

The power of a function is its ability to work with parameters. You can use **max** to find the maximum between any two **int** values. When calling a function, you need to provide arguments, which must be given in the same order as their respective parameters in the function specification. This is known as *parameter order association*. For example, the following function prints a character **n** times:

parameter order association

```
void nPrintln(char ch, int n)
{
  for (int i = 0; i < n; i++)
    cout << ch;
}
```

You can use **nPrintln('a', 3)** to print **'a'** three times. The **nPrintln('a', 3)** statement passes the actual string parameter, **'a'**, to the parameter, **ch**; passes **3** to **n**; and prints **'a'** three times. However, the statement **nPrintln(3, 'a')** would have a different meaning. It passes **3** to **ch** and **'a'** to **n**.

**Caution**

The arguments must match the parameters in *order*, *number*, and *compatible type*, as defined in the function signature. Compatible type means that you can pass an argument to a parameter without explicit casting, such as passing an **int** value argument to a **double** value parameter.

## 5.5 Passing Parameters by Values

When you invoke a function with a parameter, the value of the argument is passed to the parameter. This is referred to as *pass-by-value*. If the argument is a variable rather than a literal value, the value of the variable is passed to the parameter. The variable is not affected, regardless of the changes made to the parameter inside the function.

pass-by-value

As shown in Listing 5.3, the value of **x** (**1**) is passed to the parameter **n** to invoke the **increment** function (line 13). **n** is incremented by **1** in the function (line 5), but **x** is not changed regardless what the function does.

### LISTING 5.3 Increment.cpp

```
 1 #include <iostream>
 2 using namespace std;
 3
 4 void increment(int n) {
 5   n++;
 6   cout << "n inside the function is " << n << endl;
 7 }
 8
 9 int main()
10 {
11   int x = 1;
12   cout << "Before the call, x is " << x << endl;
13   increment(x);
14   cout << "after the call, x is " << x << endl;
15
16   return 0;
17 }
```

increment **n**

invoke increment

```
Before the call, x is 1
n inside the function is 2
after the call, x is 1
```

Listing 5.4 gives another program that demonstrates the effect of passing by value. The program creates a function for swapping two variables. The **swap** function is invoked by passing two arguments. Interestingly, the values of the arguments are not changed after the function is invoked.

### LISTING 5.4 TestPassByValue.cpp

```
 1 #include <iostream>
 2 using namespace std;
 3
 4 // Swap two variables
 5 void swap(int n1, int n2)
 6 {
 7   cout << "\tInside the swap function" << endl;
 8   cout << "\t\tBefore swapping n1 is " << n1 <<
 9     " n2 is " << n2 << endl;
10
11   // Swap n1 with n2
12   int temp = n1;
13   n1 = n2;
14   n2 = temp;
15
```

swap function

```
16    cout << "\t\tAfter swapping n1 is " << n1 <<
17       " n2 is " << n2 << endl;
18 }
19
20 int main()
21 {
22    // Declare and initialize variables
23    int num1 = 1;
24    int num2 = 2;
25
26    cout << "Before invoking the swap function, num1 is "
27       << num1 << " and num2 is " << num2 << endl;
28
29    // Invoke the swap function to attempt to swap two variables
30    swap(num1, num2);
31
32    cout << "After invoking the swap function, num1 is " << num1 <<
33       " and num2 is " << num2 << endl;
34
35    return 0;
36 }
```

main function

false swap

```
Before invoking the swap function, num1 is 1 and num2 is 2
            Inside the swap function
                 Before swapping n1 is 1 n2 is 2
                 After swapping n1 is 2 n2 is 1
After invoking the swap function, num1 is 1 and num2 is 2
```

Before the swap function is invoked (line 30), num1 is 1 and num2 is 2. After the swap function is invoked, num1 is still 1 and num2 is still 2. Their values are not swapped after the swap function is invoked. As shown in Figure 5.4, the values of the arguments num1 and num2 are passed to n1 and n2, but n1 and n2 have their own memory locations independent of num1 and num2. Therefore, changes in n1 and n2 do not affect the contents of num1 and num2.

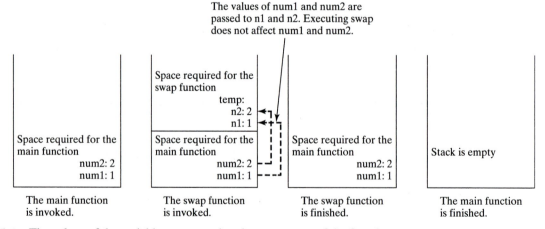

**FIGURE 5.4** The values of the variables are passed to the parameters of the function.

Another twist is to change the parameter name n1 in swap to num1. What effect does this have? No change occurs, because it makes no difference whether the parameter and the argument have the same name. The parameter is a variable in the function with its own memory space. The variable is allocated when the function is invoked, and it disappears when the function is returned to its caller.

# 5.6 Passing Parameters by References

Listing 5.4, TestPassByValue.cpp, presented a **swap** function that attempted to swap two variables. But the values of the variables are not swapped after invoking the function, because the values of variables are passed to the arguments. The original variable and arguments are independent. The values in original variables are not changed even though the values in the arguments are changed.

C++ provides a special type of variable, called a *reference variable*, which can be used as a function parameter to reference the original variable. A reference variable is an alias for another variable. Any changes made through the reference variable are actually performed on the original variable. To declare a reference variable, place the ampersand (**&**) in front of the name. For example, see Listing 5.5.

**LISTING 5.5**   TestReferenceVariable.cpp

```
 1 #include <iostream>
 2 using namespace std;
 3
 4 int main()
 5 {
 6   int count = 1;
 7   int &refCount = count;                          declare reference variable
 8   refCount++;
 9
10   cout << "count is " << count << endl;
11   cout << "refCount is " << refCount << endl;     using reference variable
12
13   return 0;
14 }
```

```
count is 2
refCount is 2
```

Line 7 declares a reference variable named **refCount** that is merely an alias for **count**. As shown in Figure 5.5(a), **refCount** and **count** reference the same value. Line 8 increments **refCount**, which in effect increments count, since they share the same value, as shown in Figure 5.5(b).

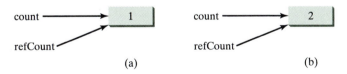

**FIGURE 5.5**   **refCount** and **count** share the same value.

**Note**

The following notations for declaring reference variables are equivalent:                   equivalent notation

```
int &refVar;
int & refVar;
int& refVar;
```

For consistency, the first notation is used throughout the book.

You can use a reference variable as a parameter in a function and pass a regular variable to invoke the function. The parameter becomes an alias for the original variable. This is known as *pass-by-reference*. When you change the value through the reference variable, the original value is actually changed. Now you can use reference parameters to implement a correct swap function, as shown in Listing 5.6.

pass-by-reference

### LISTING 5.6 TestPassByReference.cpp

```
1  #include <iostream>
2  using namespace std;
3
4  // Swap two variables
5  void swap(int &n1, int &n2)
6  {
7    cout << "\tInside the swap function" << endl;
8    cout << "\t\tBefore swapping n1 is " << n1 <<
9      " n2 is " << n2 << endl;
10
11   // Swap n1 with n2
12   int temp = n1;
13   n1 = n2;
14   n2 = temp;
15
16   cout << "\t\tAfter swapping n1 is " << n1 <<
17     " n2 is " << n2 << endl;
18 }
19
20 int main()
21 {
22   // Declare and initialize variables
23   int num1 = 1;
24   int num2 = 2;
25
26   cout << "Before invoking the swap function, num1 is "
27     << num1 << " and num2 is " << num2 << endl;
28
29   // Invoke the swap function to attempt to swap two variables
30   swap(num1, num2);
31
32   cout << "After invoking the swap function, num1 is " << num1 <<
33     " and num2 is " << num2 << endl;
34
35   return 0;
36 }
```

reference variables

main function

swap

```
Before invoking the swap function, num1 is 1 and num2 is 2
    Inside the swap function
        Before swapping n1 is 1 n2 is 2
        After swapping n1 is 2 n2 is 1
After invoking the swap function, num1 is 2 and num2 is 1
```

Before the swap function is invoked (line 30), num1 is 1 and num2 is 2. After the swap function is invoked, num1 becomes 2 and num2 becomes 1. Their values are swapped after the swap function is invoked.

**Note**

Pass-by-value and pass-by-reference are two ways of passing parameters to a function. Pass-by-value passes the value to an independent variable and pass-by-reference shares the same variable. Semantically pass-by-reference can be described as *pass-by-sharing*.

pass-by-sharing

**Caution**

When you pass an argument by reference, the formal parameter and the argument must have the same type. For example, in the following code, the reference of variable **x** is passed to the function. However, the value of variable **y** is passed to **p**, since **y** and **p** are of different types.

requires same type

```
#include <iostream>
using namespace std;

void f(double &p)
{
  p++;
}

int main()
{
  double x = 1;
  int y = 1;

  f(x);
  f(y);

  cout << "x is " << x << endl;
  cout << "y is " << y << endl;

  return 0;
}
```

```
x is 2
y is 1
```

## 5.7 Overloading Functions

The **max** function that was used earlier works only with the **int** data type. But what if you need to find which of two floating-point numbers has the maximum value? The solution is to create another function with the same name but different parameters, as shown in the following code:

```
double max(double num1, double num2)
{
  if (num1 > num2)
    return num1;
  else
    return num2;
}
```

If you call **max** with **int** parameters, the **max** function that expects **int** parameters will be invoked; if you call **max** with **double** parameters, the **max** function that expects **double** parameters will be invoked. This is referred to as *function overloading*; that is, two functions have the same name but different parameter lists within one file. The C++ compiler determines which function is used based on the function signature.

function overloading

Listing 5.7 is a program that creates three functions. The first finds the maximum integer, the second finds the maximum double, and the third finds the maximum among three double values. All three functions are named **max**.

LISTING **5.7** TestFunctionOverloading.cpp

```cpp
 1 #include <iostream>
 2 using namespace std;
 3
 4 // Return the max between two int values
 5 int max(int num1, int num2)
 6 {
 7   if (num1 > num2)
 8     return num1;
 9   else
10     return num2;
11 }
12
13 // Find the max between two double values
14 double max(double num1, double num2)
15 {
16   if (num1 > num2)
17     return num1;
18   else
19     return num2;
20 }
21
22 // Return the max among three double values
23 double max(double num1, double num2, double num3)
24 {
25   return max(max(num1, num2), num3);
26 }
27
28 int main()
29 {
30   // Invoke the max function with int parameters
31   cout << "The maximum between 3 and 4 is " << max(3, 4) << endl;
32
33   // Invoke the max function with the double parameters
34   cout << "The maximum between 3.0 and 5.4 is "
35     << max(3.0, 5.4) << endl;
36
37   // Invoke the max function with three double parameters
38   cout << "The maximum between 3.0, 5.4, and 10.14 is "
39     << max(3.0, 5.4, 10.14) << endl;
40
41   return 0;
42 }
```

max function

max function

max function

main function

invoke **max**

invoke **max**

invoke **max**

When calling `max(3, 4)` (line 31), the **max** function for finding the maximum of two integers is invoked. When calling `max(3.0, 5.4)` (line 35), the **max** function for finding the maximum of two doubles is invoked. When calling `max(3.0, 5.4, 10.14)` (line 39), the **max** function for finding the maximum of three double values is invoked.

Can you invoke the **max** function with an **int** value and a **double** value, such as `max(2, 2.5)`? If so, which of the **max** functions is invoked? The answer to the first question is yes. The answer to the second is that the **max** function for finding the maximum of two **double** values is invoked. The argument value **2** is automatically converted into a **double** value and passed to this function.

You may be wondering why the function `max(double, double)` is not invoked for the call `max(3, 4)`. Both `max(double, double)` and `max(int, int)` are possible matches for `max(3, 4)`. The C++ compiler finds the most specific function for a function invocation. Since the function `max(int, int)` is more specific than `max(double, double)`, `max(int, int)` is used to invoke `max(3, 4)`.

**Tip**
Overloading functions can make programs clearer and more readable. Functions that perform closely related tasks should be given the same name.

**Note**
Overloaded functions must have different parameter lists. You cannot overload functions based on different return types.

**Note**
Sometimes there are two or more possible matches for an invocation of a function, but the compiler cannot determine the most specific match. This is referred to as *ambiguous invocation*. Ambiguous invocation causes a compilation error. Consider the following code:

*ambiguous invocation*

```cpp
#include <iostream>
using namespace std;

int maxNumber(int num1, double num2)
{
  if (num1 > num2)
    return num1;
  else
    return num2;
}

double maxNumber(double num1, int num2)
{
  if (num1 > num2)
    return num1;
  else
    return num2;
}

int main()
{
  cout << maxNumber(1, 2) << endl;

  return 0;
}
```

Both `maxNumber(int, double)` and `maxNumber(double, int)` are possible candidates to match `maxNumber(1, 2)`. Since neither of them is more specific than the other, the invocation is ambiguous, resulting in a compilation error.

If you change `maxNumber(1,2)` to `maxNumber(1,2.0)`, it will match the first `maxNumber` function. So, there will be no compilation errors.

# 5.8 Function Prototypes

Before a function is called, it must be declared first. One way to ensure this is to place the declaration before all function calls. Another way to approach this is to declare a function prototype before the function is called. A function prototype is a function declaration without implementation. The implementation can be given later in the program.

Listing 5.8 rewrites TestFunctionOverloading.cpp in Listing 5.7 using function prototypes. Three `max` function prototypes are defined in lines 5–7. These functions are called later in the `main` function. The functions are implemented in lines 27, 36, and 45.

LISTING **5.8** TestFunctionPrototype.cpp

```
 1 #include <iostream>
 2 using namespace std;
 3
 4 // Function prototype
 5 int max(int num1, int num2);
 6 double max(double num1, double num2);
 7 double max(double num1, double num2, double num3);
 8
 9 int main()
10 {
11   // Invoke the max function with int parameters
12   cout << "The maximum between 3 and 4 is " <<
13     max(3, 4) << endl;
14
15   // Invoke the max function with the double parameters
16   cout << "The maximum between 3.0 and 5.4 is "
17     << max(3.0, 5.4) << endl;
18
19   // Invoke the max function with three double parameters
20   cout << "The maximum between 3.0, 5.4, and 10.14 is "
21     << max(3.0, 5.4, 10.14) << endl;
22
23   return 0;
24 }
25
26 // Return the max between two int values
27 int max(int num1, int num2)
28 {
29   if (num1 > num2)
30     return num1;
31   else
32     return num2;
33 }
34
35 // Find the max between two double values
36 double max(double num1, double num2)
37 {
38   if (num1 > num2)
39     return num1;
40   else
41     return num2;
42 }
43
44 // Return the max among three double values
45 double max(double num1, double num2, double num3)
46 {
47   return max(max(num1, num2), num3);
48 }
```

function prototype *(lines 5–7)*

**main** function *(line 9)*

invoke **max** *(line 13)*

invoke **max** *(line 17)*

invoke **max** *(line 21)*

function implementation *(line 27)*

function implementation *(line 36)*

function implementation *(line 45)*

 **Note**

It is not necessary to list parameter names in the prototype, only the parameter types are required. C++ compiler ignores the parameter names. The prototype tells the compiler the name of the function, its return type, number of the parameters, and the type of each parameter. So lines 5–7 can be replaced by

omitting parameter names

```
int max(int, int);
double max(double, double);
double max(double, double, double);
```

## 5.9 Default Arguments

C++ allows you to declare functions with default argument values. The default values are passed to the parameters when a function is invoked without the arguments.

Listing 5.9 demonstrates how to declare functions with default argument values and how to invoke such functions.

### LISTING 5.9  DefaultArgumentDemo.cpp

```cpp
1  #include <iostream>
2  using namespace std;
3
4  // Swap two variables
5  void printArea(double radius = 1)                          default argument
6  {
7    double area = radius * radius * 3.14159;
8    cout << "area is " << area << endl;
9  }
10
11 int main()
12 {
13   printArea();                                             invoke with default
14   printArea(4);                                            invoke with argument
15
16   return 0;
17 }
```

```
area is 3.14159
area is 50.2654
```

Line 5 declares the `printArea` function with the parameter `radius`. `radius` has a default value `1`. Line 13 invokes the function without passing an argument. In this case, the default value `1` is assigned to `radius`.

When a function contains a mixture of parameters with and without default values, the parameters with default values must be defined last. For example, the following declarations are illegal:    default arguments last

```cpp
void t1(int x, int y = 0, int z); // Illegal
void t2(int x = 0, int y = 0, int z);  // Illegal
```

However, the following declarations are fine:

```cpp
void t3(int x, int y = 0, int z = 0); // Legal
void t4(int x = 0, int y = 0, int z = 0); // Legal
```

When an argument is left out of a function, all arguments that come after it must be left out as well. For example, the following calls are illegal:

```cpp
t3(1,   , 20); // Illegal
t4(,   , 20); // Illegal
```

But the following calls are fine:

```cpp
t3(1); // Parameters y and z are assigned a default value
t4(1, 2); // Parameter z is assigned a default value
```

## 5.10 Case Study: Computing Taxes with Functions

The program in Listing 3.5, ComputeTaxWithSelectionStatement.cpp, uses **if** statements to check the filing status and computes the tax based on the filing status. This example uses functions to simplify Listing 3.5.

Each filing status has six brackets. The code for computing taxes is nearly the same for each filing status except that each filing status has different bracket ranges. For example, the single filer status has six brackets [0, 6000], (6000, 27950], (27950, 67700], (67700, 141250], (141250, 307050], (307050,∞), and the married file jointly status has six brackets [0, 12000], (12000, 46700], (46700, 112850], (112850, 171950], (171950, 307050], (307050, ∞), The first bracket of each filing status is taxed at 10%, the second at 15%, the third at 27%, the fourth at 30%, the fifth at 35%, and the sixth at 38.6%. So you can write a function with the brackets as arguments to compute the tax for the filing status. The header of the function is:

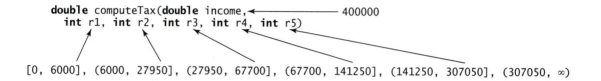

```
double computeTax(double income,                    400000
    int r1, int r2, int r3, int r4, int r5)
```
[0, 6000], (6000, 27950], (27950, 67700], (67700, 141250], (141250, 307050], (307050, ∞)

For example, you can invoke **computeTax(400000, 6000, 27950, 67700, 141250, 307050)** to compute the tax for single filers with $400,000 of taxable income.

Listing 5.10 gives the solution to the problem.

### LISTING 5.10 ComputeTaxWithFunction.cpp

function prototype

main function

input status

input income

compute tax

```cpp
 1 #include <iostream>
 2 #include <iomanip>
 3 using namespace std;
 4
 5 // Function prototype, parameter names are omitted
 6 double computeTax(int, double);
 7
 8 int main()
 9 {
10    // Prompt the user to enter filing status
11    cout << "Enter the filing status\n" <<
12       "\t(0-single, 1-joint, 2-separate, 3-head of house hold): ";
13    int status;
14    cin >> status;
15
16    // Prompt the user to enter taxable income
17    cout << "Enter the taxable income: ";
18    double income;
19    cin >> income;
20
21    // Display the result
22    cout << "Tax is " << fixed << setprecision(2)
23       << computeTax(status, income);
24
25    return 0;
26 }
```

```
27
28  double computeTax(                                              overloaded computeTax
29    double income, int r1, int r2, int r3, int r4, int r5)
30  {
31    double tax = 0;
32
33    if (income <= r1)
34      tax = income * 0.10;
35    else if (income <= r2)
36      tax = r1 * 0.10 + (income - r1) * 0.15;
37    else if (income <= r3)
38      tax = r1 * 0.10 + (r2 - r1) * 0.15 + (income - r2) * 0.27;
39    else if (income <= r4)
40      tax = r1 * 0.10 + (r2 - r1) * 0.15 + (r3 - r2) * 0.27 +
41        (income - r3) * 0.30;
42    else if (income <= r5)
43      tax = r1 * 0.10 + (r2 - r1) * 0.15 + (r3 - r2) * 0.27 +
44        (r4 - r3) * 0.30 + (income - r4) * 0.35;
45    else
46      tax = r1 * 0.10 + (r2 - r1) * 0.15 + (r3 - r2) * 0.27 +
47        (r4 - r3) * 0.30 + (r5 - r4) * 0.35 + (income - r5) * 0.386;
48
49    return tax;
50  }
51
52  double computeTax(int status, double income)                    overloaded computeTax
53  {
54    switch (status)
55    {
56      case 0:
57        return computeTax(income, 6000, 27950, 67700, 141250, 307050);
58      case 1:
59        return computeTax(income, 12000, 46700, 112850, 171950, 307050);
60      case 2:
61        return computeTax(income, 6000, 23350, 56425, 85975, 153525);
62      case 3:
63        return computeTax(income, 10000, 37450, 96700, 156600, 307050);
64      default:
65        return 0;
66    }
67  }
```

```
Enter the filing status
  (0-single, 1-joint, 2-separate, 3-head of house hold): 0  ↵Enter
Enter the taxable income: 454542  ↵Enter
Tax is 151651.91
```

This program does the same thing as the one in Listing 3.5. Instead of writing the same code for computing taxes for different filing statuses, the new program uses a function for computing taxes. Using the function not only shortens the program, it also makes the program simpler, easy to read, and easy to maintain.

The program uses two overloaded **computeTax** functions (lines 28, 52). The first **computeTax** function in line 28 computes the tax for the specified brackets and taxable income. The second **computeTax** function in line 52 computes the tax for the specified status and taxable income. Because the first **computeTax** function is invoked by the second, the first is declared before the second one. Because the second **computeTax** function is invoked from the main function, its function prototype is declared before the main function in line 6. The parameter names in the function prototype are omitted.

## 5.11 Reusing Functions by Different Programs

One of the benefits of functions is for reuse. In the preceding sections, you declared functions and used them from the same program. To make the functions available for other programs to use, you need to place the functions in a separate file, called the *header file*. By convention, the file has a .h extension. Programs use #include preprocessor directives to include header files in order to reuse the functions defined in the header file.

Listing 5.11 creates a header file named MyLib.h. This file declares a function named isEven(number) that returns **true** if the number is even.

### LISTING 5.11 MyLib.h

isEven

```
1 bool isEven(int number)
2 {
3    return (number % 2 == 0);
4 }
```

Listing 5.12 creates a file named UseMyLib.cpp. This file contains a main function for testing the isEven function.

### LISTING 5.12 UseMyLib.cpp

```
 1 #include <iostream>
 2 #include "MyLib.h"
 3
 4 using namespace std;
 5
 6 int main()
 7 {
 8    cout << isEven(4) << endl;
 9    cout << isEven(5) << endl;
10
11    return 0;
12 }
```

include MyLib.h

invoke **isEven**
invoke **isEven**

```
1
0
```

The program includes two header files iostream (line 1) and MyLib.h (line 2). iostream is a C++ standard header file and MyLib.h is a *user-defined header file.* A user-defined header file should be enclosed in double quotation marks (" ") and a *standard header file* should be enclosed in angle brackets (< >).

Header files can be placed anywhere on the disk. For example, if MyLib.h is placed under the c:\ root directory on Windows, you can include it using the absolute file name as follows:

```
#include "c:\\MyLib.h"
```

This makes your code dependent on Windows. To fix the problem, place the header in or under the same directory with the program that includes the header file, or you may compile the program using the −I option to specify the location for the header file:

```
g++ UseMyLib.cpp −I c:\ −o Main
```

user-defined header file
standard header file

placing header file

**Tip**
If you use Visual C++, please refer to Supplement II.A, "*Visual C++ Tutorial*," on the Companion Website. This supplement shows you how to include the library path in the IDE.

set include path in IDE

**Caution**
Header files are designed for reuse by other programs that likely have a main function. Because one program cannot have two main functions, you should not write a main function in header files.

no main in header file

## 5.12 Case Study: Generating Random Characters

Computer programs process numeric data and characters. You have seen many examples that involve numerical data. It is also important to understand characters and how to process them. This section presents an example for generating random characters.

As introduced in §2.11, every character has a unique ASCII code between **0** and **127**. To generate a random character is to generate a random integer between **0** and **127**. You learned how to generate a random number in §3.9. Recall that you can use the **srand(seed)** function to set a seed and use **rand()** to return a random integer. You can use it to write a simple expression to generate random numbers in any range. For example,

rand() % 10 $\longrightarrow$ Returns a random integer between 0 and 9.

50 + rand() % 50 $\longrightarrow$ Returns a random integer between 50 and 99.

In general,

a + rand() % b $\longrightarrow$ Returns a random number between a and a + b, excluding a + b.

So, you can use the following expression to generate a random integer between **0** and **127**:

rand() % **128**

Now let us consider how to generate a random lowercase letter. The ASCII for lowercase letters are consecutive integers starting from the code for **'a'**, then for **'b'**, **'c'**, ..., and **'z'**. The code for **'a'** is

static_cast<int>(**'a'**)

So, a random integer between static_cast<int>(**'a'**) and static_cast<int>(**'z'**) is

static_cast<int>(**'a'**) +
    rand() % (static_cast<int>(**'z'**) - static_cast<int>(**'a'**) + 1)

As discussed in §2.11.2, all numeric operators can be applied to the **char** operands. The **char** operand is cast into a number if the other operand is a number or a character. Thus the preceding expression can be simplified as follows:

**'a'** + rand() % (**'z'** - **'a'** + 1)

and a random lowercase letter is

static_cast<char>(**'a'** + rand() % (**'z'** - **'a'** + 1))

To generalize the foregoing discussion, a random character between any two characters **ch1** and **ch2** with **ch1** < **ch2** can be generated as follows:

static_cast<char>(ch1 + rand() % (ch2 - ch1 + 1))

This is a simple but useful discovery. Let us create a header file named RandomCharacter.h in Listing 5.13 with five overloaded functions to get a certain type of character randomly. You can use these functions in your future projects.

**LISTING 5.13** RandomCharacter.h

```cpp
 1 #include <cstdlib>
 2 using namespace std;
 3
 4 // Generate a random character between ch1 and ch2
 5 char getRandomCharacter(char ch1, char ch2)
 6 {
 7   return static_cast<char>(ch1 + rand() % (ch2 - ch1 + 1));
 8 }
 9
10 // Generate a random lowercase letter
11 char getRandomLowerCaseLetter()
12 {
13   return getRandomCharacter('a', 'z');
14 }
15
16 // Generate a random uppercase letter
17 char getRandomUpperCaseLetter()
18 {
19   return getRandomCharacter('A', 'Z');
20 }
21
22 // Generate a random digit character
23 char getRandomDigitCharacter()
24 {
25   return getRandomCharacter('0', '9');
26 }
27
28 // Generate a random character
29 char getRandomCharacter()
30 {
31   return getRandomCharacter(0, 127);
32 }
```

Listing 5.14 gives a test program that displays one hundred lowercase letters.

**LISTING 5.14** TestRandomCharacter.cpp

```cpp
 1 #include <iostream>
 2 #include "RandomCharacter.h"
 3 using namespace std;
 4
 5 int main()
 6 {
 7   const int NUMBER_OF_CHARS = 175;
 8   const int CHARS_PER_LINE = 25;
 9
10   srand(time(0)); // Set a new seed for random function
11
12   // Print random characters between '!' and '~', 25 chars per line
13   for (int i = 0; i < NUMBER_OF_CHARS; i++)
14   {
15     char ch = getRandomLowerCaseLetter();
16     if ((i + 1) % CHARS_PER_LINE == 0)
```

constants

new seed

lowercase letter

```
17        cout << ch << endl;
18     else
19        cout << ch;
20   }
21
22   return 0;
23 }
```

```
gmjsohezfkgtazqgmswfclrao
pnrunulnwmaztlfjedmpchcif
lalqdgivxkxpbzulrmqmbhikr
lbnrjlsopfxahssqhwuuljvbe
xbhdotzhpehbqmuwsfktwsoli
cbuwkzgxpmtzihgatdslvbwbz
bfesoklwbhnooygiigzdxuqni
```

Line 2 includes RandomCharacter.h, since the program invokes the function defined in this header file.

The **getRandomLowerCaseLetter()** function utilizes the **rand()** function to obtain a random character. To ensure that you get a sequence of different random numbers, **srand(time(0))** is invoked in line 10 to set a new seed for the random number generator algorithm.

Note that **getRandomLowerCaseLetter()** does not have any parameters, but you still have to use the parentheses when defining and invoking the function.

parentheses required

## 5.13 The Scope of Variables

The *scope of a variable* is the part of the program where the variable can be referenced. A variable defined inside a function is referred to as a *local variable*. C++ also allows you to use *global variables*. They are declared outside all functions and are accessible to all functions in its scope. Local variables do not have default values, but global variables are defaulted to zero.

scope
local variable
global variable

A variable must be declared before it can be used. The scope of a local variable starts from its declaration and continues to the end of the block that contains the variable. The scope of a global variable starts from its declaration and continues to the end of the program.

A *parameter* is actually a local variable. The scope of a function parameter covers the entire function.

parameter

Listing 5.15 demonstrates the scope of local and global variables.

### LISTING 5.15  VariableScopeDemo.cpp

```
1 #include <iostream>
2 using namespace std;
3
4 void t1(); // Function prototype
5 void t2(); // Function prototype
6
7 int main()
8 {
9    t1();
10   t2();
11
12   return 0;
13 }
14
```

function prototype

global variable

local variable

increment x
increment y

local variable

```
15 int y; // Global variable, default to 0
16
17 void t1()
18 {
19   int x = 1;
20   cout << "x is " << x << endl;
21   cout << "y is " << y << endl;
22   x++;
23   y++;
24 }
25
26 void t2()
27 {
28   int x = 1;
29   cout << "x is " << x << endl;
30   cout << "y is " << y << endl;
31 }
```

```
x is 1
y is 1
x is 2
y is 1
```

A global variable **y** is declared in line 15 with default value **0**. This variable is accessible in functions **t1** and **t2**, but not in the **main** function, because the **main** function is declared before **y** is declared.

When the **main** function invokes **t1()** in line 9, the global variable **y** is incremented (line 23) and becomes **1** in **t1**. When the **main** function invokes **t2()** in line 10, the global variable **y** is now **1**.

A local variable **x** is declared in **t1** in line 19 and another local variable **x** is declared in **t2** in line 28. These two variables are independent, although they are named the same. So incrementing **x** in **t1** does not effect the variable **x** defined in **t2**.

If a function has a local variable with the same name as a global variable, only the local variable can be seen from the function.

**Note**

unary scope resolution

If a local variable name is the same as a global variable name, you can access the global variable using **::globalVariable**. The **::** operator is known as the *unary scope resolution*. For example, the following code

```
#include <iostream>
using namespace std;

int v1 = 10;

int main()
{
  int v1 = 5;
  cout << "local variable v1 is " << v1 << endl;
  cout << "global variable v1 is " << ::v1 << endl;

  return 0;
}
```

displays

```
local variable v1 is 5
global variable v1 is 10
```

**Tip**

It is tempting to declare a variable globally once and use it in all functions without redeclaring it. However, this is a bad practice, because it could lead to errors that are hard to debug, when the global variables are modified. Avoid using global variables. Using global constants is fine, since constants are never changed.

*avoid global variables*

### 5.13.1 The Scope of Variables in a `for` Loop

A variable declared in the initial action part of a `for` loop header has its scope in the entire loop. But a variable declared inside a `for` loop body has its scope limited in the loop body from its declaration to the end of the block that contains the variable, as shown in Figure 5.6.

*`for` loop control variable*

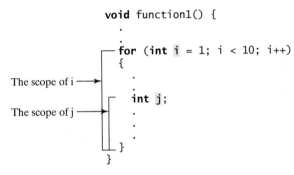

**FIGURE 5.6** A variable declared in the initial action part of a `for` loop header has its scope in the entire loop.

It is commonly acceptable to declare a local variable with the same name multiple times in different non-nesting blocks in a function, as shown in Figure 5.7(a), but it is not a good practice to declare a local variable twice in nested blocks, as shown in Figure 5.7(b). In this case, `i` is declared in the function block and also in the `for` loop. The program can compile and run, but it is easy to make mistakes. So, you should avoid declaring the same variable in nested blocks.

*multiple declarations*

It is fine to declare i in two non-nesting blocks

```
void function1()
{
    int x = 1;
    int y = 1;

    for (int i = 1; i < 10; i++)
    {
        x += i;
    }

    for (int i = 1; i < 10; i++)
    {
        y += i;
    }
}
```
(a)

It is not a good practice to declare i in two nesting blocks

```
void function2()
{
    int i = 1;
    int sum = 0;

    for (int i = 1; i < 10; i++)
    {
        sum += i;
    }

    cout << i << endl;
    cout << sum << endl;
}
```
(b)

**FIGURE 5.7** A variable can be declared multiple times in non-nested blocks, but you should avoid declaring them in nested blocks.

**Caution**

Do not declare a variable inside a block and then attempt to use it outside the block. Here is an example of a common mistake:

```
for (int i = 0; i < 10; i++)
{
}
cout << i;
```

The last statement would cause a syntax error because variable i is not defined outside of the for loop.

### 5.13.2 Static Local Variables

for loop control variable

After a function completes its execution, all its local variables are destroyed. Sometimes, it is desirable to retain the value stored in local variables so that they can be used in the next call. C++ allows you to declare static local variables. Static local variables are permanently allocated in the memory for the lifetime of the program. To declare a static variable, use the keyword static.

Listing 5.16 demonstrates using static local variables.

**LISTING 5.16** StaticVariableDemo.cpp

function prototype

invoke **t1**

static local variable
local variable
increment x
increment y

```
 1 #include <iostream>
 2 using namespace std;
 3
 4 void t1(); // Function prototype
 5
 6 int main()
 7 {
 8    t1();
 9    t1();
10
11    return 0;
12 }
13
14 void t1()
15 {
16    static int x = 1;
17    int y = 1;
18    x++;
19    y++;
20    cout << "x is " << x << endl;
21    cout << "y is " << y << endl;
22 }
```

```
x is 1
y is 1
x is 2
y is 1
```

A static local variable x is declared in line 16 with initial value 1. When t1() is invoked for the first time in line 8, x is incremented to 2 (line 18). Since x is a static local variable, x is retained in memory after this call. When t1() is invoked again in line 9, x is 2 and is incremented to 3 (line 18).

A local variable y is declared in line 17 with initial value 1. When t1() is invoked for the first time in line 8, y is incremented to 2 (line 19). Since y is a local variable, y is destroyed after this call. When t1() is invoked again in line 9, y is initialized to 1 and is incremented to 2 (line 19).

## 5.14 The Math Functions

C++ contains the functions needed to perform basic mathematical operations. You have already used the **pow(a, b)** function to compute $a^b$ in Listing 2.9, ComputeLoan.cpp. This section introduces other useful mathematical functions, summarized in Table 5.1.

**TABLE 5.1** Mathematical Functions

| Function | Description | Example |
|----------|-------------|---------|
| abs(x) | Returns the absolute value of the argument. | abs(-2) is 2 |
| ceil(x) | x is rounded up to its nearest integer and returns this integer. | ceil(2.1) is 3 <br> ceil(-2.1) is -2 |
| floor(x) | x is rounded down to its nearest integer and returns this integer. | floor(2.1) is 2 <br> floor(-2.1) is -3 |
| exp(x) | Returns the exponential function of $e^x$. | exp(1) is 2.71828 |
| pow(x, y) | Returns x raised to power y ($x^y$). | pow(2.0, 3) is 8 |
| log(x) | Returns the natural logarithm of x. | log(2.71828) is 1.0 |
| log10(x) | Returns the base-10 logarithm of x. | log10(10.0) is 1 |
| sqrt(x) | Returns the square root of x. | sqrt(4.0) is 2 |
| sin(x) | Returns the sine of x. x represents an angle in radians. | sin(3.14159 / 2) is 1 <br> sin(3.14159) is 0 |
| cos(x) | Returns the cosine of x. x represents an angle in radians. | cos(3.14159 / 2) is 0 <br> cos(3.14159) is -1 |
| tan(x) | Returns the tangent of x. x represents an angle in radians. | tan(3.14159 / 4) is 1 <br> tan(0.0) is 0 |
| fmod(x, y) | Returns the remainder of x/y as double. | fmod(2.4, 1.3) is 1.1 |
| rand() | Returns a random number. | |
| srand(seed) | Sets a new seed for random number generator. | srand(300) |

**Note**

The argument x is double. The functions **abs**, **rand**, and **srand** are in the **cstdlib** header, and all others are in the **cmath** header.

**Caution**

If you use integers to invoke Math functions (e.g., **sin(2)**), you may get ambiguous overloading error. For a discussion of this error, please see www.cs.armstrong.edu/liang/cpp/note.pdf.

ambiguous overloading

## 5.15 Function Abstraction and Stepwise Refinement

The key to developing software is to apply the concept of abstraction. You will learn many levels of abstraction from this book. *Function abstraction* is achieved by separating the use of a function from its implementation. The client can use a function without knowing how it is implemented. The details of the implementation are encapsulated in the function and hidden from the client who invokes the function. This is known as *information hiding* or *encapsulation*. If you decide to change the implementation, the client program will not be affected, provided that you do not change the function signature. The implementation of the function is hidden from the client in a "black box," as shown in Figure 5.8.

function abstraction

information hiding

Optional arguments Optional return
for Input value

Function Signature

Function body ◄——— Black Box

**FIGURE 5.8** The function body can be thought of as a black box that contains the detailed implementation for the function.

You have already used the `rand()` function to return a random number, the `time(0)` function to obtain the current time, and the `max` function to find the maximum number. You know how to write the code to invoke these functions in your program, but as a user of these functions, you are not required to know how they are implemented.

The concept of function abstraction can be applied to the process of developing programs. When writing a large program, you can use the *"divide and conquer"* strategy, also known as *stepwise refinement,* to decompose it into subproblems. The subproblems can be further decomposed into smaller, more manageable problems.

divide and conquer

stepwise refinement

Suppose you write a program that displays the calendar for a given month of the year. The program prompts the user to enter the year and the month, and then displays the entire calendar for the month, as shown in Figure 5.9.

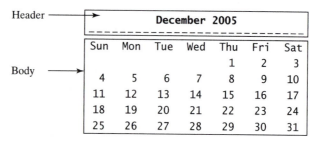

**FIGURE 5.9** After prompting the user to enter the year and the month, the program displays the calendar for that month.

Let us use this example to demonstrate the divide-and-conquer approach.

## 5.15.1 Top-Down Design

How would you get started on such a program? Would you immediately start coding? Beginning programmers often start by trying to work out the solution to every detail. Although details are important in the final program, concern for detail in the early stages may block the problem-solving process. To make problem-solving flow as smoothly as possible, this example begins by using function abstraction to isolate details from design and only later implements the details.

For this example, the problem is first broken into two subproblems: get input from the user and print the calendar for the month. At this stage, the creator of the program should be concerned with what the subproblems will achieve, not with how to get input and print the calendar for the month. You can draw a structure chart to help visualize the decomposition of the problem (see Figure 5.10(a)).

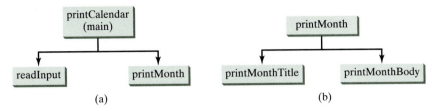

(b)

**FIGURE 5.10** The structure chart shows that the **printCalendar** problem is divided into two subproblems: **readInput** and **printMonth**, and that **printMonth** is divided into two smaller subproblems: **printMonthTitle** and **printMonthBody**.

You can use the **cin** object to read input for the year and the month. The problem of printing the calendar for a given month can be broken into two subproblems: print the month title and print the month body, as shown in Figure 5.10(b). The month title consists of three lines: month and year, a dashed line, and the names of the seven days of the week. You need to get the month name (e.g., January) from the numeric month (e.g., 1). This is accomplished in **printMonthName** (see Figure 5.11(a)).

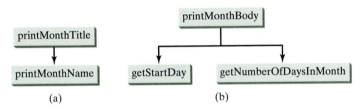

(a) (b)

**FIGURE 5.11** (a) To accomplish **printMonthTitle**, you need **printMonthName**. (b) The **printMonthBody** problem is refined into several smaller problems.

In order to print the month body, you need to know which day of the week is the first day of the month **(getStartDay)** and how many days the month has **(getNumberOfDaysInMonth)**, as shown in Figure 5.11(b). For example, December 2005 has thirty-one days, and the first of the month is Thursday, as shown in Figure 5.9.

How would you get the start day for the first date in a month? There are several ways to find the start day. Assume that you know that the start day **(startDay1800 = 3)** for January 1, 1800 was Wednesday. You could compute the total number of days **(totalNumberOfDays)** between January 1, 1800 and the first date of the calendar month. The start day for the calendar month is **(totalNumberOfDays + startDay1800) % 7**, since every week has seven days. So the **getStartDay** problem can be further refined as **getTotalNumberOfDays**, as shown in Figure 5.12(a).

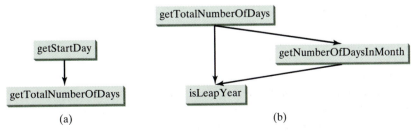

(a) (b)

**FIGURE 5.12** (a) To accomplish **getStartDay**, you need **getTotalNumberOfDays**. (b) The **getTotalNumberOfDays** problem is refined into two smaller problems.

To get the total number of days, you need to know whether a year is a leap year and the number of days in each month. So the **getTotalNumberOfDays** is further refined into two subproblems: **isLeapYear** and **getNumberOfDaysInMonth**, as shown in Figure 5.12(b). The complete structure chart is shown in Figure 5.13.

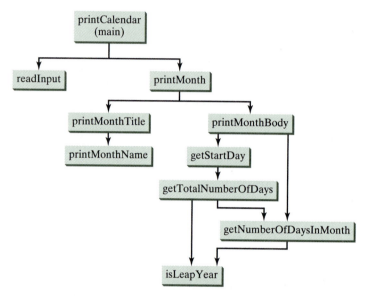

**FIGURE 5.13**   The structure chart shows the hierarchical relationship of the subproblems in the program.

### 5.15.2   Top-Down or Bottom-Up Implementation

Now we turn our attention to implementation. In general, a subproblem corresponds to a function in the implementation, although some are so simple that this is unnecessary. You would need to decide which modules to implement as functions and which to combine in other functions. Decisions of this kind should be based on whether the overall program will be easier to read as a result of your choice. In this example, the subproblem **readInput** can be simply implemented in the **main** function.

top-down approach
stub

You can use either a "top-down" approach or a "bottom-up" approach. The *top-down approach* implements one function in the structure chart at a time from the top to the bottom. Stubs can be used for the functions waiting to be implemented. A *stub* is a simple but incomplete version of a function. The use of stubs enables you to test invoking the function from a caller. Implement the **main** function first, and then use a stub for the **printMonth** function. For example, let **printMonth** display the year and the month in the stub. Thus, your program may begin like this:

```cpp
#include <iostream>
#include <iomanip>
using namespace std;

void printMonth(int year, int month);
void printMonthTitle(int year, int month);
void printMonthName(int month);
void printMonthBody(int year, int month);
int getStartDay(int year, int month);
int getTotalNumberOfDays(int year, int month);
```

```cpp
int getNumberOfDaysInMonth(int year, int month);
bool isLeapYear(int year);

int main()
{
  // Prompt the user to enter year
  cout << "Enter full year (e.g., 2001): ";
  int year;
  cin >> year;

  // Prompt the user to enter month
  cout << "Enter month in number between 1 and 12: ";
  int month;
  cin >> month;

  // Print calendar for the month of the year
  printMonth(year, month);

  return 0;
}

void printMonth(int year, int month)
{
  cout << month << "  " << year << endl;
}
```

Compile and test the program, and fix any errors. You can now implement the `printMonth` function. For functions invoked from the `printMonth` function, you can again use stubs.

The *bottom-up* approach implements one function in the structure chart at a time from the bottom to the top. For each function implemented, write a test program to test it. The top-down and bottom-up approaches are both fine. Both approaches implement functions incrementally, help to isolate programming errors, and make debugging easy. Sometimes they can be used together.

bottom-up approach

## 5.15.3 Implementation Details

The `isLeapYear(int year)` function can be implemented using the following code:

```cpp
return (year % 400 == 0 || (year % 4 == 0 && year % 100 != 0));
```

Use the following fact to implement `getTotalNumberOfDaysInMonth(int year, int month)`:

- January, March, May, July, August, October, and December have thirty-one days.

- April, June, September, and November have thirty days.

- February has twenty-eight days during a regular year and twenty-nine days during a leap year. A regular year, therefore, has 365 days, whereas a leap year has 366 days.

To implement `getTotalNumberOfDays(int year, int month)`, you need to compute the total number of days (`totalNumberOfDays`) between January 1, 1800 and the first day of the calendar month. You could find the total number of days between the year 1800 and the calendar year and then figure out the total number of days prior to the calendar month in the calendar year. The sum of these two totals is `totalNumberOfDays`.

To print a body, first add some space before the start day and then print the lines for every week, as shown for December 2005 (see Figure 5.9).

The complete program is given in Listing 5.17.

LISTING 5.17 PrintCalendar.cpp

function prototype

main function

input year

input month

print calendar

print month

print month title

```cpp
1  #include <iostream>
2  #include <iomanip>
3  using namespace std;
4
5  // Function prototypes
6  void printMonth(int year, int month);
7  void printMonthTitle(int year, int month);
8  void printMonthName(int month);
9  void printMonthBody(int year, int month);
10 int getStartDay(int year, int month);
11 int getTotalNumberOfDays(int year, int month);
12 int getNumberOfDaysInMonth(int year, int month);
13 bool isLeapYear(int year);
14
15 int main()
16 {
17   // Prompt the user to enter year
18   cout << "Enter full year (e.g., 2001): ";
19   int year;
20   cin >> year;
21
22   // Prompt the user to enter month
23   cout << "Enter month in number between 1 and 12: ";
24   int month;
25   cin >> month;
26
27   // Print calendar for the month of the year
28   printMonth(year, month);
29
30   return 0;
31 }
32
33 // Print the calendar for a month in a year
34 void printMonth(int year, int month)
35 {
36   // Print the headings of the calendar
37   printMonthTitle(year, month);
38
39   // Print the body of the calendar
40   printMonthBody(year, month);
41 }
42
43 // Print the month title, e.g., May, 1999
44 void printMonthTitle(int year, int month)
45 {
46   printMonthName(month);
47   cout << " " << year << endl;
48   cout << "-------------------------" << endl;
49   cout << " Sun Mon Tue Wed Thu Fri Sat" << endl;
50 }
51
52 // Get the English name for the month
53 void printMonthName(int month)
54 {
55   switch (month)
56   {
57     case 1:
58       cout << "January";
```

```
59        break;
60      case 2:
61        cout << "February";
62        break;
63      case 3:
64        cout << "March";
65        break;
66      case 4:
67        cout << "April";
68        break;
69      case 5:
70        cout << "May";
71        break;
72      case 6:
73        cout << "June";
74        break;
75      case 7:
76        cout << "July";
77        break;
78      case 8:
79        cout << "August";
80        break;
81      case 9:
82        cout << "September";
83        break;
84      case 10:
85        cout << "October";
86        break;
87      case 11:
88        cout << "November";
89        break;
90      case 12:
91        cout << setw(16) << "December";
92    }
93  }
94
95  // Print month body
96  void printMonthBody(int year, int month)                              print month body
97  {
98    // Get start day of the week for the first date in the month
99    int startDay = getStartDay(year, month);
100
101   // Get number of days in the month
102   int numberOfDaysInMonth = getNumberOfDaysInMonth(year, month);
103
104   // Pad space before the first day of the month
105   int i = 0;
106   for (i = 0; i < startDay; i++)
107     cout << "    ";
108
109   for (i = 1; i <= numberOfDaysInMonth; i++)
110   {
111     cout << setw(4) << i;
112
113     if ((i + startDay) % 7 == 0)
114     cout << endl;
115   }
116 }
117
```

get start day

```
118 // Get the start day of the first day in a month
119 int getStartDay(int year, int month)
120 {
121    // Get total number of days since 1//1//1800
122    int startDay1800 = 3;
123    int totalNumberOfDays = getTotalNumberOfDays(year, month);
124
125    // Return the start day
126    return (totalNumberOfDays + startDay1800) % 7;
127 }
128
```

getTotalNumberOfDays

```
129 // Get the total number of days since January 1, 1800
130 int getTotalNumberOfDays(int year, int month)
131 {
132    int total = 0;
133
134    // Get the total days from 1800 to year - 1
135    for (int i = 1800; i < year; i++)
136      if (isLeapYear(i))
137        total = total + 366;
138      else
139        total = total + 365;
140
141    // Add days from Jan to the month prior to the calendar month
142    for (int i = 1; i < month; i++)
143      total = total + getNumberOfDaysInMonth(year, i);
144
145    return total;
146 }
147
```

getNumberOfDaysInMonth

```
148 // Get the number of days in a month
149 int getNumberOfDaysInMonth(int year, int month)
150 {
151    if (month == 1 || month == 3 || month == 5 || month == 7 ||
152        month == 8 || month == 10 || month == 12)
153      return 31;
154
155    if (month == 4 || month == 6 || month == 9 || month == 11)
156      return 30;
157
158    if (month == 2) return isLeapYear(year) ? 29 : 28;
159
160    return 0; // If month is incorrect
161 }
162
```

isLeapYear

```
163 // Determine if it is a leap year
164 bool isLeapYear(int year)
165 {
166    return year % 400 == 0 || (year % 4 == 0 && year % 100 != 0);
167 }
```

The program does not validate user input. For instance, if the user enters a month not in the range between 1 and 12, or a year before 1800, the program would display an erroneous calendar. To avoid this error, add an `if` statement to check the input before printing the calendar.

This program prints calendars for a month but easily could be modified to print calendars for a whole year. Although it can only print months after January 1800, it could be modified to trace the day of a month before 1800.

**Note**

Function abstraction modularizes programs in a neat, hierarchical manner. Programs written as collections of concise functions are easier to write, debug, maintain, and modify than would otherwise be the case. This writing style also promotes function reusability.

**Tip**

When implementing a large program, use the top-down or bottom-up approach. Do not write the entire program at once. This approach seems to take more time for coding (because you are repeatedly compiling and running the program), but it actually saves time and makes debugging easier.

# 5.16 (Optional) Inline Functions

Implementing a program using functions makes the program easy to read and easy to maintain, but function calls involve runtime overhead (i.e., pushing arguments and CPU registers into the stack and transferring control to and from a function). C++ provides *inline functions* to avoid function calls. Inline functions are not called; rather, the compiler copies the function code *in line* at the point of each invocation. To specify an inline function, precede the function declaration with the **inline** keyword, as shown in Listing 5.18.

*efficiency*

**LISTING 5.18** `InlineDemo.cpp`

```
1  #include <iostream>
2  using namespace std;
3
4  inline void f(int month, int year) {
5    cout << "month is " << month << endl;
6    cout << "year is " << year << endl;
7  }
8
9  int main()
10 {
11   int month = 10, year = 2008;
12   f(month, year);  // Invoke inline function
13   f(9, 2010); // Invoke inline function
14
15   return 0;
16 }
```

*inline function*

*invoke inline function*
*invoke inline function*

As far as programming is concerned, inline functions are the same as regular functions, except that inline functions are preceded with the **inline** keyword. However, behind the scene, the C++ compiler expands the inline function call by copying the inline function code. So, Listing 5.18 is essentially equivalent to Listing 5.19.

**LISTING 5.19** `InlineDemo1.cpp`

```
1  #include <iostream>
2  using namespace std;
3
4  int main()
5  {
6    int month = 10, year = 2008;
7    cout << "month is " << month << endl;
8    cout << "year is " << year << endl;
9    cout << "month is " << 9 << endl;
10   cout << "year is " << 2010 << endl;
11
12   return 0;
13 }
```

┐
├── Inline function expanded
┘

┐
├── Inline function expanded
┘

for short functions
not for long functions
compiler decision

 **Note**

Inline functions are desirable for short functions, but are not suitable for long functions that are called in multiple places in a program, because long inline functions will dramatically increase the executable code size when it is copied in multiple places. For this reason, C++ allows the compiler to ignore the `inline` keyword if the function is too long. So, the `inline` keyword is merely a request to the compiler, and it is up to the compiler to make the decision whether to honor it or ignore it.

## KEY TERMS

## CHAPTER SUMMARY

■ Making programs modular and reusable is one of the central goals in software engineering. C++ provides many powerful constructs that help to achieve this goal. Functions are one such construct.

■ The function header specifies the *return value type, function name,* and *parameters* of the function.

■ A function may return a value. The `returnValueType` is the data type of the value that the function returns. If the function does not return a value, the `returnValueType` is the keyword `void`.

■ The *parameter list* refers to the type, order, and number of the parameters of a function. The function name and the parameter list together constitute the *function signature.* Parameters are optional; that is, a function may contain no parameters.

■ A return statement also can be used in a void function for terminating the function and returning to the function's caller. This is useful occasionally for circumventing the normal flow of control in a function.

■ The arguments that are passed to a function should have the same number, type, and order as the parameters in the function definition.

■ C++ supports two ways of passing parameters: pass-by-value and pass-by-reference. Pass-by-value is to pass the value of the argument to the parameter. Pass-by-reference is to pass the reference of the argument.

- When a program calls a function, program control is transferred to the called function. A called function returns control to the caller when its return statement is executed or when its function-ending closing brace is reached.

- A value-returning also can be invoked as a statement in C++. In this case, the caller simply ignores the return value. In the majority of cases, a call to a function with return value is treated as a value. In some cases, however, the caller is not interested in the return value.

- Each time a function is invoked, the system stores its arguments, local variables, and system registers in a space known as a *stack*. When a function calls another function, the caller's stack space is kept intact, and new space is created to handle the new function call. When a function finishes its work and returns to its caller, its associated space is released.

- A function can be overloaded. This means that two functions can have the same name as long as their function parameter lists differ.

- The *scope of a variable* is the part of the program where the variable can be referenced. C++ has global variables, local variables, and static local variables. Global variables are defined outside all functions and are accessible to all functions in its scope. Local variables are defined inside a function. After a function completes its execution, all of its local variables are destroyed. Static local variables can be defined to retain the local variables to be used by the next function call.

- *Function abstraction* is achieved by separating the use of a function from its implementation. The client can use a function without knowing how it is implemented. The details of the implementation are encapsulated in the function and hidden from the client who invokes the function. This is known as *information hiding* or *encapsulation.*

- Function abstraction modularizes programs in a neat, hierarchical manner. Programs written as collections of concise functions are easier to write, debug, maintain, and modify than would otherwise be the case. This writing style also promotes function reusability.

- When implementing a large program, use the top-down or bottom-up coding approach. Do not write the entire program at once. This approach seems to take more time for coding (because you are repeatedly compiling and running the program), but it actually saves time and makes debugging easier.

## REVIEW QUESTIONS

### Sections 5.2–5.4

**5.1**   What are the benefits of using a function? How do you declare a function? How do you invoke a function?

**5.2**   What is the `return` type of a `main` function?

**5.3**   Can you simplify the `max` function in Listing 5.1 using the conditional operator?

**5.4**   True or false? A call to a function with a `void` return type is always a statement itself, but a call to a function with a value-returning return type is always a component of an expression.

**5.5** What would be wrong with not writing a **return** statement in a value-returning function? Can you have a **return** statement in a **void** function, such as the following?

```
void p()
{
  int i;
  while (true)
  {
    // Prompt the user to enter an integer
    cout << "Enter an integer: ";
    cin >> i;
    if (i == 0)
      return;
    cout << "i is " << i << endl;
  }
}
```

Does the **return** statement in the following function cause syntax errors?

```
void p(double x, double y)
{
  cout << x << " " << y << endl;
  return x + y;
}
```

**5.6** Describe the terms parameter, argument, and function signature.

**5.7** Write a function header for the following functions:

- Computing a sales commission, given the sales amount and the commission rate.
- Printing the calendar for a month, given the month and year.
- Computing a square root.
- Testing whether a number is even, and returning **true** if it is.
- Printing a character a specified number of times.
- Computing the monthly payment, given the loan amount, number of years, and annual interest rate.
- Finding the corresponding uppercase letter, given a lowercase letter.

**5.8** Identify and correct the errors in the following program:

```
1 int xFunction(int n)
2 {
3    cout << n;
4 }
5
6 function1(int n, m)
7 {
8    n += m;
9    xFunction(3.4);
10 }
```

### Sections 5.5–5.6

**5.9** What is pass-by-value? What is pass-by-reference? Show the result of the following programs:

```
#include <iostream>
using namespace std;

void maxValue(int value1, int value2, int max)
{
  if (value1 > value2)
    max = value1;
  else
    max = value2;
}

int main()
{
  int max = 0;
  maxValue(1, 2, max);
  cout << "max is " << max << endl;

  return 0;
}
```

(a)

```
#include <iostream>
using namespace std;

void maxValue(int value1, int value2, int &max)
{
  if (value1 > value2)
    max = value1;
  else
    max = value2;
}

int main()
{
  int max = 0;
  maxValue(1, 2, max);
  cout << "max is " << max << endl;

  return 0;
}
```

(b)

```
#include <iostream>
using namespace std;

void f(int i, int num)
{
  for (int j = 1; j <= i; j++)
  {
    cout << num << " ";
    num *= 2;
  }

  cout << endl;
}

int main()
{
  int i = 1;
  while (i <= 6)
  {
    f(i, 2);
    i++;
  }

  return 0;
}
```

(c)

```
#include <iostream>
using namespace std;

void f(int &i, int num)
{
  for (int j = 1; j <= i; j++)
  {
    cout << num << " ";
    num *= 2;
  }

  cout << endl;
}

int main()
{
  int i = 1;
  while (i <= 6)
  {
    f(i, 2);
    i++;
  }

  return 0;
}
```

(d)

**5.10** For (a) in the preceding question, show the contents of the stack just before the function **max** is invoked, just entering **max**, just before **max** is returned, and right after **max** is returned.

**5.11** Show the output of the following code:

```
#include <iostream>
using namespace std;

void f(double &p)
{
  p += 2;
}
```

```
int main()
{
  double x = 10;
  int y = 10;

  f(x);
  f(y);

  cout << "x is " << x << endl;
  cout << "y is " << y << endl;

  return 0;
}
```

## Section 5.7 Overloading Functions

**5.12** What is function overloading? Is it possible to define two functions that have the same name but different parameter types? Is it possible to define two functions in one program that have identical function names and parameter lists but with different return value types?

**5.13** What is wrong in the following program?

```
void p(int i)
{
  cout << i << endl;
}

int p(int j)
{
  cout << j << endl;
}
```

**5.14** What is wrong in the following program?

```
#include <iostream>
using namespace std;

void p(int &i)
{
  cout << i << endl;
}

int p(int j)
{
  cout << j << endl;
}

int main()
{
  int k = 5;
  p(k);

  return 0;
}
```

## Section 5.9 Default Arguments

**5.15** Which of the following function declarations are illegal?

```
void t1(int x, int y = 0, int z);
void t2(int x = 0, int y = 0, int z);
```

```
void t3(int x, int y = 0, int z = 0);
void t4(int x = 0, int y = 0, int z = 0);
```

## Section 5.13 The Scope of Variables

**5.16** Identify global variables and local variables in the following program. Does a global variable have a default value? Does a local variable have a default value? What will be the output of the following code?

```cpp
#include <iostream>
using namespace std;

int j;

int main()
{
  int i;
  cout << "i is " << i << endl;
  cout << "j is " << j << endl;
}
```

**5.17** Identify global variables, local variables and static local variables in the following program. What will be the output of the following code?

```cpp
#include <iostream>
using namespace std;
int j = 40;

void p()
{
  int i = 5;
  static int j = 5;
  i++;
  j++;

  cout << "i is " << i << endl;
  cout << "j is " << j << endl;
}

int main()
{
  p();
  p();
}
```

**5.18** Identify and correct the errors in the following program:

```cpp
1 void p(int i)
2 {
3    int i = 5;
4
5    cout << "i is " << i << endl;
6 }
```

## Section 5.14 The Math Functions

**5.19** True or false? The argument for trigonometric functions represents an angle in radians.

**5.20** Write an expression that returns a random integer between **34** and **55**. Write an expression that returns a random integer between **0** and **999**. Write an expression that returns a random lowercase letter.

**5.21** Assume PI is 3.14159 and E is 2.71828. Evaluate the following function calls:

| | |
|---|---|
| A. sqrt(4.0) | J. floor(-2.5) |
| B. sin(2 * PI) | K. abs(-2.5f) |
| C. cos(2 * PI) | L. log10(100.0) |
| D. pow(2, 2) | M. cos(PI) |
| E. log(E) | N. ceil(2.5) |
| F. exp(1.0) | O. floor(2.5) |
| G. max(2, min(3,4)) | P. pow(2.0, 4) |
| H. fmod(2.5, 2.3) | Q. fmod(4.2, 3.5) |
| I. ceil(-2.5) | R. ceil(abs(-2.5)) |

# PROGRAMMING EXERCISES

### Sections 5.2–5.11

**5.1** (*Converting an uppercase letter to lowercase*) Write a function that converts an uppercase letter to a lowercase letter. Use the following function header:

```
char upperCaseToLowerCase(char ch)
```

For example, upperCaseToLowerCase('B') returns b. See Exercise 2.7 on how to convert an uppercase letter to lowercase.

**5.2**\* (*Summing the digits in an integer*) Write a function that computes the sum of the digits in an integer. Use the following function header:

```
int sumDigits(long n)
```

For example, sumDigits(234) returns 2 + 3 + 4 = 9.

**Hint**

Use the % operator to extract digits and the / operator to remove the extracted digit. For instance, to extract 4 from 234, use 234 % 10 (=4). To remove 4 from 234, use 234 / 10 (=23). Use a loop to repeatedly extract and remove the digit until all the digits are extracted.

**5.3**\* (*Displaying an integer reversed*) Write the following function to display an integer in reverse order:

```
void reverse(int number)
```

For example, reverse(3456) displays 6543.

**5.4**\*\* (*Returning an integer reversed*) Write the following function to return an integer reversed:

```
int reverse(int number)
```

For example, reverse(3456) returns 6543.

**5.5**\* (*Sorting three numbers*) Write the following function to sort three numbers in increasing order:

```
void sort(double &num1, double &num2, double &num3)
```

**5.6**\* (*Displaying patterns*) Write the following function to display a pattern as follows:

```
void displayPattern(int n)
```

```
        1
      2 1
    3 2 1
 ...
 n n-1 ... 3 2 1
```

**5.7*** (*Financial application: computing the future investment value*) Write a function that computes future investment value at a given interest rate for a specified number of years. The future investment is determined using the formula in Exercise 2.11.

Use the following function header:

```
double futureInvestmentValue(
    double investmentAmount, double monthlyInterestRate, int years)
```

For example, `futureInvestmentValue(10000, 0.05/12, 5)` returns 12833.59.

Write a test program that prompts the user to enter the investment amount (e.g., **1000**) and the interest rate (e.g., 9%), and print a table that displays the future value for the years from **1** to **30**, as shown below:

```
The amount invested: 1000
Annual interest rate: 9%
Years                   Future Value

1                       1093.8
2                       1196.41
...
29                      13467.25
30                      14730.57
```

**5.8** (*Conversions between Celsius and Fahrenheit*) Write a header file that contains the following two functions:

```
/* Converts from Celsius to Fahrenheit */
double celsiusToFahrenheit(double celsius)

/* Converts from Fahrenheit to Celsius */
double fahrenheitToCelsius(double fahrenheit)
```

The formula for the conversion is:

```
fahrenheit = (9.0 / 5) * celsius + 32
```

Implement the header file and write a test program that invokes these functions to display the following tables:

| Celsius | Fahrenheit | | Fahrenheit | Celsius |
|---|---|---|---|---|
| 40.0 | 105.0 | | 120.0 | 48.89 |
| 39.0 | 102.2 | | 110.0 | 43.33 |
| ... | | | | |
| 32.0 | 89.6 | | 40.0 | 5.44 |
| 31.0 | 87.8 | | 30.0 | -1.11 |

**5.9** (*Conversions between feet and meters*) Write a header file that contains the following two functions:

```
/* Converts from feet to meters */
double footToMeter(double foot)

/* Converts from meters to feet */
double meterToFoot(double meter)
```

The formula for the conversion is:

```
meter = 0.305 * foot
```

Implement the header file and write a test program that invokes these functions to display the following tables:

| Feet | Meters | | Meters | Feet |
|------|--------|---|--------|------|
| 1.0  | 0.305  | | 20.0   | 65.574 |
| 2.0  | 0.61   | | 25.0   | 81.967 |
| ...  |        | |        |      |
| 9.0  | 2.745  | | 60.0   | 195.721 |
| 10.0 | 3.05   | | 65.0   | 213.115 |

**5.10** (*Computing GCD*) Write a function that returns the greatest common divisor between two positive integers using the following header:

```
int gcd(int m, int n)
```

Write a test program that computes gcd(24, 16) and gcd(255, 25).

**5.11** (*Financial application: computing commissions*) Write a function that computes the commission using the scheme in Listing 4.7, FindSalesAmount.cpp. The header of the function is as follows:

```
double computeCommission(double salesAmount)
```

Write a test program that displays the following table:

| SalesAmount | Commission |
|-------------|------------|
| 10000       | 900.0      |
| 15000       | 1500.0     |
| ...         |            |
| 95000       | 11100.0    |
| 100000      | 11700.0    |

**5.12** (*Displaying characters*) Write a function that prints characters using the following header:

```
void printChars(char ch1, char ch2, int numberPerLine)
```

This function prints the characters between ch1 and ch2 with the specified numbers per line. Write a test program that prints ten characters per line from '1' and 'Z'.

**5.13*** (*Summing series*) Write a function to compute the following series:

$$m(i) = \frac{1}{2} + \frac{2}{3} + \cdots + \frac{i}{i+1}$$

Write a test program that displays the following table:

```
i          m(i)

2          0.5
3          1.1667
...
19         15.4523
20         16.4023
```

**5.14*** (*Computing series*) Write a function to compute the following series:

$$m(i) = 4\left(1 - \frac{1}{3} + \frac{1}{5} - \frac{1}{7} + \frac{1}{9} - \frac{1}{11} + \frac{1}{13} - \cdots - \frac{1}{2i-1} + \frac{1}{2i+1}\right)$$

**5.15*** (*Financial application: printing a tax table*) Use the **computeTax** functions in Listing 5.10, ComputeTaxWithFunction.cpp, to write a program that prints a 2002 tax table for taxable income from $50,000 to $60,000 with intervals of $50 for all four statuses, as follows:

| Taxable Income | Single | Married Joint | Married Separate | Head of a House |
|---|---|---|---|---|
| 50000 | 9846 | 7296 | 10398 | 8506 |
| 50050 | 9859 | 7309 | 10411 | 8519 |
| ... | | | | |
| 59950 | 12532 | 9982 | 13190 | 11192 |
| 60000 | 12546 | 9996 | 13205 | 11206 |

**5.16*** (*Revising Listing 4.11 PrimeNumber.cpp*) Write a program that meets the following requirements:

- Declare a function to determine whether an integer is a prime number. Use the following function header:

**bool** isPrime(**int** num)

An integer greater than $1$ is a *prime number* if its only divisor is $1$ or itself. For example, **isPrime(11)** returns **true**, and **isPrime(9)** returns **false**.

- Use the **isPrime** function to find the first thousand prime numbers and display every ten prime numbers in a row, as follows:

```
2    3    5    7    11   13   17   19   23   29
31   37   41   43   47   53   59   61   67   71
73   79   83   89   97   ...
...
```

**5.17*** (*Displaying matrix of 0s and 1s*) Write a function that displays an n by n matrix using the following header:

**void** printMatrix(**int** n)

Each element is 0 or 1, which is generated randomly. Write a test program that prints a 3 by 3 matrix that may look like this:

```
0 1 0
0 0 0
1 1 1
```

### Section 5.12

**5.18**[*] (*Generating random characters*) Use the functions in **RandomCharacter** in List-ing 5.13 to print one hundred uppercase letters and then one hundred single digits, and print ten per line.

### Section 5.14 The Math Functions

**5.19** (*Using the **sqrt** function*) Write a program that prints the following table using the **sqrt** function:

```
Number      SquareRoot
  0            0.0000
  2            1.4142
...
 18            5.2426
 20            5.4721
```

**5.20**[*] (*The **MyTriangle** header file*) Create a header file named **MyTriangle.h** that contains the following two functions:

```
/* Returns true if the sum of any two sides is
 * greater than the third side. */
bool isValid(double side1, double side2, double side3)

/* Returns the area of the triangle. */
double area(double side1, double side2, double side3)
```

The formula for computing the area is

$$s = (side1 + side2 + side3)/2;$$
$$area = \sqrt{s(s - side1)(s - side2)(s - side3)}$$

Implement the header file and write a test program that reads three sides for a tri-angle and computes the area if the input is valid. Otherwise, display that the input is invalid.

**5.21** (*Using trigonometric functions*) Print the following table to display the **sin** value and **cos** value of degrees from **0** to **360** with increments of **10** degrees. Round the value to keep four digits after the decimal point.

```
Degree    Sin        Cos
0         0.0        1.0
10        0.1736     0.9848
...
350       -0.1736    0.9848
360       0.0        1.0
```

**5.22**[**] (*Financial application: computing mean and standard deviation*) In business appli-cations, you are often asked to compute the mean and standard deviation of data. The mean is simply the average of the numbers. The standard deviation is a statis-tic that tells you how tightly all the various data are clustered around the mean in a set of data. For example, what is the average age of the students in a class? How close are the ages? If all the students are the same age, the deviation is **0**. Write a program that generates ten random numbers between **0** and **1000**, and computes the mean and standard deviations of these numbers using the following formula:

$$mean = \frac{\sum_{i=1}^{n} x_i}{n} = \frac{x_1 + x_2 + \cdots + x_n}{n} \qquad deviation = \sqrt{\frac{\sum_{i=1}^{n} x_i^2 - \frac{\left(\sum_{i=1}^{n} x_i\right)^2}{n}}{n - 1}}$$

**5.23**[**] (*Approximating the square root*) Implement the `sqrt` function. The square root of a number, `num`, can be approximated by repeatedly performing a calculation using the following formula:

```
nextGuess = (lastGuess + (num / lastGuess)) / 2
```

When `nextGuess` and `lastGuess` are almost identical, `nextGuess` is the approximated square root.

The initial guess will be the starting value of `lastGuess`. If the difference between `nextGuess` and `lastGuess` is less than a very small number, such as `0.0001`, you can claim that `nextGuess` is the approximated square root of `num`.

**5.24**[***] (*Displaying current date and time*) Listing 2.11, ShowCurrentTime.cpp, displays the current time. Improve this example to display the current date and time. The calendar example in §5.15, "Function Abstraction and Stepwise Refinement," should give you some ideas on how to find the year, month, and day.

**5.25**[**] (*Emirp*) An *emirp* (prime spelled backwards) is a prime number whose reversal is also a prime. For example, `17` is a prime and `71` is a prime. So `17` and `71` are emirps. Write a program that displays the first `100` emirps. Display `10` numbers per line and align the numbers properly, as follows:

```
 2   3   5   7   11   13   17   31   37   71
73  79  97  101  107  113  131  149  151  157
. . .
```

**5.26**[**] (*Palindromic prime*) A *palindromic prime* is simultaneous a prime number and palindromic. For example, `131` is a prime and also a palindromic. So `17` and `71` are emirps. Write a program that displays the first `100` emirps. Display `10` numbers per line and align the numbers properly, as follows:

```
  2    3    5    7   11   101   131   151   181   191
313  353  373  383  727   757   787   797   919   929
. .
```

**5.27**[**] (*Mersenne prime*) A prime number is called a *Mersenne prime* if it can be written in the form of $2^p - 1$ for some positive integer $p$. Write a program that finds all Mersenne primes with $p \leq 31$ and displays the output as follows:

```
p          2^p - 1

2            3
3            7
5           31
. . .
```

**5.28**[**] (*Twin primes*) Twin primes are a pair of two prime numbers that differ by `2`. For example, `3` and `5` are twin primes, `5` and `7` are twin primes, and `11` and `13` are twin primes. Write a program to find all twin primes less than `1000`. Display the output as follows:

```
(3, 5)
(5, 7)
. . .
```

CHAPTER **6**

# ARRAYS

## Objectives

- To describe why an array is necessary in programming (§6.1).

- To learn how to declare an array (§6.2.1).

- To access array elements using indexed variables (§6.2.2).

- To initialize the values in an array (§6.2.3).

- To develop and invoke functions with array arguments (§§6.3–6.4).

- To search elements using the linear (§6.5.1) or binary search algorithm (§6.5.2).

- To sort an array using the selection sort (§6.6.1).

- (Optional) To sort an array using the insertion sort (§6.6.2).

- To declare and create two-dimensional arrays (§6.7).

- (Optional) To declare and create multidimensional arrays (§6.8).

# 6.1 Introduction

why array?

Often you will have to store a large number of values during the execution of a program. Suppose, for instance, that you want to read one hundred numbers, compute their average, and find out how many numbers are above the average. Your program first reads the numbers and computes their average, and then compares each number with the average to determine whether it is above the average. The numbers all must be stored in variables in order to accomplish this task. You have to declare one hundred variables and repeatedly write almost identical code one hundred times. From the standpoint of practicality, it is impossible to write a program this way. An efficient, organized approach is needed. C++ and all other high-level languages provide a data structure, the *array,* which stores a fixed-size sequential collection of elements of the same type.

array

# 6.2 Array Basics

An array is used to store a collection of data, but it is often more useful to think of an array as a collection of variables of the same type. Instead of declaring individual variables, such as **number0**, **number1**, ..., and **number99**, you declare one array variable such as **numbers** and use **numbers[0]**, **numbers[1]**, ..., and **numbers[99]** to represent individual variables. This section introduces how to declare array variables, create arrays, and process arrays using indexed variables.

## 6.2.1 Declaring Arrays

To declare an array, you need to specify its element type and size using the following syntax:

```
dataType arrayName[arraySize];
```

The **arraySize** must be an integer greater than zero. For example, the following statement declares an array of ten **double** values:

```
double myList[10];
```

arbitrary initial values

The compiler allocates the space for ten **double** elements for array **myList**. When an array is created, its elements are assigned with *arbitrary values.* To assign values to the elements using the syntax:

```
arrayName[index] = value;
```

For example, the following code initializes the array:

```
myList[0] = 5.6;
myList[1] = 4.5;
myList[2] = 3.3;
myList[3] = 13.2;
myList[4] = 4.0;
myList[5] = 34.33;
myList[6] = 34.0;
myList[7] = 45.45;
myList[8] = 99.993;
myList[9] = 11123;
```

The array is pictured in Figure 6.1.

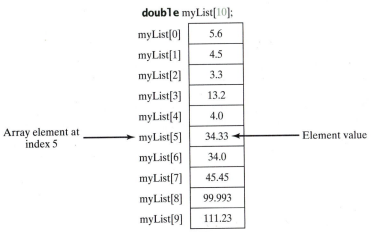

**FIGURE 6.1** The array **myList** has ten elements of **double** type and **int** indices from **0** to **9**.

**Note**

C++ requires that the array size used to declare an array must be a constant expression. For example, the following code is illegal:

```
int size = 4;
double myList[size]; // Wrong
```

But it would be OK, if **SIZE** is a constant as follows:                                                constant size

```
const int SIZE = 4;
double myList[SIZE]; // Correct
```

**Note**

When an array is created, its elements are assigned with arbitrary values.                                arbitrary initial values

**Tip**

If arrays have the same element type, they can be declared together, as follows:                         declaring together

```
datatype arrayName1[size1], arrayName2[size2], …, arrayNamen[sizen];
```

The variables are separated by commas. For example,

```
double list1[10], list2[25];
```

## 6.2.2 Array Indexed Variables

The array elements are accessed through the index. Array indices are *0-based;* that is, they         array index
start from **0** to **arraySize-1**. In the example in Figure 6.1, **myList** holds ten **double** values    0-based
and the indices are from **0** to **9**.

Each element in the array is represented using the following syntax, known as an *indexed*         indexed variables
*variable:*

```
arrayName[index];
```

For example, **myList[9]** represents the last element in the array **myList**.

**Caution**

Some languages use parentheses to reference an array element, as in `myList(9)`. But C++ uses brackets, as in `myList[9]`.

no bound checking

**Caution**

C++ does not check the array's boundary. So, accessing array elements using subscripts beyond the boundary (e.g., `myList[-1]` and `myList[11]`) does not cause syntax errors, but the operating system might report a memory access violation.

After an array is declared, an indexed variable can be used in the same way as a regular variable. For example, the following code adds the values in `myList[0]` and `myList[1]` to `myList[2]`:

```
myList[2] = myList[0] + myList[1];
```

The following loop assigns 0 to `myList[0]`, 1 to `myList[1]`, ..., and 9 to `myList[9]`:

```
for (int i = 0; i < 10; i++)
{
  myList[i] = i;
}
```

### 6.2.3 Array Initializers

array initializer

C++ has a shorthand notation, known as the *array initializer,* which combines declaring an array and initializing in one statement using the following syntax:

```
dataType arrayName[arraySize] = {value0, value1, ..., valuek};
```

For example,

```
double myList[4] = {1.9, 2.9, 3.4, 3.5};
```

This statement declares and initializes the array `myList` with four elements, which is equivalent to the statements shown below:

```
double myList[4];
myList[0] = 1.9;
myList[1] = 2.9;
myList[2] = 3.4;
myList[3] = 3.5;
```

**Caution**

Using an array initializer, you have to declare, and initialize the array all in one statement. Splitting it would cause a syntax error. Thus the next statement is wrong:

```
double myList[4];
myList = {1.9, 2.9, 3.4, 3.5};
```

**Note**

implicit size

C++ allows you to omit the array size when declaring and creating an array using an initialzer. For example, the following declaration is fine:

```
double myList[] = {1.9, 2.9, 3.4, 3.5};
```

C++ automatically figures out how many elements are in the array.

**Note**

C++ allows you to initialize a part of the array. For example, the following statement assigns values 1.9, 2.9 to the first two elements of the array. The other two elements will be set to zero. Note that if an array is declared, but not initialized, all its elements will contain "garbage," like all other local variables.

partial initialization

```
double myList[4] = {1.9, 2.9};
```

## 6.2.4   Initializing Character Arrays

You can initialize a character array using an initializer just like any other arrays. For example, the following code initializes the array `city`:

```
char city[] = {'D', 'a', 'l', 'l', 'a', 's'};
```

C++ allows you to initialize a character array simply with a string. For example,

```
char city[] = "Dallas";
```

This statement is equivalent to the preceding statement, except that C++ adds the character '\0', called the *null terminator,* to indicate the end of the string, as shown in Figure 6.2. Recall that a character that begins with the backslash symbol (\\) is an escape character.

| 'D' | 'a' | 'l' | 'l' | 'a' | 's' | '\0' |
|------|------|------|------|------|------|------|
| city[0] | city[1] | city[2] | city[3] | city[4] | city[5] | city[6] |

**FIGURE 6.2**   A character array can be initialized with a string.

## 6.2.5   Processing Arrays

When processing array elements, you will often use a `for` loop. Here are the reasons why:

■ All of the elements in an array are of the same type. They are evenly processed in the same fashion by repeatedly using a loop.

■ Since the size of the array is known, it is natural to use a `for` loop.

Assume the array is declared as follows:

```
const int ARRAY_SIZE = 10;
double myList[ARRAY_SIZE];
```

Here are some examples of processing arrays:

1. (*Initializing arrays with random values*) The following loop initializes the array `myList` with random values between 0 and 99:

```
for (int i = 0; i < ARRAY_SIZE; i++)
{
   myList[i] = rand() % 100;
}
```

2. (*Printing arrays*) To print an array, you have to print each element in the array using a loop like the following:

```
for (int i = 0; i < ARRAY_SIZE; i++)
{
   cout << myList[i] << " ";
}
```

print character array

 **Tip**

For a character array, it can be printed using one print statement. For example, the following code displays Dallas:

```
char city[] = "Dallas";
cout << city;
```

3. (*Copying arrays*) Can you copy array using a syntax like this?

```
list = myList;
```

This is not allowed in C++. You have to copy individual elements from one array to the other as follows:

```
for (int i = 0; i < ARRAY_SIZE; i++)
{
  list[i] = myList[i];
}
```

4. (*Summing all elements*) Use a variable named **total** to store the sum. Initially, **total** is **0**. Add each element in the array to **total** using a loop like this:

```
double total = 0;
for (int i = 0; i < ARRAY_SIZE; i++)
{
  total += myList[i];
}
```

5. (*Finding the largest element*) Use a variable named **max** to store the largest element. Initially **max** is **myList[0]**. To find the largest element in the array **myList**, compare each element in **myList** with **max**, then update **max** if the element is greater than **max**.

```
double max = myList[0];
for (int i = 1; i < ARRAY_SIZE; i++)
{
  if (myList[i] > max) max = myList[i];
}
```

6. (*Finding the smallest index of the largest element*) Often you need to locate the largest element in an array. If an array has more than one largest element, find the smallest index of such an element. Suppose the array **myList** is {1, 5, 3, 4, 5, 5}. So, the largest element is **5** and the smallest index for **5** is **1**. Use a variable named **max** to store the largest element and a variable named **indexOfMax** to denote the index of the largest element. Initially **max** is **myList[0]** and **indexOfMax** is **0**. Compare each element in **myList** with **max**, then update **max** and **indexOfMax** if the element is greater than **max**.

```
double max = myList[0];
int indexOfMax = 0;

for (int i = 1; i < ARRAY_SIZE; i++)
{
  if (myList[i] > max)
  {
    max = myList[i];
    indexOfMax = i;
  }
}
```

What is the consequence if **(myList[i] > max)** is replaced by **(myList[i] >= max)**?

## 6.2.6 Example: Testing Arrays

This section presents a program that reads six integers, finds the largest of them, and counts its occurrences. Suppose that you entered 3, 5, 2, 5, 5, 5; the program finds that the largest is 5 and the occurrence count for 5 is 4.

An intuitive solution is to first read the numbers and store them in an array, then find the largest number in the array, and finally count the occurrences of the largest number in the array. The program is given in Listing 6.1.

**LISTING 6.1** TestArray.cpp

```cpp
 1 #include <iostream>
 2 using namespace std;
 3
 4 int main()
 5 {
 6   const int TOTAL_NUMBERS = 6;                          array size
 7   int numbers[TOTAL_NUMBERS];                           declare array
 8
 9   // Read all numbers
10   for (int i = 0; i < TOTAL_NUMBERS; i++)
11   {
12     cout << "Enter a number: ";
13     cin >> numbers[i];                                 enter number
14   }
15
16   // Find the largest
17   int max = numbers[0];
18   for (int i = 1; i < TOTAL_NUMBERS; i++)
19   {
20     if (max < numbers[i])
21       max = numbers[i];                                update max
22   }
23
24   // Find the occurrence of the largest number
25   int count = 0;
26   for (int i = 0; i < TOTAL_NUMBERS; i++)
27   {
28     if (numbers[i] == max) count++;                    count occurrence
29   }
30
31   // Display the result
32   cout << "The array is ";
33   for (int i = 0; i < TOTAL_NUMBERS; i++)
34   {
35     cout << numbers[i] << " ";                         display output
36   }
37
38   cout << "\nThe largest number is " << max;
39   cout << "\nThe occurrence count of the largest number is "
40        << count;
41
42   return 0;
43 }
```

```
Enter a number:  5  ⏎Enter
Enter a number:  2  ⏎Enter
```

```
Enter a number: 5 ↵Enter
Enter a number: 5 ↵Enter
Enter a number: 5 ↵Enter
The array is 3 5 2 5 5 5
The largest number is 5
The occurrence count of the largest number is 4
```

The program declares an array of six integers (line 7) and enters the element from the keyboard (lines 10–14). It finds the largest number in the array (lines 17–22), counts its occurrences (lines 25–29), and displays the result (lines 32–40). To display the array, you need to display each element in the array using a loop.

Without using the **numbers** array, you would have to declare a variable for each number entered, because all the numbers are compared to the largest number to count its occurrences after it is found.

**Caution**

off-by-one error

Programmers often mistakenly reference the first element in an array with index **1**, so that the index of the tenth element becomes **10**. This is called the *off-by-one error*.

**Tip**

checking subscripts

Since C++ does not check the array's boundary, you should pay special attention to ensure the subscripts are within the range. Check the first and the last iteration in a loop to see whether the subscripts are in the permissible range.

**Tip**

debugging in IDE

If you use Visual C++, please refer to Supplement II.B, "*Learning C++ Effectively with Visual C++*," on the Companion Website. This supplement shows you how to use a debugger to inspect arrays.

### 6.2.7 Example: Assigning Grades

This example writes a program that reads student scores, gets the best score, and then assigns grades based on the following scheme:

Grade is A if score is $>=$ best $-$ 10;

Grade is B if score is $>=$ best $-$ 20;

Grade is C if score is $>=$ best $-$ 30;

Grade is D if score is $>=$ best $-$ 40;

Grade is F otherwise.

The program reads the scores, finds the best score, and finally assigns grades to the students based on the preceding scheme. For simplicity, assume that there are five students. Listing 6.2 gives the solution to the problem.

### LISTING 6.2 AssignGrade.cpp

```
1 #include <iostream>
2 using namespace std;
3
4 int main()
5 {
```

```
6     // Maximum number of students
7     const int NUMBER_OF_STUDENTS = 5;
8     int scores[NUMBER_OF_STUDENTS]; // Array scores
9     int best = 0; // The best score
10    char grade; // The grade
11
12    // Read scores and find the best score
13    for (int i = 0; i < NUMBER_OF_STUDENTS; i++)
14    {
15      cout << "Please enter a score: ";
16      cin >> scores[i];
17      if (scores[i] > best)
18        best = scores[i];
19    }
20
21    // Assign and display grades
22    for (int i = 0; i < NUMBER_OF_STUDENTS; i++)
23    {
24      if (scores[i] >= best - 10)
25        grade = 'A';
26      else if (scores[i] >= best - 20)
27        grade = 'B';
28      else if (scores[i] >= best - 30)
29        grade = 'C';
30      else if (scores[i] >= best - 40)
31        grade = 'D';
32      else
33        grade = 'F';
34
35      cout << "Student " << i << " score is " << scores[i] <<
36        " and grade is " << grade << "\n";
37    }
38
39    return 0;
40  }
```

*constant*

*declare array*

*enter score*

*update best*

*assign grade*

*display output*

```
Please enter a score: 4  ↵Enter
Please enter a score: 40 ↵Enter
Please enter a score: 50 ↵Enter
Please enter a score: 60 ↵Enter
Please enter a score: 70 ↵Enter
Student 0 score is 4 and grade is F
Student 1 score is 40 and grade is C
Student 2 score is 50 and grade is B
Student 3 score is 60 and grade is A
Student 4 score is 70 and grade is A
```

The program declares **scores** as an array of **int** type in order to store the students' scores (line 8).

The array is not needed to find the best score, but it is needed to keep all of the scores so that grades can be assigned later on, and it is needed when scores are printed along with the students' grades.

# 6.3 Passing Arrays to Functions

Just as you can pass single values to a function, you also can pass an entire array to a function. Listing 6.3 gives an example to demonstrate how to declare and invoke this type of function.

LISTING 6.3 PassArrayDemo.cpp

function prototype

declare array
invoke function

function implementation

```
1 #include <iostream>
2 using namespace std;
3
4 void printArray(int list[], int arraySize); // Function prototype
5
6 int main()
7 {
8    int numbers[5] = {1, 4, 3, 6, 8};
9    printArray(numbers, 5);
10
11   return 0;
12 }
13
14 void printArray(int list[], int arraySize)
15 {
16   for (int i = 0; i < arraySize; i++)
17   {
18     cout << list[i] << " ";
19   }
20 }
```

```
1 4 3 6 8
```

In the function header (line 14), `int list[]` indicates that the parameter is an integer array of any size. So you can pass any integer array to invoke this function (line 9).

Note that the parameter names in function prototypes can be omitted. So the function prototype may be declared without the parameter name `list` and `arraySize` as follows:

```
void printArray(int [], int arraySize); // Function prototype
```

**Note**

passing size along with array

Normally when you pass an array to a function, you should also pass its size in another argument. So the function knows how many elements are in the array. Otherwise, you will have to hard code this into the function or declare it in a global variable. Neither is flexible or robust.

You can pass a primitive data type variable or an array to a function. However, there are important differences between them.

pass-by-value

■ Passing a variable of a primitive type means that the value of the variable is passed to a formal parameter. Changing the value of the local parameter inside the function does not affect the value of the variable outside the function. This is *pass-by-value*.

pass-by-reference

■ Passing an array means that the starting address of the array is passed to the formal parameter. The parameter inside the function references to the same array that is passed to the function. No new arrays are created. This is *pass-by-reference*.

Listing 6.4 gives an example that demonstrates the differences between pass-by-value and pass-by-reference.

LISTING 6.4 PassByReferenceDemo.cpp

```
1 #include <iostream>
2 using namespace std;
3
```

```
 4 void m(int, int []);                                      function prototype
 5
 6 int main()
 7 {
 8   int x = 1; // x represents an int value
 9   int y[10]; // y represents an array of int values
10   y[0] = 1; // Initialize y[0]
11
12   m(x, y); // Invoke m with arguments x and y            pass array y
13
14   cout << "x is " << x << endl;
15   cout << "y[0] is " << y[0] << endl;
16
17   return 0;
18 }
19
20 void m(int number, int numbers[])
21 {
22   number = 1001; // Assign a new value to number
23   numbers[0] = 5555; // Assign a new value to numbers[0]   modify array
24 }
```

```
x is 1
y[0] is 5555
```

You will see that after function m is invoked, x remains 1, but y[0] is 5555. This is because the value of x is copied to number, and x and number are independent variables, but y and numbers reference to the same array numbers can be considered as an alias for array y.

Passing arrays by reference makes sense for performance reasons. If an array is passed by value, all its elements must be copied into a new array. For large arrays, it could take some time and additional memory space. However, passing arrays by reference could lead to errors if your function changes the array accidentally. To prevent it from happening, you can put the const keyword before the array parameter to tell the compiler that the array cannot be changed. The compiler will report errors if the code in the function attempts to modify the array.

Listing 6.5 gives an example that declares a const array argument list in the function p (line 4). The function attempts to modify the first element in the array in line 7. This error is detected by the compiler, as shown in the sample output.

## Listing 6.5   ConstArrayDemo.cpp

```
 1 #include <iostream>
 2 using namespace std;
 3
 4 void p(const int list[], int arraySize)                   const array argument
 5 {
 6   // Modify array accidentally
 7   list[0] = 100; // Compile error!                         attempt to modify
 8 }
 9
10 int main()
11 {
12   int numbers[5] = {1, 4, 3, 6, 8};
```

```
13    p(numbers, 5);
14
15    return 0;
16 }
```

Compiled using
Visual C++

```
error C2166: l-value specifies const object
```

Compiling using
GNU C++ compiler

```
ConstArrayDemo.cpp:1:error: assignment of read-only location
```

Both Visual C++ and the GNU compiler report the error. L-value means the left value on the left side of an assignment statement. Since the l-value is declared **const**, it cannot be changed.

 **Note**

cascading **const** parameters

If you define a **const** parameter in a function **f1** and this parameter is passed to another function **f2**, then the corresponding parameter in function **f2** should be declared **const** for consistency. Consider the following code:

```
void f2 (int list[], int size)
{
  // Do something
}

void f1(const int list[], int size)
{
  // Do something
  f2(list, size);
}
```

The compiler reports an error, because **list** is **const** in **f1** and it is passed to **f2**, but it is not **const** in **f2**. The function declaration for **f2** should be

```
void f2(const int list[], int size)
```

## 6.4 Returning Arrays from Functions

You can declare a function to return a primitive type value. For example,

```
// Return the sum of the elements in the list
int sum(int list[], int size)
```

Can you return an array from a function using a similar syntax? For example, you may attempt to declare a function that returns a new array that is a reversal of an array as follows:

```
// Return the reversal of list
int[] reverse(const int list[], int size)
```

This is not allowed in C++. However, you can circumvent this restriction by passing two array arguments in the function, as follows:

```cpp
// newList is the reversal of list
void reverse(const int list[], list newList[], int size)
```

The program is given in Listing 6.6.

### LISTING 6.6  ReverseArray.cpp

```cpp
 1 #include <iostream>
 2 using namespace std;
 3
 4 // newList is the reversal of list
 5 void reverse(const int list[], int newList[], int size)
 6 {
 7   for (int i = 0, j = size - 1; i < size; i++, j--)
 8   {
 9     newList[j] = list[i];
10   }
11 }
12
13 void printArray(const int list[], int size)
14 {
15   for (int i = 0; i < size; i++)
16     cout << list[i] << " ";
17 }
18
19 int main()
20 {
21   int size = 6;
22   int list[] = {1, 2, 3, 4, 5, 6};
23   int newList[6];
24
25   reverse(list, newList, size);
26
27   cout << "The original array: ";
28   printArray(list, 6);
29   cout << endl;
30
31   cout << "The reversed array: ";
32   printArray(newList, 6);
33   cout << endl;
34
35   return 0;
36 }
```

*reverse function*

*reverse to **newList***

*print array*

*declare original array*
*declare new array*

*invoke reverse*

*print original array*

*print reversed array*

```
The original array: 1 2 3 4 5 6
The reversed array: 6 5 4 3 2 1
```

The **reverse** function uses a loop (lines 7–10) to copy the first element, second, ..., and so on in the original array to the last element, second last, ..., into the new array, respectively, as shown in the following diagram:

To invoke this function (line 25), you have to pass three arguments. The first argument is the original array whose contents are not changed in the function. The second argument is the new array whose contents are changed in the function. The third argument indicates the size of the array.

## 6.5 Searching Arrays

*Searching* is the process of looking for a specific element in an array; for example, discovering whether a certain score is included in a list of scores. Searching is a common task in computer programming. There are many algorithms and data structures devoted to searching. In this section, two commonly used approaches are discussed, *linear search* and *binary search*.

### 6.5.1   The Linear Search Approach

linear search

The linear search approach compares the key element **key** sequentially with each element in the array. The function continues to do so until the key matches an element in the array or the array is exhausted without a match being found. If a match is made, the linear search returns the index of the element in the array that matches the key. If no match is found, the search returns –1. The **linearSearch** function in Listing 6.7 gives the solution:

### LISTING 6.7   LinearSearch.h

```
 1 int linearSearch(int list[], int key, int arraySize)
 2 {
 3    for (int i = 0; i < arraySize; i++)
 4    {
 5      if (key == list[i])
 6        return i;
 7    }
 8
 9    return -1;
10 }
```

[0] [1] [2] ...

list

key Compare key with list[i] for i = 0, 1, ...

Please trace the function using the following statements:

```
int list[] = {1, 4, 4, 2, 5, -3, 6, 2};
int i = linearSearch(list, 4, 8);   // Returns 1
int j = linearSearch(list, -4, 8);  // Returns -1
int k = linearSearch(list, -3, 8);  // Returns 5
```

The linear search function compares the key with each element in the array. The elements in the array can be in any order. On average, the algorithm will have to compare half of the elements in an array before finding the key if it exists. Since the execution time of a linear search increases linearly as the number of array elements increases, linear search is inefficient for a large array.

### 6.5.2   The Binary Search Approach

binary search

Binary search is the other common search approach for a list of values. For binary search to work, the elements in the array already must be ordered. Without loss of generality, assume that the array is in ascending order. The binary search first compares the key with the element in the middle of the array. Consider the following three cases:

■ If the key is less than the middle element, you only need to continue to search for the key in the first half of the array.

■ If the key is equal to the middle element, the search ends with a match.

■ If the key is greater than the middle element, you only need to continue to search for the key in the second half of the array.

Clearly, the binary search function eliminates half of the array after each comparison. Suppose that the array has *n* elements. For convenience, let n be a power of 2. After the first comparison, there are n/2 elements left for further search; after the second comparison, there are (n/2)/2 elements left for further search. After the $k^{th}$ comparison, there are $n/2^k$ elements left for further search. When $k = log_2n$, only one element is left in the array, and you only need one more comparison. Therefore, in the worst case, you need $log_2n+1$ comparisons to find an element in the sorted array when using the binary search approach. For a list of 1024 ($2^{10}$) elements, binary search requires only eleven comparisons in the worst case, whereas a linear search would take 1024 comparisons in the worst case.

The portion of the array being searched shrinks by half after each comparison. Let low and high denote, respectively, the first index and last index of the array that is currently being searched. Initially, low is 0 and high is listSize-1. Let mid denote the index of the middle element. So mid is (low + high)/2. Figure 6.3 shows how to find key 11 in the list {2, 4, 7, 10, 11, 45, 50, 59, 60, 66, 69, 70, 79} using binary search.

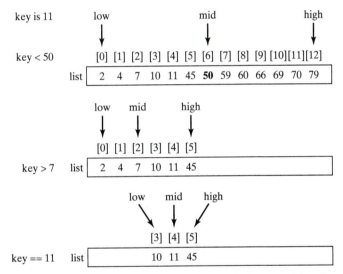

**FIGURE 6.3** Binary search eliminates half of the list from further consideration after each comparison.

The binary search returns the index of the search key if it is contained in the list. Otherwise, it returns -(insertion point + 1). The insertion point is the point at which the key would be inserted into the list. For example, the insertion point for key 5 is 2, so the binary search returns −3; the insertion point for key 51 is 7, so the binary search returns −8.

You know how the binary approach works. The task now is to implement it in C++, as shown in Listing 6.8.

## LISTING 6.8 BinarySearch.h

```
1  int binarySearch(int list[], int key, int arraySize)
2  {
3    int low = 0;
4    int high = arraySize - 1;
5
6    while (high >= low)
7    {
8      int mid = (low + high) / 2;
9      if (key < list[mid])
10       high = mid - 1;
```

```
11        else if (key == list[mid])
12          return mid;
13        else
14          low = mid + 1;
15    }
16
17    return -low - 1;
18 }
```

You start to compare the key with the middle element in the list whose low index is 0 and high index is listSize-1. If key < list[mid], set the high index to mid-1; if key == list[mid], a match is found and return mid; if key > list[mid], set the low index to mid+1. Continue the search until low > high or a match is found. If low > high, return -1 - low, where low is the insertion point.

What happens if (high >= low) in line 6 is replaced by (high > low)? The search would miss a possible matching element. Consider a list with just one element. The search would miss the element, because high and low are both 0 in this case.

Does the function still work if there are duplicate elements in the list? Yes, as long as the elements are sorted in increasing order in the list. The function returns the index of one of the matching elements if the element is in the list.

To help understand this function, trace it with the following statements and identify low and high when the function returns:

```
int list[] = {2, 4, 7, 10, 11, 45, 50, 59, 60, 66, 69, 70, 79};
int i = binarySearch(list, 2, 13); // Returns 0
int j = binarySearch(list, 11, 13); // Returns 4
int k = binarySearch(list, 12, 13); // Returns -6
int l = binarySearch(list, 1); // Returns -1
int m = binarySearch(list, 3); // Returns -2
```

Here is the table that lists the low and high values when the function exits and the value returned from invoking the function.

| Function | low | high | Value Returned |
|---|---|---|---|
| binarySearch(list, 2) | 0 | 1 | 0 |
| binarySearch(list, 11) | 3 | 5 | 4 |
| binarySearch(list, 12) | 5 | 4 | -6 |
| binarySearch(list, 1) | 0 | -1 | -1 |
| binarySearch(list, 3) | 1 | 0 | -2 |

why -low - 1?

If the key matches an element in the list, the function returns the index of the element. This index is a non-negative integer (*including* 0). If the key is not in the list, low is the index where the element would be inserted. In this case, the function returns -low - 1. It would be more intuitive to return just -low. But this would be wrong. Suppose the key is smaller than list[0] (e.g., binarySearch(list, 1)). When the function exits, low is 0. Returning -low would be -0. There is no difference between -0 and 0. -0 would indicate that the element is not in the list, while 0 indicates that the key matches the first element in the list (e.g., binarySearch(list, 2)). So, returning -low for a non-matching case could conflict with returning 0 for the matching case on list[0]. For this reason, the function is designed to return -low - 1 for a non-matching case.

**Note**

Linear search is useful for finding an element in a small array or an unsorted array, but it is inefficient for large arrays. Binary search is more efficient, but requires that the array be pre-sorted.

# 6.6 Sorting Arrays

Sorting, like searching, is also a common task in computer programming. It would be used, for instance, if you wanted to display the grades from Listing 6.2, AssignGrade.cpp, in alphabetical order. Many different algorithms have been developed for sorting. This section introduces two simple, intuitive sorting algorithms: selection sort and insertion sort.

## 6.6.1 Selection Sort

Suppose that you want to sort a list in ascending order. Selection sort finds the largest number in the list and places it last. It then finds the largest number remaining and places it next to last, and so on, until the list contains only a single number. Figure 6.4 shows how to sort the list {2, 9, 5, 4, 8, 1, 6} using selection sort.

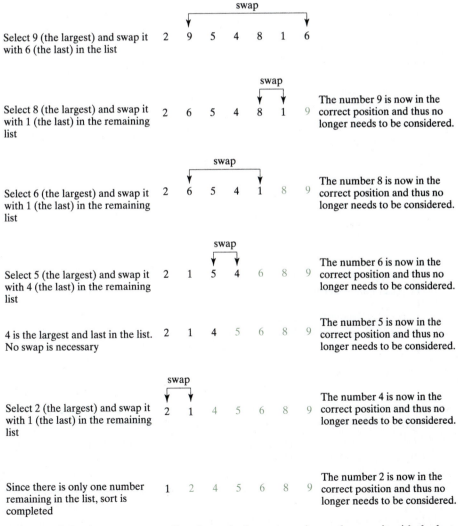

**FIGURE 6.4** Selection sort repeatedly selects the largest number and swaps it with the last number in the list.

You know how the selection sort approach works. The task now is to implement it in C++. For beginners, it is difficult to develop a complete solution on the first attempt. You may start to write the code for the first iteration to find the largest element in the list and swap it with the last element, and then observe what would be different for the second iteration, the third, and so on. The insight this gives will enable you to write a loop that generalizes all the iterations.

The solution can be described as follows:

```
for (int i = listSize - 1; i >= 1; i--)
{
  select the largest element in list[0..i];
  swap the largest with list[i], if necessary;
  // list[i] is in its correct position.
  // The next iteration apply on list[0..i-1]
}
```

Listing 6.9 implements the solution.

## LISTING 6.9 SelectionSort.h

```
1 void selectionSort(double list[], int arraySize)
2 {
3   for (int i = arraySize - 1; i >= 1; i--)
4   {
5     // Find the maximum in the list[0..i]
6     double currentMax = list[0];
7     int currentMaxIndex = 0;
8
9     for (int j = 1; j <= i; j++)
10    {
11      if (currentMax < list[j])
12      {
13        currentMax = list[j];
14        currentMaxIndex = j;
15      }
16    }
17
18    // Swap list[i] with list[currentMaxIndex] if necessary;
19    if (currentMaxIndex != i)
20    {
21      list[currentMaxIndex] = list[i];
22      list[i] = currentMax;
23    }
24  }
25 }
```

The `selectionSort(double list[])` function sorts any array of double elements. The function is implemented with a nested **for** loop. The outer loop (with the loop control variable **i**) (line 3) is iterated in order to find the largest element in the list, which ranges from `list[0]` to `list[i]`, and exchange it with the current last element, `list[i]`.

The variable **i** is initially `listSize-1`. After each iteration of the outer loop, `list[i]` is in the right place. Eventually, all the elements are put in the right place; therefore, the whole list is sorted.

To help understand this function, trace it with the following statements:

```
double list[] = {1, 9, 4.5, 6.6, 5.7, -4.5};
selectionSort(list, 6);
```

## 6.6.2    (Optional) Insertion Sort

Suppose that you want to sort a list in ascending order. The insertion-sort algorithm sorts a list of values by repeatedly inserting a new element into a sorted sublist until the whole list is sorted. Figure 6.5 shows how to sort the list {2, 9, 5, 4, 8, 1, 6} using insertion sort.

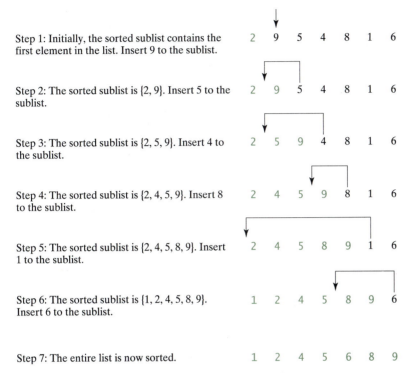

Step 1: Initially, the sorted sublist contains the first element in the list. Insert 9 to the sublist.

Step 2: The sorted sublist is {2, 9}. Insert 5 to the sublist.

Step 3: The sorted sublist is {2, 5, 9}. Insert 4 to the sublist.

Step 4: The sorted sublist is {2, 4, 5, 9}. Insert 8 to the sublist.

Step 5: The sorted sublist is {2, 4, 5, 8, 9}. Insert 1 to the sublist.

Step 6: The sorted sublist is {1, 2, 4, 5, 8, 9}. Insert 6 to the sublist.

Step 7: The entire list is now sorted.

**FIGURE 6.5**    Insertion sort repeatedly inserts a new element into a sorted sublist.

The algorithm can be described as follows:

```
for (int i = 1; i < listSize; i++) {
  insert list[i] into a sorted sublist list[0..i-1] so that
  list[0..i] is sorted.
}
```

To insert `list[i]` into `list[0..i-1]`, save `list[i]` into a temporary variable, say `currentElement`. Move `list[i-1]` to `list[i]` if `list[i-1]` > `currentElement`, move `list[i-2]` to `list[i-1]` if `list[i-2]` > `currentElement`, and so on, until `list[i-k]` <= `currentElement`. Assign `currentElement` to `list[i-k+1]`. For example, to insert 4 into {2, 5, 9} in Step 3 in Figure 6.6, move `list[2]` (9) to `list[3]` since 9 > 4, move `list[1]` (5) to `list[2]` since 5 > 4. Finally move `currentElement` (4) to `list[1]`, as shown in Figure 6.6.

The algorithm can be expanded and implemented in Listing 6.10.

## LISTING 6.10    InsertionSort.h

```
1 void insertionSort(double list[], int arraySize)
2 {
3   for (int i = 1; i < arraySize; i++)
4   {
5     /* Insert list[i] into a sorted sublist list[0..i-1] so that
6        list[0..i] is sorted. */
```

```
7      double currentElement = list[i];
8      int k;
9      for (k = i - 1; k >= 0 && list[k] > currentElement; k--)
10     {
11        list[k + 1] = list[k];
12     }
13
14     // Insert the current element into list[k+1]
15     list[k + 1] = currentElement;
16  }
17 }
```

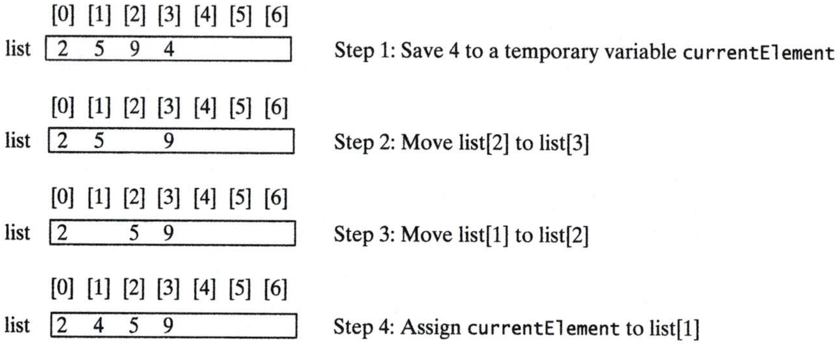

[0] [1] [2] [3] [4] [5] [6]

list  | 2 | 5 | 9 | 4 |   |   |   |          Step 1: Save 4 to a temporary variable currentElement

[0] [1] [2] [3] [4] [5] [6]

list  | 2 | 5 |   | 9 |   |   |   |          Step 2: Move list[2] to list[3]

[0] [1] [2] [3] [4] [5] [6]

list  | 2 |   | 5 | 9 |   |   |   |          Step 3: Move list[1] to list[2]

[0] [1] [2] [3] [4] [5] [6]

list  | 2 | 4 | 5 | 9 |   |   |   |          Step 4: Assign currentElement to list[1]

**FIGURE 6.6**  A new element is inserted into a sorted sublist.

The `insertionSort(double list[], int arraySize)` function sorts any array of double elements. The function is implemented with a nested **for** loop. The outer loop (with the loop control variable `i`) (line 3) is iterated in order to obtain a sorted sublist, which ranges from `list[0]` to `list[i]`. The inner loop (with the loop control variable `k`) inserts `list[i]` into the sublist from `list[0]` to `list[i-1]`.

To help understand this function, trace it with the following statements:

```
double list[] = {1, 9, 4.5, 6.6, 5.7, -4.5};
insertionSort(list, 6);
```

# 6.7 Two-Dimensional Arrays

Thus far, you have used one-dimensional arrays to model linear collections of elements. You can use a two-dimensional array to represent a matrix or a table.

## 6.7.1 Declaring Two-Dimensional Arrays

Here is the syntax for declaring a two-dimensional array:

```
dataType arrayName[rowSize][columnSize];
```

As an example, here is how you would declare a two-dimensional array variable `matrix` of **int** values:

```
int matrix[5][5];
```

Two subscripts are used in a two-dimensional array, one for the row, and the other for the column. As in a one-dimensional array, the index for each subscript is of the **int** type and starts from `0`, as shown in Figure 6.7(a).

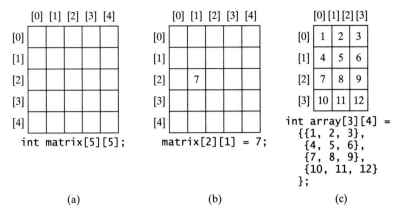

(a)                          (b)                          (c)

**FIGURE 6.7**    The index of each subscript of a two-dimensional array is an `int` value starting from 0.

To assign the value 7 to a specific element at row 2 and column 1, as shown in Figure 6.7(b), you can use the following:

```
matrix[2][1] = 7;
```

 **Caution**

It is a common mistake to use `matrix[2, 1]` to access the element at row 2 and column 1. In C++, each subscript must be enclosed in a pair of square brackets.

You also can use an array initializer to declare, create, and initialize a two-dimensional array. For example, the following code in (a) creates an array with the specified initial values, as shown in Figure 6.7(c). This is equivalent to the code in (b).

```
int array[4][3] =
  {{1, 2, 3},
   {4, 5, 6},
   {7, 8, 9},
   {10, 11, 12}
  };
```

Equivalent

```
int array[4][3];
array[0][0] = 1; array[0][1] = 2; array[0][2] = 3;
array[1][0] = 4; array[1][1] = 5; array[1][2] = 6;
array[2][0] = 7; array[2][1] = 8; array[2][2] = 9;
array[3][0] = 10; array[3][1] = 11; array[3][2] = 12;
```

(a)                                                    (b)

## 6.7.2    Processing Two-Dimensional Arrays

Suppose an array `matrix` is declared as follows:

```
const int ROW_SIZE = 10;
const int COLUMN_SIZE = 10;
int matrix[ROW_SIZE][COLUMN_SIZE];
```

Here are some examples of processing two-dimensional arrays:

1. (*Initializing arrays with random values*) The following loop initializes the array with random values between 0 and 99:

```
for (int row = 0; row < ROW_SIZE; row++)
{
  for (int column = 0; column < COLUMN_SIZE; column++)
  {
    matrix[row][column] = rand() % 100;
  }
}
```

2. (*Printing arrays*) To print a two-dimensional array, you have to print each element in the array using a loop like the following:

```cpp
for (int row = 0; row < ROW_SIZE; row++)
{
  for (int column = 0; column < COLUMN_SIZE; column++)
  {
    cout << matrix[row][column] << " ";
  }

  cout << endl;
}
```

3. (*Summing all elements*) Use a variable named **total** to store the sum. Initially **total** is **0**. Add each element in the array to **total** using a loop like this:

```cpp
int total = 0;
for (int row = 0; row < ROW_SIZE; row++)
{
  for (int column = 0; column < COLUMN_SIZE; column++)
  {
    total += matrix[row][column];
  }
}
```

4. (*Summing elements by column*) For each column, use a variable named **total** to store its sum. Add each element in the column to **total** using a loop like this:

```cpp
for (int column = 0; column < COLUMN_SIZE; column++)
{
  int total = 0;
  for (int row = 0; row < ROW_SIZE; row++)
    total += matrix[row][column];
  cout << "Sum for column " << column << " is " << total << endl;
}
```

5. (*Which row has the largest sum?*) Use variables **maxRow** and **indexOfMaxRow** to track the largest sum and index of the row. For each row, compute its sum and update **maxRow** and **indexOfMaxRow** if the new sum is greater.

```cpp
int maxRow = 0;
int indexOfMaxRow = 0;

// Get sum of the first row in maxRow
for (int column = 0; column < COLUMN_SIZE; column++)
  maxRow += matrix[0][column];

for (int row = 1; row < ROW_SIZE; row++)
{
  int totalOfThisRow = 0;
  for (int column = 0; column < COLUMN_SIZE; column++)
  {
    totalOfThisRow += matrix[row][column];
    if (totalOfThisRow > maxRow) {
      maxRow = totalOfThisRow;
      indexOfMaxRow = row;
    }
  }
}

cout << "Row " << indexOfMaxRow
  << " has the maximum sum" << " of " << maxRow << endl;
```

### 6.7.3   Passing Two-Dimensional Arrays to Functions

You can pass a two-dimensional array to a function; however, C++ requires that the column size be specified in the function declaration. Listing 6.11 gives an example with a function that returns the sum of all the elements in a matrix.

**LISTING 6.11**   PassTwoDimensionalArray.cpp

```
 1  #include <iostream>
 2  using namespace std;
 3
 4  const int COLUMN_SIZE = 3;
 5
 6  int sum(const int a[][COLUMN_SIZE], int rowSize)          fixed column size
 7  {
 8    int total = 0;
 9    for (int row = 0; row < rowSize; row++)
10    {
11      for (int column = 0; column < COLUMN_SIZE; column++)
12      {
13        total += a[row][column];
14      }
15    }
16
17    return total;
18  }
19
20  int main()
21  {
22    int array[4][3] = {
23      {1, 2, 3},
24      {4, 5, 6},
25      {7, 8, 9},
26      {10, 11, 12}
27    };
28
29    cout << "Sum of all elements is " << sum(array, 4) << endl;    pass array
30    return 0;
31  }
```

```
Sum of all elements is 78
```

The function **sum** (line 6) has two parameters. The first parameter specifies a two-dimensional array with a fixed column size. The second parameter specifies the row size for the two-dimensional array.

### 6.7.4   Example: Grading a Multiple-Choice Test

This example presents a program that grades multiple-choice tests. Suppose there are eight students and ten questions, and the answers are stored in a two-dimensional array. Each row records a student's answers to the questions. For example, the following array stores the test:

Students' Answers to the Questions:

|  | 0 | 1 | 2 | 3 | 4 | 5 | 6 | 7 | 8 | 9 |
|---|---|---|---|---|---|---|---|---|---|---|
| Student 0 | A | B | A | C | C | D | E | E | A | D |
| Student 1 | D | B | A | B | C | A | E | E | A | D |
| Student 2 | E | D | D | A | C | B | E | E | A | D |
| Student 3 | C | B | A | E | D | C | E | E | A | D |
| Student 4 | A | B | D | C | C | D | E | E | A | D |
| Student 5 | B | B | E | C | C | D | E | E | A | D |
| Student 6 | B | B | A | C | C | D | E | E | A | D |
| Student 7 | E | B | E | C | C | D | E | E | A | D |

The key is stored in a one-dimensional array, as follows:

Key to the Questions:

|  | 0 | 1 | 2 | 3 | 4 | 5 | 6 | 7 | 8 | 9 |
|---|---|---|---|---|---|---|---|---|---|---|
| key | D | B | D | C | C | D | A | E | A | D |

Your program grades the test and displays the result. The program compares each student's answers with the key, counts the number of correct answers, and displays it. Listing 6.12 gives the program.

### LISTING 6.12 GradeExam.cpp

```cpp
 1  #include <iostream>
 2  using namespace std;
 3
 4  int main()
 5  {
 6    const int NUMBER_OF_STUDENTS = 8;
 7    const int NUMBER_OF_QUESTIONS = 10;
 8
 9    // Students' answers to the questions
10    char answers[NUMBER_OF_STUDENTS][NUMBER_OF_QUESTIONS] =
11    {
12      {'A', 'B', 'A', 'C', 'C', 'D', 'E', 'E', 'A', 'D'},
13      {'D', 'B', 'A', 'B', 'C', 'A', 'E', 'E', 'A', 'D'},
14      {'E', 'D', 'D', 'A', 'C', 'B', 'E', 'E', 'A', 'D'},
15      {'C', 'B', 'A', 'E', 'D', 'C', 'E', 'E', 'A', 'D'},
16      {'A', 'B', 'D', 'C', 'C', 'D', 'E', 'E', 'A', 'D'},
17      {'B', 'B', 'E', 'C', 'C', 'D', 'E', 'E', 'A', 'D'},
18      {'B', 'B', 'A', 'C', 'C', 'D', 'E', 'E', 'A', 'D'},
19      {'E', 'B', 'E', 'C', 'C', 'D', 'E', 'E', 'A', 'D'}
20    };
21
22    // Key to the questions
23    char keys[] = {'D', 'B', 'D', 'C', 'C', 'D', 'A', 'E', 'A', 'D'};
24
25    // Grade all answers
26    for (int i = 0; i < NUMBER_OF_STUDENTS; i++)
27    {
```

two-dimensional array

array

```
28      // Grade one student
29      int correctCount = 0;
30      for (int j = 0; j < NUMBER_OF_QUESTIONS; j++)
31      {
32        if (answers[i][j] == keys[j])
33          correctCount++;
34      }
35
36      cout << "Student " << i << "'s correct count is " <<
37        correctCount << endl;
38    }
39
40    return 0;
41 }
```

```
Student 0's correct count is 7
Student 1's correct count is 6
Student 2's correct count is 5
Student 3's correct count is 4
Student 4's correct count is 8
Student 5's correct count is 7
Student 6's correct count is 7
Student 7's correct count is 7
```

The statement in lines 10–20 declares and initializes a two-dimensional array of characters. The statement in line 23 declares and initializes an array of **char** values.

Each row in the array **answers** stores a student's answer, which is graded by comparing it with the key in the array **keys**. The result is displayed immediately after a student's answer is graded.

### 6.7.5   (Optional) Example: Computing Taxes

Listing 5.10, ComputeTaxWithFunction.cpp, simplified Listing 3.5, ComputeTaxWithSelectionStatement.cpp. Listing 5.10 can be further improved using arrays. For each filing status, there are six tax rates. Each rate is applied to a certain bracket. For example, from the taxable income of $400,000 for a single filer, $6000 is taxed at 10%, $(27950 - 6000)$ at 15%, $(67700 - 27950)$ at 27%, $(141250 - 67700)$ at 30%, $(307050 - 141250)$ at 35%, and $(400000 - 307050)$ at 38.6%. The six rates are the same for all filing statuses, which can be represented in the following array:

```
double rates[] = {0.10, 0.15, 0.27, 0.30, 0.35, 0.386};
```

The brackets for each rate for all the filing statuses can be represented in a two-dimensional array as follows:

```
int brackets[4][5] =
{
  {6000, 27950, 67700, 141250, 307050}, // Single filer
  {12000, 46700, 112850, 171950, 307050}, // Married jointly
  {6000, 23350, 56425, 85975, 153525}, // Married separately
  {10000, 37450, 96700, 156600, 307050} // Head of household
};
```

Suppose the taxable income is $400,000 for single filers, the tax can be computed as follows:

```
brackets[0][0] * rates[0] +
(brackets[0][1] - brackets[0][0]) * rates[1] +
```

```
(brackets[0][2] - brackets[0][1]) * rates[2] +
(brackets[0][3] - brackets[0][2]) * rates[3] +
(brackets[0][4] - brackets[0][3]) * rates[4] +
(400000 - brackets[0][4]) * rates[5]
```

Listing 6.13 gives the solution to the program.

**LISTING 6.13** ComputeTax.cpp

```
 1 #include <iostream>
 2 #include <iomanip>
 3 using namespace std;
 4
 5 double computeTax(int, double);
 6
 7 int main()
 8 {
 9    // Prompt the user to enter filing status
10    cout << "(0-single filer, 1-married jointly,\n" <<
11      "2-married separately, 3-head of household\n" <<
12      "Enter the filing status: ";
13    int status;
14    cin >> status;
15
16    // Prompt the user to enter taxable income
17    cout << "Enter the taxable income: ";
18    double income;
19    cin >> income;
20
21    // Compute and display the result
22    cout << "Tax is " << fixed << setprecision(2) <<
23      computeTax(status, income);
24
25    return 0;
26 }
27
28 double computeTax(int status, double income)
29 {
30    const int BRACKET_SIZE = 6;
31    double rates[] = {0.10, 0.15, 0.27, 0.30, 0.35, 0.386};
32
33    int brackets[4][5] =
34    {
35      {6000, 27950, 67700, 141250, 307050}, // Single filer
36      {12000, 46700, 112850, 171950, 307050}, // Married jointly
37      {6000, 23350, 56425, 85975, 153525}, // Married separately
38      {10000, 37450, 96700, 156600, 307050} // Head of household
39    };
40
41    double tax = 0; // Tax to be computed
42
43    // Compute tax in the first bracket
44    if (income <= brackets[status][0])
45      return tax = income * rates[0]; // Done
46    else
47      tax = brackets[status][0] * rates[0];
48
49    // Compute tax in the 2nd, 3rd, 4th, and 5th brackets, if needed
50    for (int i = 1; i < BRACKET_SIZE; i++)
```

*function prototype* (line 5)

*input status* (line 14)

*input income* (line 19)

*compute tax* (line 23)

*brackets* (line 33)

*return tax* (line 45)

```
51  {
52    if (income > brackets[status][i])
53      tax += (brackets[status][i] - brackets[status][i - 1]) *
54        rates[i];
55    else
56    {
57      tax += (income - brackets[status][i - 1]) * rates[i];
58      return tax; // Done
59    }
60  }
61
62    // Compute tax in the last (i.e., 6th) bracket
63    return  tax += (income - brackets[status][4]) * rates[5];
64  }
```

return tax

return tax

```
0-single filer, 1-married jointly,
2-married separately, 3-head of household
Enter the filing status: 0  ↵Enter
Enter the taxable income: 12534  ↵Enter
Tax is 1580.10
```

The **computeTax** function computes the tax for the taxable income of a given filing status. The tax for the first bracket (**0** to **brackets[status][0]**) is computed in lines 44–47. The taxes for the second, third, fourth, and fifth brackets are computed in the loop in lines 50–60. The tax for the last bracket is computed in line 63.

## 6.8 (Optional) Multidimensional Arrays

In the preceding section, you used a two-dimensional array to represent a matrix or a table. Occasionally, you will need to represent *n*-dimensional data structures. In C++, you can create *n*-dimensional arrays for any integer *n*.

The way to declare a two-dimensional array can be generalized to declare an *n*-dimensional array for $n >= 3$. For example, the following syntax declares a three-dimensional array **scores**:

```
double scores[10][5][2];
```

### 6.8.1   Example: Computing Student Scores

Listing 6.14 gives a program that calculates the total score for the students in a class. Suppose the scores are stored in a three-dimensional array named **scores**. The first index in **scores** refers to a student, the second refers to an exam, and the third refers to a part of the exam. Suppose there are seven students, five exams, and each exam has two parts: a multiple-choice part and a programming part. **scores[i][j][0]** represents the score on the multiple-choice part for the **i**'s student on the **j**'s exam. **scores[i][j][1]** represents the score on the programming part for the **i**'s student on the **j**'s exam. The program processes the **scores** array for all the students. For each student, it adds the two scores from all exams to **totalScore** and displays **totalScore**. Your program displays the total score for each student, as shown in the sample output.

### LISTING 6.14   TotalScore.cpp

```
1 #include <iostream>
2 using namespace std;
3
```

```
 4 double computeTax(int, double);
 5
 6 int main()
 7 {
 8   const int NUMBER_OF_STUDENTS = 7;
 9   const int NUMBER_OF_EXAMS = 5;
10   const int NUMBER_OF_PARTS_IN_EXAM = 2;
11
12   double scores
13     [NUMBER_OF_STUDENTS][NUMBER_OF_EXAMS][NUMBER_OF_PARTS_IN_EXAM] =
14   {
15     {{7.5, 20.5}, {9.0, 22.5}, {15, 33.5}, {13, 21.5}, {15, 2.5}},
16     {{4.5, 21.5}, {9.0, 22.5}, {15, 34.5}, {12, 20.5}, {14, 9.5}},
17     {{6.5, 30.5}, {9.4, 10.5}, {11, 33.5}, {11, 23.5}, {10, 2.5}},
18     {{6.5, 23.5}, {9.4, 32.5}, {13, 34.5}, {11, 20.5}, {16, 7.5}},
19     {{8.5, 26.5}, {9.4, 52.5}, {13, 36.5}, {13, 24.5}, {16, 2.5}},
20     {{9.5, 20.5}, {9.4, 42.5}, {13, 31.5}, {12, 20.5}, {16, 6.5}},
21     {{1.5, 29.5}, {6.4, 22.5}, {14, 30.5}, {10, 30.5}, {16, 6.0}}
22   };
23
24   // Calculate and display total score for each student
25   for (int i = 0; i < NUMBER_OF_STUDENTS; i++)
26   {
27     double totalScore = 0;
28     for (int j = 0; j < NUMBER_OF_EXAMS; j++)
29       for (int k = 0; k < NUMBER_OF_PARTS_IN_EXAM; k++)
30         totalScore += scores[i][j][k];
31
32     cout << "Student " << i << "'s score is " <<
33       totalScore << endl;
34   }
35
36   return 0;
37 }
```

*three-dimensional array* (margin note, line 12)

```
Student 0's score is 160
Student 1's score is 163
Student 2's score is 148.4
Student 3's score is 174.4
Student 4's score is 202.4
Student 5's score is 181.4
Student 6's score is 166.9
```

To understand this example, it is essential to know how data in the three-dimensional array are interpreted. scores[0] is a two-dimensional array that stores all the exam scores for the first student. scores[0][0] is {7.5, 20.5}, a one-dimensional array, which stores two scores for two parts of the first student's first exam. scores[0][0][0] is 7.5, which is the score for the first part of the first student's first exam. scores[5] is a two-dimensional array that stores all the exam scores for the sixth student. scores[5][4] is {16, 6.5}, a one-dimensional array, which stores two scores for two parts of the sixth student's fifth exam. scores[5][4][1] is 6.5, which is the score for the second part of the sixth student's fifth exam.

The statement in lines 12–22 declares and initializes a three-dimensional array of **double** values.

The scores for each student are added in lines 27–30, and the result is displayed in lines 32–33. The **for** loop in line 25 process the scores for all the students.

## 6.8.2 Example: Guessing Birth Dates

Listing 3.2, GuessBirthDate.cpp, gives a program that guesses a birth date. The program can be simplified by storing the numbers in five sets in a three-dimensional array and prompts the user for the answers using a loop, as shown in Listing 6.15.

LISTING 6.15 GuessBirthDateUsingArray.cpp

```cpp
 1 #include <iostream>
 2 using namespace std;
 3
 4 int main()
 5 {
 6    int date = 0; // Date to be determined
 7    char answer;
 8
 9    int dates[5][4][4] = {                              three-dimensional array
10      {{16, 17, 18, 19},
11       {20, 21, 22, 23},
12       {24, 25, 26, 27},
13       {28, 29, 30, 31}},
14      {{ 8,  9, 10, 11},
15       {12, 13, 14, 15},
16       {24, 25, 26, 27},
17       {28, 29, 30, 31}},
18      {{ 1,  3,  5,  7},
19       { 9, 11, 13, 15},
20       {17, 19, 21, 23},
21       {25, 27, 29, 31}},
22      {{ 2,  3,  6,  7},
23       {10, 11, 14, 15},
24       {18, 19, 22, 23},
25       {26, 27, 30, 31}},
26      {{ 4,  5,  6,  7},
27       {12, 13, 14, 15},
28       {20, 21, 22, 23},
29       {28, 29, 30, 31}}};
30
31    for (int i = 0; i < 5; i++) {
32      cout << "Is your birth date in Set" << (i + 1) << "?" << endl;    Set 1, 2, 3, 4, 5?
33      for (int j = 0; j < 4; j++) {
34        for (int k = 0; k < 4; k++)
35          cout << dates[i][j][k] << " ";
36        cout << endl;
37      }
38      cout << "\nEnter N for No and Y for Yes: ";
39      cin >> answer;
40      if (answer == 1)
41        date += dates[i][0][0];
42    }
43
44    cout << "Your birth date is " << date << endl;
45
46    return 0;
47 }
```

A three-dimensional array `dates` is created in lines 9–29. This array stores five sets of numbers. Each set is a **4** by **4** two-dimensional array.

The loop starting from line 31 displays the numbers in each set and prompts the user to answer whether the date is in the set (lines 38–39). If the date is in the set, the first number (`dates[i][0][0]`) in the set is added to variable `date` (line 41).

## KEY TERMS

| | |
|---|---|
| array 182 | indexed variable 183 |
| array index 182 | insertion sort 199 |
| array initializer 184 | linear search 194 |
| binary search 194 | multidimensional array 207 |
| const array 191 | selection sort 197 |

## CHAPTER SUMMARY

- An array represents a list of values of the same type. An array is created using the syntax `dataType arrayName[size]`.

- Each element in the array is represented using the syntax `arrayName[index]`. An index must be an integer or an integer expression. Array index is 0-based, meaning that the index for the first element is 0.

- Programmers often mistakenly reference the first element in an array with index `1`, so that the index of the tenth element becomes `10`. This is called the *index off-by-one error*.

- C++ has a shorthand notation, known as the *array initializer,* which combines creating an array and initializing in one statement using the syntax: `dataType arrayName[]` = `{value0, value1, ..., valuek}`.

- When you pass an array argument to a function, you are actually passing the reference of the array; that is, the called function can modify the elements in the caller's original array.

- When you pass an array argument to a function, often you also should pass the size in another argument, so the function knows how many elements are in the functions.

- You can specify `const` array parameters to prevent arrays from being modified accidentally.

- You can use arrays of arrays to form multidimensional arrays. For example, a two-dimensional array is declared as an array of arrays using the syntax `dataType arrayName[size1][size2]`.

## REVIEW QUESTIONS

### Section 6.2 Array Basics

6.1 How do you declare and create an array?

6.2 How do you access elements of an array? Can you copy an array **a** to **b** using **b** = **a**?

6.3 Is memory allocated when an array is declared? What is the printout of the following code?

```
int numbers[30];
cout << "number[0] is " << number[0];
cout << "number[30] is " << number[30];
```

**6.4** Indicate true or false for the following statements:

- Every element in an array has the same type.
- The array size is fixed after it is created.
- The array size used to declare an array must be a constant expression.
- The array elements are initialized when an array is created.

**6.5** Which of the following statements are valid array declarations?

```
double d[30];
char[30] r;
int i[] = (3, 4, 3, 2);
float f[] = {2.3, 4.5, 6.6};
```

**6.6** What is the array index type? What is the lowest index?

**6.7** What is the representation of the third element in an array named **a**?

**6.8** What happens when your program attempts to access an array element with an invalid index?

**6.9** Identify and fix the errors in the following code:

```
1 int main()
2 {
3   double[100] r;
4
5   for (int i = 0; i < 100; i++);
6     r(i) = rand() % 100;
7 }
```

## Section 6.3 Passing Arrays to Functions

**6.10** When an array is passed to a function, a new array is created and passed to the function. Is this true?

**6.11** Show the output of the following two programs:

```
#include <iostream>
using namespace std;

void m(int x, int y[])
{
  x = 3;
  y[0] = 3;
}

int main()
{
  int number = 0;
  int numbers[1];

  m(number, numbers);

  cout << "number is " << number
    << " and numbers[0] is " << numbers[0];

  return 0;
}
```

(a)

```
#include <iostream>
using namespace std;

void reverse(int list[], int size)
{
  for (int i = 0; i < size / 2; i++)
  {
    int temp = list[i];
    list[i] = list[size - 1 - i];
    list[size - 1 - i] = temp;
  }
}

int main()
{
  int list[] = {1, 2, 3, 4, 5};
  int size = 5;
  reverse(list, size);
  for (int i = 0; i < size; i++)
    cout << list[i] << " ";

  return 0;
}
```

(b)

**6.12** How do you prevent the array from being modified accidentally in a function?

### Section 6.5 Searching Arrays

**6.13**    Use Figure 6.3 as an example to show how to apply the binary search approach to search for key **10** and key **12** in list {2, 4, 7, 10, 11, 45, 50, 59, 60, 66, 69, 70, 79}.

### Section 6.6 Sorting Arrays

**6.14**    Use Figure 6.4 as an example to show how to apply the selection sort approach to sort {3.4, 5, 3, 3.5, 2.2, 1.9, 2}.

**6.15**    Use Figure 6.5 as an example to show how to apply the insertion sort approach to sort {3.4, 5, 3, 3.5, 2.2, 1.9, 2}.

**6.16**    How do you modify the `selectionSort` function in Listing 6.9 to sort numbers in decreasing order?

**6.17**    How do you modify the `insertionSort` function in Listing 6.10 to sort numbers in decreasing order?

### Section 6.7 Two-Dimensional Arrays

**6.18**    Declare and create a **4** × **5 int** matrix.

**6.19**    What is the output of the following code?

```
int array[5][6];
int x[] = {1, 2};
array[0][1] = x[1];
cout << "array[0][1] is " << array[0][1];
```

**6.20**    Which of the following statements are valid array declarations?

```
int r[2];
```

```
int x[];
```

```
int y[3][];
```

**6.21**    Which of the following function declarations are wrong?

```
int f(int[][] a, int rowSize, int columnSize);
int f(int a[][], int rowSize, int columnSize);
int f(int a[][3], int rowSize);
```

## PROGRAMMING EXERCISES

### Section 6.2 Array Basics

**6.1**    (*Analyzing input*) Write a program that reads ten numbers, computes their average, and finds out how many numbers are above the average.

**6.2**    (*Alternative solution to Listing 6.1, TestArray.java*) The solution of Listing 6.1 counts the occurrences of the largest number by comparing *each number* with the largest. So you have to use an array to store all the numbers. Another way to solve the problem is to maintain two variables, **max** and **count**. **max** stores the current max number, and **count** stores its occurrences. Initially, assign the first number to **max** and **1** to **count**. Compare each subsequent number with **max**. If the number is greater than **max**, assign it to **max** and reset **count** to **1**. If the number is equal to **max**, increment **count** by **1**. Use this approach to rewrite Listing 6.1.

**6.3**    (*Reversing the numbers entered*) Write a program that reads ten integers and displays them in reverse order in which they were read.

**6.4**   (*Analyzing scores*) Write a program that reads an unspecified number of scores and determines how many scores are above or equal to the average and how many scores are below the average. Enter a negative number to signify the end of the input. Assume that the maximum number of scores is 100.

**6.5**\*\*   (*Printing distinct numbers*) Write a program that reads in ten numbers and displays distinct numbers (i.e., if a number appears multiple times, it is displayed only once).

**Hint**

Read a number and store it to an array if it is new. If the number is already in the array, discard it. After the input, the array contains the distinct numbers.

**6.6**\*   (*Revising Listing 4.11, PrimeNumber.java*) Listing 4.11 determines whether a number **n** is prime by checking whether **2, 3, 4, 5, 6, ..., n/2** is a divisor. If a divisor is found, **n** is not prime. A more efficient approach to determine whether **n** is prime is to check whether any of the prime numbers less than or equal to $\sqrt{n}$ can divide **n** evenly. If not, **n** is prime. Rewrite Listing 4.11 to display the first fifty prime numbers using this approach. You need to use an array to store the prime numbers and later use them to check whether they are possible divisors for **n**.

**6.7**\*   (*Counting single digits*) Write a program that generates one hundred random integers between **0** and **9** and displays the count for each number.

**Hint**

Use **rand()** % **10** to generate a random integer between **0** and **9**. Use an array of ten integers, say **counts**, to store the counts for the number of **0**'s, **1**'s, ..., **9**'s.

## Sections 6.3–6.4

**6.8**   (*Averaging an array*) Write two overloaded functions that return the average of an array with the following headers:

```
int average(int array[], int size);
double average(double array[], int size);
```

Use {1, 2, 3, 4, 5, 6} and {6.0, 4.4, 1.9, 2.9, 3.4, 3.5} to test the functions.

**6.9**   (*Finding the smallest element*) Write a function that finds the smallest element in an array of integers. Use {1, 2, 4, 5, 10, 100, 2, −22} to test the function.

**6.10**   (*Finding the index of the smallest element*) Write a function that returns the index of the smallest element in an array of integers. If there are more than one such element, return the smallest index. Use {1, 2, 4, 5, 10, 100, 2, −22} to test the function.

**6.11**\*   (*Computing deviation*) Exercise 5.22 computes the standard deviation of numbers. This exercise uses a different but equivalent formula to compute the standard deviation of **n** numbers.

$$mean = \frac{\sum_{i=1}^{n} x_i}{n} = \frac{x_1 + x_2 + \cdots + x_n}{n} \qquad deviation = \sqrt{\frac{\sum_{i=1}^{n}(x_i - mean)^2}{n - 1}}$$

To compute deviation with this formula, you have to store the individual numbers using an array, so that they can be used after the mean is obtained. Use {1, 2, 3, 4, 5, 6, 7, 8, 9, 10} to test the function.

Your program should contain following functions:

```
/** Function for computing mean of an array of double values */
double mean(double x[], int size)
```

```
/** Function for computing mean of an array of int values */
double mean(int x[], int size)

/** Function for computing deviation of double values */
double deviation(double x[], int size)

/** Function for computing deviation of int values */
double deviation(int x[], int size)
```

**6.12*** *(Reversing an array)* Write a function that reverses an array using the following header:

```
void reverse(int source[], int size)
```

### Sections 6.5–6.6

**6.13** *(Finding the sales amount)* Rewrite Listing 4.7, FindSalesAmount.cpp, using the binary search approach. Since the sales amount is between `1` and `COMMISSION_SOUGHT/0.08`, you can use a binary search to improve Listing 4.7.

**6.14** *(Timing execution)* Write a program that randomly generates an array of `100000` integers and a key. Estimate the execution time of invoking the `linearSearch` function in Listing 6.7. Sort the array and estimate the execution time of invoking the `binarySearch` function in Listing 6.8. You may use the following code template to obtain the execution time:

```
long startTime = time(0);
perform the task;
long endTime = time(0);
long executionTime = endTime - startTime;
```

**6.15*** *(Revising selection sort)* In §6.6.1, you used selection sort to sort an array. The selection sort function repeatedly finds the largest number in the current array and swaps it with the last number in the array. Rewrite this example by finding the smallest number and swapping it with the first number in the array.

**6.16**** *(Bubble sort)* Write a sort function that uses the bubble-sort algorithm. The bubble-sort algorithm makes several passes through the array. On each pass, successive neighboring pairs are compared. If a pair is in decreasing order, its values are swapped; otherwise, the values remain unchanged. The technique is called a *bubble sort* or *sinking sort* because the smaller values gradually "bubble" their way to the top and the larger values sink to the bottom.

The algorithm can be described as follows:

```
bool changed = true;
do
{
  changed = false;
  for (int j = 0; j < listSize - 1; j++)
    if (list[j] > list[j + 1])
    {
      swap list[j] with list[j + 1];
      changed = true;
    }
} while (changed);
```

Clearly, the list is in increasing order when the loop terminates. It is easy to show that the do loop executes at most `listSize - 1` times.

Use {6.0, 4.4, 1.9, 2.9, 3.4, 2.9, 3.5} to test the function.

### Section 6.7 Two-Dimensional Arrays

**6.17**ˣ  (*Summing all the numbers in a matrix*) Write a function that sums all the integers in a matrix of integers. Use {{1, 2, 4, 5}, {6, 7, 8, 9}, {10, 11, 12, 13}, {14, 15, 16, 17}} to test the function.

**6.18**ˣ  (*Summing the major diagonal in a matrix*) Write a function that sums all the integers in the major diagonal in a matrix of integers. Use {{1, 2, 4, 5}, {6, 7, 8, 9}, {10, 11, 12, 13}, {14, 15, 16, 17}} to test the function.

**6.19**ˣ  (*Sorting students on grades*) Rewrite Listing 6.12, GradeExam.cpp, to display the students in increasing order of the number of correct answers.

**6.20**ˣ  (*Computing the weekly hours for each employee*) Suppose the weekly hours for all employees are stored in a two-dimensional array. Each row records an employee's seven-day work hours with seven columns. For example, the following array stores the work hours for eight employees. Write a program that displays employees and their total hours in decreasing order of the total hours.

|  | Su | M | T | W | H | F | Sa |
|---|---|---|---|---|---|---|---|
| Employee 0 | 2 | 4 | 3 | 4 | 5 | 8 | 8 |
| Employee 1 | 7 | 3 | 4 | 3 | 3 | 4 | 4 |
| Employee 2 | 3 | 3 | 4 | 3 | 3 | 2 | 2 |
| Employee 3 | 9 | 3 | 4 | 7 | 3 | 4 | 1 |
| Employee 4 | 3 | 5 | 4 | 3 | 6 | 3 | 8 |
| Employee 5 | 3 | 4 | 4 | 6 | 3 | 4 | 4 |
| Employee 6 | 3 | 7 | 4 | 8 | 3 | 8 | 4 |
| Employee 7 | 6 | 3 | 5 | 9 | 2 | 7 | 9 |

**6.21**  (*Adding two matrices*) Write a function to add two matrices. The header of the function is as follows:

```
void addMatrix(int a[][COLUMN_SIZE], int b[][COLUMN_SIZE],
  int c[][COLUMN_SIZE], int rowSize)
```

In order to be added, two matrices must have the same dimensions and the same or compatible types of elements. As shown below, two matrices are added by adding the two elements of the arrays with the same index:

$$\begin{pmatrix} a_{11} & a_{12} & a_{13} & a_{14} & a_{15} \\ a_{21} & a_{22} & a_{23} & a_{24} & a_{25} \\ a_{31} & a_{32} & a_{33} & a_{34} & a_{35} \\ a_{41} & a_{42} & a_{43} & a_{44} & a_{45} \\ a_{51} & a_{52} & a_{53} & a_{54} & a_{55} \end{pmatrix} + \begin{pmatrix} b_{11} & b_{12} & b_{13} & b_{14} & b_{15} \\ b_{21} & b_{22} & b_{23} & b_{24} & b_{25} \\ b_{31} & b_{32} & b_{33} & b_{34} & b_{35} \\ b_{41} & b_{42} & b_{43} & b_{44} & b_{45} \\ b_{51} & b_{52} & b_{53} & b_{54} & b_{55} \end{pmatrix}$$

$$= \begin{pmatrix} a_{11} + b_{11} & a_{12} + b_{12} & a_{13} + b_{13} & a_{14} + b_{14} & a_{15} + b_{15} \\ a_{21} + b_{21} & a_{22} + b_{22} & a_{23} + b_{23} & a_{24} + b_{24} & a_{25} + b_{25} \\ a_{31} + b_{31} & a_{32} + b_{32} & a_{33} + b_{33} & a_{34} + b_{34} & a_{35} + b_{35} \\ a_{41} + b_{41} & a_{42} + b_{42} & a_{43} + b_{43} & a_{44} + b_{44} & a_{45} + b_{45} \\ a_{51} + b_{51} & a_{52} + b_{52} & a_{53} + b_{53} & a_{54} + b_{54} & a_{55} + b_{55} \end{pmatrix}$$

**6.22**<sup></sup> *(Multiplying two matrices)* Write a function to multiply two matrices. The header of the function is as follows:

```
void multiplyMatrix(int a[][COLUMN_SIZE],
  int b[][COLUMN_SIZE], int c[][COLUMN_SIZE], int rowSize)
```

To multiply matrix **a** by matrix **b**, the number of columns in **a** must be the same as the number of rows in **b**, and the two matrices must have elements of the same or compatible types. Let **c** be the result of the multiplication, and **a**, **b**, and **c** are denoted as follows:

$$\begin{pmatrix} a_{11} & a_{12} & a_{13} & a_{14} & a_{15} \\ a_{21} & a_{22} & a_{23} & a_{24} & a_{25} \\ a_{31} & a_{32} & a_{33} & a_{34} & a_{35} \\ a_{41} & a_{42} & a_{43} & a_{44} & a_{45} \\ a_{51} & a_{52} & a_{53} & a_{54} & a_{55} \end{pmatrix} \times \begin{pmatrix} b_{11} & b_{12} & b_{13} & b_{14} & b_{15} \\ b_{21} & b_{22} & b_{23} & b_{24} & b_{25} \\ b_{31} & b_{32} & b_{33} & b_{34} & b_{35} \\ b_{41} & b_{42} & b_{43} & b_{44} & b_{45} \\ b_{51} & b_{52} & b_{53} & b_{54} & b_{55} \end{pmatrix}$$

$$= \begin{pmatrix} c_{11} & c_{12} & c_{13} & c_{14} & c_{15} \\ c_{21} & c_{22} & c_{23} & c_{24} & c_{25} \\ c_{31} & c_{32} & c_{33} & c_{34} & c_{35} \\ c_{41} & c_{42} & c_{43} & c_{44} & c_{45} \\ c_{51} & c_{52} & c_{53} & c_{54} & c_{55} \end{pmatrix}$$

where $c_{ij} = a_{i1} \times b_{1j} + a_{i2} \times b_{2j} + a_{i3} \times b_{3j} + a_{i4} \times b_{4j} + a_{i5} \times b_{5j}$.

**6.23**<sup></sup> *(TicTacToe board)* Write a program that randomly fills in 0s and 1s into a Tic-TacToe board, prints the board, and finds the rows, columns, or diagonals with all 0s or 1s. Use a two-dimensional array to represent a TicTacToe board. Here is a sample run of the program:

```
001
001
111
All 1s on row 2
All 1s on column 2
```

**6.24**<sup></sup> *(Checker board)* Write a program that randomly fills in 0s and 1s into an 8 × 8 checker board, prints the board, and finds the rows, columns, or diagonals with all 0s or 1s. Use a two-dimensional array to represent a checker board. Here is a sample run of the program:

```
10101000
10100001
11100011
10100001
11100111
10000001
10100111
00100001
All 0s on subdiagonal
```

**6.25**\*\*\*    (*Playing a TicTacToe game*) In a game of TicTacToe, two players take turns marking an available cell in a **3** × **3** grid with their respective tokens (either X or O). When one player has placed three tokens in a horizontal, vertical, or diagonal row on the grid, the game is over and that player has won. A draw (no winner) occurs when all the cells on the grid have been filled with tokens and neither player has achieved a win. Create a program for playing TicTacToe, as follows:

1. The program prompts the first player to enter an X token, and then prompts the second player to enter an O token. Whenever a token is entered, the program refreshes the board and determines the status of the game (win, draw, or unfinished).
2. To place a token, prompt the user to enter the row and the column for the token.

## Comprehensive

**6.26**\*\*\*    (*LCM*) Write a program that prompts the user to enter two integers and finds their least common multiple. The least common multiple (LCM) of two numbers is the smallest number that is a multiple of both. For example, the LCM for **8** and **12** is **24**, for **15** and **25** is **75**, and for **120** and **150** is **600**. There are many ways to find the LCM. In this exercise, you will use the approach described as follows.

To find the LCM of two numbers, first create a prime factor table for each number. The first column of the table consists of all the prime factors and the second column tracks the occurrence of the corresponding prime factor in the number. For example, the prime factors for **120** are **2, 2, 2, 3, 5**, so the prime factor table for number **120** is shown as follows:

| prime factors for 120 | # of occurrence | | |
|---|---|---|---|
| 2 | 3 | table[0][0] = 2 | table[0][1] = 3 |
| 3 | 1 | table[1][0] = 3 | table[1][1] = 1 |
| 5 | 1 | table[2][0] = 5 | table[2][1] = 1 |

The prime factors for **150** are **2, 3, 5, 5**, so the prime factor table for number **150** is shown as follows:

| prime factors for 120 | # of occurrence | | |
|---|---|---|---|
| 2 | 1 | table[0][0] = 2 | table[0][1] = 1 |
| 3 | 1 | table[1][0] = 3 | table[1][1] = 1 |
| 5 | 2 | table[2][0] = 5 | table[2][1] = 2 |

The LCM of the two numbers consists of the factors with the largest occurrence in the two numbers. So the LCM for **120** and **150** is **2** × **2** × **2** × **3** × **5** × **5**, where **2** appears three times in **120**, **3** one time in **120**, and **5** two times in **150**.

**Hint**

The prime factor table can be represented using a two-dimensional array. Write a function named `int getPrimeFactors(int number, int table[][2])` that stores the prime factors for `number` in the table and returns the number of the prime factors.

**6.27**[**] (*Locker puzzle*) A school has **100** lockers and **100** students. All lockers are closed on the first day of school. As the students enter, the first student, denoted S1, opens every locker. Then the second student, S2, begins with the second locker, denoted L2, and closes every other locker. Student S3 begins with the third locker and changes every third locker (closes it if it was open, and opens it if it is closed). Student S4 begins with locker L4 and changes every fourth locker. Student S5 starts with L5 and changes every fifth locker, etc. until student S100 changes L100.

After all the students have passed through the building and changed the lockers, which lockers are open? Write a program to find your answer.

**Hint**

Use an array of **100** elements, each of which stores the number of the times a locker has changed. If a locker changes an even number of times, it is closed; otherwise, it is open.

## CHAPTER 7

# POINTERS AND C-STRINGS

## Objectives

- To describe what a pointer is (§7.1).

- To learn how to declare a pointer and assign a value to it (§7.2).

- To access elements via pointers (§7.2).

- To pass arguments by reference with pointers (§7.3).

- To understand the relationship between arrays and pointers (§7.4).

- To know how to access array elements using pointers (§7.4).

- To declare constant pointers and constant data (§7.5).

- To learn how to return pointers from functions (§7.6).

- To use the **new** operator to allocate persistent memory dynamically (§7.7).

- To test and convert characters using the character functions (§7.9.1).

- To store and access strings using arrays and pointers (§7.9.2).

- To read strings from the keyboard (§7.9.3).

- To process strings using the C-string functions (§7.9.4).

## 7.1 Introduction

The preceding chapter introduced arrays. You can pass an array to a function, but you cannot return an array from a function. Often it is desirable to return an array from a function. How can this be done? You can use pointers to accomplish that task. Pointer is a powerful feature in C++ that enables you to directly manipulate computer memory. A single pointer can be used to reference an array, a string, an integer, or any other variable.

why pointers?

## 7.2 Pointer Basics

*Pointer variables,* simply called *pointers,* are designed to hold memory addresses as their values. Normally, a variable contains a data value, e.g., an integer, a floating-point value, and a character. However, a pointer contains the memory address of a variable that in turn contains a data value.

Like any other variables, pointers must be declared before they can be used. To declare a pointer, use the following syntax:

declare pointer

```
dataType *pVarName;
```

Each variable being declared as a pointer must be preceded by an asterisk (*). For example, the following statement declares a pointer variable named **pCount** that can point to an **int** variable:

```
int *pCount;
```

You can now assign the address of a variable to **pCount**. For example, the following code assigns the address of variable **count** to **pCount**:

```
int count = 5;
pCount = &count;
```

assign address

address operator

The ampersand (&) symbol is called the *address operator* when placed in front of a variable. It is a unary operator that returns the address of the variable.

Listing 7.1 gives a complete example.

### LISTING 7.1 TestPointer.cpp

```
1  #include <iostream>
2  using namespace std;
3
4  int main()
5  {
6      int count = 5;
7      int *pCount = &count;
8
9      cout << "The address of count is " << &count << endl;
10     cout << "The address of count is " << pCount << endl;
11     cout << "The value of count is " << count << endl;
12     cout << "The value of count is " << *pCount << endl;
13
14     return 0;
15  }
```

declare variable
declare pointer

accessing **&count**
accessing **pCount**
accessing **count**
accessing ***pCount**

```
The address of count is 1245064
The address of count is 1245064
The value of count is 5
The value of count is 5
```

Line 6 declares a variable named **count** with an initial value **5**. Line 7 declares a pointer variable named **pCount** and initialized with the address of variable **count**. A pointer can be initialized when it is declared or using an assignment statement. However, if you assign an address to a pointer, the syntax is

```
pCount = &count; // Correct
```

rather than

```
*pCount = &count; // Wrong
```

Line 9 displays the address of **count** using **&count**. Line 10 displays the value stored in **pCount** which is same as **&count**. The value stored in **count** is retrieved directly from **count** in line 11 and is retrieved indirectly through a pointer variable using **\*pCount** in line 12. Figure 7.1 shows the relationship between **count** and **pCount**.

**FIGURE 7.1**    The **pCount** contains the address of variable **count**.

Suppose **pX** and **pY** are two pointer variables for variables **x** and **y**, as shown in Figure 7.2. To understand the relationships between the variables and their pointers, let us examine the effect of assigning **pY** to **pX** and **\*pY** to **\*pX**.

effect of assignment =

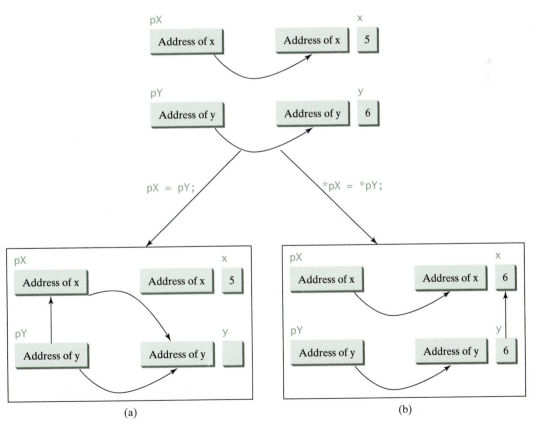

**FIGURE 7.2**    (a) **pY** is assigned to **pX**; (b) **\*pY** is assigned to **\*pX**.

The statement **pX** = **pY** assigns the content of **pY** to **pX**. The content of **pY** is the address of variable **y**. So after this assignment, **pX** and **pY** contain the same content, as pictured in Figure 7.2(a).

Now consider \***pX** = \***pY**. With the asterisk symbol in front of **pX** and **pY**, you are dealing with the variables pointed by **pX** and **pY**. \***pX** refers to the contents in **x** and \***pY** refers to the contents in **y**. So the statement \***pX** = \***pY** assigns **6** to \***pX**, as pictured in Figure 7.2(b).

Referencing a value through a pointer is often called *indirection*. The syntax for referencing a value from a pointer is

indirect referencing

```
*pointer
```

For example, you can increase **count** using

```
count++; // Direct reference
```

or

```
(*pCount)++; // Indirect reference
```

indirection operator
dereferenced operator
dereferenced

The asterisk (\*) used in the preceding statement is known as the *indirection operator or dereference operator* (dereference means indirect reference). When a pointer is *dereferenced*, the value at the address stored in the pointer is retrieved.

**Note**

\* in three forms

You have used the asterisk (\*) in three different ways:

- As a multiplication operator, such as

  ```
  double area = radius * radius * 3.14159;
  ```
- To declare a pointer variable, such as

  ```
  int *pCount = &count;
  ```
- To use as the indirection operator, such as

  ```
  (*pCount)++;
  ```

**Caution**

pointer type

A pointer variable is declared with a type such as **int**, **double**, etc. You have to assign the address of the variable of the same type. It is a syntax error if the type of the variable does not match the type of the pointer. For example, the following code is wrong:

```
int area = 1;
double *pArea = &area; // Wrong
```

**Tip**

naming pointers

Pointers are variables. So the naming conventions for variables are applied to pointers. This book names pointers with prefix **p**, such as **pCount** and **pCity**. There are some exceptions, however. Soon you will know that an array can also function as a pointer. In this case, the variable may be declared as an array or a pointer.

**Tip**

initializing pointer

Like a local variable, a local pointer is assigned an arbitrary value if you don't initialize it. A pointer may be initialized to **0**, which is a special value for a pointer to indicate that the pointer points to nothing. You should always initialize pointers to prevent errors. Dereferencing a pointer that is not initialized could cause a fatal runtime error, or it could accidentally modify important data.

## Caution

You can declare two variables on the same line. For example, the following line declares two `int` variables:

```
int i = 0, j = 1;
```

Can you declare two pointer variables on the same line as follows?

```
int* pI, pJ;
```

No, this line is equivalent to

```
int *pI, pJ;
```

## Tip

If you use Visual C++, please refer to Supplement II.B, "*Learning C++ Effectively with Visual C++*," on the Companion Website. This supplement shows you how to use a debugger to inspect pointers.

debugging in IDE

## 7.3 Passing Arguments by References with Pointers

There are three ways to pass arguments to a function in C++: *pass-by-value, pass-by-reference with reference arguments,* and *pass-by-reference with pointers.* Listing 5.4. TestPassBy-Value.cpp, demonstrated the effect of pass-by-value. Listing 5.5. TestReferenceVariable.cpp, demonstrated the effect of pass-by-reference with reference variables. Both examples used the `swap` function to demonstrate the effect. Let us rewrite the `swap` function using pointers, as shown in Listing 7.2.

**LISTING 7.2**  TestPointerArgument.cpp

```
 1 #include <iostream>
 2 using namespace std;
 3
 4 // Swap two variables
 5 void swap(int *pValue1, int *pValue2)
 6 {
 7    // Swap n1 with n2
 8    int temp = *pValue1;
 9    *pValue1 = *pValue2;
10    *pValue2 = temp;
11 }
12
13 int main()
14 {
15    // Declare and initialize variables
16    int num1 = 1;
17    int num2 = 2;
18
19    cout << "Before invoking the swap function, num1 is "
20      << num1 << " and num2 is " << num2 << endl;
21
22    // Invoke the swap function to attempt to swap two variables
23    swap(&num1, &num2);
```

pointers

indirect accessing

passing address

```
24
25    cout << "After invoking the swap function, num1 is " << num1 <<
26      " and num2 is " << num2 << endl;
27
28    return 0;
29 }
```

```
Before invoking the swap function, num1 is 1 and num2 is 2
After invoking the swap function, num1 is 2 and num2 is 1
```

The **swap** function has two pointer parameters (line 5). You invoke this function by passing the address of **num1** to **pValue1** and **num2** to **pValue2** (line 23). The **swap** function swaps the values pointed by the two pointers. After invoking the function, the values in variables **num1** and **num2** are swapped.

## 7.4 Arrays and Pointers

Recall that an array variable without a bracket and a subscript actually represents the starting address of the array. In this sense, an array variable is essentially a pointer. Suppose you declare an array of **int** value as follows:

```
int list[6] = {11, 12, 13, 14, 15, 16};
```

Figure 7.3 shows the array in the memory. C++ allows you to access the elements in the array using the indirection operator. To access the first element, use **\*list**, and other elements can be accessed using **\*(list + 1)**, **\*(list + 2)**, **\*(list + 3)**, **\*(list + 4)**, and **\*(list + 5)**.

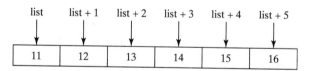

| list | list + 1 | list + 2 | list + 3 | list + 4 | list + 5 |
|------|----------|----------|----------|----------|----------|
| 11 | 12 | 13 | 14 | 15 | 16 |

**FIGURE 7.3**   **list** points to the first element in the array.

An integer may be added or subtracted from a pointer. The pointer is incremented or decremented by that integer times the size of the element to which the pointer points.

**list** points to the starting address of the array. Suppose this address is **1000**. Will **list + 1** be **1001**? No. It is **1000 + sizeof(int)**. Why? Since **list** is declared as an array of **int** elements, C++ automatically calculates the address for the next element by adding **sizeof(int)**. Recall that **sizeof(type)** is the size of a data type (see §2.9, "Numeric Data Types and Operations"). The size of each data type is machine-dependent. On Windows, the size of the **int** type is usually **4**.

Listing 7.3 gives a complete program that uses pointers to access array elements.

## LISTING 7.3  ArrayPointer.cpp

```
1 #include <iostream>
2 using namespace std;
3
```

```
4 int main()
5 {
6   int list[6] = {11, 12, 13, 14, 15, 16};
7
8   for (int i = 0; i < 6; i++)
9     cout << "address: " << (list + i) <<
10      " value: " << *(list + i) << " " <<
11      " value: " << list[i] << endl;
12
13    return 0;
14 }
```

declare array

incrementing address
dereference operator
array indexed variable

```
address: 1245040 value: 11   value: 11
address: 1245044 value: 12   value: 12
address: 1245048 value: 13   value: 13
address: 1245052 value: 14   value: 14
address: 1245056 value: 15   value: 15
address: 1245060 value: 16   value: 16
```

As shown in the sample output, the address of the array `list` is 1245040. So `(list + 1)` is actually 1245040 + 4, and `(list + 2)` is 1245040 + 2 × 4 (line 9). Line 11 accesses the elements using pointers. For example, `*list` returns 11 and `*(list + 1)` returns 12. Line 11 accesses the elements using indexed variable `list[i]`, which is equivalent to `*(list + i)`.

**Caution**

`*(list + 1)` is different from `*list + 1`. The dereference operator (`*`) has precedence over `+`. So, `*list + 1` adds 1 to the value of the first element in the array, while `*(list + 1)` dereferences the element at address `(list + 1)` in the array.

operator precedence

**Note**

Pointers can be compared using relational operators (=, !=, <, <=, >, >=) to determine their order.

compare pointers

Arrays and pointers form close relationships. An array is essentially a pointer. A pointer for an array can be used just like an array. You can even use indexed variables with pointers. Listing 7.4 gives such an example:

**LISTING 7.4  PointerWithIndex.cpp**

```
1 #include <iostream>
2 using namespace std;
3
4 int main()
5 {
6   int list[6] = {11, 12, 13, 14, 15, 16};
7   int *pList = list;
8
9   for (int i = 0; i < 6; i++)
10    cout << "address: " << (list + i) <<
11      " value: " << *(list + i) << " " <<
12      " value: " << list[i] << " " <<
13      " value: " << *(pList + i) << " " <<
14      " value: " << pList[i]) << endl;
15
16    return 0;
17 }
```

declare array
declare pointer

incrementing address
dereference operator
array indexed variable
dereference operator
pointer indexed variable

```
address: 1245036 value: 11   value: 11   value: 11   value: 11
address: 1245040 value: 12   value: 12   value: 12   value: 12
address: 1245044 value: 13   value: 13   value: 13   value: 13
address: 1245048 value: 14   value: 14   value: 14   value: 14
address: 1245052 value: 15   value: 15   value: 15   value: 15
address: 1245056 value: 16   value: 16   value: 16   value: 16
```

Line 7 declares an **int** pointer assigned with the address of the array. Note that the address operator (**&**) is not needed to assign the address of the array to the pointer, because the name of the array is already the starting address of the array. This line is equivalent to

```
int *pList = &list[0];
```

Here, **&list[0]** represents the address of **list[0]**.

The element can be accessed using **\*(list + i)**, **list[i]**, **\*(pList + i)**, and **pList[i]** (lines 11–14). So, arrays are used as pointers, and pointers are used as arrays. However, there is one difference. You cannot change the address of the array once an array is declared. For example, the following statement is illegal:

```
int list1[10], list2[10];
list1 = list2; // Wrong
```

In this sense, an array is a constant pointer.

## 7.5 Using **const** with Pointers

You learned how to declare a constant using the **const** keyword. A constant cannot be changed once it is declared. You can declare a *constant pointer*. For example, see the following code:

*constant pointer*

```
double radius = 5;
double * const pValue = &radius;
```

Here **pValue** is a constant pointer. It must be declared and initialized in the same statement. You cannot assign a new address to **pValue** later. Though **pValue** is a constant, the data pointed by **pValue** is not constant. You can change it. For example, the following statement change the radius to **10**:

```
*pValue = 10;
```

*constant data*

Can you declare that dereferenced data be constant? Yes. You can add the **const** keyword in front of the data type, as follows:

Constant data    Constant pointer

```
const double * const pValue = &radius;
```

In this case, the pointer is a constant, and the data pointed by the pointer is also a constant. If you declare the pointer as

```
const double * pValue = &radius;
```

then the pointer is not a constant, but the data pointed by the pointer is a constant. For example, see the following code:

```cpp
double radius = 5;
double * const pValue = &radius;
double length = 5;
*pValue = 6; // OK
pValue = &length; // Wrong because pValue is a constant pointer


const double *pValue1 = &radius;
*pValue1 = 6; // Wrong because pValue1 points to a constant data
pValue1 = &length; // OK


const double * const pValue2 = &radius;
*pValue2 = 6; // Wrong because pValue2 points to a constant data
*pValue2 = &length; // Wrong because pValue2 is a constant pointer
```

The **const** keyword is particularly useful for declaring parameters in functions. If a value does not change, you should declare it **const** to prevent it from being modified accidentally. Listing 7.5 gives such an example:

**LISTING 7.5** **ConstParameter.cpp**

```cpp
 1 #include <iostream>
 2 using namespace std;
 3
 4 void printArray(const int *, const int);          // function prototype
 5
 6 int main()
 7 {
 8   int list[6] = {11, 12, 13, 14, 15, 16};          // declare array
 9   printArray(list, 6);                             // invoke printArray
10
11   return 0;
12 }
13
14 void printArray(const int * list, const int size)
15 {
16   for (int i = 0; i < size; i++)
17     cout << list[i] << " ";
18 }
```

```
11 12 13 14 15 16
```

The **printArray** function declares an array parameter with constant data (line 4). This ensures that the contents of the array will not be changed. Note that the **size** parameter also is declared **const**. This usually is not necessary, since an **int** parameter is passed-by-value. Even though **size** is modified in the function, it does not affect the original size value outside this function.

# 7.6 Returning Pointers from Functions

You can use pointers as parameters in a function. Can you return a pointer from a function? The answer is yes.

Suppose you want to write a function that passes an array argument and returns a new array that is the reversal of the array argument. An algorithm for the function can be described as follows:

1. Let the original array be `list`.

2. Declare a new array named `result` that has the same size as the original array.

3. Write a loop to copy the first element, second, ..., and so on in the original array to the last element, second last, ..., into the new array, as shown in the following diagram:

4. Return `result` as a pointer.

The function prototype can be specified like this:

```
int * reverse(int const * list, const int size)
```

The return value type is an `int` pointer. How do you declare a new array in Step 2? You may attempt to declare it as

```
int result[size];
```

But C++ does not allow the size to be a variable. To avoid this limitation, let us assume that the array size is **6**. So, you can declare it as

```
int result[6];
```

You can now implement the code in Listing 7.6, but you will soon find out that it is not working correctly.

### LISTING 7.6 WrongReverse.cpp

```cpp
 1 #include <iostream>
 2 using namespace std;
 3
 4 int * reverse(int const * list, const int size)
 5 {
 6   int result[6];
 7
 8   for (int i = 0, j = size - 1; i < size; i++, j--)
 9   {
10     result[j] = list[i];
11   }
12
13   return result;
14 }
15
16 void printArray(int const *list, const int size)
17 {
18   for (int i = 0; i < size; i++)
19     cout << list[i] << " ";
20 }
21
```

reverse function

declare result array

reverse to result

return result

print array

```
22 int main()
23 {
24     int list[] = {1, 2, 3, 4, 5, 6};
25     int *pList = reverse(list, 6);
26     printArray(pList, 6);
27
28     return 0;
29 }
```

invoke reverse
print array

```
6 4462476 4419772 1245016 4199126 4462476
```

The sample output is incorrect. Why? The reason is that the array `result` is a local variable. Local variables don't persist; when the function returns, the local variables are thrown away from the call stack. Attempting to use the pointer will result in erroneous and unpredictable results. To fix this problem, you have to allocate persistent storage for the `result` array so that it can be accessed after the function returns.

## 7.7 Dynamic Memory Allocation

C++ supports dynamic memory allocation, which enables you to allocate persistent storage dynamically. The memory is created using the **new** operator. For example,

```
int *pValue = new int;
```

Here, **new int** tells the computer to allocate memory space for an `int` variable at runtime, and the address of the variable is assigned to the pointer `pValue`. So you can access the memory through the pointer. Here is another example:

```
int *list = new int[10];
```

Here, **new int[10]** tells the computer to allocate memory space for an `int` array of ten elements, and the address of the array is assigned to `list`.

Now you can fix the problem in the preceding example by creating a new array dynamically in the **reverse** function. Listing 7.7 gives the new program.

### LISTING 7.7 CorrectReverse.cpp

```
 1 #include <iostream>
 2 using namespace std;
 3
 4 int * reverse(const int * list, int size)
 5 {
 6     int *result = new int[size];
 7
 8     for (int i = 0, j = size - 1; i < size; i++, j--)
 9     {
10         result[j] = list[i];
11     }
12
13     return result;
14 }
15
16 void printArray(const int *list, int size)
17 {
18     for (int i = 0; i < size; i++)
```

reverse function

create array

reverse to result

return result

print array

```
19      cout << list[i] << " ";
20 }
21
22 int main()
23 {
24    int list[] = {1, 2, 3, 4, 5, 6};
25    int *pList = reverse(list, 6);
26    printArray(pList, 6);
27
28    return 0;
29 }
```

invoke reverse
print array

```
6 5 4 3 2 1
```

Listing 7.7 is almost identical to Listing 7.6 except that the new result array is created using the **new** operator dynamically. The size can be a variable when creating an array using the **new** operator.

heap

C++ allocates local variables in the stack, but the memory reserved by the **new** operator in an area of memory is called the *heap*. The memory reserved remains available until you explicitly free it or the program terminates. If you reserve memory while in a function, the memory is still available after the function returns. The result array is created in the function (line 6). After the function returns in line 25, the result array is intact. So, you can access it in line 26 to print all the elements in the result array.

To explicitly free the memory created by the new operator, use the **delete** keyword before the pointer. For example,

```
delete pValue;
```

If the memory is allocated for an array, the **[]** symbol must be placed between the **delete** keyword and the pointer to the array. For example,

delete a dynamic array

```
delete [] list;
```

**Caution**

delete dynamic memory

You should use the **delete** keyword only with the pointer that points to the memory created by the new operator. Otherwise, it may cause unexpected problems.

**Caution**

You might inadvertently reassign a pointer before deleting the memory to which it points. Consider the following code:

```
1 int *pValue = new int;
2 *pValue = 45;
3 pValue = new int;
```

Line 1 declares a pointer assigned with a memory space for an **int** value. Line 2 assigns **45** to the value. Line 3 assigns a new memory space to **pValue**. The original memory space that holds value **45** is not accessible, because it is not pointed to by any pointer. This memory cannot be

memory leak

accessed and cannot be deleted. This is a *memory leak*.

# 7.8 Case Studies: Counting the Occurrences of Each Letter

This section presents a program that counts the occurrences of each letter in an array of characters. The program does the following:

1. Generate one hundred lowercase letters randomly and assign them to an array of characters. You can obtain a random letter by using the **getRandomLowerCaseLetter()** function in the RandomCharacter.h header file in Listing 5.13.

2. Count the occurrences of each letter in the array. To count the occurrences of each letter in the array, create an array, say **counts** of twenty-six **int** values, each of which counts the occurrences of a letter, as shown in Figure 7.4. That is, **counts[0]** counts the number of **a**'s, **counts[1]** counts the number of **b**'s, and so on.

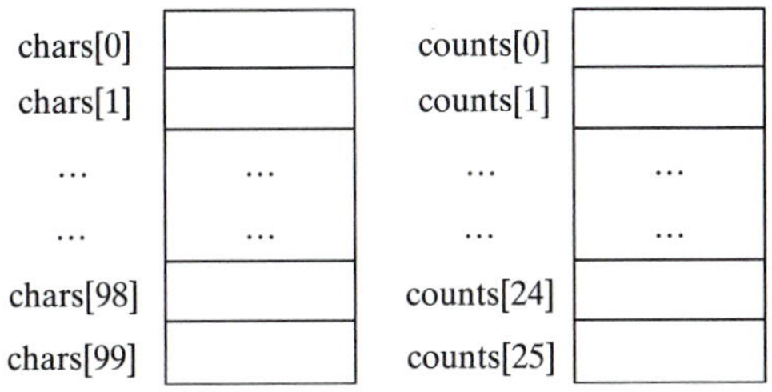

**FIGURE 7.4**  The **chars** array stores **100** characters and the **counts** array stores **26** counts; each counts the occurrences of a letter.

Listing 7.8 gives the complete program.

## LISTING 7.8  CountLettersInArray.cpp

```
 1 #include <iostream>
 2 #include "RandomCharacter.h"                    include header file
 3 using namespace std;
 4
 5 const int NUMBER_OF_LETTERS = 100;              hundred letters
 6 char * createArray();                           function prototypes
 7 void displayArray(char []);
 8 int * countLetters(char []);
 9 void displayCounts(int []);
10
11 int main()
12 {
13   // Declare and create an array
14   char * chars = createArray();                 character array
15
16   // Display the array
17   cout << "The lowercase letters are: " << endl;   pass array
18   displayArray(chars);                          display array
19
20   // Count the occurrences of each letter
21   int * counts = countLetters(chars);           count letters
22
```

```
23    // Display counts
24    cout << endl;
25    cout << "The occurrences of each letter are: " << endl;
```

display counts

```
26    displayCounts(counts);
27
28    return 0;
29 }
30
31 // Create an array of characters
32 char * createArray()
33 {
34    // Declare an array of characters and create it
```

create array

```
35    char *chars = new char[NUMBER_OF_LETTERS];
36
37    // Create lowercase letters randomly and assign
38    // them to the array
```

set a new seed

```
39    srand(time(0));
40    for (int i = 0; i < NUMBER_OF_LETTERS; i++)
```

random letter

```
41      chars[i] = getRandomLowerCaseLetter();
42
43    // Return the array
```

return pointer

```
44    return chars;
45 }
46
47 // Display the array of characters
48 void displayArray(char chars[])
49 {
50    // Display the characters in the array 20 on each line
51    for (int i = 0; i < NUMBER_OF_LETTERS; i++)
52    {
53      if ((i + 1) % 20 == 0)
54        cout << chars[i] << " " << endl;
55      else
56        cout << chars[i] << " ";
57    }
58 }
59
60 // Count the occurrences of each letter
61 int * countLetters(char chars[])
62 {
63    // Declare and create an array of 26 int
```

create array

```
64    int *counts = new int[26];
65
66    // Initialize the array
67    for (int i = 0; i < NUMBER_OF_LETTERS; i++)
68      counts[i] = 0;
69
70    // For each lowercase letter in the array, count it
71    for (int i = 0; i < 26; i++)
```

count letter

```
72      counts[chars[i] - 'a'] ++;
73
```

return pointer

```
74    return counts;
75 }
76
77 // Display counts
78 void displayCounts(int counts[])
79 {
80    for (int i = 0; i < 26; i++)
81    {
```

```
82      if ((i + 1) % 10 == 0)
83        cout << counts[i] << " " << static_cast<char>(i + 'a') << endl;      cast to char
84      else
85        cout << counts[i] << " " << static_cast<char>(i + 'a') << " ";
86   }
87 }
```

```
The lowercase letters are:
p y a o u n s u i b t h y g w q l b y o
x v b r i g h i x w v c g r a s p y i z
n f j v c j c a c v l a j r x r d t w q
m a y e v m k d m e m o j v k m e v t a
r m o u v d h f o o x d g i u w r i q h

The occurrences of each letter are:
6 a 3 b 4 c 4 d 3 e 2 f 4 g 4 h 6 i 4 j
2 k 2 l 6 m 2 n 6 o 2 p 3 q 6 r 2 s 3 t
4 u 8 v 4 w 4 x 5 y 1 z
```

The **createArray** function (lines 32–45) generates an array of one hundred random lowercase letters. Line 14 invokes the function and assigns the array to pointer **chars**. What would be wrong if you rewrote the code as follows?

```
char * chars = new char[100];
chars = createArray();
```

You would be creating two arrays. The first line would create an array by using **new char[100]**. The second line would create an array by invoking **createArray()** and assign the reference of the array to **chars**. The array created in the first line would cause memory leak because it is no longer referenced and cannot be deleted.

Invoking **getRandomLowerCaseLetter()** (line 41) returns a random lowercase letter. This function is defined in the **RandomCharacter** header file in Listing 5.13. This header file is included in line 2.

The **countLetters** function (lines 61–75) returns an array of twenty-six **int** values, each of which stores the number of occurrences of a letter. The function processes each letter in the array and increases its count by one. A brute-force approach to count the occurrences of each letter might be as follows:

```
for (int i = 0; i < NUMBER_OF_LETTERS; i++)
  if (chars[i] == 'a')
    counts[0]++;
  else if (chars[i] == 'b')
    counts[1]++;
  ...
```

But a better solution is given in lines 71–72:

```
for (int i = 0; i < NUMBER_OF_LETTERS; i++)
  counts[chars[i] - 'a']++;
```

If the letter (**chars[i]**) is **'a'**, the corresponding count is **counts['a' - 'a']** (i.e., **counts[0]**). If the letter is **'b'**, the corresponding count is **counts['b' - 'a']** (i.e., **counts[1]**) since the ASCII code of **'b'** is one more than that of **'a'**. If the letter is **'z'**, the corresponding count is **counts['z' - 'a']** (i.e., **counts[25]**) since the ASCII code of **'z'** is 25 more than that of **'a'**.

Figure 7.5 shows the call stack and heap *during* and *after* executing `createArray`.

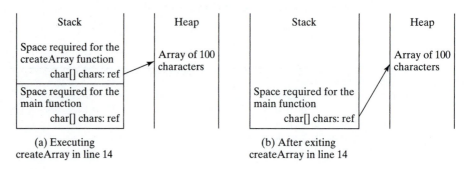

(a) Executing
createArray in line 14

(b) After exiting
createArray in line 14

**FIGURE 7.5** (a) An array of one hundred characters is created when executing `createArray`. (b) This array is returned and assigned to the variable `chars` in the `main` function.

## 7.9 Characters and Strings

pointer-based string

C-string

Strings are used often in programming. You have used string literals. A *string* is a sequence of characters. There are two ways to process strings in C++. One way is to treat strings as arrays of characters. This is known as *pointer-based strings* or *C-strings*. The other way is to process strings using the `string` class. The `string` class will be introduced in §9.8, "The C++ `string` Class." This section introduces pointer-based strings.

### 7.9.1 Character Functions

C++ provides several functions for testing a character in the `<cctype>` header file as shown in Table 7.1. These functions tests a single character and returns `true` or `false`. Note that these functions actually return an `int` value. A nonzero integer corresponds to `true` and zero corresponds to `false`. C++ also provides two functions for converting cases, as shown in Table 7.2.

Listing 7.9 gives a program to test character functions.

### LISTING 7.9 CharacterFunctions.cpp

```cpp
1 #include <iostream>
2 using namespace std;
3
4 int main()
5 {
6   cout << "Enter a character: ";
7   char ch;
8   cin >> ch;
9
10   cout << "You entered " << ch << endl;
11
12   if (islower(ch))
13   {
14     cout << "It is a lowercase letter " << endl;
15     cout << "Its equivalent uppercase letter is " <<
16       static_cast<char>(toupper(ch)) << endl;
17   }
18   else if (isupper(ch))
```

input character

is lowercase?

convert to uppercase

is uppercase?

```
19   {
20      cout << "It is an uppercase letter " << endl;
21      cout << "Its equivalent lowercase letter is " <<
22         static_cast<char>(tolower(ch)) << endl;
23   }
24   else if (isdigit(ch))
25   {
26      cout << "It is a digit character " << endl;
27   }
28
29   return 0;
30 }
```

convert to lowercase

is digit?

**TABLE 7.1**  Character Test Functions

| Function | Description | Example |
|---|---|---|
| isdigit(c) | Returns true if c is a digit. | isdigit('7') is true<br>isdigit('a') is false |
| isalpha(c) | Returns true if c is a letter. | isalpha('7') is false<br>isalpha('a') is true |
| isalnum(c) | Returns true if c is a letter or a digit. | isalnum('7') is true<br>isalnum('a') is true |
| islower(c) | Returns true if c is a lowercase letter. | islower('7') is false<br>islower('a') is true |
| isupper(c) | Returns true if c is an uppercase letter. | isupper('a') is false<br>isupper('A') is true |
| isspace(c) | Returns true if c is a whitespace character. | isspace('\t') is true<br>isspace('A') is false |
| isprint(c) | Returns true if c is a printable character including space ' '. | isprint(' ') is true<br>isprint('A') is true |
| isgraph(c) | Returns true if c is a printable character excluding space ' '. | isgraph(' ') is false<br>isgraph('A') is true |
| ispunct(c) | Returns true if c is a printable character other than a digit, letter, or space. | ispunct('*') is true<br>ispunct(',') is true<br>ispunct('A') is false |
| iscntrl(c) | Returns true if c is a control character such as '\n', '\f', '\v', '\a', and '\b'. | iscntrl('*') is false<br>iscntrl('\n') is true<br>iscntrl('\f') is true |

**TABLE 7.2**  Case Conversion Functions

| Function | Description | Example |
|---|---|---|
| tolower(c) | Returns the lowercase equivalent of c, if c is an uppercase letter. Otherwise, return c itself. | tolower('A') returns 'a'<br>tolower('a') returns 'a'<br>tolower('\t') returns '\t' |
| toupper(c) | Returns the uppercase equivalent of c, if c is a lowercase letter. Otherwise, return c itself. | toupper('A') returns 'A'<br>toupper('a') returns 'A'<br>toupper('\t') returns '\t' |

```
Enter a character: a  ↵Enter
You entered a
It is a lowercase letter
Its equivalent uppercase letter is A

Enter a character: T  ↵Enter
You entered T
It is an uppercase letter
Its equivalent lowercase letter is t

Enter a character: 8  ↵Enter
You entered 8
It is a digit character
```

### 7.9.2  Storing and Accessing Strings

null terminator

A pointer-based string in C++ is an array of characters ending in the *null terminator* (`'\0'`), which indicates where a string terminates in memory. An array can be accessed via a pointer. So a string can also be accessed via a pointer, which points to the first character in the string. So you can declare a string variable using an array or a pointer. For example, the following two declarations are both fine:

```
char city[7] = "Dallas"; // Option 1
char *pCity = "Dallas";   // Option 2
```

Each declaration creates a sequence that contain characters `'D'`, `'a'`, `'l'`, `'l'`, `'a'`, `'s'`, and `'\0'`.

array syntax
pointer syntax

You can access `city` or `pCity` using the array syntax or pointer syntax. For example,

```
cout << city[1] << endl;
cout << *(city + 1) << endl;
cout << pCity[1] << endl;
cout << *(pCity + 1) << endl;
```

each displays character `a` (the second element in the string).

**Note**

There is a subtle difference between the two declarations. For the first array declaration, you cannot reassign the array `city` after it is declared. But you can reassign a new address to the pointer `pCity` for the second declaration. If you add the `const` keyword in the second declaration as follows:

```
char * const pCity = "Dallas";
```

`pCity` becomes a constant pointer and cannot be reassigned.

**Tip**

You can display all characters in a string using

```
cout << city;
```

or

```
cout << pCity;
```

Note that

```
cout << *pCity;
```

would print `D`, the first character in the string pointed by `pCity`.

### 7.9.3    Reading Strings

You can read a string from the keyboard using the `cin` object. For example, see the following code:

```
1 cout << "Enter a city: ";
2 cin >> city; // Read to array city
3 cout << "You entered " << city << endl;
```

string to array
string to pointer

Line 2 reads a string to an array and line 3 reads a string to a pointer.

**Caution**

When you read a string to array `city`, make sure to leave room for the `null` terminator character. Since `city` has a size `7`, your input should not exceed `6` characters.

input size

This approach to read a string is simple, but there is a problem. The input ends with a whitespace character. Suppose you want to enter New York, you have to use an alternative approach. C++ provides the `cin.getline` function in the `iostream` header file, which reads a string into an array. The syntax of the function is:

```
cin.getline(char array[], int size, char delimitChar)
```

The function stops reading characters when the delimiter character is encountered or when the `size - 1` number of characters are read. The last character in the array is reserved for the null terminator (`'\0'`). If the delimiter is encountered, it is read, but not stored in the array. The third argument `delimitChar` has a default value (`'\n'`).

The following code uses the `cin.getline` function to read a string:

```
1 char city[30];
2 cout << "Enter a city: ";
3 cin.getline(city, 30, '\n'); // Read to array city
4 cout << "You entered " << city << endl;
```

declare array

string to array

Since the default value for the third argument in the `cin.getline` function is `'\n'` line 3 can be replaced by

```
cin.getline(city, 30); // Read to array city
```

**Note**

The syntax for the `cin.getline` function is new. The `getline` is actually a function in the `cin` object. You will better understand the syntax in Chapter 9, "Classes and Objects." For now, just accept that this is how to read input from the keyboard.

`cin.getline`

### 7.9.4    C-string Functions

C++ provides several useful and powerful functions for testing and processing strings, as shown in Table 7.3. To use these functions, your program needs to include the `cstring` header file.

**Note**

`size_t` is a C++ type. For most compilers, it is the same as `unsigned int`.

type **size_t**

Functions `strcpy` and `strncpy` can be used to copy a source string in the second argument to a target string in the first argument. The target string already must have been allocated with sufficient memory for the function to work. Function `strncpy` is equivalent to `strcpy` except that `strncpy` specifies the number of characters to be copied from the source. Listing 7.10 gives a program to demonstrate these two functions.

copying strings

**strcpy** and **strncpy**

**TABLE 7.3** String Functions

| Function | Description |
|---|---|
| `int strlen(char *s1)` | Returns the length of the string, i.e., the number of the characters before the null terminator. |
| `char *strcpy(char *s1, const char *s2)` | Copies the string s2 to string s1. The value in s1 is returned. |
| `char *strncpy(char *s1, const char *s2, size_t n)` | Copies at most n characters from string s2 to string s1. The value in s1 is returned. |
| `char *strcat(char *s1, const char *s2)` | Appends string s2 to s1. The first character of s2 overwrites the null terminator in s1. The value in s1 is returned. |
| `char *strncat(char *s1, const char *s2, size_t n)` | Appends at most n characters from string s2 to s1. The first character of s2 overwrites the null terminator in s1 and appends a null terminator to the result. The value in s1 is returned. |
| `int *strcmp(char *s1, const char *s2)` | Returns a value greater than 0, 0, or less than 0 if s1 is greater than, equal to, or less than s2 based on the numeric code of the characters. |
| `int *strncmp(char *s1, const char *s2, size_t n)` | Returns a value greater than 0, 0, or less than 0 if the n characters in s1 is greater than, equal to, or less than the first n characters in s2 based on the numeric code of the characters. |
| `int atoi(char *s1)` | Converts the string to an `int` value. |
| `double atof(char *s1)` | Converts the string to a `double` value. |
| `long atol(char *s1)` | Converts the string to a `long` value. |
| `void itoa(int value, char *s1, int radix)` | Converts the value to a string based on a specified radix. |

LISTING 7.10 CopyString.cpp

```cpp
1 #include <iostream>
2 #include <cstring>
3 using namespace std;
4
5 int main()
6 {
7     char s1[20];
8     char s2[] = "Dallas, Texas"; // Let C++ figure out the size of s2
9     char s3[] = "AAAAAAAAAA"; // Let C++ figure out the size of s3
10
11     strcpy(s1, s2);
12     strncpy(s3, s2, 6);
13     s3[6] = '\0'; // Insert null terminator
14
15     cout << "The string in s1 is " << s1 << endl;
16     cout << "The string in s2 is " << s2 << endl;
17     cout << "The string in s3 is " << s3 << endl;
18     cout << "The length of string s3 is " << strlen(s3) << endl;
19
20     return 0;
21 }
```

include **cstring** header (line 2)

declare three strings (lines 7–9)

copy **s2** to **s1** (line 11)
copy **s2** to **s3** (line 12)
terminating string (line 13)

string length (line 18)

```
The string in s1 is Dallas, Texas
The string in s2 is Dallas, Texas
The string in s3 is Dallas
The length of string s3 is 6
```

Three strings **s1**, **s2**, and **s3** are declared in lines 7–9. Line 11 copies **s2** to **s1** using the **strcpy** function. Line 12 copies the first 6 characters from **s2** to **s1** using the **strncpy** function. Note that the *null terminator* character is not copied in this case. To terminate the string properly, a null terminator is manually inserted at **s3[6]** (the end of the new string). What would happen if you run the program without line 13? String **s3** would become **DallasAAAA**.

null terminator

**Note**

Both **strcpy** and **strncpy** functions return a string value. But they are invoked as statements in lines 11–12. Recall that a value-returning function may be invoked as a statement if you are not interested in the return value of the function. In this case, the return value is simply ignored.

ignoring return value

Functions **strcat** and **strncat** can be used to append the string in the second argument to the string in the first argument. The first string must have already been allocated with sufficient memory for the function to work. Function **strncat** is equivalent to **strcat** except that **strncat** specifies the number of characters to be appended from the second string. Listing 7.11 gives a program to demonstrate these two functions.

combining strings

**strcat** and **strncat**

## LISTING 7.11 CombineString.cpp

```
1  #include <iostream>
2  #include <cstring>
3  using namespace std;
4
5  int main()
6  {
7    char s1[20] = "Dallas";
8    char s2[] = "Texas, USA";
9    char s3[] = "Dallas";
10
11   strcat(strcat(s1, ", "), s2);
12   strncat(strcat(s3, ", "), s2, 5);
13
14   cout << "The string in s1 is " << s1 << endl;
15   cout << "The string in s2 is " << s2 << endl;
16   cout << "The string in s3 is " << s3 << endl;
17   cout << "The length of string s1 is " << strlen(s1) << endl;
18   cout << "The length of string s3 is " << strlen(s3) << endl;
19
20   return 0;
21 }
```

include **cstring** header

declare three strings

append strings to **s1**
append strings to **s3**

string **s1** length
string **s3** length

```
The string in s1 is Dallas, Texas, USA
The string in s2 is Texas, USA
The string in s3 is Dallas, Texas
The length of string s1 is 18
The length of string s3 is 13
```

Three strings **s1**, **s2**, and **s3** are declared in lines 7–9. Line 11 invokes **strcat** twice. First, **strcat(s1, ", ")** appends **", "** to **s1** and returns new **s1**. Second, **strcat(strcat(s1, ", "), s2)** appends **s2** to the new **s1**. So, **s1** is **Dallas, Texas, USA**. Similarly, line 12 appends, **", "** and the first five characters in **s2** to **s3**. So, **s3** is **Dallas, Texas**.

comparing strings
**strcmp** and **strncmp**

Functions **strcmp** and **strncmp** can be used to compare two strings. How do you compare two strings? You compare their corresponding characters according to their numeric code. Most compilers use the ASCII code for characters.

The function returns the value **0** if **s1** is equal to **s2**, a value less than **0** if **s1** is less than **s2**, and a value greater than **0** if **s1** is greater than **s2**. For example, suppose **s1** is **"abc"** and **s2** is **"abg"**, and **strcmp(s1, s2)** returns **-4**. The first two characters (**a** versus **a**) from **s1** and **s2** are compared. Because they are equal, the second two characters (**b** versus **b**) are compared. Because they are also equal, the third two characters (**c** versus **g**) are compared. Since the character **c** is **4** less than **g**, the comparison returns **-4**.

Listing 7.12 gives a program to demonstrate these two functions.

### Listing 7.12   CompareString.cpp

```
 1  #include <iostream>
 2  #include <cstring>
 3  using namespace std;
 4
 5  int main()
 6  {
 7      char *s1 = "abcdefg";
 8      char *s2 = "abcdg";
 9      char *s3 = "abcdg";
10
11      cout << "strcmp(s1, s2) is " << strcmp(s1, s2) << endl;
12      cout << "strcmp(s2, s1) is " << strcmp(s2, s1) << endl;
13      cout << "strcmp(s2, s3) is " << strcmp(s2, s3) << endl;
14      cout << "strncmp(s1, s2, 3) is " << strncmp(s1, s2, 3) << endl;
15
16      return 0;
17  }
```

include **cstring** header

declare three strings

compare **s1** with **s2**
compare **s2** with **s1**

```
strcmp(s1, s2) is -2
strcmp(s2, s1) is 2
strcmp(s2, s3) is 0
strncmp(s1, s2, 3) is 0
```

return string

Three strings **s1**, **s2**, and **s3** are declared in lines 7–9. Line 11 invokes **strcmp(s1, s2)**, which returns **-2**, because **'e'** - **'g'** is **-2**, Line 12 invokes **strcmp(s2, s1)**, which returns **2**, because **'g'** - **'e'** is **2**. Line 13 invokes **strcmp(s2, s3)**, which returns **0**, because the two strings are identical. Line 14 invokes **strncmp(s1, s2, 3)**, which returns **0**, because the first three character substrings in both **s1** and **s2** are identical.

  **Note**

1, 0, or –1 ?

With some compilers, functions **strcmp** and **strncmp** always return **1, 0, or –1**.

conversion functions

Functions **atoi**, **atof**, and **atol** convert a string to a numeric value. Function **itoa** converts an integer to a string.

Listing 7.13 gives a program to demonstrate these functions.

LISTING 7.13  StringConversion.cpp

```
1  #include <iostream>
2  #include <cstring>                                      include cstring header
3  using namespace std;
4
5  int main()
6  {
7    cout << atoi("4") + atoi("5") << endl;                string to int
8    cout << atof("4.5") + atof("5.5") << endl;            string to double
9
10   char s[10];
11   itoa(42, s, 8);                                       int to string
12   cout << s << endl;
13
14   itoa(42, s, 10);                                      int to string
15   cout << s << endl;
16
17   itoa(42, s, 16);                                      int to string
18   cout << s << endl;
19
20   return 0;
21 }
```

```
9
10
52
42
2a
```

Invoking `atoi("4")` returns an `int` value `4` in line 7. Invoking `atof("4.5")` returns a `double`    **atoi**
value `4.5` in line 8. Invoking `itoa (42, s, 8)` converts an `int` value `42` to a string based    **atof**
radix `8` in line 11. Invoking `itoa (42, s, 10)` converts an `int` value `42` to a string based radix    **itoa**
`10` in line 14. Invoking `itoa (42, s, 16)` converts an `int` value `42` to a string based radix `8`
in line 17.

### 7.9.5  Example: Obtaining Substrings

Often it is useful to obtain a substring from a string. But there is no such function in the
`<cstring>` header. You can develop your own function for extracting substrings. The header
of the function can be specified as:

```
char * substring(char *s, int start, int end)
```

This function returns a string which is a substring in `s` from index `start` to index `end - 1`.
For example, invoking

```
substring("Welcome to C++", 2, 6)
```

returns `"lcom"`.

Listing 7.14 defines and implements the function in a header file.

### LISTING 7.14  Substring.h

```
1  char * substring(const char * const s, int start, int end)      function header
2  {
3    char * pNewString = new char[end - start + 1];                 create a new array
```

copy

null terminator

```
4
5    int j = 0;
6    for (int i = start; i < end; i++, j++)
7    {
8       pNewString[j] = s[i];
9    }
10
11   pNewString[j] = '\0'; // Set a null terminator
12
13   return pNewString;
14 }
```

A new string with the size **end** – **start** + 1 is created in line 3. **end** – **start** is the number of characters extracted from the original string to hold the substring. The extra **+1** is for the null terminator. The substring from index **start** to **end** is copied to **pNewString** (lines 6–9). The null terminator is set in line 11.

Listing 7.15 gives a test program for this function.

### LISTING 7.15 TestSubstring.h

include header

invoke substring

```
1  #include <iostream>
2  #include "Substring.h"
3  using namespace std;
4
5  int main()
6  {
7    char *s = "Atlanta, Georgia";
8    cout << substring(s, 0, 7);
9
10   return 0;
11 }
```

```
Atlanta
```

release dynamic memory

**Caution**

The substring returned from this function is created using the **new** operator. The user of the **substring** function should delete the string after it finishes using it to release the memory occupied by this substring. Otherwise, the string exists as long as the program is alive. It is better to redesign the function to pass the result substring as a parameter as follows:

```
void substring(const char * const s, int start,
  int end, char * substr)
```

## 7.10 Case Studies: Checking Palindromes

A string is a palindrome if it reads the same forward and backward. The words "mom," "dad," and "noon," for example, are all palindromes.

How do you write a program to check whether a string is a palindrome? One solution is to check whether the first character in the string is the same as the last character. If so, check whether the second character is the same as the second- to-last character. This process continues until a mismatch is found or all the characters in the string are checked, except for the middle character if the string has an odd number of characters.

To implement this idea, use two variables, say **low** and **high**, to denote the position of two characters at the beginning and the end in a string **s**, as shown in Listing 7.16 (lines 26 and 29). Initially, **low** is **0** and **high** is **strlen(s)** – 1. If the two characters at these positions match, increment `low` by 1 and decrement `high` by 1 (lines 36–37). This process continues until `(low >= high)` or a mismatch is found.

## LISTING 7.16 CheckPalindrome.cpp

```
1 #include <iostream>
2 #include <cstring>                                      include cstring header
3 using namespace std;
4
5 // Check if a string is a palindrome
6 bool isPalindrome(const char *);                        function prototype
7
8 int main()
9 {
10   // Prompt the user to enter a string
11   cout << "Enter a string: ";
12   char s[80];
13   cin.getline(s, 80);                                   input string
14
15   if (isPalindrome(s))                                  check palindrome
16     cout << s << " is a palindrome" << endl;
17   else
18     cout << s << " is not a palindrome" << endl;
19
20   return 0;
21 }
22
23 bool isPalindrome(const char * const s)
24 {
25   // The index of the first character in the string
26   int low = 0;                                          low index
27
28   // The index of the last character in the string
29   int high = strlen(s) - 1;                             high index
30
31   while (low < high)
32   {
33     if (s[low] != s[high])
34       return false; // Not a palindrome
35
36     low++;                                              update indices
37     high--;
38   }
39
40   return true; // The string is a palindrome
41 }
```

```
Enter a string: abccba  ⏎Enter
abccba is a palindrome
Enter a string: abca  ⏎Enter
abca is not a palindrome
```

Line 12 declares an array with a size 80. Line 13 reads a string to the array. Line 15 invokes the `isPalindrome` function to check whether the string is a palindrome.

The `isPalindrome` function is declared in lines 23–41 to return a Boolean value. The address of the string is passed to the pointer `s`. The length of the string is determined by invoking `strlen(s)` in line 29.

## KEY TERMS

| | | | |
|---|---|---|---|
| address operator (&) | 220 | indirection operator | 222 |
| C-string | 234 | memory leak | 230 |
| delete operator | 230 | new operator | 230 |
| dereference operator (*) | 222 | null terminator ('\0') | 236 |
| heap | 230 | pointer-based string | 234 |

## CHAPTER SUMMARY

- Pointers are variables that store the memory address of other variables.

- The declaration

  ```
  int *pCount;
  ```

  declares pCount to be a pointer that can point to an int variable.

- The ampersand (&) symbol is called the *address operator* when placed in front of a variable. It is a unary operator that returns the address of the variable.

- A pointer variable is declared with a type such as int, double, etc. You have to assign the address of the variable of the same type.

- Like a local variable, a local pointer is assigned an arbitrary value if you don't initialize it. A pointer may be initialized to 0, which is a special value for a pointer to indicate that the pointer points to nothing.

- The asterisk (*) placed before a pointer is known as the indirection operator or dereference operator (dereference means indirect reference). When a pointer is dereferenced, the value at the address stored in the pointer is retrieved.

- There are three ways to pass arguments to a function in C++: *pass-by-value, pass-by-reference with reference arguments,* and *pass-by-reference with pointers.*

- An array variable without a bracket and a subscript actually represents the starting address of the array.

- You can access array elements using pointers or index variables.

- An integer may be added or subtracted from a pointer. The pointer is incremented or decremented by that integer times the size of the element to which the pointer points.

- The const keyword can be used to declare a constant pointer and constant data.

- A pointer may be returned from a function. But you should not return the address of a local variable from a function, because a local variable is destroyed after the function is returned.

- The new operator can be used to allocate persistent memory on the heap. You should use the delete operator to release this memory, when it is no longer needed.

- C++ provides useful functions for testing characters and converting letters: `isdigit(c)`, `isalpha(c)`, `isalnum(c)`, `islower(c)`, `isupper(c)`, `isspace(c)`, `isprint(c)`, `isgraph(c)`, `ispunct(c)`, and `iscntrl(c)`.

- A string can be initialized using a string literal. A null terminator character (`'\0'`) is automatically inserted.

- The `cin.getline` function can be used to read a string from the keyboard.

- C++ provides useful functions for processing C-strings: `strlen(s)`, `strcpy(s1, s2)`, `strncpy(s1, s2, n)`, `strcat(s1, s2)`, `strncat(s1, s2, n)`, `strcmp(s1, s2)`, `strncmp(s1, s2, n)`, `isgraph(c)`, `ispunct(c)`, and `iscntrl(c)`.

## REVIEW QUESTIONS

### Section 7.2 Pointer Basics

**7.1** How do you declare a pointer variable? Does a local pointer variable have a default value?

**7.2** How do you assign a variable's address to a pointer variable? What is wrong in the following code?

```cpp
int x = 30;
int *pX = x;
cout << "x is " << x << endl;
cout << "x is " << px;
```

**7.3** What is wrong in the following code?

```cpp
double x = 3.0;
int *pX = &x;
```

**7.4** Suppose you create a dynamic array and later you need to release it. Identify two errors in the following code:

```cpp
double x[] = new double[30];
...
delete x;
```

### Section 7.3 Passing Arguments by References with Pointers

**7.5** What is the output of the following code?

```cpp
#include <iostream>
using namespace std;

void f1(int x, int &y, int *z)
{
  x++;
  y++;
  (*z)++;
}

int main()
{
  int i = 1, j = 1, k = 1;
  f1(i, j, &k);
```

```
        cout << "i is " << i << endl;
        cout << "j is " << j << endl;
        cout << "k is " << k << endl;

        return 0;
      }
```

## Section 7.4 Arrays and Pointers

**7.6**   Assume you declared `int *p` and `p`'s current value is `100`. What is `p + 1`?

**7.7**   Assume you declared `int *p`. What are the differences among `p++`, `*p++`, and `(*p)++`?

**7.8**   Assume you declared `int p[4] = {1, 2, 3, 4}`. What is `*p`, `*(p+1)`, `p[0]`, and `p[1]`?

## Section 7.5 Using const with Pointers

**7.9**   What is wrong in the following code?

```
int x;
int * const p = &x;
int y;
p = &y;
```

**7.10**   What is wrong in the following code?

```
int x;
const int * p = &x;
int y;
p = &y;
*p = 5;
```

## Section 7.6 Returning Pointers from Functions

**7.11**   Can you guarantee that `p[0]` displays `1` and `p[1]` displays `2` in the following `main` function?

```
#include <iostream>
using namespace std;

int * f()
{
  int list[] = {1, 2, 3, 4};
  return list;
}

int main()
{
  int *p = f();
  cout << p[0] << endl;
  cout << p[1] << endl;

  return 0;
}
```

## Section 7.7 Dynamic Memory Allocation

**7.12**   How do you create the memory space for a **double** value? How do you access this **double** value? How do you release this memory?

**7.13**   Is the dynamic memory destroyed when the program exits?

**7.14**   Explain memory leak.

### Section 7.9 Characters and Strings

**7.15**   Which function do you use to test whether a character is a digit? A letter? A lowercase letter? An uppercase letter? Or a digit or a letter?

**7.16**   Which function do you use to convert a letter to lowercase or to uppercase?

**7.17**   What is the last character in a C-string?

**7.18**   How do you read a string from the keyboard?

**7.19**   How do you find the length of a string? How do you copy a string? How do you combine two strings? How do you compare two strings? How do you convert a string to an **int** value? How do you convert a string to a **double** value? How do you convert an **int** value to a string?

**7.20**   What is the printout of the following statements?

```
char * const pCity = "Dallas";
cout << pCity << endl;
cout << *pCity << endl;
cout << *(pCity + 1) << endl;
cout << *(pCity + 2) << endl;
cout << *(pCity + 3) << endl;
```

**7.21**   What is wrong in the following code?

```
char *pCity;
cout << "Enter a city: ";
cin >> pCity; // Read to pointer pCity
cout << "You entered " << pCity << endl;
```

**7.22**   What is wrong in the following code?

```
char *pCity;
char s2[20] = "New York";
strcpy(pCity, s2);
```

## PROGRAMMING EXERCISES

### Sections 7.2–7.8

**7.1**   (*Analyzing input*) Use pointers on array to write a program that reads ten numbers, computes their average, and finds out how many numbers are above the average.

**7.2**\*\*   (*Printing distinct numbers*) Use pointers on array to write a program that reads in ten numbers and displays distinct numbers (i.e., if a number appears multiple times, it is displayed only once).

**Hint**
Read a number and store it to an array if it is new. If the number is already in the array, discard it.
After the input, the array contains the distinct numbers.

**7.3**\*   (*Increasing array size*) Once an array is created, its size is fixed. Occasionally, you need to add more values to an array, but the array is full. In this case, you may create a new larger array to replace the existing array. Write a function with the following header:

```
* doubleCapacity(int *list, int size)
```

The function returns a new array that doubles the size of the parameter `list`.

**7.4** (*Averaging an array*) Write two overloaded functions that return the average of an array with the following headers:

```
int average(int * array, int size);
double average(double * array, int size);
```

Use {1, 2, 3, 4, 5, 6} and {6.0, 4.4, 1.9, 2.9, 3.4, 3.5} to test the functions.

**7.5** (*Finding the smallest element*) Use pointers to write a function that finds the smallest element in an array of integers. Use {1, 2, 4, 5, 100, 2, –22} to test the function.

**7.6*** (*Sorting*) Implement a sort function that returns a new sorted array. The function header is

```
int * sort(const int * const array, int size);
```

## Section 7.9 Characters and Strings

**7.7*** (*Checking palindrome*) Revise Listing 7.16 to ignore case.

**7.8*** (*Checking substrings*) Write the following function to checks whether string `s1` is a substring of string `s2`. The function returns the first index in `s2` if there is a match. Otherwise, return `-1`.

```
int indexOf(const char *s1, const char *s2)
```

Write a test program that reads two strings and checks whether the one string is a substring of the other.

**7.9*** (*Occurrences of a specified character*) Write a function that finds the number of occurrences of a specified character in the string using the following header:

```
int count(const char * const str, char a)
```

For example, `count("Welcome", 'e')` returns `2`.

**7.10*** (*Occurrences of each digit in a string*) Write a function that counts the occurrence of each digit in a string using the following header:

```
int * count(const char * const s)
```

The function counts how many times a digit appears in the string. The return value is an array of ten elements, each of which holds the count for a digit. For example, after executing `int counts[] = count("12203AB3")`, `counts[0]` is `1`, `counts[1]` is `1`, `counts[2]` is `2`, `counts[3]` is `2`.

Write a `main` function to display the count for `"SSN is 343 32 4545 and ID is 434 34 4323"`.

Redesign the function to pass the `count` array in a parameter as follows:

```
void count(const char * const s, int * counts, int size)
```

where `size` is the size of the `counts` array. In this case, it is `10`.

**7.11**\* (*Counting the letters in a string*) Write a function that counts the number of letters in the string using the following header:

```
int countLetters(const char * const s)
```

Write a `main` function to invoke `countLetters("C++ and Java in 2008")` and display its return value.

**7.12**\* (*Counting occurrence of each letter in a string*) Write a function that counts the occurrence of each letter in the string using the following header:

```
int *count(const char * const s)
```

This function returns the counts as an array of **26** elements.

For example, after invoking

```
int counts[] = count("ABcaB")
```

`counts[0]` is **2**, `counts[1]` is **2**, and `counts[2]` is **1**.

Write a `main` function to invoke `count("ABcaBaddeekjdfefdeg,TTew44Tt")` and display the counts.

Redesign the function to pass the count array in a parameter as follows:

```
void count(const char * const s, int * counts, int size)
```

where `size` is the size of the `counts` array. In this case, it is **26**.

**7.13**\* (*Hex to decimal*) Write a function that parses a hex number as a string into a decimal integer. The function header is as follows:

```
int parseHex(const char * const hexString)
```

For example, `hexString` A5 is 165 ($10 \times 16 + 5 = 165$) and FAA is 4100 ($15 \times 16^2 + 10 \times 16 + 10 = 4100$). So, `parseHex("A5")` returns 165 and `parseHex("FAA")` returns 4100. Use hex strings ABC and 10A to test the function.

**7.14**\* (*Binary to decimal*) Write a function that parses a binary number as a string into a decimal integer. The function header is as follows:

```
int parseBinary(const char * const binaryString)
```

For example, `binaryString` 10001 is 17 ($1 \times 2^4 + 0 \times 2^3 + 0 \times 2^2 + 0 \times 2 + 1 = 17$). So, `parseBinary("10001")` returns 17. Use binary string 11111111 to test the function.

**7.15**\*\* (*Decimal to hex*) Write two overloaded functions that parse a decimal number into a hex number as a string. The function headers are as follows:

```
char * convertDecimalToHex(int value)
void convertDecimalToHex(int value, char * s)
```

See §1.5, "Number Systems," for converting a decimal into a hex. Use decimals 298 and 9123 to test the function.

**7.16**\*\* (*Decimal to binary*) Write two overloaded functions that parse a decimal number into a binary number as a string. The function headers are as follows:

```
char * convertDecimalToBinary(int value)
void convertDecimalToBinary(int value, char * s)
```

See §1.5, "Number Systems," for converting a decimal into a binary. Use decimals 298 and 9123 to test the function.

**7.17**\*\* (*Sorting characters in a string*) Write two overloaded functions that return a sorted string using the following header:

```
char * sort(char *s)
void sort(const char * const s, char * s1)
```

For example, `sort("acb")` returns `abc`.

**7.18**\*\* (*Anagrams*) Write a function that checks whether two words are anagrams. Two words are anagrams if they contain the same letters in any order. For example, "silent" and "listen" are anagrams. The header of the function is as follows:

```
bool isAnagram(const char * const s1, const char * const s2)
```

Write a `main` function to invoke `isAnagram("silent",  "listen")`, `isAnagram("garden",  "ranged")`, and `isAnagram("split",  "lisp")`.

**7.19**\*\* (*Guessing the capitals*) Write a program that repeatedly prompts the user to enter a capital for a state. Upon receiving the user input, the program reports whether the answer is correct. A sample output is shown below:

```
What is the capital of Alabama? Montgomery  ↵Enter
Your answer is correct.
What is the capital of Alaska? Anchorage  ↵Enter
The capital of Alaska is Juneau
```

Assume that ten states and their capitals are stored in a two-dimensional array, as shown in Figure 7.6. The program prompts the user to answer all ten states' capitals and displays the total correct count.

```
Alabama    Montgomery
Alaska     Juneau
Arizona    Phoenix
...        ...
```

**FIGURE 7.6**   A two-dimensional array stores states and their capitals.

**7.20**\* (*Common prefix*) Write a function that returns the common prefix of two strings. For example, the common prefix of `"distance"` and `"disjoint"` is `"dis"`. The header of the function is as follows:

```
char * prefix(const char * const s1, const char * const s2)
```

If the two strings have no common prefix, the function returns an empty string.

Write a `main` function that prompts the user to enter two strings and display their common prefix.

## CHAPTER 8

# RECURSION

## Objectives

- To know what is a recursive function and the benefits of using recursive functions (§8.1).
- To determine the base cases in a recursive function (§§8.2–8.6).
- To understand how recursive function calls are handled in a call stack (§§8.2–8.6).
- To solve problems using recursion (§§8.2–8.6).
- To use an overloaded helper function to derive a recursive function (§8.5).
- To understand the relationship and difference between recursion and iteration (§8.7).

## 8.1 Introduction

recursive function

A *recursive function* is a function that invokes itself directly or indirectly. Recursion is a useful programming technique. In some cases, using recursion enables you to develop a natural, straightforward, simple solution to a problem that would otherwise be difficult to solve. This chapter introduces the concepts and techniques of recursive programming and demonstrates how to "think recursively" using examples.

## 8.2 Example: Factorials

Many mathematical functions are defined using recursion. The factorial of a number n can be recursively defined as follows:

```
0! = 1;
n! = n  (n - 1)!; n > 0
```

How do you find n! for a given n? It is easy to find 1! because you know 0! and 1! is 1 × 0!. Assuming that you know (n-1)!, n! can be obtained immediately using n × (n-1)!. Thus, the problem of computing n! is reduced to computing (n-1)!. When computing (n-1)!, you can apply the same idea recursively until n is reduced to 0.

Let factorial(n) be the function for computing n!. If you call the function with n = 0, it immediately returns the result. The function knows how to solve the simplest case, which is referred to as the *base case* or the *stopping condition*. If you call the function with n > 0, it reduces the problem into a subproblem for computing the factorial of n - 1. The subproblem is essentially the same as the original problem, but is simpler or smaller than the original. Because the subproblem has the same property as the original, you can call the function with a different argument, which is referred to as a *recursive call*.

base case or stopping condition

recursive call

The recursive algorithm for computing factorial(n) can be simply described as follows:

```
if (n == 0)
    return 1;
else
    return n * factorial(n - 1);
```

A recursive call can result in many more recursive calls because the function is dividing a subproblem into new subproblems. For a recursive function to terminate, the problem must eventually be reduced to a stopping case. When it reaches a stopping case, the function returns a result to its caller. The caller then performs a computation and returns the result to its own caller. This process continues until the result is passed back to the original caller. The original problem can now be solved by multiplying n with the result of factorial(n-1).

Listing 8.1 gives a complete program that prompts the user to enter a non-negative integer and displays the factorial for the number.

### LISTING 8.1 ComputeFactorial.cpp

```cpp
1 #include <iostream>
2 using namespace std;
3
4 // Return the factorial for a specified number
5 int factorial(int);
6
7 int main()
8 {
9     // Prompt the user to enter an integer
10    cout << "Please enter a non-negative integer: ";
```

8.2 Example: Factorials

```
11   int n;
12   cin >> n;
13
14   // Display factorial
15   cout << "Factorial of " << n << " is " << factorial(n);
16
17   return 0;
18 }
19
20 // Return the factorial for a specified number
21 int factorial(int n)
22 {
23   if (n == 0) // Base case
24     return 1;
25   else
26     return n * factorial(n - 1); // Recursive call
27 }
```

base case

recursion

```
Please enter a non-negative integer: 5 ↵Enter
Factorial of 5 is 120
```

The **factorial** function (lines 21–27) is essentially a direct translation of the recursive mathematical definition for the factorial into C++ code. The call to **factorial** is recursive because it calls itself. The parameter passed to **factorial** is decremented until it reaches the base case of **0**.

Figure 8.1 illustrates the execution of the recursive calls, starting with n = 4. The use of stack space for recursive calls is shown in Figure 8.2.

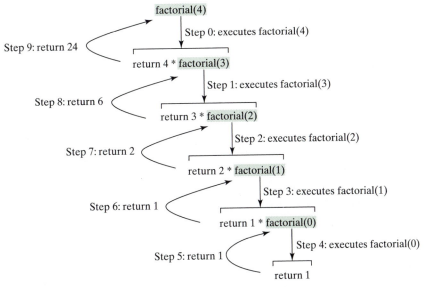

**FIGURE 8.1** Invoking **factorial(4)** spawns recursive calls to **factorial**.

**Caution**

*Infinite recursion* can occur if recursion does not reduce the problem in a manner that allows it to eventually converge into the base case. For example, if you mistakenly write the **factorial** function as follows:

infinite recursion

```
int factorial(int n)
{
  return n * factorial(n - 1);
}
```

The function runs infinitely and causes the stack overflow.

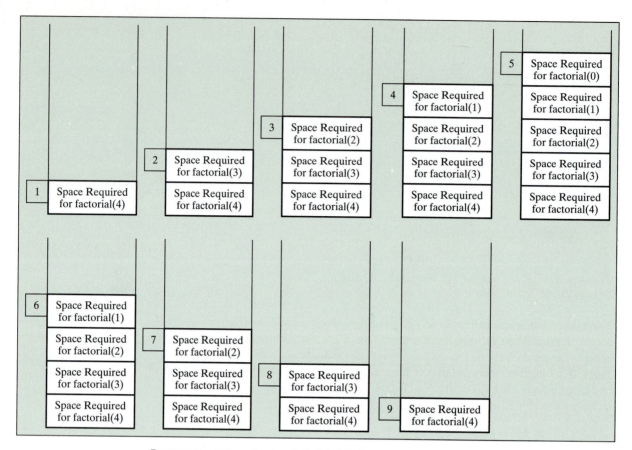

**FIGURE 8.2** When `factorial(4)` is being executed, the `factorial` function is called recursively, causing memory space to dynamically change.

 **Pedagogical Note**

It is simpler and more efficient to implement the `factorial` function using a loop. However, the recursive `factorial` function is a good example to demonstrate the concept of recursion.

## 8.3 Example: Fibonacci Numbers

The `factorial` function in the preceding section easily could be rewritten without using recursion. In some cases, however, using recursion enables you to give a natural, straightforward, simple solution to a program that would otherwise be difficult to solve. Consider the well known Fibonacci series problem, as follows:

| The series: | 0 | 1 | 1 | 2 | 3 | 5 | 8 | 13 | 21 | 34 | 55 | 89 | ... |
|---|---|---|---|---|---|---|---|---|---|---|---|---|---|
| indices: | 0 | 1 | 2 | 3 | 4 | 5 | 6 | 7 | 8 | 9 | 10 | 11 | |

The Fibonacci series begins with 0 and 1, and each subsequent number is the sum of the preceding two numbers in the series. The series can be defined recursively as follows:

```
fib(0) = 0;
fib(1) = 1;
fib(index) = fib(index - 2) + fib(index - 1); index >= 2
```

The Fibonacci series was named for Leonardo Fibonacci, a medieval mathematician, who originated it to model the growth of the rabbit population. It can be applied in numeric optimization and in various other areas.

How do you find `fib(index)` for a given `index`? It is easy to find `fib(2)` because you know `fib(0)` and `fib(1)`. Assuming that you know `fib(index-2)` and `fib(index-1)`, `fib(index)` can be obtained immediately. Thus, the problem of computing `fib(index)` is reduced to computing `fib(index-2)` and `fib(index-1)`. When computing `fib(index-2)` and `fib(index-1)`, you apply the idea recursively until `index` is reduced to `0` or `1`.

The base case is `index=0` or `index=1`. If you call the function with `index=0` or `index=1`, it immediately returns the result. If you call the function with `index>=2`, it divides the problem into two subproblems for computing `fib(index-1)` and `fib(index-2)` using recursive calls. The recursive algorithm for computing `fib(index)` can be simply described as follows:

```cpp
if (index == 0)
  return 0;
else if (index == 1)
  return 1;
else
  return fib(index - 1) + fib(index - 2);
```

Listing 8.2 gives a complete program that prompts the user to enter an index and computes the Fibonacci number for the index.

## LISTING 8.2  ComputeFibonacci.cpp

```cpp
 1 #include <iostream>
 2 using namespace std;
 3
 4 // The function for finding the Fibonacci number
 5 int fib(int);
 6
 7 int main()
 8 {
 9   // Prompt the user to enter an integer
10   cout << "Enter an index for the Fibonacci number: ";
11   int index;
12   cin >> index;
13
14   // Display factorial
15   cout << "Fibonacci number at index " << index << " is "
16     << fib(index) << endl;
17
18   return 0;
19 }
20
21 // The function for finding the Fibonacci number
22 int fib(int index)
23 {
24   if (index == 0) // Base case            base case
25     return 0;
26   else if (index == 1) // Base case       base case
27     return 1;
28   else // Reduction and recursive calls
29     return fib(index - 1) + fib(index - 2);   recursion
30 }
```

```
Enter an index for the Fibonacci number: 7  ⏎Enter
Fibonacci number at index 7 is 13
```

The program does not show the considerable amount of work done behind the scenes by the computer. Figure 8.3, however, shows successive recursive calls for evaluating **fib(4)**. The original function, **fib(4)**, makes two recursive calls, **fib(3)** and **fib(2)**, and then returns **fib(3) + fib(2)**. But in what order are these functions called? In C++, operands for the binary + operator may be evaluated in any order. Assume it is evaluated from left to right. The labels in Figure 8.3 show the order in which functions are called.

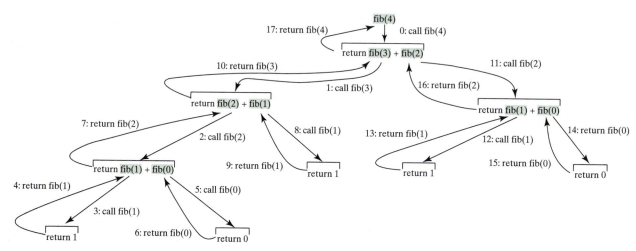

**FIGURE 8.3** Invoking **fib(4)** spawns recursive calls to **fib**.

As shown in Figure 8.3, there are many duplicated recursive calls. For instance, **fib(2)** is called twice, **fib(1)** is called three times, and **fib(0)** is called twice. In general, computing **fib(index)** requires twice as many recursive calls as are needed for computing **fib(index - 1)**. As you try larger index values, the number of calls substantially increases.

Besides the large number of recursive calls, the computer requires more time and space to run recursive functions.

 **Pedagogical Note**

The recursive implementation of the **fib** function is very simple and straightforward, but not efficient. See Exercise 8.2 for an efficient solution using loops. The recursive **fib** function is a good example to demonstrate how to write recursive functions, though it is not practical.

## 8.4 Problem Solving Using Recursion

recursion characteristics

The preceding sections presented two classic recursion examples. All recursive functions have the following characteristics:

if-else

- The function is implemented using an **if-else** or a **switch** statement that leads to different cases.

base cases

- One or more *base cases* (the simplest case) are used to stop recursion.

reduction

- Every recursive call reduces the original problem, bringing it increasingly closer to a base case until it becomes that case.

In general, to solve a problem using recursion, you break it into subproblems. If a subproblem resembles the original problem, you can apply the same approach to solve the subproblem recursively. This subproblem is almost the same as the original problem in nature with a smaller size.

Let us consider a simple problem of printing a message for n times. You can break the problem into two subproblems: one is to print the message one time and the other is to print the message for n-1 times. The second problem is the same as the original problem with a smaller size. The base case for the problem is n==0. You can solve this problem using recursion as follows:

```cpp
void nPrintln(char * message, int times)
{
  if (times >= 1)
  {
    cout << message << endl;
    nPrintln(message, times - 1);
  } // The base case is n == 0
}
```

recursive call

Note that the `fib` function in the preceding example returns a value to its caller, but the `nPrintln` function is `void` and does not return a value to its caller.

Many of the problems presented in the early chapters can be solved using recursion if you *think recursively*. Consider the palindrome problem in Listing 7.16. Recall that a string is a palindrome if it reads the same from the left and from the right. For example, mom and dad are palindromes, but uncle and aunt are not. The problem to check whether a string is a palindrome can be divided into two subproblems:

think recursively

- Check whether the first character and the last character of the string are equal.

- Ignore these two end characters and check whether the rest of the substring is a palindrome.

The second subproblem is the same as the original problem with a smaller size. There are two base cases: (1) the two end characters are not the same; (2) the string size is 0 or 1. In case 1, the string is not a palindrome; and in case 2, the string is a palindrome. The recursive function for this problem can be implemented in Listing 8.3.

## LISTING 8.3 RecursivePalindrome1.cpp

```cpp
 1 #include <iostream>
 2 #include <cstring>
 3 #include "Substring.h"
 4 using namespace std;
 5
 6 bool isPalindrome(const char * const s)
 7 {
 8   if (strlen(s) <= 1) // Base case
 9     return true;
10   else if (s[0] != s[strlen(s) - 1]) // Base case
11     return false;
12   else
13     return isPalindrome(substring(s, 1, strlen(s) - 1));
14 }
15
16 int main()
17 {
18   cout << "Enter a string: ";
19   char s[80];
20   cin.getline(s, 80);
21
22   if (isPalindrome(s))
23     cout << s << " is a palindrome" << endl;
24   else
```

include header file

function header

string length

recursive call

input string

```
25        cout << s << " is not a palindrome" << endl;
26
27     return 0;
28 }
```

```
Enter a string: aba  ⏎Enter
aba is a palindrome
```

```
Enter a string: abab  ⏎Enter
abab is not a palindrome
```

Line 3 includes the header file for the **substring** function, introduced in Listing 7.14. The **strlen(s)** function returns the length of string. This function was introduced in §7.9.4, "String Functions."

Invoking **substring(s, 1, strlen(s) - 1)** returns a new string that is a substring of **s** from index **1** to index **strlen(s) - 2**.

## 8.5 Recursive Helper Functions

The preceding recursive **isPalindrome** function is not efficient, because it creates a new string for every recursive call. To avoid creating new strings, you can use the **low** and **high** indices to indicate the range of the substring. These two indices must be passed to the recursive function. Since the original function is **isPalindrome(const char * const s)**, you have to create a new function **isPalindrome(const char * const s, int low, int high)** to accept additional information on the string, as shown in Listing 8.4.

### LISTING 8.4 RecursivePalindrome2.cpp

```
1 #include <iostream>
2 #include <cstring>
3 using namespace std;
4
5 bool isPalindrome(const char * const s, int low, int high)
6 {
7    if (high <= low) // Base case
8      return true;
9    else if (s[low] != s[high]) // Base case
10     return false;
11   else
12       return isPalindrome(s, low + 1, high - 1);
13 }
14
15 bool isPalindrome(const char * const s)
16 {
17     return isPalindrome(s, 0, strlen(s) - 1);
18 }
19
20 int main()
21 {
22   cout << "Enter a string: ";
23   char s[80];
24   cin.getline(s, 80);
25
26   if (isPalindrome(s))
27     cout << s << " is a palindrome" << endl;
28   else
29     cout << s << " is not a palindrome" << endl;
```

*helper function* (line 5)

*recursive call* (line 12)

*function header* (line 15)

*invoke helper function* (line 17)

*input string* (line 24)

```
30
31    return 0;
32 }
```

```
Enter a string: aba  ↵Enter
aba is a palindrome
```

```
Enter a string: abab  ↵Enter
abab is not a palindrome
```

Two overloaded `isPalindrome` functions are declared. The function `isPalindrome(char * s)` (line 15) checks whether a string is a palindrome and the second function `isPalindrome(char * s, int low, int high)` (line 5) checks whether a substring `s(low..high)` is a palindrome. The first function passes the string `s` with `low = 0` and `high = strlen(s) - 1` to the second function. The second function can be invoked recursively to check a palindrome in an ever-shrinking substring. It is a common design technique in recursive programming to declare a second function that receives additional parameters. Such a function is known as a *recursive helper function*.

recursive helper function

Helper functions are very useful to design recursive solutions for the problems involving strings and arrays. The following sections present two more examples.

### 8.5.1 Selection Sort

Selection sort was introduced in §6.6.1. This section introduces a recursive selection sort for characters in a string. Recall that selection sort finds the largest element in the list and places it last. It then finds the largest element remaining and places it next to last, and so on, until the list contains only a single element. The problem can be divided into two subproblems:

■ Find the largest element in the list and swap it with the last element.

■ Ignore the last element and sort the remaining smaller list recursively.

The base case is that the list contains only one element. Listing 8.5 gives the recursive sort function.

### LISTING 8.5 RecursiveSelectionSort.cpp

```cpp
1 #include <iostream>
2 #include <cstring>
3 using namespace std;
4
5 void sort(char list[], int high)
6 {
7   if (high > 0)
8   {
9     // Find the largest element and its index
10    int indexOfMax = 0;
11    char max = list[0];
12    for (int i = 1; i <= high; i++)
13    {
14      if (list[i] > max)
15      {
16        max = list[i];
17        indexOfMax = i;
18      }
19    }
20
```

helper sort function

```
21      // Swap the largest with the last element in the list
22      list[indexOfMax] = list[high];
23      list[high] = max;
24
25      // Sort the remaining list
26      sort(list, high - 1);
27    }
28 }
29
30 void sort(char list[])
31 {
32    sort(list, strlen(list) - 1);
33 }
34
35 int main()
36 {
37    cout << "Enter a string: ";
38    char s[80];
39    cin.getline(s, 80);
40
41    sort(s);
42
43    cout << "The sorted string is " << s << endl;
44
45    return 0;
46 }
```

*recursive call* (line 26)

*sort function* (line 30)

*invoke helper function* (line 32)

*input string* (line 39)

```
Enter a string: ghfdacb  ⏎Enter
The sorted string is abcdfgh
```

Two overloaded `sort` functions are declared. The function `sort(char list[])` sorts characters in `list[0..strlen(list) - 1]`, and the second function `sort(double list[], int high)` sorts characters in `list[0..high]`. The helper function can be invoked recursively to sort an ever-shrinking subarray.

### 8.5.2   Binary Search

Binary search was introduced in §6.5.2. For binary search to work, the elements in the array must be ordered already. The binary search first compares the key with the element in the middle of the array. Consider the following three cases:

■ **Case 1:** If the key is less than the middle element, recursively search the key in the first half of the array.

■ **Case 2:** If the key is equal to the middle element, the search ends with a match.

■ **Case 3:** If the key is greater than the middle element, recursively search the key in the second half of the array.

Case 1 and Case 3 reduce the search in a smaller list. Case 2 is a base case when there is a match. Another base case is that the search is exhausted without a match. Listing 8.6 gives a clear, simple solution for the binary search problem using recursion.

### LISTING 8.6   RecursiveBinarySearch.cpp

```
1 #include <iostream>
2 using namespace std;
3
```

```
 4  int binarySearch(const int list[], int key, int low, int high)      helper function
 5  {
 6    if (low > high)   // The list has been exhausted without a match
 7      return -low - 1; // Return -insertion point - 1                  base case
 8
 9    int mid = (low + high) / 2;
10    if (key < list[mid])
11      return binarySearch(list, key, low, mid - 1);                    recursive call
12    else if (key == list[mid])
13      return mid;                                                      base case
14    else
15      return binarySearch(list, key, mid + 1, high);                   recursive call
16  }
17
18  int binarySearch(const int list[], int key, int size)               binarySearch function
19  {
20    int low = 0;
21    int high = size - 1;
22    return binarySearch(list, key, low, high);                         call helper function
23  }
24
25  int main()
26  {
27    int list[] = {2, 4, 7, 10, 11, 45, 50, 59, 60, 66, 69, 70, 79};
28    int i = binarySearch(list, 2, 13); // Returns 0
29    int j = binarySearch(list, 11, 13); // Returns 4
30    int k = binarySearch(list, 12, 13); // Returns -6
31
32    cout << "binarySearch(list, 2, 13) returns " << i << endl;
33    cout << "binarySearch(list, 11, 13) returns " << j << endl;
34    cout << "binarySearch(list, 12, 13) returns " << k << endl;
35
36    return 0;
37  }
```

```
binarySearch(list, 2, 13) returns 0
binarySearch(list, 11, 13) returns 4
binarySearch(list, 12, 13) returns -6
```

The binarySearch function in line 18 finds a key in the whole list. The helper binarySearch function in line 4 finds a key in the list with index from low to high.

The binarySearch function in line 18 passes the initial array with low = 0 and high = size - 1 to the helper binarySearch function. The helper function is invoked recursively to find the key in an ever-shrinking subarray.

## 8.6 Towers of Hanoi

The Towers of Hanoi problem is another classic recursion example. The problem can be solved easily using recursion, but is difficult to solve without using recursion.

The problem involves moving a specified number of disks of distinct sizes from one tower to another while observing the following rules:

■ There are $n$ disks labeled 1, 2, 3, ..., $n$, and three towers labeled A, B, and C.

■ No disk can be on top of a smaller disk at any time.

■ All the disks are initially placed on tower A.

■ Only one disk can be moved at a time, and it must be the top disk on the tower.

The objective of the problem is to move all the disks from A to B with the assistance of C. For example, if you have three disks, the steps to move all of the disks from A to B are shown in Figure 8.4.

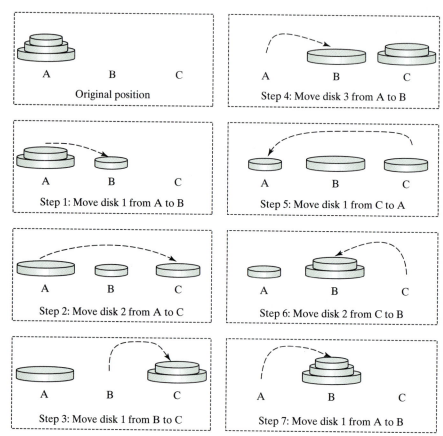

**FIGURE 8.4** The goal of the Towers of Hanoi problem is to move disks from tower A to tower B without breaking the rules.

 **Note**

The Towers of Hanoi is a classic computer science problem. There are many Websites devoted to this problem. The Website `www.cut-the-knot.com/recurrence/hanoi.html` is worth seeing.

In the case of three disks, you can find the solution manually. However, the problem is quite complex for a larger number of disks—even for four. Fortunately, the problem has an inherently recursive nature, which leads to a straightforward recursive solution.

The base case for the problem is `n = 1`. If `n == 1`, you could simply move the disk from A to B. When `n > 1`, you could split the original problem into three subproblems and solve them sequentially.

1. Move the first `n - 1` disks from A to C with the assistance of tower B, as shown in Step 1 in Figure 8.5.

2. Move disk `n` from A to B, as shown in Step 2 in Figure 8.5.

3. Move `n - 1` disks from C to B with the assistance of tower A, as shown in Step 3 in Figure 8.5.

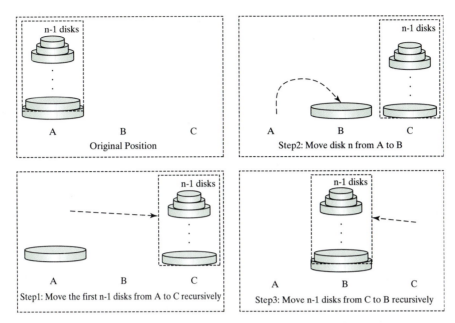

**FIGURE 8.5**    The Towers of Hanoi problem can be decomposed into three subproblems.

The following function moves *n* disks from the fromTower to the toTower with the assistance of the auxTower:

```
void moveDisks(int n, char fromTower, char toTower, char auxTower)
```

The algorithm for the function can be described as follows:

```
if (n == 1) // Stopping condition
  Move disk 1 from the fromTower to the toTower;
else
{
  moveDisks(n - 1, fromTower, auxTower, toTower);
  Move disk n from the fromTower to the toTower;
  moveDisks(n - 1, auxTower, toTower, fromTower);
}
```

Listing 8.7 gives a program that prompts the user to enter the number of disks and invokes the recursive function **moveDisks** to display the solution for moving the disks.

## LISTING 8.7  TowersOfHanoi.cpp

```
 1 #include <iostream>
 2 using namespace std;
 3
 4 /* The function for finding the solution to move n disks
 5    from fromTower to toTower with auxTower */
 6 void moveDisks(int n, char fromTower,                         recursive function
 7   char toTower, char auxTower)
 8 {
 9   if (n == 1) // Stopping condition
10     cout << "Move disk " << n << " from " <<
11       fromTower << " to " << toTower << endl;
12   else
13   {
14     moveDisks(n - 1, fromTower, auxTower, toTower);          recursion
15     cout << "Move disk " << n << " from " <<
16       fromTower << " to " << toTower << endl;
```

recursion

```
17        moveDisks(n - 1, auxTower, toTower, fromTower);
18    }
19  }
20
21  int main()
22  {
23    // Read number of disks, n
24    cout << "Enter number of disks: ";
25    int n;
26    cin >> n;
27
28    // Find the solution recursively
29    cout << "The moves are: " << endl;
30    moveDisks(n, 'A', 'B', 'C');
31
32    return 0;
33  }
```

```
Enter number of disks: 4 ⏎Enter
The moves are:
Move disk 1 from A to C
Move disk 2 from A to B
Move disk 1 from C to B
Move disk 3 from A to C
Move disk 1 from B to A
Move disk 2 from B to C
Move disk 1 from A to C
Move disk 4 from A to B
Move disk 1 from C to B
Move disk 2 from C to A
Move disk 1 from B to A
Move disk 3 from C to B
Move disk 1 from A to C
Move disk 2 from A to B
Move disk 1 from C to B
```

This problem is inherently recursive. Using recursion makes it possible to find a natural, simple solution. It would be difficult to solve the problem without using recursion.

Consider tracing the program for n=3. The successive recursive calls are shown in Figure 8.6. As you can see, writing the program is easier than tracing the recursive calls. The system uses stacks to trace the calls behind the scenes. To some extent, recursion provides a level of abstraction that hides iterations and other details from the user.

## 8.7 Recursion versus Iteration

Recursion is an alternative form of program control. It is essentially repetition without a loop control. When you use loops, you specify a loop body. The repetition of the loop body is controlled by the loop-control structure. In recursion, the function itself is called repeatedly. A selection statement must be used to control whether to call the function recursively or not.

Recursion bears substantial overhead. Each time the program calls a function, the system must assign space for all of the function's local variables and parameters. This can consume considerable memory and requires extra time to manage the additional space.

Any problem that can be solved recursively can be solved nonrecursively with iterations. Recursion has many negative aspects: it uses up too much time and too much memory. Why, then, should you use it? In some cases, using recursion enables you to specify a clear, simple solution that would otherwise be difficult to obtain.

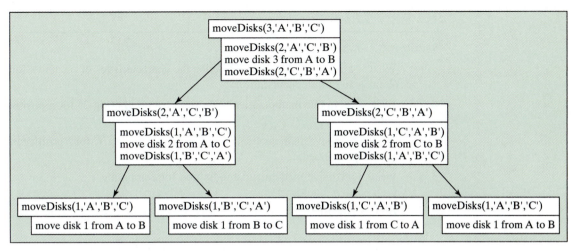

**FIGURE 8.6** Invoking `moveDisks(3, 'A', 'B', 'C')` spawns calls to `moveDisks` recursively.

The decision whether to use recursion or iteration should be based on the nature of the problem you are trying to solve and your understanding of the problem. The rule of thumb is to use whichever of the two approaches can best develop an intuitive solution that naturally mirrors the problem. If an iterative solution is obvious, use it. It generally will be more efficient than the recursive option.

**Note**

Your recursive program could run out of memory, causing a *stack overflow* runtime error.

stack overflow

**Tip**

If you are concerned about your program's performance, avoid using recursion, because it takes more time and consumes more memory than iteration.

performance concern

## KEY TERMS

base case    252
infinite recursion    253
recursive function    252

recursive helper function    259
stopping condition    252

## CHAPTER SUMMARY

- A recursive function is a function that invokes itself directly or indirectly. For a recursive function to terminate, there must be one or more base cases.

- Recursion is an alternative form of program control. It is essentially repetition without a loop control. It can be used to specify simple, clear solutions for inherently recursive problems that would otherwise be difficult to solve.

- Sometimes the original function needs to be modified to receive additional parameters in order to be invoked recursively. A recursive helper function can be declared for this purpose.

- Recursion bears substantial overhead. Each time the program calls a function, the system must assign space for all of the function's local variables and parameters. This can consume considerable memory and requires extra time to manage the additional space.

## REVIEW QUESTIONS

### Sections 8.1–8.3

**8.1** What is a recursive function? Describe the characteristics of recursive functions. What is an infinite recursion?

**8.2** Write a recursive mathematical definition for computing $2^n$ for a positive integer $n$.

**8.3** Write a recursive mathematical definition for computing $x^n$ for a positive integer $n$ and a real number $x$.

**8.4** Write a recursive mathematical definition for computing $1 + 2 + 3 + \cdots + n$ for a positive integer.

**8.5** How many times is the `factorial` function in Listing 8.1 is invoked for `factorial(6)`?

**8.6** How many times is the `fib` function in Listing 8.2 is invoked for `fib(6)`?

**8.7** Show the output of the following program:

```cpp
#include <iostream>
using namespace std;

int f(int n)
{
  if (n == 1)
    return 1;
  else
    return n + f(n - 1);
}

int main()
{
  cout << "Sum is " << f(5) << endl;

  return 0;
}
```

```cpp
#include <iostream>
using namespace std;

void f(int n)
{
  if (n > 0)
  {
    cout << n % 10;
    f(n / 10);
  }
}

int main()
{
  f(1234567);

  return 0;
}
```

**8.8** Show the output of the following two programs:

```cpp
#include <iostream>
using namespace std;

void f(int n)
{
  if (n > 0)
  {
    cout << n << " ";
    f(n - 1);
  }
}

int main()
{
  f(5);

  return 0;
}
```

```cpp
#include <iostream>
using namespace std;

void f(int n)
{
  if (n > 0)
  {
    f(n - 1);
    cout << n << " ";
  }
}

int main()
{
  f(5);

  return 0;
}
```

**8.9**    What is wrong in the following function?

```cpp
#include <iostream>
using namespace std;

void f(double n)
{
  if (n != 0)
  {
    cout << n;
    f(n / 10);
  }
}

int main()
{
  f(1234567);

  return 0;
}
```

## Sections 8.4-8.5

**8.10**   Show the call stack for `isPalindrome("abcba")` using the functions declared in Listing 8.3 and Listing 8.4, respectively.

**8.11**   Show the call stack for `selectionSort("abcba")` using the function declared in Listing 8.5.

**8.12**   What is a recursive helper function?

## Section 8.6 Towers of Hanoi

**8.13**   How many times the `moveDisks` function in Listing 8.7 is invoked for `moveDisks(5, 'A', 'B', 'C')`?

## Section 8.7 Recursion versus Iteration

**8.14**   Which of the following statements are true?

  ■ Any recursive function can be converted into a non-recursive function.
  ■ Recursive function takes more time and memory to execute than non-recursive functions.
  ■ Recursive functions are *always* simpler than non-recursive functions.
  ■ There is always a condition statement in a recursive function to check whether a base case is reached.

**8.15**   What is the cause for the stack overflow exception?

## PROGRAMMING EXERCISES

### Sections 8.2–8.3

**8.1**    (*Computing factorials*) Rewrite the `factorial` function in Listing 8.1 using iterations.

**8.2**\*   (*Fibonacci numbers*) Rewrite the `fib` function in Listing 8.2 using iterations.

**Hint**

To compute `fib(n)` without recursion, you need to obtain `fib(n-2)` and `fib(n-1)` first. Let `f0` and `f1` denote the two previous Fibonacci numbers. The current Fibonacci number would then be `f0 + f1`. The algorithm can be described as follows:

```
f0 = 0; // For fib(0)
f1 = 1; // For fib(1)

for (int i = 1; i <= n; i++)
{
  currentFib = f0 + f1;
  f0 = f1;
  f1 = currentFib;
}

// After the loop, currentFib is fib(n)
```

**8.3**\* (*Computing greatest common divisor using recursion*) The `gcd(m, n)` can also be defined recursively as follows:

- If `m % n` is `0`, `gcd (m, n)` is `n`.
- Otherwise, `gcd(m, n)` is `gcd(n, m % n)`.

Write a recursive function to find the GCD. Write a test program that computes `gcd(24, 16)` and `gcd(255, 25)`.

**8.4** (*Summing series*) Write a recursive function to compute the following series:

$$m(i) = 1 + \frac{1}{2} + \frac{1}{3} + \cdots + \frac{1}{i}$$

**8.5** (*Summing series*) Write a recursive function to compute the following series:

$$m(i) = \frac{1}{3} + \frac{2}{5} + \frac{3}{7} + \frac{4}{9} + \frac{5}{11} + \frac{6}{13} + \cdots + \frac{i}{2i + 1}$$

**8.6**\*\* (*Summing the series*) Write a recursive function to compute the following series:

$$m(i) = \frac{1}{2} + \frac{2}{3} + \cdots + \frac{i}{i + 1}$$

**8.7**\* (*Fibonacci series*) Modify Listing 8.2, ComputeFibonacci.cpp, so that the program finds the number of times the `fib` function is called. (*Hint*: Use a global variable and increment it every time the function is called.)

## Section 8.4 Problem Solving Using Recursion

**8.8**\*\* (*Printing the digits in an integer reversely*) Write a recursive function that displays an `int` value reversely on the console using the following header:

**void** reverseDisplay(**int** value)

For example, `reverseDisplay(12345)` displays `54321`.

**8.9**\*\* (*Printing the characters in a string reversely*) Write a recursive function that displays a string reversely on the console using the following header:

```
void reverseDisplay(const char * const s)
```

For example, `reverseDisplay("abcd")` displays **dcba**.

**8.10**\* (*Occurrences of a specified character in a string*) Write a recursive function that finds the number of occurrences of a specified letter in a string using the following function header:

```
int count(const char * const str, char a)
```

For example, `count("Welcome", 'e')` returns **2**.

**8.11**\*\* (*Summing the digits in an integer using recursion*) Write a recursive function that computes the sum of the digits in an integer. Use the following function header:

```
int sumDigits(long n)
```

For example, `sumDigits(234)` returns $2 + 3 + 4 = 9$.

## Section 8.5 Recursive Helper Functions

**8.12**\*\* (*Printing the characters in a string reversely*) Rewrite Exercise 8.9 using a helper function to pass the substring high index to the function. The helper function header is:

```
void reverseDisplay(const char * const s, int high)
```

**8.13**\*\* (*Finding the largest number in an array*) Write a recursive function that returns the largest integer in an array.

**8.14**\* (*Finding the number of uppercase letters in a string*) Write a recursive function to return the number of uppercase letters in a string.

**8.15**\* (*Occurrences of a specified character in a string*) Rewrite Exercise 8.10 using a helper function to pass the substring high index to the function. You need to declare the following two functions. The second one is a recursive helper function.

```
int count(const char * const s, char a)
int count(const char * const s, char a, int high)
```

## Sections 8.6 Towers of Hanoi

**8.16**\* (*Towers of Hanoi*) Modify Listing 8.7, TowersOfHanoi.cpp, so that the program finds the number of moves needed to move *n* disks from tower A to tower B. (*Hint*: Use a global variable and increment it every time the function is called.)

## Comprehensive

**8.17**\*\*\* (*String permutation*) Write a recursive function to print all permutations of a string. For example, for a string **abc**, the printout is

abc
acb
bac
bca
cab
cba

**Hint**

Declare the following two functions. The second is a helper function.

**void** displayPermutations(**const char** \* **const** s)
**void** displayPermutations(**const char** \* **const** s1, **const char** \* **const** s2)

The first function simply invokes `displayPermutations("", s)`. The second function uses a loop to move a character from s2 to s1 and recursively invokes it with a new s1 and s2. The base case is that s2 is empty and prints s1 to the console.

# PART 2

# OBJECT-ORIENTED PROGRAMMING

In Part 1, "Fundamentals of Programming," you learned how to write simple C++ programs using primitive data types, control statements, functions, arrays, pointers, and recursion, all of which are features commonly available in procedural programming languages. C++, however, is an object-oriented programming language that uses abstraction, encapsulation, inheritance, and polymorphism to provide great flexibility, modularity, and reusability for developing software. In this part of the book you will learn how to define, extend, and work with classes and their objects.

## Prerequisites for Part 2

I/O

I/O in Chapter 12, "File Input and Output," can be covered after Chapter 9, "Objects and Classes."

operator overloading

Operator overloading in Chapter 13, "Operator Overloading," can be covered after Chapter 9, "Objects and Classes."

exception

Exception handling in Chapter 14, "Exception Handling," can be covered after Chapter 12, "Inheritancec and Polymorphism."

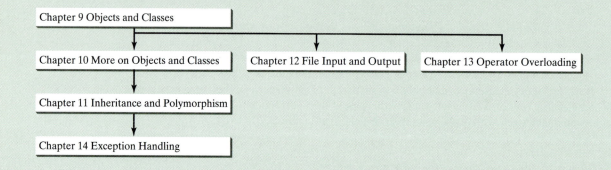

## CHAPTER 9

# OBJECTS AND CLASSES

## Objectives

- To understand objects and classes, and use classes to model objects (§9.2).

- To use UML graphical notations to describe classes and objects (§9.2).

- To understand the role of constructors when creating objects (§9.3).

- To learn how to declare a class and how to create an object of a class (§9.4).

- To know how to separate a class declaration from a class implementation (§9.5).

- To access object members using pointers (§9.6).

- To create objects using the `new` operator on the heap (§9.7).

- To process strings using the C++ `string` class (§9.8).

- To declare private data fields with appropriate `get` and `set` functions for data field encapsulation to make classes easy to maintain (§9.9).

- To understand the scope of data fields (§9.10).

- To reference hidden data fields using the `this` pointer (§9.11).

- To develop functions with object arguments (§9.12).

- To store and process objects in arrays (§9.13).

- To apply class abstraction to develop software (§§9.14–9.15).

- To initialize data fields with a constructor initializer list (§9.16).

## 9.1 Introduction

why OOP?

Programming in procedural languages like C, Pascal, BASIC, Ada, and COBOL involves choosing data structures, designing algorithms, and translating algorithms into code. An object-oriented language like C++ combines the power of procedural languages with an added dimension that provides more flexibility, modularity, clarity, and reusability through abstraction, encapsulation, inheritance, and polymorphism.

OOP vs. procedural programming

In procedural programming, data and operations on the data are separate, and this methodology requires sending data to procedures and functions. Object-oriented programming places data and the operations that pertain to them within a single entity called an *object*; this approach solves many of the problems inherent in procedural programming. The object-oriented programming approach organizes programs in a way that mirrors the real world, in which all objects are associated with both attributes and activities. Using objects improves software reusability and makes programs easier to develop and easier to maintain. Object-oriented programming involves thinking in terms of objects; a program can be viewed as a collection of cooperating objects.

This chapter introduces declaring classes, creating objects, manipulating objects, and making objects work together.

## 9.2 Defining Classes for Objects

object

Object-oriented programming (OOP) involves programming using objects. An *object* represents an entity in the real world that can be distinctly identified. For example, a student, a desk, a circle, a button, and even a loan can all be viewed as objects. An object has a unique identity, state, and behaviors.

state

- The *state* of an object is represented by *data fields* (also known as *properties*) with their current values.

behavior

- The *behavior* of an object is defined by a set of functions. Invoking a function on an object is to ask the object to perform a task.

A circle object, for example, has a data field, `radius`, which is the property that characterizes a circle. One behavior of a circle is that its area can be computed using the function `getArea()`.

Objects of the same type are defined using a common class. A class is a template or a blueprint that defines what an object's data and functions will be. An object is an instance of a class. You can create many instances of a class. Creating an instance is referred to as

instantiation
object
instance

*instantiation*. The terms *object* and *instance* are often interchangeable. The relationship between classes and objects is analogous to the relationship between apple pie recipes and apple pies. You can make as many apple pies as you want from a single recipe. Figure 9.1 shows a class named `Circle` and its three objects.

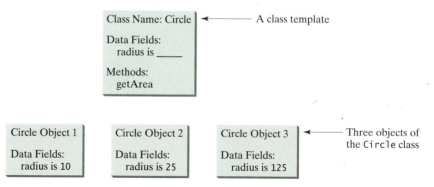

**FIGURE 9.1** A class is a template for creating objects.

A C++ *class* uses variables to define *data fields* and *functions* to define behaviors. Additionally, a class provides functions of a special type, known as *constructors,* which are invoked when a new object is created. A constructor is a special kind of function. A constructor can perform any action, but constructors are designed to perform initializing actions, such as initializing the data fields of objects. Figure 9.2 shows an example of the class for `Circle` objects.

class
data field
function
constructor

```cpp
class Circle
{
public:
  // The radius of this circle
  double radius;            ──────────── Data field

  // Construct a circle object
  Circle()
  {
    radius = 1;
  }
                                         Constructors
  // Construct a circle object
  Circle(double newRadius)
  {
    radius = newRadius;
  }

  // Return the area of this circle
  double getArea()          ──────────── Function
  {
    return radius * radius * 3.14159;
  }
};
```

**FIGURE 9.2**  A class is a construct that defines objects of the same type.

The illustration of class templates and objects in Figure 9.1 can be standardized using the UML (Unified Modeling Language) notations. This notation, as shown in Figure 9.3, is called a *UML class diagram,* or simply *class diagram.* In the class diagram, the data field is denoted as

class diagram

`dataFieldName: dataFieldType`

The constructor is denoted as

`ClassName(parameterName: parameterType)`

The function is denoted as

`functionName(parameterName: parameterType): returnType`

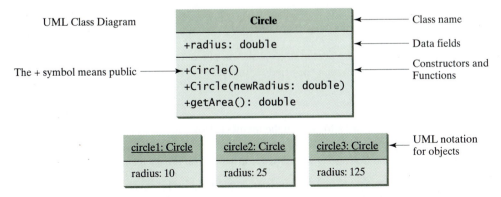

**FIGURE 9.3**  Classes and objects can be represented using UML notations.

## 9.3 Constructors

overloading constructors

The constructor has exactly the same name as the defining class. Like regular functions, *constructors can be overloaded* (i.e., multiple constructors with the same name but different signatures), making it easy to construct objects with different initial data values.

no-arg constructor

A class normally provides a constructor without arguments (e.g., `Circle()`). Such a constructor is called a *no-arg* or *no-argument constructor.*

default constructor

A class may be declared without constructors. In this case, a no-arg constructor with an empty body is implicitly declared in the class. This constructor, called a *default constructor,* is provided automatically *only if no constructors are explicitly declared in the class.*

 **Note**

Constructors are a special kind of function, with three differences:

constructor's name
no return type
invoke constructor

- Constructors must have the same name as the class itself.
- Constructors do not have a return type—not even **void**.
- Constructors are invoked when an object is created. Constructors play the role of initializing objects.

 **Caution**

It is a common mistake to put the **void** keyword in front of a constructor. For example,

```
void Circle()
{
}
```

Most C++ compilers will report an error, but some will treat this as a regular function, not as a constructor.

## 9.4 Object Names

constructing objects

In C++, you can assign a name when creating an object. A constructor is invoked when an object is created. The syntax to create an object using the no-arg constructor is

invoking no-arg constructor

```
ClassName variableName;
```

For example, the following declaration creates an object named `circle1` by invoking the `Circle` class's no-arg constructor:

```
Circle circle1;
```

The syntax to declare an object using a constructor with arguments is

constructing with args

```
ClassName variableName(arguments);
```

For example, the following declaration creates an object named `circle2` by invoking the `Circle` class's constructor with a specified radius `5.5`:

```
Circle circle2(5.5);
```

access operator

Newly created objects are allocated in the memory. How can they be accessed? Objects are accessed via object names. After an object is created, its data can be accessed and its functions invoked using the dot operator ( `.` ), also known as the *object member access operator*:

- `objectName.dataField` references a data field in the object.
- `objectName.function(arguments)` invokes a function on the object.

For example, `circle1.radius` references the radius in `circle1`, and `circle1.getArea()` invokes the `getArea` function on `circle1`. Functions are invoked as operations on objects.

The data field `radius` is referred to as an *instance variable*, because it is dependent on a specific instance. For the same reason, the function `getArea` is referred to as an *instance function*, because you can only invoke it on a specific instance. The object on which an instance function is invoked is called a *calling object*.

instance variable
instance function

calling object

Listing 9.1 gives a program that demonstrates classes and objects. The program constructs a circle object with radius 1 (line 31) and an object with radius 5 (line 32) and displays the radius and area of each of the two circles (lines 34–37). Change the radius of the second object to 100 (line 40) and display its new radius and area (lines 41–42).

## LISTING 9.1  TestCircle.cpp

```cpp
 1 #include <iostream>
 2 using namespace std;
 3
 4 class Circle
 5 {
 6 public:
 7   // The radius of this circle
 8   double radius;
 9
10   // Construct a default circle object
11   Circle()
12   {
13     radius = 1;
14   }
15
16   // Construct a circle object
17   Circle(double newRadius)
18   {
19     radius = newRadius;
20   }
21
22   // Return the area of this circle
23   double getArea()
24   {
25     return radius * radius * 3.14159;
26   }
27 };   // Must place a semicolon here
28
29 int main()
30 {
31   Circle circle1;
32   Circle circle2(5.0);
33
34   cout << "The area of the circle of radius "
35     << circle1.radius << " is " << circle1.getArea() << endl;
36   cout << "The area of the circle of radius "
37     << circle2.radius  << " is " << circle2.getArea() << endl;
38
39   // Modify circle radius
40   circle2.radius = 100;
41   cout << "The area of the circle of radius "
42     << circle2.radius << " is " << circle2.getArea() << endl;
43
44   return 0;
45 }
```

declare class

data field

no-arg constructor

second constructor

function

don't omit ;!

**main** function

using no-arg constructor
using constructor

accessing radius
invoking **getArea**

modify radius

```
The area of the circle of radius 1 is 3.14159
The area of the circle of radius 5 is 78.5397
The area of the circle of radius 100 is 31415.9
```

ending class declaration
**public**

private by default
initialize data field

The class is defined in lines 4–27. Don't forget that the semicolon (`;`) in line 27 is required.

The **public** keyword in line 6 denotes that all data fields, constructors, and functions can be accessed from the objects of the class. If you don't use the **public** keyword, the visibility is private by default. Private visibility will be introduced in §9.9, "Data Field Encapsulation."

The data field **radius** does not have an initial value. So, it must be initialized in the constructor (lines 13 and 19). Note that a variable (local or global) can be declared and initialized in one statement, but as a class member, a data field cannot be initialized when it is declared. For example, it would be wrong to replace line 5 by

```
double radius = 5; // Wrong for data field declaration
```

The **main** function (lines 29–45) creates two objects. The constructor **Circle()** was used to create **circle1** with a radius of **1.0** (line 31), and the constructor **Circle(5.0)** was used to create **circle2** with a radius of **5.0** (line 32).

These two objects (referenced by **circle1** and **circle2**) have different data but share the same functions. Therefore, you can compute their respective areas by using the **getArea()** function.

To write the **getArea** function in a procedural programming language like Pascal, you would pass radius as an argument to the function. But in object-oriented programming, **radius** and **getArea** are defined for the object. The **radius** is a data member in a circle object, which is accessible from the **getArea** function. In procedural programming languages, data and functions are separated, but in an object-oriented programming language, data and functions are grouped together.

The **getArea** function is an instance function that is always invoked by an instance in which the **radius** is specified.

#### Note

naming classes

When you declare a custom class, capitalize the first letter of each word in a class name; for example, the class names **Circle**, **Rectangle**, and **Desk**. The class names in the C++ library are named in lowercase. The objects are named like variables.

naming objects

#### Note

class is a type

You can use primitive data types to define variables. You can also use class names to declare object names. In this sense, a class is also a data type.

#### Note

memberwise copy

In C++, you can also use the assignment operator = to copy the contents from one object to the other. By default, each data field of one object is copied to its counterpart in the other object. For example,

```
circle2 = circle1;
```

copies the **radius** in **circle1** to **circle2**. After the copy, **circle1** and **circle2** are still two different objects, but with the same radius.

#### Note

constant object name

Object names are like array names. Once an object name is declared, it represents an object. It cannot be reassigned to represent another object. In this sense, an object name is a constant, although the contents of the object may change. Memberwise copy can change the contents of an object, but not the name of the object.

**Note**

Most of the time, you create a named object and later access the members of the object through its name. Occasionally, you may create an object and use it only once. In this case, you don't have to name the object. Such objects are called *anonymous objects*.

anonymous object

The syntax to create an anonymous object using the no-arg constructor is

```
ClassName()
```

The syntax to create an anonymous object using the constructor with arguments is

```
ClassName(arguments)
```

For example,

```
circle1 = Circle();
```

creates a `Circle` object using the no-arg constructor and copies its contents to `circle1`.

```
circle1 = Circle(5);
```

creates a `Circle` object with radius 5 and copies its contents to `circle1`.

For example, the following code creates `Circle` objects and invokes their `getArea()` function:

```
cout << "Area is " << Circle().getArea() << endl;
cout << "Area is " << Circle(5).getArea() << endl;
```

As you see from these examples, you may create an anonymous object if the object will not be referenced later.

**Caution**

Please note that in C++, to create an anonymous object using the *no-arg constructor*, you have to add parentheses following the constructor name (e.g., `Circle()`). To create a named object using the no-arg constructor, the parentheses cannot be used following the constructor name (e.g., `Circle circle1`, rather than `Circle circle1()`). This is just the syntax that you have to accept.

no-arg constructor

**Tip**

If you use Visual C++, please refer to Supplement II.B, *"Learning C++ Effectively with Visual C++,"* on the Companion Website. This supplement shows you how to use a debugger to inspect objects.

debugging in IDE

**Note**

The C language has the `struct` type for representing records. For example, you may define a `struct` type for representing students as shown in (a).

**class** replaces **struct**

```
struct student
{
  int id;
  char firstName[30];
  char mi;
  char lastName[30];
};
```
(a)

```
class student
{
public:
  int id;
  char firstName[30];
  char mi;
  char lastName[30];
};
```
(b)

The `struct` type is replaced by the C++ class. A `struct` is essentially a class with all public data fields but no functions (although some compilers support functions). The `struct` type defined in (a) can be replaced by the class defined in (b).

## 9.5 Separating Declaration from Implementation

The preceding example declares the class along with the main `function` that uses the class in the same file. You cannot reuse the class in other programs. To make the class reusable, you should declare the class in a separate header file.

C++ allows you to separate class declaration from implementation. The class declaration describes the contract of the class and the class implementation implements the contract. The class declaration simply lists all the data fields, constructor prototypes, and the function prototypes. The class implementation implements the constructors and functions. The class declaration and implementation are in two separate files. Both files should have the same name, but with different extension names. The class declaration file has an extension name `.h` and the class implementation file has an extension name `.cpp`.

Listings 9.2 and 9.3 present the `Circle` class declaration and implementation.

### LISTING 9.2 `Circle.h`

```
1 class Circle
2 {
3 public:
4     // The radius of this circle
5     double radius;
6
7     // Construct a default circle object
8     Circle();
9
10    // Construct a circle object
11    Circle(double);
12
13    // Return the area of this circle
14    double getArea();
15 };  ←── Semicolon required
```

data field — line 5
no-arg constructor — line 8
second constructor — line 11
function prototype — line 14
semicolon required — line 15

> **Caution**
>
> don't omit semicolon
>
> It is a common mistake to omit the semicolon ( ; ) at the end of the header file.

### LISTING 9.3 `Circle.cpp`

```
1 #include "Circle.h"
2
3 // Construct a default circle object
4 Circle::Circle()
5 {
6     radius = 1;
7 }
8
9 // Construct a circle object
10 Circle::Circle(double newRadius)
11 {
12     radius = newRadius;
13 }
14
15 // Return the area of this circle
16 double Circle::getArea()
17 {
18     return radius * radius * 3.14159;
19 };
```

include class declaration — line 1
implement constructor — line 4
implement constructor — line 10
implement function — line 16

Note that `Circle::` preceding each constructor and function in the `Circle` class tells the compiler that these are defined in the `Circle` class. The `::` symbol is called the *binary scope resolution operator* in C++.

binary scope resolution operator

Listing 9.4 gives a client program that uses the `Circle` class.

## LISTING 9.4 TestCircleWithDeclaration.cpp

```
1 #include <iostream>
2 #include "Circle.h"
3 using namespace std;
4
5 int main()
6 {
7   Circle circle1;
8   Circle circle2(5.0);
9
10  cout << "The area of the circle of radius "
11    << circle1.radius << " is " << circle1.getArea() << endl;
12  cout << "The area of the circle of radius "
13    << circle2.radius << " is " << circle2.getArea() << endl;
14
15  // Modify circle radius
16  circle2.radius = 100;
17  cout << "The area of the circle of radius "
18    << circle2.radius << " is " << circle2.getArea() << endl;
19
20  return 0;
21 }
```

include class declaration

construct circle
construct circle

set a new radius

```
The area of the circle of radius 1 is 3.14159
The area of the circle of radius 5 is 78.5397
The area of the circle of radius 100 is 31415.9
```

**Note**
To compile a main program from the command line, you need to add all its supporting files in the command. For example, to compile TestCircleWithDeclaration.cpp using a GNU C++ compiler, the command is

compiling from command line

```
g++ Circle.cpp TestCircleWithDeclaration.cpp -o Main
```

**Note**
If the main program uses other programs, all of these program source files must be present in the project pane in the IDE. Otherwise, you may get linking errors.

compiling from IDE

**Note**
§5.16, "Inline Functions," introduced how to improve function efficiency using *inline functions*. Inline functions play an important role in class declarations. When a function is implemented inside a class declaration, it automatically becomes an inline function. For example, in the following declaration for class **A**, the constructor and function **f1** are automatically inline functions, but function **f2** is a regular function.

inline functions

```
class A
{
public:
```

```
A()
{
  // Do something;
}

double f1()
{
  // Return a number
}

double f2();
};
```

There is another way to declare inline functions for classes. You may declare inline functions in the class' implementation file. For example, to declare function **f2** as an inline function, precede the inline keyword in the function header as follows:

```
// Implement function as inline
inline double A::f2()
{
  // Return a number
}
```

As noted in §5.16, short functions are good candidates for inline functions, but long functions are not.

## 9.6 Accessing Object Members via Pointers

Object names cannot be changed once they are declared. However, you can create pointers for objects and assign the addresses of objects to pointers whenever necessary. For example,

declare object
assign to pointer

```
1 Circle circle1;
2 Circle *pCircle = &circle1;
```

Line 1 declares a circle object. Line 2 declares a pointer for the circle object and assigns **circle1**'s address to **pCircle**. Later you may assign the address of another **Circle** object to the pointer.

To access object members via a pointer, you must dereference the pointer and use the dot ( **.** ) operator to access object's members. For example,

access radius
invoke **getArea**

set a new radius
access radius
invoke **getArea**

```
1 cout << "The radius is " << (*pCircle).radius << endl;
2 cout << "The area is " << (*pCircle).getArea() << endl;
3
4 (*pCircle).radius = 5.5;
5 cout << "The radius is " << (*pCircle).radius << endl;
6 cout << "The area is " << (*pCircle).getArea() << endl;
```

C++ also provides a shorthand member selection operator for accessing object members from a pointer: arrow (**->**) operator, which is a dash (**-**) immediately followed by the greater than (**>**) symbol. For example,

access radius
invoke **getArea**

set a new radius
access radius
invoke **getArea**

```
1 cout << "The radius is " << pCircle->radius << endl;
2 cout << "The area is " << pCircle->getArea() << endl;
3
4 pCircle->radius = 5.5;
5 cout << "The radius is " << pCircle->radius << endl;
6 cout << "The area is " << pCircle->getArea() << endl;
```

# 9.7 Creating Dynamic Objects on Heap

When you declare a circle object in a function, it is created in the stack. When the function returns, the object is destroyed. To retain the object, you may create it dynamically on the heap using the **new** operator.

*constructing objects*

```
ClassName *pObject = new ClassName();
```

creates an object using the no-arg constructor and assigns the object address to the pointer.

*create dynamic object*

```
ClassName *pObject = new ClassName(arguments);
```

creates an object using the constructor with arguments and assigns the object address to the pointer.

For example, see the following code:

```
// Create an object using the no-arg constructor
Circle *pCircle1 = new Circle();

// Create an object using the constructor with arguments
Circle *pCircle2 = new Circle(5.9);
```

The objects are destroyed when the program is terminated. To explicitly destroy an object, invoke

```
delete pObject;
```

*delete dynamic object*

# 9.8 The C++ **string** Class

Listing 9.1 declared the **Circle** class and created objects from the class. You will frequently use the classes in the C++ library to develop programs. This section introduces the **string** class in the C++ library.

You learned how to store strings using arrays of characters and how to process strings using the C-string functions. C++ also provides the **string** class. You can use it to create string objects and process strings using its member functions. The **string** class supports more features than the C-string functions.

Some frequently used constructors and functions in the **string** class are shown in the UML diagram in Figure 9.4.

**Note**

Many functions in the **string** class return a string such as **append**, **assign**, **erase**, **substr**, **replace**, and **insert**. In this case, the resulting new string is returned.

*return string*

## 9.8.1 Constructing a String

You can create an *empty string* using string's no-arg constructor like this one:

*empty string*

```
string newString;
```

You can create a string object from a string value or from an array of characters. To create a string from a string literal, use a syntax like this one:

```
string newString(stringLiteral);
```

The argument **stringLiteral** is a sequence of characters enclosed inside double quotes. The following statement creates a **string** object **message** for the string literal **"Welcome to C++"**:

```
string message("Welcome to C++");
```

| string | |
|---|---|
| +string() | Constructs an empty string. |
| +string(value: string) | Constructs a string with the specified string literal value. |
| +string(value: char[]) | Constructs a string with the specified character array. |
| +string(ch: char, n: int) | Constructs a string initialized with the specified character n times. |
| +append(s: string): string | Appends string s into this string object. |
| +append(s: string, index: int, n: int): string | Appends n number of characters in s starting at the position index to this string. |
| +append(s[]: char, n: int): string | Appends the first n number of characters in s to this string. |
| +append(n: int, ch: char): string | Appends n copies of character ch to this string. |
| +assign(s[]: char): string | Assigns array of characters or a string s to this string. |
| +assign(s: string, index: int, n: int): string | Assigns n number of characters in s starting at the position index to this string. |
| +assign(s: string, n: int): string | Assigns the first n number of characters in s to this string. |
| +assign(n: int, ch: char): string | Assigns n copies of character ch to this string. |
| +at(index: int): char | Returns the character at the position index from this string. |
| +length(): int | Returns the number of characters in this string. |
| +size(): int | Same as length(). |
| +capacity(): int | Returns the size of the storage allocated for this string. |
| +clear(): void | Removes all characters in this string. |
| +erase(index: int, n: int): string | Removes n characters from this string starting at position index. |
| +empty(): bool | Returns true if this string is empty. |
| +compare(s: string): int | These two compare functions are like the strcmp function in §7.9.4, "String Function," with the same return value. |
| +compare(index: int, n: int, s: string): int | |
| +copy(s[]: char, n: int, index: int): void | Copies n characters into s starting at position index. |
| +data(): char* | Returns a character array from this string. |
| +substr(index: int, n: int): string | Returns a substring of n characters from this starting at position index. |
| +substr(index: int): string | Returns a substring of this string starting at position index. |
| +swap(s: string): void | Swaps this string with s. |
| +find(ch: char): int | Returns the position of the first matching character for ch. |
| +find(ch: char, index: int): int | Returns the position of the first matching character for ch at or from the position index. |
| +find(s: string): int | Returns the position of the first matching substring s. |
| +find(s: string, index: int): int | Returns the position of the first matching substring s starting at or from the position index. |
| +replace(index: int, n: int, s: string): string | Replaces the n characters starting at position index in this string with the string s. |
| +insert(index: int, s: string): string | Inserts the string s into this string at position index. |
| +insert(index: int, n: int, ch: char): string | Inserts the character ch n times into this string at position index. |

**FIGURE 9.4** The `string` class provides the functions for processing a string.

You can also create a string from an array of characters. For example, the following statements create the string "Good Day":

```
char charArray[] = {'G', 'o', 'o', 'd', ' ', 'D', 'a', 'y', '\0'};
string message(charArray):
```

### 9.8.2 Appending a String

You can use several overloaded functions to add new contents to a string. For example, see the following code:

```
string s1("Welcome");
s1.append(" to C++"); // Appends " to C++" to s1
cout << s1 << endl; // s1 now becomes Welcome to C++
```

```cpp
string s2("Welcome");
s2.append(" to C and C++", 0, 5); // Appends " to C" to s2
cout << s2 << endl; // s2 now becomes Welcome to C

string s3("Welcome");
s3.append(" to C and C++", 5); // Appends " to C" to s3
cout << s3 << endl; // s3 now becomes Welcome to C

string s4("Welcome");
s4.append(4, 'G'); // Appends "GGGG" to s4
cout << s4 << endl; // s4 now becomes WelcomeGGGG
```

**Note**

On most compilers, the capacity is automatically increased to accommodate more characters for the functions **append**, **assign**, **insert**, and **replace**. If the capacity is fixed and is too small, the function will copy as many characters as possible.

*too small capacity?*

### 9.8.3 Assigning a String

You can use several overloaded functions to assign new contents to a string. For example, see the following code:

```cpp
string s1("Welcome");
s1.assign("Dallas"); // Assigns "Dallas" to s1
cout << s1 << endl; // s1 now becomes Dallas

string s2("Welcome");
s2.assign("Dallas, Texas", 0, 5); // Assigns "Dalla" to s2
cout << s2 << endl; // s2 now becomes Dalla

string s3("Welcome");
s3.assign("Dallas, Texas", 5); // Assigns "Dalla" to s3
cout << s3 << endl; // s3 now becomes Dalla

string s4("Welcome");
s4.assign(4, 'G'); // Assigns "GGGG" to s4
cout << s4 << endl; // s4 now becomes GGGG
```

### 9.8.4 Functions **at**, **clear**, **erase**, and **empty**

You can use the **at(index)** function to retrieve a character at a specified index, **clear()** to clear the string, **erase(index, n)** to delete part of the string, and **empty()** to test if a string is empty. For example, see the following code:

```cpp
string s1("Welcome");
cout << s1.at(3) << endl; // s1.at(3) returns c
cout << s1.erase(2, 3) << endl; // s1 is now Weme
s1.clear(); // s1 is now empty
cout << s1.empty() << endl; // s1.empty returns 1 (means true)
```

### 9.8.5 Functions **length**, **size**, and **capacity**

You can use the functions **length()**, **size()**, and **capacity()** to obtain string's length, size, and capacity. For example, see the following code:

```cpp
1 string s1("Welcome");
2 cout << s1.length() << endl; // Length is 7
```

*create string*

```
3 cout << s1.size() << endl; // Size is 7
4 cout << s1.capacity() << endl; // Capacity is still 7
5
6 s1.erase(1, 2);
7 cout << s1.length() << endl; // Length is now 5
8 cout << s1.size() << endl; // Size is now 5
9 cout << s1.capacity() << endl; // Capacity is still 7
```

erase two characters

**Note**

capacity?

The *capacity* is set to 7 when string s1 is created in line 1. After erasing two characters in line 6, the capacity is still 7, but the length and size become 5.

### 9.8.6 Comparing Strings

Often, in a program, you need to compare the contents of two strings. You can use the compare function. This function works in the same way as the C-string strcmp function and returns a value greater than 0, 0, or less than 0. For example, see the following code:

```
string s1("Welcome");
string s2("Welcomg");
cout << s1.compare(s2) << endl; // Returns -2
cout << s2.compare(s1) << endl; // Returns 2
cout << s1.compare("Welcome") << endl; // Returns 0
```

### 9.8.7 Obtaining Substrings

You can obtain a single character from a string using the at function. You also can obtain a substring from a string using the substr function. For example, see the following code:

```
string s1("Welcome");
cout << s1.substr(0, 1) << endl; // Returns W
cout << s1.substr(3) << endl; // Returns come
cout << s1.substr(3, 3) << endl; // Returns com
```

### 9.8.8 Searching in a String

You can use the find function to search for a substring or a character in a string. For example, see the following code:

```
string s1("Welcome to HTML");
cout << s1.find("co") << endl; // Returns 3
cout << s1.find("co", 6) << endl; // Returns -1
cout << s1.find('o') << endl; // Returns 4
cout << s1.find('o', 6) << endl; // Returns 9
```

### 9.8.9 Inserting and Replacing Strings

Here are the examples to use the insert and replace functions:

```
string s1("Welcome to HTML");
s1.insert(11, "C++ and ");
cout << s1 << endl; // s1 becomes Welcome to C++ and HTML
```

```
string s2("AA");
s2.insert(1, 4, 'B');
cout << s2 << endl; // s2 becomes to ABBBBA

string s3("Welcome to HTML");
s3.replace(11, 4, "C++");
cout << s3 << endl; // s3 becomes Welcome to C++
```

### 9.8.10  String Operators

C++ supports string operators to simplify string operations. Table 9.1 lists the string operators.

**TABLE 9.1**    String Operators

| Operator | Description |
|----------|-------------|
| [] | Accesses characters using the array subscript operators. |
| = | Copies the contents of one string to the other. |
| + | Concatenates two strings into a new string. |
| += | Appends the contents of one string to the other. |
| << | Inserts a string to a stream |
| >> | Extracts characters from a stream to a string delimited by a whitespace or the null terminator character. |
| ==, !=, <, <=, >, >= | Six relational operators for comparing strings. |

Here are the examples to use these operators:

```
string s1 = "ABC"; // The = operator                         =
string s2 = s1;  // The = operator
for (int i = s2.size() - 1; i >= 0; i--)
  cout << s2[i]; // The [] operator                          []

string s3 = s1 + "DEFG"; // The + operator                   +
cout << s3 << endl; // s3 becomes ABCDEFG                    <<

s1 += "ABC";                                                 +=
cout << s1 << endl; // s1 becomes ABCABC

s1 = "ABC";
s2 = "ABE";
cout << (s1 == s2) << endl; // Displays 0 (means false)      ==
cout << (s1 != s2) << endl; // Displays 1 (means true)       !=
cout << (s1 > s2) << endl; // Displays 0 (means false)       >
cout << (s1 >= s2) << endl; // Displays 0 (means false)      >=
cout << (s1 < s2) << endl; // Displays 1 (means true)        <
cout << (s1 <= s2) << endl; // Displays 1 (means true)       <=
```

## 9.9  Data Field Encapsulation

The data fields `radius` in the `Circle` class in Listing 9.1 can be modified directly (e.g., `circle1.radius = 5`). This is not a good practice for two reasons:

- First, data may be tampered with.
- Second, it makes the class difficult to maintain and vulnerable to bugs. Suppose you want to modify the `Circle` class to ensure that the radius is non-negative after other

client

programs have already used the class? You have to change not only the `Circle` class, but also the programs that use the `Circle` class. Such programs are often referred to as *clients*. This is because the clients may have modified the radius directly (e.g., `myCircle.radius = -5`).

data field encapsulation

To prevent direct modifications of properties, you should declare the field private, using the `private` keyword. This is known as *data field encapsulation*. Making the radius data field private in the `Circle` class, the class declaration can be declared as follows:

```cpp
class Circle
{
public:
  Circle();
  Circle(double);
  double getArea();

private:
  double radius;
};
```

A private data field cannot be accessed by an object through a direct reference outside the class that defines the private field. But often a client needs to retrieve and modify a data field. To make a private data field accessible, provide a *get* function to return the value of the data field. To enable a private data field to be updated, provide a *set* function to set a new value.

 **Note**

Colloquially, a `get` function is referred to as a *getter* (or *accessor*), and a `set` function is referred to as a *setter* (or *mutator*).

accessor
mutator

A `get` function has the following signature:

`returnType getPropertyName()`

bool accessor

If the `returnType` is `bool`, the `get` function should be defined as follows by convention:

`bool isPropertyName()`

A set function has the following signature:

`public void setPropertyName(dataType propertyValue)`

Let us create a new circle class with a private data field radius and its associated accessor and mutator functions. The class diagram is shown in Figure 9.5. The new circle class is declared in Listing 9.5.

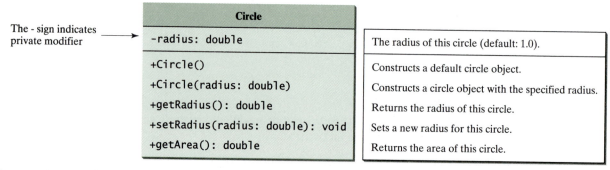

The - sign indicates private modifier

| Circle |
| --- |
| -radius: double |
| +Circle() |
| +Circle(radius: double) |
| +getRadius(): double |
| +setRadius(radius: double): void |
| +getArea(): double |

The radius of this circle (default: 1.0).

Constructs a default circle object.
Constructs a circle object with the specified radius.
Returns the radius of this circle.
Sets a new radius for this circle.
Returns the area of this circle.

**FIGURE 9.5** The `Circle` class encapsulates circle properties and provides get/set and other functions.

**LISTING 9.5**   `Circle2.h`

```
 1 class Circle
 2 {
 3 public:                              public
 4   Circle();
 5   Circle(double);
 6   double getArea();
 7   double getRadius();                 access function
 8   void setRadius(double);             mutator function
 9
10 private:                             private
11   double radius;
12 };
```

Listing 9.6 implements the class contract specified in Listing 9.5.

**LISTING 9.6**   `Circle2.cpp`

```
 1 #include "Circle2.h"                         include header file
 2
 3 // Construct a default circle object
 4 Circle::Circle()                             constructor
 5 {
 6   radius = 1;
 7 }
 8
 9 // Construct a circle object
10 Circle::Circle(double newRadius)             constructor
11 {
12   radius = newRadius;
13 }
14
15 // Return the area of this circle
16 double Circle::getArea()                     get area
17 {
18   return radius * radius * 3.14159;
19 }
20
21 // Return the radius of this circle
22 double Circle::getRadius()                   get radius
23 {
24   return radius;
25 }
26
27 // Set a new radius
28 void Circle::setRadius(double newRadius)     set radius
29 {
30   radius = (newRadius >= 0) ? newRadius : 0;
31 }
```

The `getRadius()` function (lines 22–25) returns the radius, and the `setRadius`
`(newRadius)` function (lines 28–31) sets a new radius into the object. If the new radius is
negative, `0` is set to the radius in the object. Since these functions are the only ways to read
and modify radius, you have total control over how the **radius** property is accessed. If you
have to change the implementation of these functions, you need not change the client programs. This makes the class easy to maintain.

Listing 9.7 is a client program that uses the **Circle** class to create a **Circle** object and modifies the radius using the **setRadius** function.

**LISTING 9.7** TestCircle2.cpp

```
 1 #include <iostream>
 2 #include "Circle2.h"
 3 using namespace std;
 4
 5 int main()
 6 {
 7    Circle circle1;
 8    Circle circle2(5.0);
 9
10    cout << "The area of the circle of radius "
11      << circle1.getRadius() << " is " << circle1.getArea() << endl;
12    cout << "The area of the circle of radius "
13      << circle2.getRadius() << " is " << circle2.getArea() << endl;
14
15    // Modify circle radius
16    circle2.setRadius(100);
17    cout << "The area of the circle of radius "
18      << circle2.getRadius() << " is " << circle2.getArea() << endl;
19
20    return 0;
21 }
```

*include header file* (line 2)
*construct object* (line 7)
*construct object* (line 8)
*get radius* (line 11)
*set radius* (line 16)

```
The area of the circle of radius 1 is 3.14159
The area of the circle of radius 5 is 78.5397
The area of the circle of radius 100 is 31415.9
```

The data field **radius** is declared private. Private data can be accessed only within their defining class. You cannot use **circle1.radius** in the client program. A compilation error would occur if you attempted to access private data from a client.

Since **radius** is private, it cannot be modified. This prevents tampering. For example, the user cannot set **radius** to **-100**.

**Tip**
To prevent data from being tampered with and to make the class easy to maintain, the data fields in this book will be private.

## 9.10 The Scope of Variables

Chapter 5, "Functions," discussed the scope of global variables, local variables, static local variables. Global variables are declared outside all functions and are accessible to all functions in its scope. The scope of a global variable starts from its declaration and continues to the end of the program. Local variables are defined inside functions. The scope of a local variable starts from its declaration and continues to the end of the block that contains the variable. Static local variables are permanently stored in the program so they can be used in the next call of the function.

The data fields are declared as variables and are accessible to all constructors and functions in the class. In this sense, data fields are like global variables. However, data fields and functions can be declared in any order in a class. For example, all the following declarations are the same:

```
class Circle
{
public:
  Circle();
  Circle(double);
  double getArea();
  double getRadius();
  void setRadius(double);

private:
  double radius;
};
```
(a)

```
class Circle
{
public:
  Circle();
  Circle(double);

private:
  double radius;

public:
  double getArea();
  double getRadius();
  void setRadius(double);
};
```
(b)

```
class Circle
{
private:
  double radius;

public:
  double getArea();
  double getRadius();
  void setRadius(double);

public:
  Circle();
  Circle(double);
};
```
(c)

 **Tip**

Though the class members can be declared in any order, The preferred style in C++ is to declare public members first and then the private members.

*public first*

This section discusses the scope rules of all the variables in the context of a class.

You can declare a variable for a data field only once, but you can declare the same variable name in a function many times in different functions.

Local variables are declared and used inside a function locally. If a local variable has the same name as a data field, the local variable takes precedence and the data field with the same name is hidden. For example, in the following program in Listing 9.8, x is defined as a data field and as a local variable in the function.

## LISTING 9.8  HideDataField.cpp

```
 1 #include <iostream>
 2 using namespace std;
 3
 4 class Foo
 5 {
 6 public:
 7   int x; // Data field
 8   int y; // Data field
 9
10   Foo()
11   {
12     x = 10;
13     y = 10;
14   }
15
16   void p()
17   {
18     int x = 20; // Local variable
19     cout << "x is " << x << endl;
20     cout << "y is " << y << endl;
21   }
22 };
23
24 int main()
25 {
26   Foo foo;
27   foo.p();
28
29   return 0;
30 }
```

*data field x*
*data field y*

*no-arg constructor*

*local variable*

*create object*
*invoke function*

```
x is 20
y is 10
```

Why is the printout **20** for **x** and **10** for **y**? Here is why:

- **x** is declared as a data field in the **Foo** class, but is also defined as a local variable in the function **p()** with an initial value of **20**. The latter **x** is displayed to the console in line 19.

- **y** is declared as a data field, so it is accessible inside function **p()**.

**Tip**

As demonstrated in the example, it is easy to make mistakes. To avoid confusion, do not declare the same variable name twice in a class, except for function parameters.

## 9.11 The **this** Pointer

*hidden variable*

Sometimes you need to reference a class's hidden data field in a function. For example, a data field name is often used as the parameter name in a set function for the data field. In this case, you need to reference the hidden data field name in the function in order to set a new value to it. A hidden data field can be accessed by using the **this** keyword, which is a special built-in pointer that references to the calling object. You can rewrite the **Circle** class implementation in Listing 9.9 using the **this** pointer.

### LISTING **9.9** Circle3.cpp

*include header file*

```
 1  #include "Circle2.h"
 2
 3  // Construct a default circle object
 4  Circle::Circle()
 5  {
 6    radius = 1;
 7  }
 8
 9  // Construct a circle object
10  Circle::Circle(double radius)
11  {
12    this->radius = radius; // or (*this).radius  = radius;
13  }
14
15  // Return the area of this circle
16  double Circle::getArea()
17  {
18    return radius * radius * 3.14159;
19  }
20
21  // Return the radius of this circle
22  double Circle::getRadius()
23  {
24    return radius;
25  }
26
27  // Set a new radius
28  void Circle::setRadius(double radius)
29  {
30    this->radius = (radius >= 0) ? radius : 0;
31  }
```

*this pointer* (line 12)

*this pointer* (line 30)

The parameter named `radius` in the constructor (line 10) is a local variable. To reference the data field `radius` in the object, you have to use `this->radius` (line 12). The parameter named `radius` in the `setRadius` function (line 28) is a local variable. To reference the data field `radius` in the object, you have to use `this->radius` (line 30).

## 9.12 Passing Objects to Functions

So far, you have learned how to pass arguments of primitive types and array types to functions. You can also pass objects to functions. You can pass objects by value or by reference. Listing 9.10 gives an example that passes an object by value.

LISTING **9.10** `PassObjectByValue.cpp`

```
1  #include <iostream>
2  #include "Circle2.h"                                    include header file
3  using namespace std;
4
5  void printCircle(Circle c)                              object parameter
6  {
7    cout << "The area of the circle of "
8      << c.getRadius() << " is " << c.getArea() << endl;  access circle
9  }
10
11 int main()
12 {
13   Circle myCircle(5.0);                                 create circle
14   printCircle(myCircle);                                pass object
15
16   return 0;
17 }
```

```
The area of the circle of 5 is 78.5397
```

The `Circle` class defined Circle2.h from Listing 9.5 is included in line 2. The parameter for the `printCircle` function is declared as `Circle` (line 5). The `main` function creates a `Circle` object `myCircle` (line 13) and passes it to the `printCircle` function by value (line 14). Passing an object argument by value is to copy the object to the function parameter. So the object `c` in the `printCircle` function has the same content as the object `myCircle` in the `main` function, as shown in Figure 9.6(a).

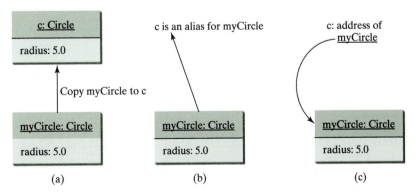

**FIGURE 9.6** You can pass an object to a function in three ways: (a) pass-by-value, (b) pass-by-reference, (c) pass-by-reference via pointer.

Listings 9.11 gives an example that passes an object by reference.

### LISTING 9.11 PassObjectByReference.cpp

include header file

reference parameter

access circle

create circle
pass reference

```
 1 #include <iostream>
 2 #include "Circle2.h"
 3 using namespace std;
 4
 5 void printCircle(Circle &c)
 6 {
 7   cout << "The area of the circle of "
 8     << c.getRadius() << " is " << c.getArea() << endl;
 9 }
10
11 int main()
12 {
13   Circle myCircle(5.0);
14   printCircle(&myCircle);
15
16   return 0;
17 }
```

```
The area of the circle of 5 is 78.5397
```

A reference parameter of the **Circle** type is declared in the **printCircle** function (line 5). The **main** function creates a **Circle** object **myCircle** (line 13) and passes the reference of the object to the **printCircle** function (line 14). So the object **c** in the **printCircle** function is essentially an alias of the object **myCircle** in the **main** function, as shown in Figure 9.6(b).

Listings 9.12 gives an example that passes an object by reference via a pointer.

### LISTING 9.12 PassObjectToPointer.cpp

include header file

pointer parameter

access circle

create circle
pass address

```
 1 #include <iostream>
 2 #include "Circle2.h"
 3 using namespace std;
 4
 5 void printCircle(Circle *c)
 6 {
 7   cout << "The area of the circle of "
 8     << c->getRadius() << " is " << c->getArea() << endl;
 9 }
10
11 int main()
12 {
13   Circle myCircle(5.0);
14   printCircle(&myCircle);
15
16   return 0;
17 }
```

```
The area of the circle of 5 is 78.5397
```

A pointer parameter of the **Circle** type is declared in the **printCircle** function (line 5). The **main** function creates a **Circle** object **myCircle** (line 13) and passes the address of the object to the **printCircle** function (line 14). So the object **c** in the **printCircle** function points to the object **myCircle** in the main function, as shown in Figure 9.6(c).

**Tip**
Though you can pass an object to a function by value, by reference, or by reference via a pointer parameter, passing an object by reference is preferred for two reasons: (1) it takes time and additional memory space to pass an object by value; (2) using an object reference parameter is simpler than using a pointer parameter.

pass an object by reference

## 9.13 Array of Objects

In Chapter 6, "Arrays," arrays of primitive type elements were created. You also can create arrays of objects. For example, the following statement declares and creates an array of ten Circle objects:

```
Circle circleArray[10]; // Declare array of ten Circle objects
```

The name of the array is `circleArray` and the no-arg constructor is called to initialize each element in the array. So, `circleArray[0].getRadius()` returns 1, because the no-arg constructor assigns 1 to `radius`.

You also can use the array initializer to declare and initialize an array using a constructor with arguments. For example,

```
Circle circleArray[3] = {Circle(3), Circle(4), Circle(5)};
```

Listing 9.13 gives an example that demonstrates how to use an array of objects. The program summarizes the areas of an array of circles. The program creates `circleArray`, an array composed of ten Circle objects; it then sets circle radii with radius 1, 2, 3, 4, ..., and 10, and displays the total area of the circles in the array.

LISTING **9.13** TotalArea.cpp

```
 1  #include <iostream>
 2  #include "Circle2.h"                                    include header file
 3  using namespace std;
 4
 5  // Add circle areas
 6  double sum(Circle circleArray[], int size)              array of objects
 7  {
 8    // Initialize sum
 9    double sum = 0;
10
11    // Add areas to sum
12    for (int i = 0; i < size; i++)
13      sum += circleArray[i].getArea();                    get area
14
15    return sum;
16  }
17
18  // Print an array of circles and their total area
19  void printCircleArray(Circle circleArray[], int size)   array of objects
20  {
21    cout << "Radius\t\t\t\t" << "Area" << endl;
22    for (int i = 0; i < size; i++)
23    {
24      cout << circleArray[i].getRadius() << "\t\t" <<
25        circleArray[i].getArea() << endl;
26    }
27
28    cout << "--------------" << endl;
29
```

```
30    // Compute and display the result
31    cout << "The total areas of circles is \t" <<
32      sum(circleArray, size) << endl;
33 }
34
35 int main()
36 {
37    const int SIZE = 10;
38
39    // Create a Circle object with radius 1
40    Circle circleArray[SIZE];
41
42    for (int i = 0; i < SIZE; i++)
43    {
44      circleArray[i].setRadius(i + 1);
45    }
46
47    printCircleArray(circleArray, SIZE);
48
49    return 0;
50 }
```

create array

new radius

pass array

| Radius | Area |
|--------|------|
| 1 | 3.14159 |
| 2 | 12.5664 |
| 3 | 28.2743 |
| 4 | 50.2654 |
| 5 | 78.5397 |
| 6 | 113.097 |
| 7 | 153.938 |
| 8 | 201.062 |
| 9 | 254.469 |
| 10 | 314.159 |

```
------------------------------------
The total areas of circles is 1209.51
```

The program creates an array of ten `Circle` objects (line 40). Two `Circle` classes were introduced in this chapter. This example uses the `Circle` class defined in Listing 9.5.

Each object element in the array is created using the `Circle`'s no-arg constructor. A new radius for each circle is set in lines 42–45. `circleArray[i]` refers to a `Circle` object in the array. `circleArray[i].setRadius(i + 1)` sets a new radius in the `Circle` object (line 44). The array is passed to the `printCircleArray` function, which displays the radii of the total area of the circles.

The sum of the areas of the circle is computed using the `sum` function (line 32), which takes the array of `Circle` objects as the argument and returns a `double` value for the total area.

## 9.14  Class Abstraction and Encapsulation

In Chapter 5, "Functions," you learned about function abstraction and used it in stepwise program development. C++ provides many levels of abstraction. *Class abstraction* is the separation of class implementation from the use of a class. The creator of a class provides a description of the class and lets the user know how the class can be used. The collection of functions and fields that are accessible from outside the class, together with the description of how these members are expected to behave, serves as the *class's contract.* As shown in Figure 9.7, the user of the class does not need to know how the class is implemented. The details of implementation are encapsulated and hidden from the user. This is known as *class encapsulation.* For example, you can create a `Circle` object and find the area of the circle without knowing how the area is computed.

class abstraction

class encapsulation

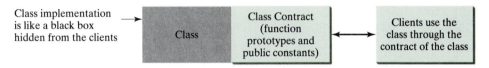

**FIGURE 9.7**  Class abstraction separates class implementation from the use of the class.

Class abstraction and encapsulation are two sides of the same coin. There are many real-life examples that illustrate the concept of class abstraction. Consider building a computer system, for instance. Your personal computer is made up of many components, such as a CPU, CD-ROM, floppy disk, motherboard, fan, and so on. Each component can be viewed as an object that has properties and functions. To get the components to work together, all you need to know is how each component is used and how it interacts with the others. You don't need to know how it works internally. The internal implementation is encapsulated and hidden from you. You can build a computer without knowing how a component is implemented.

The computer-system analogy precisely mirrors the object-oriented approach. Each component can be viewed as an object of the class for the component. For example, you might have a class that models all kinds of fans for use in a computer, with properties like fan size and speed, and functions like start, stop, and so on. A specific fan is an instance of this class with specific property values.

Consider getting a loan, for another example. A specific loan can be viewed as an object of a **Loan** class. Interest rate, loan amount, and loan period are its data properties, and computing monthly payment and total payment are its functions. When you buy a car, a loan object is created by instantiating the class with your loan interest rate, loan amount, and loan period. You can then use the functions to find the monthly payment and total payment of your loan. As a user of the **Loan** class, you don't need to know how these functions are implemented.

## 9.15  Case Study: The **Loan** Class

Let us use the **Loan** class as an example to demonstrate the creation and use of classes. **Loan** has the data fields: `annualInterestRate`, `numberOfYears`, and `loanAmount`, and the functions `getAnnualInterestRate`, `getNumberOfYears`, `getLoanAmount`, `setAnnualInterestRate`, `setNumberOfYears`, `setLoanAmount`, `getMonthlyPayment`, and `getTotalPayment`, as shown in Figure 9.8.

The UML diagram in Figure 9.8 serves as the contract for the **Loan** class. Throughout the book, you will play the role of both class user and class writer. The user can use the class without knowing how the class is implemented. Assume that the **Loan** class is available, with the header file, as shown in Listing 9.14. Let us begin by writing a test program that uses the **Loan** class in Listing 9.15.

| Loan |
|---|
| -annualInterestRate: double |
| -numberOfYears: int |
| -loanAmount: double |
| +Loan() |
| +Loan(annualInterestRate: double, numberOfYears: int, loanAmount: double) |
| +getAnnualInterestRate(): double |
| +getNumberOfYears(): int |
| +getLoanAmount(): double |
| +setAnnualInterestRate( annualInterestRate: double): void |
| +setNumberOfYears( numberOfYears: int): void |
| +setLoanAmount( loanAmount: double): void |
| +getMonthlyPayment(): double |
| +getTotalPayment(): double |

The annual interest rate of the loan (default: 2.5).
The number of years for the loan (default: 1)
The loan amount (default: 1000).

Constructs a default loan object.
Constructs a loan with specified interest rate, years, and loan amount.

Returns the annual interest rate of this loan.
Returns the number of the years of this loan.
Returns the amount of this loan.
Sets a new annual interest rate to this loan.

Sets a new number of years to this loan.

Sets a new amount to this loan.

Returns the monthly payment of this loan.
Returns the total payment of this loan.

**FIGURE 9.8** The **Loan** class models the properties and behaviors of loans.

## LISTING 9.14 Loan.h

public functions

private fields

```cpp
1  class Loan
2  {
3  public:
4    Loan();
5    Loan(double annualInterestRate, int numberOfYears,
6      double loanAmount);
7    double getAnnualInterestRate();
8    int getNumberOfYears();
9    double getLoanAmount();
10   void setAnnualInterestRate(double annualInterestRate);
11   void setNumberOfYears(int numberOfYears);
12   void setLoanAmount(double loanAmount);
13   double getMonthlyPayment();
14   double getTotalPayment();
15
16 private:
17   double annualInterestRate;
18   int numberOfYears;
19   double loanAmount;
20 };
```

## LISTING 9.15 TestLoanClass.cpp

include **Loan** header

```cpp
1  #include <iostream>
2  #include <iomanip>
3  #include "Loan.h"
4  using namespace std;
5
6  int main()
7  {
8    // Enter annual interest rate
9    cout << "Enter yearly interest rate, for example 8.25: ";
10   double annualInterestRate;
```

```
11     cin >> annualInterestRate;
12
13     // Enter number of years
14     cout << "Enter number of years as an integer, for example 5: ";
15     int numberOfYears;
16     cin >> numberOfYears;                                          input number of years
17
18     // Enter loan amount
19     cout << "Enter loan amount, for example 120000.95: ";
20     double loanAmount;
21     cin >> loanAmount;                                             input loan amount
22
23     // Create Loan object
24     Loan loan(annualInterestRate, numberOfYears, loanAmount);      create Loan object
25
26     // Display results
27     cout << fixed << setprecision(2);
28     cout << "The monthly payment is " << loan.getMonthlyPayment()  monthly payment
29         << endl;
30     cout << "The total payment is " << loan.getTotalPayment() << endl;  total payment
31
32     return 0;
33 }
```

The **main** function reads interest rate, payment period (in years), and loan amount (lines 8–21); creates a **Loan** object (line 24); and then obtains the monthly payment (line 28) and total payment (line 30) using the instance functions in the **Loan** class.

The **Loan** class can be implemented in Listing 9.16.

## LISTING 9.16    Loan.cpp

```
 1 #include "Loan.h"
 2 #include <cmath>
 3 using namespace std;
 4
 5 Loan::Loan()                                                       no-arg constructor
 6 {
 7    annualInterestRate = 9.5;
 8    numberOfYears = 30;
 9    loanAmount = 100000;
10 }
11
12 Loan::Loan(double annualInterestRate, int numberOfYears,          constructor
13    double loanAmount)
14 {
15    this->annualInterestRate = annualInterestRate;                 this pointer
16    this->numberOfYears = numberOfYears;
17    this->loanAmount = loanAmount;
18 }
19
20 double Loan::getAnnualInterestRate()                              accessor function
21 {
22    return annualInterestRate;
23 }
24
25 int Loan::getNumberOfYears()                                      accessor function
26 {
27    return numberOfYears;
28 }
29
```

accessor function

```
30 double Loan::getLoanAmount()
31 {
32   return loanAmount;
33 }
34
35 void Loan::setAnnualInterestRate(double annualInterestRate)
36 {
37   this->annualInterestRate = annualInterestRate;
38 }
39
```

accessor function

```
40 void Loan::setNumberOfYears(int numberOfYears)
41 {
42   this->numberOfYears = numberOfYears;
43 }
44
```

accessor function

```
45 void Loan::setLoanAmount(double loanAmount)
46 {
47   this->loanAmount = loanAmount;
48 }
49
```

compute monthly payment

```
50 double Loan::getMonthlyPayment()
51 {
52   double monthlyInterestRate = annualInterestRate / 1200;
53   return loanAmount * monthlyInterestRate / (1 -
54     (pow(1 / (1 + monthlyInterestRate), numberOfYears * 12)));
55 }
56
```

compute total payment

```
57 double Loan::getTotalPayment()
58 {
59   return getMonthlyPayment() * numberOfYears * 12;
60 }
```

From a class developer's perspective, a class is designed for use by many different customers. In order to be useful in a wide range of applications, a class should provide a variety of ways for customization through constructors, properties, and functions.

The **Loan** class contains two constructors, three get functions, three set functions, and the functions for finding monthly payment and total payment. You can construct a **Loan** object by using the no-arg constructor or the one with three parameters: annual interest rate, number of years, and loan amount. The three get functions, **getAnnualInterest**, **getNumberOfYears**, and **getLoanAmount**, return annual interest rate, payment years, and loan amount, respectively.

 **Important Pedagogical Tip**

The UML diagram for the **Loan** class is shown in Figure 9.8. Students should begin by writing a test program that uses the **Loan** class even though they don't know how the **Loan** class is implemented. This has three benefits:

- It demonstrates that developing a class and using a class are two separate tasks.
- It enables you to skip the complex implementation of certain classes without interrupting the sequence of the book.
- It is easier to learn how to implement a class if you are familiar with the class through using it.

For all the examples from now on, you may first create an object from the class and try to use its functions and then turn your attention to its implementation.

# 9.16  Constructor Initializer Lists

Data fields may be initialized in the constructor using an initializer list in the following syntax:

```
ClassName(parameterList)
  : datafield1(value1), datafield2(value2) // initializer list
{
  // Additional statements if needed
}
```

The initializer list initializes **datafield1** with **value1** and **datafield2** with **value2**.
   For example,

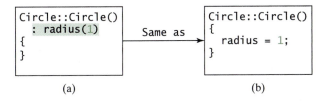

```
Circle::Circle()
  : radius(1)
{
}
```
(a)

Same as

```
Circle::Circle()
{
  radius = 1;
}
```
(b)

(b) is actually simpler than (a) without using an initializer list. However, using an initializer
list is necessary to initialize object data fields that don't have a no-arg constructor.

**Note**

In C++, you can declare an object data field. For example, **name** is declared a **string** object in
the following code:

*object data field vs. local object*

```
class Student
{
public:
  Student();

private:
  string name;
};
```

However, declaring an object data field in a class is different from declaring a local object in a
function like this:

```
int main()
{
  string name;

};
```

As an object data field, the object is not created when it is declared. As an object declared in a
function, the object is created when it is declared.

**Note**

In C++, data fields (primitive or object type) cannot be declared with an initial value. For example, the following code is wrong:

*initialize data field*

```
class Student
{
public:
  Student();

private:
  int age = 5; // Cannot initialize a class member
```

```
    string name("Peter"); // Cannot initialize a class member
};
```

The correct declaration is

```
class Student
{
public:
  Student();

private:
  int age; // Declare a data field of the int type
  string name; // Declare a data field of the string type
};
```

When an object of the Student class is created, the constructor automatically invokes the string class's no-arg constructor to create an object for name. However, the primitive data field age is not automatically initialized. You have to explicitly initialize it in the constructor. For example,

```
class Student
{
public:
  Student()
  {
    age = 5; // Initialize age
  };

private:
  int age; // Declare a data field of the int type
  string name; // Declare a data field of the string type
};
```

If a data field is of an object type, the no-arg constructor for the object type is automatically invoked to construct an object for the data field. If the no-arg constructor does not exist, a compilation error will be reported. For example, the code in Listing 9.17 has an error, because the time data field (line 24) in the Action class is of the Time class that does not have a no-arg constructor.

LISTING 9.17 NoDefaultConstructor1.cpp

Time class
```
1 class Time
2 {
3 public:
```
Time class constructor
```
4   Time(int hour, int minute, int second)
5   {
6     // Code omitted
7   }
8
9 private:
10    int hour;
11    int minute;
12    int second;
13 };
14
```
Action class
```
15 class Action
16 {
17 public:
18   Action(int hour, int minute, int second)
19   {
```

```
20      time = Time(hour, minute, second);
21    }
22
23 private:
24    Time time;
25 };
```

time data field

To fix this error, you have to use the constructor initializer list as shown in Listing 9.18. The data field `time` is initialized in the constructor initializer (line 19).

## LISTING 9.18 NoDefaultConstructor2.cpp

```
 1 class Time
 2 {
 3 public:
 4    Time(int hour, int minute, int second)
 5    {
 6       // Code omitted
 7    }
 8
 9 private:
10    int hour;
11    int minute;
12    int second;
13 };
14
15 class Action
16 {
17 public:
18    Action(int hour, int minute, int second)
19      :time(hour, minute, second)
20    {
21    }
22
23 private:
24    Time time;
25 };
```

**Time** class constructor

initializer

time data field

Using the constructor initializer list also can improve efficiency. Note that an object data field is automatically initialized with an object created using its no-arg constructor if you don't use a construction initializer list. Sometimes you wish to initialize the data field using a different constructor. In this case, you have to create a new object. So, two objects are created in the process. Using a constructor initializer list, you need to create only one object.

improve efficiency

## KEY TERMS

accessor function (getter)   288
arrow operator (`->`)   282
class   275
class abstraction   297
class encapsulation   297
class's contract   297
constructor   276
data field encapsulation   278
default constructor   276
dot operator (`.`)   276
instance   274
instance function   277

instance variable   277
instantiation   274
mutator function (setter)   288
no-arg constructor   276
object-oriented programming
   (OOP)   274
Unified Modeling Language
   (UML)   275
private   288
public   288
scope resolution operator (`::`)   281
`this` keyword   292

## CHAPTER SUMMARY

- A class is a template for objects. It defines the generic properties of objects, and provides constructors for creating objects and functions for manipulating them.

- A class is also a data type. You can use it to declare object names. An object is an instance of a class. You use the dot (`.`) operator to access members of that object through its name.

- You can separate class declaration from class implementation by defining class declaration in a header file and class implementation in a separate file.

- Visibility keywords specify how the class, function, and data are accessed. A `public` function or data is accessible to all clients. A `private` function or data is only accessible inside the class.

- You can provide a get function or a set function to enable clients to see or modify the data. Colloquially, a get function is referred to as a *getter* (or *accessor*), and a set function is referred to as a *setter* (or *mutator*).

- A get function has the signature `returnType getPropertyName()`. If the `returnType` is `bool`, the get function should be defined as `bool isPropertyName()`. A set function has the signature `void setPropertyName(dataType propertyValue)`.

- The scope of data fields is the entire class, regardless of where the data fields are declared. The class members can be declared anywhere in the class.

- The keyword `this` can be used as a pointer to the calling object.

- You can pass an object to a function by value, by reference, or by reference via a pointer. For performance and simplicity, passing by reference is preferred.

## REVIEW QUESTIONS

### Sections 9.2–9.4

**9.1**   Describe the relationship between an object and its defining class. How do you declare a class? How do you declare and create an object?

**9.2**   What are the differences between constructors and functions?

**9.3**   How do you declare an object using a no-arg constructor? How do you declare an object using a constructor with arguments?

**9.4**   Once an object name is declared, can it be reassigned to reference another object?

**9.5**   What is wrong in the following code? (Use the `Circle` class defined in Listing 9.1, TestCircle.cpp.)

```
int main()
{
  Circle c1();
  cout << c1.getRadius() << endl;

  return 0;
}
```
(a)

```
int main()
{
  Circle c1(5);
  Circle c1(6);

  return 0;
}
```
(b)

**9.6** What is wrong in the following code?

```
1 class Circle
2 {
3 public:
4   Circle();
5   Circle(double);
6   double getArea();
7
8 private:
9   double radius = 1;
10 };
```

## Section 9.5 Separating Declaration from Implementation

**9.7** How do you separate class declaration from implementation?

**9.8** What is the output of the following code? (Use the `Circle` class defined in Listing 9.5, Circle2.h.)

```
int main()
{
  Circle c1;
  Circle c2(6);
  c1 = c2;
  cout << c1.getRadius() << endl;

  return 0;
}
```
(a)

```
int main()
{
  cout << Circle(8).getRadius()
    << endl;

  return 0;
}
```
(b)

**9.9** How do you implement all functions inline for Circle2.h in Listing 9.5?

## Section 9.6 Accessing Object Members via Pointers

**9.10** What is wrong in the following code?

```
int main()
{
  Circle c1;
  Circle *p = c1;

  return 0;
}
```
(a)

```
int main()
{
  Circle c1;
  Circle *p = new Circle;

  return 0;
}
```
(b)

**9.11** How do you create an object dynamically? How do you delete an object?

## Sections 9.8 The C++ `string` Class

**9.12** Suppose that `s1` and `s2` are two strings, given as follows:

```
string s1("I have a dream");
string s2("Computer Programming");
```

Assume that each expression is independent. What are the results of the following expressions?

(1) s1.append(s2)
(2) s1.append(s2, 9, 7)
(3) s1.append("NEW", 3)
(4) s1.append(3, 'N')

(13) s1.erase(1, 2)
(14) s1.compare(s3)
(15) s1.compare(0, 10, s3)
(16) s1.data()

```
(5) s1.assign(3, 'N')          (17) s1.substr(4, 8)
(6) s1.assign(s2, 9, 7)        (18) s1.substr(4)
(7) s1.assign("NEWNEW", 3)     (19) s1.find('A')
(8) s1.assign(3, 'N')          (20) s1.find('a', 9)
(9) s1.at(0)                   (21) s1.replace(2, 4, "NEW")
(10) s1.length()               (22) s1.insert(4, "NEW")
(11) s1.size()                 (23) s1.insert(6, 8, 'N')
(12) s1.capacity()             (24) s1.empty()
```

**9.13** Suppose that **s1** and **s2** are given as follows:

```
string s1("I have a dream");
string s2("Computer Programming");
char s3[] = "ABCDEFGHIJKLMN";
```

Assume that each expression is independent. What are the results of **s1**, **s2**, and **s3** after each of the following statements?

```
(1) s1.clear()
(2) s1.copy(s3, 5, 2)
(3) s1.swap(s2)
```

**9.14** Suppose that **s1** and **s2** are given as follows:

```
string s1("I have a dream");
string s2("Computer Programming");
```

Assume that each expression is independent. What are the results of the following expressions?

```
(1) s1[0]                      (6) s1 >= s2
(2) s1 = s2                    (7) s1 < s2
(3) s1 = "C++ " + s2           (8) s1 <= s2
(4) s2 += "C++ "               (9) s1 == s2
(5) s1 > s2                    (10) s1 != s2
```

### Section 9.9 Data Field Encapsulation

**9.15** What is an accessor function? What is a mutator function? What are the naming conventions for accessor functions and mutator functions?

**9.16** What are the benefits of data field encapsulation?

### Section 9.10 The Scope of Variables

**9.17** Can data fields and functions be declared in any order in a class?

### Section 9.11 The **this** Pointer

**9.18** What is wrong in the following code? How can it be fixed?

```
// Construct a circle object
Circle::Circle(double radius)
{
  radius = radius;
}
```

### Section 9.12 Passing Objects to Functions

**9.19** Describe the three ways to pass an object to a function.

**9.20** What is the printout of the following code?

```
#include <iostream>
using namespace std;
```

```
class Count
{
public:
  int count;

  Count(int c)
  {
    count = c;
  }

  Count()
  {
    count = 0;
  }
};

void increment(Count c, int times)
{
  c.count++;
  times++;
}

int main()
{
  Count myCount;
  int times = 0;

  for (int i = 0; i < 100; i++)
    increment(myCount, times);
  cout << "myCount.count is " << myCount.count;
  cout << " times is " << times;

  return 0;
}
```

**9.21**    If the highlighted code in Question 9.20 is changed to

```
void increment(Count &c, int times)
```

What will be the printout?

**9.22**    If the highlighted code in Question 9.20 is changed to

```
void increment(Count &c, int &times)
```

What will be the printout?

## Section 9.13 Array of Objects

**9.23**    How do you declare an array of ten string objects?

**9.24**    What is the output in the following code?

```
1 int main()
2 {
3   string cities[] = {"Atlanta", "Dallas", "Savannah"};
4   cout << cities[0] << endl;
5   cout << cities[1] << endl;
6
7   return 0;
8 }
```

# PROGRAMMING EXERCISES

**Pedagogical Note**

The exercises in Part 2 achieve *three objectives:*

1. Design and draw UML for classes.
2. Implement classes from the UML.
3. Use classes to develop applications.

Solutions for the UML diagrams for the even-numbered exercises can be downloaded from the Student Website and all others can be downloaded from the Instructor Website.

### Sections 9.2–9.11

**9.1** (*The* `Rectangle` *class*) Design a class named `Rectangle` to represent a rectangle. The class contains:

- Two `double` data fields named `width` and `height` that specify the width and height of the rectangle. The default values are `1` for both `width` and `height`.
- A no-arg constructor that creates a default rectangle.
- A constructor that creates a rectangle with the specified `width` and `height`.
- The accessor and mutator functions for all the data fields.
- A function named `getArea()` that returns the area of this rectangle.
- A function named `getPerimeter()` that returns the perimeter.

Draw the UML diagram for the class. Implement the class. Write a test program that creates two `Rectangle` objects. Assign width `4` and height `40` to the first object and width `3.5` and height `35.9` to the second object. Display the properties of both objects and find their areas and perimeters.

**9.2** (*The* `Fan` *class*) Design a class named `Fan` to represent a fan. The class contains:

- An `int` data field named `speed` that specifies the speed of the fan. A fan has three speeds indicated with a value `1`, `2`, or `3`. The default value is `1`.
- A `bool` data field named `on` that specifies whether the fan is on (default `false`).
- A `double` data field named `radius` that specifies the radius of the fan (default `5`).
- A string data field named `color` that specifies the color of the fan (default `blue`).
- A no-arg constructor that creates a default fan.
- The accessor and mutator functions for all the data fields.

Draw the UML diagram for the class. Implement the class. Write a test program that creates two `Fan` objects. Assign speed `3`, radius `10`, color `yellow`, and turn it on to the first object. Assign speed `2`, radius `5`, color `blue`, and turn it off to the second object. Invoke the accessor functions to display the fan properties.

**9.3** (*The* `Account` *class*) Design a class named `Account` that contains:

- An `int` data field named `id` for the account (default `0`).
- A `double` data field named `balance` for the account (default `0`).
- A `double` data field named `annualInterestRate` that stores the current interest rate (default `0`).
- A no-arg constructor that creates a default account.
- The accessor and mutator functions for `id`, `balance`, and `annualInterestRate`.
- A function named `getMonthlyInterestRate()` that returns the monthly interest rate.

■ A function named `withDraw` that withdraws a specified amount from the account.

■ A function named `deposit` that deposits a specified amount to the account.

Draw the UML diagram for the class. Implement the class. Write a test program that creates an `Account` object with an account ID of `1122`, a balance of `20000`, and an annual interest rate of `4.5%`. Use the `withdraw` function to withdraw `$2500`, use the `deposit` function to deposit `$3000`, and print the balance, the monthly interest, and the date when this account was created.

**9.4**    (*The `Stock` class*) Design a class named `Stock` that contains:

■ A string data field named `symbol` for the stock's symbol.

■ A string data field named `name` for the stock's name.

■ A `double` data field named `previousClosingPrice` that stores the stock price for the previous day.

■ A `double` data field named `currentPrice` that stores the stock price for the current time.

■ A constructor that creates a stock with specified symbol and name.

■ The accessor functions for all data fields.

■ The mutator functions for `previousClosingPrice` and `currentPrice`.

■ A function named `changePercent()` that returns the percentage changed from `previousClosingPrice` to `currentPrice`.

Draw the UML diagram for the class. Implement the class. Write a test program that creates a `Stock` object with the stock symbol SUNW, the name Sun Microsystems Inc, and the previous closing price of `100`. Set a new current price to `90` and display the price-change percentage.

**9.5***    (*The `Time` class*) Design a class named `Time`. The class contains:

■ Data fields `hour`, `minute`, and `second` that represents a time.

■ A no-arg constructor that creates a `Time` object for the current time. (The data fields value will represent the current time.)

■ A constructor that constructs a `Time` object with a specified elapse time since the middle of night, Jan 1, 1970 in seconds. (The data fields value will represent this time.)

■ Three get functions for the data fields `hour`, `minute`, and `second`, respectively.

Draw the UML diagram for the class. Implement the class. Write a test program that creates two `Time` objects (using `Time()` and `Time(555550)`) and display their hour, minute, and second.

**Hint**

The current time can be obtained using `time(0)`, as shown in Listing 2.11, ShowCurrent-Time.cpp. The other constructor sets the hour, minute, and second for the specified elapse time. For example, if the elapse time is `555550` seconds, the hour is `10`, the minute is `19`, and the second is `10`.

**9.6**    (*The `MyPoint` class*) Design a class named `MyPoint` to represent a point with `x` and `y`-coordinates. The class contains:

■ Two data fields `x` and `y` that represent the coordinates.

■ A no-arg constructor that creates a point (`0`, `0`).

■ A constructor that constructs a point with specified coordinates.

■ Two get functions for data fields `x` and `y`, respectively.

■ A function named `distance` that returns the distance from this point to another point of the `MyPoint` type.

Draw the UML diagram for the class. Implement the class. Write a test program that creates two points $(0, 0)$ and $(10, 30.5)$ and displays the distance between the two points.

**9.7**\*\* (*Implementing the string class*) The **string** class is provided in the C++ library. Provide your own implementation for the following functions (name the new class **MyString1**):

```
MyString1();
MyString1(char * chars);
MyString1(char chars[], int size);
MyString1 append(MyString1 s);
MyString1 append(MyString1 s, int index, int n);
MyString1 assign(char chars[]);
MyString1 assign(MyString1 s, int index, int n);
char at(int index);
int length();
void clear();
MyString1 erase(int index, int n);
bool empty();
int compare(MyString1 s);
void copy(char s[], int index, int n);
char * data();
MyString1 substr(int index, int n);
void swap(MyString1 s);
int find(char ch);
```

**9.8**\*\* (*Implementing the string class*) The **string** class is provided in the C++ library. Provide your own implementation for the following functions (name the new class **MyString2**):

```
MyString2(char chars[], int size);
MyString2 append(int n, char ch);
MyString2 assign(MyString2 s, int n);
MyString2 assign(int n, char ch);
int compare(int index, int n, MyString2 s);
void copy(char s[], int index, int n);
char * data();
MyString2 substr(int index);
int find(char ch, int index);
```

**9.9**\* (*Sorting characters in a string*) Write a function that returns a sorted string using the following header:

```
string sort(string &s)
```

**9.10**\* (*Anagrams*) Rewrite Exercise 7.18 using the **string** class with the following function header:

```
bool isAnagram(string const &s1, string const &s2)
```

# CHAPTER 10

# MORE ON OBJECTS AND CLASSES

## Objectives

- To create immutable objects from immutable classes (§10.2).

- To prevent multiple declarations using the `#ifndef` inclusion guard directive (§10.3).

- To understand the difference between instance and static variables and functions (§10.4).

- To implement destructors to perform customized operations (§10.5).

- To create objects using copy constructors with initial data copied from another object of the same type (§10.6).

- To customize copy constructors to perform deep copy (§10.7).

- To enable friend functions and friend classes to access a class's private members (§10.8).

- To develop classes for modeling composition relationships (§§10.9–10.11).

- To use the C++ **vector** class as a resizable array (§10.12).

## 10.1 Introduction

Chapter 9 introduced the concept of classes and objects. You learned how to design and develop simple classes. This chapter introduced more advanced features on classes and objects.

## 10.2 Immutable Objects and Classes

immutable object
immutable class

If the contents of an object cannot be changed (except through memberwise copy) once the object is created, the object is called an *immutable object* and its class is called an *immutable class*. If you delete the set function in the **Circle** class in the preceding example, the class would be immutable because **radius** is private and cannot be changed without a set function.

A class with all private data fields and no mutators is not necessarily immutable. To demonstrate this, let us define two classes: **Person** and **Date**. Figures 10.1 and 10.2 give the UML class diagrams of these two classes.

| **Person** | |
|---|---|
| -id: int<br>-birthDate: Date* | The id of this person.<br>The birth date of this person. |
| +Person(id: int, year: int,<br>    month: int, day: int)<br>+getId(): int<br>+getBirthDate(): Date* | Constructs a Person with the specified id, year, month,<br>    and day.<br>Returns the id of this person.<br>Returns the birth date of this person. |

**FIGURE 10.1** The **Person** class encapsulates the id and birth date of a person.

| **Date** | |
|---|---|
| -year: int<br>-month: int<br>-day: int | The year of this date.<br>The month of this date.<br>The day of this date. |
| +Date(newYear: int, newMonth:<br>    int, newDay: int)<br>+getYear(): int<br>+setYear(newYear: int): void | Constructs a Date with the specified year, month, and<br>    day.<br>Returns the year of this date.<br>Sets a new year for this date. |

**FIGURE 10.2** The **Date** class encapsulates the year, month, and day.

The **Person** class declaration and implementation are shown in Listings 10.1 and 10.2. The **Date** class declaration and implementation are shown in Listings 10.3 and 10.4.

## LISTING 10.1 Person.h

include header file

construct object

get birth date

```
1  #include "Date.h"
2
3  class Person
4  {
5  public:
6    Person(int id, int year, int month, int day);
7    int getId();
8    Date* getBirthDate(); // Return the pointer of the object
```

```
 9
10 private:
11    int id;
12    Date* birthDate; // The pointer of the object
13 };
```

person birth date

## LISTING 10.2  Person.cpp

```
 1 #include "Person.h"
 2
 3 Person::Person(int id, int year, int month, int day)
 4 {
 5    this->id = id;
 6    birthDate = new Date(year, month, day);
 7 }
 8
 9 int Person::getId()
10 {
11    return id;
12 }
13
14 Date* Person::getBirthDate()
15 {
16    return birthDate; // Return the pointer of the object
17 }
```

include header file

construct birth date

get birth date

## LISTING 10.3  Date.h

```
 1 class Date
 2 {
 3 public:
 4    Date(int newYear, int newMonth, int newDay);
 5    int getYear();
 6    void setYear(int newYear);
 7
 8 private:
 9    int year;
10    int month;
11    int day;
12 };
```

construct birth date
get year
set year

## LISTING 10.4  Date.cpp

```
 1 #include "Date.h"
 2
 3 Date::Date(int newYear, int newMonth, int newDay)
 4 {
 5    year = newYear;
 6    month = newMonth;
 7    day = newDay;
 8 }
 9
10 int Date::getYear()
11 {
12    return year;
13 }
14
15 void Date::setYear(int newYear)
16 {
17    year = newYear;
18 }
```

include header file

constructor

get year

set year

The **Person** class has all private data fields and no mutators, but it is mutable. As shown in the client program in Listing 10.5, the data field **birthDate** is returned using the **getBirthDate()** function. This is a pointer to a **Date** object. Through this pointer, the year of the birth date is changed, which effectively changes the contents of the **Person** object.

**LISTING 10.5** TestPerson.cpp

include header file

construct person

set new date

```
 1 #include <iostream>
 2 #include "Person.h"
 3 using namespace std;
 4
 5 int main()
 6 {
 7    Person person(111223333, 1970, 5, 3);
 8    cout << "birth year before the change is " <<
 9       person.getBirthDate()->getYear() << endl;
10    Date *pDate = person.getBirthDate();
11    pDate->setYear(2010);
12    cout << "birth year after the change is " <<
13       person.getBirthDate()->getYear() << endl;
14
15    return 0;
16 }
```

```
birth year before the change is 1970
birth year after the change is 2010
```

For a class to be immutable, it must mark all data fields private and provide no mutator functions and no accessor functions that would return a reference or a pointer to a mutable data field object.

## 10.3 Preventing Multiple Declarations

It is a common mistake to include the same header file in a program multiple times inadvertently. For example, you may also add the header file for the **Date** class, as shown in Listing 10.6, because **Date** is used in this program. If so, you would get a compile error to indicate that there are multiple declarations for **Date**.

**LISTING 10.6** TestPerson1.cpp

Wrong

```
 1 #include <iostream>
 2 #include "Person.h"
 3 #include "Date.h"   // Wrong
 4 using namespace std;
 5
 6 int main()
 7 {
 8    Person person(111223333, 1970, 5, 3);
 9    Date *pDate = person.getBirthDate();
10    pDate->setYear(2010);
11    cout << person.getBirthDate()->getYear() << endl;
12
13    return 0;
14 }
```

Why wrong? Recall that the C++ preprocessor inserts the contents of the header file at the position where the header is included. Since the header file for **Date** is already included in **Person.h** (see line 1 in Listing 10.1), the preprocessor will add the declaration for the **Date** class twice in this case, which causes the multiple declaration errors.

The C++ **#ifndef** directive can be used to prevent a header file from being included multiple times. This is known as *inclusion guard*. To make this work, you have to add three lines to the header file. Listing 10.7, Date1.h, adds the inclusion guard to Date.h in Listing 10.3. The three lines are highlighted in the listing.

*inclusion guard*

### LISTING 10.7  Date1.h

```
1 #ifndef DATE_H
2 #define DATE_H
3
4 class Date
5 {
6 public:
7   Date(int newYear, int newMonth, int newDay);
8   int getYear();
9   void setYear(int newYear);
10
11 private:
12   int year;
13   int month;
14   int day;
15 };
16
17 #endif
```

test constant
define constant

end test

Recall that the statements preceded by the pound sign (#) are preprocessor directives. They are interpreted by the C++ preprocessor. The preprocessor directive **#ifndef** stands for "if not defined." Line 1 tests whether constant **DATE_H** is already defined. If so, this header file will be skipped. If not, define the constant in line 2 and include the header file; otherwise, skip the header file. The **#endif** directive is needed to indicate the end of the header file.

The new Date1.cpp given in Listing 10.8 is the same as Date.cpp in Listing 10.4 except that you need to include Date1.h.

### LISTING 10.8  Date1.cpp

```
1 #include "Date1.h"
2
3 Date::Date(int newYear, int newMonth, int newDay)
4 {
5   year = newYear;
6   month = newMonth;
7   day = newDay;
8 }
9
10 int Date::getYear()
11 {
12   return year;
13 }
14
15 void Date::setYear(int newYear)
16 {
17   year = newYear;
18 }
```

include Date1.h

# 10.4 Instance and Static Members

*instance variable*

The data fields used in the classes so far are known as *instance data fields, or instance variables.* An instance variable is tied to a specific instance of the class; it is not shared among objects of the same class. For example, suppose that you create the following objects using the `Circle` class in Listing 9.5, Circle2.h:

```
Circle circle1;
Circle circle2(5);
```

The `radius` in `circle1` is independent of the `radius` in `circle2`, and is stored in a different memory location. Changes made to `circle1`'s `radius` do not affect `circle2`'s `radius`, and vice versa.

*static variable*
*static function*

If you want all the instances of a class to share data, use *static variables,* also known as *class variables.* Static variables store values for the variables in a common memory location. Because of this common location, all objects of the same class are affected if one object changes the value of a static variable. C++ supports static functions as well as static variables. *Static functions* can be called without creating an instance of the class.

Let us modify the `Circle` class by adding a static variable `numberOfObjects` to count the number of circle objects created. When the first object of this class is created, `numberOfObjects` is 1. When the second object is created, `numberOfObjects` becomes 2. The UML of the new circle class is shown in Figure 10.3. The `Circle` class defines the instance variable `radius` and the static variable `numberOfObjects`, the instance functions `getRadius`, `setRadius`, and `getArea`, and the static function `getNumberOfObjects`. (Note that static variables and functions are underlined in the UML diagram.)

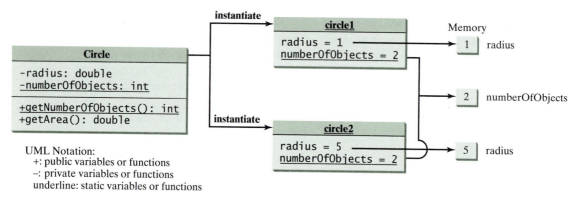

**UML Notation:**
+: public variables or functions
−: private variables or functions
underline: static variables or functions

**Figure 10.3** The instance variables, which belong to the instances, have memory storage independent of one another. The static variables are shared by all the instances of the same class.

To declare a static variable or a static function, put the modifier **static** in the variable or function declaration. So the static variable `numberOfObjects` and the static function `getNumberOfObjects()` can be declared as follows:

*declare static variable*

```
static int numberOfObjects;
```

*declare static function*

```
static int getNumberObjects();
```

The new circle class is declared in Listing 10.9.

## Listing 10.9 Circle5.h

```
1 #ifndef CIRCLE_H
2 #define CIRCLE_H
3
```

```
 4 class Circle
 5 {
 6 public:
 7   Circle();
 8   Circle(double);
 9   double getArea();
10   double getRadius();
11   void setRadius(double);
12   static int getNumberOfObjects();
13
14 private:
15   double radius;
16   static int numberOfObjects;
17 };
18
19 #endif
```

static function

static variable

A static function **getNumberOfObjects** is declared in line 12 and a static variable **numberOfObjects** is declared in line 16 as a private data field in the class.

Listing 10.10 gives the implementation of the Circle class.

## LISTING 10.10 Circle5.cpp

```cpp
 1 #include "Circle5.h"
 2
 3 int Circle::numberOfObjects = 0;
 4
 5 // Construct a circle object
 6 Circle::Circle()
 7 {
 8   radius = 1;
 9   numberOfObjects++;
10 }
11
12 // Construct a circle object
13 Circle::Circle(double radius)
14 {
15   this->radius = radius;
16   numberOfObjects++;
17 }
18
19 // Return the area of this circle
20 double Circle::getArea()
21 {
22   return radius * radius * 3.14159;
23 }
24
25 // Return the radius of this circle
26 double Circle::getRadius()
27 {
28   return radius;
29 }
30
31 // Set a new radius
32 void Circle::setRadius(double radius)
33 {
34   this->radius = (radius >= 0) ? radius : 0;
35 }
36
37 // Return the number of circle objects
38 int Circle::getNumberOfObjects()
```

include header

initialize static variable

increment **numberOfObjects**

increment **numberOfObjects**

return **numberOfObjects**

```
39 {
40    return numberOfObjects;
41 }
```

The static data field **numberOfObjects** is initialized in line 3. When a `Circle` object is created, **numberOfObjects** is incremented (lines 9 and 16).

Instance functions (e.g., `getArea()`) and instance data fields (e.g., **radius**) belong to instances and only can be used after the instances are created. They are accessed from a specific instance. Static functions (e.g., `getNumberOfObjects()`) and static data fields (e.g., **numberOfObjects**) can be accessed from any instance of the class, as well as from their class name.

The following program in Listing 10.11 demonstrates how to use instance and static variables and functions, and illustrates the effects of using them.

### LISTING 10.11  TestCircle5.cpp

include header

invoke instance function
invoke static function

invoke static function

modify radius

invoke static function

invoke static function

```cpp
1 #include <iostream>
2 #include "Circle5.h"
3 using namespace std;
4
5 int main()
6 {
7    cout << "Number of circle objects created: "
8      << Circle::getNumberOfObjects() << endl;
9
10   Circle circle1;
11   cout << "The area of the circle of radius "
12     << circle1.getRadius() << " is " << circle1.getArea() << endl;
13   cout << "Number of circle objects created: "
14     << Circle::getNumberOfObjects() << endl;
15
16   Circle circle2(5.0);
17   cout << "The area of the circle of radius "
18     << circle2.getRadius() << " is " << circle2.getArea() << endl;
19   cout << "Number of circle objects created: "
20       << Circle::getNumberOfObjects() << endl;
21
22   circle1.setRadius(3.3);
23   cout << "The area of the circle of radius "
24     << circle1.getRadius() << " is " << circle1.getArea() << endl;
25
26   cout << "circle1.getNumberOfObjects() returns "
27     << circle1.getNumberOfObjects() << endl;
28   cout << "circle2.getNumberOfObjects() returns "
29     << circle2.getNumberOfObjects() << endl;
30
31   return 0;
32 }
```

```
Number of circle objects created: 0
The area of the circle of radius 1 is 3.14159
Number of circle objects created: 1
The area of the circle of radius 5 is 78.5397
Number of circle objects created: 2
The area of the circle of radius 3.3 is 34.2119
circle1.getNumberOfObjects() returns 2
circle2.getNumberOfObjects() returns 2
```

The `main` function creates two circles, `circle1` and `circle2` (lines 10 and 16). The instance variable `radius` in `circle1` is modified to become `3.3` (line 22). This change does not affect the instance variable `radius` in `circle2`, since these two instance variables are independent. The static variable `numberOfObjects` becomes `1` after `circle1` is created (line 10), and it becomes `2` after `circle2` is created (line 16).

You can access static data fields and functions from the instances of the class, e.g., `circle1.getNumberOfObjects()` in line 27 and `circle2.getNumberOfObjects()` in line 29. But it is better to access them from the class name, e.g., `Circle::` Note that `circle1.getNumberOfObjects()` and `circle2.getNumberOfObjects()` could be replaced by `Circle::getNumberOfObjects()` in lines 27 and 29. This improves readability because the reader can easily recognize the static function `getNumberOfObjects()`.

**Tip**

Use `ClassName::functionName(arguments)` to invoke a static function and `ClassName::staticVariable`. This improves readability because the user can easily recognize the static function and data in the class.

*use class name*

**Tip**

How do you decide whether a variable or function should be instance or static? A variable or function that is dependent on a specific instance of the class should be an instance variable or function. A variable or function that is not dependent on a specific instance of the class should be a static variable or function. For example, every circle has its own radius. Radius is dependent on a specific circle. Therefore, `radius` is an instance variable of the `Circle` class. Since the `getArea` function is dependent on a specific circle, it is an instance function. Since `numberOfObjects` is not dependent on any specific instance, it should be declared static.

*instance or static?*

## 10.5 Destructors

Destructors are the opposite of constructors. A constructor is invoked when an object is created and a destructor is invoked when the object is destroyed. Every class has a default destructor if the destructor is not explicitly defined. Sometimes, it is desirable to implement destructors to perform customized operations. Destructors are named the same as constructors, but you must put a tilde character (~) in front of it. Listing 10.12 shows a `Circle` class with a destructor defined.

**LISTING 10.12** `Circle6.h`

```
1  #ifndef CIRCLE6_H
2  #define CIRCLE6_H
3
4  class Circle
5  {
6  public:
7    Circle();
8    Circle(double);
9    ~Circle();
10   double getArea();
11   double getRadius();
12   void setRadius(double);
13   static int getNumberOfObjects();
14
15 private:
16   double radius;
17   static int numberOfObjects;
18 };
19
20 #endif
```

*destructor*

A destructor for the **Circle** class is defined in line 9. Destructors have no return type and no arguments.

Listing 10.13 gives the implementation of the **Circle** class.

### LISTING 10.13 Circle6.cpp

include header

```cpp
1  #include "Circle6.h"
2
3  int Circle::numberOfObjects = 0;
4
5  // Construct a default circle object
6  Circle::Circle()
7  {
8    radius = 1;
9    numberOfObjects++;
10 }
11
12 // Construct a circle object
13 Circle::Circle(double radius)
14 {
15   this->radius = radius;
16   numberOfObjects++;
17 }
18
19 // Return the area of this circle
20 double Circle::getArea()
21 {
22   return radius * radius * 3.14159;
23 }
24
25 // Return the radius of this circle
26 double Circle::getRadius()
27 {
28   return radius;
29 }
30
31 // Set a new radius
32 void Circle::setRadius(double radius)
33 {
34   this->radius = (radius >= 0) ? radius : 0;
35 }
36
37 // Return the number of circle objects
38 int Circle::getNumberOfObjects()
39 {
40   return numberOfObjects;
41 }
42
43 // Destruct a circle object
44 Circle::~Circle()
45 {
46   numberOfObjects--;
47 }
```

implement destructor

The implementation is identical to Circle5.cpp in Listing 10.10, except that the destructor is implemented to decrement **numberOfObjects** in lines 42–45.

The following program in Listing 10.14 demonstrates the effects of destructors.

**LISTING 10.14** `TestCircle6.cpp`

```
1  #include <iostream>
2  #include "Circle6.h"
3  using namespace std;
4
5  int main()
6  {
7    Circle *pCircle1 = new Circle();
8    Circle *pCircle2 = new Circle();
9    Circle *pCircle3 = new Circle();
10
11   cout << "Number of circle objects created: "
12     << Circle::getNumberOfObjects() << endl;
13
14   delete pCircle1;
15
16   cout << "Number of circle objects created: "
17     << Circle::getNumberOfObjects() << endl;
18
19   return 0;
20 }
```

include header

create **pCircle1**
create **pCircle2**
create **pCircle3**

display **numberOfObjects**

destroy **pCircle1**

display **numberOfObjects**

```
Number of circle objects created: 3
Number of circle objects created: 2
```

All objects are destroyed when the program terminates. However, you cannot write the code to destroy an object if it is created on the stack. If an object is created dynamically on the heap, it can be explicitly destroyed using the `delete` operator.

The program creates three `Circle` objects using the `new` operator in lines 7–9. Afterwards, **numberOfObjects** becomes 3. The program deletes a `Circle` object in line 14. After this, **numberOfObjects** becomes 2.

Destructors are useful for deleting memory and other resources allocated by the object. The **Person** class in Listing 10.2 creates a **Date** object for the birth date dynamically in the **Person**'s constructor. When a **Person** object is destroyed, you should also destroy its **Date** object to avoid memory leak. To accomplish this, you can add a destructor as follows:

```
Person::~Person()
{
  delete birthDate;
}
```

# 10.6 Copy Constructors

Each class may define several overloaded constructors and one destructor. Additionally, every class has a *copy constructor*. The signature of the copy constructor is:

```
ClassName(ClassName &)
```

For example, the copy constructor for the `Circle` class is

```
Circle(Circle &)
```

The copy constructor can be used to create an object initialized with another object's data. By default, the copy constructor simply copies each data field in one object to its counterpart in the other object. Listing 10.15 demonstrates this.

**LISTING 10.15** CopyConstructorDemo.cpp

include header

```
 1 #include <iostream>
 2 #include "Circle6.h"
 3 using namespace std;
 4
 5 int main()
 6 {
 7   Circle circle1(5);
 8   Circle circle2(circle1);
 9
10   cout << "After creating circle2 from circle1:" << endl;
11   cout << "\tcircle1.getRadius() returns "
12     << circle1.getRadius() << endl;
13   cout << "\tcircle2.getRadius() returns "
14     << circle2.getRadius() << endl;
15
16   circle1.setRadius(10.5);
17   circle2.setRadius(20.5);
18
19   cout << "After modifying circle1 and circle2: " << endl;
20   cout << "\tcircle1.getRadius() returns "
21     << circle1.getRadius() << endl;
22   cout << "\tcircle2.getRadius() returns "
23     << circle2.getRadius() << endl;
24
25   return 0;
26 }
```

create **circle1**
create **circle2**

display **circle1**

display **circle2**

modify **circle1**
modify **circle2**

display **circle1**

display **circle2**

```
After creating circle2 from circle1:
  circle1.getRadius() returns 5
  circle2.getRadius() returns 5
After modifying circle1 and circle2:
  circle1.getRadius() returns 10.5
  circle2.getRadius() returns 20.5
```

The program creates two **Circle** objects: **circle1** and **circle2** (lines 7–8). **circle2** is created using the copy constructor by copying **circle1**'s data.

The program then modifies the radius in **circle1** and **circle2** (lines 16–17) and displays their new radius in lines 20–23.

shallow copy

deep copy

The default copy constructor or assignment operator for copying objects performs a *shallow copy*, rather than a *deep copy*, meaning that if the field is a pointer to some object, the address of the pointer is copied rather than its contents. Listing 10.16 demonstrates this.

**LISTING 10.16** ShallowCopyDemo.cpp

include **Person** header

```
 1 #include <iostream>
 2 #include "Person.h"
 3 using namespace std;
 4
 5 void displayPerson(Person &person1, Person &person2)
 6 {
 7   cout << "\tperson1 id: " << person1.getId() << endl;
 8   cout << "\tperson1 birth year: " <<
 9     person1.getBirthDate()->getYear() << endl;
10   cout << "\tperson2 id: " << person2.getId() << endl;
11   cout << "\tperson2 birth year: " <<
12     person2.getBirthDate()->getYear() << endl;
13 }
```

display **person1**

display year
display **person2**

display year

```
14
15  int main()
16  {
17    Person person1(111, 1970, 5, 3);                      create person1
18    Person person2(222, 2000, 11, 8);                     create person2
19
20    cout << "After creating person1 and person2" << endl;
21    displayPerson(person1, person2);
22
23    person1 = Person(person2); // Copy person2 to person1  copy person2 to person1
24
25    cout << "\nAfter copying person2 to person1" << endl;
26    displayPerson(person1, person2);
27
28    person2.getBirthDate()->setYear(1963);                modify person2's year
29
30    cout << "\nAfter modifying person2's birthDate" << endl;
31    displayPerson(person1, person2);
32
33    cout << "\n" << (person1.getBirthDate() == person2.getBirthDate());
34
35    return 0;
36  }
```

```
After creating person1 and person2
  person1 id: 111
  person1 birth year: 1970
  person2 id: 222
  person2 birth year: 2000

After copying person2 to person1
  person1 id: 222
  person1 birth year: 2000
  person2 id: 222
  person2 birth year: 2000

After modifying person2's birthDate
  person1 id: 222
  person1 birth year: 1963
  person2 id: 222
  person2 birth year: 1963


1
```

The program creates two **Person** objects: **person1** and **person2** (lines 17–18), as shown in Figure 10.4. The **Person** class was declared in Listing 10.1. It has two data fields: **id** and **birthDate**. The **birthDate** field is a pointer type. When copying **person2** to **person1** (line 23), the **id** in **person2** is copied to **person1** and the address of **birthDate** in **person2** is copied to **birthDate** in **person1**, as shown in Figure 10.5.

Now the **birthDate** data field in **person1** and **person2** point to the same object. Line 28 sets a new birth year **1963** for **person2**, the birth year for **person1** is also **1963** now. Both **person1.getBirthDate()** and **person2.getBirthDate()** are the same, so

```
person1.getBirthDate() == person2.getBirthDate()
```

is **true**.

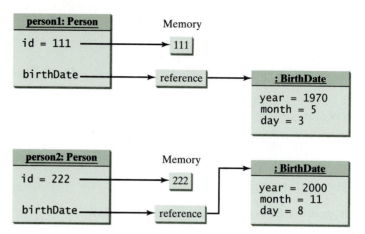

**FIGURE 10.4** Before **person2** is copied to **person1**, the **birthDate** field of **person1** and **person2** point to two different **Date** objects.

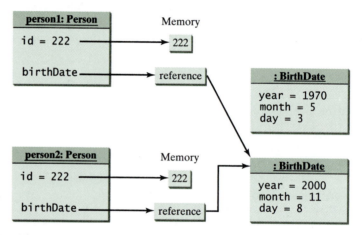

**FIGURE 10.5** After **person2** is copied to **person1**, the **birthDate** field of **person1** and **person2** point to the same **Date** object.

 **Note**

memberwise copy

**person1 = Person(person2);** // Copy using the copy constructor

has the same effect as

**person1 = person2;** // Copy using the assignment operator

The former creates an anonymous object and copies the contents to **person1**. The latter directly copies the contents of **person2** to **person1**. Using the direct assignment is more efficient and simpler.

## 10.7 Customizing Copy Constructors

As discussed in the preceding section, the default copy constructor or assignment operator = performs a shallow copy. To perform a deep copy, you can implement the copy constructor. Listing 10.17 revises the declaration for the **Person** class to declare a copy constructor in line 7.

### LISTING 10.17 Person1.h

include header file

```
1 #include "Date1.h"
2
```

```
 3 class Person
 4 {
 5 public:
 6    Person(int id, int year, int month, int day);
 7    Person(Person &);                                          copy constructor
 8    Person::~Person()                                          destructor
 9    int getId();
10    Date * getBirthDate(); // Return the pointer of the object
11
12 private:
13    int id;
14    Date *birthDate; // The pointer of the object
15 };
```

Listing 10.18 implements the new copy constructor in lines 9–14. Line 11 copies the `id` field and line 13 creates a new `Date` object using the copy constructor of the `Date` class. This new `Date` object is initialized with the `birthDate` in `person`.

## LISTING 10.18  Person1.cpp

```
 1 #include "Person1.h"                                          include header file
 2
 3 Person::Person(int id, int year, int month, int day)
 4 {
 5    this->id = id;
 6    birthDate = new Date(year, month, day);                    construct birth date
 7 }
 8
 9 Person::Person(Person &person)
10 {
11    id = person.id;
12    Date *p = person.getBirthDate();
13    birthDate = new Date(*p);
14 }
15
16 Person::~Person()                                             destructor
17 {
18    delete birthDate;
19 }
20
21 int Person::getId()
22 {
23    return id;
24 }
25
26 Date * Person::getBirthDate()                                 get birth date
27 {
28    return birthDate; // Return the pointer of the object
29 }
```

Listing 10.19 gives a test program for the custom copy constructor. The program creates a `Person` object `person1` in line 17 and creates `person2` that is a copy of `person1`. Both objects have the same contents when displayed in line 21. The birth year in `person2` is changed to `1963` (line 23). It does not affect `person1`, because `person1`'s `birthDate` field is different from `person2`'s, as displayed in line 28.

## LISTING 10.19  CustomCopyConstructor.cpp

```
1 #include <iostream>
2 #include "Person1.h"                                           include header Person1.h
3 using namespace std;
```

```
4
5  void displayPerson(Person &person1, Person &person2)
6  {
7    cout << "\tperson1 id: " << person1.getId() << endl;
8    cout << "\tperson1 birth year: " <<
9      person1.getBirthDate()->getYear() << endl;
10   cout << "\tperson2 id: " << person2.getId() << endl;
11   cout << "\tperson2 birth year: " <<
12     person2.getBirthDate()->getYear() << endl;
13 }
14
15 int main()
16 {
17   Person person1(111, 1970, 5, 3);
18   Person person2(person1);
19
20   cout << "After creating person1 and person2" << endl;
21   displayPerson(person1, person2);
22
23   person2.getBirthDate()->setYear(1963);
24
25   cout << "\nAfter modifying person2's birthDate" << endl;
26   displayPerson(person1, person2);
27
28   cout << '\n' << (person1.getBirthDate() == person2.getBirthDate());
29
30   Person person3(111, 1970, 5, 3);
31   Person person4 = person3;
32   cout << '\n' << (person3.getBirthDate() == person3.getBirthDate());
33
34   return 0;
35 }
```

use copy constructor — (line 18)

same **birthDate**? — (line 28)

```
After creating person1 and person2
   person1 id: 111
   person1 birth year: 1970
   person2 id: 111
   person2 birth year: 1970

After modifying person2's birthDate
   person1 id: 111
   person1 birth year: 1970
   person2 id: 111
   person2 birth year: 1963

0
1
```

**Note**

assignment copy

The custom copy constructor does not change the behavior of the *assignment copy* operator = by default. As shown in this example, **person3** is copied to **person4** using the assignment operator (line 31), but **person3**'s **birthDate** is still the same as **person4**'s (line 32).

## 10.8  `friend` Functions and `friend` Classes

Private members of a class cannot be accessed from outside of the class. Occasionally, it is convenient to allow some trusted functions and classes to access a class's private members.

C++ enables you to use the **friend** keyword to declare **friend** functions and **friend** classes so these functions and classes can access the class's private members.

Listing 10.20 revises the **Date** class header file to add the **AccessDate** class as a friend. So, you can directly access private data fields **year**, **month**, and **day** from the **AccessDate** class in Listing 10.21.

**friend** class

## LISTING 10.20 Date2.h

```
1 class Date
2 {
3 public:
4     friend class AccessDate;
5
6 private:
7     int year;
8     int month;
9     int day;
10 };
```

a **friend** class

## LISTING 10.21 TestFriendClass.cpp

```
1 #include <iostream>
2 #include "Date2.h"
3 using namespace std;
4
5 class AccessDate
6 {
7 public:
8     static void p()
9     {
10        Date birthDate;
11        birthDate.year = 2000;
12        cout << birthDate.year;
13     }
14 };
15
16 int main()
17 {
18     AccessDate::p();
19
20     return 0;
21 }
```

header Date1.h

static function

create a **Date**
modify private data
access private data

invoke static function

The **AccessDate** class is declared in lines 5–14. A **Date** object is created in the class. Since **AccessDate** is a friend class of the **Date** class, the private data in **Date** object can be accessed from a **Date** object in the **AccessDate** class (lines 11–12). The main function invokes the static function **AccessDate::p()** in line 18.

Listing 10.22 gives an example on how to use a friend function. The program declares the **Date** class with a friend function **p** (line 6). Function **p** is not a member of the **Date** class, but can access the private data in **Date**. In function **p**, a **Date** object is created in line 16, and the private field data **year** is modified in line 17 and retrieved in line 18.

friend function

## LISTING 10.22 TestFriendFunction.cpp

```
1 #include <iostream>
2 using namespace std;
3
4 class Date
5 {
6     friend void p();
7
```

declare **friend** function

```
 8 private:
 9   int year;
10   int month;
11   int day;
12 };
13
14 void p()
15 {
16   Date date;
17   date.year = 2000;
18   cout << date.year;
19 }
20
21 int main()
22 {
23   p();
24
25   return 0;
26 }
```

modify private data
access private data

invoke **friend** function

## 10.9 Object Composition

An object can contain another object. The relationship between the two is called *composition*. In Listing 10.1, you defined the **Person** class to contain a **Date** data field. A **Person** object contains a **Date** object. The relationship between **Person** and **Date** is composition.

Composition is actually a special case of the aggregation relationship. Aggregation models *has-a* relationships and represents an ownership relationship between two objects. The owner object is called an *aggregating object* and its class an *aggregating class*. The subject object is called an *aggregated object* and its class an *aggregated class*.

composition

An object may be owned by several other aggregating objects. If an object is exclusively owned by an aggregating object, the relationship between the object and its aggregating object is referred to as *composition*. For example, "a student has a name" is a composition relationship between the **Student** class and the **Name** class, whereas "a student has an address" is an aggregation relationship between the **Student** class and the **Address** class, since an address may be shared by several students. In UML, a filled diamond is attached to an aggregating class (e.g., **Student**) to denote the composition relationship with an aggregated class (e.g., **Name**): an empty diamond is attached to an aggregating class (e.g., **Student**) to denote the aggregation relationship with an aggregated class (e.g., **Address**), as shown in Figure 10.6.

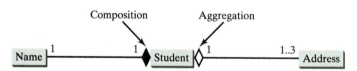

**FIGURE 10.6** A student has a name and an address.

multiplicity

Each class involved in a relationship may specify a *multiplicity*. A multiplicity could be a number or an interval that specifies how many objects of the class are involved in the relationship. The character * means an unlimited number of objects, and the interval m..n means that the number of objects should be between m and n, inclusive. In Figure 10.6, each student has only one address, and each address may be shared by up to 3 students. Each student has one name, and a name is unique for each student.

An aggregation relationship usually is represented as a data field in the aggregating class. For example, the relationship in Figure 10.6 can be represented as follows:

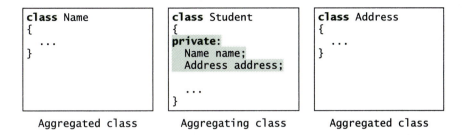

| Aggregated class | Aggregating class | Aggregated class |

Aggregation may exist between objects of the same class. For example, a person may have a supervisor. This is illustrated in Figure 10.7.

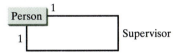

**FIGURE 10.7**    A person may have a supervisor.

In the relationship "a person has a supervisor," as shown in Figure 10.7, a supervisor can be represented as a data field in the **Person** class, as follows:

```
class Person
{
private:
Person supervisor;   // The type for the data is the class itself

   ...
}
```

If a person may have several supervisors, as shown in Figure 10.8, you may use an array to store supervisors (for example, 10 supervisors).

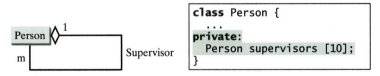

**FIGURE 10.8**    A person may have several supervisors.

**Note**

Since aggregation and composition relationships are represented using classes in similar ways, many texts don't differentiate them and call both compositions.

*aggregation or composition*

# 10.10  Case Study: The **Course** Class

This section uses the **Course** class to demonstrate the creation and use of classes. The UML diagram for the class is shown in Figure 10.9.

| Course |
| --- |
| -courseN: string<br>-courseN: string<br>-numberOfStudents: int |
| +Course(name: &string)<br>+getcourseName: string<br>+addStudent(student: &string): void<br>+getStudents(): string*<br>+getNumberOfStudents(): int |

The name of the course.
The students who take the course.
The number of students (default: 0).

Creates a Course with the specified name.
Returns the course name.
Adds a new student to the course list.
Returns the array of students for the course.
Returns the number of students for the course.

**FIGURE 10.9** The Course class models the courses.

A Course object can be created using the constructor Course(string courseName) by passing a course name. You can add students to the course using the addStudent(string student) function and return all the students for the course using the getStudents() function. The Course class uses an array to store the students for the course. For simplicity, assume the course enrollment is a maximum of 100. So, the array is created using string[100]. The addStudent function adds a student to the array. Whenever a new student is added to the course, numberOfStudents is increased. The getStudents function returns the array.

Suppose the class is declared as shown in Listing 10.23. Listing 10.24 gives a test class that creates two courses and adds students to the courses.

**LISTING 10.23** Course.h

using string class

Course class

public members

private members

```
1  #ifndef COURSE_H
2  #define COURSE_H
3
4  #include <string>
5  using namespace std;
6
7  class Course
8  {
9  public:
10    Course(const string &courseName);
11    string getCourseName();
12    void addStudent(const string &student);
13    string * getStudents();
14    int getNumberOfStudents();
15
16  private:
17    string courseName;
18    string students[100];
19    int numberOfStudents;
20  };
21
22  #endif
```

**LISTING 10.24** TestCourse.cpp

Course header

```
1  #include <iostream>
2  #include "Course.h"
3  using namespace std;
4
5  int main()
6  {
```

```
7    Course course1("Data Structures");                                    create course1
8    Course course2("Database Systems");                                   create course2
9
10   course1.addStudent("Peter Jones");                                    add a student
11   course1.addStudent("Brian Smith");
12   course1.addStudent("Anne Kennedy");
13
14   course2.addStudent("Peter Jones");
15   course2.addStudent("Steve Smith");
16
17   cout << "Number of students in course1: " <<                          number of students
18     course1.getNumberOfStudents() << "\n";
19   string * students = course1.getStudents();                            return students
20   for (int i = 0; i < course1.getNumberOfStudents(); i++)
21     cout << students[i] << ", ";                                        display a student
22
23   cout << "\nNumber of students in course2: "
24     << course2.getNumberOfStudents() << "\n";
25   students = course2.getStudents();
26   for (int i = 0; i < course2.getNumberOfStudents(); i++)
27     cout << students[i] << ", ";
28
29   return 0;
30 }
```

```
Number of students in course1: 3
Peter Jones, Brian Smith, Anne Kennedy,
Number of students in course2: 2
Peter Jones, Steve Smith,
```

The **Course** class is implemented in Listing 10.25. The **Course** constructor initializes **numberOfStudents** to **0** (line 7) and sets a new course name (line 8).

The **addStudent** function adds a student to the array (line 25). This function first checks whether the number of students in the class exceeds the maximum **100**. If so, the program terminates by invoking the **exit** function (line 22). The **exit** function is a function in the standard library. It terminates the program immediately. Whenever a new student is added to the course, **numberOfStudents** is increased (line 26). The **getStudents** function returns the address of the array **students**.

## LISTING 10.25  Course.cpp

```
1  #include <iostream>
2  #include "Course.h"                                                     Course header
3  using namespace std;
4
5  Course::Course(const string &courseName)
6  {
7    numberOfStudents = 0;                                                 initialize data field
8    this->courseName = courseName ;                                       set course name
9  }
10
11 string Course::getCourseName()
12 {
13   return courseName;
14 }
15
```

```
16 void Course::addStudent(const string &student)
17 {
18   if (numberOfStudents >= 100)
19   {
20     cout << "The maximum size of array exceeded" << endl;
21     cout << "Program terminates now" << endl;
22     exit(0);
23   }
24
25   students[numberOfStudents] = student;
26   numberOfStudents++;
27 }
28
29 string * Course::getStudents()
30 {
31   return students;
32 }
33
34 int Course::getNumberOfStudents()
35 {
36   return numberOfStudents;
37 }
```

*terminate program* (line 22)

*add a student* (line 25)
*increase number of students* (line 26)

*return students* (line 31)

**Note**

When you create a **Course** object, an array of **100** strings, **students**, is created. Each element has a default string value created by the **string** class' no-arg constructor.

**Note**

The user can create a **Course** and manipulate it through the public functions **addStudent**, **getNumberOfStudents**, and **getStudents**. However, the user doesn't need to know how these functions are implemented. The **Course** class encapsulates the internal implementation. This example uses an array to store students. You may use a different data structure to store students. The program that uses **Course** does not need to change as long as the contract of the public functions remains unchanged.

## 10.11 Case Study: The **StackOfIntegers** Class

This section gives another example to demonstrate the creation and use of classes. Let us create a class for stacks.

*stack*

A *stack* is a data structure that holds objects in a last-in first-out fashion, as illustrated in Figure 10.10. It has many applications. For example, the compiler uses a stack to process function invocations. When a function is invoked, the parameters and local variables of the function are pushed into a stack. When a function calls another function, the new function's

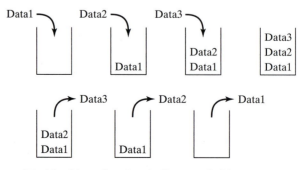

**FIGURE 10.10** A stack holds objects in a last-in first-out fashion.

parameters and local variables are pushed into the stack. When a function finishes its work and returns to its caller, its associated space is released from the stack.

For simplicity, assume the stack holds the `int` values. So, name the stack class as `StackOfIntegers`. The UML diagram for the class is shown in Figure 10.11.

Suppose that the class is available, as declared in Listing 10.26. Let us write a test program in Listing 10.27 that uses the class to create a stack (line 7), stores ten integers 0, 1, 2, ..., and 9 (lines 9–10), and displays them in reverse order (lines 12–13).

| **StackOfIntegers** | |
|---|---|
| -elements[100]: int <br> -size: int | An array to store integers in the stack. <br> The number of integers in the stack. |
| +StackOfIntegers() <br> +empty(): bool <br> +peek(): int <br><br> +push(value: int): void <br> +pop(): int <br> +getSize(): int | Constructs an empty stack. <br> Returns true if the stack is empty. <br> Returns the integer at the top of the stack without <br> removing it from the stack. <br> Stores an integer into the top of the stack. <br> Removes the integer at the top of the stack and returns it. <br> Returns the number of elements in the stack. |

**FIGURE 10.11**   The `StackOfIntegers` class encapsulates the stack storage and provides the operations for manipulating the stack.

## LISTING 10.26   StackOfIntegers.h

```
1  #ifndef STACK_H
2  #define STACK_H
3
4  class StackOfIntegers
5  {
6  public:                                    public members
7    StackOfIntegers();
8    bool isEmpty();
9    int peek();
10   void push(int value);
11   int pop();
12   int getSize();
13
14 private:                                   private members
15   int elements[100];
16   int size;                                element array
17 };
18
19 #endif
```

## LISTING 10.27   TestStackOfIntegers.cpp

```
1  #include <iostream>
2  #include "StackOfIntegers.h"               StackOfIntegers header
3  using namespace std;
4
5  int main()
6  {
7    StackOfIntegers stack;                   create a stack
8
```

push to stack

stack empty?
pop from stack

```
 9    for (int i = 0; i < 10; i++)
10      stack.push(i);
11
12    while (!stack.isEmpty())
13      cout << stack.pop() << " ";
14
15    return 0;
16 }
```

```
9 8 7 6 5 4 3 2 1 0
```

How do you implement the **StackOfIntegers** class? The elements in the stack are stored in an array named **elements**. When you create a stack, the array is also created. The no-arg constructor initializes **size** to **0**. The variable **size** counts the number of elements in the stack, and **size** − **1** is the index of the element at the top of the stack, as shown in Figure 10.12. For an empty stack, **size** is **0**.

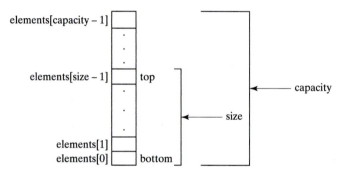

**FIGURE 10.12** The **StackOfIntegers** class encapsulates the stack storage and provides the operations for manipulating the stack.

The **StackOfIntegers** class is implemented in Listing 10.28.

### LISTING 10.28 StackOfIntegers.cpp

**StackOfIntegers** header

constructor

initialize **size**

```
 1 #include "StackOfIntegers.h"
 2
 3 StackOfIntegers::StackOfIntegers()
 4 {
 5   size = 0;
 6 }
 7
 8 bool StackOfIntegers::isEmpty()
 9 {
10   return (size == 0);
11 }
12
13 int StackOfIntegers::peek()
14 {
15   return elements[size - 1];
16 }
17
18 void StackOfIntegers::push(int value)
19 {
```

```
20    elements[size++] = value;
21 }
22
23 int StackOfIntegers::pop()
24 {
25    return elements[--size];
26 }
27
28 int StackOfIntegers::getSize()
29 {
30    return size;
31 }
```

## 10.12 The C++ **vector** Class

The preceding two examples use arrays to store students and **int** values. There is a serious limitation: the array size is fixed in the class declaration. C++ provides the **vector** class, which is more flexible than arrays. You can use a **vector** object just like an array, but a vector's size can grow automatically if needed.

To create a vector, use the syntax:

```
vector<dataType> vectorName;
```

For example,

```
vector<int> intVector;
```

creates a vector to store **int** values.

```
vector<string> stringVector;
```

creates a vector to store **string** objects.

Figure 10.13 lists several frequently used methods in the vector class in a UML class diagram.

| vector<dataType> | |
|---|---|
| +vector<dataType>() | Constructs an empty vector with the specified element type. |
| +push_back(element: dataType): void | Appends the element in this vector. |
| +pop_back(): void | Removes the last element from this vector. |
| +size(): unsigned int | Returns the number of the elements in this vector. |
| +at(index: int): dataType | Returns the element at the specified index in this vector. |
| +empty(): bool | Returns true if this vector is empty. |
| +clear(): void | Removes all elements from this vector. |
| +swap(v2: vector): void | Swaps the contents of this vector with the specified vector. |

**FIGURE 10.13**   The **vector** class functions as a resizable array.

A vector can be accessed using the array subscript operator []. For example,

```
cout << intVector[0];
```

displays the first element in the vector.

**Caution**

To use the array subscript operator [] , the element must already exist in the vector. Like array, the index is 0-based in a vector, i.e., the index of the first element in the vector is 0.

Listing 10.29 gives an example of using vectors.

LISTING 10.29 TestVector.cpp

```cpp
 1  #include <iostream>
 2  #include <vector>
 3  #include <string>
 4  using namespace std;
 5
 6  int main()
 7  {
 8    vector<int> intVector;
 9
10    // Store numbers 1, 2, 3, 4, 5, ..., 10 to the vector
11    for (int i = 0; i < 10; i++)
12      intVector.push_back(i + 1);
13
14    // Display the numbers in the vector
15    cout << "Numbers in the vector: ";
16    for (int i = 0; i < intVector.size(); i++)
17      cout << intVector[i] << " ";
18
19    vector<string> stringVector;
20
21    // Store strings into the vector
22    stringVector.push_back("Dallas");
23    stringVector.push_back("Houston");
24    stringVector.push_back("Austin");
25    stringVector.push_back("Norman");
26
27    // Display the string in the vector
28    cout << "\nStrings in the string vector: ";
29    for (int i = 0; i < stringVector.size(); i++)
30      cout << stringVector[i]  << " ";
31
32    stringVector.pop_back(); // Remove the last element
33
34    vector<string> v2;
35    v2.swap(stringVector);
36    v2[0] = "Atlanta";
37
38    // Redisplay the string in the vector
39    cout << "\nStrings in the vector v2: ";
40    for (int i = 0; i < v2.size(); i++)
41      cout << v2.at(i) << " ";
42
43    return 0;
44  }
```

Margin notes:
- vector header (line 2)
- string header (line 3)
- create a vector (line 8)
- append **int** value (line 12)
- vector size (line 16)
- vector subscript (line 17)
- create a vector (line 19)
- append **string** (line 21)
- vector size (line 29)
- vector subscript (line 30)
- remove element (line 32)
- create vector (line 34)
- swap vector (line 35)
- assign string (line 36)
- vector size (line 40)
- **at** function (line 41)

```
Numbers in the vector: 1 2 3 4 5 6 7 8 9 10
Strings in the string vector: Dallas Houston Austin Norman
Strings in the vector v2: Atlanta Houston Austin
```

Since the vector class is used in the program, line 2 includes its header file. Since the string class also is used, line 3 includes the string class header file.

A vector for storing int values is created in line 8. The int values are appended to the vector in line 12. There is no limit on the size of the vector. The size grows automatically as more elements are added into the vector. The program displays all the int values in the vector in lines 15–17. Note the array subscript operator [] is used to retrieve an element in line 17.

A vector for storing strings is created in line 19. Four strings are added to the vector (lines 22–25). The program displays all the strings in the vector in lines 29–30. Note the array subscript operator `[]` is used to retrieve an element in line 30.

Line 32 removes the last string from the vector. Line 34 creates another vector `v2`. Line 35 swaps `v2` with `stringVector`. Line 36 assigns a new string to the `v2[0]`. The program displays the strings in `v2`. Note that the `at` function is used to retrieve the elements. You also can use the subscript operator `[]` to retrieve the elements.

## KEY TERMS

aggregation    328
composition    328
copy constructor    321
deep copy    322
destructor    319
friend keyword    327
has-a relationship    328
immutable class    312
immutable object    312

inclusion guard    315
instance field    316
instance function    319
mutator function    316
shallow copy    322
static field    316
static function    316
vector    335

## CHAPTER SUMMARY

■ If the contents of an object cannot be changed (except through memberwise copy) once the object is created, the object is called an *immutable object* and its class is called an *immutable class*.

■ For a class to be immutable, it must mark all data fields private and provide no mutator functions and no accessor functions that would return a pointer to a mutable data field object.

■ The C++ `#ifndef` directive can be used to prevent a header file from being included multiple times.

■ An instance variable or function belongs to an instance of a class. Its use is associated with individual instances. A static variable is a variable shared by all instances of the same class. A static function is a function that can be invoked without using instances.

■ Every instance of a class can access the class's static variables and functions. However, it is better to invoke static variables and functions using `ClassName::static-Variable` and `ClassName::functionName(arguments)` for clarity.

■ Destructors are the opposite of constructors. Constructors are invoked to create objects and destructors are invoked automatically when the object is destroyed. Every class has a default destructor if the destructor is not explicitly defined.

■ Each class may define several overloaded constructors and one destructor. Additionally, every class has a *copy constructor*. You may use the default copy constructor, or redefine it. By default, the copy constructor simply copies each data field in one object to its counterpart in the other object.

■ The `friend` keyword can be used to give the trusted functions and classes access to a class's private members.

■ The array size is fixed after it is created. C++ provides the `vector` class, which is more flexible than arrays. You can use a `vector` object just like an array, but a vector's size can grow automatically if needed.

## REVIEW QUESTIONS

### Section 10.2 Immutable Objects and Classes

**10.1** Is the following class immutable?

```
class A
{
public:
  int x;
  int getX();
};
```

```
class B
{
public:
  int getX();

private:
  int x;
};
```

```
class C
{
public:
  int getX();
  void setX(int x);

private:
  int x;
};
```

**10.2** Is the following class immutable?

```
#include "Date.h"

class A
{
public:
  Date getBirthDate();

private:
  Date birthDate;
};
```

```
#include "Date.h"

class B
{
public:
  Date * getBirthDate();

private:
  Date * birthDate;
};
```

**10.3** Is the following class immutable?

```
class A
{
public:
  A()
  {
    name = "ABC";
  }

  string getName()
  {
    return name;
  }

private:
  string name;
};
```

```
class B
{
public:
  B()
  {
    name = new string ("ABC");
  }

  string * getName()
  {
    return name;
  }

private:
  string * name;
};
```

**10.4** If a class contains only private data fields and no set functions, is the class immutable?

### Section 10.3 Preventing Multiple Declarations

**10.5** What might cause a multiple declarations error? How do you prevent multiple declarations?

**10.6** What is the **#define** directive for?

### Section 10.4 Instance and Static Members

**10.7**  A data field and function can be declared as instance or static. What are the criteria to decide it?

**10.8**  Where do you initialize a static data field?

**10.9**  Suppose function `f()` is static defined in class `C` and `c` is an object of the `C` class. Can you invoke `c.f()`, `C::f()`, or `c::f()`?

### Section 10.5 Destructors

**10.10**  Does every class have a destructor? How is a destructor named? Can it be overloaded? Can you redefine a destructor? Can you invoke destructor explicitly?

**10.11**  What is the output of the following code?

```cpp
#include <iostream>
using namespace std;

class A
{
public:
  A(int id)
  {
    this->id = id;
  }

  ~A()
  {
    cout << "object with id " << id << " is destroyed" << endl;
  }

private:
  int id;
};

int main()
{
  A a1(1);
  A a2(2);
  A a3(3);

  return 0;
}
```

**10.12**  Why does the following class need a destructor? Add a destructor in the class.

```cpp
class B
{
public:
  B()
  {
    name = new string("ABC");
  }

  string* getName()
  {
    return name;
  }

private:
  string* name;
};
```

### Section 10.6 Copy Constructors

**10.13** Does every class have a copy constructor? How is a copy constructor named? Can it be overloaded? Can you redefine a copy constructor? How do you invoke a copy constructor?

**10.14** What is the output of the following code?

```cpp
#include <iostream>
#include <string>
using namespace std;

int main()
{
  string s1("ABC");
  string s2("DEFG");
  s1 = string(s2);
  cout << s1 << endl;
  cout << s2 << endl;

  return 0;
}
```

**10.15** Is the highlighted code in the preceding exercise the same as

```cpp
s1 = s2;
```

Which is better?

**10.16** What are a deep copy and a shallow copy? Give an example of a shallow copy.

### Section 10.8 `friend` Functions and `friend` Classes

**10.17** How do you declare a friend function to access a class's private members?

**10.18** How do you declare a friend class to access a class's private members?

### Section 10.9 Object Composition

**10.19** What is the output of the following code? (Use the **Loan** class defined in Listing 9.14, Loan.h.)

```cpp
#include <iostream>
#include "Loan.h"
using namespace std;

class A
{
public:
  Loan loan;
  int i;
};

int main()
{
  A a;
  cout << a.loan.getLoanAmount() << endl;

  return 0;
}
```

### Section 10.12 The C++ `vector` Class

**10.20** How do you declare a vector to store `double` values? How do you append a double to a vector? How do you find the size of a vector? How do you remove an element from a vector?

**10.21** What is wrong in the following code?

```
vector<int> v;
v[0] = 4;
```

## PROGRAMMING EXERCISES

### Sections 10.2–10.6

**10.1**[*] (*The MyInteger class*) Design a class named `MyInteger`. The class contains:

- An `int` data field named `value` that stores the `int` value represented by this object.
- A constructor that creates a `MyInteger` object for the specified `int` value.
- A get function that returns the `int` value.
- Functions `isEven()`, `isOdd()`, `isPrime()` that return `true` if the value is even, odd, or prime, respectively.
- Static functions `isEven(int)`, `isOdd(int)`, `isPrime(int)` that return `true` if the specified value is even, odd, or prime, respectively.
- Static functions `isEven(MyInteger)`, `isOdd(MyInteger)`, `isPrime(MyInteger)` that return `true` if the specified value is even, odd, or prime, respectively.
- Functions `equals(int)` and `equals(MyInteger)` that return `true` if the value in the object is equal to the specified value.
- A static function `parseInt(string)` that converts a string to an `int` value.

Draw the UML diagram for the class. Implement the class. Write a client program that tests all functions in the class.

**10.2** (*Modifying the Loan class*) Rewrite the `Loan` class to add two static functions for computing monthly payment and total payment, as follows:

```
public static double getMonthlyPayment(double annualInterestRate,
    int numberOfYears, double loanAmount)
public static double getTotalPayment(double annualInterestRate,
    int numberOfYears, double loanAmount)
```

Write a client program to test these two functions.

**10.3**[*] (*Displaying the prime factors*) Write a program that receives a positive integer and displays all its smallest factors in decreasing order. For example, if the integer is 120, the smallest factors are displayed as 5, 3, 2, 2, 2. Use the `StackOfIntegers` class to store the factors (e.g., 2, 2, 2, 3, 5) and retrieve and display the factors in reverse order.

**10.4**[*] (*Displaying the prime numbers*) Write a program that displays all the prime numbers less than 120 in decreasing order. Use the `StackOfIntegers` class to store the prime numbers (e.g., 2, 3, 5, ...) and retrieve and display them in reverse order.

**10.5** (*The StackOfIntegers class*) Rewrite the `StackOfIntegers` class in Listing 10.28. Use a `vector` to replace an array to store integers.

**10.6** (*The Course class*) Rewrite the `Course` class in Listing 10.25. Use a `vector` to replace an array to store students.

# CHAPTER 11

# INHERITANCE AND POLYMORPHISM

## Objectives

- To develop a derived class from a base class through inheritance (§11.2).

- To enable generic programming by passing objects of derived type to a parameter of a base class type (§11.3).

- To understand constructor and destructor chaining (§11.4).

- To know how to invoke the base class' constructors with arguments (§11.4).

- To redefine functions in the derived class (§11.5).

- To distinguish differences between redefining and overloading (§11.5).

- To understand polymorphism and dynamic binding using virtual functions (§11.6).

- To distinguish differences between redefining and overriding (§11.6).

- To distinguish differences between static matching and dynamic binding (§11.6).

- To access protected members of the base class from derived classes (§11.7).

- To declare abstract classes that contain pure virtual functions (§11.8).

- To cast an object of a base class type to a derived type using the `dynamic_cast` operator (§11.9).

## 11.1 Introduction

inheritance

Object-oriented programming allows you to derive new classes from existing classes. This is called *inheritance.* This chapter introduces the concept of inheritance. Specifically, it discusses base classes and derived classes, constructor and destructor chaining, protected data members, virtual functions, and polymorphism.

## 11.2 Base Classes and Derived Classes

derived class
base class

In C++ terminology, a class **C1** extended from another class **C2** is called a *derived class,* and **C2** is called a *base class.* A base class also is referred to as a *parent class,* and a derived class as an *extended class* or a *derived class.* A derived class inherits accessible data fields and functions from its base class, and may also add new data fields and functions.

Consider geometric objects. Suppose you want to design the classes to model geometric objects like circles and rectangles. Geometric objects have many common properties and behaviors. They can be drawn in a certain color, filled or unfilled. Thus, a general class **GeometricObject** can be used to model all geometric objects. This class contains the properties **color** and **filled** and their appropriate get and set functions. Assume that this class also contains the **toString()** function, which returns a string representation for the object. Since a circle is a special type of geometric object, it shares common properties and functions with other geometric objects. Thus, it makes sense to define the **Circle** class that extends the **GeometricObject** class. Likewise, **Rectangle** also can be declared as a derived class of **GeometricObject**. Figure 11.1 shows the

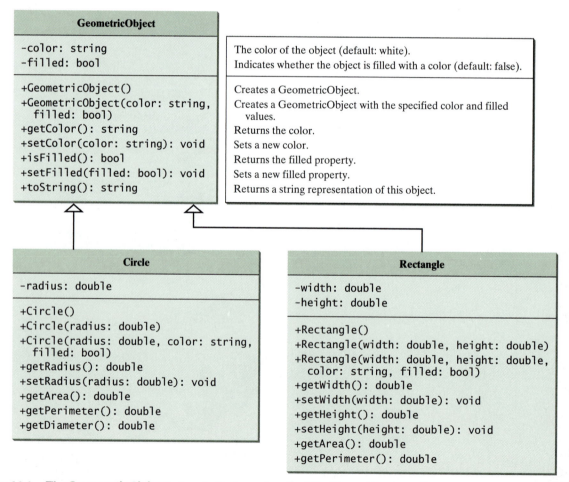

**FIGURE 11.1** The **GeometricObject** class is the base class for **Circle** and **Rectangle**.

relationship among these classes. An arrow pointing to the base class is used to denote the inheritance relationship between the two classes involved.

The **Circle** class inherits all accessible data fields and functions from the **GeometricObject** class. In addition, it has a new data field, **radius**, and its associated get and set functions. It also contains the **getArea()**, **getPerimeter()**, and **getDiameter()** functions for returning the area, perimeter, and diameter of the circle.

The **Rectangle** class inherits all accessible data fields and functions from the **GeometricObject** class. In addition, it has data fields **width** and **height**, and its associated **get** and **set** functions. It also contains the **getArea()** and **getPerimeter()** functions for returning the area and perimeter of the rectangle.

The class declaration for **GeometricObject** is shown in Listing 11.1. The preprocessor directives in lines 2 and 3 guard to prevent multiple declarations. The C++ **string** class header is included in line 3 to support the use of the **string** class in **GeometricObject**. The **isFilled()** function is the accessor for the **filled** data field. Since this data field is the **bool** type, the accessor function is named **isFilled()** by convention.

## LISTING 11.1 GeometricObject.h

```
1  #ifndef GEOMETRICOBJECT_H
2  #define GEOMETRICOBJECT_H
3  #include <string>
4  using namespace std;
5
6  class GeometricObject
7  {
8  public:
9     GeometricObject();
10    GeometricObject(string color, bool filled);
11    string getColor();
12    void setColor(string color);
13    bool isFilled();
14    void setFilled(bool filled);
15    string toString();
16
17 private:
18    string color;
19    bool filled;
20 }; // Must place semicolon here
21
22 #endif
```

inclusion guard

public members

private members

The **GeometricObject** class is implemented in Listing 11.2. The **toString** function (lines 35–39) returns a string that describes the object. The **string** operator + is used to concatenate two strings and returns a new **string** object.

## LISTING 11.2 GeometricObject.cpp

```
1  #include "GeometricObject.h"
2
3  GeometricObject::GeometricObject()
4  {
5     color = "white";
6     filled = false;
7  }
8
9  GeometricObject::GeometricObject(string color, bool filled)
10 {
11    this->color = color;
```

header file

no-arg constructor

no-arg constructor

getColor

setColor

isFilled

setFilled

toString

```
12    this->filled = filled;
13  }
14
15  string GeometricObject::getColor()
16  {
17    return color;
18  }
19
20  void GeometricObject::setColor(string color)
21  {
22    this->color = color;
23  }
24
25  bool GeometricObject::isFilled()
26  {
27    return filled;
28  }
29
30  void GeometricObject::setFilled(bool filled)
31  {
32    this->filled = filled;
33  }
34
35  string GeometricObject::toString()
36  {
37    return "Geometric object color " + color +
38      " filled " + ((filled) ? "true" : "false");
39  }
```

The class declaration for **Circle** is shown in Listing 11.3. Line 3 declares that the **Circle** class is derived from the base class **GeometricObject**. The syntax

tells the compiler that the class is derived from the base class. So, all public members in **GeometricObject** are inherited in **Circle**.

### LISTING 11.3 DerivedCircle.h

inclusion guard

extends **GeometricObject**

public members

```
1  #ifndef DERIVEDCIRCLE_H
2  #define DERIVEDCIRCLE_H
3  #include "GeometricObject.h"
4
5  class Circle: public GeometricObject
6  {
7  public:
8    Circle();
9    Circle(double);
10   Circle(double radius, string color, bool filled);
11   double getRadius();
12   void setRadius(double);
13   double getArea();
14   double getPerimeter();
15   double getDiameter();
16
```

```
17 private:
18   double radius;
19 };  // Must place semicolon here
20
21 #endif
```

The `Circle` class is implemented in Listings 11.4. Note that the constructor `Circle (double radius, string color, bool filled)` will be implemented in §11.4.1.

## LISTING 11.4  DerivedCircle.cpp

```
1 #include "DerivedCircle.h"
2
3 // Construct a default circle object
4 Circle::Circle()
5 {
6    radius = 1;
7 }
8
9 // Construct a circle object with specified radius
10 Circle::Circle(double radius)
11 {
12    this->radius = radius;
13 }
14
15 // Return the radius of this circle
16 double Circle::getRadius()
17 {
18    return radius;
19 }
20
21 // Set a new radius
22 void Circle::setRadius(double radius)
23 {
24    this->radius = (radius >= 0) ? radius : 0;
25 }
26
27 // Return the area of this circle
28 double Circle::getArea()
29 {
30    return radius * radius * 3.14159;
31 }
32
33 // Return the perimeter of this circle
34 double Circle::getPerimeter()
35 {
36    return 2 * radius * 3.14159;
37 }
38
39 // Return the diameter of this circle
40 double Circle::getDiameter()
41 {
42    return 2 * radius;
43 }
```

Circle header

no-arg constructor

constructor

getRadius

setRadius

getArea

getPerimeter

getDiameter

The class declaration for **Rectangle** is shown in Listing 11.5. Line 3 declares that the **Rectangle** class is derived from the base class **GeometricObject**. So, all public members in **GeometricObject** are inherited in **Rectangle**.

### LISTING 11.5 Rectangle.h

```
1 #ifndef RECTANGLE_H
2 #define RECTANGLE_H
3 #include "GeometricObject.h"
4
5 class Rectangle: public GeometricObject
6 {
7 public:
8   Rectangle();
9   Rectangle(double width, double height);
10  Rectangle(double width, double height, string color, bool filled);
11  double getWidth();
12  void setWidth(double);
13  double getHeight();
14  void setHeight(double);
15  double getArea();
16  double getPerimeter();
17
18 private:
19  double width;
20  double height;
21 };  // Must place semicolon here
22
23 #endif
```

*inclusion guard* — lines 1-3

*extends GeometricObject* — line 5

*public members* — line 7

*private members* — line 18

The **Rectangle** class is implemented in Listing 11.6. Note that the constructor **Rectangle(double width, double height, string color, bool filled)** is not implemented. You will know how to implement it in §11.4.1.

### LISTING 11.6 Rectangle.cpp

```
1 #include "Rectangle.h"
2
3 // Construct a default rectangle object
4 Rectangle::Rectangle()
5 {
6   width = 1;
7   height = 1;
8 }
9
10 // Construct a rectangle object with specified width and height
11 Rectangle::Rectangle(double width, double height)
12 {
13   this->width = width;
14   this->height = height;
15 }
16
17 // Return the width of this rectangle
18 double Rectangle::getWidth()
19 {
20   return width;
21 }
22
23 // Set a new radius
24 void Rectangle::setWidth(double width)
25 {
26   this->width = (width >= 0) ? width : 0;
27 }
28
```

*Rectangle header* — line 1

*no-arg constructor* — line 4

*constructor* — line 11

*getWidth* — line 18

*setWidth* — line 24

```
29  // Return the height of this rectangle
30  double Rectangle::getHeight()
31  {
32    return height;
33  }
34
35  // Set a new height
36  void Rectangle::setHeight(double height)
37  {
38    this->height = (height >= 0) ? height : 0;
39  }
40
41  // Return the area of this rectangle
42  double Rectangle::getArea()
43  {
44    return width * height;
45  }
46
47  // Return the perimeter of this rectangle
48  double Rectangle::getPerimeter()
49  {
50    return 2 * (width + height);
51  }
```

*getHeight*

*setHeight*

*getArea*

*getPerimeter*

Listing 11.7 gives a test program that uses these three classes GeometricObject, Circle, and Rectangles.

## LISTING 11.7  TestGeometricObject.cpp

```
1  #include "GeometricObject.h"
2  #include "DerivedCircle.h"
3  #include "Rectangle.h"
4  #include <iostream>
5  using namespace std;
6
7  int main()
8  {
9    GeometricObject shape;
10   shape.setColor("red");
11   shape.setFilled(true);
12   cout << shape.toString() << endl;
13
14   Circle circle(5);
15   circle.setColor("black");
16   circle.setFilled(false);
17   cout << " Circle radius: " << circle.getRadius()
18     << " area: " << circle.getArea()
19     << " perimeter: " << circle.getPerimeter() << endl;
20   cout << circle.toString() << endl;
21
22   Rectangle rectangle(2, 3);
23   rectangle.setColor("orange");
24   rectangle.setFilled(true);
25   cout << " Rectangle width: " << rectangle.getWidth()
26     << " height: " << rectangle.getHeight()
27     << " area: " << rectangle.getArea()
28     << " perimeter: " << rectangle.getPerimeter() << endl;
29   cout << rectangle.toString() << endl;
30
31   return 0;
32 }
```

**GeometricObject** header
**Circle** header
**Rectangle** header

create a **GeometricObject**

create a **Circle**

create a **Rectangle**

```
Geometric object color red filled true
  Circle radius: 5 area: 78.5397 perimeter: 31.4159
Geometric object color black filled false
  Rectangle width: 2 height: 3 area: 6 perimeter: 10
Geometric object color orange filled true
```

The program creates a `GeometricObject` and invokes its functions `setColor`, `setFilled`, and `toString` in lines 9–12.

The program creates a `Circle` object and invokes its functions `setColor`, `setFilled`, `getRadius`, `getArea`, `getPerimeter`, and `toString` in lines 14–20. Note that the `set-Color`, `setFilled`, and `toString` functions are defined in the `GeometricObject` class and inherited in the `Circle` class.

The program creates a `Rectangle` object and invokes its functions `setColor`, `setFilled`, `getRadius`, `getArea`, `getPerimeter`, and `toString` in lines 22–29. Note that the `setColor`, `setFilled`, and `toString` functions are defined in the `GeometricObject` class and inherited in the `Rectangle` class.

**Caution**

no blind extension

Inheritance is used to model the *is-a* relationship. Do not blindly extend a class just for the sake of reusing functions. For example, it makes no sense for a `Tree` class to extend a `Person` class. A derived class and its base class must have the is-a relationship.

## 11.3 Generic Programming

An object of a derived class can be used wherever an object of a base-type is required. This enables a function to be used generically for a wide range of object arguments. This is known as *generic programming*. If a function's parameter type is a base class (e.g., `GeometricObject`), you may pass an object to this function of any of the parameter's derived classes (e.g., `Circle` or `Rectangle`).

For example, if you declare a function as follows:

```
void displayGeometricObject(GeometricObject shape)
{
  cout << shape.toString() << endl;
}
```

The parameter type is `GeometricObject`. You can invoke this function in the following code:

```
displayGeometricObject(GeometricObject("black", true));
displayGeometricObject(Circle(5));
displayGeometricObject(Rectangle(2, 3));
```

Each statement creates an anonymous object and passes it to invoke `displayGeometric-Object`. Since `Circle` and `Rectangle` are derived from `GeometricObject`, you can pass a `Circle` object or a `Rectangle` object to the `GeometricObject` parameter type in the `displayGeometricObject` function.

## 11.4 Constructors and Destructors

A derived class inherits accessible data fields and functions from its base class. Does it inherit constructors or destructors? Can base class constructors and destructors be invoked from derived classes? This section addresses these questions and their ramification.

## 11.4.1   Calling Base Class Constructors

A constructor is used to construct an instance of a class. Unlike data fields and functions, the constructors of a base class are not inherited in the derived class. They only can be invoked from the constructors of the derived classes to initialize the data fields in the base class. The syntax to invoke it is as follows:

```
DerivedClass(parameterList): BaseClass()
{
  // Perform initialization
}
```

or

```
DerivedClass(parameterList): BaseClass(argumentList)
{
  // Perform initialization
}
```

The former invokes the no-arg constructor of its base class, and the latter invokes the base class constructor with the specified arguments.

You can only invoke the base class' constructor in the class implementation, not in the class declaration. For example, the `Circle(double radius, string color, bool filled)` constructor in the `Circle` class can be implemented as follows:

```
1 // Construct a circle object with specified radius, color and filled
2 Circle::Circle(double radius, string color, bool filled)
3   : GeometricObject(color, filled)            invoke base constructor
4 {
5   this->radius = radius;
6 }
```

This implements the `Circle` class' constructor to invoke the `GeometricObject` class' constructor with the specified `color` and `filled` values.

**Note**

A constructor in a derived class must always invoke a constructor in its base class. If a base constructor is not invoked explicitly, the base class' no-arg constructor is invoked by default. For example,

```
public Circle()
{
  radius = 1;
}
```
is equivalent to
```
public Circle(): GeometricObject()
{
  radius = 1;
}
```

```
public Circle(double radius)
{
  this->radius = radius;
}
```
is equivalent to
```
public Circle(double radius)
  : GeometricObject()
{
  this->radius = radius;
}
```

## 11.4.2   Constructor and Destructor Chaining

Constructing an instance of a class invokes the constructors of all the base classes along the inheritance chain. A base class' constructor is called before the derived class' constructor. Conversely, the destructors automatically are invoked in reverse order, with the derived class' destructor invoked first. This is called *constructor and destructor chaining*.

Consider the following code.

### LISTING 11.8 ChainingDemo.cpp

**Person** class

**Employee** class

**Faculty** class

create a **Faculty**

```cpp
1  #include <iostream>
2  using namespace std;
3
4  class Person
5  {
6  public:
7    Person()
8    {
9      cout << "Person's constructor is invoked" << endl;
10   }
11
12   ~Person()
13   {
14     cout << "Person's destructor is invoked" << endl;
15   }
16 };
17
18 class Employee: public Person
19 {
20 public:
21   Employee()
22   {
23     cout << "Employee's constructor is invoked" << endl;
24   }
25
26   ~Employee()
27   {
28     cout << "Employee's destructor is invoked" << endl;
29   }
30 };
31
32 class Faculty: public Employee
33 {
34 public:
35   Faculty()
36   {
37     cout << "Faculty's constructor is invoked" << endl;
38   }
39
40   ~Faculty()
41   {
42     cout << "Faculty's destructor is invoked" << endl;
43   }
44 };
45
46 int main()
47 {
48   Faculty faculty;
49
50   return 0;
51 }
```

```
Person's constructor is invoked
Employee's constructor is invoked
Faculty's constructor is invoked
```

```
Faculty's destructor is invoked
Employee's destructor is invoked
Person's destructor is invoked
```

The program creates an instance of **Faculty** in line 48. Since **Faculty** is derived from **Employee** and **Employee** is derived from **Person**, **Person**'s constructor is called first, then **Employee**'s, and finally **Faculty**'s. When the program exits, the **Faculty** object is destroyed. So the **Faculty**'s destructor is called, then **Employee**'s, and finally **Person**'s.

### Caution

If a class is designed to be extended, it is better to provide a *no-arg constructor* to avoid programming errors. Consider the following code:

no-arg constructor

```
 1 class Fruit
 2 {
 3 public:
 4    Fruit(int id)
 5    {
 6    }
 7 };
 8
 9 class Apple: public Fruit
10 {
11 public:
12    Apple()
13    {
14    }
15 };
```

Since no constructor explicitly is defined in **Apple**, **Apple**'s default no-arg constructor is declared implicitly. Since **Apple** is a derived class of **Fruit**, **Apple**'s default constructor automatically invokes **Fruit**'s no-arg constructor. However, **Fruit** does not have a no-arg constructor, because **Fruit** has an explicit constructor defined. Therefore, the program cannot be compiled.

## 11.5 Redefining Functions

The **toString()** function is defined in the **GeometricObject** class to return a string description of a **GeometricObject**. You can redefine this function in the **Circle** and **Rectangle** classes to return a more specific description that is tailored to a **Circle** or a **Rectangle** object.

To redefine a base class' function in the derived class, you need to add the function's prototype in the derived class' header file, and provide a new implementation for the function in the derived class' implementation file.

For example, to redefine **toString** in **Circle**, add the function's prototype to the **Circle** declaration and implement it as follows:

```
// Redefine the toString function
string Circle::toString()
{
  return "Circle object";
}
```

So the following code

create **GeometricObject**
invoke **toString**

```
1 GeometricObject shape;
2 cout << "shape.toString() returns " << shape.toString() << endl;
3
```

create **Circle**
invoke **toString**

```
4 Circle circle(5);
5 cout << "circle.toString() returns " << circle.toString() << endl;
```

displays:

```
shape.toString() returns Geometric object color white filled false
circle.toString() returns Circle object
```

The code creates a **GeometricObject** in line 1. The **toString** function defined in **GeometricObject** is invoked in line 2, since **shape**'s type is **GeometricObject**.

The code creates a **Circle** object in line 3. The **toString** function defined in **Circle** is invoked in line 5, since **circle**'s type is **Circle**.

invoke function in the base

If you wish to invoke the **toString** function defined in the **GeometricObject** class on the calling object **circle**, use the scope resolution operator (::) with the base class name as follows:

```
circle.GeometricObject::toString()
```

### Note

redefining vs. overloading

You have learned about overloading functions in §5.7, "Overloading Functions." Overloading a function is a way to provide more than one function with the same name but with different signatures to distinguish them. To redefine a function, the function must be defined in the derived class using the same signature and same return type as in its base class.

## 11.6 Polymorphism and Virtual Functions

Before introducing polymorphism, let us begin with an example in Listing 11.9 to demonstrate the need for polymorphism.

### LISTING 11.9 WhyPolymorphismDemo.cpp

class **C**

define **toString** function

class **B**

redefine **toString** function

```
 1 #include <iostream>
 2 using namespace std;
 3
 4 class C
 5 {
 6 public:
 7   string toString()
 8   {
 9     return "class C";
10   }
11 };
12
13 class B: public C
14 {
15   string toString()
16   {
17     return "class B";
18   }
19 };
20
```

```
21 class A: public B                                    class A
22 {
23   string toString()                                  redefine toString function
24   {
25     return "class A";
26   }
27 };
28
29 void displayObject(C x)                              displayObject
30 {
31   cout << x.toString().data() << endl;               invoke toString
32 }
33
34 int main()
35 {
36   displayObject(A());                                invoke displayObject
37   displayObject(B());                                invoke displayObject
38   displayObject(C());                                invoke displayObject
39
40   return 0;
41 }
```

```
class C
class C
class C
```

The program declares three classes **A**, **B**, and **C**. **A** is derived from **B**, and **B** is derived from **C**. The **displayObject** function is invoked in lines 36–38 by passing anonymous objects **A()**, **B()**, and **C()**.

The argument of the **displayObject** function (lines 29–32) is an object of the **C** class or **C**'s derived classes. The function invokes the **toString()** function on the object (line 31). The **toString()** function defined in class **C** is invoked. So, the output is the same for the three function calls.

It would be nice to invoke the **toString()** function defined in **A** when invoking **display-Object(A())**, the **toString()** function defined in **B** when invoking **displayObject(B())**, and the **toString()** function defined in **C** when invoking **displayObject(C())**. This can be done by modifying Listing 11.9 using virtual functions and pointer variables. The new program is shown in Listing 11.10.

## LISTING 11.10  PolymorphismDemo.cpp

```
1 #include <iostream>
2 using namespace std;
3
4 class C                                               class C
5 {
6 public:
7   virtual string toString()                           virtual function toString
8   {
9     return "class C";
10   }
11 };
12
13 class B: public C                                     class B
14 {
15   string toString()                                  override toString function
```

```
16    {
17       return "class B";
18    }
19 };
20
21 class A: public B
22 {
23    string toString()
24    {
25       return "class A";
26    }
27 };
28
29 void displayObject(C *p)
30 {
31    cout << p->toString().data() << endl;
32 }
33
34 int main()
35 {
36    A a = A();
37    B b = B();
38    C c = C();
39    displayObject(&a);
40    displayObject(&b);
41    displayObject(&c);
42
43    return 0;
44 }
```

class A

override **toString** function

**displayObject**

invoke **toString**

invoke **displayObject**
invoke **displayObject**
invoke **displayObject**

```
class A
class B
class C
```

virtual
pointer

Line 7 defines **toString** to be a *virtual* function using the keyword **virtual**. Line 29 defines a *pointer* parameter **p** whose type is class **C**. When invoking **displayObject(&a)** in line 39, the address of object **A()** is passed to **p**. When invoking **p->toString()** in line 31, C++ dynamically determines which **toString()** to use. Since **p** points to an object of class **A**, the **toString** function defined in class **A** is invoked. The capability of determining which function to invoke at runtime is known as *dynamic binding*. It also is known commonly as *polymorphism* (from a Greek word meaning "many forms") because one function has many implementations.

dynamic binding
polymorphism

redefining vs. overriding

 **Note**

In C++, *redefining* a virtual function in a derived class is called *overriding a function*.

To enable dynamic binding for a function, you need to do two things:

■ The function must be declared **virtual** in the base class.

■ The variable that references the object for the function must contain the address of the object.

Listing 11.10 passes the address of the object to a pointer (lines 29–43); alternatively, you can rewrite lines 29–43 by passing the object to a base class reference, as follows:

```
void displayObject(C &p)
{
   cout << p.toString().data() << endl;
}
```

```
int main()
{
  A a = A();
  B b = B();
  C c = C();
  displayObject(a);
  displayObject(b);
  displayObject(c);

  return 0;
}
```

**Note**

If a function is defined `virtual` in a base class, it is automatically `virtual` in all its derived classes. It is not necessary to add the keyword `virtual` in the function declaration in the derived class.

`virtual`

**Note**

Matching a function signature and binding a function implementation are two separate issues. The *declared type* of the variable decides which function to match at compile time. The compiler finds a matching function according to parameter type, number of parameters, and order of the parameters at compile time. A virtual function may be implemented in several derived classes. C++ dynamically binds the implementation of the function at runtime, decided by the *actual class* of the object referenced by the variable.

static matching vs. dynamic binding

**Tip**

If a function defined in a base class needs to be redefined in its derived classes, you should declare it virtual to avoid confusions and mistakes. On the other hand, if a function will not be redefined, it is more efficient without declaring it virtual, because it takes more time and system resource to bind virtual functions dynamically at runtime.

use virtual functions?

## 11.7 The **protected** Keyword

So far you have used the **private** and **public** keywords to specify whether data fields and functions can be accessed from the outside of the class. Private members only can be accessed from the inside of the class, and public members can be accessed from any other classes. A protected data field or a protected function in a base class can be accessed by name in its derived classes.

The keywords **private**, **protected**, and **public** are known as *visibility* or *accessibility keywords* because they specify how class and class members are accessed. The visibility of these modifiers increases in this order:

visibility keyword

Visibility increases
→
private, protected, public

Listing 11.11 demonstrates how to use **protected** keywords.

**LISTING 11.11** VisibilityDemo.cpp

```
1 #include <iostream>
2 using namespace std;
3
4 class B
5 {
```

public

protected

private

```
 6  public:
 7    int i;
 8
 9  protected:
10    int j;
11
12  private:
13    int k;
14  };
15
16  class A: public B
17  {
18  public:
19    void display()
20    {
21      cout << i << endl; // Fine, can access it
22      cout << j << endl; // Fine, can access it
23      cout << k << endl; // Wrong, cannot access it
24    }
25  };
26
27  int main()
28  {
29    A a;
30    cout << a.i << endl; // Fine, can access it
31    cout << a.j << endl; // Wrong, cannot access it
32    cout << a.k << endl; // Wrong, cannot access it
33
34    return 0;
35  }
```

Since **A** is derived from **B** and **j** is protected, **j** can be accessed from class **A** in line 22. Since **k** is private, **k** cannot be accessed from class **A**.

Since **i** is public, **i** can be accessed from **a.i** in line 30. Since **j** and **k** are not public, they cannot be accessed from the object **a** in lines 31–32.

## 11.8 Abstract Classes and Pure Virtual Functions

In the inheritance hierarchy, classes become more specific and concrete *with each new derived class*. If you move from a derived class back up to its parent and ancestor classes, the classes become more general and less specific. Class design should ensure that a base class contains common features of its derived classes. Sometimes a base class is so abstract that it cannot have any specific instances. Such a class is referred to as an *abstract class*.

abstract class

**GeometricObject** was declared as the base class for **Circle** and **Rectangle** in §11.2, "Base Classes and Derived Classes." **GeometricObject** models common features of geometric objects. Both **Circle** and **Rectangle** contain the **getArea()** and **getPerimeter()** functions for computing the area and perimeter of a circle and a rectangle. Since you can compute areas and perimeters for all geometric objects, it is better to declare the **getArea()** and **getPerimeter()** functions in the **GeometricObject** class. However, these functions cannot be implemented in the **GeometricObject** class, because their implementation is dependent on the specific type of geometric object. Such functions are referred to as *abstract*

abstract function

*functions*. After you declare the functions in **GeometricObject**, **GeometricObject** becomes an abstract class. The new **GeometricObject** class is shown in Figure 11.2. In UML graphic notation, the names of abstract classes and their abstract functions are italicized, as shown in Figure 11.2.

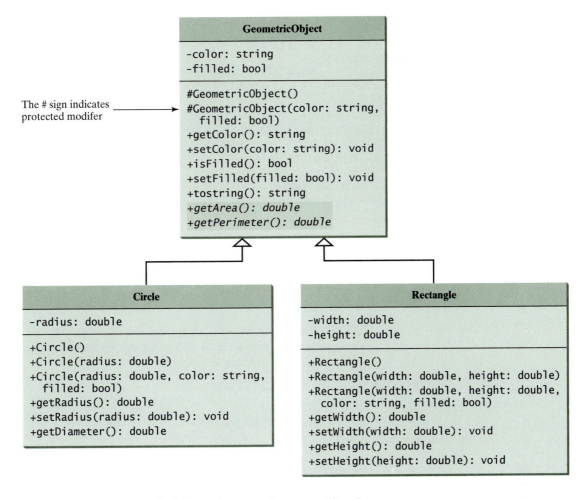

The # sign indicates
protected modifer

**FIGURE 11.2**   The new `GeometricObject` class contains abstract functions.

In C++, abstract functions are called *pure virtual functions*. A class that contains pure vir-      pure virtual function
tual functions becomes an abstract class. A pure virtual function is declared in a manner sim-
ilar to the following:

Indicating pure virtual function

```
virtual double getArea() = 0;
```

The = 0 notation indicates that **getArea** is a pure virtual function. A pure virtual function
does not have a body or implementation in the base class.

Listing 11.12 defines the new abstract `GeometricObject` class with two pure virtual
functions in lines 18–19.

## LISTING 11.12  AbstractGeometricObject.h

```
1 #ifndef ABSTRACTGEOMETRICOBJECT_H
2 #define ABSTRACTGEOMETRICOBJECT_H
3 #include <string>
4 using namespace std;
5
```

```
 6 class GeometricObject
 7 {
 8 protected:
 9   GeometricObject();
10   GeometricObject(string color, bool filled);
11
12 public:
13   string getColor();
14   void setColor(string color);
15   bool isFilled();
16   void setFilled(bool filled);
17   string toString();
18   virtual double getArea() = 0;
19   virtual double getPerimeter() = 0;
20
21 private:
22   string color;
23   bool filled;
24 }; // Must place semicolon here
25
26 #endif
```

pure virtual function (line 18)
pure virtual function (line 19)

GeometricObject is just like a regular class, except that you cannot create objects from GeometricObject because it is an abstract class. If you attempt to create an object from GeometricObject, the compile will generate an error.

Listing 11.13 gives an implementation of the GeometricObject class.

### LISTING 11.13 AbstractGeometricObject.cpp

include header

```
1 #include "AbstractGeometricObject.h"
2
3 // Same as lines 3-39 in GeometricObject.cpp in Listing 11.2
```

Listings 11.14, 11.15, and 11.16 show the files for the new Circle and Rectangle classes derived from the abstract GeometricObject.

### LISTING 11.14 DerivedCircle2.h

inclusion guard

**AbstractGeometricObject** header

```
1 #ifndef DERIVEDCIRCLE2_H
2 #define DERIVEDCIRCLE2_H
3 #include "AbstractGeometricObject.h"
4
5 // Same as lines 5-21 in DerivedCircle.h in Listing 11.3
```

### LISTING 11.15 DerivedCircle2.cpp

inclusion guard

**AbstractGeometricObject** header

```
1 #include "DerivedCircle2.h"
2
3 // Same as lines 3-43 in DerivedCircle.cpp in Listing 11.4
```

### LISTING 11.16 Rectangle2.h

inclusion guard

**AbstractGeometricObject** header

```
1 #ifndef RECTANGLE2_H
2 #define RECTANGLE2_H
3 #include "AbstractGeometricObject.h"
4
5 // Same as lines 5-23 in Rectangle.h in Listing 11.5
```

## LISTING 11.17  Rectangle2.cpp

```
1 #include "Rectangle2.h"                                          inclusion guard
2
3 // Same as lines 3-51 in Rectangle.cpp in Listing 11.6          AbstractGeometricObject
                                                                   header
```

You may be wondering whether the abstract functions **getArea** and **getPerimeter** should be removed from the **GeometricObject** class. The following example shows the benefits of retaining them in the **GeometricObject** class.

This example in Listing 11.18 presents a program that creates two geometric objects (a circle and a rectangle), invokes the **equalArea** function to check whether the two objects have equal areas, and invokes the **displayGeometricObject** function to display the objects.

## LISTING 11.18  TestGeometricObject2.cpp

```
1 #include "AbstractGeometricObject.h"                        include header file
2 #include "DerivedCircle2.h"
3 #include "Rectangle2.h"
4 #include <iostream>
5 using namespace std;
6
7 // A function for comparing the areas of two geometric objects
8 bool equalArea(GeometricObject &object1,
9   GeometricObject &object2)
10 {
11   return object1.getArea() == object2.getArea();             dynamic binding
12 }
13
14 // A function for displaying a geometric object
15 void displayGeometricObject(GeometricObject &object)
16 {
17   cout << "The area is " << object.getArea() << endl;        dynamic binding
18   cout << "The perimeter is " << object.getPerimeter() << endl;  dynamic binding
19 }
20
21 int main()
22 {
23   Circle circle(5);
24   Rectangle rectangle(5, 3);
25
26   cout << "Circle info: " << endl;
27   displayGeometricObject(circle);
28
29   cout << "\nRectangle info: " << endl;
30   displayGeometricObject(rectangle);
31
32   cout << "\nThe two objects have the same area? " <<
33     (equalArea(circle, rectangle) ? "Yes" : "No") << endl;
34
35   return 0;
36 }
```

```
Circle info:
The area is 78.5397
The perimeter is 31.4159
```

```
Rectangle info:
The area is 15
The perimeter is 16

The two objects have the same area? No
```

The program creates a **Circle** object and a **Rectangle** object in lines 23–24.

The pure virtual functions **getArea()** and **getPerimeter()** defined in the **Geometric-Object** class are overridden in the **Circle** class and the **Rectangle** class.

When invoking **displayGeometricObject(circle1)** (line 27), the functions **getArea** and **getPerimeter** defined in the **Circle** class are used, and when invoking **display-GeometricObject(rectangle)** (line 29), the functions **getArea** and **getPerimeter** defined in the **Rectangle** class are used. C++ dynamically determines which of these functions to invoke at runtime, depending on the type of object.

Similarly, when invoking **equalArea(object1, object2)** (line 33), the **getArea** function defined in the **Circle** class is used for **object1.getArea()**, since **object1** is a circle. Also, the **getArea** function defined in the **Rectangle** class is used for **object2.getArea()**, since **object2** is a rectangle.

Note that if the **getArea** and **getPerimeter** functions were not defined in **Geometric-Object**, you cannot define the **equalArea** and **displayObject** functions in this program. So, you now see the benefits of defining the abstract functions in **GeometricObject**.

## 11.9 Dynamic Casting

**dynamic_cast** operator The header for the **displayGeometricObject** function in Listing 11.18 is

```
void displayGeometricObject(GeometricObject &object)
```

Suppose you wish to modify this function to display radius, diameter, area, and perimeter if the object is a circle. How can this be done?

You can use the **dynamic_cast** operator to cast a parameter of the **GeometricObject** type into a **Circle** type, and then invoke the **getRadius()** and **getDiameter()** functions defined in the **Circle** class, as shown in the following code:

create a pointer

```
1 GeometricObject *p = &object;
2 Circle *p1 = dynamic_cast<Circle*>(p);
3
4 if (p1 != NULL) // NULL is a C++ constant same as 0
5 {
6   cout << "The radius is " << p1->getRadius() << endl;
7   cout << "The diameter is " << p1->getDiameter() << endl;
8 }
```

Line 1 creates a pointer for the **object** parameter. The **dynamic_cast** operator (line 2) checks whether pointer **p** points to a **Circle** object. If so, the object's address is assigned to **p1**, otherwise **p1** is NULL. If **p1** is not NULL, the **getRadius()** and **getDiameter()** functions of the **Circle** object (pointed by **p1**) are invoked in lines 6–7.

**Note**

**NULL** NULL is a C++ constant for **0**, which indicates that a pointer does not point to any object. The definition of **NULL** is in a number of standard libraries including **<iostream>** and **<cstddef>**.

**Note**

upcasting Assigning a pointer of a derived class type to a pointer of its base class type is called *upcasting* and assigning a pointer of a base class type to a pointer of its derived class type is called

*downcasting*. Upcasting can be performed implicitly without using the **dynamic_cast** operator. For example, the following code is correct:

```cpp
GeometricObject *p = new Circle(1);
Circle *p1 = new Circle(2);
p = p1;
```

downcasting

However, downcasting must be performed explicitly. For example, to assign **p** to **p1**, you
have to use

```cpp
p1 = dynamic_cast<Circle>(p);
```

Listing 11.19 gives a complete program that modifies the **displayGeometricObject**
function to display information for **Circle** and **Rectangle** objects.

## LISTING 11.19  DynamicCastingDemo.cpp

```cpp
 1 #include "AbstractGeometricObject.h"
 2 #include "DerivedCircle2.h"
 3 #include "Rectangle2.h"
 4 #include <iostream>
 5 using namespace std;
 6
 7 // A function for displaying a geometric object
 8 void displayGeometricObject(GeometricObject &object)
 9 {
10   cout << "The area is " << object.getArea() << endl;
11   cout << "The perimeter is " << object.getPerimeter() << endl;
12
13   GeometricObject *p = &object;
14   Circle *p1 = dynamic_cast<Circle*>(p);
15   Rectangle *p2 = dynamic_cast<Rectangle*>(p);
16
17   if (p1 != NULL)
18   {
19     cout << "The radius is " << p1->getRadius() << endl;
20     cout << "The diameter is " << p1->getDiameter() << endl;
21   }
22
23   if (p2 != NULL)
24   {
25     cout << "The width is " << p2->getWidth() << endl;
26     cout << "The height is " << p2->getHeight() << endl;
27   }
28 }
29
30 int main()
31 {
32   Circle circle(5);
33   Rectangle rectangle(5, 3);
34
35   cout << "Circle info: " << endl;
36   displayGeometricObject(circle);
37
38   cout << "\nRectangle info: " << endl;
39   displayGeometricObject(rectangle);
40
41   return 0;
42 }
```

include header file

casting to **Circle**
casting to **Rectangle**

```
Circle info:
The area is 78.5397
The perimeter is 31.4159
The radius is 5
The diameter is 10

Rectangle info:
The area is 15
The perimeter is 16
The width is 5
The height is 3
```

The program invokes the `displayGeometricObject` function to display a `Circle` object in line 36 and a `Rectangle` object in line 39. The function casts the `object` parameter into a `Circle` pointer `p1` in line 14 and a `Rectangle` pointer `p2` in line 15. If it is a `Circle` object, the object's `getRadius()` and `getDiameter()` functions are invoked in lines 19–20. If it is a `Rectangle` object, the object's `getWidth()` and `getHeight()` functions are invoked in lines 25–26.

The function also invokes `GeometricObject`'s `getArea()` and `getPerimeter()` functions in lines 10–11. Since these two functions are defined in the `GeometricObject` class, there is no need to downcast the object parameter to `Circle` or `Rectangle` in order to invoke these two functions.

### Tip

`typeid` operator

Occasionally, it is useful to obtain the information about the class of the object. You can use the `typeid` operator to return a reference to an object of class `type_info`. For example, you can use the following statement to display the class name for object `x`.

```
string x;
cout << typeid(x).name()  << endl;
```

It displays string, because `x` is an object of the `string` class.

## KEY TERMS

abstract class    358
abstract function    358
base class    344
constructor chaining    351
derived class    344
destructor chaining    351
downcasting    363
dynamic binding    356
generic programming    350

inheritance    344
is-a relationship    350
override    356
polymorphism    356
protected    357
pure virtual function    359
redefine    356
upcasting    363
virtual function    356

## CHAPTER SUMMARY

■   You can derive a new class from an existing class. This is known as *class inheritance*. The new class is called a *derived class, child class,* or *extended class.* The existing class is called a *base class* or *parent class.*

- An object of a derived class can be used wherever an object of a based type is required. This enables a function to be used generically for a wide range of object arguments. This is known as *generic programming*.

- A constructor is used to construct an instance of a class. Unlike data fields and functions, the constructors of a base class are not inherited in the derived class. They can only be invoked from the constructors of the derived classes to initialize the data fields in the base class.

- A child class constructor always invokes its base class' constructor. If a base constructor is not invoked explicitly, the base class' no-arg constructor is invoked by default.

- Constructing an instance of a class invokes the constructors of all the base classes along the inheritance chain. A base class' constructor is called before the derived class' constructor. Conversely, the destructors automatically are invoked in reverse order, with the derived class' destructor invoked first. This is called *constructor and destructor chaining*.

- A function defined in the base class may be redefined in the derived class. A redefined function must match the signature and return type of the function in the base class.

- A virtual function enables dynamic binding. A virtual function often is redefined in the derived classes. The compiler decides which function implementation to use dynamically at runtime.

- If a function defined in a base class needs to be redefined in its derived classes, you should declare it virtual to avoid confusions and mistakes. On the other hand, if a function will not be redefined, it is more efficient without declaring it virtual, because it takes more time and system resource to bind virtual functions dynamically at runtime.

- A protected data field or a protected function in a base class can be accessed by name in its derived classes.

- A pure virtual function also is called an abstract function. If a class contains a pure virtual function, the class is called an abstract class. You cannot create instances from an abstract class, but abstract classes can be used as data types for parameters in a function to enable generic programming.

- You can use the `dynamic_cast` operator to cast an object of a base class type to a pointer of a derived class type in order to invoke the functions defined in the derived classes.

## REVIEW QUESTIONS

### Sections 11.2–11.5

11.1     What is the printout from running the program in (a)? What problem arises in compiling the program in (b)?

```
#include <iostream>
using namespace std;

class A
{
public:
  A()
  {
    cout <<
      "A's no-arg constructor is invoked";
  }
};

class B: public A
{
};

int main()
{
  B b;

  return 0;
}
```

(a)

```
#include <iostream>
using namespace std;

class A
{
public:
  A(int x)
  {
  }
};

class B: public A
{
};

int main()
{
  B b;

  return 0;
}
```

(b)

**11.2** True or false? (1) A derived class is a subset of a base class. (2) When invoking a constructor from a derived class, its base class's no-arg constructor is always invoked. (3) You can override a private function defined in a base class. (4) You can override a static function defined in a base class. (5) Can you override a constructor.

**11.3** Identify the problems in the following classes.

```
 1 class Circle
 2 {
 3 public:
 4   Circle(double radius)
 5   {
 6     radius = radius;
 7   }
 8
 9   double getRadius()
10   {
11     return radius;
12   }
13
14   double getArea()
15   {
16     return radius * radius * 3.14159;
17   }
18
19 private:
20   double radius;
21 };
22
23 class B : Circle
24 {
25 public:
26   B(double radius, double length): Circle(radius)
27   {
28     length = length;
29   }
30
```

```
31   // Returns Circle's getArea * length
32   double getArea()
33   {
34     return getArea() * length;
35   }
36
37 private:
38   double length;
39 };
```

**11.4**  Explain the difference between function overloading and function overriding.

**11.5**  Show the output of the following code:

```cpp
#include <iostream>
using namespace std;

class A
{
public:
  A()
  {
    cout << "A's no-arg constructor is invoked" << endl;
  }

  ~A()
  {
    cout << "A's destructor is invoked" << endl;
  }
};


class B: public A
{
public:
  B()
  {
    cout << "B's no-arg constructor is invoked" << endl;
  }

  ~B()
  {
    cout << "B's destructor is invoked" << endl;
  }
};

int main()
{
  B b1;
  B b2;

  return 0;
}
```

## Section 11.6 Polymorphism and Virtual Functions

**11.6**  Show the output of the following code.

```cpp
#include <iostream>
using namespace std;
```

```cpp
class A
{
public:
  void f()
  {
    cout << "invoke f from A" << endl;
  }
};

class B: public A
{
public:
  void f()
  {
    cout << "invoke f from B" << endl;
  }
};

void p(A a)
{
  a.f();
}

int main()
{
  A a;
  a.f();
  p(a);

  B b;
  b.f();
  p(b);

  return 0;
}
```

11.7 Show the output of the following code:

```cpp
#include <iostream>
using namespace std;

class A
{
public:
  virtual void f()
  {
    cout << "invoke f from A" << endl;
  }
};

class B: public A
{
public:
  void f()
  {
    cout << "invoke f from B" << endl;
  }
};

void p(A a)
{
```

```
    a.f();
}

int main()
{
  A a;
  a.f();
  p(a);

  B b;
  b.f();
  p(b);

  return 0;
}
```

If you replace p(A a) by p(A &a), what will be the output?

**11.8**  Is declaring virtual functions enough to enable dynamic binding?

**11.9**  Is it a good practice to declare all functions virtual?

## Section 11.7 The **protected** Keyword

**11.10**  If a member is declared private in a class, can it be accessed from other classes? If a member is declared protected in a class, can it be accessed from other classes? If a member is declared public in a class, can it be accessed from other classes?

## Section 11.8 Abstract Classes and Pure Virtual Functions

**11.11**  How do you declare a pure virtual function?

**11.12**  What is wrong in the following code?

```
class A
{
public:
  virtual void f() = 0;
};

int main()
{
  A a;

  return 0;
}
```

**11.13**  Can you compile and run the following code? What will be the output?

```
#include <iostream>
using namespace std;

class A
{
public:
  virtual void f() = 0;
};

class B: public A
{
public:
  void f()
  {
    cout << "invoke f from B" << endl;
  }
};
```

```
class C: public B
{
public:
  virtual void m() = 0;
};

class D: public C
{
public:
  virtual void m()
  {
    cout << "invoke m from D" << endl;
  }
};

void p(A &a)
{
  a.f();
}

int main()
{
  D d;
  p(d);
  d.m();

  return 0;
}
```

11.14 The **getArea** and **getPerimeter** methods may be removed from the **Geometric-Object** class. What are the benefits of defining **getArea** and **getPerimeter** as abstract methods in the **GeometricObject** class?

11.15 What is upcasting? What is downcasting?

11.16 When do you need to downcast an object from a base class type to a derived class type?

11.17 What will be the value in **p1** after the following statements?

```
GeometricObject *p = new Rectangle(2, 3);
Circle *p1 = new Circle(2);
p1 = dynamic_cast<Circle>(p);
```

## PROGRAMMING EXERCISES

11.1 (*The Triangle class*) Design a class named **Triangle** that extends **Geometric-Object**. The class contains:

- Three **double** data fields named **side1**, **side2**, and **side3** with default values **1.0** to denote three sides of the triangle.
- A no-arg constructor that creates a default triangle.
- A constructor that creates a rectangle with the specified **side1**, **side2**, and **side3**.
- The accessor functions for all three data fields.
- A function named **getArea()** that returns the area of this triangle.
- A function named **getPerimeter()** that returns the perimeter of this triangle.

Draw the UML diagram that involving the classes **Triangle** and **Geometric-Object**. Implement the class. Write a test program that creates a **Triangle** object with sides **1**, **1.5**, **1**, setting color **yellow** and filled **true**, and displaying the area, perimeter, color, and whether filled or not.

**11.2** (*The Person, Student, Employee, Faculty, and Staff classes*) Design a class named **Person** and its two derived classes named **Student** and **Employee**. Make **Faculty** and **Staff** derived classes of **Employee**. A person has a name, address, phone number, and e-mail address. A student has a class status (freshman, sophomore, junior, or senior). Define the status as a constant. An employee has an office, salary, and date hired. Define a class named **MyDate** that contains the fields **year**, **month**, and **day**. A faculty member has office hours and a rank. A staff member has a title. Override the **toString** function in each class to display the class name and the person's name.

Draw the UML diagram for the classes. Implement the classes. Write a test program that creates a **Person**, **Student**, **Employee**, **Faculty**, and **Staff**, and invokes their **toString()** functions.

**11.3** (*Extending MyPoint*) In Exercise 9.6, the **MyPoint** class was created to model a point in a two-dimensional space. The **MyPoint** class has the properties **x** and **y** that represent **x**- and **y**-coordinates, two get functions for **x** and **y**, and the function for returning the distance between two points. Create a class named **3DPoint** to model a point in a three-dimensional space. Let **3DPoint** be derived from **MyPoint** with the following additional features:

- A data field named **z** that represents the **z**-coordinate.
- A no-arg constructor that constructs a point with coordinates (**0**, **0**, **0**).
- A constructor that constructs a point with three specified coordinates.
- A get function that returns the **z** value.
- Override the **distance** function to return the distance between two points in the three-dimensional space.

Draw the UML diagram for the classes involved. Implement the classes. Write a test program that creates two points (**0**, **0**, **0**) and (**10**, **30**, **25.5**) and display the distance between the two points.

**11.4** (*Derived classes of Account*) In Exercise 9.3, the **Account** class was created to model a bank account. An account has the properties account number, balance, and annual interest rate, date created, and functions to deposit and withdraw. Create two derived classes for checking and saving accounts. A checking account has an overdraft limit, but a savings account cannot be overdrawn.

Draw the UML diagram for the classes. Implement the classes. Write a test program that creates objects of **Account**, **SavingsAccount**, and **Checking-Account**, invokes their **toString()** functions.

## CHAPTER 12

# FILE INPUT AND OUTPUT

## Objectives

- To use `ofstream` for output (§12.2.1) and `ifstream` for input (§12.2.2).

- To test whether a file exists (§12.2.3).

- To test the end of a file (§12.2.4).

- To write data in a desired format (§12.3).

- To read and write data using the `getline`, `get`, and `put` functions (§12.4).

- To use an `fstream` object to read and write data (§12.5).

- To open a file with specified modes (§12.5).

- To use the `eof()`, `fail()`, `bad()`, and `good()` functions to test stream states (§12.6).

- To understand the difference between text I/O and binary I/O (§12.7).

- To write binary data using the `write` function (§12.7.1).

- To read binary data using the `read` function (§12.7.2).

- To cast primitive type values and objects to character arrays using the `reinterpret_cast` operator (§12.7).

- To read/write arrays and objects (§§12.7.3–12.7.4).

- To use the `seekp` and `seekg` functions to move the file pointers for random file access (§12.8).

- To open a file for both input and output to update files (§12.9).

## 12.1 Introduction

Data stored in variables, arrays, and objects are temporary; they are lost when the program terminates. To permanently store the data created in a program, you need to save them in a file on a disk or a CD. The file can be transported and can be read later by other programs. §4.10, "Simple File Input and Output," introduced simple text I/O involving numeric values. This chapter introduces I/O in detail.

C++ defines the **ifstream**, **ofstream**, and **fstream** for processing and manipulating files. These classes are all defined in the **<fstream>** header file. The **ifstream** class is for reading data from a file, the **ofstream** class is for writing data to a file, and the **fstream** class can be used for updating data in a file.

## 12.2 Text I/O

This section demonstrates how to perform simple text input and output. Let us first consider output.

### 12.2.1 Writing Data to a File

The **ofstream** class can be used to write primitive data type values, arrays, strings, and objects to a text file. Listing 12.1 demonstrates how to write data. The program creates an instance of **ofstream** and writes two lines to the file "scores.txt". Each line consists of first name (a string), middle name initial (a character), last name (a string), and score (an integer).

**LISTING 12.1** TextFileOutput.cpp

include **fstream** header

declare object

open file

output to file

close file

```
 1  #include <iostream>
 2  #include <fstream>
 3  using namespace std;
 4
 5  int main()
 6  {
 7    ofstream output;
 8
 9    // Create a file
10    output.open("scores.txt");
11
12    // Write two lines
13    output << "John" << " " << "T" << " " << "Smith"
14      << " " << 90 << endl;
15    output << "Eric" << " " << "K" << " " << "Jones"
16      << " " << 85;
17
18    output.close();
19
20    cout << "Done" << endl;
21
22    return 0;
23  }
```

scores.txt

```
John T Smith 90

Eric K Jones 85
```

including **<fstream>** header
create object
open file

cout

close file

Since the **ofstream** class is defined in the **fstream** header file, line 2 includes this header file.

Line 7 creates an object, **output**, from the **ofstream** class using its no-arg constructor.

Line 10 opens a file named scores.txt for the **output** object. If the file does not exist, a new file is created. If the file already exists, its contents are destroyed without warning.

You can write data to the **output** object using the stream insertion operator (<<) in the same way that you send data to the **cout** object. The **cout** object is a predefined object for output to the console. Lines 13–16 write strings and numeric values to **output**, as shown in Figure 12.1.

The **close()** function (line 18) must be used to close the stream for the object. If this function is not invoked, the data may not be saved properly in the file.

```
output << "John" << " " << "T" << "Smith" << " " << 90 << endl;
```

scores.txt
file

John T Smith 90
Eric K Jones 85

```
output << "Eric" << " " << "K" << "Jones" << " " << 85 << endl;
```

**FIGURE 12.1**    The output stream sends data to the file.

### Caution
If a file already exists, the contents of the file will be destroyed without warning.

file exists?

### Note
Every file is placed in a directory in the file system. An *absolute file* name contains a file name with its complete path and drive letter. For example, **c:\example\scores.txt** is the absolute file name for the file **scores.txt** on the Windows operating system. Here **c:\example** is referred to as the *directory path* for the file. Absolute file names are machine-dependent. On UNIX, the absolute file name may be **/home/liang/example/scores.txt**, where **/home/liang/example** is the directory path for the file **scores.txt**.

absolute file name

### Caution
The directory separator for Windows is a backslash (\\). The backslash is a special character in C++ and should be written as \\\\ in a string literal (see Table 2.5). For example,

\\ in file names

```
output.open("c:\\example\\scores.txt");
```

### Note
An absolute file name is platform dependent. It is better to use a *relative file name* without drive letters. The directory of the relative filename can be specified in the IDE if you use an IDE to run C++. For example, the default directory for data files is the same directory with the source code in Visual C++.

relative filename

## 12.2.2    Reading Data from a File

The **ifstream** class can be used to read data from a text file. Listing 12.2 demonstrates how to read data. The program creates an instance of **ifstream** and reads data from the file scores.txt. scores.txt was created in the preceding example.

### LISTING 12.2    TextFileInput.cpp

```
1 #include <iostream>
2 #include <fstream>
3 using namespace std;
4
5 int main()
6 {
7   ifstream input;
8
9   // Open a file
10  input.open("scores.txt");
11
12  // Read data
13  char firstName[80];
14  char mi;
```

include **fstream** header

declare object

open file

```
15   char lastName[80];
16   int score;
```
input from file

```
17   input >> firstName >> mi >> lastName >> score;
18   cout << firstName << " " << mi << " " << lastName << " "
19     << score << endl;
20
```
input from file

```
21   input >> firstName >> mi >> lastName >> score;
22   cout << firstName << " " << mi << " " << lastName << " "
23     << score << endl;
24
```
close file

```
25   input.close();
26
27   cout << "Done" << endl;
28
29   return 0;
30 }
```

```
John T Smith 90
Eric K Jones 85
Done
```

including **<fstream>** header

Since the **ifstream** class is defined in the **fstream** header file, line 2 includes this header file.

create object

Line 7 creates an object, **input**, from the **ifstream** class using its no-arg constructor.

open file

Line 10 opens a file named scores.txt for the **input** object.

**cin**

You can read data from the **input** object using the stream extraction operator (>>) in the same way that you read data from the **cin** object. The **cin** object is a predefined object for input from the console. Lines 17 and 21 read strings and numeric values from the input file, as shown in Figure 12.2.

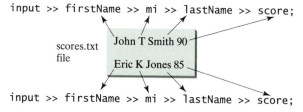

**FIGURE 12.2** The input stream reads data from the file.

close file

The **close()** function (line 25) must be used to close the stream for the object. It is not necessary to close the input file, but it is a good practice to do so to release the resources occupied by the file.

 **Note**

input stream

output stream

An input object reads a stream of data. For convenience, an input object is also called an *input stream*. For the same reason, an output object is called an *output stream*.

### 12.2.3  Testing File Existence

file not exist?

If the file does not exist, your program will run and produce incorrect results. Can your program check whether a file exists? Yes. You can invoke the **fail()** function immediately after invoking the **open** function. If **fail()** returns **true**, it would indicate that the file does not exist.

```
1 // Open a file
2 input.open("scores.txt");
3
4 if (input.fail())
5 {
6   cout << "File does not exist" << endl;
7   cout << "Exit program" << endl;
8
9   return 0;
10 }
```

check file operation

### 12.2.4  Testing End of File

Listing 12.2 reads two lines from the data file. If you don't know how many lines are in the file and want to read them all, how do you know the end of file? You can invoke the **eof()** function on the input object to detect it. Listing 12.3 revises Listing 12.2 to read all lines from the file scores.txt.

**eof** function

### LISTING 12.3  TestEndOfFile.cpp

```
1 #include <iostream>
2 #include <fstream>
3 using namespace std;
4
5 int main()
6 {
7   ifstream input;
8
9   // Open a file
10   input.open("scores.txt");
11
12   if (input.fail())
13   {
14     cout << "File does not exist" << endl;
15     cout << "Exit program" << endl;
16     return 0;
17   }
18
19   // Read data
20   char firstName[80];
21   char mi;
22   char lastName[80];
23   int score;
24
25   while (!input.eof()) // Continue if not end of file
26   {
27     input >> firstName >> mi >> lastName >> score;
28     cout << firstName << " " << mi << " " << lastName
29       << " " << score << endl;
30   }
31
32   input.close();
33
34   cout << "Done" << endl;
35
36   return 0;
37 }
```

include **fstream** header

declare object

open file

file exist?

end of file?

input from file
display data

close file

```
John T Smith 90
Eric K Jones 85
Done
```

The program reads data in a loop (lines 25–30). Each iteration of the loop reads one student record that consists of first name, middle name initial, last name, and score. The loop terminates when the input reaches the end of file.

end of file?

How does the program know the end of file? When there is nothing more to read, **eof()** returns **true**. How does the program know there is nothing to read? This information is obtained from the operating system. When the program reads the last item 85 in the last line of the file, it attempts to read beyond 5, as shown in following diagram.

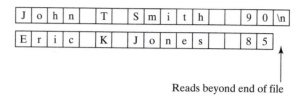

Reads beyond end of file

The operating system notifies the program that the end of file is reached. When you invoke **eof()** now, it returns **true**.

**Caution**

Ctrl+Z or Ctrl+D

If the data is read from the console, you can use Ctrl+Z on Windows or Ctrl+D on UNIX to signify the end of file.

**Caution**

know data format

To read data correctly, you need to know exactly how data is stored. For example, the program in Listing 12.3 would not work if the score is a **double** value with a decimal point.

## 12.3 Formatting Output

You have used the stream manipulators to format output to the console in §3.12, "Formatting Output." You can use the same stream manipulator to format output to a file. Listing 12.4 gives an example that formats the student records to the file named formattedscores.txt.

**LISTING 12.4 WriteFormatData.cpp**

include **iomanip** header
include **fstream** header

declare object

output with format

output with format

close file

```cpp
 1 #include <iostream>
 2 #include <iomanip>
 3 #include <fstream>
 4 using namespace std;
 5
 6 int main()
 7 {
 8   ofstream output;
 9
10   // Create a file
11   output.open("formattedscores.txt");
12
13   // Write two lines
14   output << setw(6) << "John" << setw(2) << "T" << setw(6) << "Smith"
15     << " " << setw(4) << 90 << endl;
16   output << setw(6) << "Eric" << setw(2) << "K" << setw(6) << "Jones"
17     << " " << setw(4) << 85;
18
19   output.close();
20
```

```
21   cout << "Done" << endl;
22
23   return 0;
24 }
```

The contents in the file are shown below:

```
|   |   | J | o | h | n |   | T |   | S | m | i | t | h |   |   | 9 | 0 | \n |
|   |   | E | r | i | c |   | K |   | J | o | n | e | s |   |   | 8 | 5 |
```

# 12.4 Member Functions: **getline**, **get**, and **put**

There is a problem to read data using the stream extraction operator (>>). Data are delimited by whitespace. What happens if the whitespace characters are part of a string? In §7.9.3, "Reading Strings," you learned how to use the **getline** function to read a string with white-space. You can use the same function to read strings from a file. Recall that the syntax for the **getline** function is

```
getline(char array[], int size, char delimitChar)
```
**getline**

The function stops reading characters when the delimiter character or end-of-file is encountered, or when the **size - 1** number of characters are read. The last character in the array is reserved for the null terminator ('\0'). If the delimiter is encountered, it is read, but not stored in the array. The third argument **delimitChar** has a default value ('\n').

Suppose a file named state.txt is created that contains the state names delimited by the pound (#) symbol. The following diagram shows the contents in the file:

```
| N | e | w |   | Y | o | r | k | # | N | e | w |   | M | e | x | i | c | o |
| # | T | e | x | a | s | # | I | n | d | i | a | n | a |
```

Listing 12.5 shows the program that reads the states from the file.

## LISTING 12.5   ReadCity.cpp

```
1 #include <iostream>
2 #include <fstream>                           include fstream header
3 using namespace std;
4
5 int main()
6 {
7    ifstream input;                           input object
8
9    // Open a file
10   input.open("state.txt");                  open file
11
12   if (input.fail())                         file exist?
13   {
14      cout << "File does not exist" << endl;
15      cout << "Exit program" << endl;
16      return 0;
17   }
18
19   // Read data
20   char city[40];                            string city
21
```

end of file?

input from file
display data

close file

```
22   while (!input.eof()) // Continue if not end of file
23   {
24     input.getline(city, 40, '#');
25     cout << city << endl;
26   }
27
28   input.close();
29
30   cout << "Done" << endl;
31
32   return 0;
33 }
```

```
New York
New Mexico
Texas
Indiana
Done
```

Invoking `getline(state, 40, '#')` (line 24) reads characters to the array `state` until it encounters the # character or the end-of-file is encountered or when the **39** characters are read.

Two other useful functions are `get` and `put`. You can invoke the `get` function on an input object to read a character and invoke the `put` function on an output object to write a character.

The `get` function has three versions:

```
char get() // Returns a char
istream * get(char &ch) // Read a character to ch
char get(char array[], int size, char delimitChar) // Read into array
```

The first version returns a character from the input. The second version passes a character reference argument, reads a character from the input, and stores it in `ch`. This function also returns the reference to the input object being used. The third version is almost identical to the `getline` function, except that it does not insert the null terminator character (`'\0'`) in the character array. Note that `istream` is a base class for `ifstream`.

The header for the `put` function is

```
void put(char ch)
```

It writes the specified character to the output object.

Listing 12.6 gives an example of using these two functions. The program prompts the user to enter a file and copies it to a new file.

## LISTING 12.6 CopyFile.cpp

include **fstream** header

enter input filename

```
1  #include <iostream>
2  #include <fstream>
3  using namespace std;
4
5  int main()
6  {
7    const int FILENAME_SIZE = 40;
8
9    // Enter a source file
10   cout << "Enter a source file name: ";
11   char inputFilename[FILENAME_SIZE];
12   cin >> inputFilename;
13
14   // Enter a target file
15   cout << "Enter a target file name: ";
```

```
16    char outputFilename[FILENAME_SIZE];
17    cin >> outputFilename;
18
19    ifstream input;
20    ofstream output;
21
22    // Open a file
23    input.open(inputFilename);
24    output.open(outputFilename);
25
26    if (input.fail())
27    {
28      cout << inputFilename << " does not exist" << endl;
29      cout << "Exit program" << endl;
30      return 0;
31    }
32
33    while (!input.eof()) // Continue if not end of file
34    {
35      output.put(input.get());
36    }
37
38    input.close();
39    output.close();
40
41    cout << "\nCopy Done" << endl;
42
43    return 0;
44  }
```

enter output filename

input object
output object

open input file
open output file

file exist?

end of file?

**get** function
**put** function

close file
close file

```
Enter a source file name: c:\example\CopyFile.cpp ↵Enter
Enter a target file name: c:\example\temp.txt ↵Enter
Copy Done
```

The program prompts the user to enter a source filename in line 12 and enter a target filename in line 17. A file input object is created in line 19 and a file output object is created in line 20. Files are associated with input objects and output objects in lines 23–24.

Lines 26–31 check whether the input file exists. Lines 33–36 read characters repeatedly one at a time using the **get** function and write the character to the output file using the **put** function.

There is a problem in this program. If you check the size of the two files, you will find that the new file is one byte larger than the original file. The new file contains an extra garbage character at the end. The reason is that when the last character is read from the input file using `input.get()`, `input.eof()` is still **false**. Afterwards, the program attempts to read another character, `input.eof()` now becomes **true**. However, the extraneous garbage character is already sent to the output file.

To fix this problem, replace the `while` loop (lines 33–36) with the following code:

```
char ch = input.get();
while (!input.eof()) // Continue if not end of file
{
  output.put(ch);
  ch = input.get(); // Check eof before copying this character
}
```

The revised code reads a character and checks `eof()`. If `eof()` is **true**, the character is not put to **output**; otherwise, the character is copied. This process continues until `eof()` returns **true**.

## 12.5 `fstream` and File Open Modes

In the preceding sections, you used the `ofstream` to write data and the `ifstream` to read data. Alternatively, you can also use the `fstream` class to create an input stream or output stream. It is convenient to use `fstream` if your program needs to use the same stream object for both input and output. To open an `fstream` file, you have to specify a file mode to tell C++ how the file will be used. The file modes are listed in Table 12.1.

**TABLE 12.1** File Modes

| Mode | Description |
|------|-------------|
| `ios::in` | Opens a file for input. |
| `ios::out` | Opens a file for output. |
| `ios::app` | Appends all output to the end of the file. |
| `ios::ate` | Opens a file for output. If the file already exists, move to the end of the file. Data can be written anywhere in the file. |
| `ios::truct` | Discards the file's contents if the file already exists. (This is the default action for `ios:out`.) |
| `ios::binary` | Opens a file for binary input and output. |

**Note**

Some of the file modes also can be used with `ifstream` and `ofstream` objects to open a file. For example, you may use the `ios:app` mode to open a file with an `ofstream` object so you can append data to the file. However, for consistency and simplicity, it is better to use the file modes with the `fstream` objects.

**Note**

combining modes

Several modes can be combined together using the | operator. This is a bitwise inclusive OR operator. See Appendix D, "Bit Operations," for more details. For example, to open an output file named city.txt for appending data, you can use the following statement:

```
stream.open("city.txt", ios::out | ios::app);
```

Listing 12.7 gives a program that creates a new file named city.txt (line 10) and writes data to the file. The program then closes the file and reopens it to append new data (line 18), rather than overrides it. Finally, the program reads all data from the file.

### LISTING 12.7 AppendFile.cpp

```
 1  #include <iostream>
 2  #include <fstream>
 3  using namespace std;
 4
 5  int main()
 6  {
 7    fstream inout;
 8
 9    // Create a file
10    inout.open("city.txt", ios::out);
11
12    // Write cities
13    inout << "Dallas" << " " << "Houston" << " " << "Atlanta" << " ";
14
15    inout.close();
```

include **fstream** header

**fstream** object

open output file

write data

close stream

```
16
17    // Append to the file
18    inout.open("city.txt", ios::out | ios::app );          open output for append
19
20    // Write cities
21    inout << "Savannah" << " " << "Austin" << " " << "Chicago";    write data
22
23    inout.close();                                          close stream
24
25    char city[20];
26
27    // Open the file
28    inout.open("city.txt", ios::in );                       open for input
29    while (!inout.eof()) // Continue if not end of file     end of file?
30    {
31      inout >> city;                                        read data
32      cout << city << " ";
33    }
34
35    inout.close();                                          close stream
36
37    return 0;
38 }
```

```
Dallas Houston Atlanta Savannah Austin Chicago
```

The program creates a `fstream` object in line 7 and opens the file city.txt for output using the file mode `ios::out` in line 10. After writing data in line 13, the program closes the stream in line 15.

The program uses the same stream object to reopen the text file with the combined modes `ios::out | ios::app` in line 18. The program then appends new data to the end of the file in line 21 and closes the stream in line 23.

Finally the program uses the same stream object to reopen the text file with the input mode `ios::in` in line 28. The program then reads all data from the file (lines 29–33).

## 12.6 Testing Stream States

You have used the `eof()` function and `fail()` function to test the states of a stream. C++ provides several more functions in a stream for testing stream states. Each stream object contains a set of bits that act as flags. These bit values (0 or 1) indicate the state of a stream. Table 12.2 lists these bits.

**TABLE 12.2**   Stream State Bit Values

| Bit | Description |
|-----|-------------|
| ios::eofbit | Set when the end of an input stream is reached. |
| ios::failbit | Set when an operation failed. |
| ios::hardfail | Set when an unrecoverable error occurred. |
| ios::badbit | Set when an invalid operation has been attempted. |
| ios::goodbit | Set when an operation is successful. |

The states of the I/O operations are represented in these bits. It is not convenient to directly access these bits. C++ provides member functions in the IO stream object to test these bits. These functions are listed in Table 12.3.

**TABLE 12.3** Stream State Functions

| Function | Description |
|----------|-------------|
| eof() | Returns true if the eofbit flag is set. |
| fail() | Returns true if the failbit or hardfail flag is set. |
| bad() | Returns true if the badbit is set. |
| good() | Returns true if the goodbit is set. |
| clear() | Clears all flags. |

Listing 12.8 gives an example to detect the stream states.

**LISTING 12.8** ShowStreamState.cpp

```
 1 #include <iostream>
 2 #include <fstream>
 3 using namespace std;
 4
 5 void showState(fstream &);
 6
 7 int main()
 8 {
 9   fstream inout;
10
11   // Create an output file
12   inout.open("temp.txt", ios::out);
13   inout << "Dallas";
14   cout << "Normal operation (no errors)" << endl;
15   showState(inout);
16   inout.close();
17
18   // Create an output file
19   inout.open("temp.txt", ios::in);
20
21   // Read a string
22   char city[6];
23   inout >> city;
24   cout << "End of file (no errors)" << endl;
25   showState(inout);
26
27   inout.close();
28
29   // Attempt to read after file closed
30   inout >> city;
31   cout << "Bad operation (errors)" << endl;
32   showState(inout);
33
34   return 0;
35 }
36
37 void showState(fstream & stream)
38 {
39   cout << "Stream status: " << endl;
40   cout << "  eof(): " << stream.eof() << endl;
41   cout << "  fail(): " << stream.fail() << endl;
42   cout << "  bad(): " << stream.bad() << endl;
43   cout << "  good(): " << stream.good() << endl;
44 }
```

Margin notes:
- include **fstream** header (line 2)
- function prototype (line 5)
- input object (line 9)
- open input file (line 12)
- show state (line 15)
- close file (line 16)
- open output file (line 19)
- read city (line 23)
- show state (line 25)
- close file (line 27)
- show state (line 32)
- show state (line 37)

```
Normal operation (no errors)
Stream status:
  eof(): 0
  fail(): 0
  bad(): 0
  good(): 1
End of file (no errors)

Stream status:
  eof(): 1
  fail(): 0
  bad(): 0
  good(): 0

Bad operation (errors)
Stream status:
  eof(): 1
  fail(): 1
  bad(): 0
  good(): 0
```

The program creates a `fstream` object using its no-arg constructor in line 9, opens temp.txt for output in line 12, and writes a string Dallas in line 13. The state of the stream is displayed in line 15. There are no errors so far.

The program then closes the stream in line 16, reopens temp.txt for input in line 19, and reads a string Dallas in line 23. The state of the stream is displayed in line 25. There are no errors so far, but the end of the file is reached.

Finally, the program closes the stream in line 27 and attempts to read data after the file is closed in line 30, which causes an error. The state of the stream is displayed in line 32.

When invoking the `showState` function in lines 15, 25, and 32, the stream object is passed to the function by reference.

## 12.7 Binary I/O

So far you have used text files. Data stored in a *text file* are represented in human-readable form. Data stored in a *binary file* are represented in binary form. You cannot read binary files. They are designed to be read by programs. For example, the C++ source programs are stored in text files and can be read by a text editor, but the C++ executable files are stored in binary files and are read by the operating system. The advantage of binary files is that they are more efficient to process than text files.

Although it is not technically precise and correct, you can envision a text file as consisting of a sequence of characters and a binary file as consisting of a sequence of bits. For example, the decimal integer 199 is stored as the sequence of three characters, `'1'`, `'9'`, `'9'`, in a text file, and the same integer is stored as a `byte`-type value `C7` in a binary file, because decimal **199** equals hex `C7` ($199 = 12 \times 16^1 + 7$).

text file

binary file

### Note

Computers do not differentiate binary files and text files. All files are stored in binary format, and thus all files are essentially binary files. Text I/O is built upon binary I/O to provide a level of abstraction for character encoding and decoding.

text vs. binary I/O

ios::binary

Binary I/O does not require conversions. If you write a numeric value to a file using binary I/O, the exact value in the memory is copied into the file. To perform binary I/O in C++, you have to open a file using the binary mode **ios::binary**. By default, a file is opened in text mode.

You used the **<<** operator and **put** function to write data to a text file and the **>>** operator, **get**, and **getline** functions to read data from a text file. To read/write data from/to a binary file, you have to use the **read** and **write** functions on a stream.

### 12.7.1 The **write** Function

The syntax for the **write** function is

write function

```
streamObject.write(char * address, int size)
```

Listing 12.9 shows an example of using the **write** function.

### LISTING 12.9 BinaryCharOutput.cpp

```
 1 #include <iostream>
 2 #include <fstream>
 3 using namespace std;
 4
 5 int main()
 6 {
 7   fstream binaryio;
 8   binaryio.open("city.dat", ios::out | ios::binary);
 9   char s[] = "Atlanta";
10   binaryio.write(s, 5);
11   binaryio.close();
12
13   cout << "Done" << endl;
14
15   return 0;
16 }
```

fstream object
open binary file
character array
write data
close file

Line 8 opens the binary file city.dat for output. Invoking **binaryio.write(s, 5)** (line 10) writes five characters from the array to the file.

Often you need to write data other than characters. How can you accomplish it? C++ provides the **reinterpret_cast** for this purpose. You can use this operator to cast the address of a primitive type value or an object to a character array pointer for binary I/O. The syntax of this type of casting is:

```
reinterpret_cast<dataType>(address)
```

where **address** is the starting address of the data (primitive, array, or object) and **dataType** is the data type you are converting to. In this case for binary I/O, it is **char \***.

For example, see the following code in Listing 12.10.

### LISTING 12.10 BinaryIntOutput.cpp

```
 1 #include <iostream>
 2 #include <fstream>
 3 using namespace std;
 4
 5 int main()
 6 {
 7   fstream binaryio;
 8   binaryio.open("temp.dat", ios::out | ios::binary);
 9   int value = 199;
10   binaryio.write(reinterpret_cast<char *>(&value), sizeof(value));
11   binaryio.close();
```

fstream object
open binary file
**int** value
binary output
close file

```
12
13    cout << "Done" << endl;
14
15    return 0;
16 }
```

Line 10 writes the content in variable **value** to the file. **reinterpret_cast<char \*>-(&value)** (line 10) cast the address of the **int** value to the type **char \*. sizeof(value)** returns the storage size for the value variable, which is **4**, since it is an **int** type variable.

**Note**

For consistency, this book uses the extension **.txt** to name text files and **.dat** to name binary files.

**.txt** and **.dat**

## 12.7.2    The **read** Function

The syntax for the **read** function is

```
streamObject.read(char * address, int size)
```

**write** function

Assume the file city.dat was created in Listing 12.9. Listing 12.11 reads the characters using the **read** function.

### LISTING 12.11    BinaryCharInput.cpp

```
 1 #include <iostream>
 2 #include <fstream>
 3 using namespace std;
 4
 5 int main()
 6 {
 7    fstream binaryio;
 8    binaryio.open("city.dat", ios::in | ios::binary);
 9    char s[10];
10    binaryio.read(s, 5);
11    s[5] = '\0';
12    cout << s;
13    binaryio.close();
14
15    return 0;
16 }
```

**fstream** object
open binary file
character array
write data
close file

```
Atlan
```

Line 8 opens the binary file city.dat for input. Invoking **binaryio.read(s, 5)** (line 10) reads five characters from the file to the array.

Similarly, to read data other than characters, you need to use the **reinterpret_cast** operator. Assume that the file temp.dat was created in Listing 12.10. Listing 12.12 reads the integer using the **read** function.

### LISTING 12.12    BinaryIntInput.cpp

```
 1 #include <iostream>
 2 #include <fstream>
 3 using namespace std;
 4
 5 int main()
 6 {
```

```
 7   fstream binaryio;
 8   binaryio.open("temp.dat", ios::in | ios::binary);
 9   int value;
10   binaryio.read(reinterpret_cast<char *>(&value), sizeof(value));
11   cout << value;
12   binaryio.close();
13
14   return 0;
15 }
```

fstream object
open binary file
int value
binary output
close file

```
199
```

Line 10 reads an **int** from the file to the variable **value**.

### 12.7.3 Example: Binary Array I/O

This section gives an example in Listing 12.13 to write an array of **double** values to a binary file and read it back from the file.

**LISTING 12.13** BinaryArrayIO.cpp

```
 1 #include <iostream>
 2 #include <fstream>
 3 using namespace std;
 4
 5 int main()
 6 {
 7   const int SIZE = 5;  // Array size
 8
 9   fstream binaryio; // Create stream object
10
11   // Write array to the file
12   binaryio.open("array.dat", ios::out | ios::binary);
13   double array[SIZE] = {3.4, 1.3, 2.5, 5.66, 6.9};
14   binaryio.write(reinterpret_cast<char *>(&array), sizeof(array));
15   binaryio.close();
16
17   // Read array from the file
18   binaryio.open("array.dat", ios::in | ios::binary);
19   double result[SIZE];
20   binaryio.read(reinterpret_cast<char *>(&result), sizeof(result));
21   binaryio.close();
22
23   // Display array
24   for (int i = 0; i < SIZE; i++)
25     cout << result[i] << " ";
26
27   return 0;
28 }
```

constant array size
fstream object
open binary file
create array
write to file
close file
open input file
create array
read from file
close file

```
3.4 1.3 2.5 5.66 6.9
```

The program creates a stream object in line 9, opens the file array.dat for binary output in line 12, writes an array of **double** values to the file in line 14, and closes the file in line 15.

The program then opens the file array.dat for binary input in line 18, reads an array of **double** values from the file in line 20, and closes the file in line 21.

Finally, the program displays the contents in the array **result** (lines 24–25).

### 12.7.4 Example: Binary Object I/O

This section gives an example to write objects to a binary file and read the objects back from the file.

Listing 12.1 writes student records into a text file. A student record consists of first name, middle name initial, last name, and score. These fields are written to the file separately. A better way to process it is to declare a class to model records. Each record is an object of the Student class.

**Note**

You may define records using the **struct** keyword. However, it is better to use classes. In C++, **struct** is obsolete and replaced by the class.

**struct** obsolete

Let the class be named Student with the data fields firstName, mi, lastName, and score, their supporting accessors and mutators, and two constructors. The class UML diagram is shown in Figure 12.3.

| Student |
|---|
| -firstName: string |
| -mi: char |
| -lastName: string |
| -score: double |
| +Student() |
| +Student(firstName: string, mi: char, lastName: string, score: int) |
| +getFirstName(): string |
| +getMi(): char |
| +getLastName(): string |
| +getScore(): int |
| +setFirstName(s: string): void |
| +setMi(ch: char): void |
| +setLastName(s: string): void |
| +setScore(score: int): void |

| |
|---|
| The first name of this student. |
| The middle name initial of this student. |
| The last name of this student. |
| The score of this student. |
| Constructs a default Student object. |
| Constructs a student with specified first name, mi, last name, and score |
| Returns the first name of this student. |
| Returns the mi of this student. |
| Returns the last name of this student. |
| Returns the score of this student. |
| Sets a new first name of this student. |
| Sets a new mi of this student. |
| Sets a new last name of this student. |
| Sets a new score for this student. |

**FIGURE 12.3**  The Student class describes student information.

Listing 12.14 declares the Student class in the header file, and Listing 12.15 implements the class.

### LISTING 12.14  Student.h

```
1 #include <string>
2 using namespace std;
3
4 class Student
5 {
6 public:
7   Student();
8   Student(string firstName, char mi, string lastName, int score);
9   void setFirstName(string s);
```

public members
no-arg constructor
constructor
mutator function

```
10    void setMi(char mi);
11    void setLastName(string s);
12    void setScore(int score);
```
accessor function
```
13    string getFirstName();
14    char getMi();
15    string getLastName();
16    int getScore();
17
```
private data fields
```
18  private:
19    string firstName;
20    char mi;
21    string lastName;
22    int score;
23 };
```

## LISTING 12.15   Student.cpp

include header file
```
1 #include "Student.h"
2
3 // Construct a default student
```
no-arg constructor
```
4 Student::Student()
5 {
6 }
7
8 // Construct a Student object with specified data
```
constructor
```
9 Student::Student
10   (string firstName, char mi, string lastName, int score)
11 {
12   setFirstName(firstName);
13   setMi(mi);
14   setLastName(lastName);
15   setScore(score);
16 }
17
```
setFirstName
```
18 void Student::setFirstName(string s)
19 {
20   firstName = s;
21 }
22
23 void Student::setMi(char mi)
24 {
25   this->mi = mi;
26 }
27
28 void Student::setLastName(string s)
29 {
30   lastName = s;
31 }
32
33 void Student::setScore(int score)
34 {
35   this->score = score;
36 }
37
38 string Student::getFirstName()
39 {
40   return firstName;
41 }
42
```

```
43 char Student::getMi()
44 {
45   return mi;
46 }
47
48 string Student::getLastName()
49 {
50   return lastName;
51 }
52
53 int Student::getScore()
54 {
55   return score;
56 }
```
getFirstName

Listing 12.16 gives a program that creates two **Student** objects, writes them to a file named object.dat, and reads them back from the file.

## LISTING 12.16  BinaryObjectIO.cpp

```
 1 #include <iostream>
 2 #include <fstream>
 3 #include "Student.h"
 4 using namespace std;
 5
 6 void displayStudent(Student student)
 7 {
 8   cout << student.getFirstName() << " ";
 9   cout << student.getMi() << " ";
10   cout << student.getLastName() << " ";
11   cout << student.getScore() << endl;
12 }
13
14 int main()
15 {
16   fstream binaryio; // Create stream object
17   binaryio.open("object.dat", ios::out | ios::binary);
18
19   Student student1("John", 'T', "Smith", 90);
20   Student student2("Eric", 'K', "Jones", 85);
21
22   binaryio.write(reinterpret_cast<char *>
23     (&student1), sizeof(Student));
24   binaryio.write(reinterpret_cast<char *>
25     (&student2), sizeof(Student));
26
27   binaryio.close();
28
29   // Read student back from the file
30   binaryio.open("object.dat", ios::in | ios::binary);
31
32   Student studentNew;
33
34   binaryio.read(reinterpret_cast<char *>
35     (&studentNew), sizeof(Student));
36
37   displayStudent(studentNew);
38
39   binaryio.read(reinterpret_cast<char *>
40     (&studentNew), sizeof(Student));
41
```

include **Student** header

display **Student** data

**fstream** object
open output file

create **student1**
create **student2**

write **student1**

write **student2**

close file

open input file

create student

read from file

display student

```
42    displayStudent(studentNew);
43
44    binaryio.close();
45
46    return 0;
47 }
```

```
John T Smith 90
Eric K Jones 85
```

The program creates a stream object in line 16, opens the file object.dat for binary output in line 17, creates two **Student** objects in lines 19–20, writes them to the file in lines 22–25, and closes the file in line 27.

The statement to write an object to the file is

```
binaryio.write(reinterpret_cast<char *>
  (&student1), sizeof(Student));
```

The address of object **student1** is cast into the type **char** *. The size of an object is determined by the data fields in the object.

The program opens the file object.dat for binary input in line 30, creates a **Student** object using its no-arg construction in line 32, reads a **Student** object from the file in lines 34–35, and displays the object's data in line 37. The program continues to read another object (lines 39–40) and displays its data in line 42.

Finally, the program closes the file in line 44.

## 12.8 Random Access File

file pointer

A file consists of a sequence of bytes. There is a special marker called a *file pointer* that is positioned at one of these bytes. A read or write operation takes place at the location of the file pointer. When a file is opened, the file pointer is set at the beginning of the file. When you read or write data to the file, the file pointer moves forward to the next data item. For example, if you read a character using the **get()** function, C++ reads one byte from the file pointer, and now the file pointer is 1 byte ahead of the previous location, as shown in Figure 12.4.

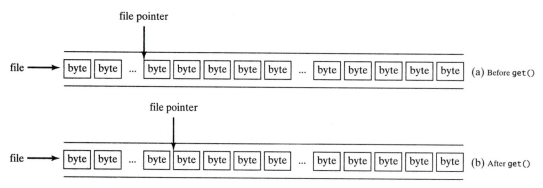

**FIGURE 12.4** After reading a character, the file pointer is moved one byte ahead.

All the programs you have developed so far read/write data sequentially, i.e., the file pointer always moves forward. If a file is open for input, it starts to read data from the beginning to the end. If a file is open for output, it writes data one item after the other from the beginning or from the end (with the append mode **ios::app**).

The problem with sequential access is that, in order to read a byte in a specific location, all the bytes that precede it must be read. This is not efficient. C++ enables the file pointer to jump backward or forward freely using the **seekp** and **seekg** member functions on a stream object. This capability is known as *random file access.*

The **seekp** ("seek put") function is for the output stream and the **seekg** ("seek get") function is for the input stream. Each function has two versions with one argument or two arguments. With one argument, the argument is the absolute location. For example,

**seekp** function<br>**seekg** function

```
input.seekg(0);
output.seekp(0);
```

moves the file pointer to the beginning of the file.

With two arguments, the first argument is a long integer that indicates an offset and the second argument, known as the *seek base,* specifies where to calculate the offset from. Table 12.4 lists the three possible seek base arguments.

**TABLE 12.4**   Seek Base

| Seek Base | Description |
|-----------|-------------|
| ios::beg | Calculates the offset from the beginning of the file. |
| ios::end | Calculates the offset from the end of the file. |
| ios::cur | Calculates the offset from the current file pointer. |

Table 12.5 gives some examples of using the **seekp** and **seekg** functions.

**TABLE 12.5**   **seekp** and **seekg** Examples

| Statement | Description |
|-----------|-------------|
| seekg(100L, ios::beg); | Moves the file pointer to the 100th byte from the beginning of the file. |
| seekg(-100L, ios::end); | Moves the file pointer to the 100th byte backward from the end of the file. |
| seekp(42L, ios::cur); | Moves the file pointer to the 42nd byte forward from the current file pointer. |
| seekp(-42L, ios::cur); | Moves the file pointer to the 42nd byte backward from the current file pointer. |
| seekp(100L); | Moves the file pointer to the 100th byte in the file. |

You also can use the **tellp** and **tellg** functions to return the position of the file pointer in the file.

**tellp** function<br>**tellg** function

Listing 12.17 demonstrates how to access a file randomly. The program first stores 10 student objects into the file and then retrieves the third student from the file.

## LISTING 12.17   RandomAccessFile.cpp

```
1 #include <iostream>
2 #include <fstream>
3 #include "Student.h"
4 using namespace std;
5
6 void displayStudent(Student student)
7 {
```

```
 8    cout << student.getFirstName() << " ";
 9    cout << student.getMi() << " ";
10    cout << student.getLastName() << " ";
11    cout << student.getScore() << endl;
12  }
13
14  int main()
15  {
16    fstream binaryio; // Create stream object
17    binaryio.open("object1.dat", ios::out | ios::binary);
18
19    Student student1("Student1", 'T', "Smith", 90);
20    Student student2("Student2", 'T', "Smith", 90);
21    Student student3("Student3", 'T', "Smith", 90);
22    Student student4("Student4", 'T', "Smith", 90);
23    Student student5("Student5", 'T', "Smith", 90);
24    Student student6("Student6", 'T', "Smith", 90);
25    Student student7("Student7", 'T', "Smith", 90);
26    Student student8("Student8", 'T', "Smith", 90);
27    Student student9("Student9", 'T', "Smith", 90);
28    Student student10("Student10", 'T', "Smith", 90);
29
30    binaryio.write(reinterpret_cast<char *>
31      (&student1), sizeof(Student));
32    binaryio.write(reinterpret_cast<char *>
33      (&student2), sizeof(Student));
34    binaryio.write(reinterpret_cast<char *>
35      (&student3), sizeof(Student));
36    binaryio.write(reinterpret_cast<char *>
37      (&student4), sizeof(Student));
38    binaryio.write(reinterpret_cast<char *>
39      (&student5), sizeof(Student));
40    binaryio.write(reinterpret_cast<char *>
41      (&student6), sizeof(Student));
42    binaryio.write(reinterpret_cast<char *>
43      (&student7), sizeof(Student));
44    binaryio.write(reinterpret_cast<char *>
45      (&student8), sizeof(Student));
46    binaryio.write(reinterpret_cast<char *>
47      (&student9), sizeof(Student));
48    binaryio.write(reinterpret_cast<char *>
49      (&student10), sizeof(Student));
50
51    binaryio.close();
52
53    // Read student back from the file
54    binaryio.open("object1.dat", ios::in | ios::binary);
55
56    Student studentNew;
57
58    binaryio.seekg(2 * sizeof(Student));
59
60    cout << "Current position is " << binaryio.tellg() << endl;
61
62    binaryio.read(reinterpret_cast<char *>
63      (& studentNew), sizeof(Student));
64
65    displayStudent(studentNew);
66
```

Margin labels:
- open output file (line 17)
- create students (line 19)
- output students (line 30)
- close file (line 51)
- open input file (line 54)
- create student (line 56)
- move to 3rd student (line 58)
- read student (line 62)
- display student (line 65)

```
67    cout << "Current position is " << binaryio.tellg() << endl;
68
69    binaryio.close();
70
71    return 0;
72 }
```

```
Current position is 136
Student3 T Smith 90
Current position is 204
```

The program creates a stream object in line 16, opens the file object1.dat for binary output in line 17, creates ten **Student** objects in lines 19–28, writes them to the file in lines 30–49, and closes the file in line 51.

The program opens the file object1.dat for binary input in line 54, creates a **Student** object using its no-arg construction in line 56, and moves the file pointer to the address of the third student in the file in line 58. The current position is now at **136**. (Note that the size of each **Student** object is 68.) After the third object is read, the file pointer is moved to the fourth object. So, the current position becomes **204**.

## 12.9 Updating Files

Often you need to update the contents of the file. You can open a file for both input and output. For example,

```
binaryio.open("object1.dat", ios::in | ios::out | ios::binary);
```

This statement opens the binary file object1.dat for both input and output.

Listing 12.18 demonstrates how to update a file. Suppose file object1.dat already has been created with ten **Student** objects from Listing 10.17. The program first reads the third student from the file, changes the last name, writes the revised object back to the file, and reads the new object back from the file.

### LISTING 12.18 UpdateFile.cpp

```
1  #include <iostream>
2  #include <fstream>                                          include header file
3  #include "Student.h"
4  using namespace std;
5
6  void displayStudent(Student student)
7  {
8     cout << student.getFirstName() << " ";
9     cout << student.getMi() << " ";
10    cout << student.getLastName() << " ";
11    cout << student.getScore() << endl;
12 }
13
14 int main()
15 {
16    fstream binaryio; // Create stream object
17
18    // Open file for input and output
19    binaryio.open("object1.dat", ios::in | ios::out | ios::binary);    open input/output
20
21    Student student1;                                          student1
22    binaryio.seekg(2 * sizeof(Student));
23    binaryio.read(reinterpret_cast<char *>                     read student1
```

display **student1**

update **student1**

**student2**

read **student2**

display **student2**

```
24       (&student1), sizeof(Student));
25    displayStudent(student1);
26
27    student1.setLastName("Peterson");
28    binaryio.seekp(2 * sizeof(Student));
29    binaryio.write(reinterpret_cast<char *>
30       (&student1), sizeof(Student));
31
32    Student student2;
33    binaryio.seekg(2 * sizeof(Student));
34    binaryio.read (reinterpret_cast<char *>
35       (&student2), sizeof(Student));
36    displayStudent(student2);
37
38    binaryio.close();
39
40    return 0;
41 }
```

```
Student3 T Smith 90
Student3 T Peterson 90
```

The program creates a stream object in line 16 and opens the file object1.dat for binary input and output in line 19.

The program first reads the third object from the file (lines 23–24), displays it (line 25), changes its last name (line 27), and writes the revised object back to the file (lines 29–30).

The program then reads the third object back from the file (lines 34–35) and displays it (line 36). You will see that the last name of this object has been changed in the sample output.

## KEY TERMS

absolute file name    375
binary I/O    385
file open mode    382
file pointer    392
fstream    382
ifstream    375
ofstream    374

random access file    392
relative file name    375
sequential access file    392
stream    376
stream state    383
text I/O    385

## CHAPTER SUMMARY

■   C++ provides the classes ofstream, ifstream, and fstream for facilitating file input and output. You can use the ofstream class to write data to a file, use ifstream to read data from a file, and use the fstream class to read and write data.

■   You can use the open function to open a file, the close function to close a file, the fail function to test if a file exists, and the eof function to test whether the end of the file is reached.

■   The stream manipulators (e.g., setw, precision, left, and right) can be used to format output.

■   You can use the getline function to read a line from a file, the get function to read a character from a file, and the put function to write a character to a file.

- The file open modes (`iso::in`, `iso::out`, `iso::app`, `iso::truct`, and `iso::binary`) can be used to specify how a file is opened.

- File I/O can be classified into text I/O and binary I/O. Text I/O interprets data in sequences of characters. Binary I/O interprets data as raw binary values. How text is stored in a file is dependent on the encoding scheme for the file. C++ automatically performs encoding and decoding for text I/O. To perform binary I/O, open the file using the `iso::binary` mode.

- For binary output, use the `write` function. For binary input, use the `read` function. You can use the `reinterpret_cast` operator to cast any type of data into an array of bytes for binary input and output.

- You can process a file sequentially or in a random manner. The `seekp` and `seekg` functions can be used to move the file access pointer anywhere in the file before invoking the `put` and `get` functions.

## REVIEW QUESTIONS

### Section 12.2 Simple Text I/O

**12.1**  How do you declare and open a file for output? How do you declare and open a file for input?

**12.2**  Why should you always close a file after it is processed?

**12.3**  How do you detect whether a file exists?

**12.4**  How do you detect whether the end of a file is reached?

### Section 12.3 Formatting Output

**12.5**  Can you use the stream manipulators to format text output?

### Section 12.4 Member Functions: `getline`, `get`, and `put`

**12.6**  What are the differences between `getline` and `get` functions?

**12.7**  What function do you use to write a character?

### Section 12.5 `fstream` and File Open Modes

**12.8**  How do you open a file so that you can append data into the file?

**12.9**  What is the file open mode `ios::truct`?

### Section 12.6 Testing Stream States

**12.10**  How do you determine the state of I/O operations?

### Section 12.7 Binary I/O

**12.11**  What is a text file, and what is a binary file? Can you view a text file or a binary file using a text editor?

**12.12**  How do you open a file for binary I/O?

**12.13**  The `write` function can write only an array of bytes. How do you write a primitive type value or an object into a binary file?

**12.14**  If you write string `"ABC"` to an ASCII text file, what values are stored in a file?

**12.15**  If you write string `"100"` to an ASCII text file, what values are stored in a file? If you write a numeric byte-type value `100` using binary I/O, what values are stored in a file?

### Section 12.8 Random Access File

**12.16** What is the file pointer?

**12.17** What are the differences between **seekp** and **seekg**?

## PROGRAMMING EXERCISES

### Sections 12.2–12.6

**12.1**[*] (*Creating a text file*) Write a program to create a file named **Exercise12_1.txt** if it does not exist. If it exists, append new data to it. Write one hundred integers created randomly into the file using text I/O. Integers are separated by a space.

**12.2**[*] (*Counting characters*) Write a program that will count the number of characters in a file.

**12.3**[*] (*Processing scores in a text file*) Suppose that a text file **Exercise12_3.txt** contains an unspecified number of scores. Write a program that reads the scores from the file and displays their total and average. Scores are separated by blanks.

**12.4**[*] (*Writing/Reading data*) Write a program to create a file named **Exercise12_4.txt** if it does not exist. Write one hundred integers created randomly into the file using text I/O. Integers are separated by spaces in the file. Read the data back from the file and display the sorted data.

### Section 12.7 Binary I/O Classes

**12.5**[*] (*Creating a binary data file*) Write a program to create a file named **Exercise12_5.dat** if it does not exist. If it exists, append new data to it. Write one hundred integers created randomly into the file using binary I/O.

**12.6**[*] (*Storing Loan objects*) Write a program that creates five **Loan** objects and stores them in a file named **Exercise12_6.dat**. The **Loan** class was introduced in §9.15, "Case Study: The **Loan** Class."

**12.7**[*] (*Restoring objects from a file*) Suppose a file named **Exercise12_6.dat** has been created from the preceding exercise. Write a program that reads the **Loan** objects from the file and computes the total of the loan amount. Suppose you don't know how many **Loan** objects are in the file. Use the **eof()** to detect the end of the file.

### Section 12.8 Random Access File

**12.8**[*] (*Updating count*) Suppose you want to track how many times a program has been executed. You may store an **int** to count the file. Increase the count by 1 each time this program is executed. Let the program be **Exercise12_8** and store the count in **Exercise12_8.dat**.

# CHAPTER 13

# OPERATOR OVERLOADING

## Objectives

- To define the `Rational` class to represent rational numbers (§13.2).

- To understand in general how an operator can be overloaded in C++ (§13.3).

- To know how to overload the relational operators and arithmetic operators (§13.3).

- To know how to overload the shorthand operators (§13.4).

- To know how to overload the array subscript operator `[]` (§13.5).

- To know how to overload the unary operators (§13.6).

- To know how to overload the prefix and postfix `++` and `--` operators (§13.7).

- To know how to overload the stream insertion and extraction operators `<<` and `>>` (§13.8).

- To define operator functions to perform object conversion (§13.9).

- To overload the `=` operator to perform a deep copy (§13.11).

## 13.1 Introduction

In §9.8.10, "String Operators," you learned how to use the operators to simplify string operations. You can use the + operator to concatenate two strings, the relational operators (==, !=, <, <=, >, and >=) to compare two strings, and the array subscript operator [] to access a character. In §10.12, "The C++ vector Class," you learned how to use the [] operator to access individual elements in a vector. You can define operators in custom classes. This chapter uses the Rational class as an example to demonstrate how to define and use operators. First you will learn how to create a Rational class for supporting rational number operations and then define convenient operators for these operations.

## 13.2 The Rational Class

A rational number is a number with a numerator and a denominator in the form a/b, where a is the numerator and b is the denominator. For example, 1/3, 3/4, and 10/4 are rational numbers.

A rational number cannot have a denominator of 0, but a numerator of 0 is fine. Every integer a is equivalent to a rational number a/1. Rational numbers are used in exact computations involving fractions; for example, 1/3 = 0.33333.... This number cannot be represented precisely in floating-point format using data type double or float. To obtain the exact result, it is necessary to use rational numbers.

C++ provides data types for integers and floating-point numbers, but not for rational numbers. This section shows how to design a class to represent rational numbers.

A Rational number can be represented using two data fields: numerator and denominator. You can create a Rational number with specified numerator and denominator or create a default Rational number with numerator 0 and denominator 1. You can add, subtract, multiply, divide, and compare rational numbers. You also can convert a rational number into an integer, floating-point value, or string. The UML class diagram for the Rational class is given in Figure 13.1.

 **Note**

pass reference

The Rational parameter is passed by reference using the syntax &secondRational. This improves performance by preventing the compiler from making a copy of the object being passed into the function.

A rational number consists of a numerator and a denominator. There are many equivalent rational numbers; for example, 1/3 = 2/6 = 3/9 = 4/12. For convenience, 1/3 is used in this example to represent all rational numbers that are equivalent to 1/3. The numerator and the denominator of 1/3 have no common divisor except 1, so 1/3 is said to be in *lowest terms*.

lowest term

To reduce a rational number to its lowest terms, you need to find the greatest common divisor (GCD) of the absolute values of its numerator and denominator, and then divide both numerator and denominator by this value. You can use the function for computing the GCD of two integers n and d, as suggested in Listing 4.6, GreatestCommonDivisor.cpp. The numerator and denominator in a Rational object are reduced to their lowest terms.

As usual, you can first write a test program to create two Rational objects and test its functions. Listing 13.1 shows the header file for the Rational class and Listing 13.2 is a test program.

### LISTING 13.1 Rational.h

include guard
define constant

```
1 #ifndef RATIONL_H
2 #define RATIONL_H
3 #include <string>
4 using namespace std;
5
6 class Rational
7 {
```

```
 8 public:                                                      public members
 9   Rational();
10   Rational(long numerator, long denominator);
11   long getNumerator();
12   long getDenominator();
13   Rational add(Rational &secondRational);
14   Rational subtract(Rational &secondRational);
15   Rational multiply(Rational &secondRational);
16   Rational divide(Rational &secondRational);
17   int compareTo(Rational &secondRational);
18   bool equals(Rational &secondRational);
19   int intValue();
20   double doubleValue();
21   string toString();
22
23 private:                                                     private members
24   long numerator;
25   long denominator;
26   static long gcd(long n, long d);                           static function
27 };
28
29 #endif
```

| Rational | |
|---|---|
| -numerator: long | The numerator of this rational number. |
| -denominator: long | The denominator of this rational number. |
| +Rational() | Creates a rational number with numerator 0 and denominator 1. |
| +Rational(numerator: long, denominator: long) | Creates a rational number with specified numerator and denominator. |
| +getNumerator(): long | Returns the numerator of this rational number. |
| +getDenominator(): long | Returns the denominator of this rational number. |
| +add(&secondRational: Rational): Rational | Returns the addition of this rational with another. |
| +subtract(&secondRational: Rational): Rational | Returns the subtraction of this rational with another. |
| +multiply(&secondRational: Rational): Rational | Returns the multiplication of this rational with another. |
| +divide(&secondRational: Rational): Rational | Returns the division of this rational with another. |
| +compareTo(&secondRational: Rational): int | Returns an int value -1, 0, or 1 to indicate whether this rational number is less than, equal to, or greater than the specified number. |
| +equals(&secondRational: Rational): bool | Returns true if this rational number is equal to the specified number. |
| +intValue(): int | Returns the numerator / denominator. |
| +doubleValue(): double | Returns the 1.0 * numerator / denominator. |
| +toString(): string | Returns a string in the form "numerator / denominator." Returns numerator if denominator is 1. |
| -gcd(n: long, d: long): long | Returns the greatest common divisor between n and d. |

**FIGURE 13.1** The properties, constructors, and functions of the `Rational` class are illustrated in UML.

**LISTING 13.2** TestRationalClass.cpp

include **Rational**

create **Rational**

invoke **toString**
invoke **add**

invoke **subtract**

invoke **multiply**

invoke **divide**

invoke **intValue**
invoke **doubleValue**

invoke **compareTo**

invoke **equal**

```cpp
 1  #include <iostream>
 2  #include "Rational.h"
 3  using namespace std;
 4
 5  int main()
 6  {
 7    // Create and initialize two rational numbers r1 and r2.
 8    Rational r1(4, 2);
 9    Rational r2(2, 3);
10
11    // Test toString, add, subtract, multiply, and divide
12    cout << r1.toString() << " + " << r2.toString() << " = "
13      << r1.add(r2).toString() << endl;
14    cout << r1.toString() << " - " << r2.toString() << " = "
15      << r1.subtract(r2).toString() << endl;
16    cout << r1.toString() << " * " << r2.toString() << " = "
17      << r1.multiply(r2).toString() << endl;
18    cout << r1.toString() << " / " << r2.toString() << " = "
19      << r1.divide(r2).toString() << endl;
20
21    // Test intValue and double
22    cout << "r2.intValue()" << " is " << r2.intValue() << endl;
23    cout << "r2.doubleValue()" << " is " << r2.doubleValue() << endl;
24
25    // Test compareTo and equal
26    cout << "r1.compareTo(r2) is " << r1.compareTo(r2) << endl;
27    cout << "r2.compareTo(r1) is " << r2.compareTo(r1) << endl;
28    cout << "r1.compareTo(r1) is " << r1.compareTo(r1) << endl;
29    cout << "r1.equals(r1) is " << r1.equals(r1) << endl;
30    cout << "r1.equals(r2) is " << r1.equals(r2) << endl;
31
32    return 0;
33  }
```

```
2 + 2/3 = 8/3
2 − 2/3 = 4/3
2*2/3 = 4/3
2 / 2/3 = 3
r2.intValue() is 0
r2.doubleValue() is 0.666667
r1.compareTo(r2) is 1
r2.compareTo(r1) is −1
r1.compareTo(r1) is 0
r1.equals(r1) is 1
r1.equals(r2) is 0
```

The **main** function creates two rational numbers, **r1** and **r2** (lines 8–9), and displays the results of **r1 + r2, r1 - r2, r1 x r2**, and **r1 / r2** (lines 12–19). To perform **r1 + r2**, invoke **r1.add(r2)** to return a new **Rational** object. Similarly, **r1.subtract(r2)** returns a new **Rational** object for **r1 - r2**, **r1.multiply(r2)** for **r1 x r2** , and **r1.divide(r2)** for **r1 / r2**.

The **intValue()** function displays the **int** value of **r1** (line 22). The **doubleValue()** function displays the **double** value of **r2** (line 23).

Invoking `r1.compareTo(r2)` (line 26) returns 1 since `r1` is greater than `r2`. Invoking `r2.compareTo(r1)` (line 27) returns −1 since `r2` is less than `r1`. Invoking `r1.compareTo(r1)` (line 28) returns 0 since `r1` is equal to `r1`. Invoking `r1.equals(r1)` (line 29) returns 1 (`true`) since `r1` is equal to `r1`. Invoking `r1.equals(r2)` (line 30) returns 0 (`false`) since `r1` and `r2` are not equal.

The `Rational` class is implemented in Listing 13.3.

## LISTING 13.3  Rational.cpp

```
1  #include "Rational.h"
2
3  Rational::Rational()
4  {
5    numerator = 0;
6    denominator = 1;
7  }
8
9  Rational::Rational(long numerator, long denominator)
10 {
11   long factor = gcd(numerator, denominator);
12   this->numerator = ((denominator > 0) ? 1 : -1) * numerator / factor;
13   this->denominator = abs(denominator) / factor;
14 }
15
16 long Rational::getNumerator()
17 {
18   return numerator;
19 }
20
21 long Rational::getDenominator()
22 {
23   return denominator;
24 }
25
26 // Find GCD of two numbers
27 long Rational::gcd(long n, long d)
28 {
29   long n1 = abs(n);
30   long n2 = abs(d);
31   int gcd = 1;
32
33   for (int k = 1; k <= n1 && k <= n2; k++)
34   {
35     if (n1 % k == 0 && n2 % k == 0)
36       gcd = k;
37   }
38
39   return gcd;
40 }
41
42 Rational Rational::add(Rational &secondRational)
43 {
44   long n = numerator * secondRational.getDenominator() +
45     denominator * secondRational.getNumerator();
46   long d = denominator * secondRational.getDenominator();
47   return Rational(n, d);
48 }
49
```

**Rational** header

no-arg constructor

initialize data fields

constructor

initialize data fields

**gcd**

**add**
$$\frac{a}{b} + \frac{c}{d} = \frac{ad + bc}{bd}$$

**subtract**

$$\frac{a}{b} - \frac{c}{d} = \frac{ad - bc}{bd}$$

```
50 Rational Rational::subtract(Rational &secondRational)
51 {
52    long n = numerator * secondRational.getDenominator()
53      - denominator * secondRational.getNumerator();
54    long d = denominator * secondRational.getDenominator();
55    return Rational(n, d);
56 }
57
```

**multiply**

$$\frac{a}{b} \times \frac{c}{d} = \frac{ac}{bd}$$

```
58 Rational Rational::multiply(Rational &secondRational)
59 {
60    long n = numerator * secondRational.getNumerator();
61    long d = denominator * secondRational.getDenominator();
62    return Rational(n, d);
63 }
64
```

**divide**

$$\frac{a}{b} \div \frac{c}{d} = \frac{ad}{bc}$$

```
65 Rational Rational::divide(Rational &secondRational)
66 {
67    long n = numerator * secondRational.getDenominator();
68    long d = denominator * secondRational.numerator;
69    return Rational(n, d);
70 }
71
```

**compareTo**

```
72 int Rational::compareTo(Rational &secondRational)
73 {
74    Rational temp = this->subtract(secondRational);
75    if (temp.getNumerator() < 0)
76      return -1;
77    else if (temp.getNumerator() == 0)
78      return 0;
79    else
80      return 1;
81 }
82
```

**equal**

```
83 bool Rational::equals(Rational &secondRational)
84 {
85    if (this->compareTo(secondRational) == 0)
86      return true;
87    else
88      return false;
89 }
90
```

**intValue**

```
91 int Rational::intValue()
92 {
93    return getNumerator() / getDenominator();
94 }
95
```

**doubleValue**

```
96 double Rational::doubleValue()
97 {
98    return 1.0 * getNumerator() / getDenominator();
99 }
100
```

**toString**

```
101 string Rational::toString()
102 {
103    char s1[20], s2[20];
104    itoa(numerator, s1, 10); // Convert int to string s1
105    itoa(denominator, s2, 10); // Convert int to string s2
106
107    if (denominator == 1)
108      return string(s1);
109    else
110      return string(strcat(strcat(s1, "/"), s2));
111 }
```

The rational number is encapsulated in a `Rational` object. Internally, a rational number is represented in its lowest terms (lines 14–15), and the numerator determines its sign (line 14). The denominator is always positive (line 15).

The `gcd()` function (lines 27–40) is private; it is not intended for use by clients. The `gcd()` function is only for internal use by the `Rational` class. The `gcd()` function is also static, since it is not dependent on any particular `Rational` object.

The `abs(x)` function (lines 29–30) is defined in the standard C++ library that returns the absolute value of `x`.

Two `Rational` objects can interact with each other to perform add, subtract, multiply, and divide operations. These functions return a new `Rational` object (lines 42–70).

The `compareTo(&secondRational)` function (lines 72–81) compares this rational number to the other rational number. It first subtracts this rational by the second rational and saves the result in `temp` (line 74). Return $-1$, $0$, or $1$, if `temp`'s numerator is less than, equal to, or greater than $0$.

The `equals(&secondRational)` function (lines 83–89) utilizes the `compareTo` function to compare this rational number to the other rational number. If this function returns $0$, the `equals` function returns true; otherwise, it returns false.

The functions `intValue` and `doubleValue` return an `int` and `double` value for this rational number (lines 91–99), respectively.

The `toString()` function (lines 101–111) returns a string representation of a `Rational` object in the form `numerator/denominator` or simply `numerator` if `denominator` is $1$. The C string function `itoa` is used to convert the `int` value numerator and denominator to a C-string `s1` and `s2` (lines 104–105). The C string function `strcat` (line 110) is used to concatenate C strings into a new C-string. This new C-string is passed to the constructor of the C++ string class to create a `string` object. C string functions were introduced in §7.9.4, "String Functions."

**Tip**
The get functions for the properties `numerator` and `denominator` are provided in the `Rational` class, but the set functions are not provided, so the contents of a `Rational` object cannot be changed once the object is created. The `Rational` class is *immutable*.

*immutable*

**Tip**
The numerator and denominator are represented using two variables. It is possible to use an array of two integers to represent the numerator and denominator. See Exercise 13.2. The signatures of the public functions in the `Rational` class are not changed, although the internal representation of a rational number is changed. This is a good example to illustrate the idea that the data fields of a class should be kept private so as to *encapsulate* the implementation of the class from the use of the class.

*encapsulation*

## 13.3 Operator Functions

It is convenient to compare two string objects using an intuitive syntax like:

```
string1 < string2
```

Can you compare two `Rational` objects using a similar syntax like

```
r1 < r2
```

Yes. You can define a special function called the *operator function* in the class. The function is just like a regular function, except that the function must be named with word `operator` followed by the actual operator. For example, the following function header:

```
bool operator<(Rational &secondRational)
```

defines the < operator function that returns **true** if this **Rational** object is less than the specified **Rational**. You can invoke the function using

```
r1.operator< (r2)
```

or simply

```
r1 < r2
```

To use this operator, you have to add the function header in the Rational.h header file and implement the function in the Rational.cpp file as follows:

function operator

invoke **compareTo**

```
1 bool Rational::operator<(Rational &secondRational)
2 {
3   if (this->compareTo(secondRational) < 0)
4     return true;
5   else
6     return false;
7 }
```

So, the following code:

```
Rational r1(4, 2);
Rational r2(2, 3);
cout << "r1 < r2 is " << r1.operator<(r2) << endl;
cout << "r1 < r2 is " << (r1 < r2) << endl;
cout << "r2 < r1 is " << r2.operator<(r1) << endl;
```

displays

```
r1 < r2 is 0
r1 < r2 is 0
r2 < r1 is 1
```

overloadable operators

C++ allows you to overload most of the operators, as shown in Table 13.1. Table 13.2 shows the four operators that cannot be overloaded. C++ does not allow you to create new operators. The only operators you can overload are in Table 13.1.

**TABLE 13.1**   Operators That Can Be Overloaded

| | | | | | | | | | | |
|---|---|---|---|---|---|---|---|---|---|---|
| + | – | * | / | % | ^ | & | \| | ~ | ! | = |
| < | > | += | -= | *= | /= | %= | ^= | &= | \|= | << |
| >> | >>= | <<= | == | != | <= | >= | && | \|\| | ++ | – |
| ->* | , | -> | [] | () | new | delete | | | | |

**TABLE 13.2**   Operators That Cannot Be Overloaded

| | | | |
|---|---|---|---|
| ?: | . | .* | :: |

**Note**

precedence and associativity

C++ defines the operator precedence and associativity (see §3.13, "Operator Precedence and Associativity"). You cannot change the operator precedence and associativity by overloading.

**Note**

Most operators are binary operators. Some are unary. You cannot change the number of operands by overloading. For example, the / divide operator is binary and ++ is unary.

number of operands

Here is another example that overloads the addition operator in the `Rational` class.

```
1 Rational Rational::operator+ (Rational &secondRational)
2 {
3   return this->add(secondRational);
4 }
```

+ function operator

invoke **add**

So, the following code:

```
Rational r1(4, 2);
Rational r2(2, 3);
cout << "r1 + r2 is " << (r1 + r2).toString() << endl;
```

displays

```
r1 + r2 is 8/3
```

## 13.4 Overloading the Shorthand Operators

C++ has shorthand operators +=, -=, *=, /= and %= for adding, subtracting, multiplying, dividing, and modulus a value in a variable. You can overload these operators in the `Rational` class.

Here is an example that overloads the addition assignment operator +=.

```
1 Rational Rational::operator+=    (Rational &secondRational)
2 {
3   *this = this->add(secondRational);
4   return (*this);
5 }
```

+= function operator

add to calling object
return calling object

The expression `this->add(secondRational)` invokes the **add** function to add the calling `Rational` object with the second `Rational` object. The result is copied to the calling object *this in line 3. The calling object is returned in line 4.

For example, the following code:

```
1 Rational r1(2, 4);
2 Rational r2 = r1 += Rational(2, 3);
3 cout << "r1 is " << r1.toString() << endl;
4 cout << "r2 is " << r2.toString() << endl;
```

+= function operator

displays

```
r1 is 7/6
r2 is 7/6
```

## 13.5 Overloading the [] Operators

In C++, the array subscript [] is an operator. You can overload this operator to access the contents of the object using the array-like syntax if desirable. For example, you may wish to access the numerator and denominator using `r[0]` and `r[1]`.

To enable a `Rational` object to access its numerator and denominator using the array subscript, declare the following function header in the Rational.h header file:

```
long operator[](const int &index);
```

Implement the function in Rational.cpp as follows:

[] function operator

access numerator

access denominator

```
 1 long Rational::operator[](const int &index)
 2 {
 3    if (index == 0)
 4       return numerator;
 5    else if (index == 1)
 6       return denominator;
 7    else
 8    {
 9       cout << "subscript error" << endl;
10       exit(0);
11    }
12 }
```

So, the following code:

```
Rational r2(2, 3);
cout << "r2[0] is " << r2[0] << endl;
cout << "r2[1] is " << r2[1] << endl;
```

displays

```
r2[0] is 2
r2[1] is 3
```

Can you set a new numerator or denominator like an array assignment such as

```
r2[0] = 5;
r2[1] = 6;
```

If you compile it, you will get the following error:

```
Lvalue required in function main()
```

Lvalue
Rvalue

*Lvalue* (short for left value) refers to anything that can appear on the left side of the assignment operator and Rvalue (short for right value) refers to anything that can appear on the right side of the assignment operator (=). How can you make **r2[0]** and **r2[1]** an Lvalue so that you can assign a value to **r2[0]** and **r2[1]**? The answer is to declare the **[]** operator to return a reference as follows:

redeclare function header

```
long & operator[](const int &index);
```

So, the following code:

assign to **r2[0]**
assign to **r2[1]**

```
1 Rational r2(2, 3);
2 r2[0] = 5; // Set numerator to 5
3 r2[1] = 6; // Set denominator to 6
```

```
4 cout << "r2[0] is " << r2[0] << endl;
5 cout << "r2[1] is " << r2[1] << endl;
6 cout << "r2.doubleValue() is " << r2.doubleValue() << endl;
```

displays

```
r2[0] is 5
r2[1] is 6
r2.doubleValue() is 0.833333
```

In **r2[0]**, **r2** is an object and **0** is the argument to the member function **[]**. When **r2[0]** is used as an expression, it returns a value for the numerator. When **r2[0]** is used on the left side of the assignment operator, it denotes the address for the numerator. So, **r2[0] = 5** is to assign **5** to numerator.

**Note**

The **[]** operator functions as both accessor and mutator. For example, you use **r2[0]** as an accessor to retrieve the numerator in an expression, and use **r2[0] = value** as a mutator. After adding this operator to the **Rational** class, the **Rational** class is mutable.

**[]** accessor and mutator

## 13.6 Overloading the Unary Operators

The **+** and **-** are unary operators. They can be overloaded too. Since the unary operator operates on one operand that is the calling object itself, the unary function operator has no parameters.

The **-** operator in the **Rational** class can be implemented as follows:

```
1 Rational Rational::operator-()
2 {
3     numerator *= -1;
4     return *this;
5 }
```

negate numerator
return calling object

Negating a **Rational** object is the same as negating its numerator (line 3). Line 4 returns the calling object.

So, the following code:

```
1 Rational r2(2, 3);
2 -r2; // Negate r2
3 cout << "r2 is " << r2.toString() << endl;
```

unary - operator

displays

```
r2 is -2/3
```

## 13.7 Overloading the ++ and -- Operators

The **++** and **--** operators may be prefix or postfix. The prefix **++var** or **--var** first adds or subtracts **1** from the variable and then evaluates to the new value in the **var**. The postfix **var++** or **var--** adds or subtracts **1** from the variable, but evaluates to the old value in the **var**.

If the `++` and `--` are implemented correctly, the following code:

```
1 Rational r2(2, 3);
2 Rational r3 = ++r2; // Prefix increment
3 cout << "r3 is " << r3.toString() << endl;
4 cout << "r2 is " << r2.toString() << endl;
5
6 Rational r1(2, 3);
7 Rational r4 = r1++; // Postfix increment
8 cout << "r1 is " << r1.toString() << endl;
9 cout << "r4 is " << r4.toString() << endl;
```

assign to **r2[0]**
assign to **r2[1]**

should display

```
r3 is 5/3

r2 is 5/3

r1 is 5/3

r4 is 2/3 ◄──────── r4 stores the original value of r1
```

How does C++ distinguish the prefix `++` or `--` function operators from the postfix `++` or `--` function operators? C++ declares postfix `++`/`--` function operators with a special dummy parameter of the **int** type and the prefix `++` function operator defined with no parameters as follows:

prefix `++` operator

```
Rational operator++();
```

postfix `++` operator

```
Rational operator++(int dummy)
```

These two functions can be implemented as follows:

$$\frac{a}{b} + 1 = \frac{a + b}{b}$$
return calling object

```
1 Rational Rational::operator++()
2 {
3     numerator += denominator;
4     return *this;
5 }
6
7 Rational Rational::operator++(int dummy)
8 {
9     Rational temp(numerator, denominator);
10    numerator += denominator;
11    return temp;
12 }
```

create temp
$$\frac{a}{b} + 1 = \frac{a + b}{b}$$
return temp object

In the prefix `++` function, line 3 adds the denominator to the numerator. This is the new numerator for the calling object after adding 1 to the **Rational** object. Line 4 returns the calling object.

In the postfix `++` function, line 9 creates a temporary **Rational** object to store the original calling object. Line 10 increments the calling object. Line 11 returns the original calling object.

## 13.8 Overloading the `<<` and `>>` Operators

Note that you have to invoke the **toString()** function to return a string representation for a **Rational** object in order to print to the console. For example,

```
cout << r1.toString();
```

Wouldn't it be nice to be able to display a **Rational** object directly using a syntax like

```
cout << r1;
```

C++ allows you to overload the stream insertion operator (<<) for sending an object to **cout** and overload the stream extraction operator (>>) for reading values from **cin**. Overloading these two operators is different from other operators you have seen in this chapter. Since the first parameter **cout** (**cin**) of the << (>>) operator is an instance of **ostream** (**istream**), these two operators are defined in the **ostream** and **istream** classes, not in the **Rational** class. However, overloading these two operators requires access to the private members of the **Rational** class, so you need to declare the function operators as friends of the **Rational** class in the Rational.h header file:

```
friend ostream &operator<<(ostream &stream, Rational &rational);
```

Implement this function in Rational.cpp as follows:

```
ostream &operator<<(ostream &stream, Rational &rational)
{
  stream << rational.numerator << " / " << rational.denominator;
  return stream;
}
```

To overload the >> operator, declare the following function header in the Rational.h header file:

```
friend istream &operator>>(istream &stream, Rational &rational);
```

Implement this function in Rational.cpp as follows:

```
istream &operator>>(istream &stream, Rational &rational)
{
  cout << "Enter numerator: ";
  stream >> rational.numerator;

  cout << "Enter denominator: ";
  stream >> rational.denominator;
  return stream;
}
```

The following code gives a test program that uses the overloaded << and >> functions operators:

```
 1 #include <iostream>
 2 #include "Rational.h"
 3 using namespace std;
 4
 5 int main()
 6 {
 7   Rational r1, r2;
 8   cout << "Enter first rational number" << endl;
 9   cin >> r1;
10
11   cout << "Enter second rational number" << endl;
12   cin >> r2;
13
14   cout << "r1 + r2 is " << r1 + r2 << endl;
15
16   return 0;
17 }
```

Rational header

>> operator

>> operator

<< operator

```
Enter first rational number
Enter numerator: 1 ⏎Enter
Enter denominator: 2 ⏎Enter
Enter second rational number
Enter numerator: 3 ⏎Enter
Enter denominator: 4 ⏎Enter
r1 + r2 is 5/4
```

Line 8 sends a string to `cout`. Line 9 reads values to a rational object from `cin`. In line 14, `r1 + r2` is evaluated to a new rational number, which is then sent to `cout`.

## 13.9 Object Conversion

You can add an `int` value with a `double` value such as

```
4 + 5.5
```

In this case, C++ performs automatic type conversion to convert an `int` value `4` to a double value `4.0`.

Can you add a rational number with an `int` or a `double` value? Yes. You have to define a function operator to convert an object into `int` or `double`. Here is the implementation of the function to convert a `Rational` object to a `double` value.

```
Rational::operator double()
{
  return doubleValue();
}
```

Don't forget that you have to add the member function header in the Rational.h header file.

```
operator double();
```

**Note**

conversion function syntax

This is a special syntax for defining conversion functions in C++. There is no return type. The function name is the type that you want the object to be converted to.

So, the following code:

add rational with double

```
1 Rational r1(1, 4);
2 double d = r1 + 5.1;
3 cout << "r1 + 5.1 is " << d << endl;
```

displays

```
r1 + 5.1 is 5.35
```

The statement in line 2 adds a rational number `r1` with a `double` value `5.1`. Since the conversion function is defined to convert a rational number to a `double`, `r1` is converted to a `double` value `0.25`, which is then added with `5.1`.

# 13.10 The New **Rational** Class

The preceding sections introduced how to overload function operators. You are ready to give a new **Rational** class with all appropriate function operators. Listings 13.4 and 13.5 show the new Rational.h and Rational.cpp.

**LISTING 13.4** NewRational.h

```cpp
1 #ifndef NEWRATIONL_H
2 #define NEWRATIONL_H
3 #include <iostream>
4 using namespace std;
5
6 class Rational
7 {
8 public:
9   Rational();
10   Rational(long numerator, long denominator);
11   long getNumerator();
12   long getDenominator();
13   Rational add(Rational &secondRational);
14   Rational subtract(Rational &secondRational);
15   Rational multiply(Rational &secondRational);
16   Rational divide(Rational &secondRational);
17   int compareTo(Rational &secondRational);
18   bool equals(Rational &secondRational);
19   int intValue();
20   double doubleValue();
21   string toString();
22
23   // Define function operators for relational operators
24   bool operator<(Rational &secondRational);
25   bool operator<=(Rational &secondRational);
26   bool operator>(Rational &secondRational);
27   bool operator>=(Rational &secondRational);
28   bool operator!=(Rational &secondRational);
29   bool operator==(Rational &secondRational);
30
31   // Define function operators for arithmetic operators
32   Rational operator+(Rational &secondRational);
33   Rational operator-(Rational &secondRational);
34   Rational operator*(Rational &secondRational);
35   Rational operator/(Rational &secondRational);
36
37   // Define function operators for shorthand operators
38   Rational operator+=(Rational &secondRational);
39   Rational operator-=(Rational &secondRational);
40   Rational operator*=(Rational &secondRational);
41   Rational operator/=(Rational &secondRational);
42
43   // Define function operator []
44   long& operator[](const int &index);
45
46   // Define function operators for prefix ++ and --
47   Rational operator++();
48   Rational operator--();
49
```

relational operators

arithmetic operators

shorthand operators

subscript operator

prefix ++ operator

postfix ++ operator

```
50    // Define function operators for postfix ++ and --
51    Rational operator++(int dummy);
52    Rational operator--(int dummy);
53
```

unary + operator

```
54    // Define function operators for unary + and -
55    Rational operator+();
56    Rational operator-();
57
```

<< operator

```
58    // Define the output and input operator
59    friend ostream &operator<<(ostream &stream, Rational &rational);
60    friend istream &operator>>(istream &stream, Rational &rational);
61
```

convert to **double**

```
62    // Define function operator for conversion
63    operator double();
64
65 private:
66    long numerator;
67    long denominator;
68    static long gcd(long n, long d);
69 };
70
71 #endif
```

## LISTING 13.5  NewRational.cpp

include Rational header

```
 1 #include "NewRational.h"
 2
 3 Rational::Rational()
 4 {
 5    numerator = 0;
 6    denominator = 1;
 7 }
 8
 9 Rational::Rational(long numerator, long denominator)
10 {
11    long factor = gcd(numerator, denominator);
12    this->numerator = ((denominator > 0) ? 1 : -1) * numerator / factor;
13    this->denominator = abs(denominator) / factor;
14 }
15
16 long Rational::getNumerator()
17 {
18    return numerator;
19 }
20
21 long Rational::getDenominator()
22 {
23    return denominator;
24 }
25
26 // Find GCD of two numbers
27 long Rational::gcd(long n, long d) {
28    long n1 = abs(n);
29    long n2 = abs(d);
30    int gcd = 1;
31
32    for (int k = 1; k <= n1 && k <= n2; k++)
33    {
34       if (n1 % k == 0 && n2 % k == 0)
```

```
35        gcd = k;
36    }
37
38    return gcd;
39 }
40
41 Rational Rational::add(Rational &secondRational)
42 {
43    long n = numerator * secondRational.getDenominator() +
44      denominator * secondRational.getNumerator();
45    long d = denominator * secondRational.getDenominator();
46    return Rational(n, d);
47 }
48
49 Rational Rational::subtract(Rational &secondRational)
50 {
51    long n = numerator * secondRational.getDenominator()
52      - denominator * secondRational.getNumerator();
53    long d = denominator * secondRational.getDenominator();
54    return Rational(n, d);
55 }
56
57 Rational Rational::multiply(Rational &secondRational)
58 {
59    long n = numerator * secondRational.getNumerator();
60    long d = denominator * secondRational.getDenominator();
61    return Rational(n, d);
62 }
63
64 Rational Rational::divide(Rational &secondRational)
65 {
66    long n = numerator * secondRational.getDenominator();
67    long d = denominator * secondRational.numerator;
68    return Rational(n, d);
69 }
70
71 int Rational::compareTo(Rational &secondRational)
72 {
73    Rational temp = this->subtract(secondRational);
74    if (temp.getNumerator() < 0)
75      return -1;
76    else if (temp.getNumerator() == 0)
77      return 0;
78    else
79      return 1;
80 }
81
82 bool Rational::equals(Rational &secondRational)
83 {
84    if (this->compareTo(secondRational) == 0)
85      return true;
86    else
87      return false;
88 }
89
90 int Rational::intValue()
91 {
92    return getNumerator() / getDenominator();
93 }
94
```

```
 95 double Rational::doubleValue()
 96 {
 97   return 1.0 * getNumerator() / getDenominator();
 98 }
 99
100 string Rational::toString()
101 {
102   char s1[20], s2[20];
103   itoa(numerator, s1, 10); // Convert int to string s1
104   itoa(denominator, s2, 10); // Convert int to string s2
105
106   if (denominator == 1)
107     return string(s1);
108   else
109     return string(strcat(strcat(s1, "/"), s2));
110 }
111
```

relational operators

```
112 // Define function operators for relational operators
113 bool Rational::operator<(Rational &secondRational)
114 {
115   return (this->compareTo(secondRational) < 0);
116 }
117
118 bool Rational::operator<=(Rational &secondRational)
119 {
120   return (this->compareTo(secondRational) <= 0);
121 }
122
123 bool Rational::operator>(Rational &secondRational)
124 {
125   return (this->compareTo(secondRational) > 0);
126 }
127
128 bool Rational::operator>=(Rational &secondRational)
129 {
130   return (this->compareTo(secondRational) >= 0);
131 }
132
133 bool Rational::operator!=(Rational &secondRational)
134 {
135   return (this->compareTo(secondRational) != 0);
136 }
137
138 bool Rational::operator==(Rational &secondRational)
139 {
140   return (this->compareTo(secondRational) == 0);
141 }
142
```

arithmetic operators

```
143 // Define function operators for arithmetic operators
144 Rational Rational::operator+(Rational &secondRational)
145 {
146   return this->add(secondRational);
147 }
148
149 Rational Rational::operator-(Rational &secondRational)
150 {
151   return this->subtract(secondRational);
152 }
153
```

```
154 Rational Rational::operator*(Rational &secondRational)
155 {
156    return this->multiply(secondRational);
157 }
158
159 Rational Rational::operator/(Rational &secondRational)
160 {
161    return this->divide(secondRational);
162 }
163
164 // Define function operators for shorthand operators
165 Rational Rational::operator+=(Rational &secondRational)
166 {
167    *this = this->add(secondRational);
168    return (*this);
169 }
170
171 Rational Rational::operator-=(Rational &secondRational)
172 {
173    *this = this->subtract(secondRational);
174    return (*this);
175 }
176
177 Rational Rational::operator*=(Rational &secondRational)
178 {
179    *this = this->multiply(secondRational);
180    return (*this);
181 }
182
183 Rational Rational::operator/=(Rational &secondRational)
184 {
185    *this = this->divide(secondRational);
186    return *this;
187 }
188
189 // Define function operator []
190 long& Rational::operator[](const int &index)
191 {
192    if (index == 0)
193      return numerator;
194    else if (index == 1)
195      return denominator;
196    else
197    {
198      cout << "subscript error" << endl;
199      exit(0);
200    }
201 }
202
203 // Define function operators for prefix ++ and --
204 Rational Rational::operator++()
205 {
206    numerator += denominator;
207    return *this;
208 }
209
210 Rational Rational::operator--()
211 {
212    numerator -= denominator;
213    return *this;
```

shorthand operators

[] operator

prefix ++

```
214 }
215
216 // Define function operators for postfix ++ and --
217 Rational Rational::operator++(int dummy)
218 {
219   Rational temp(numerator, denominator);
220   numerator += denominator;
221   return temp;
222 }
223
224 Rational Rational::operator--(int dummy)
225 {
226   Rational temp(numerator, denominator);
227   numerator -= denominator;
228   return temp;
229 }
230
231 // Define function operators for unary + and -
232 Rational Rational::operator+()
233 {
234   return *this;
235 }
236
237 Rational Rational::operator-()
238 {
239   numerator *= -1;
240   return *this;
241 }
242
243 // Define the output and input operator
244 ostream &operator<<(ostream &str, const Rational &rational)
245 {
246   str << rational.numerator << " / " << rational.denominator;
247   return str;
248 }
249
250 istream &operator>>(istream &str, Rational &rational)
251 {
252   cout << "Enter numerator: ";
253   str >> rational.numerator;
254
255   cout << "Enter denominator: ";
256   str >> rational[1];
257   return str;
258 }
259
260 // Define function operator for conversion
261 Rational::operator double()
262 {
263   return doubleValue();
264 }
```

postfix ++ (line 217)

unary + operator (line 232)

<< operator (line 244)

convert to **double** (line 261)

Listing 13.6 gives a program for testing the new **Rational** class.

## LISTING 13.6 TestNewRationalClass.cpp

```
1 #include <iostream>
2 #include <string>
```

include new **Rational**

```
3  #include "NewRational.h"
4  using namespace std;
5
6  int main()
7  {
8    // Create and initialize two rational numbers r1 and r2.
9    Rational r1(4, 2);
10   Rational r2(2, 3);
11
12   // Test relational operators
13   cout << r1 << " > " << r2 << " is " << (r1 > r2) << endl;
14   cout << r1 << " < " << r2 << " is " << (r1 < r2) << endl;
15   cout << r1 << " == " << r2 << " is " << (r1 == r2) << endl;
16   cout << r1 << " != " << r2 << " is " << (r1 != r2) << endl;
17
18   // Test toString, add, subtract, multiply, and divide operators
19   cout << r1 << " + " << r2 << " = " << r1 + r2 << endl;
20   cout << r1 << " - " << r2 << " = " << r1 - r2 << endl;
21   cout << r1 << " * " << r2 << " = " << r1 * r2 << endl;
22   cout << r1 << " / " << r2 << " = " << r1 / r2 << endl;
23
24   // Test shorthand operators
25   Rational r3(1, 2);
26   r3 += r1;
27   cout << "r3 is " << r3 << endl;
28
29   // Test function operator []
30   Rational r4(1, 2);
31   r4[0] = 3; r4[1] = 4;
32   cout << "r4 is " << r4 << endl;
33
34   // Test function operators for prefix ++ and --
35   r3 = r4++;
36   cout << "r3 is " << r3 << endl;
37   cout << "r4 is " << r4 << endl;
38
39   // Test function operator for conversion
40   cout << "1 + " << r4 << " is " << (1 + r4) << endl;
41
42   return 0;
43 }
```

relational operator

arithmetic operator

postfix ++

array subscript []

conversion operator

```
2 / 1 > 2 / 3 is 1
2 / 1 < 2 / 3 is 0
2 / 1 == 2 / 3 is 0
2 / 1 != 2 / 3 is 1
2 / 1 + 2 / 3 = 2.66667
2 / 1 - 2 / 3 = 1.33333
2 / 1*2 / 3 = 1.33333
2 / 1 / 2 / 3 = 3
r3 is 5 / 2
r4 is 3 / 4
r3 is 3 / 4
r4 is 7 / 4
1 + 7 / 4 is 2.75
```

# 13.11 Overloading the = Operators

By default, the = operator performs a memberwise copy from one object to the other. For example, the following code copies **r2** to **r1**:

copy **r2** to **r1**

```
1 Rational r1(1, 2);
2 Rational r2(4, 5);
3 r1 = r2;
4 cout << "r1 is " << r1.toString() << endl;
5 cout << "r2 is " << r2.toString() << endl;
```

So, the output is

```
r1 is 4/5
r2 is 4/5
```

shallow copy

The behavior of the = operator is the same as the default copy constructor. It performs a *shallow copy,* meaning that if the data field is a pointer to some object, the address of the pointer is copied rather than its contents. In §10.7, "Customizing Copy Constructors," you learned how to customize the copy constructor to perform a deep copy. However, customizing the copy constructor does not change the default behavior of the assignment copy operator =. For example, the **Person** class defined in Figure 10.1 has a pointer data field named **birthDate** which points to a **Date** object. The **Date** class is defined in Figure 10.2. If you run the following code using the assignment operator to assign **person2** to **person1**, as shown in line 23 in Listing 13.7, both **person1** and **person2** point to the same **birthDate**, as shown in Figure 10.5.

## LISTING 13.7 DefaultAssignmentDemo.cpp

```
 1 #include <iostream>
 2 #include "Person.h"
 3 using namespace std;
 4
 5 void displayPerson(Person &person1, Person &person2)
 6 {
 7   cout << "\tperson1 id: " << person1.getId() << endl;
 8   cout << "\tperson1 birth year: " <<
 9     person1.getBirthDate()->getYear()   << endl;
10   cout << "\tperson2 id: " << person2.getId() << endl;
11   cout << "\tperson2 birth year: " <<
12     person2.getBirthDate()->getYear() << endl;
13 }
14
15 int main()
16 {
17   Person person1(111, 1970, 5, 3);
18   Person person2(222, 2000, 11, 8);
19
20   cout << "After creating person1 and person2" << endl;
21   displayPerson(person1, person2);
22
23   person1 = person2; // Copy person2 to person1
24
25   cout << "\nAfter copying person2 to person1" << endl;
26   displayPerson(person1, person2);
27
```

include **Person** header
display **person1**
display year
display **person2**
display year
create **person1**
create **person2**
copy **person2** to **person1**

```
28   person2.getBirthDate()->setYear(1963);
29
30   cout << "\nAfter modifying person2's birthDate" << endl;
31   displayPerson(person1, person2);
32
33   cout << "\n" << (person1.getBirthDate() == person2.getBirthDate());
34   return 0;
35 }
```

modify **person2**'s year

```
After creating person1 and person2

  person1 id: 111
  person1 birth year: 1970
  person2 id: 222
  person2 birth year: 2000

After copying person2 to person1

  person1 id: 222
  person1 birth year: 2000
  person2 id: 222
  person2 birth year: 2000

After modifying person2's birthDate

  person1 id: 222
  person1 birth year: 1963
  person2 id: 222
  person2 birth year: 1963

1
```

To change the way the default assignment operator = works, you need to overload the = operator. In the Person.h file, define

**const** Person **operator=** (**const** Person &person)

Why is the return type **Person** not **void**? C++ allows multiple assignments such as:

person1 = person2 = person3;

In this statement, **person3** is copied to **person2**, and then returns **person2**, and then **person2** is copied to **person1**. So the = operator must have a valid return value type.

In the Person.cpp, implement the function as follows:

```
1 const Person operator=(const Person &person)
2 {
3   id = person.id;
4   Date *p = person.getBirthDate();
5   birthDate = new Date(*p); // Create a new Date object
6   return *this;
7 }
```

copy id

copy date
return calling object

Line 6 returns the calling object using *this. Note that this is the pointer to the calling object, so *this refers to the calling object.

If you run Listing 13.7 now, person1 and person2 will have their independent Date objects for birthDate.

## CHAPTER SUMMARY

- C++ allows you to overload operators to simplify operations for objects.

- You can overload nearly all operators except **?:**, **.**, **.***, and **::**. You cannot change the operator precedence and associativity by overloading.

- In C++, the array subscript **[]** is an operator. You can overload this operator to access the contents of the object using the array-like syntax if desirable.

- You can overload the prefix and postfix **++** and **--**.

- You can overload the **<<** and **>>** operators for input and output.

- You can implement a cast operator to convert an object to a primitive type value.

## REVIEW QUESTIONS

### Section 13.3 Operator Functions

**13.1** How do you define an operator function for overloading an operator?

**13.2** List the operators that cannot be overloaded?

**13.3** Can you change the operator precedence or associativity by overloading?

### Section 13.4 Overloading the Shorthand Operators

**13.4** When you overload a shorthand operator such as **+=**, should the function be void or nonvoid?

### Section 13.5 Overloading the [] Operators

**13.5** What should be the function signature for the **[]** operator?

### Section 13.6 Overloading the Unary Operators

**13.6** What should be the function signature for the unary **+** operator?

### Section 13.7 Overloading the ++ and -- Operators

**13.7** What should be the function signature for the prefix **++** operator? What should be the function signature for the postfix **++** operator?

### Section 13.8 Overloading the << and >> Operators

**13.8** What should be the function signature for the **<<** operator? What should be the function signature for the **>>** operator?

**13.9** If you overload the **<<** operator as follows,

```
ostream &operator<<(ostream &stream, Rational &rational)
{
  stream << rational.getNumerator() << " / " <<
    rational.getDenominator();
  return stream;
}
```

do you still need to declare it in the **Rational** class as follows:

```
friend ostream &operator<<(ostream
  &stream, Rational &rational)
```

**Section 13.9 Object Conversion**

**13.10** What should be the function signature for converting an object to the `int` type?

# PROGRAMMING EXERCISES

**13.1** (*Using the Rational class*) Write a program that will compute the following summation series using the `Rational` class:

$$\frac{1}{2} + \frac{2}{3} + \frac{3}{4} + \cdots + \frac{98}{99} + \frac{99}{100}$$

**13.2**\* (*Demonstrating the benefits of encapsulation*) Rewrite the `Rational` class in §13.2 using a new internal representation for the numerator and denominator. Declare an array of two integers as follows:

`long r[2];`

Use `r[0]` to represent the numerator and `r[1]` to represent the denominator. The signatures of the functions in the `Rational` class are not changed, so a client application that uses the previous `Rational` class can continue to use this new `Rational` class without any modifications.

**13.3**\* (*The Circle class*) Implement the relational operators (`<`, `<=`, `==`, `!=`, `>`, `>=`) in the `Circle` class in Listing 9.5 to order the `Circle` objects according to their radii.

**13.4**\* (*The StackOfIntegers class*) §10.11 defined the `StackOfIntegers` class. Implement the subscript operator `[]` in this class to access the elements via the `[]` operator.

**13.5**\*\* (*Implementing string operators*) The `string` class in the C++ standard library supports the overloaded operators, as shown in Table 9.1. Implement the following operators: `[]`, `+`, `<<`, `<`, and `<=` in the `MyString1` class in Exercise 9.7.

**13.6**\*\* (*Implementing string operators*) The `string` class in the C++ standard library supports the overloaded operators, as shown in Table 9.1. Implement the following operators: `+=`, `>>`, `==`, `!=`, `>`, and `>=` in the `MyString2` class in Exercise 9.8.

## CHAPTER 14

# EXCEPTION HANDLING

## Objectives

- To understand exceptions and exception handling (§14.2).
- To know how to throw an exception and how to catch it (§14.2).
- To understand the advantages of using exception handling (§14.3).
- To create exceptions using C++ standard exception classes (§14.4).
- To create custom exception classes (§14.5).
- To catch multiple exceptions (§14.6).
- To explain how an exception is propagated (§14.7).
- To rethrow exceptions in a **catch** block (§14.8).
- To declare functions with an exception throw list (§14.9).
- To use exception handling appropriately (§14.10).

## 14.1 Introduction

An exception indicates an unusual situation that may occur during a program's execution. For example, suppose your program uses a vector **v** to store elements. The program accesses an element in the vector using **v[i]**, assuming that the element at the index **i** exists. The exceptional situation occurs when the element at the index **i** does not exist. You should write the code in the program to deal with this exceptional case. This chapter introduces the concept of exception handling in C++. You will learn how to throw, catch, and process an exception.

## 14.2 Exception-Handling Overview

To demonstrate exception-handling, let us begin with an example in Listing 14.1 that reads in two integers and displays their quotient.

### LISTING 14.1 Quotient.cpp

```
 1 #include <iostream>
 2 using namespace std;
 3
 4 int main()
 5 {
 6   // Read two integers
 7   cout << "Enter two integers: ";
 8   int number1, number2;
 9   cin >> number1 >> number2;
10
11   cout << number1 << " / " << number2 << " is "
12     << (number1 / number2) << endl;
13
14   return 0;
15 }
```

reads two integers

integer division

```
Enter two integers: 5 2  ⏎ Enter
5 / 2 is 2
```

If you enter **0** for the second number, a runtime error would occur, because you cannot divide an integer by **0**. A simple way to fix the error is to add an **if** statement to test the second number as shown in Listing 14.2.

### LISTING 14.2 QuotientWithIf.cpp

```
 1 #include <iostream>
 2 using namespace std;
 3
 4 int main()
 5 {
 6   // Read two integers
 7   cout << "Enter two integers: ";
 8   int number1, number2;
 9   cin >> number1 >> number2;
10
11   if (number2 != 0)
12   {
13     cout << number1 << " / " << number2 << " is "
14       << (number1 / number2) << endl;
15   }
16   else
17   {
```

reads two integers

test **number2**

```
18       cout << "Divisor cannot be zero" << endl;
19    }
20
21    return 0;
22 }
```

```
Enter two integers: 5 0 ↵Enter
Divisor cannot be zero
```

Listing 14.2 can be rewritten using exception handling as shown in Listing 14.3. Listing 14.2 is simpler than Listing 14.3. You should not use exception handling in this case. However, the purpose of Listing 14.3 is to give a simple example to demonstrate the concept of exception handling. Later you will see the advantages of using exception handling.

### LISTING 14.3  QuotientWithException.cpp

```
 1 #include <iostream>
 2 using namespace std;
 3
 4 int main()
 5 {
 6   // Read two integers
 7   cout << "Enter two integers: ";
 8   int number1, number2;
 9   cin >> number1 >> number2;                          reads two integers
10
11   try                                                  try block
12   {
13     if (number2 == 0)
14       throw number1;
15
16     cout << number1 << " / " << number2 << " is "
17       << (number1 / number2) << endl;
18   }
19   catch (int e)                                        catch block
20   {
21     cout << "Exception: an integer " << e <<
22       " cannot be divided by zero" << endl;
23   }
24
25   cout << "Execution continues ..." << endl;
26
27   return 0;
28 }
```

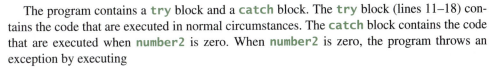

```
Enter two integers: 5 3 ↵Enter
5 / 3 is 1
Execution continues ...
```

```
Enter two integers: 5 0 ↵Enter
Exception: an integer 5 cannot be divided by zero
Execution continues ...
```

The program contains a **try** block and a **catch** block. The **try** block (lines 11–18) contains the code that are executed in normal circumstances. The **catch** block contains the code that are executed when **number2** is zero. When **number2** is zero, the program throws an exception by executing

```
throw number1;
```
                                                         **throw** statement

exception
throwing exception

The value thrown, in this case `number1`, is called an *exception*. The execution of a throw statement is called *throwing an exception.* You can throw a value of any type. In this case, it is the `int` type.

When an exception is thrown, the normal execution flow is interrupted. As the name suggests, "throw exception" is to pass the exception from one place to another. The exception is caught by the `catch` block. The code in the `catch` block is executed to *handle the exception.* Afterwards, the statement (line 25) after the `catch` block is executed.

handle exception

The `throw` statement is analogous to a function call, but instead of calling a function, it calls a `catch` block. In this sense, a `catch` block is like a function definition with a parameter that matches the type of the value being thrown. Unlike a function, after executing the `catch` block, the program control does not return back to the `throw` statement, instead it executes the next statement after the `catch` block.

The identifier `e` in the `catch` block header

```
catch (int e)
```

catch block parameter

acts very much like a parameter in a function. So this parameter is referred to as a `catch` block parameter. The type (e.g., `int`) preceding `e` specifies what kind of exception that `catch` block can catch. Once the exception is caught, you can access the thrown value from this parameter in the body of a `catch` block.

In summary, a template for a `try-throw-catch` block may look like this:

```
try
{
  Code to try;
  Throw an exception with a throw statement or
    from function if necessary;
  More code to try;
}
catch (type e)
{
  Code to process the exception;
}
```

An exception may be thrown directly using a `throw` statement in a `try` block or from invoking a function that may throw an exception.

 **Note**

omit **catch** block parameter

If you are not interested in the contents of an exception object, the `catch` block parameter may be omitted. For example, the following `catch` block is legal:

```
try
{
  // ...
}
catch (type)
{
  cout << "Error occurred " << endl;
}
```

## 14.3 Exception-Handling Advantages

The purpose of Listing 14.3 is to give a simple example to demonstrate exception handling. It does not show any real advantages. This section uses functions to demonstrate the advantages of using exception handling.

Listing 14.4 rewrites Listing 14.3 to compute quotient using a function.

**LISTING 14.4**  QuotientWithFunction.cpp

```
 1 #include <iostream>
 2 using namespace std;
 3
 4 int quotient(int number1, int number2)
 5 {
 6   if (number2 == 0)
 7     throw number1;
 8
 9   return number1 / number2;
10 }
11
12 int main()
13 {
14   // Read two integers
15   cout << "Enter two integers: ";
16   int number1, number2;
17   cin >> number1 >> number2;
18
19   try
20   {
21     int result = quotient(number1, number2);
22     cout << number1 << " / " << number2 << " is "
23       << result << endl;
24   }
25   catch (int e)
26   {
27     cout << "Exception from function: an integer " << e <<
28       " cannot be divided by zero" << endl;
29   }
30
31   cout << "Execution continues ..." << endl;
32
33   return 0;
34 }
```

quotient function

throw exception

reads two integers

try block

invoke function

catch block

```
Enter two integers: 5 3  ⏎Enter
5 / 3 is 1
Execution continues ...
```

```
Enter two integers: 5 0  ⏎Enter
Exception from function: an integer 5 cannot be divided by zero
Execution continues ...
```

Function quotient (lines 4–10) returns the quotient of two integers. If number2 is 0, it cannot return a value. So an exception is thrown in line 7.

The main function invokes the quotient function (line 21). If the quotient function executes normally, it returns a value to the caller. If the quotient function encounters an exception, it throws the exception back to its caller. The caller's catch block handles the exception.

Now you see the *advantages* of using exception handling. It enables a function to throw an exception to its caller. Without this capability, a function must handle the exception or terminate the program.

advantage

# 14.4 Exception Classes

The catch block parameter in the preceding examples is the int type. A class type is often more useful, because an object can contain more information that you want to throw to a

**catch** block. C++ provides a number of predefined classes that can be used for creating exception objects. These classes are shown in Figure 14.1.

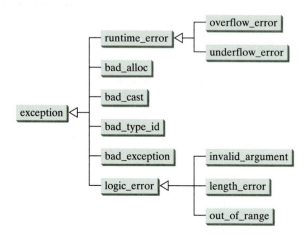

**FIGURE 14.1** You can use standard library classes to create exception objects.

**exception**
**what()**
**runtime_error**

The root class in this hierarchy is **exception** (defined in header **<exception>**). It contains the virtual function **what()** that returns an exception object's error message.

The **runtime_error** class (defined in header **<stdexcept>**) is a base class for several standard exception classes that describes runtime errors. Class **overflow_error** describes an arithmetic overflow, i.e., a value is too large to be stored. Class **underflow_error** describes an arithmetic underflow, i.e., a value is too small to be stored.

**logic_error**

The **logic_error** class (defined in header **<stdexcept>**) is a base class for several standard exception classes that describes logic errors. Class **invalid_argument** indicates that an invalid argument has been passed to a function. Class **length_error** indicates that an object's length has exceeded the maximum allowed length. Class **out_of_range** indicates a value has exceeded its allowed range.

**bad_alloc**
**bad_cast**
**bad_typeid**

**bad_exception**

Classes **bad_alloc**, **bad_cast**, **bad_type_id**, and **bad_exception** describe the exceptions thrown by C++ operators. For example, a **bad_alloc** exception is thrown by the **new** operator if the memory cannot be allocated. A **bad_cast** exception is thrown by the **dynamic_cast** operator as the result of a failed cast to a reference type. A **bad_typeid** exception is thrown by the **typeid** operator when the operand for **typeid** is a **NULL** pointer. The **bad_exception** class describes an exception that can be thrown from an unexpected handler. C++ requires that **unexpected** is called when a function throws an exception that is not on its throw list.

These classes are used by some functions in the C++ standard library to throw exceptions. You also can use these classes to throw exceptions in your programs. Listing 14.5 shows an example that handles the **bad_alloc** exception.

### LISTING 14.5 ExceptionDemo1.cpp

**try** block

```
1 #include <iostream>
2 using namespace std;
3
4 int main()
5 {
6     try
7     {
8         for (int i = 1; i <= 100; i++)
```

```
 9    {
10        new int[70000000];                                      create a large array
11        cout << i << " arrays have been created" << endl;
12    }
13  }
14  catch (bad_alloc &e)                                          catch block
15  {
16    cout << "Exception: " << e.what() << endl;                  invoke e.what()
17  }
18
19    return 0;
20 }
```

```
1 arrays have been created
2 arrays have been created
3 arrays have been created
4 arrays have been created
5 arrays have been created
6 arrays have been created
Exception: bad alloc exception thrown
```

The output shows that the program created six arrays before it failed on the seventh **new** operator. When it fails, a **bad_alloc** exception is thrown and caught in the **catch** block, which displays the message returned from **e.what()**.

Listing 14.6 shows an example that handles the **bad_cast** exception.

## LISTING 14.6  ExceptionDemo2.cpp

```
 1 #include "DerivedCircle.h"                                     include typeinfo
 2 #include "Rectangle.h"
 3 #include <iostream>
 4 using namespace std;
 5
 6 int main()
 7 {
 8   try                                                          try block
 9   {
10     Rectangle r(3, 4);
11     Circle & c = dynamic_cast<Circle&>(r);                     cast
12   }
13   catch (bad_cast &e)                                          catch block
14   {
15     cout << "Exception: " << e.what() << endl;                 invoke e.what()
16   }
17
18     return 0;
19 }
```

```
Exception: Bad Dynamic_cast!
```

Dynamic casting was introduced in §11.9. In line 11, a reference of a **Rectangle** object is cast to a **Circle** reference type, which is illegal and a **bad_cast** exception is thrown. The exception is caught in the **catch** block in line 13.

Listing 14.7 shows an example that creates a **runtime_error** exception.

LISTING 14.7 ExceptionDemo3.cpp

include **typeinfo**

```cpp
 1 #include <typeinfo>
 2 #include <iostream>
 3 #include <stdexcept>
 4 using namespace std;
 5
 6 int quotient(int number1, int number2)
 7 {
 8   if (number2 == 0)
 9     throw runtime_error("Runtime error in quotient");
10
11   return number1 / number2;
12 }
13
14 int main()
15 {
16   // Read two integers
17   cout << "Enter two integers: ";
18   int number1, number2;
19   cin >> number1 >> number2;
20
21   try
22   {
23     int result = quotient(number1, number2);
24     cout << number1 << " / " << number2 << " is "
25       << result << endl;
26   }
27   catch (exception &e)
28   {
29     cout << "Exception: " << e.what() << endl;
30     cout << "Exception type: " << typeid(e).name() << endl;
31   }
32
33   cout << "Execution continues ..." << endl;
34
35   return 0;
36 }
```

throw **runtime_error** (line 9)

**try** block (line 21)

invoke **quotient** (line 23)

**catch** block (line 27)

invoke **e.what()** (line 29)

```
Enter two integers: 5 4 ⏎Enter
5 / 4 is 1
Execution continues ...
```

```
Enter two integers: 5 0 ⏎Enter
Exception: Runtime error in quotient
Exception type: _STL::runtime_error

Execution continues ...
```

In the sample output, the program prompts the user to enter two integers 5 and 0. Invoking **quotient(5, 0)** (line 23) causes a **runtime_error** exception to be thrown (line 9). This exception is caught in the **catch** block in line 27. Note that the **catch-b**lock parameter type is **exception** that is a base class for **runtime_error**. So, it can catch a **runtime_error**.

The **<typeinfo>** header is included in line 1. This header file is needed to use the **typeid** function in line 30.

## 14.5 Custom Exception Classes

C++ provides quite a few exception classes. Use them whenever possible instead of creating your own exception classes. However, if you run into a problem that cannot be adequately described by the predefined exception classes, you can create your own exception class. This class is just like any C++ class, but often it is desirable to derive it from **exception** or a derived class of **exception** so you can utilize the common features (e.g., the **what()** function) in the **exception** class.

Let us consider the **Triangle** class for modeling triangles. The class UML diagram is shown in Figure 14.2. The class is derived from the **GeometricObject** class, which is an abstract class introduced in §11.8.

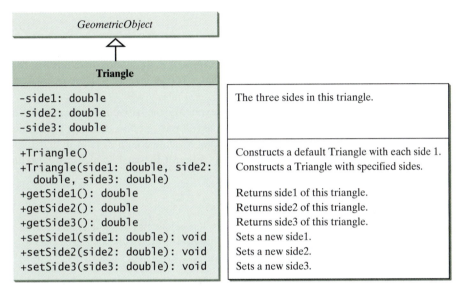

**FIGURE 14.2**    The **Triangle** class models triangles.

A triangle is valid if the sum of any two sides is greater than the third side. When you attempt to create a triangle, or change a side of a triangle, you need to ensure that this property is not violated. If it is violated, an exception should be thrown. You can define the **TriangleException** class in Listing 14.8 to model this exception.

## LISTING 14.8  TriangleException.h

```
1  #include <stdexcept>
2  using namespace std;
3
4  class TriangleException: public logic_error
5  {
6  public:
7    TriangleException(double side1, double side2, double side3)
8      : logic_error("Invalid triangle")
9    {
10     this->side1 = side1;
11     this->side2 = side2;
12     this->side3 = side3;
13   }
14
15   double getSide1()
16   {
17     return side1;
18   }
19
```

*include* **stdexcept**

*extend* **logic_error**

*invoke base constructor*

```
20    double getSide2()
21    {
22      return side2;
23    }
24
25    double getSide3()
26    {
27      return side3;
28    }
29
30 private:
31    double side1, side2, side3;
32 }; // Semicolon required
```

The **TriangleException** class describes a logic error so it is appropriate to define this class to extend the standard **logic_error** class in line 4. Since **logic_error** is in the **<stdexcept>** header file, this header is included in line 1.

Recall that if a base constructor is not invoked explicitly, the base class' no-arg constructor is invoked by default. However, since the base class **logic_error** does not have a no-arg constructor, you must invoke a base class' constructor to avoid compile errors in line 8. Invoking **logic_error("Invalid triangle")** sets an error message, which can be returned from invoking **what()** on an **exception** object.

**Note**

A custom exception class is just like a regular class. It is not necessary to extend from a base class, but it is a good practice to extend from the standard **exception** or a derived class of **exception** so your custom exception class can use the functions from the standard classes.

**Note**

The header file TriangleException.h contains the implementation for the class. Recall that this is the inline implementation. For short functions, using inline implementation is efficient.

The **Triangle** class can be implemented as follows.

## LISTING 14.9 Triangle.h

header for **GeometricObject**
header for
  **TriangleException**
header for **cmath**
extend **GeometricObject**

no-arg constructor

constructor

throw **TriangleException**

```
 1 #include "AbstractGeometricObject.h"
 2 #include "TriangleException.h"
 3 #include <cmath>
 4
 5 class Triangle : public GeometricObject
 6 {
 7 public:
 8   Triangle()
 9   {
10     side1 = side2 = side3 = 1;
11   }
12
13   Triangle(double side1, double side2, double side3)
14   {
15     if (!isValid(side1, side2, side3))
16       throw TriangleException(side1, side2, side3);
17
18     this->side1 = side1;
19     this->side2 = side2;
20     this->side3 = side3;
21   }
```

```
22
23    double getSide1()
24    {
25       return side1;
26    }
27
28    double getSide2()
29    {
30       return side2;
31    }
32
33    double getSide3()
34    {
35       return side3;
36    }
37
38    void setSide1(double side1)
39    {
40       if (!isValid(side1, side2, side3))
41          throw TriangleException(side1, side2, side3);         throw TriangleException
42
43       this->side1 = side1;
44    }
45
46    void setSide2(double side2)
47    {
48       if (!isValid(side1, side2, side3))
49          throw TriangleException(side1, side2, side3);         throw TriangleException
50
51       this->side2 = side2;
52    }
53
54    void setSide3(double side3)
55    {
56       if (!isValid(side1, side2, side3))
57          throw TriangleException(side1, side2, side3);         throw TriangleException
58
59       this->side3 = side3;
60    }
61
62    double getPerimeter()                                        override getPerimeter()
63    {
64       return side1 + side2 + side3;
65    }
66
67    double getArea()                                             override getArea()
68    {
69       double s = getPerimeter() / 2;
70       return sqrt(s * (s - side1) * (s - side2) * (s - side3));
71    }
72
73 private:
74    double side1, side2, side3;
75
76    bool isValid(double side1, double side2, double side3)       check sides
77    {
78       return (side1 < side2 + side3) && (side2 < side1 + side3) &&
79          (side3 < side1 + side2);
80    }
81 };
```

The `Triangle` class extends `GeometricObject` (line 5) and overrides the pure virtual functions `getPerimeter` and `getArea` defined in the `GeometricObject` class (lines 62–71).

The `isValid` function (lines 76–80) checks whether a triangle is valid. This function is declared private for use inside the `Triangle` class.

When constructing a `Triangle` object with three specified sides, the constructor invokes the `isValid` function (line 15) to check the validity. If not valid, a `TriangleException` object is created and thrown in line 16. The validity also is checked when the functions `setSide1`, `setSide2`, and `setSide3` are invoked. When invoking `setSide1(side1)`, `isValid(side1, side2, side3)` is invoked. Here `side1` is the new `side1` to be set, not the current `side1` in the object.

Listing 14.10 gives a test program that creates a `Triangle` object using its no-arg constructor (line 9), displays its perimeter and area (lines 10–11), and changes its `side3` to `4` (line 13), which causes a `TriangleException` to be thrown. The exception is caught in the `catch` block (lines 17–22).

**LISTING 14.10** TestTriangle.cpp

**Triangle** header

create object

set new side

**catch** block

invoke **ex.what()**
invoke **ex.getSide1()**

```cpp
 1  #include <iostream>
 2  #include "Triangle.h"
 3  using namespace std;
 4
 5  int main()
 6  {
 7    try
 8    {
 9      Triangle triangle;
10      cout << "Perimeter is " << triangle.getPerimeter() << endl;
11      cout << "Area is " << triangle.getArea() << endl;
12
13      triangle.setSide3(4);
14      cout << "Perimeter is " << triangle.getPerimeter() << endl;
15      cout << "Area is " << triangle.getArea() << endl;
16    }
17    catch (TriangleException &ex)
18    {
19      cout << ex.what();
20      cout << " three sides are " << ex.getSide1() << " "
21        << ex.getSide2() << " " << ex.getSide3() << endl;
22    }
23
24    return 0;
25  }
```

```
Perimeter is 3
Area is 0.433013
Invalid triangle three sides are 1 1 4
```

The `what()` function is defined in the `exception` class, since `TriangleException` is derived from `logic_error` that is derived from `exception`, you can invoke `what()` (line 19) to display an error message on a `TriangleException` object. The `TriangleException` object contains the information pertinent to a triangle. This information is useful for handling the exception.

## 14.6 Multiple Catches

Most of time, a **try** block should run without exceptions. But occasionally, it may throw an exception. The exception can be of differing types. For example, you may consider a non-positive value for a side in a triangle in the preceding example in Listing 14.10 as another type of exception different from a TriangleException. So, the **try** block may throw a non-positive side exception or a TriangleException, depending on the occasion. One **catch** block can catch only one type of exception. C++ allows you to add multiple **catch** blocks after a **try** block in order to catch multiple types of exceptions.

Let us revise the example in the preceding section by creating a new exception class named NonPositiveSideException and incorporating this exception in the Triangle class. The NonPositiveSideException class is shown in Listing 14.11, and the new Triangle class is given in Listing 14.12.

LISTING 14.11   NonPositiveSideException.h

```cpp
1 #include <stdexcept>
2 using namespace std;
3
4 class NonPositiveSideException : public logic_error
5 {
6 public:
7   NonPositiveSideException(double side)
8     : logic_error("Non-positive side")
9   {
10     this->side = side;
11   }
12
13   double getSide()
14   {
15     return side;
16   }
17
18 private:
19   double side;
20 };
```

include **stdexcept**

extend **logic_error**

invoke base constructor

The NonPositiveSideException class describes a logic error so it is appropriate to define this class to extend the standard **logic_error** class in line 4.

LISTING 14.12   NewTriangle.h

```cpp
1 #include "AbstractGeometricObject.h"
2 #include "TriangleException.h"
3 #include "NonPositiveSideException.h"
4 #include <cmath>
5
6 class Triangle: public GeometricObject
7 {
8 public:
9   Triangle()
10   {
11     side1 = side2 = side3 = 1;
12   }
13
14   Triangle(double side1, double side2, double side3)
15   {
16     check(side1);
```

header for **GeometricObject**

header for **TriangleException**

**NonPositiveSideException**

header for **cmath**

extend **GeometricObject**

no-arg constructor

constructor

check **side1**

```
17        check(side2);
18        check(side3);
19
20        if (!isValid(side1, side2, side3))
21          throw TriangleException(side1, side2, side3);
22
23        this->side1 = side1;
24        this->side2 = side2;
25        this->side3 = side3;
26      }
27
28      double getSide1()
29      {
30        return side1;
31      }
32
33      double getSide2()
34      {
35        return side2;
36      }
37
38      double getSide3()
39      {
40        return side3;
41      }
42
43      void setSide1(double side1)
44      {
45        check(side1);
46        if (!isValid(side1, side2, side3))
47          throw TriangleException(side1, side2, side3);
48
49        this->side1 = side1;
50      }
51
52      void setSide2(double side2)
53      {
54        check(side2);
55        if (!isValid(side1, side2, side3))
56          throw TriangleException(side1, side2, side3);
57
58        this->side2 = side2;
59      }
60
61      void setSide3(double side3)
62      {
63        check(side3);
64        if (!isValid(side1, side2, side3))
65          throw TriangleException(side1, side2, side3);
66
67        this->side3 = side3;
68      }
69
70      double getPerimeter()
71      {
72        return side1 + side2 + side3;
73      }
74
75      double getArea()
76      {
```

throw **TriangleException**

check **side1**

check **side1**

```
77        double s = getPerimeter() / 2;
78        return sqrt(s * (s - side1) * (s - side2) * (s - side3));
79      }
80
81 private:
82      double side1, side2, side3;
83
84      bool isValid(double side1, double side2, double side3)
85      {
86        return (side1 < side2 + side3) && (side2 < side1 + side3) &&
87          (side3 < side1 + side2);
88      }
89
90      void check(double side)
91      {
92        if (side <= 0)
93          throw NonPositiveSideException(side);                         throw
94      }                                                                 NonPositiveSide-
95 };                                                                    Exception
```

The new **Triangle** class is identical to the one in Listing 14.9, except that it also checks non-positive sides. When a **Triangle** object is created, all of its sides are checked by invoking the **check** function (lines 16–18). The **check** function checks whether a side is non-positive (line 92): it throws a **NonPositiveSideException** (line 93).

Listing 14.13 gives a test program that prompts the user to enter three sides (lines 9–11) and creates a **Triangle** object (line 12).

## LISTING 14.13   MultipleCatchDemo.cpp

```
 1 #include <iostream>
 2 #include "NewTriangle.h"                                              new Triangle class
 3 using namespace std;
 4
 5 int main()
 6 {
 7    try
 8    {
 9      cout << "Enter three sides: ";
10      double side1, side2, side3;
11      cin >> side1 >> side2 >> side3;
12      Triangle triangle(side1, side2, side3);                          create object
13      cout << "Perimeter is " << triangle.getPerimeter() << endl;
14      cout << "Area is " << triangle.getArea() << endl;
15    }
16    catch (NonPositiveSideException &ex)                               catch block
17    {
18      cout << ex.what();
19      cout << " the side is " << ex.getSide() << endl;
20    }
21    catch (TriangleException &ex)                                      catch block
22    {
23      cout << ex.what();
24      cout << " three sides are " << ex.getSide1() << " "
25        << ex.getSide2() << " " << ex.getSide3() << endl;
26    }
27
28    return 0;
29 }
```

```
Enter three sides: 2 2.5 2.5    ↵Enter    ←———— Normal execution
Perimeter is 7
Area is 2.29129
```

```
Enter three sides: -1 1 1    ↵Enter    ←———— Non-positive side -1
Non-positive side the side is -1
```

```
Enter three sides: 1 2 1    ↵Enter    ←———— Invalid triangle
Invalid triangle three sides are 1 2 1
```

As shown in the sample output, if you enter three sides 2, 2.5, and 2.5, it is a legal triangle. The program displays the perimeter and area of the triangle (lines 13–14). If you enter -1, 1, and 1, the constructor (line 12) throws a NonPositiveSideException. This exception is caught by the **catch** block in line 16 and processed in lines 18–19. If you enter 1, 2, and 1, the constructor (line 12) throws a TriangleException. This exception is caught by the **catch** block in line 21 and processed in lines 23–25.

**catch** block

### Note

Various exception classes can be derived from a common base class. If a **catch** block catches exception objects of a base class, it can catch all the exception objects of the derived classes of that base class.

order of exception handlers

### Note

The order in which exceptions are specified in **catch** blocks is important. A **catch** block for a base class type should appear after a **catch** block for a derived class type. Otherwise, the exception of a derived class is always caught by the **catch** block for the base class. For example, the ordering in (a) is erroneous, because TriangleException is a derived class of logic_error. The correct ordering should be as shown in (b). In (a), a TriangleException occurred in the **try** block is caught by the **catch** block for logic_error.

```
try
{
    ...
}
catch (logic_error &ex)
{
    ...
}
catch (TriangleException &ex)
{
    ...
}
```

(a) Wrong order

```
try
{
    ...
}
catch (TriangleException &ex)
{
    ...
}
catch (logic_error &ex)
{
    ...
}
```

(b) Correct order

## 14.7 Exception Propagation

You now know how to declare an exception and how to throw an exception. When an exception is thrown, it can be caught and handled in a **try-catch** block, as follows:

```
try
{
    statements;  // Statements that may throw exceptions
}
catch (Exception1 &exVar1)
{
```

```
    handler for exception1;
}
catch (Exception2 &exVar2)
{
    handler for exception2;
}
...
catch (ExceptionN &exVar3)
{
    handler for exceptionN;
}
```

If no exceptions arise during the execution of the **try** block, the **catch** blocks are skipped.

If one of the statements inside the **try** block throws an exception, C++ skips the remaining statements in the **try** block and starts the process of finding the code to handle the exception. The code that handles the exception is called the *exception handler*; it is found by propagating the exception backward through a chain of function calls, starting from the current function. Each **catch** block is examined in turn, from first to last, to see whether the type of the exception object is an instance of the exception class in the **catch** block. If so, the exception object is assigned to the variable declared, and the code in the **catch** block is executed. If no handler is found, C++ exits this function, passes the exception to the function that invoked the function, and continues the same process to find a handler. If no handler is found in the chain of functions being invoked, the program terminates and prints an error message on the console. The process of finding a handler is called *catching an exception*.

> exception handler

> catching exception

Suppose the **main** function invokes **function1**, **function1** invokes **function2**, **function2** invokes **function3**, and an exception occurs in **function3**, as shown in Figure 14.3. Consider the following scenario:

- If **function3** cannot handle the exception, **function3** is aborted, and the control is returned to **function2**. If the exception type is **Exception3**, it is caught by the **catch** block for handling exception **ex3** in **function2**. **statement5** is skipped, and **statement6** is executed.

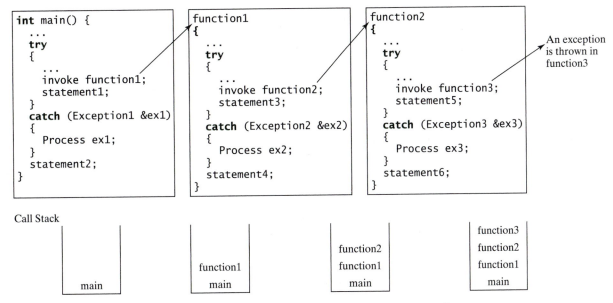

**FIGURE 14.3** If an exception is not caught in the current function, it is passed to its caller. The process is repeated until the exception is caught or passed to the **main** function.

- If the exception type is Exception2, function2 is aborted, the control is returned to function1, and the exception is caught by the catch block for handling exception ex2 in function1. statement3 is skipped, and statement4 is executed.

- If the exception type is Exception1, function1 is aborted, the control is returned to the main function, and the exception is caught by the catch block for handling exception ex1 in the main function. statement1 is skipped, and statement2 is executed.

- If the exception type is not Exception1, Exception2, or Exception3, the exception is not caught and the program terminates. statement1 and statement2 are not executed.

## 14.8 Rethrowing Exceptions

C++ allows an exception handler to rethrow the exception if the handler cannot process the exception or the handler simply wants to let its caller be notified of the exception. The syntax may look like this:

```
try
{
  statements;
}
catch (TheException &ex)
{
  perform operations before exits;
  throw;
}
```

The statement throw rethrows the exception so that other handlers get a chance to process the exception.

Listing 14.14 gives an example that demonstrates how to rethrow exceptions.

LISTING 14.14 RethrowExceptionDemo.cpp

```
 1 #include <iostream>
 2 #include <stdexcept>
 3 using namespace std;
 4
 5 int f1()
 6 {
 7   try
 8   {
 9     throw runtime_error("Exception in f1");
10   }
11   catch (exception &ex)
12   {
13     cout << "Exception caught in function f1" << endl;
14     cout << ex.what() << endl;
15     throw; // Rethrow the exception
16   }
17 }
18
19 int main()
20 {
21   try
22   {
23     f1();
24   }
```

*throw an exception*

**catch** block

*rethrow exception*

*invoke* **f1**

```
25   catch (exception &ex)
26   {
27     cout << "Exception caught in function main" << endl;
28     cout << ex.what() << endl;
29   }
30
31   return 0;
32 }
```

**catch** block

```
Exception caught in function f1   ←———— Handler in function f1
Exception in f1

Exception caught in function main ←———— Handler in function main
Exception in f1
```

The program invokes function **f1** in line 23, which throws an exception in line 9. This exception is caught in the **catch** block in line 11, and it is rethrown to the **main** function in line 15. The **catch** block in the **main** function catches the rethrown exception and processes it in lines 27–28.

## 14.9 Exception Specification

An *exception specification*, also known as *throw list*, lists exceptions that a function can throw. So far, you have seen the function defined without a throw list. In this case, the function can throw any exception. So, it is attempting to omit exception specification. However, this is not a good practice. A function should warn the programmers that any exceptions it might throw, so the programmers can write a robust program to deal with these potential exceptions in a **try-catch** block.

throw list

The syntax for exception specification is as follows:

```
returnType functionName(parameterList) throw (exceptionList)
```

The exceptions are declared in the function header. For example, you should revise the **check** function and the **Triangle** constructor in Listing 14.12 to specify appropriate exceptions as follows:

```
1 void check(double side) throw (NonPositiveSideException)
2 {
3   if (side <= 0)
4     throw NonPositiveSideException(side);
5 }
6
7 Triangle(double side1, double side2, double side3)
8     throw (NonPositiveSideException, TriangleException)
9 {
10   check(side1);
11   check(side2);
12   check(side3);
13
14   if (!isValid(side1, side2, side3))
15     throw TriangleException(side1, side2, side3);
16
17   this->side1 = side1;
18   this->side2 = side2;
19   this->side3 = side3;
20 }
```

throw list

throw
  **NonPositiveSide-
  Exception**

throw list

throw **TriangleException**

Function **check** declares to throw NonPositiveSideException and constructor Triangle declares to throw NonPositiveSideException and TriangleException.

empty exception specification

**Note**

Placing **throw()** after a function header, known as an *empty exception specification*, declares that the function does not throw any exceptions. If a function attempts to throw an exception, a standard C++ function **unexpected** in invoked, which normally terminates the program.

undeclared exception

**Note**

Throwing an exception that is not declared in the throw list will cause the function **unexpected** to be invoked. However, a function without exception specification can throw any exception and will not cause **unexpected** to be invoked.

## 14.10 When to Use Exceptions

The **try** block contains the code that are executed in normal circumstances. The **catch** block contains the code that are executed in exceptional circumstances. Exception handling separates error-handling code from normal programming tasks, thus making programs easier to read and to modify. Be aware, however, that exception handling usually requires more time and resources, because it requires instantiating a new exception object, rolling back the call stack, and propagating the exception through the chain of functions invoked to search for the handler.

An exception occurs in a function. If you want the exception to be processed by its caller, you should throw it. If you can handle the exception in the function where it occurs, there is no need to throw or use exceptions.

In general, common exceptions that may occur in multiple classes in a project are candidates for exception classes. Simple errors that may occur in individual functions are best handled locally without throwing exceptions.

Exception handling is for dealing with unexpected error conditions. Do not use a **try-catch** block to deal with simple, expected situations. Which situations are exceptional and which are expected is sometimes difficult to decide. The point is not to abuse exception handling as a way to deal with a simple logic test.

A general paradigm for exception handling is that you declare to throw an exception in a function as shown in (a), and use the function in a **try-catch** block as shown in (b).

```
returnType function1(parameterList)
  throw (exceptionList)
{
  ...
  if (an exception condition)
    throw AnException(arguments);
  ...
}
```

(a)

```
returnType function2(parameterList)
{
  try
  {
    ...
    function1 (arguments);
    ...
  }
  catch (AnException &ex)
  {
    Handler;
  }
  ...
}
```

(b)

## KEY TERMS

## CHAPTER SUMMARY

- Exception handling makes programs robust. Exception handling separates error-handling code from normal programming tasks, thus making programs easier to read and to modify. Another important advantage of exception handling is that it enables a function to throw an exception to its caller.

- C++ allows you to use the `throw` statement to throw a value of any type (primitive or class type) when an exception occurs. This value is passed to a `catch` block as an argument so that the `catch` block can utilize this value to process the exception.

- When an exception is thrown, the normal execution flow is interrupted. If the exception value matches a `catch` block parameter type, the control is transferred to a `catch` block. Otherwise, the function is exited and the exception is thrown to the function's caller. If the exception is not handled in the `main` function, the program is aborted.

- C++ provides a number of predefined classes that can be used for creating exception objects. You can use the `exception` class or its derived classes `runtime_error` and `logic_error` to create exception objects.

- You can also create custom exception classes if the predefined classes cannot adequately describe exceptions. This class is just like any C++ class, but often it is desirable to derive it from `exception` or a derived class of `exception` so you can utilize the common features (e.g., the `what()` function) in the `exception` class.

- A `try` block may be followed by multiple `catch` blocks. The order in which exceptions are specified in `catch` blocks is important. A `catch` block for a base class type should appear after a `catch` block for a derived class type.

- If a function throws an exception, you should declare the type of the exception in the function header to tell the programmers to deal with the potential exceptions.

- Exception handling should not be used to replace simple tests. You should test simple exceptions whenever possible and reserve exception handling for dealing with situations that cannot be handled with `if` statements.

## REVIEW QUESTIONS

**Sections 14.2–14.3**

14.1 Show the output of the following code with input `120`:

```cpp
#include <iostream>
using namespace std;

int main()
{
  cout << "Enter a temperature: ";
  double temperature;
  cin >> temperature;

  try
  {
    cout << "Start of try block ..." << endl;
```

```
      if (temperature > 95)
        throw temperature;

      cout << "End of try block ..." << endl;
    }
    catch (double temperature)
    {
      cout << "The temperature is " << temperature << endl;
      cout << "It is too hot" << endl;
    }

    cout << "Continue ..." << endl;

    return 0;
  }
```

14.2  What will be the output for the preceding code if the input is **80**?

14.3  Will it be an error if you change

```
catch (double temperature)
{
  cout << "The temperature is " << temperature << endl;
  cout << "It is too hot" << endl;
}
```

in the preceding code to

```
catch (double)
{
  cout << "It is too hot" << endl;
}
```

### Sections 14.4–14.5

14.4  Describe the C++ **exception** class and its derived classes. Give examples of using **bad_alloc** and **bad_cast**. Why is it a good practice to declare custom exception classes derived from a standard exception class?

14.5  Show the output of the following code with input **10**, **60**, and **120**, respectively:

```cpp
#include <iostream>
using namespace std;

int main()
{
  cout << "Enter a temperature: ";
  double temperature;
  cin >> temperature;

  try
  {
    cout << "Start of try block ..." << endl;

    if (temperature > 95)
      throw runtime_error("Exceptional temperature");

    cout << "End of try block ..." << endl;
  }
  catch (runtime_error &ex)
  {
    cout << ex.what() << endl;
```

```
            cout << "It is too hot" << endl;
        }

        cout << "Continue ..." << endl;

        return 0;
    }
```

## Sections 14.4–14.10

**14.6** Can you throw multiple exceptions in one **throw** statement? Can you have multiple **catch** blocks in a **try-catch** block?

**14.7** Suppose that **statement2** causes an exception in the following **try-catch** block:

```
try
{
    statement1;
    statement2;
    statement3;
}
catch (Exception1 ex1)
{
}
catch (Exception2 ex2)
{
}

statement4;
```

Answer the following questions:

- Will **statement3** be executed?
- If the exception is not caught, will **statement4** be executed?
- If the exception is caught in the **catch** block, will **statement4** be executed?
- If the exception is passed to the caller, will **statement4** be executed?

**14.8** Suppose that **statement2** causes an exception in the following statement:

```
try {
    statement1;
    statement2;
    statement3;
}
catch (Exception1 ex1)
{
}
catch (Exception2 ex2)
{
}
catch (Exception3 ex3)
{
    statement4;
    throw;
}
statement5;
```

Answer the following questions:

- Will **statement5** be executed if the exception is not caught?
- If the exception is of type **Exception3**, will **statement4** be executed, and will **statement5** be executed?

**14.9** What is the purpose of exception specifications? How do you declare a throw list? Can you declare multiple exceptions in a function declaration?

## PROGRAMMING EXERCISES

**14.1**\* (*runtime_error*) Exercise 7.13 specifies the **parseHex(char \*hexString)** function that converts a hex string into a decimal number. Implement the **parseHex** function to throw a **runtime_error** exception if the string is not a hex string. Write a test program that prompts the user to enter a hex number as a string and display the number in decimal format.

**14.2**\* (*runtime_error*) Exercise 7.14 specifies the **parseBinary (char \*binaryString)** function that converts a binary string into a decimal number. Implement the **parseBinary** function to throw a **runtime_error** exception if the string is not a binary string. Write a test program that prompts the user to enter a binary number as a string and display the number in decimal format.

**14.3**\* (*Modify Rational class*) In §13.5, "Overloading the **[]** Operators," introduced how to overload the **[]** array subscript operator in the **Rational** class. If the subscript is neither **0** nor **1**, the function terminates the program by invoking **exit(0)**, which obviously is not a good implementation. You should not let this operator terminate the program. To fix this problem, define a custom exception called **IllegalSubscriptException** and let the function operator throw an **IllegalSubscriptException** if the subscript is neither **0** nor **1**. Write a test program with a **try-catch** block to handle this type of exception.

**14.4**\* (*Modify StackOfIntegers class*) §10.11, "Case Study: The **StackOfIntegers**" Class," defined a stack class for integers. Define a custom exception class named **EmptyStackException** and let the **pop** function throw an **EmptyStackException** if the stack is empty. Write a test program with a **try-catch** block to handle this type of exception.

**14.5**\* (*HexFormatException*) Implement the **parseHex** function in Exercise 14.1 to throw a **HexFormatException** if the string is not a hex string. Define a custom exception class named **HexFormatException**. Write a test program that prompts the user to enter a hex number as a string and display the number in decimal.

**14.6**\* (*BinaryFormatException*) Implement the **parseBinary** function in Exercise 14.2 to throw a **BinaryFormatException** if the string is not a binary string. Define a custom exception class named **BinaryFormatException**. Write a test program that prompts the user to enter a binary number as a string and display the number in decimal.

# PART 3

# DATA STRUCTURES

The design and implementation of efficient data structures is an important subject in computer science. Data structures such as lists, stacks, queues, sets, maps, heaps, and binary trees have many applications in compiler construction, computer operating systems, and file management. C++ provides vectors, deques, lists, stacks, queues, sets, and maps in the Standard Template Library (STL). This part of the book introduces the main subjects in a typical data structures course.

## Prerequisites for Part 3

templates

Chapter 15, "Templates," introduces the concept of the templates. This chapter is a prerequisite for all other chapters in Part 3.

implementation

Chapter 16, "Linked Lists, Stacks, and Queues," and Chapter 17, "Trees, Heaps, and Priority Queues," discuss the implementation of the basic data structures. Chapter 18, "Algorithm Efficiency and Sorting," is optional and can be covered after Chapter 15. Chapter 19, "STL Containers," and Chapter 20, "STL Algorithms," introduce the data structures provided in the C++ library. Chapters 19 and 20 can be covered independently from Chapters 16 and 17.

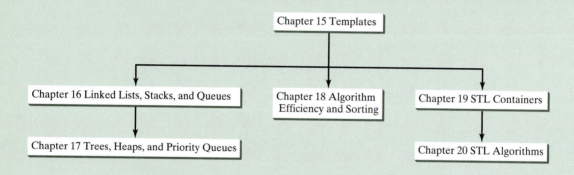

# TEMPLATES

## 15.1 Introduction

templates

C++ provides functions and classes for developing reusable software. *Templates* provide the capability to parameterize types in functions and classes. With this capability, you can define one function or one class with a generic type that can be substituted for a concrete type by the compiler. For example, you may define one function for finding the maximum number between two numbers of a generic type. If you invoke this function with two `int` arguments, the generic type is substituted by the `int` type. If you invoke this function with two `double` arguments, the generic type is substituted by the `double` type.

This chapter introduces the concept of templates, and you will learn how to define function templates and class templates and use the templates with concrete types.

## 15.2 Templates Basics

Let us begin with a simple example to demonstrate the need for templates. Suppose you want to find the maximum of two integers, two doubles, and two characters. You might write three overloaded functions as follows:

`int` type

```
 1  int maxValue (int value1, int value2)
 2  {
 3    if (value1 > value2)
 4      return value1;
 5    else
 6      return value2;
 7  }
 8
```

`double` type

```
 9  double maxValue(double value1, double value2)
10  {
11    if (value1 > value2)
12      return value1;
13    else
14      return value2;
15  }
16
```

`char` type

```
17  char maxValue(char value1, char value2)
18  {
19    if (value1 > value2)
20      return value1;
21    else
22      return value2;
23  }
```

These three functions are almost identical, except that each uses a different type. The first function uses the `int` type in three places, the second uses the `double` type in three places, and the third uses the `char` type in three places. It would save typing, save space, and make the program easy to maintain if you could simply define one function with a generic type as follows:

generic type

```
GenericType maxValue(
  GenericType value1, GenericType value2)
{
  if (value1 > value2)
    return value1;
  else
    return value2;
}
```

This `GenericType` applies to all types such as `int`, `double`, and `char`.

C++ enables you to define a function template with generic types. Listing 15.1 defines a template function for finding a maximum value between two values of a generic type.

## LISTING 15.1  GenericMaxValue.cpp

```cpp
 1 #include <iostream>
 2 #include <string>
 3 using namespace std;
 4
 5 template<typename T>
 6 T maxValue(T value1, T value2)
 7 {
 8   if (value1 > value2)
 9     return value1;
10   else
11     return value2;
12 }
13
14 int main()
15 {
16   cout << "Maximum between 1 and 3 is " << maxValue(1, 3) << endl;
17   cout << "Maximum between 1.5 and 0.3 is "
18     << maxValue(1.5, 0.3) << endl;
19   cout << "Maximum between 'A' and 'N' is "
20     << maxValue('A', 'N') << endl;
21   cout << "Maximum between \"ABC\" and \"ABD\" is "
22     << maxValue("ABC", "ABD") << endl;
23
24   return 0;
25 }
```

template prefix<br>type parameter

invoke **maxValue**

invoke **maxValue**

invoke **maxValue**

invoke **maxValue**

```
Maximum between 1 and 3 is 3
Maximum between 1.5 and 0.3 is 1.5
Maximum between 'A' and 'N' is N
Maximum between "ABC" and "ABD" is ABD
```

The definition for the function template begins with the keyword `template` followed by a list of parameters. Each parameter must be preceded by the interchangeable keywords `typename` or `class` in the form `<typename typeParameter>` or `<class typeParameter>`. For example, line 5

```
template<typename T>
```

begins the definition of the function template for `maxValue`. This line is also known as the *template prefix*. Here `T` is a *type parameter*. By convention, a single capital letter such as `T` is used to denote a type parameter.

template prefix<br>type parameter

The `maxValue` function is defined in lines 6–12. A type parameter can be used in the function just like a regular type. You can use it to specify the return type of a function, declare function parameters, or declare variables in the function.

The `maxValue` function is invoked to return the maximum `int`, `double`, `char`, and `string` in lines 16–22. For the function call `maxValue(1, 3)`, the compiler recognizes that the parameter type is `int` and replaces the type parameter `T` with `int` to invoke the `maxValue` function with a concrete `int` type. For the function call `maxValue("ABC", "ABD")`, the compiler recognizes that the parameter type is `string` and replaces the type parameter `T` with `string` to invoke the `maxValue` function with a concrete `string` type.

invoke a function

**Caution**

The generic `maxValue` function can be used to return a maximum of two values of *any type*, provided that

- The two values have the same type;
- The two values can be compared using the > operator.

match parameter

For example, if one value is `int` and the other is `double` (e.g., `maxValue(1, 3.5)`), the compiler will report a syntax error because it cannot find a match for the call. If you invoke `maxValue(Circle(1), Circle(2))`, the compiler will report a syntax error because the > operator is not defined in the `Circle` class.

**Tip**

**<typename T> preferred**

You can use either `<typename T>` or `<class T>` to specify a type parameter. Using `<typename T>` is better because `<typename T>` is descriptive. `<class T>` could be confused with class declaration.

**Note**

multiple type parameters

Occasionally, a template function may have more than one parameter. In this case, place the parameters together inside the brackets, separated by commas, such as `<typename T1, typename T2, typename T3>`.

## 15.3 Example: A Generic Sort

Listing 6.9, SelectionSort.h, gives a function to sort an array of **double** values. Here is a copy of the function:

**double** type

```
1  void selectionSort(double list[], int arraySize)
2  {
3    for (int i = arraySize - 1; i >= 1; i--)
4    {
5      // Find the maximum in the list[0..i]
6      double currentMax = list[0];
7      int currentMaxIndex = 0;
8
9      for (int j = 1; j <= i; j++)
10     {
11       if (currentMax < list[j])
12       {
13         currentMax = list[j];
14         currentMaxIndex = j;
15       }
16     }
17
18     // Swap list[i] with list[currentMaxIndex] if necessary;
19     if (currentMaxIndex != i)
20     {
21       list[currentMaxIndex] = list[i];
22       list[i] = currentMax;
23     }
24   }
25 }
```

**double** type

It is easy to modify this function to write new overloaded functions for sorting an array of **int** values, **char** values, **string** values, etc. All you need to do is to replace the word **double** by **int**, **char**, or **string** in two places (lines 1 and 6).

Instead of writing several overloaded sort functions, you can define just one template function that works for any type. Listing 15.2 defines a generic function for sorting an array of elements.

## LISTING 15.2  GenericSort.cpp

```
 1 #include <iostream>
 2 #include <string>
 3 using namespace std;
 4
 5 template<typename T T>                                          template prefix
 6 void sort(T list[], int arraySize)                             type parameter
 7 {
 8   for (int i = arraySize - 1; i >= 1; i--)
 9   {
10     // Find the maximum in the list[0..i]
11     T currentMax = list[0];                                    type parameter
12     int currentMaxIndex = 0;
13
14     for (int j = 1; j <= i; j++)
15     {
16       if (currentMax < list[j])
17       {
18         currentMax = list[j];
19         currentMaxIndex = j;
20       }
21     }
22
23     // Swap list[i] with list[currentMaxIndex] if necessary;
24     if (currentMaxIndex != i)
25     {
26       list[currentMaxIndex] = list[i];
27       list[i] = currentMax;
28     }
29   }
30 }
31
32 template<typename T>                                            template prefix
33 void printArray(T list[], int arraySize)                       type parameter
34 {
35   for (int i = 0; i < arraySize; i++)
36   {
37     cout << list[i] << " ";
38   }
39   cout << endl;
40 }
41
42 int main()
43 {
44   int list1[] = {3, 5, 1, 0, 2, 8, 7};
45   sort(list1, 7);                                              invoke sort
46   printArray(list1, 7);                                        invoke printArray
47
48   double list2[] = {3.5, 0.5, 1.4, 0.4, 2.5, 1.8, 4.7};
49   sort(list2, 7);
50   printArray(list2, 7);
51
52   string list3[] = {"Atlanta", "Denver", "Chicago", "Dallas"};
53   sort(list3, 4);
54   printArray(list3, 4);
55
56   return 0;
57 }
```

```
0 1 2 3 5 7 8
0.4 0.5 1.4 1.8 2.5 3.5 4.7
Atlanta Chicago Dallas Denver
```

Two template functions are defined in this program. The template function `sort` (lines 5–30) uses the type parameter `T` to specify the element type in an array. This function is identical to the `selectionSort` function except that the parameter `double` is replaced by a generic type `T`.

The template function `printArray` (lines 32–40) uses the type parameter `T` to specify the element type in an array. This function displays all the elements in the array to the console.

The `main` function invokes the `sort` function to sort an array of `int`, `double`, and `string` values (lines 45, 49, and 53) and invokes the `printArray` function to display these arrays (lines 46, 50, and 54).

developing generic function

 **Tip**

When you define a generic function, it is better to start with a non-generic function, debug and test it, and then convert it to a generic function.

## 15.4 Class Templates

In the preceding sections, you defined template functions with type parameters for the function. You also can define template classes with type parameters for the class. The type parameters can be used everywhere in the class where a regular type appears.

Recall that the `StackOfIntegers` class, defined in §10.11, can be used to create a stack for `int` values. Here is a copy of the class with its UML class diagram, as shown in Figure 15.1(a).

```
1  #ifndef STACK_H
2  #define STACK_H
3
4  class StackOfIntegers
5  {
6  public:
7    StackOfIntegers();
8    bool empty();
9    int peek();
10   void push(int value);
11   int pop();
12   int getSize();
13
14 private:
15   int elements[100];
16   int size;
17 };
18
19 StackOfIntegers::StackOfIntegers()
20 {
21   size = 0;
22 }
23
24 bool StackOfIntegers::empty()
25 {
26   return (size == 0);
27 }
28
```

int type
int type
int type

int type

```
29 int  StackOfIntegers::peek()
30 {
31    return elements[size - 1];
32 }
33
34 void StackOfIntegers::push(int value)
35 {
36    elements[size++] = value;
37 }
38
39 int StackOfIntegers::pop()
40 {
41    return elements[--size];
42 }
43
44 int StackOfIntegers::getSize()
45 {
46    return size;
47 }
48
49 #endif
```

| **StackOfIntegers** | **Stack\<T>** |
|---|---|
| -elements[100]: int<br>-size: int | -elements[100]: T<br>-size: int |
| +StackOfIntegers()<br>+empty(): bool<br>+peek(): int<br>+push(value: int): void<br>+pop(): int<br>+getSize(): int | +Stack()<br>+empty(): bool<br>+peek(): T<br>+push(value: T): void<br>+pop(): T<br>+getSize(): int |
| (a) | (b) |

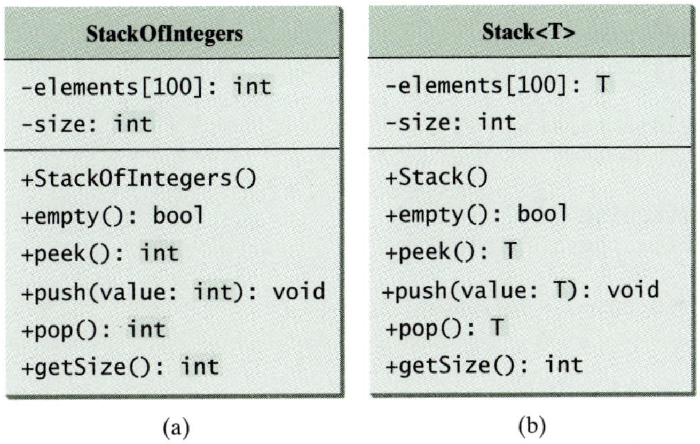

**FIGURE 15.1**    Stack\<T> is a generic version of the Stack class.

By replacing the highlighted **int** in the preceding code with **double**, **char**, or **string**, you easily can modify this class to define classes such as **StackOfDouble**, **StackOfChar**, and **StackOfString** for representing a stack of **int**, **double**, and **string** values. But, instead of writing almost identical code for these classes, you can define just one template class that works for the element of any type. Figure 15.1(b) shows the UML class diagram for the new generic **Stack** class. Listing 15.3 defines a generic stack class for storing elements of certain types.

## LISTING 15.3  GenericStack.h

```
1 #ifndef STACK_H
2 #define STACK_H
3
4 template<typename T>                        template prefix
5 class Stack
6 {
```

type parameter
type parameter
type parameter

```
 7 public:
 8   Stack();
 9   bool empty();
10   T peek();
11   void  push(T value);
12   T pop();
13   int getSize();
14
15 private:
16   T elements[100];
17   int size;
18 };
19
```

function template

```
20 template<typename T>
21 Stack<T>::Stack()
22 {
23   size = 0;
24 }
25
```

function template

```
26 template<typename T>
27 bool Stack<T>::empty()
28 {
29   return (size == 0);
30 }
31
```

function template

```
32 template<typename T>
33 T Stack<T>::peek()
34 {
35   return elements[size - 1];
36 }
37
```

function template

```
38 template<typename T>
39 void Stack<T>::push(T value)
40 {
41   elements[size++] = value;
42 }
43
```

function template

```
44 template<typename T>
45 T Stack<T>::pop()
46 {
47   return elements[--size];
48 }
49
```

function template

```
50 template<typename T>
51 int Stack<T>::getSize()
52 {
53   return size;
54 }
55
56 #endif
```

template prefix

The syntax for class templates is basically the same as that for function templates. You place the *template prefix* before the class declaration (line 4), just like you place the template prefix before the function template.

```
template<typename T>
```

The type parameter can be used in the class just like any regular data type. Here, the type `T` is used to declare functions `peek()` (line 10), `push(T value)` (line 11), and `pop()` (line 12). `T` also is used to declare array `elements` in line 16.

The constructors and functions are defined the same way for regular classes, except that the constructors and functions themselves are templates. So you have to place the template prefix before the constructor and function header. For example,

defining constructors
defining functions

```cpp
template<typename T>
Stack<T>::Stack()
{
  size = 0;
}

template<typename T>
bool Stack<T>::empty()
{
  return (size == 0);
}

template<typename T>
T Stack<T>::peek()
{
  return elements[size - 1];
}
```

Also, please note that the class name before the scope resolution operator :: is Stack<T> not Stack.

**Tip**

compile issue

GenericStack.h combines class declaration and class implementation into one file. Normally, you put class declaration and class implementation into two separate files. However, it is safer to put them together for class templates, because some compliers cannot compile them separately.

Listing 15.4 gives a test program that creates a stack for int values in line 9 and a stack for strings in line 18.

## LISTING 15.4   TestGenericStack.cpp

```cpp
1 #include <iostream>
2 #include <string>
3 #include "GenericStack.h"
4 using namespace std;
5
6 int main()
7 {
8   // Create a stack of int values
9   Stack<int> intStack;
10  for (int i = 0; i < 10; i++)
11    intStack.push(i);
12
13  while (!intStack.empty())
14    cout << intStack.pop() << " ";
15  cout << endl;
16
17  // Create a stack of strings
18  Stack<string> stringStack;
19  stringStack.push("Chicago");
20  stringStack.push("Denver");
21  stringStack.push("London");
22
```

generic **Stack**

**int** stack

**string** stack

```
23    while (!stringStack.empty())
24      cout << stringStack.pop() << " ";
25    cout << endl;
26
27    return 0;
28 }
```

```
9 8 7 6 5 4 3 2 1 0
London Denver Chicago
```

declaring objects

To declare an object from a template class, you have to specify a concrete type for the type parameter T. For example,

```
Stack<int> intStack;
```

This declaration replaces the type parameter T with int. So, intStack is a stack for int values. The object intStack is just like any other object. The program invokes the push function on intStack to add ten int values to the stack (lines 10–11) and displays the elements from the stack (lines 13–14).

The program declares a stack object for storing strings in line 18, adds three strings in the stack (lines 19–21), and displays the strings from the stack (line 23–24).

Note the code in lines 13–15:

```
while (!intStack.empty())
  cout << intStack.pop() << " ";
cout << endl;
```

and in lines 23–25:

```
while (!stringStack.empty())
  cout << stringStack.pop() << " ";
cout << endl;
```

These two fragments are almost identical. The difference is that the former operates on **intStack** and the latter is on **stringStack**. You can define a function with a stack parameter to display the elements in the stack. The new program is shown in Listing 15.5.

### LISTING 15.5  TestGenericStack1.cpp

generic **Stack**

Stack<T> parameter

```
1 #include <iostream>
2 #include <string>
3 #include "GenericStack.h"
4 using namespace std;
5
6 template<typename T>
7 void printStack(Stack<T> &stack)
8 {
9   while (!stack.empty())
10      cout << stack.pop() << " ";
11    cout << endl;
12 }
13
14 int main()
```

```
15 {
16   // Create a stack of int values
17   Stack<int> intStack;
18   for (int i = 0; i < 10; i++)
19     intStack.push(i);
20   printStack(intStack);                                    invoke printStack
21
22   // Create a stack of strings
23   Stack<string> stringStack;
24   stringStack.push("Chicago");
25   stringStack.push("Denver");
26   stringStack.push("London");
27   printStack(stringStack);                                 invoke printStack
28
29   return 0;
30 }
```

The generic class name **Stack\<T>** is used as a parameter type in a template function (line 7).

**Note**

C++ allows you to assign a *default type* for a type parameter in a class template. For example, you may assign **int** as a default type in the generic **Stack** class as follows:

**default type**

```
template<typename T = int>
class Stack
{
  ...
};
```

You now can declare an object using the default type like this:

```
Stack<> stack;  // stack is a stack for int values
```

You can use default type only in class templates, not in function templates.

**Note**

You also can use *nontype parameters* along with type parameters in a template prefix. For example, you may declare the array capacity as a parameter for the **Stack** class as follows:

**nontype parameter**

```
template<typename T, int capacity>
class Stack
{
  ...
private:
  T elements[capacity];
  int size;
};
```

So, when you create a stack, you can specify the capacity for the array. For example,

```
Stack<string, 500> stack;
```

declares a stack that can hold up to **500** strings.

**Note**

A nontemplate class can be derived from a class template specialization. A class template can be derived from a nontemplate class. A class template can be derived from a class template.

**templates and inheritance**

**Note**

Friends are used exactly the same for template and nontemplate classes.

**template class friends**

**Note**

You can define *static members* in a template class. Each template specialization has its own copy of a static data field.

## 15.5 Improving the **Stack** Class

There is a problem in the **Stack** class. The elements of the stack are stored in an array with a fixed size **100** (see line 16 in Listing 15.3). So, you cannot store more than **100** elements in a stack. You may change **100** to a larger number. But this would waste space if the actual stack is small. One way to resolve this dilemma is to allocate more memory when needed.

The **size** property in the **Stack<T>** class represents the number of elements in the stack. Let us add a new property named **capacity** that represents the current size of the array for storing the elements. The no-arg constructor of **Stack<T>** creates an array with capacity **16**. When you add a new element to the stack, you may need to increase the array size in order to store the new element if the current capacity is full.

How do you increase the array capacity? You cannot increase the array capacity once the array is declared. To circumvent this restriction, you may create a new, larger size array, copy the contents of the old array to this new array, and delete the old array.

The improved **Stack<T>** class is shown in Listing 15.6.

**LISTING 15.6** **ImprovedStack.h**

```
1  #ifndef IMPROVEDSTACK_H
2  #define IMPROVEDSTACK_H
3
4  template<typename T>
5  class Stack
6  {
7  public:
8    Stack();
9    bool empty();
10   T peek();
11   void push(T value);
12   T pop();
13   int getSize();
14
15 private:
16   T *elements;
17   int size;
18   int capacity;
19   void ensureCapacity();
20 };
21
22 template<typename T>
23 Stack<T>::Stack(): size(0), capacity(16)
24 {
25   elements = new T[capacity];
26 }
27
28 template<typename T>
29 bool Stack<T>::empty()
30 {
31   return (size == 0);
32 }
33
```

```
34 template<typename T>
35 T Stack<T>::peek()
36 {
37   return elements[size - 1];
38 }
39
40 template<typename T>
41 void Stack<T>::push(T value)
42 {
43   ensureCapacity();
44   elements[size++] = value;
45 }
46
47 template<typename T>
48 void Stack<T>::ensureCapacity()
49 {
50   if (size >= capacity)
51   {
52     T *old = elements;
53     capacity = 2 * size;
54     elements = new T[size * 2];
55
56     for (int i = 0; i < size; i++)
57       elements[i] = old[i];
58
59     delete old;
60   }
61 }
62
63 template<typename T>
64 T Stack<T>::pop()
65 {
66   ·return elements[--size];
67 }
68
69 template<typename T>
70 int Stack<T>::getSize()
71 {
72   return size;
73 }
74
75 #endif
```

The **push(T value)** function (lines 40–45) adds a new element to the stack. This function first invokes **ensureCapacity()** (line 43), which ensures that there is a space in the array for the new element.

The **ensureCapacity()** function (lines 47–61) checks whether the array is full. If so, create a new array that doubles the current array size, set the new array as the current array, copy the old array to the new array, and delete the old array (line 59).

## KEY TERMS

## CHAPTER SUMMARY

- Templates provide the capability to parameterize types in functions and classes. With this capability, you can define one function or one class with a generic type that can be substituted for a concrete type by the compiler.

- The definition for the function template begins with the keyword `template` followed by a list of parameters. Each parameter must be preceded by the interchangeable keywords `class` or `typename` in the form `<typename typeParameter>` or `<class typeParameter>`.

- When you define a generic function, it is better to start with a non-generic function, debug and test it, and then convert it to a generic function.

- The syntax for class templates is basically the same as that for function templates. You place the template prefix before the class declaration, just like you place the template prefix before the function template.

- The constructors and functions are defined the same way for regular classes, except that the constructors and functions themselves are templates. So, you have to place the template prefix before the constructor and function header.

## REVIEW QUESTIONS

### Section 15.2 Templates Basics

**15.1** For the `maxValue` function in Listing 15.1, can you invoke it with two arguments of different types, such as `maxValue(1, 1.5)`?

**15.2** For the `maxValue` function in Listing 15.1, can you invoke it with two arguments of strings, such as `maxValue("ABC", "ABD")`? Can you invoke it with two arguments of circles, such as `maxValue(Circle(2), Circle(3))`?

**15.3** Can `template<typename T>` be replaced by `template<class T>`?

**15.4** Can a type parameter be named using any identifier other than a keyword?

**15.5** Can a type parameter be of a primitive type or an object type?

**15.6** What is wrong in the following code?

```
 1 #include <iostream>
 2 #include <string>
 3 using namespace std;
 4
 5 template<typename T>
 6 T maxValue(T value1, T value2)
 7 {
 8   int result;
 9   if (value1 > value2)
10     result = value1;
11   else
12     result = value2;
13   return result;
14 }
15
```

```
16 int main()
17 {
18    cout << "Maximum between 1 and 3 is "
19      << maxValue(1, 3) << endl;
20    cout << "Maximum between 1.5 and 0.3 is "
21      << maxValue(1.5, 0.3) << endl;
22    cout << "Maximum between 'A' and 'N' is "
23     << maxValue('A', 'N') << endl;
24    cout << "Maximum between \"ABC\" and \"ABD\" is "
25     << maxValue("ABC", "ABD") << endl;
26
27    return 0;
28 }
```

15.7   If you define the `maxValue` function as follows:

```
template<typename T1, typename T2>
T1 maxValue(T1 value1, T2 value2)
{
  if (value1 > value2)
    return value1;
  else
    return value2;
}
```

what would be the return value from invoking `maxValue(1, 2.5)`, `maxValue(1.4, 2.5)`, and `maxValue(1.5, 2)`?

15.8   If you define the `swap` function as follows:

```
template<typename T>
void swap(T &var1, T &var2)
{
  T temp = var1;
  var1 = var2;
  var2 = temp;
}
```

What is wrong in the following code?

```
 1 int main()
 2 {
 3    int v1 = 1;
 4    int v2 = 2;
 5    swap(v1, v2);
 6
 7    double d1 = 1;
 8    double d2 = 2;
 9    swap(d1, d2);
10
11    swap(v1, d2);
12    swap(1, 2);
13
14    return 0;
15 }
```

### Section 15.4 Class Templates

15.9   Do you have to use the template prefix for each function in the class declaration? Do you have to use the template prefix for each function in the class implementation?

**15.10**  What is wrong in the following code?

```
template<typename T = int>
void printArray(T list[], int arraySize)
{
  for (int i = 0; i < arraySize; i++)
  {
    cout << list[i] << " ";
  }
  cout << endl;
}
```

**15.11**  What is wrong in the following code?

```
1 template<typename T>
2 class Foo
3 {
4 public:
5   Foo();
6   T f1(T value);
7   T f2();
8 };
9
10 Foo::Foo()
11 {
12   ...
13 }
14
15 T Stack::f1(T value)
16 {
17   ...
18 }
19
20 T Stack::f2()
21 {
22   ...
23 };
```

**15.12**  Suppose the template prefix for the **Stack** class is

```
template<typename T = string>
```

Can you create a stack of strings using

```
Stack stack;
```

## PROGRAMMING EXERCISES

**15.1**  (*Maximum in array*) Design a generic function that returns a maximum element from an array. The function should have two parameters. One is the array of a generic type and the other is the size of the array. Test the function with the array of `int`, `double`, `string`, and rational values.

**15.2**  (*Binary search*) Rewrite the binary search function in Listing 6.8, BinarySearch.h, to use a generic type for array elements. Test the function with array of `int`, `double`, `string`, and rational values.

**15.3**  (*Recursive binary search*) Rewrite the recursive binary search function in Listing 8.6, RecursiveBinarySearch.cpp, to use a generic type for array elements. Test the function with array of `int`, `double`, `string`, and rational values.

**15.4** (*Insertion sort*) Rewrite the insertion search function in Listing 6.10, Insertion-Sort.h, to use a generic type for array elements. Test the function with array of `int`, `double`, `string`, and rational values.

**15.5** (*Swap values*) Write a generic function that swap values in two variables. Your function should have two parameters of the same type. Test the function with `int`, `double`, `string`, and rational values.

**15.6*** (*Function printStack*) Add the `printStack` function into the `Stack` class as an instance function to display all the elements in the stack. The `Stack` class was introduced in Listing 15.3, GenericStack.h.

**15.7*** (*Function contains*) Add the `contains(T element)` function into the `Stack` class as an instance function to check whether the element is in the stack. The `Stack` class was introduced in Listing 15.3, GenericStack.h.

**15.8*** (*Implementing vector class*) The `vector` class is provided in the standard C++ library. Implement the `vector` class as an exercise. The standard `vector` class has many functions. For this exercise, implement only the functions defined in the UML class diagram, as shown in Figure 10.13.

**15.9** (*Implementing a stack class using inheritance*) In Listing 15.3, `GenericStack` is implemented using arrays. Create a new stack class that extends `vector`. Draw the UML diagram for the classes. Implement it.

# CHAPTER 16

# LINKED LISTS, STACKS, AND QUEUES

## Objectives

- To create nodes to store elements in a linked list (§16.2).

- To access the nodes in a linked list via pointers (§16.3).

- To declare a `LinkedList` class for storing and processing data in a list (§16.4).

- To add an element to the head of a list (§16.4.1).

- To add an element to the end of a list (§16.4.2).

- To insert an element into a list (§16.4.3).

- To remove the first element from a list (§16.4.4).

- To remove the last element from a list (§16.4.5).

- To remove an element at a specified position in a list (§16.4.6).

- To know the variations of linked lists (§16.5).

- To implement the `Stack` class using a linked list (§16.6).

- To implement the `Queue` class using a linked list (§16.7).

- (Optional) To implement iterators for traversing the elements in various types of containers (§16.8).

## 16.1 Introduction

The preceding chapter introduced a generic **Stack** class. The elements in the stack are stored in an array. The array size is fixed. If the array is too small, the elements cannot be stored in the stack. If the array is too large, a lot of space will be wasted. A possible solution to fix this problem was proposed in §15.5, "Improving the **Stack** Class." Initially, the stack uses a small array. When there is no room to add a new element, the stack creates a new array that doubles the size of the old array, copies the contents from the old array to this new array, and discards the old array. It is time-consuming to copy the array.

*linked list*

This chapter introduces a new data structure, called *linked list*. A linked list is efficient for storing and managing a varying number of elements. This chapter will also discuss how to implement stacks and queues using linked lists.

## 16.2 Nodes

In a linked list, each element is contained in a structure, called the *node*. When a new element is added to the list, a node is created to contain the element. All the nodes are chained through pointers, as shown in Figure 16.1.

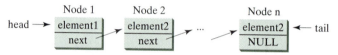

**FIGURE 16.1**    A linked list consists of any number of nodes chained together.

Nodes can be defined using structs or classes in C++. Using classes are preferred. The class definition for a node can be as follows:

*template class*

```
1  template<typename T>
2  class Node
3  {
4  public:
```

*element type*
*node pointer*

```
5    T element;  // Element contained in the node
6    Node *next; // Pointer to the next node
7
```

*no-arg constructor*

```
8    Node() // No-arg constructor
9    {
10     next = NULL;
11   }
12
```

*no-arg constructor*

```
13   Node(T element) // Constructor
14   {
15     this->element = element;
16     next = NULL;
17   }
18 };
```

**Node** is declared as a template class with a type parameter **T** for specifying the element type.

By convention, pointer variables named **head** and **tail** are used to point to the first node and last node in the list, as shown in Figure 16.1. They are declared as

```
Node<string> *head, *tail;
```

*NULL is 0*

If the list is empty, both **head** and **tail** should be **NULL**. Recall that **NULL** is a C++ constant for **0**, which indicates that a pointer does not point to any node. The definition of **NULL** is in a number of standard libraries including **<iostream>** and **<cstddef>**. Here are the examples to add three strings to the list.

```
 1 // Create a node to store the first string
 2 head = new Node<string>("Chicago");
 3 tail = head;
 4
 5 // Create a node to store the second string
 6 tail->next = new Node<string>("Denver");
 7 tail = tail->next;
 8
 9 // Create a node to store the third string
10 tail->next = new Node<string>("Dallas");
11 tail = tail->next;
```

create a node
new tail

create a node
new tail

create a node
new tail

Each new node is created dynamically using the **new** operator. The process of creating a new linked list and adding three nodes is shown in Figure 16.2. Initially, the **head** and **tail** are **NULL**. When you add the first node, both **head** and **tail** point to this node. When you add the second node, it is pointed to by the tail node's **next** pointer. Since this new node becomes the last node in the list, **tail** now points to this new node. **head** still points to the same node, but **tail** now points to this new node (line 7).

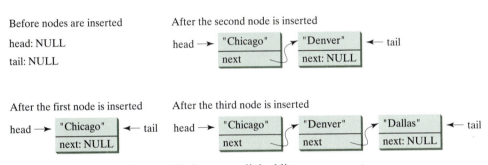

**FIGURE 16.2** Three nodes are added to a new linked list.

Each node contains the element and a pointer that points to the next element. If the node is the last in the list, its pointer data field **next** contains the value **NULL**. You can use this property to detect the last node. For example, you may write the following loop to traverse all the nodes in the list.

```
1 Node<string> *current = head;
2 while (current != NULL )
3 {
4   cout << current->element << endl;
5   current = current->next;
6 }
```

current pointer
check last node

next node

The **current** pointer points to the first node in the list initially (line 1). In the loop, the element of the current node is retrieved (line 4), and then **current** points to the next node (line 5). The loop continues until the current node is **NULL**.

## 16.3 The **LinkedList** Class

Linked list is a popular data structure for storing data in sequential order. For example, a list of students, a list of available rooms, a list of cities, and a list of books all can be stored using lists. The operations listed here are typical of most lists:

- Retrieve an element from a list.
- Insert a new element to a list.

■ Delete an element from a list.

■ Find how many elements are in a list.

■ Find whether an element is in a list.

■ Find whether a list is empty.

Figure 16.3 gives the class diagram for `LinkedList`. `LinkedList` is a class template with type parameter `T` that represents the type of the elements stored in the list.

| LinkedList<T> | |
|---|---|
| -head: Node<T>*<br>-tail: Node<T>*<br>-size: int | The head of the list.<br>The tail of the list.<br>The size of the list. |
| +LinkedList()<br>+addFirst(element: T): void<br>+addLast(element: T): void<br>+getFirst(): T<br>+getLast(): T<br>+removeFirst(): T<br>+removeLast(): T<br>+add(element: T): void<br>+add(index: int, element: T): void<br>+clear(): void<br>+contains(element: T): bool<br>+get(index: int): T<br>+indexOf(element: T): int<br>+isEmpty(): bool<br>+lastIndexOf(element: T): int<br>+remove(element: T): void<br>+getSize(): int<br>+removeAt(index: int): T<br><br>+set(index: int, element: T): T | Creates a default linked list.<br>Adds the element to the head of the list.<br>Adds the element to the tail of the list.<br>Returns the first element in the list.<br>Returns the last element in the list.<br>Removes the first element from the list.<br>Removes the last element from the list.<br>Appends a new element at the end of this list.<br>Adds a new element at the specified index in this list.<br>Removes all the elements from this list.<br>Returns true if this list contains the specified element.<br>Returns the element from this list at the specified index.<br>Returns the index of the first matching element in this list.<br>Returns true if this list contains no elements.<br>Returns the index of the last matching element in this list.<br>Removes the specified element from this list.<br>Returns the number of elements in this list.<br>Removes the element at the specified index and returns the removed element.<br>Sets the element at the specified index and returns the element being replaced. |

**FIGURE 16.3** `LinkedList` implements a list using a linked list of nodes.

You can get an element from the list using `get(int index)`. The index is 0-based, i.e., the node at the head of the list has `index 0`. Assume that the `LinkedList` class is available in the header file LinkedList.h. Let us begin by writing a test program that uses the `LinkedList` class in Listing 16.1. The program creates a list using `LinkedList` (line 18). It uses the `add` function to add strings to the list and the `remove` function to remove strings from the list.

## LISTING 16.1 `TestLinkedList.cpp`

include class

```
1 #include <iostream>
2 #include <string>
3 #include "LinkedList.h"
4 using namespace std;
```

```
5
6  void printList(LinkedList<string> list)                                        print list
7  {
8     for (int i = 0; i < list.getSize(); i++)                                    list size
9     {
10       cout << list.get(i) << " ";                                              get element
11    }
12    cout << endl;
13 }
14
15 int main()
16 {
17    // Create a list for strings
18    LinkedList <string> list;                                                   create list
19
20    // Add elements to the list
21    list.add("America"); // Add it to the list                                  append element
22    cout << "(1) ";
23    printList(list);                                                            invoke printList
24
25    list.add(0, "Canada"); // Add it to the beginning of the list               insert element
26    cout << "(2) ";
27    printList(list);
28
29    list.add("Russia"); // Add it to the end of the list                        append element
30    cout << "(3) ";
31    printList(list);
32
33    list.add("France"); // Add it to the end of the list                        append element
34    cout << "(4) ";
35    printList(list);
36
37    list.add(2, "Germany"); // Add it to the list at index 2                    insert element
38    cout << "(5) ";
39    printList(list);
40
41    list.add(5, "Norway"); // Add it to the list at index 5                     insert element
42    cout << "(6) ";
43    printList(list);
44
45    list.add(0, "Netherlands"); // Same as list.addFirst("Netherlands")         insert element
46    cout << "(7) ";
47    printList(list);
48
49    // Remove elements from the list
50    list.removeAt(0); // Same as list.remove("Netherlands") in this case        remove element
51    cout << "(8) ";
52    printList(list);
53
54    list.removeAt(2); // Remove the element at index 2                          remove element
55    cout << "(9) ";
56    printList(list);
57
58    list.removeAt(list.getSize() - 1); // Remove the last element              remove element
59    cout << "(10) ";
60    printList(list);
61
62    return 0;
63 }
```

```
(1) America
(2) Canada America
(3) Canada America Russia
(4) Canada America Russia France
(5) Canada America Germany Russia France
(6) Canada America Germany Russia France Norway
(7) Canada America Germany Russia France Norway
(8) Canada America Germany Russia France Norway
(9) Canada America Russia France Norway
(10) Canada America Russia France
```

## 16.4 Implementing LinkedList

Now let us turn our attention to implementing the LinkedList class. Some functions are easy to implement. For example, the isEmpty() function simply returns head == NULL, and the clear() function simply deletes all nodes in the list and sets head and tail to NULL. The addLast(T element) function is same as the add(T element) function. The reason that both are defined is for convenience.

### 16.4.1 Implementing addFirst(T element)

The addFirst(T element) function can be implemented as follows:

```
1 template<typename T>
2 void LinkedList<T>::addFirst(T element)
3 {
4     Node<T> *newNode = new Node<T>(element);
5     newNode->next = head;
6     head = newNode;
7     size++;
8
9     if (tail == NULL)
10        tail = head;
11 }
```

create a node
link with head
head to new node
increase size

was empty?

The addFirst(T element) function creates a new node (line 4) to store the element and insert the node to the beginning of the list (line 5). After the insertion, head should point to this new element node (line 6), as shown in Figure 16.4.

If the list is empty (line 9), both head and tail will point to this new node (line 10). After the node is created, the size should be increased by 1 (line 7).

### 16.4.2 Implementing addLast(T element)

The addLast(T element) function creates a node to hold an element and inserts the node at the end of the list. It can be implemented as follows:

```
1 template<typename T>
2 void LinkedList<T>::addLast(T element)
3 {
4     if (tail == NULL)
5     {
6         head = tail = new Node<T>(element);
7     }
8     else
9     {
10        tail->next = new Node<T>(element);
11        tail = tail->next;
```

create a node

create a node

```
12   }
13
14   size++;                                        increase size
15 }
```

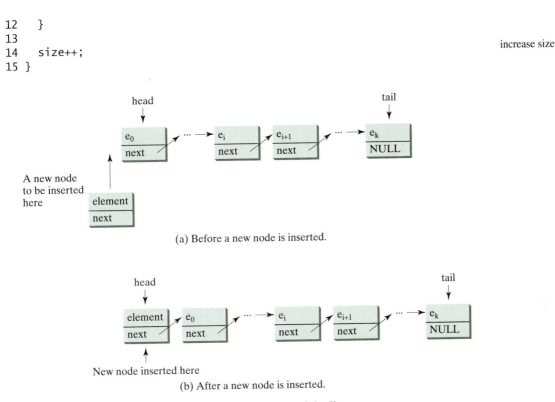

(a) Before a new node is inserted.

(b) After a new node is inserted.

**FIGURE 16.4** A new element is added to the beginning of the list.

Consider two cases:

1. If the list is empty (line 4), both **head** and **tail** will point to this new node (line 6);

2. Otherwise, insert the node at the end of the list (line 10). After the insertion, **tail** should refer to this new element node (line 11), as shown in Figure 16.5.

In any case, after the node is created, the size should be increased by **1** (line 14).

## 16.4.3 Implementing **add(int index, T element)**

The **add(int index, T element)** function adds an element to the list at the specified index. It can be implemented as follows:

```
1 template<typename T>
2 void LinkedList<T>::add(int index, T element)
3 {
4   if (index == 0)
5     addFirst(element);                          insert first
6   else if (index >= size)
7     addLast(element);                           insert last
8   else
9   {
10    Node<T> *current = head;
11    for (int i = 1; i < index; i++)
12      current = current->next;
13    Node<T> *temp = current->next;
14    current->next = new Node<T>(element);        create a node
15    (current->next)->next = temp;
16    size++;                                      increase size
17  }
18 }
```

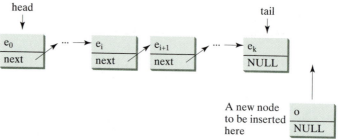

(a) Before a new node is inserted.

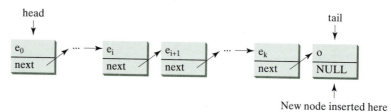

(b) After a new node is inserted.

**FIGURE 16.5** A new element is added at the end of the list.

Consider three cases:

1. If **index** is **0**, invoke **addFirst(element)** (line 5) to insert the element at the beginning of the list;

2. If **index** is greater than or equal to **size**, invoke **addLast(element)** (line 7) to insert the element at the end of the list;

3. Otherwise, create a new node to store the new element and locate where to insert it. As shown in Figure 16.6, the new node is to be inserted between the nodes **current** and **temp**. The function assigns the new node to **current.next** and assigns **temp** to the new node's **next**. The size is now increased by **1** (line 16).

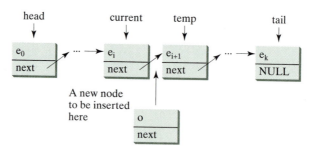

(a) Before a new node is inserted.

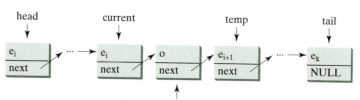

New node inserted here
(b) After a new node is inserted.

**FIGURE 16.6** A new element is inserted in the middle of the list.

### 16.4.4 Implementing removeFirst()

The removeFirst() function can be implemented as follows:

```
1 template<typename T>
2 T LinkedList<T>::removeFirst() throw (runtime_error)
3 {
4   if (size == 0)
5     throw runtime_error("No elements in the list");
6   else
7   {
8     Node<T> *temp = head;
9     head = head->next;
10     size--;
11     if (head == NULL) tail = NULL;
12     T element = temp->element;
13     delete temp;
14     return element;
15   }
16 }
```

- throw exception
- keep old head
- new head
- decrease **size**
- destroy the node

Consider three cases:

1. If the list is empty, an exception is thrown (line 5);

2. Otherwise, remove the first node from the list by pointing **head** to the second node, as shown in Figure 16.7. The size is reduced by 1 after the deletion (line 10);

3. If there is one element, after removing the element, **tail** should be set to NULL (line 11).

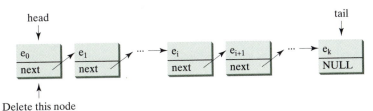

(a) Before the node is deleted.

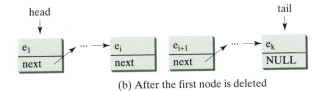

(b) After the first node is deleted

**FIGURE 16.7** The first node is deleted from the list.

### 16.4.5 Implementing removeLast()

The removeLast() function can be implemented as follows:

```
1 template<typename T>
2 T LinkedList<T>::removeLast() throw (runtime_error)
3 {
4   if (size == 0)
5     throw runtime_error("No elements in the list");
6   else if (size == 1)
```

- throw exception
- size 1?

```
                  7    {
                  8      Node<T> *temp = head;
head and tail NULL 9      head = tail = NULL;
size is 1         10     size = 0;
                  11     T element = temp->element;
destroy the node  12     delete temp;
return element    13     return element;
                  14   }
size > 1?         15   else
                  16   {
                  17     Node<T> *current = head;
                  18
                  19     for (int i = 0; i < size - 2; i++)
                  20       current = current->next;
                  21
move tail         22     Node<T> *temp = tail;
                  23     tail = current;
reduce size       24     tail->next = NULL;
                  25     size--;
destroy the node  26     T element = temp->element;
return element    27     delete temp;
                  28     return element;
                  29   }
                  30 }
```

Consider three cases:

1. If the list is empty, an exception is thrown (line 5);

2. If the list contains only one node, this node is destroyed, **head** and **tail** both become **NULL**;

3. Otherwise, the last node is destroyed (line 26) and the **tail** is repositioned to point to the second to last node, as shown in Figure 16.8.

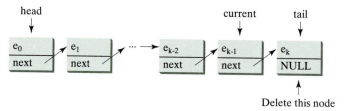

(a) Before the node is deleted.

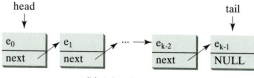

(b) After the last node is deleted.

**Figure 16.8** The last node is deleted from the list.

For the last two cases, the size is reduced by 1 after the deletion (lines 12, 27) and the element value of the deleted node is returned (lines 13, 28).

## 16.4.6 Implementing removeAt(int index)

The removeAt(int index) function finds the node at the specified index and then removes it. It can be implemented as follows:

```
1  template<typename T>
2  T LinkedList<T>::removeAt(int index) throw (runtime_error)
3  {
4    if (index < 0 || index >= size)
5      throw runtime_error("Index out of range");              throw exception
6    else if (index == 0)
7      return removeFirst();                                    remove first
8    else if (index == size - 1)
9      return removeLast();                                     remove last
10   else
11   {
12     Node<T> *previous = head;
13
14     for (int i = 1; i < index; i++)                          locate previous
15     {
16       previous = previous->next;
17     }
18
19     Node<T> *current = previous->next;                       locate current
20     previous->next = current->next;                          remove from list
21     size--;                                                  reduce size
22     T element = current->element;
23     delete current;                                          destroy the node
24     return element;                                          return element
25   }
26 }
```

Consider four cases:

1. If index is beyond the range of the list (i.e., index < 0 || index >= size), throw an exception (line 5);

2. If index is 0, invoke removeFirst() to remove the first node (line 7);

3. If index is size - 1, invoke removeLast() to remove the last node (line 9);

4. Otherwise, locate the node at the specified index. Let current denote this node and previous denote the node before this node, as shown in Figure 16.9. Assign current.next to previous.next to eliminate the current node.

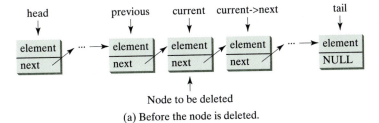

(a) Before the node is deleted.

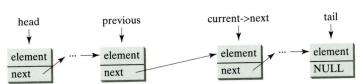

(b) After the node is deleted.

**FIGURE 16.9** A node is deleted from the list.

Listing 16.2 gives the implementation of `LinkedList`. The implementation of `lastIndexOf(T element)`, `remove(T element)`, `contains(T element)`, and `set(int index, Object o)` is omitted and left as an exercise.

### LISTING 16.2 LinkedList.h

```cpp
1  #ifndef LINKEDLIST_H
2  #define LINKEDLIST_H
3  #include <stdexcept>
4  using namespace std;
5
6  template<typename T>
7  class Node
8  {
9  public:
10   T element;  // Element contained in the node
11   Node<T> *next; // Pointer to the next node
12
13   Node() // No-arg constructor
14   {
15     next = NULL;
16   }
17
18   Node(T element) // Constructor
19   {
20     this->element = element;
21     next = NULL;
22   }
23 };
24
25 template<typename T>
26 class LinkedList
27 {
28 public:
29   LinkedList();
30   void addFirst(T element);
31   void addLast(T element);
32   T getFirst();
33   T getLast();
34   T removeFirst() throw (runtime_error);
35   T removeLast();
36   void add(T element);
37   void add(int index, T element);
38   void clear();
39   bool contains(T element);
40   T get(int index);
41   int indexOf(T element);
42   bool isEmpty();
43   int lastIndexOf(T element);
44   void remove(T element);
45   int getSize();
46   T removeAt(int index);
47   T set(int index, T element);
48
49 private:
50   Node<T> *head, *tail;
51   int size;
52 };
53
```

runtime_error header

class template
class **Node**

class template
class **LinkedList**

```
54  template<typename T>
55  LinkedList<T>::LinkedList()                                       constructor
56  {
57    head = tail = NULL;
58    size = 0;
59  }
60
61  template<typename T>
62  void LinkedList<T>::addFirst(T element)                           addFirst
63  {
64    Node<T> *newNode = new Node<T>(element);
65    newNode->next = head;
66    head = newNode;
67    size++;
68
69    if (tail == NULL)
70      tail = head;
71  }
72
73  template<typename T>
74  void LinkedList<T>::addLast(T element)                            addLast
75  {
76    if (tail == NULL)
77    {
78      head = tail = new Node<T>(element);
79    }
80    else
81    {
82      tail->next = new Node<T>(element);
83      tail = tail->next;
84    }
85
86    size++;
87  }
88
89  template<typename T>
90  T LinkedList<T>::getFirst()                                       getFirst
91  {
92    if (size == 0)
93      throw runtime_error("Index out of range");
94    else
95      return head->element;
96  }
97
98  template<typename T>
99  T LinkedList<T>::getLast()                                        getLast
100 {
101   if (size == 0)
102     throw runtime_error("Index out of range");
103   else
104     return tail->element;
105 }
106
107 template<typename T>
108 T LinkedList<T>::removeFirst() throw (runtime_error)              removeFirst
109 {
110   if (size == 0)
111     throw runtime_error("No elements in the list");
112   else
113   {
114     Node<T> *temp = head;
115     head = head->next;
```

```
116      if (head == NULL) tail = NULL;
117      size--;
118      T element = temp->element;
119      delete temp;
120      return element;
121   }
122 }
123
124 template<typename T>
125 T LinkedList<T>::removeLast()
126 {
127   if (size == 0)
128     throw runtime_error("No elements in the list");
129   else if (size == 1)
130   {
131     Node<T> *temp = head;
132     head = tail = NULL;
133     size = 0;
134     T element = temp->element;
135     delete temp;
136     return element;
137   }
138   else
139   {
140     Node<T> *current = head;
141
142     for (int i = 0; i < size - 2; i++)
143       current = current->next;
144
145     Node<T> *temp = tail;
146     tail = current;
147     tail->next = NULL;
148     size--;
149     T element = temp->element;
150     delete temp;
151     return element;
152   }
153 }
154
155 template<typename T>
156 void LinkedList<T>::add(T element)
157 {
158   addLast(element);
159 }
160
161 template<typename T>
162 void LinkedList<T>::add(int index, T element)
163 {
164   if (index == 0)
165     addFirst(element);
166   else if (index >= size)
167     addLast(element);
168   else
169   {
170     Node<T> *current = head;
171     for (int i = 1; i < index; i++)
172       current = current->next;
173     Node<T> *temp = current->next;
174     current->next = new Node<T>(element);
175     (current->next)->next = temp;
```

**removeLast**

**add**

**add**

```
176        size++;
177      }
178  }
179
180  template<typename T>                                          clear
181  void LinkedList<T>::clear()
182  {
183    while (head != NULL)
184    {
185      Node<T> *temp = head;
186      delete temp;
187      head = head->next;
188    }
189
190    tail = NULL;
191  }
192
193  template<typename T>                                          get
194  T LinkedList<T>::get(int index)
195  {
196    if (index < 0 || index > size - 1)
197      throw runtime_error("Index out of range");
198
199    Node<T> *current = head;
200    for (int i = 0; i < index; i++)
201      current = current->next;
202
203    return current->element;
204  }
205
206  template<typename T>                                          indexOf
207  int LinkedList<T>::indexOf(T element)
208  {
209    // Implement it in this exercise
210    Node<T> *current = head;
211    for (int i = 0; i < size; i++)
212    {
213      if (current->element == element)
214        return i;
215      current = current->next;
216    }
217
218    return -1;
219  }
220
221  template<typename T>                                          isEmpty
222  bool LinkedList<T>::isEmpty()
223  {
224    return head == NULL;
225  }
226
227  template<typename T>                                          getSize
228  int LinkedList<T>::getSize()
229  {
230    return size;
231  }
232
233  template<typename T>                                          removeAt
234  T LinkedList<T>::removeAt(int index)
235  {
```

```
236    if (index < 0 || index >= size)
237      throw runtime_error("Index out of range");
238    else if (index == 0)
239      return removeFirst();
240    else if (index == size - 1)
241      return removeLast();
242    else
243    {
244      Node<T> *previous = head;
245
246      for (int i = 1; i < index; i++)
247      {
248        previous = previous->next;
249      }
250
251      Node<T> *current = previous->next;
252      previous->next = current->next;
253      size--;
254      T element = current->element;
255      delete current;
256      return element;
257    }
258  }
259
260    // The functions remove(T element), lastIndexOf(T element),
261    // contains(T element), and set(int index, T element) are
262    // left as an exercise
263
264  #endif
```

 **Tip**

array vs. linked list

You can use an array or a linked list to store elements. If you don't know the number of elements in advanced, it is more efficient to use a linked list, because a linked list can grow and shrink dynamically. If your application requires frequent insertion and deletion anywhere, it is more efficient to store elements using a linked list, because inserting an element into an array would require all the elements in the array after the insertion point to be moved. If the number of the elements in an application is fixed and the application does not require random insertion and deletion, it is simple and efficient to use an array to store the elements.

## 16.5 Variations of Linked Lists

The linked list introduced in the preceding section is known as a *singly linked list*. It contains a pointer to the list's first node, and each node contains a pointer to the next node sequentially. Several variations of the linked list are useful in certain applications.

A *circular, singly linked list* is like a singly linked list, except that the pointer of the last node points back to the first node.

A doubly linked list contains the nodes with two pointers. One points to the next node and the other points to the previous node. These two pointers are conveniently called *a forward pointer* and *a backward pointer*. So, a doubly linked list can be traversed forward and backward.

A circular, doubly linked list is a doubly linked list, except that the forward pointer of the last node points to the first node and the backward pointer of the first pointer points to the last node.

The implementation of these linked lists is given as exercises.

## 16.6 Implementing Stack Using a LinkedList

The **Stack** class in the preceding chapter was implemented using an array. It is more efficient to implement the **Stack** class using a linked list. Listing 16.3 presents a new implementation using a linked list.

## LISTING 16.3  StackWithLinkedList.h

```
 1 #ifndef STACKWITHLINKEDLIST_H
 2 #define STACKWITHLINKEDLIST_H
 3 #include "LinkedList.h"
 4
 5 template<typename T>
 6 class Stack
 7 {
 8 public:
 9   Stack();
10   bool isEmpty();
11   T peek();
12   void push(T value);
13   T pop();
14   int getSize();
15
16 private:
17   LinkedList<T> list;
18 };
19
20 template<typename T>
21 Stack<T>::Stack()
22 {
23 }
24
25 template<typename T>
26 bool Stack<T>::isEmpty()
27 {
28   return list.isEmpty();
29 }
30
31 template<typename T>
32 T Stack<T>::peek() throw (runtime_error)
33 {
34   return list.getLast();
35 }
36
37 template<typename T>
38 void Stack<T>::push(T value)
39 {
40   list.addLast(value);
41 }
42
43 template<typename T>
44 T Stack<T>::pop() throw (runtime_error)
45 {
46   return list.removeLast();
47 }
48
49 template<typename T>
50 int Stack<T>::getSize()
51 {
52   return list.getSize();
53 }
54
55 #endif
```

include **LinkedList**

class template

linked list

constructor

empty

peek

push

pop

getSize

The interface (e.g., public functions and constructors) for the **Stack** class remains unchanged, as shown in Figure 15.1(b). Rather than implementing a stack using an array, a linked list is used (line 17). The implementation is rather simple. To test whether a stack is empty, return `list.isEmpty()` (line 28). To peek an element on the stack, return `list.getLast()` (line 34). To push an element to the stack, invoke `list.addLast(value)` (line 40). To delete an element from the stack, return `list.removeLast()` (line 46). To find the size of the stack, return `list.getSize()` (line 52).

## 16.7 Queues

A queue represents a waiting list. A queue can be viewed as a special type of list whose elements are inserted into the end (tail) of the queue and are accessed and deleted from the beginning (head) of the queue, as shown in Figure 16.10.

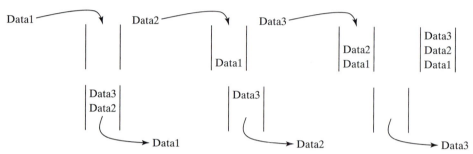

**FIGURE 16.10**  A queue holds objects in a first-in first-out fashion.

There are two ways to design the queue class:

inheritance

- ■ **Using inheritance:** You can declare a queue class by extending the linked list class.

composition

- ■ **Using composition:** You can declare a linked list as a data field in the queue class.

Both designs are fine, but using composition is better, because it enables you to declare a completely new queue class without inheriting the unnecessary and inappropriate functions from the linked list.

Figure 16.11 shows the UML class diagram for the queue. Its implementation is shown in Listing 16.4.

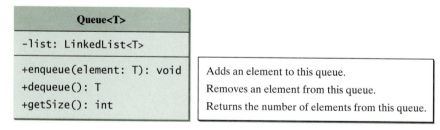

**FIGURE 16.11**  Queue uses a linked list to provide a first-in first-out data structure.

### LISTING 16.4  Queue.h

include **LinkedList**

class template

```
1 #ifndef QUEUE_H
2 #define QUEUE_H
3 #include "LinkedList.h"
4 #include <stdexcept>
5 using namespace std;
```

```
 6
 7 template<typename T>
 8 class Queue
 9 {
10 public:
11   Queue();
12   void enqueue(T element);
13   T dequeue() throw (runtime_error);
14   int getSize();
15
16 private:
17   LinkedList<T> list;
18 };
19
20 template<typename T>
21 Queue<T>::Queue()
22 {
23 }
24
25 template<typename T>
26 void Queue<T>::enqueue(T element)
27 {
28   list.addLast(element);
29 }
30
31 template<typename T>
32 T Queue<T>::dequeue() throw (runtime_error)
33 {
34   return list.removeFirst();
35 }
36
37 template<typename T>
38 int Queue<T>::getSize()
39 {
40   return list.getSize();
41 }
42
43 #endif
```

linked list

constructor

**enqueue**

**dequeue**

**getSize**

A linked list is created to store the elements in a queue (line 17). The **enqueue(T element)** function (lines 25–29) adds elements into the tail of the queue. The **dequeue()** function (lines 31–35) removes an element from the head of the queue and returns the removed element. The **getSize()** function (lines 37–41) returns the number of elements in the queue.

Listing 16.5 gives an example that creates a queue for **int** values (line 17) and a queue for strings (line 24) using the **Queue** class. It uses the **enqueue** function to add elements to the queues (lines 19, 25–27) and the **dequeue** function to remove int values and strings from the queue.

## LISTING 16.5   TestQueue.cpp

```
1 #include <iostream>
2 #include "Queue.h"
3 #include <string>
4 using namespace std;
5
6 template<typename T>
7 void printQueue(Queue<T> &queue)
8 {
```

include **Queue**

class template

**printQueue** function

```
queue size?       9    while (queue.getSize() > 0)
dequeue          10      cout << queue.dequeue()  << " ";
                 11    cout << endl;
                 12 }
                 13
                 14 int main()
                 15 {
                 16    // Queue of int values
create a queue   17    Queue<int> intQueue;
                 18    for (int i = 0; i < 10; i++)
enqueue int      19      intQueue.enqueue(i);
                 20
invoke printQueue 21   printQueue(intQueue);
                 22
                 23    // Queue of strings
create a queue   24    Queue<string> stringQueue;
enqueue          25    stringQueue.enqueue("New York");
                 26    stringQueue.enqueue("Boston");
                 27    stringQueue.enqueue("Denver");
                 28
invoke printQueue 29   printQueue(stringQueue);
                 30
                 31    return 0;
                 32 }
```

```
0 1 2 3 4 5 6 7 8 9
New York Boston Denver
```

 ## 16.8 (Optional) Iterators

An iterator is an important construct in C++. It provides a uniform way for traversing elements in various types of containers. The Standard Template Library (STL) uses iterators to access the elements in the containers. The STL will be introduced in Chapters 19 and 20. This section creates an iterator class for traversing the elements in a linked list. The objectives of this section are twofold:

1. To provide an example on how to create an iterator class.

2. To become familiar with iterators and how to use them to traverse the elements in a container.

Iterators can be viewed as encapsulated pointers. In a linked list, you can use pointers to traverse the list. But iterators have more functions than pointers. Iterators are objects. Iterators contain functions for accessing and manipulating elements. §16.3, "The LinkedList Class," introduced the LinkedList class. Let us create an iterator class for LinkedList, as shown in Figure 16.12.

| Iterator<T> |
|---|
| -current: Node<T>* |
| +Iterator(p: Node<T>*) |
| +operator++(): Iterator |
| +operator*(): T |
| +operator==(itr: Iterator<T>&): bool |
| +operator!=(itr: Iterator<T>&): bool |

| |
|---|
| Current pointer in the iterator. |
| Constructs an iterator with a specified pointer. |
| Obtains the iterator for the next pointer. |
| Returns the element from the node pointed by the iterator. |
| Returns true if this iterator is the same as the iterator itr. |
| Returns true if this iterator is different from the iterator itr. |

**FIGURE 16.12** Iterator encapsulates pointers with additional functions.

To obtain iterators from a linked list, let us modify the `LinkedList` class by adding two new functions:

```
Iterator<T> begin();
Iterator<T> end();
```

The `begin()` function returns the iterator for the first element in the list and the `end()` function returns the iterator that passes the last element in the list.

For convenience, we define a header file named NewLinkedList.h. This new header file contains all lines in LinkedList.h in Listing 16.2 and two new functions `begin()` and `end()` (lines 83–93) in the `LinkedList` class and the `Iterator` class (lines 25–57) , as shown in Listing 16.6.

## LISTING 16.6 NewLinkedList.h

```
 1 #ifndef LINKEDLIST_H
 2 #define LINKEDLIST_H
 3 #include <stdexcept>
 4 using namespace std;
 5
 6 template<typename T>
 7 class Node
 8 {
 9 public:
10   T element;  // Element contained in the node
11   Node<T> *next; // Pointer to the next node
12
13   Node() // No-arg constructor
14   {
15     next = NULL;
16   }
17
18   Node(T element) // Constructor
19   {
20     this->element = element;
21     next = NULL;
22   }
23 };
24
25 template<typename T>
26 class Iterator                                        class Iterator
27 {
28 public:
29   Iterator(Node<T> *p)                                constructor
30   {
31     current = p;
32   };
33
34   Iterator &operator++()                              next iterator
35   {
36     current = current -> next;
37     return *this;
38   }
39
40   T operator*()                                       return element
41   {
42     return current -> element;
43   }
44
45   bool operator==(const Iterator<T> &iterator)        same iterator?
46   {
```

```
47        return current == iterator.current;
48    }
49
50    bool operator!=(const Iterator<T> &iterator)
51    {
52        return current != iterator.current;
53    }
54
55 private:
56    Node<T> *current;
57 };
58
59 template<typename T>
60 class LinkedList
61 {
62 public:
63    LinkedList();
64    void addFirst(T element);
65    void addLast(T element);
66    T getFirst();
67    T getLast();
68    T removeFirst() throw (runtime_error);
69    T removeLast();
70    void add(T element);
71    void add(int index, T element);
72    void clear();
73    bool contains(T element);
74    T get(int index);
75    int indexOf(T element);
76    bool isEmpty();
77    int lastIndexOf(T element);
78    void remove(T element);
79    int getSize();
80    T removeAt(int index);
81    T set(int index, T element);
82
83    // This function is defined inside the LinkedList class
84    Iterator<T> begin()
85    {
86        return Iterator<T>(head);
87    };
88
89    // This function is defined inside the LinkedList class
90    Iterator<T> end()
91    {
92        return Iterator<T>(tail->next);
93    };
94
95 #endif
96
97    // Copy lines 94-264 in Listing 16.2
```

different iterator?

to first element

to last element

The **Node** class is defined in Listing 6.2 and is copied in line 6. The **Iterator** class (lines 26–57) encapsulates pointers. An iterator is like a pointer, but an iterator is an object with the functions for accessing elements, comparing iterators, and obtaining the next iterator.

The functions **begin()** and **end()** (lines 84–90) are defined in the **LinkedList** class. A **LinkedList** object may invoke **begin()** or **end()** to return an **Iterator** that points to the first or last element in the list. Note that **end()** returns the **Iterator** that passes the last element in the list. In this **Iterator**, **current** is actually **NULL** (line 92).

Listing 16.7 gives an example that uses iterators to traverse the elements in a linked list. The program creates a **LinkedList** for strings in line 9, adds four strings to the list (lines 12–15), and traverses all the elements in the list using iterators (lines 18–22).

**LISTING 16.7** TestIterator.cpp

```
1 #include <iostream>
2 #include <string>
3 #include "NewLinkedList.h"
4 using namespace std;
5
6 int main()
7 {
8   // Create a list for strings
9   LinkedList<string> list;                          create list
10
11  // Add elements to the list
12  list.add("America");                              add string
13  list.add("Canada");
14  list.add("Russia");
15  list.add("France");
16
17  // Traverse a list using iterators
18  for (Iterator<string> iterator = list.begin();    traverse list
19    iterator != list.end(); iterator++)
20  {
21    cout << *iterator << " ";                        access element
22  }
23
24  return 0;
25 }
```

```
America Canada Russia France
```

## KEY TERMS

circular doubly linked list    484
circular singly linked list    484
dequeue    486
doubly linked list    484
enqueue    486
linked list    470

**peek**    485
**pop**    485
**push**    485
queue    486
singly linked list    484
stack    485

## CHAPTER SUMMARY

■ A linked list grows and shrinks dynamically. Nodes in a linked list are dynamically created using the **new** operator, and they are destroyed using the **delete** operator.

■ You can implement a stack using an array or a linked list. The public functions of the **Stack** class remain unchanged.

■ A queue represents a waiting list. A queue can be viewed as a special type of list whose elements are inserted into the end (tail) of the queue and are accessed and deleted from the beginning (head) of the queue.

- If you don't know the number of elements in advance, it is more efficient to use a linked list, because a linked list can grow and shrink dynamically.

- If your application requires frequent insertion and deletion anywhere, it is more efficient to store elements using a linked list, because inserting an element into an array would require all the elements in the array after the insertion point to be moved.

- If the elements need to be processed in a last-in first-out fashion, use a stack. If the elements need to be processed in a first-in first-out fashion, use a queue.

## REVIEW QUESTIONS

### Section 16.2 Nodes

**16.1** Are the following class declarations correct?

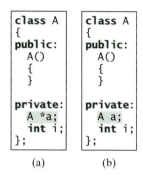

```
class A
{
public:
    A()
    {
    }

private:
    A *a;
    int i;
};
```
(a)

```
class A
{
public:
    A()
    {
    }

private:
    A a;
    int i;
};
```
(b)

**16.2** What is NULL for?

**16.3** When a node is created using the Node class, is the next pointer of this new node NULL?

### Section 16.3 The LinkedList Class

**16.4** Which of the following statements are used to insert a string s to the head of the list? Which of the following statements are used to append a string s to the end of the list?

```
list.addFirst(s);
list.add(s);
list.add(0, s);
list.add(1, s);
```

**16.5** Which of the following statements are used to remove the first element from the list? Which of the following statements are used to remove the last element from the list?

```
list.removeFirst(s);
list.removeLast(s);
list.removeFirst();
list.removeLast();
list.remove(0);
list.removeAt(0);
list.removeAt(list.getSize() - 1);
list.removeAt(list.getSize());
```

**16.6** Suppose the removeAt function is renamed as remove so there are two overloaded functions remove(T element) and remove(int index). This is incorrect. Explain the reason.

### Section 16.4 Implementing LinkedList

**16.7**   If a linked list does not contain any nodes, what are the values in **head** and **tail**?

**16.8**   If a linked list has only one node, is **head == tail** true?

**16.9**   When a new node is inserted to the head of a linked list, will the **head** pointer and the **tail** pointer be changed?

**16.10**  When a new node is inserted to the end of a linked list, will the **head** pointer and the **tail** pointer be changed?

**16.11**  When a node is removed from a linked list, what would happen if you don't explicitly use the delete operator to release the node?

**16.12**  Under what circumstances would the functions **removeFirst**, **removeLast**, and **removeAt** throw an exception?

**16.13**  Discuss the pros and cons of using arrays and linked lists.

**16.14**  If the number of elements in the program is fixed, what data structure should you use? If the number of elements in the program changes, what data structure should you use?

**16.15**  If you have to add or delete the elements anywhere in a list, should you use an array or a linked list?

**16.16**  What would happen when you run the following code?

```
1 #include <iostream>
2 #include <string>
3 #include "LinkedList.h"
4 using namespace std;
5
6 int main()
7 {
8   LinkedList<string> list;
9   list.add("abc");
10   cout << list.removeLast() << endl;
11   cout << list.removeLast() << endl;
12
13   return 0;
14 }
```

**16.17**  Show the output of the following code:

```
1 #include <iostream>
2 #include <string>
3 #include "LinkedList.h"
4 using namespace std;
5
6 int main()
7 {
8   LinkedList<string> list;
9   list.add("abc");
10
11   try
12   {
13     cout << list.removeLast() << endl;
14     cout << list.removeLast() << endl;
15   }
16   catch (runtime_error ex)
17   {
18     cout << "The list size is " <<  list.getSize() << endl;
19   }
```

```
20
21    return 0;
22 }
```

### Section 16.5 Variations of Linked Lists

**16.18** What is a circular, singly linked list? What is a doubly linked list? What is a circular, doubly linked list?

### Sections 16.6–16.7

**16.19** You can use inheritance or composition to design the data structures for stacks and queues. Discuss the pros and cons of these two approaches.

**16.20** Show the output of the following code:

```cpp
1  #include <iostream>
2  #include <string>
3  #include "StackWithLinkedList.h"
4  #include "Queue.h"
5  using namespace std;
6
7  int main()
8  {
9    Stack<string> stack;
10   Queue<int> queue;
11
12   stack.push("Georgia");
13   stack.push("Indiana");
14   stack.push("Oklahoma");
15
16   cout << stack.pop() << endl;
17   cout << "Stack's size is " << stack.getSize() << endl;
18
19   queue.enqueue(1);
20   queue.enqueue(2);
21   queue.enqueue(3);
22
23   cout << queue.dequeue() << endl;
24   cout << "Queue's size is " << queue.getSize() << endl;
25
26   return 0;
27 }
```

## PROGRAMMING EXERCISES

### Sections 16.2–16.4

**16.1**[*] (*Implementing* remove(T element)) The implementation of remove(T element) is omitted in Listing 16.2, LinkedList.h. Implement it.

**16.2**[*] (*Implementing* lastIndexOf(T element)) The implementation of lastIndexOf(T element) is omitted in Listing 16.2, LinkedList.h. Implement it.

**16.3**[*] (*Implementing* contains(T element)) The implementation of contains(T element) is omitted in Listing 16.2, LinkedList.h. Implement it.

**16.4**[*] (*Implementing* set(int index, T element)) The implementation of contains(T element) is omitted in Listing 16.2, LinkedList.h. Implement it.

**16.5**    (*Adding set-like operations in* `LinkedList`) Add and implement the following functions in `LinkedList`:

```
/* Add the elements in otherList to this list.
 */
void addAll(LinkedList<T> otherList)

/* Remove all the elements in otherList from this list
 */
void removeAll(LinkedList<T> otherList)

/* Retain the elements in this list if they are also in
otherList
 */
void retainAll(LinkedList<T> otherList)
```

Write a test program that creates two `LinkedList`s, `list1` and `list2`, with the initial values `{"Beijing", "Tokyo", "New York", "London", "Paris"}` and `{"Beijing", "Shanghai", "Paris", "Berlin", "Rome"}`, then invokes `list1.addAll(list2)`, `list1.removeAll(list2)`, and `list1.retainAll(list2)`, and displays the resulting new `list1`.

## Section 16.5 Variations of Linked Lists

**16.6**\*    (*Creating a doubly linked list*) The `LinkedList` class in the text is a singly linked list that enables one-way traversal of the list. Modify the `Node` class to add the new field name `previous` to refer to the previous node in the list, as follows:

```
template<typename T>
class Node
{
public:
  T element;  // Element contained in the node
  Node<T> *previous; // Pointer to the previous node
  Node<T> *next; // Pointer to the next node

  Node() // No-arg constructor
  {
    previous = NULL;
    next = NULL;
  }

  Node(T element) // Constructor
  {
    this->element = element;
    previous = NULL;
    next = NULL;
  }
};
```

Simplify the implementation of the `add(T element, int index)` and `removeAt(int index)` functions to take advantage of the doubly linked list.

**Sections 16.6–16.7**

**16.7** (*Implementing Stack using inheritance*) In §16.6, "Implementing Stack Using a LinkedList," Stack is implemented using composition. Create a new stack class that extends LinkedList.

**16.8** (*Implementing Queue using inheritance*) In §16.7, "Queues," Queue is implemented using composition. Create a new queue class that extends LinkedList.

## CHAPTER 17

# TREES, HEAPS, AND PRIORITY QUEUES

## Objectives

- To represent and access the elements in a binary tree (§§17.2.1–17.2.2).

- To insert an element into a binary tree (§17.2.3).

- To traverse a binary tree in inorder, postorder, and preorder (§17.2.4).

- To define and implement a binary tree class (§17.2.5).

- To know the properties of a heap (§17.3).

- To know how to add and remove elements from a heap (§§17.3.2–17.3.3).

- To implement a heap using a vector (§17.3.4).

- To implement a priority queue using a heap (§17.4).

## 17.1 Introduction

The preceding chapter introduced three basic data structures: linked lists, stacks, and queues. This chapter introduces three advanced data structures: binary trees, heaps, and priority queues.

## 17.2 Binary Trees

root
left subtree
right subtree

A list, stack, or queue is a linear structure that consists of a sequence of elements. A binary tree is a hierarchical structure. It is either empty or consists of an element, called the *root*, and two distinct binary trees, called the *left subtree* and *right subtree*. Examples of binary trees are shown in Figure 17.1.

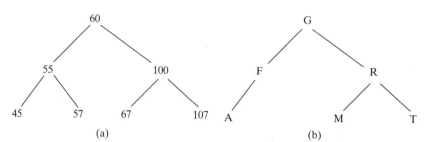

**FIGURE 17.1**   Each node in a binary tree has zero, one, or two branches.

leaf
binary search tree

The root of a left (right) subtree of a node is called a *left (right) child* of the node. A node without children is called a *leaf*. A special type of binary tree called a *binary search tree* is often useful. A binary search tree (with no duplicate elements) has the property that for every node in the tree, the value of any node in its left subtree is less than the value of the node, and the value of any node in its right subtree is greater than the value of the node. The binary trees in Figure 17.1 are all binary search trees. This section is concerned with binary search trees.

### 17.2.1   Representing Binary Trees

A binary tree can be represented using a set of linked nodes. Each node contains a value and two links named *left* and *right* that reference the left child and right child, respectively, as shown in Figure 17.2.

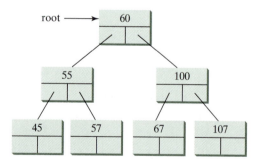

**FIGURE 17.2**   A binary tree can be represented using a set of linked nodes.

A node can be defined as a class, as follows:

```
template<typename T>
class TreeNode
```

```
{
public:
  T element; // Element contained in the node
  TreeNode<T> *left; // Pointer to the left child
  TreeNode<T> *right; // Pointer to the right child

  TreeNode() // No-arg constructor
  {
    left = NULL;
    right = NULL;
  }

  TreeNode(T element) // Constructor
  {
    this->element = element;
    left = NULL;
    right = NULL;
  }
};
```

The variable **root** refers to the root node of the tree. If the tree is empty, **root** is NULL. The following code creates the first three nodes of the tree in Figure 17.1:

```
// Create the root node
TreeNode<int> *root = new TreeNode<int>(60);

// Create the left child node
root->left = new TreeNode<int>(55);

// Create the right child node
root->right = new TreeNode<int>(100);
```

## 17.2.2  Accessing Nodes in Binary Trees

Suppose a tree with three nodes is created as in the preceding section. You can access the nodes in the tree through the **root** pointer. Here are the statements to display the elements in the tree.

```
// Display the root element
cout << root->element << endl;

// Display the element in the left child of the root
cout << (root->left)->element << endl;

// Display the element in the right child of the root
cout << (root->right)->element << endl;
```

## 17.2.3  Inserting an Element into a Binary Search Tree

As shown in the following algorithm, if a binary tree is empty, create a root node for the new element (lines 1–2). Otherwise, locate the parent node for the new element node (lines 3–19). If the new element is less than the parent element, the node for the new element becomes the left child of the parent. If the new element is greater than the parent element (line 23), the node for the new element becomes the right child of the parent (line 25).

```
1 if (root == NULL)
2    root = new TreeNode<T>(element);
3 else
4 {
5    // Locate the parent node
6    current = root;
```

```
 7   while (current != NULL)
 8     if (element < current->element)
 9     {
10       parent = current;
11       current = current->left;
12     }
13     else if (element > current->element)
14     {
15       parent = current;
16       current = current->right;
17     }
18     else
19       return false; // Duplicate node not inserted
20
21   // Create the new node and attach it to the parent node
22   if (element < parent->element)
23     parent->left = new TreeNode<T>(element);
24   else
25     parent->right = new TreeNode<T>(element);
26
27   return true; // Element inserted
28 }
```

For example, to insert 101 into the tree in Figure 17.2, the parent is the node for 107. The new node for 101 becomes the left child of the parent. To insert 59 into the tree, the parent is the node for 57. The new node for 59 becomes the right child of the parent. Both of these insertions are shown in Figure 17.3.

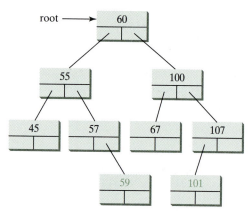

**FIGURE 17.3** Two new elements are inserted into the tree.

## 17.2.4 Tree Traversal

Tree traversal is the process of visiting each node in the tree exactly once in a certain order. There are several ways to traverse a tree. This section presents *inorder*, *preorder*, *postorder*, *depth-first*, and *breadth-first* traversals.

inorder

With *inorder* traversal, the left subtree of the current node is visited first, then the current node, and finally the right subtree of the current node. The inorder traversal displays all the nodes in a binary search tree in increasing order.

postorder

With *postorder* traversal, the left subtree of the current node is visited first, then the right subtree of the current node, and finally the current node itself.

preorder
depth-first

With *preorder* traversal, the current node is visited first, then the left subtree of the current node, and finally the right subtree of the current node. *Depth-first* traversal is the same as preorder traversal.

With *breadth-first* traversal, the nodes are visited level by level. First the root is visited, breadth-first
then all the children of the root from left to right, then the grandchildren of the root from left
to right, and so on.

For example, in the tree in Figure 17.3, the inorder is

45 55 57 59 60 67 100 101 107

The postorder is

45 59 57 55 67 101 107 100 60

The preorder is

60 55 45 57 59 100 67 107 101

The breadth-first traversal is

60 55 100 45 57 67 107 59 101

## 17.2.5 The BinaryTree Class

Let us define a binary tree class named **BinaryTree** with insert, inorder traversal, postorder
traversal, and preorder traversal, as shown in Figure 17.4. Its implementation is given in
Listing 17.1.

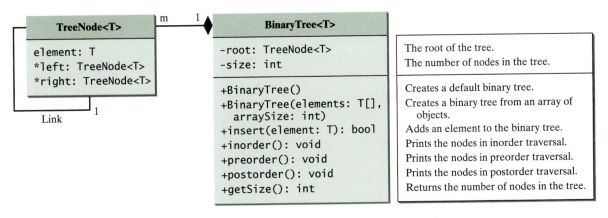

**FIGURE 17.4** BinaryTree implements a binary tree with operations insert, inorder,
preorder, and postorder.

## LISTING 17.1 BinaryTree.h

```
1 #ifndef BINARYTREE_H
2 #define BINARYTREE_H
3
4 template<typename T>
5 class TreeNode
6 {
7 public:
8   T element; // Element contained in the node
9   TreeNode<T> *left; // Pointer to the left child
10  TreeNode<T> *right; // Pointer to the right child
11
12  TreeNode() // No-arg constructor
13  {
14    left = NULL;
```

TreeNode class

left pointer
right pointer

TreeNode constructor

**TreeNode** constructor

**BinaryTree** class

constructor

function

root

private function

non-arg constructor

constructor

insert function

new root

```
15      right = NULL;
16    }
17
18    TreeNode(T element) // Constructor
19    {
20      this->element = element;
21      left = NULL;
22      right = NULL;
23    }
24  };
25
26  template<typename T>
27  class BinaryTree
28  {
29  public:
30    BinaryTree();
31    BinaryTree(T elements[], int arraySize);
32    bool insert(T element);
33    void inorder();
34    void preorder();
35    void postorder();
36    int getSize();
37
38  private:
39    TreeNode<T> *root;
40    int size;
41    void inorder(TreeNode<T> *root);
42    void postorder(TreeNode<T> *root);
43    void preorder(TreeNode<T> *root);
44  };
45
46  template<typename T >
47  BinaryTree<T>::BinaryTree()
48  {
49    root = NULL;
50    size = 0;
51  }
52
53  template<typename T>
54  BinaryTree<T>::BinaryTree(T elements[], int arraySize)
55  {
56    root = NULL;
57    size = 0;
58    for (int i = 0; i < arraySize; i++)
59    {
60      insert(elements[i]);
61    }
62  }
63
64  /* Insert element into the binary tree
65   * Return true if the element is inserted successfully
66   * Return false if the element is already in the tree
67   */
68  template<typename T>
69  bool BinaryTree<T>::insert(T element)
70  {
71    if (root == NULL)
72      root = new TreeNode<T>(element); // Create a new root
73    else
74    {
```

```
75      // Locate the parent node
76      TreeNode<T> *parent = NULL;
77      TreeNode<T> *current = root;
78      while (current != NULL)
79        if (element < current->element)
80        {
81          parent = current;
82          current = current->left;
83        }
84        else if (element > current->element)
85        {
86          parent = current;
87          current = current->right;
88        }
89        else
90          return false; // Duplicate node not inserted
91
92      // Create the new node and attach it to the parent node
93      if (element < parent->element)
94        parent->left = new TreeNode<T>(element);
95      else
96        parent->right = new TreeNode<T>(element);
97    }
98
99    size++;
100   return true; // Element inserted
101 }
102
103 /* Inorder traversal */
104 template<typename T>
105 void BinaryTree<T>::inorder()
106 {
107   inorder(root);
108 }
109
110 /* Inorder traversal from a subtree */
111 template<typename T>
112 void BinaryTree<T>::inorder(TreeNode<T> *root)
113 {
114   if (root == NULL) return;
115   inorder(root->left);
116   cout << root->element << " ";
117   inorder(root->right);
118 }
119
120 /* Postorder traversal */
121 template<typename T>
122 void BinaryTree<T>::postorder()
123 {
124   postorder(root);
125 }
126
127 /** Inorder traversal from a subtree */
128 template<typename T>
129 void BinaryTree<T>::postorder(TreeNode<T> *root)
130 {
131   if (root == NULL) return;
132   postorder(root->left);
133   postorder(root->right);
134   cout << root->element << " ";
135 }
```

locate parent

duplicate element

new left child

new right child

increase size

inorder

recursive helper function

postorder

recursive helper function

preorder

```
136
137 /* Preorder traversal */
138 template<typename T>
139 void BinaryTree<T>::preorder()
140 {
141   preorder(root);
142 }
143
144 /* Preorder traversal from a subtree */
145 template<typename T>
```

recursive helper function

```
146 void BinaryTree<T>::preorder(TreeNode<T> *root)
147 {
148   if (root == NULL) return;
149   cout << root->element << " ";
150   preorder(root->left);
151   preorder(root->right);
152 }
153
154 /* Get the number of nodes in the tree */
155 template<typename T>
```

getSize

```
156 int BinaryTree<T>::getSize()
157 {
158   return size;
159 }
160
161 #endif
```

The no-arg constructor (lines 46–51) constructs an empty binary tree with **root NULL** and **size** 0. The constructor (lines 53–62) constructs a binary tree initialized with the elements in the array.

The **insert(T element)** function (lines 68–101) creates a node for element and inserts it into the tree. If the tree is empty, the node becomes the root (line 72). Otherwise, the function finds an appropriate parent for the node to maintain the order of the tree. If the element is already in the tree, the function returns **false** (line 90); otherwise it returns **true** (line 100).

The **inorder()** function (lines 104–108) invokes **inorder(root)** to traverse the entire tree. The function **inorder(TreeNode root)** traverses the tree with the specified root. This is a recursive function. It recursively traverses the left subtree, then the root, and finally the right subtree. The traversal ends when the tree is empty.

The **postorder()** function (lines 121–125) and the **preorder()** function (lines 138–142) are implemented similarly using recursion.

Listing 17.2 gives an example that creates a binary tree for strings using **BinaryTree<string>** (line 8). Add strings into the binary tree (lines 9–15) and traverse the tree in inorder (line 18), postorder (line 21), and preorder (line 24).

## Listing 17.2 TestBinaryTree.cpp

```
1 #include <iostream>
2 #include <string>
```

include class

```
3 #include "BinaryTree.h"
4 using namespace std;
5
6 int main()
7 {
```

create **tree1**
insert string

```
8   BinaryTree<string> tree1;
9   tree1.insert("George");
10  tree1.insert("Michael");
11  tree1.insert("Tom");
12  tree1.insert("Adam");
13  tree1.insert("Jones");
```

```
14    tree1.insert("Peter");
15    tree1.insert("Daniel");
16
17    cout << "Inorder (sorted): ";                              inorder
18    tree1.inorder();
19
20    cout << "\nPostorder: ";                                   postorder
21    tree1.postorder();
22
23    cout << "\nPreorder: ";                                    preorder
24    tree1.preorder();
25
26    cout << "\nThe number of nodes is " << tree1.getSize();    getSize
27
28    int numbers[] = {2, 4, 3, 1, 8, 5, 6, 7};
29    BinaryTree<int> tree2(numbers, 8);                         create tree2
30    cout << "\nInorder (sorted): ";                            inorder
31    tree2.inorder();
32
33    return 0;
34 }
```

```
Inorder (sorted): Adam Daniel George Jones Michael Peter Tom
Postorder: Daniel Adam Jones Peter Tom Michael George
Preorder: George Adam Daniel Michael Jones Tom Peter
The number of nodes is 7
Inorder (sorted): 1 2 3 4 5 6 7 8
```

After all the string elements are inserted, **tree1** should appear as shown in Figure 17.5(a). Tree **tree2** is created as shown in Figure 17.5(b).

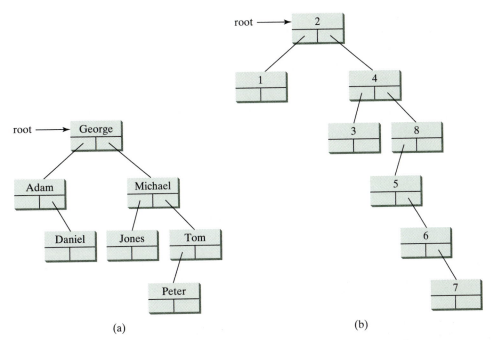

**FIGURE 17.5** The binary search trees are pictured here after they are created.

If the elements are inserted in a different order, the tree will look different. However, the inorder traversal prints elements in the same order as long as the set of elements is the same. The inorder traversal displays a sorted list.

## 17.3 Heaps

heap

*Heap* is a useful data structure for designing efficient sorting algorithms and priority queues. A *heap* is a binary tree with the following properties:

- It is a complete binary tree.

- Each node is greater than or equal to any of its children.

complete binary tree

A binary tree is *complete* if every level of the tree is full except that the last level may not be full and all the leaves on the last level are placed left-most. For example, in Figure 17.6, the binary trees in (a) and (b) are complete, but the binary trees in (c) and (d) are not complete. Further, the binary tree in (a) is a heap, but the binary tree in (b) is not a heap, because the root (39) is less than its right child (42).

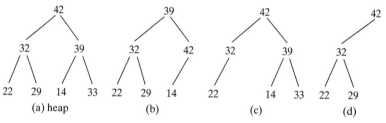

**FIGURE 17.6** A heap is a special complete binary tree.

### 17.3.1 Representing a Heap

A heap is a binary tree. So, it can be represented using a binary tree data structure. However, a more efficient representation for a heap is using an array or a vector if the heap size is known in advance. The heap in Figure 17.7(a) can be represented using an array in Figure 17.7(b). The root is at position 0, and its two children are at positions 1 and 2. For a node at position $i$, its left child is at position $2i + 1$ and its right child is at position $2i + 2$, and its parent is $(i - 1)/2$. For example, the node for element 39 is at position 4, so its left child (element 14) is at 9 ($2 \times 4 + 1$), its right child (element 33) is at 10 ($2 \times 4 + 2$), and its parent (element 42) is at 1 (($4 - 1)/2$).

If the heap size is not known in advance, it is better to use a vector to store a heap.

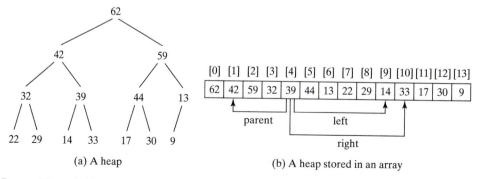

**FIGURE 17.7** A binary heap can be implemented using an array.

### 17.3.2 Removing the Root

Often, you need to remove the max element which is the root in a heap. After the root is removed, the tree must be rebuilt to maintain the heap property. The algorithm for building the tree can be described as follows:

```
Move the last node to replace the root;
Let the root be the current node;
while (the current node has children and the current node is
        smaller than one of its children)
{
  Swap the current node with the larger of its children;
  Now the current node is one level down;
}
```

Figure 17.8 shows the process of rebuilding a heap after the root 62 is removed from Figure 17.7(a). Move the last node 9 to the root, as shown in Figure 17.8(a). Swap 9 with 59, as shown in Figure 17.8(b). Swap 9 with 44, as shown in Figure 17.8(c). Swap 9 with 30, as shown in Figure 17.8(d).

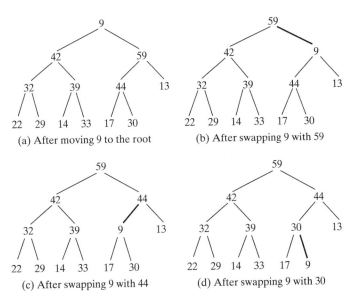

FIGURE 17.8 Rebuild the heap after the root is removed.

### 17.3.3 Adding a New Node

To add a new node to the heap, first add it to the end of the heap and then rebuild the tree as follows:

```
Let the last node be the current node;
while (the current node is greater than its parent)
{
  Swap the current node with its parent;
  Now the current node is one level up;
}
```

Figure 17.9 shows the process of rebuilding a heap after adding a new node 88 to the heap in Figure 17.8(d). Place the new node 88 at the end of the tree, as shown in Figure 17.9(a). Swap 88 with 13, as shown in Figure 17.9(b). Swap 88 with 44, as shown in Figure 17.9(c). Swap 88 with 59, as shown in Figure 17.9(d).

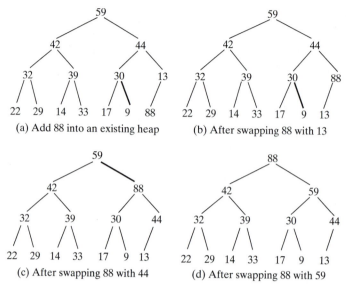

(a) Add 88 into an existing heap

(b) After swapping 88 with 13

(c) After swapping 88 with 44

(d) After swapping 88 with 59

**FIGURE 17.9** Rebuild the heap after adding a new node.

## 17.3.4 The Heap Class

Now you are ready to design and implement the **Heap** class. The class diagram is shown in Figure 17.10. Its implementation is given in Listing 17.3.

| Heap<T> |
| --- |
| -vector: vector<T> |
| +Heap() <br> +Heap(elements[]: T, arraySize: int) <br> +remove(): T <br> +add(element: T): void <br> +getSize(): int |

Creates a default heap.
Creates a heap with the specified objects.
Removes the root from the heap and returns it.
Adds a new object to the heap.
Returns the size of the heap.

**FIGURE 17.10** **Heap** provides operations for manipulating a heap.

## LISTING 17.3 Heap.h

```
1  #ifndef HEAP_H
2  #define HEAP_H
3  #include <vector>
4  #include <stdexcept>
5  using namespace std;
6
7  template<typename T>
8  class Heap
9  {
10 public:
11   Heap();
12   Heap(T elements[], int arraySize);
13   T remove() throw (runtime_error);
14   void add(T element);
15   int getSize();
16
```

include **vector**
include **stdexcept**

**Heap** class

public constructor

public function

```
17  private:
18    vector<T> v;                                              internal heap representation
19  };
20
21  template<typename T>
22  Heap<T>::Heap()                                             no-arg constructor
23  {
24  }
25
26  template<typename T>
27  Heap<T>::Heap(T elements[], int arraySize)                  constructor
28  {
29    for (int i = 0; i < arraySize; i++)
30    {
31      add(elements[i]);                                       add a new element
32    }
33  }
34
35  /* Remove the root from the heap */
36  template<typename T>
37  T Heap<T>::remove() throw (runtime_error)                   remove the root
38  {
39    if (v.size() == 0)                                        empty heap
40      throw runtime_error("Heap is empty");
41
42    T removedElement = v[0];
43    v[0] = v[v.size() - 1]; // Move the last to root           new root
44    v.pop_back(); // Remove root                               remove the last
45
46    // Maintain the heap property
47    int currentIndex = 0;
48    while (currentIndex < v.size())                           adjust the tree
49    {
50      int leftChildIndex = 2 * currentIndex + 1;
51      int rightChildIndex = 2 * currentIndex + 2;
52
53      // Find the maximum between two children
54      if (leftChildIndex >= v.size()) break; // The tree is a heap
55      int maxIndex = leftChildIndex;
56      if (rightChildIndex < v.size())
57      {
58        if (v[maxIndex] < v[rightChildIndex])
59        {
60          maxIndex = rightChildIndex;
61        }
62      }
63
64      // Swap if the current node is less than the maximum
65      if (v[currentIndex] < v[maxIndex])
66      {
67        T temp = v[maxIndex];
68        v[maxIndex] = v[currentIndex];
69        v[currentIndex] = temp;
70        currentIndex = maxIndex;
71      }
72      else
73        break; // The tree is a heap
74    }
75
76    return removedElement;                                    return removed element
77  }
```

```
78
79 /* Insert element into the heap and maintain the heap property */
80 template<typename T>
81 void Heap<T>::add(T element)
82 {
83     v.push_back(element); // Append element to the heap
84     int currentIndex = v.size() - 1; // The index of the last node
85
86     // Maintain the heap property
87     while (currentIndex > 0)
88     {
89       int parentIndex = (currentIndex - 1) / 2;
90       // Swap if the current element is greater than its parent
91       if (v[currentIndex] > v[parentIndex])
92       {
93         T temp = v[currentIndex];
94         v[currentIndex] = v[parentIndex];
95         v[parentIndex] = temp;
96       }
97       else
98         break; // the tree is a heap now
99
100       currentIndex = parentIndex;
101     }
102 }
103
104 /* Get the number of element in the heap */
105 template<typename T>
106 int Heap<T>::getSize()
107 {
108     return v.size();
109 }
110
111 #endif
```

*(margin notes: add element — line 81; append element — line 83; adjust the tree — line 87; get size — line 106)*

A heap is represented using a vector internally (line 18). You may change it to other data structures, but the **Heap** class contract will remain unchanged (see Exercise 17.9).

The **remove()** function (lines 36–77) removes and returns the root. To maintain the heap property, the function moves the last element to the root position and swaps it with its larger child if it is less than the larger child. This process continues until the last element becomes a leaf or it is not less than its children.

The **add(T element)** function (lines 80–102) appends the element to the tree and then swaps it with its parent if it is greater than its parent. This process continues until the new element becomes the root or it is not greater than its parent.

Listing 17.4 gives an example of using a heap to sort strings and numbers. The program creates a heap in line 8, adds strings to the heap (lines 9–14), and displays all strings in the heap (lines 16–17). The program creates a heap from an array of integers (line 21) and displays all elements in the heap in decreasing order (lines 22–23).

### LISTING 17.4  TestHeap.cpp

```
1 #include <iostream>
2 #include <string>
3 #include "Heap.h"
4 using namespace std;
5
6 int main()
7 {
8 Heap<string> heap1;
```

*(margin notes: include **Heap** — line 3; create a heap — line 8)*

```
 9   heap1.add("George");                                       add to heap
10   heap1.add("Michael");
11   heap1.add("Tom");
12   heap1.add("Adam");
13   heap1.add("Jones");
14   heap1.add("Peter");
15
16   while (heap1.getSize() > 0)                                 heap size?
17     cout << heap1.remove() << " ";                           remove the root
18   cout << endl;
19
20   int numbers[] = {8, 9, 2, 3, 4, 1, 5, 6, 7};               create a heap
21   Heap<int> heap2(numbers, 9);                               heap size?
22   while (heap2.getSize() > 0)                                 remove the root
23     cout << heap2.remove() << " ";
24
25   return 0;
26 }
```

```
Tom Peter Michael Jones George Adam
9 8 7 6 5 4 3 2 1
```

## 17.4 Priority Queues

A regular queue is a first-in and first-out data structure. Elements are appended to the end of the queue and are removed from the beginning of the queue. In a priority queue, elements are assigned with priorities. The element with the highest priority is accessed or removed first. A priority queue has a largest-in, first-out behavior. For example, the emergency room in a hospital assigns patients with priority numbers; the patient with the highest priority is treated first.

A priority queue can be implemented using a heap, where the root is the element with the highest priority in the queue. The class diagram for the priority queue is shown in Figure 17.11. Its implementation is given in Listing 17.5.

| **PriorityQueue<T>** |
| --- |
| -heap: Heap<T> |
| +enqueue(element: T): void<br>+dequeue(): T<br>+getSize(): int |

Adds an element to this queue.
Removes an element from this queue.
Returns the number of elements from this queue.

**FIGURE 17.11** PriorityQueue uses a heap to provide a largest-in first-out data structure.

## LISTING 17.5 PriorityQueue.h

```
1 #ifndef PRIORITYQUEUE_H
2 #define PRIORITYQUEUE_H
3 #include "Heap.h"                                              heap for priority queue
4
5 template<typename T>
6 class PriorityQueue
7 {
8 public:
9   PriorityQueue();                                            constructor
```

```
10    void enqueue(T element);
11    T dequeue() throw (runtime_error);
12    int getSize();
13
14 private:
15    Heap<T> heap;
16 };
17
18 template<typename T>
19 PriorityQueue<T>::PriorityQueue()
20 {
21 }
22
23 template<typename T>
24 void PriorityQueue<T>::enqueue(T element)
25 {
26    heap.add(element);
27 }
28
29 template<typename T>
30 T PriorityQueue<T>::dequeue() throw (runtime_error)
31 {
32    return heap.remove();
33 }
34
35 template<typename T>
36 int PriorityQueue<T>::getSize()
37 {
38    return heap.getSize();
39 }
40
41 #endif
```

heap — line 15

add to queue — line 24

remove from queue — line 30

queue size — line 36

Listing 17.6 gives an example of using a priority queue for patients. The **Patient** class is declared in lines 5–37. Line 42 creates a priority queue. Four patients are created with associated priority values are created and enqueued in lines 43–46. Line 50 dequeues a patient from the queue.

## LISTING 17.6  TestPriorityQueue.cpp

```
1 #include <iostream>
2 #include "PriorityQueue.h"
3 using namespace std;
4
5 class Patient
6 {
7 public:
8    Patient(string name, int priority)
9    {
10       this->name = name;
11       this->priority = priority;
12    }
13
14    bool operator<(Patient &secondPatient)
15    {
16       return (this->priority < secondPatient.priority);
17    }
18
19    bool operator>(Patient &secondPatient)
```

include **PriorityQueue** — line 2

**Patient** class — line 5

**Patient** constructor — line 8

overload < operator — line 14

overload > operator — line 19

```
20    {
21        return (this->priority > secondPatient.priority);
22    }
23
24    string getName()                                              getName
25    {
26        return name;
27    }
28
29    int getPriority()                                             getPriority
30    {
31        return priority;
32    }
33
34 private:
35     string name;
36     int priority;
37 };
38
39 int main()
40 {
41     // Queue of patients
42     PriorityQueue<Patient> patientQueue;                         create a priority queue
43     patientQueue.enqueue(Patient("John", 2));                    add to queue
44     patientQueue.enqueue(Patient("Jim", 1));
45     patientQueue.enqueue(Patient("Tim", 5));
46     patientQueue.enqueue(Patient("Cindy", 7));
47
48     while (patientQueue.getSize() > 0)
49     {
50         Patient element = patientQueue.dequeue();                remove from queue
51         cout << element.getName() << " (priority: " <<
52             element.getPriority() << ") ";
53     }
54
55     return 0;
56 }
```

```
Cindy(priority: 7) Tim(priority: 5) John(priority: 2) Jim(priority: 1)
```

The < and > operators are defined the **Patient** class so two patients can be compared. You can use any class type for the elements in the heap, provided that the elements can be compared using the < and > operators.

## KEY TERMS

| | | | |
|---|---|---|---|
| binary search tree | 498 | postorder traversal | 500 |
| binary tree | 498 | preorder traversal | 500 |
| heap | 506 | priority queue | 511 |
| inorder traversal | 500 | tree traversal | 500 |

## CHAPTER SUMMARY

■ A binary tree can be implemented using linked nodes. Each node contains the element value and two pointers that point to the left and right children.

■ Tree traversal is the process of visiting each node in the tree exactly once in a certain order. There are several ways to traverse a tree.

■ With inorder traversal, the left subtree of the current node is visited first, then the current node, and finally the right subtree of the current node. The inorder traversal displays all the nodes in a binary search tree in increasing order.

■ With postorder traversal, the left subtree of the current node is visited first, then the right subtree of the current node, and finally the current node itself.

■ With preorder traversal, the current node is visited first, then the left subtree of the current node, and finally the right subtree of the current node. Depth-first traversal is the same as preorder traversal.

■ With breadth-first traversal, the nodes are visited level by level. First the root is visited, then all the children of the root from left to right, then the grandchildren of the root from left to right, and so on.

■ Heap is a useful data structure for designing efficient sorting algorithms and priority queues. A *heap* is a binary tree with two properties: (1) It is a complete binary tree; (2) Each node is greater than or equal to any of its children.

■ You can implement a heap using a binary tree, an array, or a vector.

■ A regular queue is a first-in and first-out data structure. Elements are appended to the end of the queue and are removed from the beginning of the queue. In a priority queue, elements are assigned with priorities. When accessing elements, the element with the highest priority is removed first. A priority queue has a largest-in, first-out behavior.

■ A priority queue can be implemented using a heap, where the root is the element with the highest priority in the queue.

## REVIEW QUESTIONS

### Section 17.2 Binary Trees

**17.1** If a set of the same elements is inserted into a binary tree in two different orders, will the two corresponding binary trees look the same? Will the inorder traversal be the same? Will the postorder traversal be the same? Will the preorder traversal be the same?

**17.2** What is wrong if the following two highlighted lines are deleted in the following constructor for **BinaryTree**?

```
template<typename T>
BinaryTree<T>::BinaryTree(T elements[], int arraySize)
{
  root = NULL;
  size = 0;
  for (int i = 0; i < arraySize; i++)
  {
    insert(elements[i]);
  }
}
```

**17.3** Add the elements 4, 5, 1, 2, 9, 3 into a binary tree in this order. Draw the diagrams to show the binary tree as each element is added.

**17.4** Show the inorder, postorder, preorder, and breadth-first traversals for the binary tree in Figure 17.1.

## Section 17.3 Heaps

**17.5** What is a complete binary tree? What is a heap? Describe how to remove the root from a heap and how to add a new object to a heap.

**17.6** What is the return value from invoking the `remove` function if the heap is empty?

**17.7** Add the elements 4, 5, 1, 2, 9, 3 into a heap in this order. Draw the diagrams to show the heap as each element is added.

**17.8** Show the heap after the root in the heap in Figure 17.9(d) is removed.

## Section 17.6 Priority Queues

**17.9** What is a priority queue?

# PROGRAMMING EXERCISES

## Section 17.2 Binary Trees

**17.1**[*] (*Search in BinaryTree*) Add a function in `BinaryTree` to search an element in the tree.

```
/* Search element in this binary tree */
bool search(T element)
```

**17.2**[*] (*Breadth-first traversal in BinaryTree*) Add a function in `BinaryTree` to traverse the tree in breadth-first order.

```
/* Display the nodes in breadth-first traversal */
void breadthFirstTraversal()
```

**17.3**[*] (*Depth of BinaryTree*) Add a function in `BinaryTree` to return the depth of the tree.

```
/* Return the depth of this binary tree. Depth is the
 * number of the nodes in the longest path of the tree
 */
int depth()
```

**17.4**[**] (*Implementing inorder traversal using a stack*) Implement the `inorder` function in `BinaryTree` using a stack instead of recursion.

**17.5**[**] (*Implementing preorder traversal using a stack*) Implement the `preorder` function in `BinaryTree` using a stack instead of recursion.

**17.6**[**] (*Implementing postorder traversal using a stack*) Implement the `postorder` function in `BinaryTree` using a stack instead of recursion.

**17.7**[***] (*Deleting elements*) Add a function in `BinaryTree` to delete an element from the tree.

```
/* Delete the specified element from the tree
 * return true if deletion successful;
 * return false if no element is in the tree.
 */
bool deleteElement(T element)
```

Write a `main` function that inserts 10 14 16 20 27 30 40 50 80 in this order and then deletes these numbers in the same order. Display the inorder after each number is deleted.

**Section 17.3 Heaps**

17.8** (*Sorting using a heap*) Implement the following sort function using a heap:

```
void sort(int list[], int arraySize)
```

17.9* (*Implementing heap using binary tree*) Listing 17.3, Heap.cpp, implements a heap using a vector. Use a binary tree to implement it.

# CHAPTER 18

# ALGORITHM EFFICIENCY AND SORTING

## Objectives

- To estimate algorithm efficiency using the Big O notation (§18.2).

- To understand growth rates and why constants and smaller terms can be ignored in the estimation (§18.2).

- To know the examples of algorithms with constant time, logarithmic time, linear time, log-linear time, quadratic time, and exponential time (§18.2).

- To analyze linear search, binary search, selection sort, and insertion sort (§18.2).

- To design, implement, and analyze bubble sort (§18.3).

- To design, implement, and analyze merge sort (§18.4).

- To design, implement, and analyze quick sort (§18.5).

- To design, implement, and analyze heap sort (§18.6).

- To sort large data in a file (§18.7).

# 18.1 Introduction

Sorting is a classic subject in computer science. There are three reasons for studying sorting algorithms. First, sorting algorithms illustrate many creative approaches to problem solving, and these approaches can be applied to solve other problems. Second, sorting algorithms are good for practicing fundamental programming techniques using selection statements, loops, functions, and arrays. Third, sorting algorithms are excellent examples to demonstrate algorithm performance.

The data to be sorted might be integers, doubles, characters, or any generic element type. §6.6, "Sorting Arrays," presented selection sort and insertion sort for numeric values. The selection sort algorithm was extended to sort an array of the generic element type in §15.3, "Example: A Generic Sort." For simplicity, this section assumes:

1. Data to be sorted are integers,

2. Data are sorted in ascending order, and

3. Data are stored in an array.

The programs can be easily modified to sort other types of data, to sort in descending order, or to sort data in a vector or a linked list.

There are many algorithms on sorting. In order to analyze and compare the complexities of these algorithms, this chapter first introduces the Big O notation for estimating algorithm efficiency. The whole chapter is optional. No chapter in the book is dependent on this chapter.

# 18.2 Estimating Algorithm Efficiency

Suppose two algorithms perform the same task such as search (linear search versus binary search) or sort (selection sort versus insertion sort). Which one is better? One possible approach to answer this question is to implement these algorithms and run the programs to get *execution time*. But there are two problems for this approach:

1. There are many tasks running concurrently on a computer. The execution time of a particular program is dependent on the system load.

2. The execution time is dependent on specific input. Consider linear search and binary search, for example. If an element to be searched happens to be the first in the list, linear search will find the element quicker than binary search.

It is very difficult to compare algorithms by measuring their execution time. To overcome these problems, a theoretical approach was developed to analyze algorithms independent of computers and specific input. This approach approximates the effect of a change on the size of the input. In this way, you can see how fast an algorithm's execution time increases as the input size increases, so you can compare two algorithms by examining their *growth rates*.

## 18.2.1 Big O Notation

Consider linear search. The linear search algorithm compares the key with the elements in the array sequentially until the key is found or the array is exhausted. If the key is not in the array, it requires $n$ comparisons for an array of size $n$. If the key is in the array, it requires $n/2$ comparisons on average. The algorithm's execution time is proportional to the size of the array. If you double the size of the array, you will expect the number of comparisons to double. The algorithm grows at a linear rate. The growth rate has an order of magnitude of $n$. Computer scientists use the *Big O notation* to abbreviate for *"order of magnitude."* Using this notation, the complexity of the linear search algorithm is $O(n)$, pronounced as *"order of n."*

For the same input size, an algorithm's execution time may vary, depending on the input. An input that results in the shortest execution time is called the *best-case* input, and an input that results in the longest execution time is called the *worst-case* input. Best-case and worst-case are not representative, but worst-case analysis is very useful. You can show that the algorithm will never be slower than the worst-case. An *average-case* analysis attempts to determine the average amount of time among all possible input of the same size. Average-case analysis is ideal, but difficult to perform, because it is hard to determine the relative probabilities and distributions of various input instances for many problems. Worst-case analysis is easier to obtain and is thus more common. So, the analysis generally is conducted for the worst-case.

average-case

The linear search algorithm requires $n$ comparisons in the worst-case and $n/2$ comparisons in the average-case. Using the Big $O$ notation, both cases require $O(n)$ time. The multiplicative constant (1/2) can be omitted. Algorithm analysis is focused on growth rate. The multiplicative constants have no impact on growth rates. The growth rate for $n/2$ or $100n$ is the same as $n$, as illustrated in Table 18.1. Therefore, $O(n) = O(n/2) = O(100n)$.

ignoring multiplicative constants

**TABLE 18.1**    Growth Rates

| $n$ \ $f(n)$ | $n$ | $n/2$ | $100n$ | |
|---|---|---|---|---|
| 100 | 100 | 50 | 10000 | |
| 200 | 200 | 100 | 20000 | |
| | 2 | 2 | 2 | $f(200) / f(100)$ |

Consider the algorithm for finding the maximum number in an array of $n$ elements. If $n$ is 2, it takes one comparison to find the maximum number. If $n$ is 3, it takes two comparisons to find the maximum number. In general, it takes $n - 1$ times of comparisons to find the maximum number in a list of $n$ elements. Algorithm analysis is for *large input size*. If the input size is small, there is no significance to estimate an algorithm's efficiency. As $n$ grows larger, the $n$ part in the expression $n - 1$ dominates the complexity. The Big $O$ notation allows you to ignore the non-dominating part (e.g., $-1$ in the expression $n - 1$) and highlight the important part (e.g., $n$ in the expression $n - 1$). So, the complexity of this algorithm is $O(n)$.

large input size

ignoring non-dominating terms

The Big $O$ notation estimates the execution time of an algorithm in relation to the input size. If the time is not related to the input size, the algorithm is said to take *constant time* with the notation $O(1)$. For example, a function that retrieves an element at a given index in an array takes constant time, because the time does not grow as the size of the array increases.

constant time

The following two mathematical summations are often useful in algorithm analysis:

$$1 + 2 + 3 + \ldots + (n - 1) + n = \frac{n(n + 1)}{2}$$

$$a^0 + a^1 + a^2 + a^3 + \ldots + a^{(n-1)} + a^n = \frac{a^{n+1} - 1}{a - 1}$$

## 18.2.2   Examples: Determining Big-O

This section gives several examples of determining Big O for repetition, sequence, and selection statements.

## Example 1

Consider the time complexity for the following loop:

```
for (i = 1; i <= n; i++)
{
  k = k + 5;
}
```

It is a constant time, $c$, for executing

```
k = k + 5;
```

Since the loop is executed $n$ times, the time complexity for the loop is

$$T(n) = (\text{a constant } c) * n = O(n)$$

## Example 2

What is the time complexity for the following loop?

```
for (i = 1; i <= n; i++)
{
  for (j = 1; j <= n; j++)
  {
    k = k + i + j;
  }
}
```

It is a constant time, $c$, for executing

```
k = k + i + j;
```

The outer loop executes $n$ times. For each iteration in the outer loop, the inner is executed $n$ times. So, the time complexity for the loop is

$$T(n) = (\text{a constant } c) * n * n = O(n^2)$$

## Example 3

Consider the following loop:

```
for (i = 1; i <= n; i++)
{
  for (j = 1; j <= i; j++)
  {
    k = k + i + j;
  }
}
```

The outer loop executes $n$ times. For $i = 1, 2, ...$, the inner loop is executed one time, two times and $n$ times. So, the time complexity for the loop is

$$T(n) = c + 2c + 3c + 4c + \ ... \ + nc = cn(n + 1)/2 = (c/2)n^2 + (c/2)n = O(n^2)$$

## Example 4

Consider the following loop:

```
for (i = 1; i <= n; i++)
{
  for (j = 1; j <= 20; j++)
  {
    k = k + i + j;
  }
}
```

The inner loop executes 20 times, and the outer loop executes $n$ times. So, the time complexity for the loop is

$$T(n) = 20 * c * n = O(n)$$

## Example 5

Consider the following sequences:

```
for (j = 1; j <= 10; j++)
{
```

```
    k = k + 4;
  }

  for (i = 1; i <= n; i++)
  {
    for (j = 1; j <= 20; j++)
    {
      k = k + i + j;
    }
  }
```

The first loop executes 10 times, and the second loop executes 20 * n times. So, the time complexity for the loop is

$$T(n) = 10*c + 20*c*n = O(n)$$

## Example 6

Consider the following selection statement:

```
  if (list.contains(e))
  {
    System.out.println(e);
  }
  else
    for (Object t: list)
    {
      System.out.println(t);
    }
```

Suppose the list contains $n$ elements. The execution time for `list.contains(e)` is $O(n)$. The loop in the **else** clause takes $O(n)$ time. So, the time complexity for the entire statement is

$$T(n) = \text{if test time} + \text{worst-case time (if clause, else clause)} = O(n) + O(n) = O(n)$$

### 18.2.3 Analyzing Binary Search

The binary search algorithm presented in Listing 6.8, BinarySearch.h, searches a key in a sorted array. Each iteration in the algorithm contains a fixed number of operations, denoted by $c$. Let $T(n)$ denote the time complexity for a binary search on a list of $n$ elements. Without loss of generality, assume $n$ is a power of 2 and $k = \log n$. Since binary search eliminates half of the input after two comparisons,

$$T(n) = T\left(\frac{n}{2}\right) + c = T\left(\frac{n}{2^2}\right) + c + c = \ldots = T\left(\frac{n}{2^k}\right) + ck$$

$$= T(1) + c \log n = 1 + c \log n$$

$$= O(\log n)$$

Ignoring constants and smaller terms, the complexity of the binary search algorithm is $O(\log n)$. An algorithm with the $O(\log n)$ time complexity is called a *logarithmic algorithm*.  logarithmic time
The base of the log is 2, but the base does not affect a logarithmic growth rate, so it can be omitted. The logarithmic algorithm grows slowly as the problem size increases. If you square the input size, you only double the time for the algorithm.

### 18.2.4 Analyzing Selection Sort

The selection sort algorithm presented in Listing 6.9, SelectionSort.h, finds the largest number in the list and places it last. It then finds the largest number remaining and places it next to last, and so on, until the list contains only a single number. The number of comparisons is

$n - 1$ for the first iteration, $n - 2$ for the second iteration, and so on. Let $T(n)$ denote the complexity for selection sort and $c$ denote the total number of other operations such as assignments and additional comparisons in each iteration. So,

$$T(n) = (n - 1) + c + (n - 2) + c \ldots + 2 + c + 1 + c$$

$$= \frac{(n - 1)(n - 1 + 1)}{2} + c(n - 1) = \frac{n^2}{2} - \frac{n}{2} + cn - c$$

$$= O(n^2)$$

Ignoring constants and smaller terms, the complexity of the selection sort algorithm is $O(n^2)$.

**quadratic time**

An algorithm with the $O(n^2)$ time complexity is called a *quadratic algorithm*. The quadratic algorithm grows quickly as the problem size increases. If you double the input size, the time for the algorithm is quadrupled. Algorithms with two nested loops are often quadratic.

### 18.2.5 Analyzing Insertion Sort

The insertion sort algorithm presented in Listing 6.10, InsertionSort.h, sorts a list of values by repeatedly inserting a new element into a sorted partial array until the whole array is sorted. At the $k$th iteration, to insert an element to an array of size $k$, it may take $k$ comparisons to find the insertion position, and $k$ moves to insert the element. Let $T(n)$ denote the complexity for insertion sort and $c$ denote the total number of other operations, such as assignments and additional comparisons in each iteration. So,

$$T(n) = 2 + c + 2 \times 2 + c \ldots + 2 \times (n - 1) + c$$

$$= 2(1 + 2 + \ldots + n - 1) + c(n - 1)$$

$$= 2\frac{(n - 1)n}{2} + cn - c = n^2 - n + cn - c$$

$$= O(n^2)$$

Ignoring constants and smaller terms, the complexity of the insertion sort algorithm is $O(n^2)$.

### 18.2.6 Analyzing Towers of Hanoi

The Towers of Hanoi problem presented in Listing 8.7, TowersOfHanoi.cpp, moves $n$ disks from tower A to tower B with the assistance of tower C recursively, as follows:

1. Move the first $n - 1$ disks from A to C with the assistance of tower B.

2. Move disk $n$ from A to B.

3. Move $n - 1$ disks from C to B with the assistance of tower A.

Let $T(n)$ denote the complexity for the algorithm that moves $n$ disks and $c$ denote the constant time to move one disk (i.e., $T(1)$ is $c$). So,

$$T(n) = T(n - 1) + c + T(n - 1)$$

$$= 2T(n - 1) + c$$

$$= 2(2(T(n - 2) + c) + c)$$

$$= 2(2(2T(n - 3) + c + c) + c)$$

$$= 2^{n-1}T(1) + 2^{n-2}c + \ldots + 2c + c$$

$$= 2^{n-1}c + 2^{n-2}c + \ldots + 2c + c = (2^n - 1)c = O(2^n)$$

An algorithm with the $O(2^n)$ time complexity is called an *exponential algorithm.* As the $O(2^n)$ input size increases, the time for the exponential algorithm grows exponentially. The exponential algorithms are not practical for large input size.

$O(2^n)$
exponential time

## 18.2.7 Comparing Common Growth Functions

The preceding sections analyzed the complexity of several algorithms. Table 18.2 lists some common growth functions. These functions are ordered as follows:

$$O(1) < O(\log n) < O(n) < O(n \log n) < O(n^2) < O(n^3) < O(2^n)$$

**TABLE 18.2**   Common Growth Functions

| Big-O Function | Name |
| --- | --- |
| $O(1)$ | Constant time |
| $O(\log n)$ | Logarithmic time |
| $O(n)$ | Linear time |
| $O(n \log n)$ | Log-linear time |
| $O(n^2)$ | Quadratic time |
| $O(n^3)$ | Cubic time |
| $O(2^n)$ | Exponential time |

Table 18.3 shows how growth rates change as the input size doubles from $n = 25$ to $n = 50$.

**TABLE 18.3**   Change of Growth Rates

| Function | $n = 25$ | $n = 50$ | $f(50)/f(25)$ |
| --- | --- | --- | --- |
| $O(1)$ | 1 | 1 | 1 |
| $O(\log n)$ | 4.64 | 5.64 | 1.21 |
| $O(n)$ | 25 | 50 | 2 |
| $O(n \log n)$ | 116 | 282 | 2.431 |
| $O(n^2)$ | 625 | 2500 | 4 |
| $O(n^3)$ | 15625 | 125000 | 8 |
| $O(2^n)$ | $3.36 \times 10^7$ | $1.27 \times 10^{15}$ | $3.35 \times 10^7$ |

## 18.3 Bubble Sort

The bubble sort algorithm makes several passes through the array. On each pass, successive neighboring pairs are compared. If a pair is in decreasing order, its values are swapped; otherwise, the values remain unchanged. The technique is called a *bubble sort* or *sinking sort* because the smaller values gradually "bubble" their way to the top and the larger values sink to the bottom. After first pass, the last element becomes the largest in the array. After the second pass, the second to last element becomes the second largest in the array. Continue the process until all the elements are sorted.

Figure 18.1(a) shows the first pass of a bubble sort of an array of six elements (2 9 5 4 8 1). Compare the elements in the first pair (2 and 9), and no swap is needed because they are already in order. Compare the elements in the second pair (9 and 5), and swap 9 with 5

bubble sort illustration

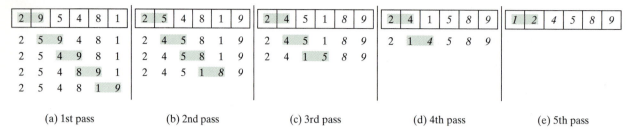

(a) 1st pass          (b) 2nd pass          (c) 3rd pass          (d) 4th pass          (e) 5th pass

**FIGURE 18.1** Each pass compares and orders the pairs of elements sequentially.

because 9 is greater than 5. Compare the elements in the third pair (9 and 4), and swap 9 with 4. Compare the elements in the fourth pair (9 and 8), and swap 9 with 8. Compare the elements in the fifth pair (9 and 1), and swap 9 with 1. The pairs being compared are highlighted and the numbers that are already sorted are italicized.

The first pass places the largest number (9) as the last in the array. In the second pass, as shown in Figure 18.1(b), you compare and order pairs of elements sequentially. There is no need to consider the last pair, because the last element in the array is already the largest. In the third pass, as shown in Figure 18.1(c), you compare and order pairs of elements sequentially except the last two elements, because they are already ordered. So in the $k$th pass, you don't need to consider the last $k - 1$ elements, because they already are ordered.

algorithm

The algorithm for bubble sort can be described as follows.

### LISTING 18.1   Bubble Sort Algorithm

```
1  for (int k = 1; k < arraySize; k++)
2  {
3     // Perform the kth pass
4     for (int i = 0; i < arraySize - k; i++)
5     {
6        if (list[i] > list[i + 1])
7           swap list[i] with list[i + 1];
8     }
9  }
```

Note that if no swap takes place in a pass, there is no need to perform the next pass, because all the elements are already sorted. You may improve the preceding algorithm by utilizing this property, as in Listing 18.2.

### LISTING 18.2   Improved Bubble Sort Algorithm

```
1  bool needNextPass = true;
2  for (int k = 1; k < arraySize && needNextPass; k++)
3  {
4     // Array may be sorted and next pass not needed
5     needNextPass = false;
6     // Perform the kth pass
7     for (int i = 0; (i < arraySize - k); i++)
8     {
9        if (list[i] > list[i + 1])
10       {
11          swap list[i] with list[i + 1];
12          needNextPass = true;// Next pass still needed
13       }
14    }
15 }
```

The algorithm can be implemented as follows.

## LISTING 18.3  BubbleSort.h

```
 1 /* The function for sorting the numbers */
 2 void bubbleSort(int list[], int arraySize)
 3 {
 4   bool needNextPass = true;
 5
 6   for (int k = 1; k < arraySize && needNextPass; k++)
 7   {
 8     // Array may be sorted and next pass not needed
 9     needNextPass = false;
10     for (int i = 0; i < arraySize - k; i++)
11     {
12       if (list[i] > list[i + 1])
13       {
14         // Swap list[i] with list[i + 1]
15         int temp = list[i];
16         list[i] = list[i + 1];
17         list[i + 1] = temp;
18
19         needNextPass = true; // Next pass still needed
20       }
21     }
22   }
23 }
```

### 18.3.1  Bubble Sort Time

In the best-case, the bubble sort algorithm needs just the first pass to find out that the array is already sorted. No next pass is needed. Since the number of comparisons is $n - 1$ in the first pass, the best-case time for bubble sort is $O(n)$.

In the worst case, the bubble sort algorithm requires $n - 1$ passes. The first pass takes $n - 1$ comparisons; the second pass takes $n - 2$ comparisons; and so on. The last pass takes one comparison. So, the total number of comparisons is:

$$(n - 1) + (n - 2) + \ldots + 2 + 1 = \frac{(n - 1)n}{2} = \frac{n^2}{2} - \frac{n}{2} = O(n^2)$$

Therefore, the worst-case time for bubble sort is $O(n^2)$.

## 18.4  Merge Sort

The merge sort algorithm can be described recursively as follows: The algorithm divides the array into two halves and applies merge sort on each half recursively. After the two halves are sorted, merge them. The algorithm is described in Listing 18.4.

## LISTING 18.4  Merge Sort Algorithm

```
 1 void mergeSort(int list[], int arraySize)
 2 {
 3   if (arraySize > 1)                                    base condition
 4   {
 5     mergeSort on list[0 ... arraySize / 2];             sort first half
 6     mergeSort on list[arraySize / 2 + 1 ... arraySize]); sort second half
 7     merge list[0 ... arraySize / 2] with               merge two halves
 8       list[arraySize / 2 + 1 ... arraySize];
 9   }
10 }
```

merge sort illustration

Figure 18.2 illustrates a merge sort of an array of eight elements (2 9 5 4 8 1 6 7). The original array is split into (2 9 5 4) and (8 1 6 7). Apply merge sort on these two subarrays recursively to split (2 9 5 4) into (2 9) and (5 4) and (8 1 6 7) into (8 1) and (6 7). This process continues until the subarray contains only one element. For example, array (2 9) is split into subarrays (2) and (9). Since array (2) contains a single element, it cannot be further split. Now merge (2) with (9) into a new sorted array (2 9), merge (5) with (4) into a new sorted array (4 5). Merge (2 9) with (4 5) into a new sorted array (2 4 5 9), and finally merge (2 4 5 9) with (1 6 7 8) into a new sorted array (1 2 4 5 6 7 8 9).

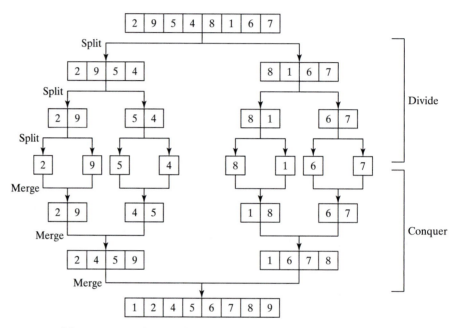

**FIGURE 18.2** Merge sort employs a divide-and-conquer approach to sort the array.

The recursive call continues dividing the array into subarrays until each subarray contains only one element. The algorithm then merges these small subarrays into larger sorted subarrays until one sorted array results. The function for merging two sorted arrays is given in Listing 18.5.

## LISTING 18.5 Function for Merging Two Arrays

```
 1 void merge(int list1[], int list1Size,
 2   int list2[], int list2Size, int temp[])
 3 {
 4   int current1 = 0; // Index in list1
 5   int current2 = 0; // Index in list2
 6   int current3 = 0; // Index in temp
 7
 8   while (current1 < list1Size && current2 < list2Size)
 9   {
10     if (list1[current1] < list2[current2])
11       temp[current3++] = list1[current1++];
12     else
13       temp[current3++] = list2[current2++];
14   }
15
```

move to temp

move to temp

```
16    while (current1 < list1Size)
17      temp[current3++] = list1[current1++];
18
19    while (current2 < list2Size)
20      temp[current3++] = list2[current2++];
21 }
```

rest to temp

rest to temp

This function merges arrays **list1** and **list2** into a new array **temp**. So, the size of **temp** should be **list1Size + list2Size**. **current1** and **current2** point to the current element to be considered in **list1** and **list2** (lines 4–5). The function repeatedly compares the current elements from **list1** and **list2** and moves the smaller one to **temp**. **current1** is increased by 1 (line 11) if the smaller one is in **list1**. **current2** is increased by 1 (line 13) if the smaller one is in **list2**. Finally, all the elements in one of the lists are moved to **temp**. If there still are unmoved elements in **list1**, copy them to **temp** (lines 16–17). If there still are unmoved elements in **list2**, copy them to **temp** (lines 19–20).

Figure 18.3 illustrates how to merge two arrays **list1** (2 4 5 9) and **list2** (1 6 7 8). Initially, the current elements to be considered in the arrays are 2 and 1. Compare them and move the smaller element 1 to **temp**, as shown in Figure 18.3(a). **current2** and **current3** are increased by 1. Continue to compare the current elements in the two arrays and move the smaller one to **temp** until one of the arrays is completely moved. As shown in Figure 18.3(b), all the elements in **list2** are moved to **temp**, and **current1** points to element 9 in **list1**. Copy 9 to **temp**, as shown in Figure 18.3(c).

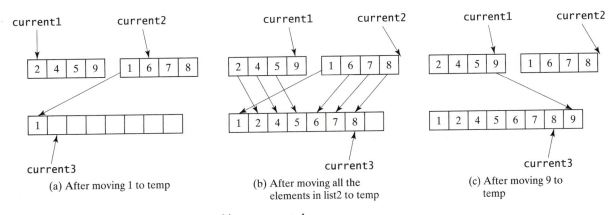

(a) After moving 1 to temp

(b) After moving all the elements in list2 to temp

(c) After moving 9 to temp

**FIGURE 18.3** Two sorted arrays are merged into one sorted array.

The merge sort algorithm is implemented in Listing 18.6.

## LISTING 18.6 MergeSort.h

```
1  // Function prototype
2  void arraycopy(int source[], int sourceStartIndex,
3    int target[], int targetStartIndex, int length);
4
5  void merge(int list1[], int list1Size,
6    int list2[], int list2Size, int temp[]);
7
8  /* The function for sorting the numbers */
9  void mergeSort(int list[], int arraySize)
10 {
11   if (arraySize > 1)
12   {
13     // Merge sort the first half
14     int *firstHalf = new int[arraySize / 2];
```

mergeSort

create **firstHalf**

sort **firstHalf**

```
15    arraycopy(list, 0, firstHalf, 0, arraySize / 2);
16    mergeSort(firstHalf, arraySize / 2);
17
18    // Merge sort the second half
19    int secondHalfLength = arraySize - arraySize / 2;
```

create **secondHalf**

```
20    int *secondHalf = new int[secondHalfLength];
21    arraycopy(list, arraySize / 2, secondHalf, 0, secondHalfLength);
```

sort **secondHalf**

```
22    mergeSort(secondHalf, secondHalfLength);
23
24    // Merge firstHalf with secondHalf
25    int *temp = new int[arraySize];
```

merge two halves

```
26    merge(firstHalf, arraySize / 2, secondHalf, secondHalfLength,
27      temp);
```

copy to original array
delete

```
28    arraycopy(temp, 0, list, 0, arraySize);
29    delete [] temp;
30    delete [] firstHalf;
31    delete [] secondHalf;
32  }
33 }
34
35 void merge(int list1[], int list1Size,
36   int list2[], int list2Size, int temp[])
37 {
38   // Same as in Listing 18.5, so omitted
39 }
40
41 void arraycopy(int source[], int sourceStartIndex,
42   int target[], int targetStartIndex, int length)
43 {
44   for (int i = 0; i < length; i++)
45   {
46     target[i + targetStartIndex] = source[i + sourceStartIndex];
47   }
48 }
```

The algorithm creates a new array **firstHalf**, which is a copy of the first half of **list** (line 14). The algorithm invokes **mergeSort** recursively on **firstHalf** (line 16). The length of the **firstHalf** is **arraySize / 2** and the length of the **secondHalf** is **arraySize - arraySize / 2**. The new array **secondHalf** was created to contain the second part of the original array **list**. The algorithm invokes **mergeSort** recursively on **secondHalf** (line 22). After **firstHalf** and **secondHalf** are sorted, they are merged to become a new sorted array in **temp** (line 26). Finally, **temp** is copied to the original array **list** (line 28). So, array **list** is now sorted.

## 18.4.1 Merge Sort Time

time analysis

Let $T(n)$ denote the time required for sorting an array of $n$ elements using merge sort. Without loss of generality, assume $n$ is a power of 2. The merge sort algorithm splits the array into two subarrays, sorts the subarrays using the same algorithm recursively, and then merges the subarrays. So,

$$T(n) = T\left(\frac{n}{2}\right) + T\left(\frac{n}{2}\right) + mergetime$$

The first $T\left(\frac{n}{2}\right)$ is the time for sorting the first half of the array, and the second $T\left(\frac{n}{2}\right)$ is the time for sorting the second half. To merge two subarrays, it takes at most $n - 1$ comparisons to compare the elements from the two subarrays and $n$ moves to move elements to the temporary array. So, the total time is $2n - 1$. Therefore,

$$T(n) = T\left(\frac{n}{2}\right) + T\left(\frac{n}{2}\right) + mergetime$$

$$= 2T\left(\frac{n}{2}\right) + 2n - 1$$

$$= 2\left(2T\left(\frac{n}{4}\right) + 2\frac{n}{2} - 1\right) + 2n - 1$$

$$= 2\left(2\left(2T\left(\frac{n}{8}\right) + 2\frac{n}{4} - 1\right) + 2\frac{n}{2} - 1\right) + 2n - 1$$

$$= 2\left(2\left(2T\left(\frac{n}{2^3}\right) + 2\frac{n}{2^2} - 1\right) + 2\frac{n}{2^1} - 1\right) + 2n - 1$$

$$= 2^k T\left(\frac{n}{2^k}\right) + 2n - 2^{k-1} + \ldots + 2n - 2 + 2n - 1$$

$$= 2^k T\left(\frac{n}{2^k}\right) + \overbrace{2n + 2n + \ldots + 2n}^{k} - 2^{k-1} + \ldots - 2 - 1$$

$$= 2^k T\left(\frac{n}{2^k}\right) + 2nk - (2^k - 1)$$

$$= 2^{\log n} T(1) + 2n(\log n) - (2^{\log n} - 1)$$

$$= n + 2n \log n - n + 1$$

$$= 2n \log n + 1 = O(n \log n)$$

The complexity of merge sort is $O(n \log n)$. This algorithm is better than selection sort, insertion sort, and bubble sort.

*$O(n \log n)$ merge sort*

## 18.5 Quick Sort

Quick sort, developed by C. A. R. Hoare (1962), works as follows: The algorithm selects an element, called the *pivot,* in the array. Divide the array into two parts, such that all the elements in the first part are less than or equal to the pivot, and all the elements in the second part are greater than the pivot. Recursively, apply the quick sort algorithm to the first part and then the second part. The algorithm is described in Listing 18.7.

### LISTING 18.7  Quick Sort Algorithm

```
1 void quickSort(int list[], int arraySize)
2 {
3    if (arraySize > 1)
4    {
```

*base condition*

select the pivot
partition the list

```
 5      select a pivot;
 6      partition list into list1 and list2 such that
 7         all elements in list1 <= pivot and all elements
 8         in list2 > pivot;
```

sort first part
sort second part

```
 9      quickSort on list1;
10      quickSort on list2;
11   }
12 }
```

pivot

| list1 | | list2 |

how to partition

Each partition places the pivot in the right place. The selection of the pivot affects the performance of the algorithm. Ideally, you should choose the pivot that divides the two parts evenly. For simplicity, assume the first element in the array is chosen as the pivot. Exercise 18.4 proposes an alternative strategy for selecting the pivot.

quick sort illustration

Figure 18.4 illustrates how to sort an array (5 2 9 3 8 4 0 1 6 7) using quick sort. Choose the first element 5 as the pivot. The array is partitioned into two parts, as shown in Figure 18.4(b). The highlighted pivot is placed in the right place in the array. Apply quick sort on two partial arrays (4 2 1 3 0) and then (8 9 6 7). The pivot 4 partitions (4 2 1 3 0) into just one partial array (0 2 1 3), as shown in Figure 18.4(c). Apply quick sort on (0 2 1 3). The pivot 0 partitions it to just one partial array (2 1 3), as shown in Figure 18.4(d). Apply quick sort on (2 1 3). The pivot 2 partitions it to (1) and (3), as shown in Figure 18.4(e). Apply quick sort on (1). Since the array contains just one element, no further partition is needed.

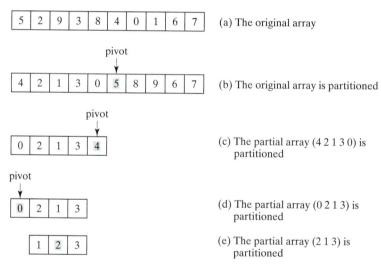

**FIGURE 18.4** The quick sort algorithm is recursively applied to partial arrays.

Now turn attention to partition. To partition an array or a partial array, search for the first element from left forward in the array that is greater than the pivot, then search for the first element from right backward in the array that is less than or equal to the pivot. Swap these two elements. Repeat the same search and swap operations until all the elements are searched. Listing 18.8 gives a function that partitions a partial array `list[first..last]`. The first element in the partial array is chosen as the pivot (line 3). Initially, `low` points to the second element in the partial array, and `high` points to the last element in the partial array. The function returns the new index for the pivot that divides the partial array into two parts.

## LISTING 18.8 Partition Function

```
1 /* Partition the array list[first..last] */
2 int partition(int list[], int first, int last)
3 {
4   int pivot = list[first]; // Choose the first element as the pivot
5   int low = first + 1; // Index for forward search
6   int high = last; // Index for backward search
7
8   while (high > low)
9   {
10    // Search forward from left
11    while (low <= high && list[low] <= pivot)
12      low++;
13
14    // Search backward from right
15    while (low <= high && list[high] > pivot)
16      high--;
17
18    // Swap two elements in the list
19    if (high > low)
20    {
21      int temp = list[high];
22      list[high] = list[low];
23      list[low] = temp;
24    }
25  }
26
27  while (high > first && list[high] >= pivot)
28    high--;
29
30  // Swap pivot with list[high]
31  if (pivot > list[high])
32  {
33    list[first] = list[high];
34    list[high] = pivot;
35    return high;
36  }
37  else
38  {
39    return first;
40  }
41 }
```

forward

backward

swap

place pivot

pivot's new index

pivot's new index

Figure 18.5 illustrates how to partition an array (5 2 9 3 8 4 0 1 6 7). Choose the first element 5 as the pivot. Initially **low** is the index that points to element 2 and **high** points to element 7, as shown in Figure 18.5(a). Advance index **low** forward to search for the first element (9) that is greater than the pivot, and move index **high** backward to search for the first element (1) that is less than or equal to the pivot, as shown in Figure 18.5(b). Swap 9 with 1, as shown in Figure 18.5(c). Continue the search, and move **low** to point to element 8 and **high** to point to element 0, as shown in Figure 18.5(d). Swap element 8 with 0, as shown in Figure 18.5(e). Continue to move **low** until it passes **high**, as shown in Figure 18.5(f). Now all the elements are examined. Swap the pivot with element 4 at index **high**. The final partition is shown in Figure 18.5(g). The index of the pivot is returned when the function is finished.

partition illustration

The quick sort algorithm is implemented in Listing 18.9 with two overloaded **quickSort** functions. The first function (line 2) is used to sort an array. The second is a helper function (line 3) that sorts a partial array with a specified range.

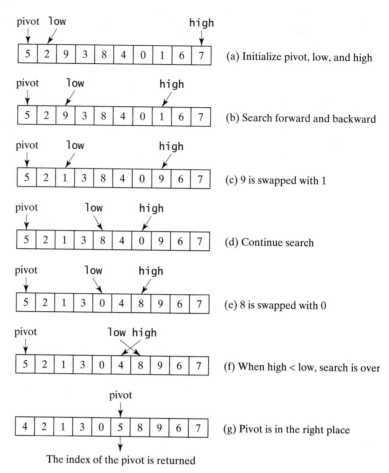

**FIGURE 18.5** The partition function returns the index of the pivot after it is put in the right place.

## LISTING 18.9 QuickSort.h

```
1  // Function prototypes
2  void quickSort(int list[], int arraySize);
3  void quickSort(int list[], int first, int last);
4  int partition(int list[], int first, int last);
5
6  void quickSort(int list[], int arraySize)
7  {
8     quickSort(list, 0, arraySize - 1);
9  }
10
11 void quickSort(int list[], int first, int last)
12 {
13    if (last > first)
14    {
15       int pivotIndex = partition(list, first, last);
16       quickSort(list, first, pivotIndex - 1);
17       quickSort(list, pivotIndex + 1, last);
18    }
19 }
20
```

Margin labels:
- sort function (line 2)
- helper function (line 3)
- partition function (line 4)
- helper function (line 6)
- call helper function (line 8)
- recursion base (line 13)
- find pivot (line 15)
- recursive call (line 16)
- recursive call (line 17)

```
21 /* Partition the array list[first..last] */
22 int partition(int list[], int first, int last)
23 {
24    // Same as in Listing 18.8, so omitted
25 }
```

### 18.5.1 Quick Sort Time

To partition an array of $n$ elements, it takes $n$ comparisons and $n$ moves in the worst case. So, the time required for partition is $O(n)$.

In the worst case, each time the pivot divides the array into one big subarray with the other empty. The size of the big subarray is one less than the one before divided. The algorithm requires $(n - 1) + (n - 2) + \ldots + 2 + 1 = O(n^2)$ time.

In the best case, each time the pivot divides the array into two parts of about the same size. Let $T(n)$ denote the time required for sorting an array of $n$ elements using quick sort. So,

*O(n) partition time*

*O(n²) worst-case time*

*O(n log n) best-case time*

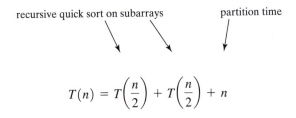

recursive quick sort on subarrays     partition time

$$T(n) = T\left(\frac{n}{2}\right) + T\left(\frac{n}{2}\right) + n$$

Similar to the merge sort analysis, $T(n) = O(n \log n)$.

On the average, each time the pivot will not divide the array into two parts of the same size nor one empty part. Statistically, the sizes of the two parts are very close. So the average time is $O(n \log n)$. The exact average-case analysis is beyond the scope of this book.

*O(n log n) average-case time*

Both merge sort and quick sort employ the divide-and-conquer approach. For merge sort, the bulk of work is to merge two sublists, which takes place *after* the sublists are sorted. For quick sort, the bulk of work is to partition the list into two sublists, which takes place *before* the sublists are sorted. Merge sort is more efficient than quick sort in the worst case, but the two are equally efficient in the average case. Merge sort requires a temporary array for merging two subarrays. Quick sort does not need additional array space. So, quick sort is more space efficient than merge sort.

*quick sort vs. merge sort*

## 18.6 Heap Sort

Heap sort uses a binary heap to sort an array. The binary heap was introduced in §17.3, "Heaps." Recall that a heap is a complete binary tree. Each node in the tree is greater than or equal to its descendants. To sort an array using a heap, first create an object using the **Heap** class, add all the elements to the heap using the **add** function, and remove all the elements from the heap using the **remove** function. The elements are removed in descending order. Listing 18.10 gives an algorithm for sorting an array of a generic type using a heap.

### LISTING 18.10 HeapSort.h

```
1 #include "Heap.h"
2
3 template<typename T>
4 void heapSort(T list[], int arraySize)
5 {
6    Heap<T> heap;
7
8    for (int i = 0; i < arraySize; i++)
9       heap.add(list[i]);
10
11   for (int i = 0; i < arraySize; i++)
```

include **Heap.h**

generic type
sort function

create a heap

add element

remove element

```
12      list[i] = heap.remove();
13 }
```

*height of a heap*

Let us turn our attention to analyzing the time complexity for the heap sort. Let $h$ denote the height for a heap of $n$ elements. Since a heap is a complete binary tree, the first level has 1 node, the second level has 2 nodes, the $k$th level has $2^{k-1}$ nodes, the $h-1$th level has $2^{h-2}$ nodes, and the $h$th level has at least one node and at most $2^{h-1}$ nodes. Therefore,

$$1 + 2 + \ldots + 2^{h-2} < n \le 1 + 2 + \ldots + 2^{h-2} + 2^{h-1}$$

i.e.,

$$2^{h-1} - 1 < n \le 2^h - 1$$

$$2^{h-1} < n + 1 \le 2^h$$

$$h - 1 < \log(n + 1) \le h$$

Thus, $h < \log(n + 1) + 1$ and $\log(n + 1) \le h$. Therefore, $\log(n + 1) \le h < \log(n + 1) + 1$. Hence, the height of the heap is $O(\log n)$.

*$O(n \log n)$ worst-case time*

Since the **add** function traces a path from a leaf to a root, it takes at most $h$ steps to add a new element to the heap. So the total time for constructing an initial heap is $O(n \log n)$ for an array of n elements. Since the **remove** function traces a path from a root to a leaf, it takes at most $h$ steps to rebuild a heap after removing the root from the heap. Since the **remove** function is invoked $n$ times, the total time for producing a sorted array from a heap is $O(n \log n)$.

*heap sort vs. merge sort*

Both merge sort and heap sort requires $O(n \log n)$ time. Merge sort requires a temporary array for merging two subarrays. Heap sort does not need additional array space. So, heap sort is more space efficient than merge sort.

## 18.7 External Sort

All the sort algorithms discussed in the preceding sections assume that all data to be sorted is available at one time in internal memory, such as an array. To sort data stored in an external file, you may first bring data to the memory, then sort it internally. However, if the file is too large, all data in the file cannot be brought to memory at one time. This section discusses how to sort data in a large external file.

For simplicity, assume that two million **int** values are stored in a binary file named largedata.dat. This file was created using the following program:

**LISTING 18.14** CreateLargeFile.cpp

```cpp
1 #include <iostream>
2 #include <fstream>
3 #include <cmath>
4 using namespace std;
5
6 int main()
7 {
8     fstream output;
9     output.open("largedata.dat", ios::out | ios::binary);
10
11    for (int i = 0; i < 2000000; i++)
12    {
13        int value = rand();
14        output.write(reinterpret_cast<char *>(&value), sizeof(value));
15    }
16
17    output.close();
18    cout << "File created" << endl;
19
```

*a binary output stream*

*random value*
*output an **int** value*

*close output*

```
20    fstream input;
21    input.open("largedata.dat", ios::in | ios::binary);
22    int value;
23
24    cout << "The first 10 numbers in the file are " << endl;
25    for (int i = 0; i < 10; i++)
26    {
27      input.read(reinterpret_cast<char *>(& value), sizeof(value));
28      cout << value << " ";
29    }
30
31    input.close();
32
33    return 0;
34 }
```

a binary output stream

read input

close input

```
File created
The first 10 numbers in the file are
130 10982 1090 11656 7117 17595 6415 22948 31126 9004
```

A variation of merge sort can be used to sort this file in two phases.

## Phase I

Repeatedly bring data from the file to an array, sort the array using an internal sorting algorithm, and output the data from the array to a temporary file. This process is shown in Figure 18.6. Ideally, you want to create a large array, but the maximum size of the array is limited. Assume that the maximum array size is of 100000 **int** values. In the temporary file, every 100000 **int** values are sorted. They are denoted as $S_1, S_2, \ldots$, and $S_k$, where the last segment, $S_k$, may contain less than 100000 values.

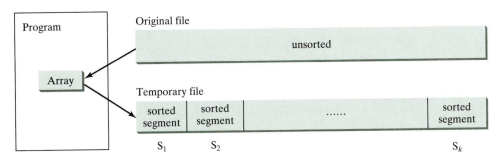

**FIGURE 18.6** The original file is sorted in segments.

## Phase II

Merge every pair of sorted segments (e.g., $S_1$ with $S_2$, $S_3$ with $S_4, \ldots$, and so on) into a larger sorted segment and save the new segment into a new temporary file. Continue the same process until one sorted segment results. Figure 18.7 shows how to merge eight segments.

**Note**

It is not necessary to merge two successive segments. For example, you may merge $S_1$ with $S_5$, $S_2$ with $S_6$, $S_3$ with $S_7$, and $S_4$ with $S_8$, in the first merge step. This observation is useful to implement Phase II efficiently.

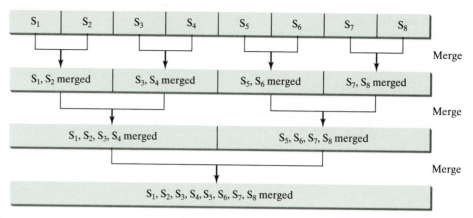

**FIGURE 18.7** Sorted segments are merged iteratively.

### 18.7.1   Implementing Phase I

Assume MAX_ARRAY_SIZE is declared as a constant 100000. Listing 18.15 gives the function that sorts every 100000 in largedata.dat and stores the sorted segments into a new file named f1.dat. The function returns the number of segments.

### LISTING 18.15   Creating Initial Sorted Segments

```
 1  /* Sort original file into sorted segments */
 2  int initializeSegments(int segmentSize, char* originalFile, char* f1)
 3  {
 4    int *list = new int[segmentSize];
 5
 6    fstream input;
 7    input.open(originalFile, ios::in | ios::binary);
 8    fstream output;
 9    output.open(f1, ios::out | ios::binary);
10
11    int numberOfSegments = 0;
12    while (!input.eof())
13    {
14      int i = 0;
15      for ( ; !input.eof() && i < segmentSize; i++)
16      {
17        input.read(reinterpret_cast<char *>
18          (&list[i]), sizeof(list[i]));
19      }
20
21      if (input.eof()) i--;
22      if (i <= 0)
23        break;
24      else
25        numberOfSegments++;
26
27      // Sort an array list[0..i-1]
28      quickSort(list, i);
29
30      // Write the array to f1.dat
31      for (int j = 0; j < i; j++)
32      {
33        output.write(reinterpret_cast<char *>
34          (&list[j]), sizeof(list[j]));
35      }
36  }
```

*a dynamic array* (line 4)

*a binary input stream* (line 7)

*a binary output stream* (line 9)

*end of file?* (line 12)

*read an int value* (lines 17–18)

*discard EOF marker* (line 21)

*sort a segment* (line 28)

*output an int value* (line 33)

```
37
38   input.close();
39   output.close();
40   delete [] list;
41   return numberOfSegments;
42 }
```
close file

return # of segments

The function declares an array with the max size in line 4, declares a data input stream for the original file in line 7, and declares a data output stream for a temporary file in line 9.

Lines 15–19 read a segment of data from the file into the array. Line 28 sorts the array. Lines 31–35 write the data in the array to the temporary file.

The number of the segments is returned in line 41. Note that every segment has `MAX_ARRAY_SIZE` number of elements except the last segment, which may have a smaller number of elements.

## 18.7.2  Implementing Phase II

In each merge step, two sorted segments are merged to form a new segment. The size of the new segment is doubled. The number of segments is reduced by half after each merge step. A segment is too large to be brought to an array in memory. To implement a merge step, copy half the number of segments from file f1.dat to a temporary file f2.dat. Then merge the first remaining segment in f1.dat with the first segment in f2.dat into a temporary file named f3.dat, as shown in Figure 18.8.

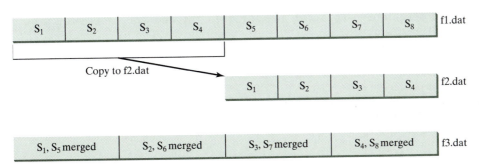

**FIGURE 18.8**  Sorted segments are merged iteratively.

**Note**
f1.dat may have one segment more than f2.dat. If so, move the last segment into f3.dat after the merge.

Listing 18.16 gives a function that copies the first half of the segments in f1.dat to f2.dat. Listing 18.17 gives a function that merges a pair of segments in f1.dat and f2.dat. Listing 18.18 gives a function that merges two segments.

## LISTING 18.16  Copying First Half Segments

```
1 /* Copy first half number of segments from f1.dat to f2.dat */
2 void copyHalfToF2(int numberOfSegments, int segmentSize,
3   fstream &f1, fstream &f2)
4 {
5   for (int i = 0; i < (numberOfSegments / 2) * segmentSize; i++)
6   {
7     int value;
8     f1.read(reinterpret_cast<char *>(& value), sizeof(value));
9     f2.write(reinterpret_cast<char *>(& value), sizeof(value));
10  }
11 }
```
input stream f1
output stream f2

segments copied

### LISTING 18.17 Merging All Segments

input stream f1 and f2
output stream f3

merge two segments

extra segment in f1

```
1  /* Merge all segments */
2  void mergeSegments(int numberOfSegments, int segmentSize,
3    fstream &f1, fstream &f2, fstream &f3)
4  {
5    for (int i = 0; i < numberOfSegments; i++)
6    {
7      mergeTwoSegments(segmentSize, f1, f2, f3);
8    }
9
10   // f1 may have one extra segment, copy it to f3
11   while (!f1.eof())
12   {
13     int value;
14     f1.read(reinterpret_cast<char *>(&value), sizeof(value));
15     if (f1.eof()) break;
16     f3.write(reinterpret_cast<char *>(&value), sizeof(value));
17   }
18 }
```

### LISTING 18.18 Merging Two Segments

input stream f1 and f2
output stream f3

read from f1

read from f2

write to f3

segment in f1 finished

write to f3

segment in f2 finished

```
1  /* Merge two segments */
2  void mergeTwoSegments(int segmentSize, fstream &f1, fstream &f2,
3    fstream &f3)
4  {
5    int intFromF1;
6    f1.read(reinterpret_cast<char *>(&intFromF1), sizeof(intFromF1));
7    int intFromF2;
8    f2.read(reinterpret_cast<char *>(&intFromF2), sizeof(intFromF2));
9    int f1Count = 1;
10   int f2Count = 1;
11
12   while (true)
13   {
14     if (intFromF1 < intFromF2)
15     {
16       f3.write(reinterpret_cast<char *>
17         (&intFromF1), sizeof(intFromF1));
18       if (f1.eof() || f1Count++ >= segmentSize)
19       {
20         if (f1.eof()) break;
21         f3.write(reinterpret_cast<char *>
22           (&intFromF2), sizeof(intFromF2));
23         break;
24       }
25       else
26       {
27         f1.read(reinterpret_cast<char *>
28           (& intFromF1), sizeof(intFromF1));
29       }
30     }
31     else
32     {
33       f3.write(reinterpret_cast<char *>
34         (&intFromF2), sizeof(intFromF2));
35       if (f2.eof() || f2Count++ >= segmentSize)
36       {
37         if (f2.eof()) break;
```

```
38            f3.write(reinterpret_cast<char *>
39               (&intFromF1), sizeof(intFromF1));
40            break;
41          }
42        else
43          {
44            f2.read(reinterpret_cast<char *>
45               (&intFromF2), sizeof(intFromF2));
46          }
47      }
48  }
49
50  while (!f1.eof() && f1Count++ < segmentSize)                    remaining f1 segment
51  {
52    int value;
53    f1.read(reinterpret_cast<char *>
54      (&value), sizeof(value));
55    if (f1.eof()) break;
56    f3.write(reinterpret_cast<char *>
57      (&value), sizeof(value));
58  }
59
60  while (!f2.eof() && f2Count++ < segmentSize)                    remaining f2 segment
61  {
62    int value;
63    f2.read(reinterpret_cast<char *>
64      (&value), sizeof(value));
65    if (f2.eof()) break;
66    f3.write(reinterpret_cast<char *>
67      (&value), sizeof(value));
68  }
69 }
```

## 18.7.3  Combining Two Phases

Listing 18.19 gives the complete program for sorting `int` values in largedata.dat and storing the sorted data in sortedlargedata.dat.

### LISTING 18.19  SortLargeFile.cpp

```
 1 #include <iostream>
 2 #include <fstream>                                              include fstream
 3 #include "QuickSort.h"                                          include quick sort
 4 using namespace std;
 5
 6 // Function prototype
 7 int initializeSegments(int segmentSize,                         function prototype
 8   char* originalFile, char* f1);
 9 void mergeTwoSegments(int segmentSize, fstream &f1, fstream &f2,
10   fstream &f3);
11 void merge(int numberOfSegments, int segmentSize,
12   char* f1, char* f2, char* f3);
13 void copyHalfToF2(int numberOfSegments, int segmentSize,
14   fstream &f1, fstream &f2);
15 void mergeOneStep(int numberOfSegments, int segmentSize,
16   char* f1, char* f2, char* f3);
17 void mergeSegments(int numberOfSegments, int segmentSize,
18   fstream &f1, fstream &f2, fstream &f3);
19 void copyFile(char * f1, char * target);
20
```

```
21 int main()
22 {
23    const int MAX_ARRAY_SIZE = 100000;
24
25    // Implement Phase 1: Create initial segments
26    int numberOfSegments =
27      initializeSegments(MAX_ARRAY_SIZE, "largedata.dat", "f1.dat");
28
29    // Implement Phase 2: Merge segments recursively
30    merge(numberOfSegments, MAX_ARRAY_SIZE,
31      "f1.dat", "f2.dat", "f3.dat");
32 }
33
34 /* Sort original file into sorted segments */
35 int initializeSegments(int segmentSize, char* originalFile, char* f1)
36 {
37    int *list = new int[segmentSize];
38
39    fstream input;
40    input.open(originalFile, ios::in | ios::binary);
41    fstream output;
42    output.open(f1, ios::out | ios::binary);
43
44    int numberOfSegments = 0;
45    while (!input.eof())
46    {
47      int i = 0;
48      for ( ; !input.eof() && i < segmentSize; i++)
49      {
50        input.read(reinterpret_cast<char *>
51          (&list[i]), sizeof(list[i]));
52      }
53
54      if (input.eof()) i--;
55      if (i <= 0)
56        break;
57      else
58        numberOfSegments++;
59
60      // Sort an array list[0..i-1]
61      quickSort(list, i);
62
63      // Write the array to f1.dat
64      for (int j = 0; j < i; j++)
65      {
66        output.write(reinterpret_cast<char *>
67          (& list[j]), sizeof(list[j]));
68      }
69    }
70
71    input.close();
72    output.close();
73    delete [] list;
74    return numberOfSegments;
75 }
76
77 /* Recursively merge sorted segments */
78 void merge(int numberOfSegments, int segmentSize,
79    char* f1, char* f2, char* f3)
80 {
81    if (numberOfSegments > 1)
```

max array size

create segments

merge recursively

recursive merge

```
82   {
83     mergeOneStep(numberOfSegments, segmentSize, f1, f2, f3);
84     merge((numberOfSegments + 1) / 2, segmentSize * 2, f3, f1, f2);
85   }
86   else
87   { // rename f1 as the final sorted file
88     copyFile(f1, "sortedlargedata.dat");
89     cout << "\nSorted into the file sortedlargedata.dat" << endl;
90   }
91 }
92
93 /* Copy file from f1 to target */
94 void copyFile(char * f1, char * target)                          copy file
95 {
96   fstream input;
97   input.open(f1, ios::in | ios::binary);
98
99   fstream output;
100  output.open(target, ios::out | ios::binary);
101
102  while (!input.eof()) // Continue if not end of file
103  {
104    int value;
105    input.read(reinterpret_cast<char *> (& value), sizeof(value));
106    if (input.eof()) break;
107    output.write(reinterpret_cast<char *> (& value), sizeof(value));
108  }
109
110  input.close();
111  output.close();
112 }
113
114 /* Merge every pair of two segments */
115 void mergeOneStep(int numberOfSegments, int segmentSize, char* f1,    merge one time
116   char* f2, char* f3)
117 {
118  fstream f1Input;
119  f1Input.open(f1, ios::in | ios::binary);
120
121  fstream f2Output;
122  f2Output.open(f2, ios::out | ios::binary);
123
124  // Copy half of the number of segments from f1.dat to f2.dat
125  copyHalfToF2(numberOfSegments, segmentSize, f1Input, f2Output);
126  f2Output.close();
127
128  // Merge remaining segments in f1 with segments in f2 into f3
129  fstream f2Input;
130  f2Input.open(f2, ios::in | ios::binary);
131  fstream f3Output;
132  f3Output.open(f3, ios::out | ios::binary);
133
134  mergeSegments(numberOfSegments / 2, segmentSize,
135    f1Input, f2Input, f3Output);
136
137  f1Input.close();
138  f2Input.close();
139  f3Output.close();
140 }
141
142 /* Copy the first half of the number of segments from f1.dat to f2.dat */
```

```
143 void copyHalfToF2(int numberOfSegments, int segmentSize,
144   fstream &f1, fstream &f2)
145 {
146   // Same as Listing 18.16, so omitted
147 }
148
149 /* Merge all segments */
150 void mergeSegments(int numberOfSegments, int segmentSize,
151   fstream &f1, fstream &f2, fstream &f3)
152 {
153   // Same as Listing 18.17, so omitted
154 }
155
156 /* Merge two segments */
157 void mergeTwoSegments(int segmentSize, fstream &f1, fstream &f2,
158   fstream &f3)
159 {
160   // Same as Listing 18.18, so omitted
161 }
```

Line 27 creates initial segments from the original array and stores the sorted segments in a new file f1.dat. Lines 30–31 produce a sorted file in sortedlargedata.dat. The `merge` function

```
merge(int numberOfSegments,
   int segmentSize, char * f1, char * f2, char * f3)
```

merges the segments in `f1` into `f3` using `f2` to assist the merge. The `merge` function is invoked recursively with many merge steps. Each merge step reduces the `numberOfSegments` by half and doubles the sorted segment size. After completing one merge step, the next merge step merges the new segments in `f3` to `f2`, using `f1` to assist the merge. So the statement to invoke the new merge function is (line 83)

```
merge((numberOfSegments + 1) / 2, segmentSize * 2, f3, f1, f2);
```

The `numberOfSegments` for the next merge step is `(numberOfSegments + 1) / 2`. For example, if `numberOfSegments` is 5, `numberOfSegments` is 3 for the next merge step, because every two segments are merged but there is one left unmerged.

The recursive `merge` function ends when `numberOfSegments` is 1. In this case, `f1` contains sorted data. Copy f1 to sortedlargedata.dat in line 88.

## 18.7.4 External Sort Analysis

In the external sort, the dominating cost is on I/O. Assume $n$ is the number of the elements to be sorted in the file. In Phase I, $n$ numbers of elements are read from the original file and output to a temporary file. So, the I/O for Phase I is $O(n)$.

In Phase II, before the first merge step, the number of sorted segments is $\frac{n}{c}$, where $c$ is MAX_ARRAY_SIZE. Each merge step reduces the number of segments by half. So, after the first merge step, the number of segments is $\frac{n}{2c}$. After the second merge step, the number of segments is $\frac{n}{2^2c}$. After the third merge step, the number of segments is $\frac{n}{2^3c}$. After $\log\left(\frac{n}{c}\right)$ merge steps, the number of segments reduced to 1. Therefore, the total number of merge steps is $\log\left(\frac{n}{c}\right)$.

In each merge step, half of the number of segments are read from file f1 and then written into a temporary file f2. The remaining segments in f1 are merged with the segments in f2.

The number of I/Os in each merge step is $O(n)$. Since the total number of merge steps is $\log\left(\dfrac{n}{c}\right)$, the total number of I/Os is

$$O(n) \times \log\left(\frac{n}{c}\right) = O(n \log n)$$

Therefore, the complexity of the external sort is $O(n \log n)$.

## KEY TERMS

| | |
|---|---|
| average-time analysis  519 | growth rate  518 |
| best-time analysis  518 | heap sort  533 |
| big O notation  518 | logarithmic time  521 |
| bubble sort  523 | merge sort  526 |
| constant time  519 | quadratic time  522 |
| exponential time  523 | quick sort  530 |
| external sort  534 | worst-time analysis  519 |

## CHAPTER SUMMARY

- The Big O notation is a theoretical approach for analyzing the performance of the algorithm. It estimates how fast an algorithm's execution time increases as the input size increases. So, you can compare two algorithms by examining their *growth rates*.

- An input that results in the shortest execution time is called the *best-case* input, and an input that results in the longest execution time is called the *worst-case* input. Best-case and worst-case are not representative, but worst-case analysis is very useful. You can show that the algorithm will never be slower than the worst-case.

- An *average-case* analysis attempts to determine the average amount of time among all possible inputs of the same size. Average-case analysis is ideal, but difficult to perform, because it is hard to determine the relative probabilities and distributions of various input instances for many problems.

- If the time is not related to the input size, the algorithm is said to take *constant time* with the notation $O(1)$.

- Linear search takes $O(n)$ time. An algorithm with the $O(n)$ time complexity is called a *linear algorithm*. Binary search takes $O(\log n)$ time. An algorithm with the $O(\log n)$ time complexity is called a *logarithmic algorithm*.

- The worst-time complexity for selection sort, insertion sort, bubble sort, and quick sort is $O(n^2)$. An algorithm with the $O(n^2)$ time complexity is called a *quadratic algorithm*.

- The average-time and worst-time complexity for merge sort and heap sort is $O(n \log n)$. The average time for quick sort is also $O(n \log n)$. An algorithm with the $O(n \log n)$ time complexity is called a log-linear time.

- A variation of merge sort can be applied to sort large data from external files.

## REVIEW QUESTIONS

### Section 18.2 Estimating Algorithm Efficiency

18.1 Put the following growth functions in order:

$$\frac{5n^3}{4032}, \quad 44 \log n, \quad 10n \log n, \quad 500, \quad 2n^2, \quad \frac{2^n}{45}, \quad 3n$$

18.2 Count the number of iterations in the following loops.

```
int count = 1;
while (count < 30)
{
    count = count * 2;
}
```
(a)

```
int count = 15;
while (count < 30)
{
    count = count * 3;
}
```
(b)

```
int count = 1;
while (count < n)
{
    count = count * 2;
}
```
(c)

```
int count = 15;
while (count < n)
{
    count = count * 3;
}
```
(d)

18.3 How many stars are displayed in the following code if n is 10? How many stars are displayed in the following code if n is 20? Use the Big O notation to estimate the time complexity.

```
for (int i = 0; i < n; i++)
{
    cout << '*';
}
```

```
for (int i = 0; i < n; i++)
{
    for (int j = 0; j < n; j++)
    {
        cout << '*';
    }
}
```

```
for (int k = 0; k < n; k++)
{
    for (int i = 0; i < n; i++)
    {
        for (int j = 0; j < n; j++)
        {
            cout << '*';
        }
    }
}
```

```
for (int k = 0; k < 10; k++)
{
    for (int i = 0; i < n; i++)
    {
        for (int j = 0; j < n; j++)
        {
            cout << '*';
        }
    }
}
```

18.4 Use the Big O notation to estimate the time complexity of the following functions:

```
void mA (int n)
{
  for (int i = 0; i < n; i++)
  {
    cout << rand();
  }
}
```

```
void mB (int n)
{
  for (int i = 0; i < n; i++)
  {
    for (int j = 0; j < i; j++)
      cout << rand();
  }
}
```

```
void mC (int m, int size)
{
  for (int i = 0; i < size; i++)
  {
    cout << m[i];
  }

  for (int i = size - 1; i >= 0; )
  {
    cout << m[i];
    i--;
  }
}
```

```
void mD (int m[], int size)
{
  for (int i = 0; i < size; i++)
  {
    for (int j = 0; j < i; j++)
      cout << m[i] * m[j];
  }
}
```

**18.5** Estimate the time complexity for adding two $n \times m$ matrices, and for multiplying an $n \times m$ matrix with a $m \times k$ matrix.

### Sections 18.3–18.7

**18.6** Use Figure 18.1 as an example to show how to apply bubble sort on {45, 11, 50, 59, 60, 2, 4, 7, 10}.

**18.7** Use Figure 18.2 as an example to show how to apply merge sort on {45, 11, 50, 59, 60, 2, 4, 7, 10}.

**18.8** Use Figure 18.4 as an example to show how to apply quick sort on {45, 11, 50, 59, 60, 2, 4, 7, 10}.

**18.9** Show the steps of creating a heap using {45, 11, 50, 59, 60, 2, 4, 7, 10}.

**18.10** Given the following heap, show the steps of removing all nodes from the heap.

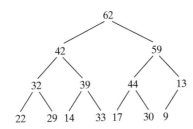

**18.11** There are 10 numbers {2, 3, 4, 0, 5, 6, 7, 9, 8, 1} stored in the external file large-data.dat. Trace the SortLargeFile program by hand with MAX_ARRAY_SIZE 2.

## PROGRAMMING EXERCISES

**18.1** (*Generic bubble sort*) Write a generic function for bubble sort.

**18.2** (*Generic merge sort*) Write a generic function for merge sort.

**18.3** (*Generic quick sort*) Write a generic function for quick sort.

**18.4** (*Improving quick sort*) The quick sort algorithm presented in the book selects the first element in the list as the pivot. Revise it by selecting the medium among the first, middle, and last elements in the list.

**18.5** (*Generic heap sort*) Write a test program that invokes the generic sort function to sort an array of **int** values, an array of **double** values, and an array of strings.

**18.6** (*Checking order*) Write the following overloaded functions that check whether an array is ordered in ascending order, or descending order. By default, the function checks ascending order. To check descending order, pass **false** to the ascending argument in the function.

```
// T is a generic type
bool ordered(T list[], int size)

// T is a generic type
bool ordered(T list[], int size, bool ascending)
```

**18.7** (*Execution time for sorting*) Write a program that obtains the execution time of selection sort, insertion sort, bubble sort, merge sort, quick sort, and heap sort for input size 500,000, 1,000,000, 1,500,000, 2,000,000, 2,500,000 and 3,000,000. Your program should print a table like this:

| Array size | Selection Sort | Insertion Sort | Bubble Sort | Merge Sort | Quick Sort | Heap Sort |
|---|---|---|---|---|---|---|
| 500000 | | | | | | |
| 1000000 | | | | | | |
| 1500000 | | | | | | |
| 2000000 | | | | | | |
| 2500000 | | | | | | |
| 3000000 | | | | | | |

 **Hint**

You can use the following code template to obtain the execution time:

```
long startTime = time(0);
perform the task;
long endTime = time(0);
long executionTime = endTime - startTime;
```

**18.8** (*Execution time for external sorting*) Write a program that obtains the execution time of external sort for integers of size 5,000,000, 10,000,000, 15,000,000, 20,000,000, 25,000,000, and 30,000,000. Your program should print a table like this:

| File size | 5000000 | 10000000 | 15000000 | 20000000 | 25000000 | 30000000 |
|---|---|---|---|---|---|---|
| Time | | | | | | |

## CHAPTER 19

# STL CONTAINERS

## Objectives

- To know the relationships among containers, iterators, and algorithms (§19.2).

- To distinguish sequence containers, associative containers, and container adapters (§19.2).

- To distinguish containers `vector`, `deque`, `list`, `set`, `multiset`, `map`, `multimap`, `stack`, `queue`, and `priority_queue` (§19.2).

- To use common features of containers (§19.2).

- To access elements in a container using iterators (§19.3).

- To distinguish iterator types: input, output, forward, bidirectional, and random access (§19.3.1).

- To manipulate iterators using operators (§19.3.2).

- To obtain iterators from containers and know the type of interators supported by containers (§19.3.3).

- To perform input and output using `istream_iterator` and `ostream_iterator` (§19.3.4).

- To store, retrieve, and process elements in sequence containers: `vector`, `deque`, and `list` (§19.4).

- To store, retrieve, and process elements in associative containers: `set`, `multiset`, `map`, and `multimap` (§19.5).

- To store, retrieve, and process elements in container adapters: `stack`, `queue`, and `priority_queue` (§19.6).

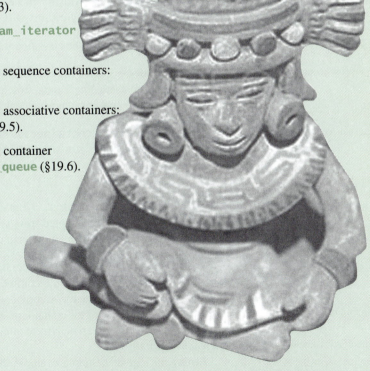

# 19.1 Introduction

Chapter 16, "Linked Lists, Stacks, and Queues," and Chapter 17, "Trees, Heaps, and Priority Queues," introduced several data structures such as linked lists, stacks, queues, heaps, and priority queues. These popular data structures are used widely in many applications. C++ provides a library known as the *Standard Template Library* (*STL*) for these and many other useful data structures. So, you can use them without having to reinvent the wheel. One example in the STL that you have learned is the **vector** class, which was introduced in §10.12. This chapter introduces the STL, and you will learn how to use the classes in the STL to simplify application development.

# 19.2 STL Basics

history of STL

The STL was developed by Alexander Stepanov and Meng Lee at Hewlett-Packard and was based on their research of generic programming in collaboration with David Musser. It is a collection of libraries written in C++. As its name suggests, the classes and functions in the STL are template classes and template functions.

three components

The STL contains three main components:

container

■ **Containers:** Classes in the STL are container classes. A container object such as a vector is used to store a collection of data, often referred to as *elements*.

iterator

■ **Iterators:** The STL container classes make extensive use of *iterators*, which are objects that facilitate traversing through the elements in a container. Iterators are like built-in pointers that provide a convenient way to access and manipulate the elements in a container.

algorithm

■ **Algorithms:** Algorithms are used in the functions to manipulate data such as sorting, searching, and comparing elements. There are about 80 algorithms implemented in the STL. Most of these algorithms use iterators to access the elements in the container. STL algorithms will be introduced in Chapter 20.

container types

The STL containers can be classified into three categories:

sequence containers

■ **Sequence containers:** The sequence containers (also known as sequential containers) represent linear data structures. The three sequence containers are **vector**, **list**, and **deque** (pronounced deck).

associative containers

■ **Associative containers:** Associative containers are non-linear containers that can locate elements stored in the container quickly. Such containers can store sets of values or *key/value* pairs. The four associative containers are **set**, **multiset**, **map**, and **multimap**.

container adapters

■ **Container adapters:** Container adapters are constrained versions of sequence containers. They are adapted from sequence containers for handling special cases. The three container adapters are **stack**, **queue**, and **priority_queue**.

Table 19.1 summarizes the container classes and their header files.

All STL containers share some common features and functions. For example, each container has a no-arg constructor, a copy constructor, a destructor, and so on. Table 19.2 lists the common functions for all containers, and Table 19.3 lists the common functions for the sequence containers and associative containers. These two containers also are known as the *first-class containers*.

common functions

first-class container

Listing 19.1 gives a simple example that demonstrates how to create a **vector**, **list**, **deque**, **set**, **multiset**, **stack**, and **queue**.

**TABLE 19.1**   Container Classes

| STL Container | Header File | Applications |
|---|---|---|
| vector | <vector> | For direct access to any element, quick insertion, and deletion at the end of the vector. |
| deque | <deque> | For direct access to any element, quick insertion, and deletion at the front and end of the deque. |
| list | <list> | For rapid insertion and deletion anywhere. |
| set | <set> | For direct lookup, no duplicated elements. |
| multiset | <set> | Same as set, except that duplicated elements allowed. |
| map | <map> | Key/value pair mapping, no duplicates allowed, and quick lookup using the key. |
| multimap | <map> | Same as map, except that keys may be duplicated |
| stack | <stack> | Last-in first-out container. |
| queue | <queue> | First-in first-out container. |
| priority_queue | <queue> | The highest-priority element is removed first. |

**TABLE 19.2**   Common Functions to All Containers

| Functions | Description |
|---|---|
| non-arg constructor | Constructs an empty container. |
| constructor with args | In addition to the no-arg constructor, every container has several constructors with args. |
| copy constructor | Creates a container by copying the elements from an existing container of the same type. |
| destructor | Performs cleanup after the container is destroyed. |
| empty() | Returns true if there are no elements in the container. |
| size() | Returns the number of elements in the container. |
| operator= | Copies one container to another. |
| Relational operators (<, <=, >, >=, ==, and !=) | The elements in the two containers are compared sequentially to determine the relation. |

**TABLE 19.3**   Common Functions to First-Class Containers

| STL Functions | Description |
|---|---|
| c1.swap(c2) | Swaps the elements of two containers c1 and c2. |
| c.max_size() | Returns the maximum number of elements a container can hold. |
| c.clear() | Erases all elements from the container. |
| c.begin() | Returns an iterator to the first element in the container. |
| c.end() | Returns an iterator that refers to the next position after the end of the container. |
| c.rbegin() | Returns an iterator to the last element in the container for processing elements in reverse order. |
| c.rend() | Returns an iterator that refers to the position before the first element in the container. |
| c.erase(beg, end) | Erases the elements in the container from beg to end-1. Both beg and end are iterators. |

**LISTING 19.1** SimpleSTLDemo.cpp

```cpp
 1 #include <iostream>
 2 #include <vector>
 3 #include <list>
 4 #include <deque>
 5 #include <set>
 6 #include <stack>
 7 #include <queue>
 8 using namespace std;
 9
10 int main()
11 {
12     vector<int> vector1, vector2;
13     list<int> list1, list2;
14     deque<int> deque1, deque2;
15     set<int> set1, set2;
16     multiset<int> multiset1, multiset2;
17     stack<int> stack1, stack2;
18     queue<int> queue1, queue2;
19
20     cout << "Vector: " << endl;
21     vector1.push_back(1);
22     vector1.push_back(2);
23     vector2.push_back(30);
24     cout << "size of vector1: " << vector1.size() << endl;
25     cout << "size of vector2: " << vector2.size() << endl;
26     cout << "maximum size of vector1: " << vector1.max_size() << endl;
27     cout << "maximum size of vector2: " << vector1.max_size() << endl;
28     vector1.swap(vector2);
29     cout << "size of vector1: " << vector1.size() << endl;
30     cout << "size of vector2: " << vector2.size() << endl;
31     cout << "vector1 < vector2? " << (vector1 < vector2)
32       << endl << endl;
33
34     cout << "List: " << endl;
35     list1.push_back(1);
36     list1.push_back(2);
37     list2.push_back(30);
38     cout << "size of list1: " << list1.size() << endl;
39     cout << "size of list2: " << list2.size() << endl;
40     cout << "maximum size of list1: " << list1.max_size() << endl;
41     cout << "maximum size of list2: " << list2.max_size() << endl;
42     list1.swap(list2);
43     cout << "size of list1: " << list1.size() << endl;
44     cout << "size of list2: " << list2.size() << endl;
45     cout << "list1 < list2? " << (list1 < list2) << endl << endl;
46
47     cout << "Deque: " << endl;
48     deque1.push_back(1);
49     deque1.push_back(2);
50     deque2.push_back(30);
51     cout << "size of deque1: " << deque1.size() << endl;
52     cout << "size of deque2: " << deque2.size() << endl;
53     cout << "maximum size of deque1: " << deque1.max_size() << endl;
54     cout << "maximum size of deque2: " << deque2.max_size() << endl;
55     deque1.swap(deque2);
56     cout << "size of deque1: " << deque1.size() << endl;
57     cout << "size of deque2: " << deque2.size() << endl;
58     cout << "deque1 < deque2? " << (deque1 < deque2) << endl << endl;
```

Margin annotations:

include vector (line 2)
include list (line 3)
include deque (line 4)
include set (line 5)
include stack (line 6)
include queue (line 7)

create vector (line 12)
create list (line 13)
create deque (line 14)
create set (line 15)
create multiset (line 16)
create stack (line 17)
create queue (line 18)

append element (line 21)

vector size (line 24)

vector max size (line 26)

compare vector (line 31)

append to list (line 35)

append to deque (line 48)

```
59
60    cout << "Set: " << endl;
61    set1.insert(1);                                              insert to set
62    set1.insert(1);
63    set1.insert(2);
64    set2.insert(30);
65    cout << "size of set1: " << set1.size() << endl;
66    cout << "size of set2: " << set2.size() << endl;
67    cout << "maximum size of set1: " << set1.max_size() << endl;
68    cout << "maximum size of set2: " << set2.max_size() << endl;
69    set1.swap(set2);
70    cout << "size of set1: " << set1.size() << endl;
71    cout << "size of set2: " << set2.size() << endl;
72    cout << "set1 < set2? " << (set1 < set2) << endl << endl;
73
74    cout << "Multiset: " << endl;
75    multiset1.insert(1);                                         insert to multiset
76    multiset1.insert(1);
77    multiset1.insert(2);
78    multiset2.insert(30);
79    cout << "size of multiset1: " << multiset1.size() << endl;
80    cout << "size of multiset2: " << multiset2.size() << endl;
81    cout << "maximum size of multiset1: " <<
82            multiset1.max_size() << endl;
83    cout << "maximum size of multiset2: " <<
84            multiset2.max_size() << endl;
85    multiset1.swap(multiset2);
86    cout << "size of multiset1: " << multiset1.size() << endl;
87    cout << "size of multiset2: " << multiset2.size() << endl;
88    cout << "multiset1 < multiset2? " <<
89            (multiset1 < multiset2) << endl << endl;
90
91    cout << "Stack: " << endl;
92    stack1.push(1);                                              push to stack
93    stack1.push(1);
94    stack1.push(2);
95    stack2.push(30);
96    cout << "size of stack1: " << stack1.size() << endl;
97    cout << "size of stack2: " << stack2.size() << endl;
98    cout << "stack1 < stack2? " << (stack1 < stack2) << endl << endl;
99
100   cout << "Queue: " << endl;
101   queue1.push(1);                                              push to queue
102   queue1.push(1);
103   queue1.push(2);
104   queue2.push(30);
105   cout << "size of queue1: " << queue1.size() << endl;
106   cout << "size of queue2: " << queue2.size() << endl;
107   cout << "queue1 < queue2? " << (queue1 < queue2) << endl << endl;
108
109   return 0;
110 }
```

```
Vector:
size of vector1: 2
size of vector2: 1
maximum size of vector1: 1073741823
```

```
maximum size of vector2: 1073741823
size of vector1: 1
size of vector2: 2
vector1 < vector2? 0


List:
size of list1: 2
size of list2: 1
maximum size of list1: 4294967295
maximum size of list2: 4294967295
size of list1: 1
size of list2: 2
list1 < list2? 0


Deque:
size of deque1: 2
size of deque2: 1
maximum size of deque1: 4294967295
maximum size of deque2: 4294967295
size of deque1: 1
size of deque2: 2
deque1 < deque2? 0


Set:
size of set1: 2
size of set2: 1
maximum size of set1: 4294967295
maximum size of set2: 4294967295
size of set1: 1
size of set2: 2
set1 < set2? 0


Multiset:
size of multiset1: 3
size of multiset2: 1
maximum size of multiset1: 4294967295
maximum size of multiset2: 4294967295
size of multiset1: 1
size of multiset2: 3
multiset1 < multiset2? 0


Stack:
size of stack1: 3
size of stack2: 1
stack1 < stack2? 1


Queue:
size of queue1: 3
size of queue2: 1
queue1 < queue2? 1
```

Each container has a no-arg constructor. The program creates vectors, lists, deques, sets, multisets, stacks, and queues in lines 12–18 using the container's no-arg constructors.

no-arg constructor

The program uses the `push_back(element)` function to append an element into a vector, list, and deque in lines 21–23, 35–37, and 48–50; the `insert(element)` function to insert an element to a set and multiset in lines 61–64 and 75–78; and the `push(element)` function to push an element into a stack and queue in lines 92–95 and 101–104.

add element

Integer 1 is inserted into `set1` twice in lines 61–62. Since a set does not allow duplicate elements, `set1` contains {1, 2} after 2 is inserted into `set1` in line 63. A multiset allows duplicates, so `multiset1` contains {1, 1, 2} after 1, 1, and 2 are inserted into `multiset1` in lines 75–77.

set vs. multiset

All containers support the *relational operators*. The program compares two containers of the same type in lines 31, 45, 58, and 72.

relational operator

## 19.3 STL Iterators

Iterators are used extensively in the first-class containers for accessing and manipulating the elements. As you already have seen in Table 19.3, several functions (e.g., `begin()` and `end()`) in the first-class containers are related to iterators. §16.8, "Iterators," presented examples on how to implement iterators in a container. It is helpful to review §16.8 before reading this section.

The `begin()` function returns the iterator that points to the first element in a container and the `end()` function returns the iterator that represents a position that passes the last element in a container, as pictured in Figure 19.1.

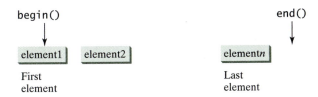

**FIGURE 19.1** `end()` represents a position that passes the last element.

Typically, you cycle through all the elements in a container using the following loop:

```
for (iterator p = c.begin(); p != c.end(); p++)
{
  processing *p; // *p is the current element
}
```

Each container has its own iterator type. The abstraction hides the detailed implementation and provides a uniform way for using iterators on all containers.

Iterators are used in the same way in all containers, so if you know how to use iterators with one container class, you can apply it to all other containers.

Listing 19.2 demonstrates using iterators in a vector and a set.

### LISTING 19.2 `IteratorDemo.cpp`

```
1 #include <iostream>
2 #include <vector>
3 #include <set>
4 using namespace std;
5
```

include vector
include set

```
     6  int main()
     7  {
     8      vector<int> intVector;
     9      intVector.push_back(10);
    10      intVector.push_back(40);
    11      intVector.push_back(50);
    12      intVector.push_back(20);
    13      intVector.push_back(30);
    14
    15      vector<int>::iterator p1;
    16      cout << "Traverse the vector: ";
    17      for (p1 = intVector.begin(); p1 != intVector.end(); p1++)
    18      {
    19          cout << *p1 << " ";
    20      }
    21
    22      set<int> intSet;
    23      intSet.insert(10);
    24      intSet.insert(40);
    25      intSet.insert(50);
    26      intSet.insert(20);
    27      intSet.insert(30);
    28
    29      set<int>::iterator p2;
    30      cout << "\nTraverse the set: ";
    31      for (p2 = intSet.begin(); p2 != intSet.end(); p2++)
    32      {
    33          cout << *p2 << " ";
    34      }
    35      cout << endl;
    36
    37      return 0;
    38  }
```

Left margin annotations: create vector (line 8), append element (line 9), declare iterator (line 15), traverse vector (line 17), get element (line 19), create set (line 22), append element (line 23), declare iterator (line 29), traverse set (line 31), get element (line 33).

```
Traverse the vector: 10 40 50 20 30
Traverse the set: 10 20 30 40 50
```

The program creates a vector for **int** values (line 8), appends five numbers (lines 9–13), and traverses the vector using an iterator (line 15–20).

An iterator **p1** is declared in line 15:

```
vector<int>::iterator p1;
```

**vector<int>** iterator

Every container has its own iterator type. Here **vector<int>::iterator** denotes the iterator type in the **vector<int>** class.

The expression (line 17)

**begin()**

```
p1 = intVector.begin();
```

obtains the iterator that points to the first element in the vector **intVector** and assigns the iterator to **p1**.

The expression (line 17)

**end()**

```
p1 != intVector.end();
```

checks whether **p1** has passed the last element in the container.

The expression (line 17)

**move iterator**

```
p1++
```

advances the iterator to the next element.

The expression (line 19)

```
*p1
```

returns the element pointed by **p1**.

Similarly, the program creates a set for **int** values (line 22), inserts five numbers (lines 23–27), and traverses the set using an iterator (line 29–34). Note that the elements in a set are sorted, so the program displays 10, 20, 30, 40, and 50 in the sample output.

From this example, you can see that an iterator functions like a pointer. An iterator variable points to an element in the container. You use the increment operator (**p++**) to move the iterator to the next element and use the dereference operator (**\*p**) to access the element.

## 19.3.1    Type of Iterators

Each container has its own iterator type. Iterators can be classified into five categories:

- **Input iterators:** An input iterator is used for reading an element from a container. It can move only in a forward direction one element at a time.

- **Output iterators:** An output iterator is used for writing an element to a container. It can move only in a forward direction one element at a time.

- **Forward iterator:** A forward iterator combines all the functionalities of input and output iterators to support both read and write operations.

- **Bidirectional iterator:** A bidirectional iterator is a forward iterator with the capability of moving backward. The iterator can be moved freely back or forth one at a time.

- **Random-access iterator:** A random-access iterator is a bidirectional iterator with the capability of accessing any element in any order, i.e., to jump forward or backward by a number of elements.

The **vector** and **deque** containers support random-access iterators, and the **list**, **set**, **multiset**, **map**, and **multimap** containers support bidirectional iterators. Note that the **stack**, **queue**, and **priority_queue** don't support iterators, as shown in Table 19.4.

**TABLE 19.4**    Iterator Types Supported by Containers

| STL Container | Type of Iterators Supported |
| --- | --- |
| vector | Random-access iterators |
| deque | Random-access iterators |
| list | Bidirectional iterators |
| set | Bidirectional iterators |
| multiset | Bidirectional iterators |
| map | Bidirectional iterators |
| multimap | Bidirectional iterators |
| stack | No iterator support |
| queue | No iterator support |
| priority_queue | No iterator support |

## 19.3.2    Iterator Operators

You can manipulate the iterators using the overloaded operators to move its position, access the element, and compare them. Table 19.5 shows the operators supported by the iterators.

**TABLE 19.5**   Operators Supported by Iterators

| Operator | Description |
| --- | --- |
| *All iterators* | |
| ++p | Pre-increment an iterator. |
| p++ | Post-increment an iterator. |
| *Input iterators* | |
| *p | Dereference an iterator (used as rvalue). |
| p1 == p2 | Evaluates **true** if **p1** and **p2** point to the same element. |
| p1 != p2 | Evaluates **true** if **p1** and **p2** point to different elements. |
| *Output iterators* | |
| *p | Dereference an iterator (used as lvalue). |
| *Bidirectional iterators* | |
| --p | Pre-decrement an iterator. |
| p-- | Post-decrement an iterator. |
| *Random-access iterators* | |
| p += i | Increment iterator **p** by *i* positions. |
| p -= i | Decrement iterator **p** by *i* positions. |
| p + i | Returns an iterator *i*th position after **p**. |
| p - i | Returns an iterator *i*th position before **p**. |
| p1 < p2 | Returns **true** if **p1** is before **p2**. |
| p1 <= p2 | Returns **true** if **p1** is before or equal to **p2**. |
| p1 > p2 | Returns **true** if **p1** is after **p2**. |
| p1 >= p2 | Returns **true** if **p1** is after **p2** or equal to **p2**. |
| p[i] | Returns the element at the position **p** offset by *i*. |

All the iterators support the pre- and post-increment operators (++p and p++). The input iterators also support the dereference operator (*) as a rvalue, equality checking operator (==), and inequality checking operator (!=). The output iterators also support the dereference operator (*) as a lvalue. The forward iterators support all functions provided in the input and output iterators. The bidirectional iterators support the pre- and post-decrement operators in addition to all the functions in the forward iterators. The random-access iterators support all the operators listed in this table.

Listing 19.3 demonstrates how to use these operators on iterators.

## LISTING 19.3   IteratorOperatorDemo.cpp

```
1 #include <iostream>
2 #include <vector>
3 using namespace std;
4
```

```
 5  int main()
 6  {
 7      vector<int> intVector;                              create vector
 8      intVector.push_back(10);                            append element
 9      intVector.push_back(20);
10      intVector.push_back(30);
11      intVector.push_back(40);
12      intVector.push_back(50);
13      intVector.push_back(60);
14
15      vector<int>::iterator p1 = intVector.begin();       obtain an iterator
16      for (; p1 != intVector.end(); p1++)                 != iterators
17      {
18        cout << *p1 << " ";                               dereferencing operator
19      }
20
21      cout << endl << *(--p1) << endl;                    pre-decrement operator
22      cout << *(p1 - 3) << endl;                          subtract operator
23      cout << p1[-3] << endl;                             offset
24      *p1 = 1234;                                         dereferencing operator
25      cout << *p1 << endl;
26
27      return 0;
28  }
```

```
10 20 30 40 50 60
60
30
30
1234
```

The **vector** class contains random-access iterators. The program creates a vector (line 7), appends six elements into it (lines 8–13), and obtains an iterator **p1** in line 15. Since the **vector** class contains the random-access iterators, all the operators in Table 19.5 can be applied to **p1**.

### 19.3.3 Predefined Iterators

The STL containers use the **typedef** keyword to predefine iterators. The **typedef** keyword is used to declare synonyms for data types. For example, the following statement declares integer as a synonym for **int**.

```
typedef int integer;
```

So, now you can declare a variable using

```
integer value = 40;
```

The predefined typedefs are **iterator**, **const_iterator**, **reverse_iterator**, and **const_reverse_iterator**. These iterators are defined in every first-class container.
For example,

```
vector<int>::iterator p1;                               typedef iterator
```

declares **p1** to be an iterator for the **vector<int>** container.

**Note**

Since **iterator** is a **typedef** defined inside a class such as **vector**, the *scope resolution* operator is needed to reference it.

scope resolution

**typedef const_iterator**

The **typedef const_iterator** is the same as **typedef iterator**, except that you cannot modify elements through a **const_iterator**. A **const_iterator** is read-only. Listing 19.4 shows the differences between **iterator** and **const_iterator**.

**LISTING 19.4** ConstIteratorDemo.cpp

```cpp
1  #include <iostream>
2  #include <vector>
3  using namespace std;
4
5  int main()
6  {
7      vector<int> intVector;
8      intVector.push_back(10);
9
10     vector<int>::iterator  p1 = intVector.begin();
11     vector<int>::const_iterator p2 = intVector.begin();
12
13     *p1 = 123; // OK
14     *p2 = 123; // Not allowed
15
16     cout << *p1 << endl;
17     cout << *p2 << endl;
18
19     return 0;
20 }
```

iterator
const_iterator

writable
read-only

read from **p1**
read from **p2**

```
Error line 14: cannot modify a const object
```

Since **p2** is a **const_iterator** (line 11), you cannot modify the element from **p2**.

You use reverse iterators to traverse containers in the reverse direction. Listing 19.5 demonstrates how to use **reverse_iterator**.

**typedef**
  **reverse_iterator**

**LISTING 19.5** ReverseIteratorDemo.cpp

```cpp
1  #include <iostream>
2  #include <vector>
3  using namespace std;
4
5  int main()
6  {
7      vector<int> intVector;
8      intVector.push_back(10);
9      intVector.push_back(30);
10     intVector.push_back(20);
11
12     vector<int>::reverse_iterator p1 = intVector.rbegin();
13     for (; p1 != intVector.rend(); p1++)
14     {
15         cout << *p1 << " ";
16     }
17
18     return 0;
19 }
```

create vector
append element

reverse_iterator
rend()

access element

```
20 30 10
```

The program declares a `reverse_iterator p1` in line 12. The function `rbegin()` returns a `reverse_iterator` that refers to the last element in the container (line 12). The function `rend()` returns a `reverse_iterator` that refers to the next element after the first element in the reversed container (line 13).

The `typedef const_reverse_iterator` is the same as `typedef reverse_iterator`, except that you cannot modify elements through a `const_reverse_iterator`. A `const_reverse_iterator` is read-only.

`typedef reverse_`
`const_iterator`

### 19.3.4 `istream_iterator` and `ostream_iterator`

Iterators are used for sequencing elements. You can use iterators to sequence the elements in a container as well as the elements in input/output streams. Listing 19.6 demonstrates how to use `istream_iterator` to input data from an input stream and `ostream_iterator` to output data to an output stream. The program prompts the user to enter three integers and displays the largest integer.

**LISTING 19.6** `InputOutputStreamIteratorDemo.cpp`

```cpp
 1 #include <iostream>
 2 #include <iterator>
 3 #include <cmath>
 4 using namespace std;
 5
 6 int main()
 7 {
 8   cout << "Enter three numbers: ";
 9   istream_iterator<int> inputIterator(cin);
10   ostream_iterator<int> outputIterator(cout);
11
12   int number1 = *inputIterator;
13   inputIterator++;
14   int number2 = *inputIterator;
15   inputIterator++;
16   int number3 = *inputIterator;
17
18   cout << "The largest number is ";
19   *outputIterator = max(max(number1, number2), number3);
20
21   return 0;
22 }
```

include iterator

input stream iterator
output stream iterator

read an integer
move to next

write an integer

```
Enter three numbers: 34 12 23  ↵Enter
The largest number is 34
```

The `istream_iterator` and `ostream_iterator` are in the `<iterator>` header, so it is included in line 2. An `istream_iterator inputIterator` is created for reading integers from the `cin` object in line 9. An `ostream_iterator outputIterator` is created for writing integers to the `cout` object in line 10.

The dereferencing operator applies on `inputIterator` (line 12) to read an integer from `cin`, and the iterator is moved to point to the next number in the input stream (line 13).

The dereferencing operator applies on `outputIterator` (line 19) to write an integer to `cout`. Here `*outputIterator` is a lvalue.

# 19.4 Sequence Containers

The STL provides three sequence containers: `vector`, `list`, and `deque`. The `vector` and `deque` containers are implemented using arrays, and the `list` container is implemented using a linked list.

- A `vector` is efficient if the elements are appended to the `vector`, but it is expensive to insert or delete elements anywhere except at the end of the `vector`.

- A `deque` is like a vector, but it is efficient for insertion at both the front and end of a `deque`. Nevertheless, it is still expensive to insert or delete elements in the middle of a `deque`.

- A `list` is good for applications that require frequent insertion and deletion in the middle of a `list`.

A vector has the least overhead, a `deque` has slightly more overhead than a `vector`, and a `list` has the most overhead.

Tables 19.2 and 19.3 listed the functions common to all the containers and first-class containers. In addition to these common functions, each sequence container has the following functions, as shown in Table 19.6.

**TABLE 19.6**    Common Functions in Sequence Containers

| Functions | Description |
| --- | --- |
| `assign(n, elem)` | Assign *n* copies of the specified element in the container. |
| `assign(beg, end)` | Assign the elements in the range from iterator `beg` to iterator `end`. |
| `push_back(elem)` | Appends an element in the container. |
| `pop_back()` | Removes the last element from the container. |
| `front()` | Returns the iterator to the first element. |
| `back()` | Returns the iterator to the last element. |
| `insert(position, elem)` | Inserts an element at the specified iterator. |

## 19.4.1   Sequence Container: `vector`

As shown in Table 19.2, every container has a no-arg constructor, a copy constructor, a destructor, and supports the functions `empty()`, `size()`, and relational operators. Every first-class container contains the functions `swap`, `max_size`, `clear`, `begin`, `end`, `rbegin`, `rend`, and `erase`, as shown in Table 19.3, and the iterators, as shown in Table 19.5. Every sequence container contains the functions `assign`, `push_back`, `pop_back`, `front`, `back`, and `insert`, as shown in Table 19.6. In addition to these common functions, the `vector` class also contains the following functions, as shown in Table 19.7.

Listing 19.7 demonstrates how to use the functions in `vector`.

**TABLE 19.7**    Functions Specific in `vector`

| Functions | Description |
| --- | --- |
| `vector(n, element)` | Constructs a vector filled with *n* copies of the same element. |
| `vector(beg, end)` | Constructs a vector initialized with elements from iterator `beg` to `end`. |
| `vector(size)` | Constructs a vector with the specified size. |
| `at(index): dataType` | Returns the element at the specified index. |

LISTING 19.7  VectorDemo.cpp

```
1 #include <iostream>
2 #include <vector>
3 using namespace std;
4
5 int main()
6 {
7   double values[] = {1, 2, 3, 4, 5, 6, 7};
8   vector<double> doubleVector(values, values + 7);
9
10  cout << "Initial contents in doubleVector: ";
11  for (int i = 0; i < doubleVector.size(); i++)
12    cout << doubleVector[i]  << " ";
13
14  doubleVector.assign(4, 11.5);
15
16  cout << "\nAfter the assign function, doubleVector: ";
17  for (int i = 0; i < doubleVector.size(); i++)
18    cout << doubleVector[i] << " ";
19
20  doubleVector.at(0) = 22.4;
21  cout << "\nAfter the at function, doubleVector: ";
22  for (int i = 0; i < doubleVector.size(); i++)
23    cout << doubleVector[i] << " ";
24
25  vector<double>::iterator itr = doubleVector.begin();
26  doubleVector.insert(itr + 1, 555);
27  doubleVector.insert(itr + 1, 666);
28  cout << "\nAfter the insert function, doubleVector: ";
29  for (int i = 0; i < doubleVector.size(); i++)
30    cout << doubleVector[i] << " ";
31
32  doubleVector.erase(itr + 2, itr + 4);
33  cout << "\nAfter the erase function, doubleVector: ";
34  for (int i = 0; i < doubleVector.size(); i++)
35    cout << doubleVector[i] << " ";
36
37  doubleVector.clear();
38  cout << "\Size is " << doubleVector.size() << endl;
39  cout << "Is empty? " <<
40      (doubleVector.empty() ? "true" : "false") << endl;
41
42  return 0;
43 }
```

include vector

create an array
create a vector

vector size
subscript operator

assign to vector

new element value

get iterator
insert an element

erase elements

clear vector

is empty?

```
Initial contents in doubleVector: 1 2 3 4 5 6 7
After the assign function, doubleVector: 11.5 11.5 11.5 11.5
After the at function, doubleVector: 22.4 11.5 11.5 11.5
After the insert function, doubleVector: 22.4 666 555 11.5 11.5 11.5
After the erase function, doubleVector: 22.4 666 11.5 11.5 Size is 0
Is empty? true
```

The program creates an array of seven elements in line 7, and creates a vector using the elements from the array. Arrays can be accessed using pointers. The pointers are like iterators, so **values** and **values + 7** point to the first element and the last element in the array.

The program displays all the elements in the vector using a **for** loop (lines 17–18). The subscript operator **[]** (line 18) can be used for a **vector** or a **deque** to access elements in the container.

The program assigns `22.4` to the first element (line 20) in the vector using

```
doubleVector.at(0) = 22.4;
```

This statement is the same as

```
doubleVector[0] = 22.4;
```

Iterators can be used to specify the positions in a container. An iterator is obtained in line 25. A new element is inserted at position `itr + 1` (line 26) and another one is inserted in the same position `itr + 1` (line 27). The program deletes the elements from `itr + 2` to `itr + 4` (line 32).

### 19.4.2 Sequence Container: deque

The term *deque* stands for *double-ended* queue. A **deque** provides efficient operations to support insertion and deletion on both ends of a **deque**. In addition to the common functions for all sequence containers, the **deque** class contains the following functions, as shown in Table 19.8. Listing 19.8 demonstrates how to use the functions in **deque**.

**TABLE 19.8** Functions Specific in deque

| Functions | Description |
|---|---|
| `deque(n, element)` | Constructs a deque filled with n copies of the same element. |
| `deque(beg, end)` | Constructs a deque initialized with elements from iterator **beg** to **end**. |
| `deque(size)` | Constructs a deque with the specified size. |
| `at(index): dataType` | Returns the element at the specified index. |
| `push_front(element)` | Inserts the element to the front of the queue. |
| `pop_front(): dataType` | Removes the element from the front of the queue. |

**LISTING 19.8** DequeDemo.cpp

include deque

create an array
create deque

```
 1 #include <iostream>
 2 #include <deque>
 3 using namespace std;
 4
 5 int main()
 6 {
 7   double values[] = {1, 2, 3, 4, 5, 6, 7};
 8   deque<double> doubleDeque(values, values + 7);
 9
10   cout << "Initial contents in doubleDeque: ";
11   for (int i = 0; i < doubleDeque.size(); i++)
12     cout << doubleDeque[i] << " ";
13
14   doubleDeque.assign(4, 11.5);
15   cout << "\nAfter the assign function, doubleDeque: ";
16   for (int i = 0; i < doubleDeque.size(); i++)
17     cout << doubleDeque[i] << " ";
18
19   doubleDeque.at(0) = 22.4;
20   cout << "\nAfter the at function, doubleDeque: ";
21   for (int i = 0; i < doubleDeque.size(); i++)
22     cout << doubleDeque[i] << " ";
```

```
23
24    deque<double>::iterator itr = doubleDeque.begin();
25    doubleDeque.insert(itr + 1, 555);
26    doubleDeque.insert(itr + 1, 666);
27    cout << "\nAfter the insert function, doubleDeque: ";
28    for (int i = 0; i < doubleDeque.size(); i++)
29      cout << doubleDeque[i] << " ";
30
31    doubleDeque.erase(itr + 2, itr + 4);
32    cout << "\nAfter the erase function, doubleDeque: ";
33    for (int i = 0; i < doubleDeque.size(); i++)
34      cout << doubleDeque[i] << " ";
35
36    doubleDeque.clear();
37    cout << "\nAfter the clear function, doubleDeque: ";
38    cout << "Size is " << doubleDeque.size() << endl;
39    cout << "Is empty? " <<
40          (doubleDeque.empty() ? "true" : "false");
41
42    doubleDeque.push_front(10.10);                              push front
43    doubleDeque.push_front(11.15);
44    doubleDeque.push_front(12.34);
45    cout << "\nAfter the insertion, doubleDeque: ";
46    for (int i = 0; i < doubleDeque.size(); i++)
47      cout << doubleDeque[i] << " ";
48
49    doubleDeque.pop_front();                                    pop front
50    doubleDeque.pop_back();
51    cout << "\nAfter the pop functions, doubleDeque: ";
52    for (int i = 0; i < doubleDeque.size(); i++)
53      cout << doubleDeque[i] << " ";
54
55    return 0;
56 }
```

```
Initial contents in doubleDeque: 1 2 3 4 5 6 7
After the assign function, doubleDeque: 11.5 11.5 11.5 11.5
After the at function, doubleDeque: 22.4 11.5 11.5 11.5
After the insert function, doubleDeque: 22.4 555 666 11.5 11.5 11.5
After the erase function, doubleDeque: 22.4 555 666 11.5
After the clear function, doubleDeque: Size is 0
Is empty? true
After the insertion, doubleDeque: 12.34 11.15 10.1
After the pop functions, doubleDeque: 11.15
```

The **deque** class contains all the functions in the **vector** class. So you can use a **deque** wherever a **vector** is used. Lines 1–42 in Listing 19.8 are almost the same as lines 1–40 in Listing 19.7.

The **push_front** function is used to add elements to the front of the deque in lines 42–44, the **pop_front()** function removes the element from the front of the deque (line 49), and the **pop_back()** function removes the element from the back of the deque (line 50).

## 19.4.3  Sequence Container: `list`

The class `list` is implemented as a doubly linked list. It supports efficient insertion and deletion operations anywhere on the list. In addition to the common functions for all sequence containers, the `list` class contains the following functions, as shown in Table 19.9.

**TABLE 19.9** Functions Specific in `list`

| Functions | Description |
| --- | --- |
| `list(n, element)` | Constructs a list filled with *n* copies of the same element. |
| `list(beg, end)` | Constructs a list initialized with elements from iterator **beg** to **end**. |
| `list(size)` | Constructs a list initialized with the specified size. |
| `push_front(element)` | Inserts the element to the front of the queue. |
| `pop_front(): dataType` | Removes the element from the front of the queue. |
| `remove(element)` | Removes all the elements that are equal to the specified element. |
| `remove_if(oper)` | Removes all the elements for which `oper(element)` is `true`. |
| `splice(pos, list2)` | All the elements of `list2` are moved to this list before the specified position. After invoking this function, `list2` is empty. |
| `splice(pos1, list2, pos2)` | All the elements of `list2` starting from **pos2** are moved to this list before **pos1**. After invoking this function, `list2` is empty. |
| `splice(pos1, list2, beg, end)` | All the elements of `list2` from iterator beg to end are moved to this list before **pos1**. After invoking this function, `list2` is empty. |
| `sort()` | Sorts the elements in the list in increasing order. |
| `sort(oper)` | Sorts the elements in the list. The sort criterion is specified by oper. |
| `merge(list2)` | Suppose the elements in this list and `list2` are sorted. Merges `list2` into this list. After the merge, `list2` is empty. |
| `merge(list2, oper)` | Suppose the elements in this list and `list2` are sorted based on sort criterion oper. Merges `list2` into this list. |
| `reverse()` | Reverse the elements in this list. |

The iterators for **vector** and **deque** are random access but are bidirectional for **list**. You cannot access the elements in a list using the subscript operator []. Listing 19.9 demonstrates how to use the functions in **list**.

**LISTING 19.9** `ListDemo.cpp`

```
1  #include <iostream>
2  #include <list>
3  using namespace std;
4
5  int main()
6  {
7    int values[] = {1, 2, 3, 4};
8    list<int> intList(values, values + 4);
9
10   cout << "Initial contents in intList: ";
11   list<int>::iterator p;
12   for (p = intList.begin(); p != intList.end(); p++)
13     cout << *p << " ";
14
15   intList.assign(4, 11);
16   cout << "\nAfter the assign function, intList: ";
17   for (p = intList.begin(); p != intList.end(); p++)
18     cout << *p << " ";
19
20   list<int>::iterator itr = intList.begin();
21   itr++;
```

include list

create an array
create **intList**

list iterator

access element

assign element

```
22    intList.insert(itr, 555);                              insert element
23    intList.insert(itr, 666);
24    cout << "\nAfter the insert function, intList: ";
25    for (p = intList.begin(); p != intList.end(); p++)
26      cout << *p << " ";
27
28    list<int>::iterator beg = intList.begin();
29    itr++;
30    intList.erase(beg, itr);                                erase element
31    cout << "\nAfter the erase function, intList: ";
32    for (p = intList.begin(); p != intList.end(); p++)
33      cout << *p << " ";
34
35    intList.clear();                                        clear element
36    cout << "\nAfter the clear function, intList: ";
37    cout << "Size is " << intList.size() << endl;
38    cout << "Is empty? " <<
39          (intList.empty() ? "true" : "false");
40
41    intList.push_front(10);
42    intList.push_front(11);
43    intList.push_front(12);
44    cout << "\nAfter the push functions, intList: ";
45    for (p = intList.begin(); p != intList.end(); p++)
46      cout << *p << " ";
47
48    intList.pop_front();
49    intList.pop_back();
50    cout << "\nAfter the pop functions, intList: ";
51    for (p = intList.begin(); p != intList.end(); p++)
52      cout << *p << " ";
53
54    int values1[] = {7, 3, 1, 2};
55    list<int> list1(values1, values1 + 4);
56    list1.sort();                                           sort
57    cout << "\nAfter the sort function, list1: ";
58    for (p = list1.begin(); p != list1.end(); p++)
59      cout << *p << " ";
60
61    list<int> list2(list1);                                 create list2
62    list1.merge(list2);                                     merge
63    cout << "\nAfter the merge function, list1: ";
64    for (p = list1.begin(); p != list1.end(); p++)
65      cout << *p << " ";
66    cout << "\nSize of list2 is " << list2.size();
67                                                            reverse
68    list1.reverse();
69    cout << "\nAfter the reverse function, list1: ";
70    for (p = list1.begin(); p != list1.end(); p++)
71      cout << *p << " ";
72
73    list1.push_back(7);
74    list1.push_back(1);
75    cout << "\nAfter the push functions, list1: ";
76    for (p = list1.begin(); p != list1.end(); p++)
77      cout << *p << " ";
78                                                            remove
79    list1.remove(7);
80    cout << "\nAfter the remove function, list1: ";
81    for (p = list1.begin(); p != list1.end(); p++)
82      cout << *p << " ";
```

```
83
84   list2.assign(7, 2);
85   cout << "\nAfter the assign function, list2: ";
86   for (p = list2.begin(); p != list2.end(); p++)
87     cout << *p << " ";
88
89   p = list2.begin();
90   p++;
91   list2.splice(p, list1);
92   cout << "\nAfter the splice function, list2: ";
93   for (p = list2.begin(); p != list2.end(); p++)
94     cout << *p << " ";
95   cout << "\nAfter the splice function, list1's size is "
96     << list1.size();
97
98   return 0;
99 }
```

```
Initial contents in intList: 1 2 3 4
After the assign function, intList: 11 11 11 11
After the insert function, intList: 11 555 666 11 11 11
After the erase function, intList: 11 11
After the clear function, intList: Size is 0
Is empty? true
After the push functions, intList: 12 11 10
After the pop functions, intList: 11
After the sort function, list1: 1 2 3 7
After the merge function, list1: 1 1 2 2 3 3 7 7
Size of list2 is 0
After the reverse function, list1: 7 7 3 3 2 2 1 1
After the push functions, list1: 7 7 3 3 2 2 1 1 7 1
After the remove function, list1: 3 3 2 2 1 1 1
After the assign function, list2: 2 2 2 2 2 2 2
After the splice function, list2: 2 3 3 2 2 1 1 1 2 2 2 2 2 2
After the splice function, list1's size is 0
```

The program creates a list `intList` and displays its contents in lines 7–13.

The program assigns four elements with value `11` to `intList` (line 15), inserts `555` and `666` into the position specified by the iteration `itr` (lines 22–23), erases the elements from the `beg` iterator to iterator `itr` (line 30), clears the list (line 35), and pushes and pops elements (lines 41–52).

The program creates a list `list1` (line 55), sorts it (line 56), and merges it with `list2` (line 62). After the merge, `list2` is empty.

The program reverses `list1` (line 68) and removes all the elements with value `7` from list1 (line 79).

The program applies the `splice` function to move all the elements from `list1` into `list2` before the iterator `p` (line 91). Afterwards, `list1` is empty.

## 19.5 Associative Containers

The STL provides four associative containers: `set`, `multiset`, `map`, and `multimap`. These containers provide fast storage and quick access to retrieve elements using *keys* (often called *search keys*). Elements in an associative container are sorted according to some sorting criterion. By default, the elements are sorted using the < operator.

The **set** and **multiset** containers are identical, except that a **multiset** allows duplicate keys and a **set** does not. The **map** and **multimap** are identical, except that a **multimap** allows duplicate keys and a **map** does not.

Tables 19.2 and 19.3 listed the functions common to all the containers and first-class containers. In addition to these common functions, each associative container supports the following functions, as shown in Table 19.10.

**TABLE 19.10** Common Functions in Associative Containers

| Functions | Description |
|---|---|
| find(key) | Returns an iterator that points to the element with the specified key in the container. |
| lower_bound(key) | Returns an iterator that points to the first element with the specified key in the container. |
| upper_bound(key) | Returns an iterator that points to the next element after the last element with the specified key in the container. |
| count(key) | Returns the number of occurrences of the element with the specified key in the container. |

## 19.5.1  Associative Containers: **set** and **multiset**

The elements are the keys stored in a **set/multiset** container. A multiset allows duplicate keys, but a set does not. Listing 19.10 demonstrates how to use the **set** and **multiset** containers.

**LISTING 19.10**  SetDemo.cpp

```cpp
1 #include <iostream>
2 #include <set>
3 using namespace std;
4
5 int main()
6 {
7   int values[] = {3, 5, 1, 7, 2, 2};
8   multiset<int> set1(values, values + 6);
9
10  cout << "Initial contents in set1: ";
11  multiset<int>::iterator p;
12  for (p = set1.begin(); p != set1.end(); p++)
13    cout << *p << " ";
14
15  set1.insert(555);
16  set1.insert(1);
17  cout << "\nAfter the insert function, set1: ";
18  for (p = set1.begin(); p != set1.end(); p++)
19    cout << *p << " ";
20
21  p = set1.lower_bound(2);
22  cout << "\nLower bound of 2 in set1: " << *p;
23  p = set1.upper_bound(2);
24  cout << "\nUpper bound of 2 in set1: " << *p;
25
26  p = set1.find(2);
27  if (p == set1.end())
28    cout << "2 is not in set1" << endl;
29  else
30    cout << "\nThe number of 2's in set1: " << set1.count(2);
31
```

include list

create an array
create **set1**

**set1** iterator

access element

insert element

lower bound

upper bound

find element

count element

erase element

```
32   set1.erase(2);
33   cout << "\nAfter the erase function, set1: ";
34   for (p = set1.begin(); p != set1.end(); p++)
35     cout << *p << " ";
36
37   return 0;
38 }
```

```
Initial contents in set1: 1 2 2 3 5 7
After the insert function, set1: 1 1 2 2 3 5 7 555
Lower bound of 2 in set1: 2
Upper bound of 2 in set1: 3
The number of 2's in set1: 2
After the erase function, set1: 1 1 3 5 7 555
```

The program creates a set `set1` and displays its contents in lines 7–13. By default, the elements in a set are sorted in increasing order. To specify a decreasing order, you may replace line 8 by

specify an order

```
multiset<int, greater<int> > set1(values, values + 6);
```

Please note that a space after `greater<int>` is needed, otherwise, C++ would be confused with the `>>` operator.

The program inserts keys `555` and `1` (lines 15–16) and displays the new elements in the set (lines 17–19).

Invoking `lower_bound(2)` (line 21) returns the iterator that points to the first occurrence of `2` in the container, and invoking `upper_bound(2)` (line 23) returns the iterator that points to the next element after the last occurrence of `2` in the container. Thus, `*p` in line 24 displays element `3`.

Invoking `find(2)` (line 26) returns the iterator that points to the first occurrence of `2` in the container. If no such element is in the container, the returned iterator is `end()` (line 27).

Invoking `erase(2)` (line 32) deletes all the elements with key value `2` from the set.

This example created a `multiset`. You can replace `multiset` by `set` as follows:

```
set<int> set1(values, values + 6);
```

Trace the program with this new statement.

### 19.5.2  Associative Containers: `map` and `multimap`

Each element in a `map/multimap` is a pair. The first value in the pair is the key, and the second value is associated with the key. A `map/multimap` provides quick access to value using the key. A `multimap` allows duplicate keys, but a `map` does not. Listing 19.11 demonstrates how to use the `map` and `multimap` containers.

### LISTING 19.11  MapDemo.cpp

include map

```
1 #include <iostream>
2 #include <map>
3 #include <string>
4 using namespace std;
5
```

```
 6 int main()
 7 {
 8    map<int, string> map1;
 9    map1.insert(map<int, string>::value_type(100, "John Smith"));
10    map1.insert(map<int, string>::value_type(101, "Peter King"));
11    map1.insert(map<int, string>::value_type(102, "Jane Smith"));
12    map1.insert(map<int, string>::value_type(103, "Jeff Reed"));
13
14    cout << "Initial contents in map1:\n";
15    map<int, string>::iterator p;
16    for (p = map1.begin(); p != map1.end(); p++)
17      cout << p->first << " " << p->second << endl;
18
19    cout << "Enter a key to serach for the name: ";
20    int key;
21    cin >> key;
22    p = map1.find(key);
23
24    if (p == map1.end())
25      cout << "  Key " << key << " not found in map1";
26    else
27      cout << "  " << p->first << " " << p->second << endl;
28
29    map1.erase(103);
30    cout << "\nAfter the erase function, map1:\n";
31    for (p = map1.begin(); p != map1.end(); p++)
32      cout << p->first << " " << p->second << endl;
33
34    return 0;
35 }
```

create **map1**
insert pairs

**map1** iterator

map1 iterator
traversing map
key/value

find key

found?

erase a pair

key/value

```
Initial contents in map1:
100 John Smith
101 Peter King
102 Jane Smith
103 Jeff Reed
Enter a key to serach for the name: 105 ⏎Enter
    Key 105 not found in map1

After the erase function, map1:
100 John Smith
101 Peter King
102 Jane Smith
```

The program creates a map **map1** using its no-arg constructor (line 8), and inserts key/value pairs to **map1** (lines 9–12). To insert an element to a map, you have to create a pair using the **value_type(key, value)** function.

The program prompts the user to enter a key (lines 19–21). Invoking **find(key)** returns the iterator that points to the element with the specified key (line 22). A pair consists of the key and the value, which can be accessed using **p->first** and **p->second** (line 27).

Invoking **erase(103)** deletes the element with key **103** (line 29).

This example created a **map**. You can replace **map** by **multipmap** as follows:

```
multimap<int, string> map1;
```

The program runs exactly the same as using a **map**.

## 19.6 Container Adapters

The STL provides three container adapters: `stack`, `queue`, and `priority_queue`. These containers are called *adapters* because they are adapted from the sequence containers for handling special cases. The STL enables the programmer to choose an appropriate sequence container for a container adapter. For example, you can create a stack with the underlying data structure `vector`, `deque`, or `list`.

Container adapters do not have iterators. Table 19.2 listed the functions common to all the containers. In addition to these common functions, each container adapter supports the `push` and `pop` functions to insert and remove an element.

### 19.6.1 Container Adapter: `stack`

A stack is a last-in first-out container. You can choose a `vector`, `deque`, or `list` to construct a `stack`. By default, a `stack` is implemented with a `deque`. The common functions on a `stack` are listed in Table 19.11.

**TABLE 19.11** Functions in `stack`

| Functions | Description |
| --- | --- |
| push(element) | Inserts the element to the top of the stack. |
| pop() | Removes an element from the top of the stack. |
| top() | Returns the top element from the stack without removing it. |
| size() | Returns the size of the stack. |
| empty() | Returns true if the stack is empty. |

Listing 19.12 gives an example on how to use `stack`.

**LISTING 19.12** StackDemo.cpp

```cpp
1  #include <iostream>
2  #include <stack>
3  #include <vector>
4  using namespace std;
5
6  template<typename T>
7  void printStack(T &stackRef)
8  {
9    while (!stackRef.empty())
10   {
11     cout << stackRef.top() << " ";
12     stackRef.pop();
13   }
14 }
15
16 int main()
17 {
18   stack<int> stack1;
19   stack<int, vector<int> > stack2;
20
21   for (int i = 0; i < 8; i++)
22   {
23     stack1.push(i);
24     stack2.push(i);
25   }
```

include stack

is empty?

get top
remove top

create **stack1**
create **stack2**

insert to **stack1**
insert to **stack2**

```
26
27    cout << "Contents in stack1: ";
28    printStack(stack1);
29
30    cout << "\nContents in stack2: ";
31    printStack(stack2);
32
33    return 0;
34 }
```

invoke **printStack**

```
Contents in stack1: 7 6 5 4 3 2 1 0
Contents in stack2: 7 6 5 4 3 2 1 0
```

This program creates a **stack** using the default implementation in line 18 and a **stack** using the **vector** implementation in line 19.

The program inserts numbers from **0** to **7** to **stack1** and **stack2** (lines 21–25) and invokes **printStack(stack1)** and **printStack(stack2)** to display and remove all the elements in **stack1** and **stack2**.

## 19.6.2  Container Adapter: queue

A queue is a first-in first-out container. You can choose a **deque** or **list** to construct a **queue**. By default, a **queue** is implemented with a **deque**. The common functions on a **queue** are listed in Table 19.12.

**TABLE 19.12**  Functions in queue

| Functions | Description |
| --- | --- |
| push(element) | Inserts the element to the top of the queue. |
| pop() | Removes an element from the top of the queue. |
| front() | Returns the front element from the queue without removing it. |
| back() | Returns the back element from the queue without removing it. |
| size() | Returns the size of the queue. |
| empty() | Returns true if the queue is empty. |

Listing 19.13 gives an example on how to use **queue**.

## LISTING 19.13  QueueDemo.cpp

```
1 #include <iostream>
2 #include <queue>
3 #include <list>
4 using namespace std;
5
6 template<typename T>
7 void printQueue(T &queue)
8 {
9    while (!queue.empty())
10   {
11     cout << queue.front() << " ";
12     queue.pop();
13   }
14 }
```

include queue

is empty?

get front
remove element

```
15
16 int main()
17 {
18   queue<int> queue1;
19   queue<int, list<int> > queue2;
20
21   for (int i = 0; i < 8; i++)
22   {
23     queue1.push(i);
24     queue2.push(i);
25   }
26
27   cout << "Contents in queue1: ";
28   printQueue(queue1);
29
30   cout << "\nContents in queue2: ";
31   printQueue(queue2);
32
33   return 0;
34 }
```

create **queue1**
create **queue2**

insert to **queue1**
insert to **queue2**

invoke **printQueue**

```
Contents in queue1: 0 1 2 3 4 5 6 7
Contents in queue2: 0 1 2 3 4 5 6 7
```

This program creates a queue using the default implementation in line 18 and a queue using the list implementation in line 19.

The program inserts numbers from 0 to 7 to queue1 and queue2 (lines 23–24) and invokes printQueue(queue1) and printQueue(queue2) to display and remove all the elements in queue1 and queue2.

### 19.6.3 Container Adapter: `priority_queue`

In a priority queue, elements are assigned with priorities. The element with the highest priority is accessed or removed first. A priority queue has a largest-in, first-out behavior.

You can choose a vector or deque to construct a priority_queue. By default, a priority_queue is implemented with a vector. The priority_queue class uses the same functions push, pop, top, size, and empty as in the stack class.

Listing 19.14 gives an example on how to use priority_queue.

### LISTING 19.14 PriorityQueueDemo.cpp

include queue

is empty?

get top
remove element

```
1 #include <iostream>
2 #include <queue>
3 #include <deque>
4 using namespace std;
5
6 template<typename T>
7 void printQueue(T &priority_queue)
8 {
9   while (!priority_queue.empty())
10  {
11    cout << priority_queue.top() << " ";
12    priority_queue.pop();
13  }
14 }
15
```

```
16 int main()
17 {
18    priority_queue<int> priority_queue1;
19    priority_queue<int, deque<int> > priority_queue2;
20
21    for (int i = 0; i < 8; i++)
22    {
23      priority_queue1.push(i);
24      priority_queue2.push(i);
25    }
26
27    cout << "Contents in priority_queue1: ";
28    printQueue(priority_queue1);
29
30    cout << "\nContents in priority_queue2: ";
31    printQueue(priority_queue2);
32
33    return 0;
34 }
```

create **queue1**
create **queue2**

insert to **queue1**
insert to **queue2**

invoke **printQueue**

```
Contents in priority_queue1: 7 6 5 4 3 2 1 0
Contents in priority_queue2: 7 6 5 4 3 2 1 0
```

This program creates a `priority_queue` using the default implementation in line 18 and a `priority_queue` using the **deque** implementation in line 19.

The program inserts numbers from 0 to 7 to queue1 and queue2 (lines 23–24) and invokes `printQueue(queue1)` and `printQueue(queue2)` to display and remove all the elements in queue1 and queue2. Since the queues are priority queues, the largest numbers are accessed and removed first.

## KEY TERMS

| | |
|---|---|
| associative container    566 | multimap    568 |
| bidirectional iterator    555 | multiset    567 |
| container    548 | ostream_iterator    559 |
| container adapter    570 | output iterator    555 |
| deque    562 | priority_queue    572 |
| first-class container    548 | random-access iterator    555 |
| forward iterator    555 | queue    571 |
| input iterator    555 | sequence container    560 |
| istream_iterator    559 | set    567 |
| iterator    553 | STL algorithm    548 |
| list    563 | vector    560 |
| map    568 | |

## CHAPTER SUMMARY

■   The *Standard Template Library (STL)* contains useful data structures. You can use them without having to reinvent the wheel.

■   A container object such as a vector is used to store a collection of data, often referred to as *elements*.

- The STL container classes make extensive use of iterators, which are objects that facilitate traversing through the elements in a container. Iterators are like built-in pointers that provide a convenient way to access and manipulate the elements in a container.

- The sequence containers (also known as sequential containers) represent linear data structures. The three sequence containers are `vector`, `list`, and `deque`.

- Associative containers are non-linear containers that can locate elements stored in the container quickly. Such containers can store sets of values or *key/value* pairs. The four associative containers are `set`, `multiset`, `map`, and `multimap`.

- Container adapters are constrained versions of sequence containers. They are adapted from sequence containers for handling special cases. The three container adapters are `stack`, `queue`, and `priority_queue`.

- An iterator is an abstraction of a pointer, and in fact, it is typically implemented using a pointer. Each container has its own iterator type. The abstraction hides the detailed implementation and provides a uniform way for using iterators on all containers.

- Iterators can be classified into five categories: input iterators, output iterators, forward iterators, bidirectional iterators, and random-access iterators.

- An input iterator is used for reading an element from a container. An output iterator is used for writing an element to a container. A forward iterator combines all the functionalities of input and output iterators to support both read and write operations. A bidirectional iterator is a forward iterator with the capability of moving backward. A random-access iterator is a bidirectional iterator with the capability of accessing any element in any order.

- The iterator type determines which operators can be used. The `vector` and `deque` containers support random-access iterators, and the `list`, `set`, `multiset`, `map`, and `multimap` containers support bidirectional iterators. The `stack`, `queue`, and `priority_queue` don't support iterators.

- A vector is efficient if the elements are appended to the vector. It is expensive to insert or delete elements in the middle of a vector.

- A deque is like a vector, but it is efficient for insertion at both the front and end of a deque. It is still expensive to insert or delete elements in the middle of a deque.

- A linked list is good for applications that require frequent insertion and deletion in the middle of a list.

- The `set` and `multiset` containers are identical, except that a `multiset` allows duplicate keys and a `set` does not.

- The `map` and `multimap` are identical, except that a `multimap` allows duplicate keys and a `map` does not.

# REVIEW QUESTIONS

## Section 19.2 STL Basics

**19.1**   What are the three main components of the STL? What are the relationships among them?

**19.2**   What are the three types of containers? What are they used for?

**19.3**   Does C++ define a base class for all containers?

**19.4**   Which of the following are the common features for all containers?

   a. Each container has a no-arg constructor.
   b. Each container has a copy constructor.
   c. Each container has the `empty()` function to check whether a container is empty.
   d. Each container has the `size()` function to return the number of elements in the container.
   e. Each container supports the relational operators (`<`, `<=`, `>`, `>=`, `==`, and `!=`).

**19.5**   What is a first-class container?

**19.6**   Which containers use iterators?

**19.7**   Which of the following are the common features for all first-class containers?

   a. Each first-class container has the `swap` function.
   b. Each first-class container has the `max_size()` function.
   c. Each first-class container has the `clear()` function.
   d. Each first-class container has the `erase` function.
   e. Each first-class container has the `add` function.

## Section 19.3 Iterators

**19.8**   Does an iterator act like a pointer to an element? How do you obtain the iterator for the first element in a container? How do you obtain the iterator that points to the next element after the last element in a container?

**19.9**   Show the output of the following code:

```
vector<int> intVector;
intVector.push_back(1);
intVector.push_back(2);
intVector.push_back(3);
intVector.push_back(4);

vector<int>::iterator p;
for (p = intVector.begin(); p != intVector.end(); p++)
{
   cout << *p << " ";
}
cout << "\nsize " << intVector.size() << " ";
```

**19.10**   List the types of iterators.

## Section 19.4 Sequence Containers

**19.11**   For what applications should you use a `vector`, a `deque`, or a `list`? What types of the iterators are supported in a `vector`, a `deque`, and a `list`?

**19.12**   What is wrong in the following code?

```
vector<int> intVector;
intVector.assign(4, 20);
intVector.insert(1, 10);
```

**19.13** How do you remove elements in a **vector**, a **deque**, or a **list**?

**19.14** Are the **sort**, **splice**, **merge,** and **reverse** functions contained in **vector**, **deque**, or **list**?

### Section 19.5 Associative Containers

**19.15** For what applications should you use a **set** or **multiset**? What are the differences between **set** and **multiset**?

**19.16** Show the output of the following code:

```
set<int> intSet;
intSet.insert(20);
intSet.insert(10);
intSet.erase(30);
intSet.insert(10);

set<int>::iterator p;
for (p = intSet.begin(); p != intSet.end(); p++)
{
  cout << *p << " ";
}
```

**19.17** Show the output of the following code:

```
multiset<int> intSet;
intSet.insert(20);
intSet.insert(10);
intSet.erase(30);
intSet.insert(10);

set<int>::iterator p;
for (p = intSet.begin(); p != intSet.end(); p++)
{
  cout << *p << " ";
}
```

**19.18** What is wrong in the following code?

```
set<int> intSet;
intSet.insert(20);
intSet.insert(10);
cout << "\nfind 40? " << (intSet.find(40) ? "true" : "false")
  << " ";
```

**19.19** For what applications should you use a **map** or **multimap**? What are the differences between **map** and **multimap**?

**19.20** Show the output of the following code:

```
map<int, string> map1;
map1.insert(map<int, string>::value_type(100, "John Smith"));
map1.insert(map<int, string>::value_type(101, "Peter King"));
map1.insert(map<int, string>::value_type(100, "Jane Smith"));

map<int, string>::iterator p;
for (p = map1.begin(); p != map1.end(); p++)
{
  cout << p->first << " " << p->second << endl;
}
```

**19.21** Show the output of the following code:

```
multimap<int, string> map1;
map1.insert(map<int, string>::value_type(100, "John Smith"));
map1.insert(map<int, string>::value_type(101, "Peter King"));
map1.insert(map<int, string>::value_type(100, "Jane Smith"));

map<int, string>::iterator p;
for (p = map1.begin(); p != map1.end(); p++)
{
  cout << p->first << " " << p->second << endl;
}
```

**19.22** What is the header file for `set`? What is the header file for `multiset`? What is the header file for `map`? What is the header file for `multimap`?

## Section 19.6 Container Adapters

**19.23** Why container adapters are called adapters? Do container adapters have iterators?

**19.24** Can you create a `stack`, `queue`, or `priority_queue` using a `vector`, `deque`, or `list`?

**19.25** How do you insert elements to a `priority_queue`? How do you remove elements from a `priority_queue`? How do you find the size of a `priority_queue`?

## PROGRAMMING EXERCISES

**19.1*** (*Maximum and minimum*) Implement the following functions that find the maximum and minimum elements in a first-class container:

```
template<typename ElementType, typename ContainerType>
ElementType maxElement(ContainerType &container)
```

```
template<typename ElementType, typename ContainerType>
ElementType minElement(ContainerType &container)
```

**19.2*** (*Position of a value*) Implement the following function that finds the position of a specified value in a first-class container. Return `-1` if there is no match.

```
template<typename ElementType, typename ContainerType>
ElementType find(ContainerType &container,
  const ElementType &value)
```

**19.3*** (*Occurrence of a value*) Implement the following function that finds the number of occurrences of a specified value in a first-class container:

```
template<typename ElementType, typename ContainerType>
int countElement(ContainerType &container, const ElementType
  &value)
```

**19.4*** (*Reversing a container*) Implement the following function that reverses the elements in a container:

```
template<typename ContainerType>
void reverse(ContainerType &container)
```

**19.5*** (*Removing elements*) Implement the following function that removes the specified values from a first-class container. The elements after the removed elements are moved to fill in for the removed elements. The total number of the elements in a container is not changed by this function.

```
template<typename ElementType, typename ContainerType>
void remove(ContainerType &container, const ElementType &value)
```

**19.6*** (*Replacing elements*) Implement the following function that replaces a given element with a new value:

```
template<typename ElementType, typename ContainerType>
void replace(ContainerType &container,
    const ElementType &oldValue, const ElementType &newValue)
```

**19.7**** (*Union of two sets*) Implement the following mathematical set union function to combine two sets s1 and s2 into a new set s3:

```
void union(set &s1, set &s2, set &s3);
```

**19.8**** (*Difference of two sets*) Implement the following mathematical set difference function to produce a new set s3 from the difference between s1 and s2:

```
void difference(set &s1, set &s2, set &s3);
```

**19.9**** (*Displaying nonduplicate words in ascending order*) Write a program that reads words from a text file and displays all the nonduplicate words in ascending order. (*Hint:* Use a set to store all the words.)

**19.10**** (*Displaying duplicate words in ascending order*) Write a program that reads words from a text file and displays all the words (duplicates allowed) in ascending order. (*Hint:* Use a multiset to store all the words.)

**19.11**** (*Counting the keywords in C++ source code*) Write a program that reads a C++ source code file and reports the number of keywords in the file. (*Hint:* Create a set to store all the C++ keywords.)

**19.12**** (*Counting the occurrences of numbers entered*) Write a program that reads an unspecified number of integers and finds the one that has the most occurrences. Your input ends when the input is 0. For example, if you entered 2 3 40 3 5 4 –3 3 3 2 0, the number 3 occurred most often. Please enter one number at a time. If not one but several numbers have the most occurrences, all of them should be reported. For example, since 9 and 3 appear twice in the list 9 30 3 9 3 2 4, both should be reported. (*Hint:* Use a map to store pairs. The first element in the pair is a number entered from the input, and the second element tracks the number of occurrences of this number.)

**19.13**** (*Counting the occurrences of words*) Write a program that counts the occurrences of words in a text and displays the words and their occurrences in ascending order of word frequency. The program uses a map to store a pair consisting of a word and its count. For each word, check whether it is already a key in the map. If not, add the key and value 1 to the map. Otherwise, increase the value for the word (key) by 1 in the map.

## CHAPTER 20

# STL Algorithms

## Objectives

- To know how to use various types of iterators with the STL algorithms (§§20.1–20.20).

- To know the four types of STL algorithms (§20.2).

- To use the copy algorithm (§20.3).

- To use the algorithms fill, fill_n, generate, and generate_n (§§20.4–20.5).

- To use the algorithms remove, remove_if, remove_copy, and remove_copy_if (§20.6).

- To use Boolean functions to specify criteria for STL algorithms (§20.6).

- To use the algorithms replace, replace_if, replace_copy, and replace_copy_if, find, find_if, find_end, and find_first_of (§§20.7–20.8).

- To use the algorithms search, search_n, sort, binary_search, adjacent_find, merge, and inplace_merge (§§20.9–20.11).

- To use function objects in STL algorithms (§20.10).

- To use the algorithms reverse, reverse_copy, rotate, rotate_copy, swap, iter_swap, and swap_range (§§20.12–20.14).

- To use the algorithms count, count_if, max_element, min_element, random_shuffle, for_each, and transform (§§20.15–20.18).

- To use set algorithms includes, set_union, set_difference, set_intersection, and set_symmetric_difference (§20.19).

- To use numeric algorithms accumulate, adjacent_sort, inner_product, and partial_sum (§20.20).

## 20.1 Introduction

Often you need to find an element in a container, replace an element with a new element in a container, remove elements from a container, fill the container with some elements, reverse the elements in a container, find the maximum or minimum element in a container, and sort the elements in a container. These functions are common to all containers. Rather than implementing them in each container, the STL supports these operations as generic algorithms that can be applied to a variety of containers as well as arrays. The algorithms operate on the elements through iterators.

Prior to the STL, algorithms were implemented in the classes with inheritance and polymorphism. The STL separates algorithms from the containers. This enables the algorithms to be applied generically to all containers through iterators. The STL makes the algorithms and containers easy to maintain.

function and algorithm

**Note**

The terms operations, algorithms, and functions are interchangeable. Functions are operations and functions are implemented using algorithms.

iterators and pointers

**Note**

Iterators are a generalization of pointers. Pointers themselves are iterators. So the array pointers can be treated as iterators. Iterators are often used with containers, but some iterators such as `istream_iterator` and `ostream_iterator` are not associated with containers at all.

## 20.2 Types of Algorithms

The STL provides approximately 80 algorithms. The algorithms can be classified into four groups:

nonmodifying algorithms

- **Nonmodifying Algorithms:** Nonmodifying algorithms do not change the contents in the container. They obtain information from the elements. The nonmodifying algorithms are listed in Table 20.1.

**TABLE 20.1** Nonmodifying Algorithms

| | | | |
|---|---|---|---|
| adjacent_find | find | lower_bound | search |
| binary_search | find_end | mismatch | search_n |
| count | find_first_of | max | upper_bound |
| count_if | find_if | max_element | |
| equal | for_each | min | |
| equal_range | includes | min_element | |

modifying algorithms

- **Modifying Algorithms:** Modifying algorithms modify the elements in the container by insertion, removing, rearranging, and changing the values of the elements. Table 20.2 lists these algorithms.

numeric algorithms

- **Numeric Algorithms:** Numeric algorithms provide four numeric operations for computing accumulate, adjacent difference, partial sum, and inner product. Table 20.3 lists these algorithms.

heap algorithms

- **Heap Algorithms:** Heap algorithms provide four operations for creating a heap, removing and inserting elements from/to a heap, and sorting a heap.

**TABLE 20.2** Modifying Algorithms

| | | |
|---|---|---|
| copy | prev_permutation | rotate_copy |
| copy_backward | random_shuffle | set_difference |
| fill | remove | set_intersection |
| fill_n | remove_copy | set_symmetric_difference |
| generate | remove_copy_if | set_union |
| generate_n | remove_if | sort |
| inplace_merge | replace | stable_partition |
| iter_swap | replace_copy | stable_sort |
| merge | replace_copy_if | swap |
| next_permutation | replace_if | swap_ranges |
| nth_element | reverse | transform |
| partial_sort | reverse_copy | unique |
| partial_sort_copy | rotate | unique_copy |
| partition | | |

**TABLE 20.3** Numeric Algorithms

| | | | |
|---|---|---|---|
| accumulate | adjacent_difference | inner_product | partial_sum |

**TABLE 20.4** Heap Algorithms

| | | | |
|---|---|---|---|
| make_heap | pop_heap | push_heap | sort_heap |

The numeric algorithms are contained in the `<numeric>` header file, and all the other algorithms are contained in the `<algorithm>` header file.

All the algorithms operate through iterators. Recall that the STL defines five types of iterators: input, output, forward, bidirectional, and random access. The containers **vector** and **deque** support random-access iterators, and **list**, **set**, **multiset**, **map**, and **multimap** support bidirectional iterators. Most of the algorithms require a forward iterator. If an algorithm works with a weak iterator, it can automatically work with a stronger iterator.

Many algorithms operate on a sequence of elements pointed by two iterators. The first iterator points to the first element of the sequence, and the second points to the element after the last element of the sequence.

The rest of the chapter gives examples to demonstrate some frequently used algorithms.

## 20.3 copy

The **copy** function can be used to copy elements in a sequence from one container to another. The syntax is

```
template<typename InputIterator, typename OutputIterator>
OuputIterator copy(InputIterator beg, InputIterator end,
  OutputIterator targetPosition)
```

copy

The function copies the elements within the ranges **beg .. end - 1** from a source container to a target container starting at **targetPosition**, where **beg** and **end** are the iterators in the source container and **targetPosition** is the iterator in the target container. The function returns an iterator that points to the next position past the last element copied.

Listing 20.1 demonstrates how to use the **copy** function.

### LISTING 20.1 CopyDemo.cpp

```
 1 #include <iostream>
 2 #include <algorithm>
 3 #include <vector>
 4 #include <list>
 5 #include <iterator>
 6 using namespace std;
 7
 8 int main()
 9 {
10   int values[] = {1, 2, 3, 4, 5, 6};
11   vector<int> intVector(5);
12   list<int> intList(5);
13
14   copy(values + 2, values + 4, intVector.begin());
15   copy(values, values + 5, intList.begin());
16
17   cout << "After initial copy intVector: ";
18   for (int i = 0; i < intVector.size(); i++)
19   {
20     cout << intVector[i] << " ";
21   }
22
23   cout << "\nAfter initial copy intList: ";
24   for (list<int>::iterator p = intList.begin();
25     p != intList.end(); p++)
26   {
27     cout << *p << " ";
28   }
29
30   intVector.insert(intVector.begin(), 747);
31   ostream_iterator<int> output(cout, " ");
32   cout << "\nAfter the insertion function, intVector: ";
33   copy(intVector.begin(), intVector.end(), output);
34
35   cout << "\nAfter the copy function, intList: ";
36   copy(intVector.begin(), intVector.begin() + 4, intList.begin());
37   copy(intVector.begin(), intVector.end(), output);
38
39   return 0;
40 }
```

*Margin notes:*
include algorithm

create a vector
create a list

copy to vector
copy to list

insert to list
iterator for ostream

copy to cout

copy to list
copy to cout

```
After initial copy intVector: 3 4 0 0 0
After initial copy intList: 1 2 3 4 5
After the insertion function, intVector: 747 3 4 0 0 0
After the copy function, intList: 747 3 4 0 5
```

The program creates an array (line 10), a vector (line 11), and a list (line 12). The **copy** function copies the elements in **values[2]** and **values[3]** to the beginning of the vector (line 14), and the elements **values[0]**, **values[1]**, **values[2]**, **values[3]**, and **values[4]** to the beginning of the list (line 15).

You can copy elements from an array to a container. You can also copy elements from a container to an array or to an output stream.

The program inserts a new element to the vector (line 30), creates an output stream iterator (line 31), and copies the vector to the output stream iterator (line 33):

```
copy(intVector.begin(), intVector.end(), output);
```

copy to output

The elements in the list are displayed similarly (line 37).

**Tip**

It is convenient to use the **copy** function to write the elements from a container to an output stream.

write elements

**Caution**

Before copying **n** elements from a source to a target, the elements in the target must already exist. Otherwise, a runtime error may occur. For example, the following code will cause a runtime error, because the vector is empty:

possible copy errors

```
int values[] = {1, 2, 3, 4, 5, 6};
vector<int> intVector;
copy(values + 2, values + 4, intVector.begin()); // Error
```

## 20.4 **fill** and **fill_n**

The **fill** function can be used to fill a container with a specified value for the elements from iterator **beg** to **end** - 1, using the following syntax:

```
template<typename ForwardIterator, typename T>
void fill(ForwardIterator beg, ForwardIterator end, const T &value)
```

fill

The **fill_n** function can be used to fill a container with a specified value for the elements from iterator **beg** to **beg** + **n** - 1, using the following syntax:

```
template<typename ForwardIterator, typename size, typename T>
void fill_n(ForwardIterator beg, size n, const T &value)
```

fill_n

Listing 20.2 demonstrates how to use these two functions.

### LISTING 20.2   FillDemo.cpp

```
1  #include <iostream>
2  #include <algorithm>
3  #include <list>
4  #include <iterator>
5  using namespace std;
6
7  int main()
8  {
9      int values[] = {1, 2, 3, 4, 5, 6};
10     list<int> intList(values, values + 6);
11
12     ostream_iterator<int> output(cout, " ");
13     cout << "Initial contents, values: ";
14     copy(values, values + 6, output);
15     cout << "\nInitial contents, intList: ";
```

include algorithm

create an array
create a list

```
16     copy(intList.begin(), intList.end(), output);
17
18     fill(values + 2, values + 4, 88);
19     fill_n(intList.begin(), 2, 99);
20
21     cout << "\nAfter the fill function, values: ";
22     copy(values, values + 6, output);
23     cout << "\nAfter the fill_n function, intList: ";
24     copy(intList.begin(), intList.end(), output);
25
26     return 0;
27 }
```

fill values
fill 2 elements

```
Initial contents, values: 1 2 3 4 5 6
Initial contents, intList: 1 2 3 4 5 6
After the fill function, values: 1 2 88 88 5 6
After the fill_n function, intList: 99 99 3 4 5 6
```

The program creates an array (line 9) and a list (line 10). The `fill` function (line 18) fills `88` to the array in `values[2]` and `values[3]`. The `fill_n` function (line 19) fills 2 elements with value `99` starting from the beginning of the list.

## 20.5 `generate` and `generate_n`

The functions **generate** and **generate_n** fill a sequence with a value returned from a function, using the following syntax:

generate

```
template<typename ForwardIterator, typename function>
void generate(ForwardIterator beg, ForwardIterator end, function gen)
```

generate_n

```
template<typename ForwardIterator, typename size, typename function>
void generate_n(ForwardIterator beg, size n, function gen)
```

Listing 20.3 demonstrates how to use these two functions.

### LISTING 20.3 GenerateDemo.cpp

include algorithm

function **nextNum**

static local variable

create an array
create a list

```
 1 #include <iostream>
 2 #include <algorithm>
 3 #include <list>
 4 #include <iterator>
 5 using namespace std;
 6
 7 int nextNum()
 8 {
 9     static int n = 20;
10     return n++;
11 }
12
13 int main()
14 {
15     int values[] = {1, 2, 3, 4, 5, 6};
16     list<int> intList(values, values + 6);
17
18     ostream_iterator<int> output(cout, " ");
19     cout << "Initial contents, values: ";
20     copy(values, values + 6, output);
```

```
21    cout << "\nInitial contents, intList: ";
22    copy(intList.begin(), intList.end(), output);
23
24    generate(values + 2, values + 4, nextNum);                    fill generated values
25    generate_n(intList.begin(), 2, nextNum);                      fill generated values
26
27    cout << "\nAfter the generate function, values: ";
28    copy(values, values + 6, output);
29    cout << "\nAfter the generate_n function, intList: ";
30    copy(intList.begin(), intList.end(), output);
31
32    return 0;
33 }
```

```
Initial contents, values: 1 2 3 4 5 6
Initial contents, intList: 1 2 3 4 5 6
After the generate function, values: 1 2 20 21 5 6
After the generate_n function, intList: 22 23 3 4 5 6
```

The program creates an array (line 15) and a list (line 16). The **generate** function (line 24) fills the array elements **values[2]** and **values[3]** with the values generated from the **nextNum** function. Note that **n** is a static local variable (line 9), so the value of **n** is persistent for the lifetime of the program. Invoking **nextNum()** returns **20** the first time, **21** the second time, and the return value is always one more for the next call.

## 20.6 **remove**, **remove_if**, **remove_copy**, and **remove_copy_if**

The function **remove** removes the elements from a sequence that matches the specified **value**, using the following syntax:

```
template<typename ForwardIterator, typename T>
ForwardIterator remove(ForwardIterator beg,                      remove
    ForwardIterator end, const T &value)
```

The function **remove_if** removes all the elements from a sequence such that **boolFunction(element)** is **true**, using the following syntax:

```
template<typename ForwardIterator, typename boolFunction>
ForwardIterator remove_if(ForwardIterator beg,                   remove_if
    ForwardIterator end, boolFunction f)
```

Both **remove** and **remove_if** return an iterator that points to the position after the last element of the new range of the elements.

The function **remove_copy** copies all the elements in the sequence to the target container, except those whose value matches the specified value, using the following syntax:

```
template<typename InputIterator, typename OutputIterator, typename T>
OutputIterator remove_copy(InputIterator beg, InputIterator end,  remove_copy
    OutputIterator targetPosition, const T &value)
```

The function **remove_copy_if** copies all the elements in the sequence to the target container, except those for which **boolFunction(element)** is **true**, using the following syntax:

```
template<typename InputIterator, typename OutputIterator,
    typename boolFunction>
OutputIterator remove_copy_if(InputIterator beg, InputIterator end,  remove_copy_if
    OutputIterator targetPosition, boolFunction f)
```

Both `remove_copy` and `remove_copy_if` return an iterator that points to the position after the last element copied.

**Note**

Boolean function

Some STL algorithms allow you to pass the pointer of a Boolean function. The Boolean function is used to check whether an element satisfies a condition. For example, you may define a function named `greaterThan3(int element)` to check whether an element is greater than 3.

**Note**

size not changed

These four functions do not change the size of the container. Elements are moved to the beginning of the container. For example, suppose a list contains elements {1, 2, 3, 4, 5, 6}, after removing 2, the list contains {1, 3, 4, 5, 6, 6}. Note that the last element is 6.

**Note**

source not changed

The `remove_copy` and `remove_copy_if` functions copy the new contents to the target container, but do not change the source container.

Listing 20.4 demonstrates how to use the functions `remove` and `remove_if`.

### LISTING 20.4 RemoveDemo.cpp

include algorithm

function **greaterThan3**

create an array
create a list

**remove** function
**remove_if** function

```cpp
1  #include <iostream>
2  #include <algorithm>
3  #include <list>
4  #include <iterator>
5  using namespace std;
6
7  bool greaterThan3(int value)
8  {
9    return value > 3;
10 }
11
12 int main()
13 {
14   int values[] = {1, 7, 3, 4, 3, 6, 1, 2};
15   list<int> intList(values, values + 8);
16
17   ostream_iterator<int> output(cout, " ");
18   cout << "Initial contents, values: ";
19   copy(values, values + 8, output);
20   cout << "\nInitial contents, intList: ";
21   copy(intList.begin(), intList.end(), output);
22
23   remove(values, values + 8, 3);
24   remove_if(intList.begin(), intList.end(), greaterThan3);
25
26   cout << "\nAfter the remove function, values: ";
27   copy(values, values + 8, output);
28   cout << "\nAfter the remove_if function, intList: ";
29   copy(intList.begin(), intList.end(), output);
30
31   return 0;
32 }
```

```
Initial contents, values: 1 7 3 4 3 6 1 2
Initial contents, intList: 1 7 3 4 3 6 1 2
After the remove function, values: 1 7 4 6 1 2 1 2
After the remove_if function, intList: 1 3 3 1 2 6 1 2
```

The program creates an array (line 14), a list (line 15), and displays their initial contents (lines 17–21). The array is {1, 7, 3, 4, 3, 6, 1, 2}. The **remove** function (line 23) removes 3 from the array. The new array is {1, 7, 4, 6, 1, 2, 1, 2}.

The **remove_if** function (line 24) removes all the elements in the list such that **greaterThan3(element)** is **true**. Before invoking the function, the list is {1, 7, 3, 4, 3, 6, 1, 2}. After invoking the function, the list becomes {1, 3, 3, 1, 2, 6, 1, 2}.

Listing 20.5 demonstrates how to use the functions **remove_copy** and **remove_copy_if**.

**LISTING 20.5**  RemoveCopyDemo.cpp

```
 1 #include <iostream>
 2 #include <algorithm>                                              include algorithm
 3 #include <list>
 4 #include <iterator>
 5 using namespace std;
 6
 7 bool greaterThan3(int value)                                      function greaterThan3
 8 {
 9   return value > 3;
10 }
11
12 int main()
13 {
14   int values[] = {1, 7, 3, 4, 3, 6, 1, 2};                        create an array
15   list<int> intList(values, values + 8);                          create a list
16
17   ostream_iterator<int> output(cout, " ");
18   cout << "Initial contents, values: ";
19   copy(values, values + 8, output);
20   cout << "\nInitial contents, intList: ";
21   copy(intList.begin(), intList.end(), output);
22
23   int newValues[] = {9, 9, 9, 9, 9, 9, 9, 9};                     create an array
24   list<int> newIntList(values, values + 8);                       create a list
25   remove_copy(values, values + 8, newValues, 3);                  remove_copy function
26   remove_copy_if(intList.begin(), intList.end(), newIntList.begin(),   remove_copy_if function
27     greaterThan3);
28
29   cout << "\nAfter the remove_copy function, values: ";
30   copy(values, values + 8, output);
31   cout << "\nAfter the remove_copy_if function, intList: ";
32   copy(intList.begin(), intList.end(), output);
33   cout << "\nAfter the remove_copy function, newValues: ";
34   copy(newValues, newValues + 8, output);
35   cout << "\nAfter the remove_copy_if function, newIntList: ";
36   copy(newIntList.begin(), newIntList.end(), output);
37
38   return 0;
39 }
```

```
Initial contents, values: 1 7 3 4 3 6 1 2
Initial contents, intList: 1 7 3 4 3 6 1 2
After the remove_copy function, values: 1 7 3 4 3 6 1 2
After the remove_copy_if function, intList: 1 7 3 4 3 6 1 2
After the remove_copy function, newValues: 1 7 4 6 1 2 9 9
After the remove_copy_if function, newIntList: 1 3 3 1 2 6 1 2
```

The `remove_copy` function (line 25) removes 3 from array `values` and copies the rest to array `newValues`. The content of the original array is not changed. Before the copy, array `values` is {1, 7, 3, 4, 3, 6, 1, 2} and `newValues` is {9, 9, 9, 9, 9, 9, 9, 9}. After the copy, array `newValue`s becomes {1, 7, 4, 6, 1, 2, 9, 9}.

The `remove_copy_if` function (line 26) removes all the elements in the list such that `greaterThan3(element)` is `true`, and copies the rest to list `newIntList`. The content of the original list is not changed. Before the copy, list `intList` is {1, 7, 3, 4, 3, 6, 1, 2} and `newIntList` is {9, 9, 9, 9, 9, 9, 9, 9}. After the copy, list `newIntList` becomes {1, 3, 3, 1, 2, 6, 1, 2}.

## 20.7 `replace`, `replace_if`, `replace_copy`, and `replace_copy_if`

The `replace` function replaces all occurrences of a given value with a new value in a sequence, using the following syntax:

**replace**

```
template<typename ForwardIterator, typename T>
void replace(ForwardIterator beg, ForwardIterator end,
    const T &oldValue, const T &newValue)
```

The `replace_if` function replaces all occurrences of the element for which `boolFunction(element)` is `true`, with a new value, using the following syntax:

**replace_if**

```
template<typename ForwardIterator, typename boolFunction, typename T>
void replace_if(ForwardIterator beg, ForwardIterator end,
    boolFunction f, const T &newValue)
```

The function `replace_copy` replaces the occurrence of a given value with a new value and copies the result to the target container, using the following syntax:

**replace_copy**

```
template<typename ForwardIterator, typename OutputIterator,
    typename T>
ForwardIterator replace_copy(ForwardIterator beg,
    ForwardIterator end, OutputIterator targetPosition,
    T &oldValue, T &newValue)
```

The function `replace_copy_if` replaces the occurrence of the element for which `boolFunction(element)` is `true`, with a new value, and copies all the elements in the sequence to the target container, using the following syntax:

**replace_copy_if**

```
template<typename ForwardIterator, typename OutputIterator,
    typename boolFunction, typename T>
ForwardIterator replace_copy_if(ForwardIterator beg,
    ForwardIterator end, OutputIterator targetPosition,
    boolFunction f, const T &newValue)
```

Both `replace_copy` and `replace_copy_if` return an iterator that points to the position after the last element copied.

 **Note**

The `replace_copy` and `replace_copy_if` functions copy the new contents to the target container, but do not change the source container.

**source not changed**

Listing 20.6 demonstrates how to use the functions `replace` and `replace_if`.

LISTING 20.6   ReplaceDemo.cpp

```
1  #include <iostream>
2  #include <algorithm>
3  #include <list>
4  #include <iterator>
5  using namespace std;
6
7  bool greaterThan3(int value)
8  {
9     return value > 3;
10 }
11
12 int main()
13 {
14    int values[] = {1, 7, 3, 4, 3, 6, 1, 2};
15    list<int> intList(values, values + 8);
16
17    ostream_iterator<int> output(cout, " ");
18    cout << "Initial contents, values: ";
19    copy(values, values + 8, output);
20    cout << "\nInitial contents, intList: ";
21    copy(intList.begin(), intList.end(), output);
22
23    replace(values, values + 8, 3, 747);
24    replace_if(intList.begin(), intList.end(), greaterThan3, 747);
25
26    cout << "\nAfter the replace function, values: ";
27    copy(values, values + 8, output);
28    cout << "\nAfter the replace_if function, intList: ";
29    copy(intList.begin(), intList.end(), output);
30
31    return 0;
32 }
```

include algorithm

function **greaterThan3**

create an array
create a list

**replace** function
**replace_if** function

```
Initial contents, values: 1 7 3 4 3 6 1 2
Initial contents, intList: 1 7 3 4 3 6 1 2
After the replace function, values: 1 7 747 4 747 6 1 2
After the replace_if function, intList: 1 747 3 747 3 747 1 2
```

The program creates an array (line 14), a list (line 15), and displays their initial contents (lines 17–21). The array is {1, 7, 3, 4, 3, 6, 1, 2}. The **replace** function (line 23) replaces 3 with 747 in the array. The new array is {1, 7, 747, 4, 747, 6, 1, 2}.

The **replace_if** function (line 24) replaces all the elements in the list such that **greaterThan3(element)** is **true**. Before invoking the function, the list is {1, 7, 3, 4, 3, 6, 1, 2}. After invoking the function, the list becomes {1, 747, 3, 747, 3, 747, 1, 2}.

Listing 20.7 demonstrates how to use the functions **replace_copy** and **replace_copy_if**.

LISTING 20.7   ReplaceCopyDemo.cpp

```
1  #include <iostream>
2  #include <algorithm>
3  #include <list>
4  #include <iterator>
```

include algorithm

function **greaterThan3**

create an array
create a list

**replace_copy** function
**replace_copy_if** function

```cpp
 5  using namespace std;
 6
 7  bool greaterThan3(int value)
 8  {
 9     return value > 3;
10  }
11
12  int main()
13  {
14     int values[] = {1, 7, 3, 4, 3, 6, 1, 2};
15     list<int> intList(values, values + 8);
16
17     ostream_iterator<int> output(cout, " ");
18     cout << "Initial contents, values: ";
19     copy(values, values + 8, output);
20     cout << "\nInitial contents, intList: ";
21     copy(intList.begin(), intList.end(), output);
22
23     int newValues[] = {9, 9, 9, 9, 9, 9, 9, 9};
24     list<int> newIntList(values, values + 8);
25     replace_copy(values + 2, values + 5, newValues, 3, 88);
26     replace_copy_if(intList.begin(), intList.end(),
27        newIntList.begin(), greaterThan3, 88);
28
29     cout << "\nAfter the replace_copy function, values: ";
30     copy(values, values + 8, output);
31     cout << "\nAfter the replace_copy_if function, intList: ";
32     copy(intList.begin(), intList.end(), output);
33     cout << "\nAfter the replace_copy function, newValues: ";
34     copy(newValues, newValues + 8, output);
35     cout << "\nAfter the replace_copy_if function, newIntList: ";
36     copy(newIntList.begin(), newIntList.end(), output);
37
38     return 0;
39  }
```

```
Initial contents, values: 1 7 3 4 3 6 1 2
Initial contents, intList: 1 7 3 4 3 6 1 2
After the replace_copy function, values: 1 7 3 4 3 6 1 2
After the replace_copy_if function, intList: 1 7 3 4 3 6 1 2
After the replace_copy function, newValues: 88 4 88 9 9 9 9 9
After the replace_copy_if function, newIntList: 1 88 3 88 3 88 1 2
```

The `replace_copy` function (line 25) replaces 3 by 88 in array `values` and copies a partial array to array `newValues`. The content of the original array is not changed. Before the replacement, array `values` is {1, 7, 3, 4, 3, 6, 1, 2} and `newValues` is {9, 9, 9, 9, 9, 9, 9, 9}. After the replacement, array `newValues` becomes {88, 4, 88, 9, 9, 9, 9, 9}. Note that only a partial array from position 2 to 4 is copied to the target starting at position 0.

The `replace_copy_if` function (line 26) replaces all the elements in the list such that `greaterThan3(element)` is `true`, and copies the rest to list `newIntList`. The content of the original list is not changed. Before the replacement, list `intList` is {1, 7, 3, 4, 3, 6, 1, 2} and `newIntList` is {9, 9, 9, 9, 9, 9, 9, 9}. After the replacement, list `newIntList` becomes {1, 88, 3, 88, 3, 88, 1, 2}.

# 20.8 **find**, **find_if**, **find_end**, and **find_first_of**

The functions **find**, **find_if**, **find_end**, and **find_first_of** can be used to find the elements in sequence.

The **find** function searches for an element, using the syntax:

```
template<typename InputIterator, typename T>
InputIterator find(InputIterator beg, InputIterator end, T &value)
```
find

The **find_if** function searches for an element such that **boolFunction(element)** is **true**, using the syntax:

```
template<typename InputIterator, typename boolFunction>
InputIterator find_if(InputIterator beg, InputIterator end,
  boolFunction f)
```
find_if

Both functions return the iterator that points to the first matching element if found; otherwise, return **end**.

Listing 20.8 demonstrates how to use the functions **find** and **find_if**.

## LISTING 20.8 FindDemo.cpp

```cpp
 1 #include <iostream>
 2 #include <algorithm>
 3 #include <vector>
 4 #include <iterator>
 5 using namespace std;
 6
 7 int main()
 8 {
 9   int values[] = {1, 7, 3, 4, 3, 6, 1, 2};
10   vector<int> intVector(values, values + 8);
11
12   ostream_iterator<int> output(cout, " ");
13   cout << "values: ";
14   copy(values, values + 8, output);
15   cout << "\nintVector: ";
16   copy(intVector.begin(), intVector.end(), output);
17
18   int key;
19   cout << "\nEnter a key: ";
20   cin >> key;
21   cout << "Find " << key << " in values: ";
22   int *p = find(values, values + 8, key);
23   if (p != values + 8)
24     cout << "found at position " << (p - values);
25   else
26     cout << "not found";
27
28   cout << "\nFind " << key << " in intVector: ";
29   vector<int>::iterator itr = find(intVector.begin(),
30     intVector.end(), key);
31   if (itr != intVector.end())
32     cout << "found at position " << (itr - intVector.begin());
33   else
34     cout << "not found";
35
36   return 0;
37 }
```

include algorithm

create an array
create a vector

enter a key

find a key
found?
position

find a key

found?
position

```
values: 1 7 3 4 3 6 1 2
intVector: 1 7 3 4 3 6 1 2
Enter a key: 4 ↵Enter
Find 4 in values: found at position 3
Find 4 in intVector: found at position 3

values: 1 7 3 4 3 6 1 2
intVector: 1 7 3 4 3 6 1 2
Enter a key: 5 ↵Enter
Find 5 in values: not found
Find 5 in intVector: not found
```

The **find** function (line 22) returns the pointer of the first element in the array that matches the **key**. If not found, **p** is **values + 8** (line 23). If found, **(p – values)** is the position of the matching element.

The **find** function (line 29) returns the pointer of the first element in the vector that matches the **key**. If not found, **itr** is **intVector.end()** (line 31). If found, **(itr – intVector.end())** is the position of the matching element.

**find_end**

The **find_end** function is used to search a subsequence. It has two versions:

```
template<typename ForwardIterator1, typename ForwardIterator2>
ForwardIterator find_end(ForwardIterator1 beg1, ForwardIterator1 end1,
    ForwardIterator2 beg2, ForwardIterator2 end2)

template<typename ForwardIterator1, typename ForwardIterator2,
    typename boolFunction>
ForwardIterator find_end(ForwardIterator1 beg1, ForwardIterator1 end1,
    ForwardIterator2 beg2, ForwardIterator2 end2, boolFunction f)
```

Both functions search in sequence **beg1 .. end1 – 1** for a match of the entire sequence **beg2 .. end2 – 1**. If successful, return the position where the last match occurs; otherwise, return **end1**. In the first version, the elements are compared for equality; in the second version, the comparison **boolFunction(elementInFirstSequence, elementInSecondSequence)** must be **true**.

Listing 20.9 demonstrates how to use the two versions of the **find_end** function.

## LISTING 20.9 FindEndDemo.cpp

```
1  #include <iostream>
2  #include <algorithm>
3  #include <vector>
4  #include <iterator>
5  using namespace std;
6
7  int main()
8  {
9      int array1[] = {1, 7, 3, 4, 3, 6, 1, 2};
10     int array2[] = {3, 6, 1};
11     vector<int> intVector(array1, array1 + 8);
12
13     ostream_iterator<int> output(cout, " ");
14     cout << "array1: ";
15     copy(array1, array1 + 8, output);
16     cout << "\nintVector: ";
17     copy(intVector.begin(), intVector.end(), output);
```

include algorithm

create **array1**
create **array2**
create a vector

```
18
19   int *p = find_end(array1, array1 + 8, array2, array2 + 1);
20   if (p != array1 + 8)
21     cout << "\nfind {3} in array1 at position " << (p - array1);
22   else
23     cout << "\nnot found";
24
25   vector<int>::iterator itr =
26     find_end(intVector.begin(), intVector.end(), array2 + 1,
27       array2 + 2);
28   if (itr != intVector.end())
29     cout << "\nfind {6, 1} in intVector at position " <<
30       (itr - intVector.begin());
31   else
32     cout << "\nnot found";
33
34   return 0;
35 }
```

find a subsequence
found?
position

find a subsequence

found?

position

```
array1: 1 7 3 4 3 6 1 2
intVector: 1 7 3 4 3 6 1 2
find {3} in array1 at position 4
find {6, 1} in intVector at position 5
```

The program creates two arrays and a vector (lines 9–11). The contents of these three containers are:

```
array1: {1, 7, 3, 4, 3, 6, 1, 2}
array2: {3, 6, 1}
intVector: {1, 7, 3, 4, 3, 6, 1, 2}
```

Invoking **find_end(array1, array1 + 8, array2, array2 + 1)** searches **array1** to match {3, 6}. The position of the last successful match is 4.

Invoking **find_end(intVector.begin(), intVector.end(), array2 + 1, array2 + 2)** searches **intVector** to match {6, 1}. The position of the last successful match is 5.

The function **find_first_of** searches the first common element in two sequences. It has two versions:

**find_first_of**

```
template<typename ForwardIterator1, typename ForwardIterator2>
ForwardIterator find_first_of(ForwardIterator1 beg1,
  ForwardIterator1 end1, ForwardIterator2 beg2,
  ForwardIterator2 end2)


template<typename ForwardIterator1, typename ForwardIterator2,
  typename boolFunction>
ForwardIterator find_first_of(ForwardIterator1 beg1,
  ForwardIterator1 end1, ForwardIterator2 beg2,
  ForwardIterator2 end2, boolFunction)
```

Both functions return a position in the first sequence if there is a match; otherwise, return **end1**. In the first version, the elements are compared for equality; in the second version, the comparison **boolFunction(elementInFirstSequence, elementInSecondSequence)** must be **true**.

Listing 20.10 demonstrates how to use the two versions of the **find_first_of** function.

**LISTING 20.10** FindFirstOfDemo.cpp

include algorithm

function **greaterThan**

create **array1**
create **array2**
create a vector

find first
found?

position

find first

found?

position

```
 1 #include <iostream>
 2 #include <algorithm>
 3 #include <vector>
 4 #include <iterator>
 5 using namespace std;
 6
 7 bool greaterThan(int e1, int e2)
 8 {
 9   return e1 > e2;
10 }
11
12 int main()
13 {
14   int array1[] = {1, 7, 3, 4, 3, 6, 1, 2};
15   int array2[] = {9, 96, 21, 3, 2, 3, 1};
16   vector<int> intVector(array1, array1 + 8);
17
18   ostream_iterator<int> output(cout, " ");
19   cout << "array1: ";
20   copy(array1, array1 + 8, output);
21   cout << "\nintVector: ";
22   copy(intVector.begin(), intVector.end(), output);
23
24   int *p = find_first_of(array1, array1 + 8, array2 + 2, array2 + 4);
25   if (p != array1 + 8)
26     cout << "\nfind first of {21, 3} in array1 at position "
27       << (p - array1);
28   else
29     cout << "\nnot found";
30
31   vector<int>::iterator itr =
32     find_first_of (intVector.begin(), intVector.end(),
33       array2 + 2, array2 + 4, greaterThan);
34   if (itr != intVector.end())
35     cout << "\nfind {21, 3} in intVector at position " <<
36       (itr - intVector.begin()) ;
37   else
38     cout << "\nnot found";
39
40   return 0;
41 }
```

```
array1: 1 7 3 4 3 6 1 2
intVector: 1 7 3 4 3 6 1 2
find first of {21, 3} in array1 at position 2
find {21, 3} in intVector at position 1
```

The program creates two arrays and a vector (lines 9–11). The contents of these three containers are:

```
array1: {1, 7, 3, 4, 3, 6, 1, 2}
array2: {9, 96, 21, 3, 2, 3, 1}
intVector: {1, 7, 3, 4, 3, 6, 1, 2}
```

Invoking `find_first_of(array1, array1 + 8, array2 + 2, array2 + 4)` searches **array1** to find the first match in {21, 3}, which is 3. The position of 3 is **2** in **array1**.

Invoking **find_first_of(intVector.begin(), intVector.end(), array2 + 2, array2 + 4, greaterThan)** searches **intVector** to find the first element greater than the element in {21, 3}.

Element 7 in **intVector** satisfies the condition. The position of 7 in **intVector** is 1.

# 20.9 **search** and **search_n**

The function **search** is similar to the function **find_end**. Both searches for a subsequence. The **find_end** finds the last match, but **search** finds the first match. The **search** function has two versions:

```
template<typename ForwardIterator1, typename ForwardIterator2>
ForwardIterator search(ForwardIterator1 beg1, ForwardIterator1 end1,
    ForwardIterator2 beg2, ForwardIterator2 end2)
```

search

```
template<typename ForwardIterator1, typename ForwardIterator2,
    typename boolFunction>
ForwardIterator search(ForwardIterator1 beg1, ForwardIterator1 end1,
    ForwardIterator2 beg2, ForwardIterator2 end2, boolFunction)
```

Both functions return a position in the first sequence if there is a match; otherwise, return **end1**. In the first version, the elements are compared for equality; in the second version, the comparison **boolFunction(elementInFirstSequence, elementInSecondSequence)** must be **true**.

The **search_n** function searches for consecutive occurrences of a value in the sequence. The **search_n** function has two versions:

```
template<typename ForwardIterator, typename size, typename T>
ForwardIterator search_n(ForwardIterator beg,
    ForwardIterator end, size count, const T &value)
```

search_n

```
template<typename ForwardIterator, typename size,
    typename boolFunction>
ForwardIterator search_n(ForwardIterator1 beg,
    ForwardIterator1 end, size count, boolFunction f)
```

Both functions return a position of the matching element in the sequence if there is a match; otherwise, return **end**. In the first version, the elements are compared for equality; in the second version, the comparison **boolFunction(element)** must be **true**.

Listing 20.11 demonstrates how to use the functions **search** and **search_n**.

## LISTING 20.11 SearchDemo.cpp

```
 1 #include <iostream>
 2 #include <algorithm>
 3 #include <vector>
 4 #include <iterator>
 5 using namespace std;
 6
 7 int main()
 8 {
 9   int array1[] = {1, 7, 3, 4, 3, 3, 1, 2};
10   int array2[] = {9, 96, 4, 3, 2, 3, 1};
11   vector<int> intVector(array1, array1 + 8);
12
13   ostream_iterator<int> output(cout, " ");
14   cout << "array1: ";
15   copy(array1, array1 + 8, output);
```

include algorithm

create an array
create an array
create a vector

```
16    cout << "\nintVector: ";
17    copy(intVector.begin(), intVector.end(), output);
18
19    int *p = search(array1, array1 + 8, array2 + 2, array2 + 4);
20    if (p != array1 + 8)
21      cout << "\nSearch {4, 3} in array1 at position "
22        << (p - array1);
23    else
24      cout << "\nnot found";
25
26    vector<int>::iterator itr =
27      search_n(intVector.begin(), intVector.end(), 2, 3);
28    if (itr != intVector.end())
29      cout << "\nSearch two occurrences of 3 in intVector at position "
30        << (itr - intVector.begin());
31    else
32      cout << "\nnot found";
33
34    return 0;
35 }
```

*search subsequence* (margin, line 19)

*search a value* (margin, lines 26–27)

```
array1: 1 7 3 4 3 3 1 2
intVector: 1 7 3 4 3 3 1 2
Search {4, 3} in array1 at position 3
Search two occurrences of 3 in intVector at position 4
```

The program creates two arrays and a vector (lines 9–11). The contents of these three containers are:

```
array1: {1, 7, 3, 4, 3, 3, 1, 2}
array2: {9, 96, 4, 3, 2, 3, 1}
intVector: {1, 7, 3, 4, 3, 3, 1, 2}
```

Invoking **search(array1, array1 + 8, array2 + 2, array2 + 4)** searches **array1** to find the sequence {4, 3}. The matching position is 3 in **array1**.

Invoking **search_n(intVector.begin(), intVector.end(), 2, 3)** searches for two consecutive 3. The matching position is 4 in **array1**.

## 20.10 **sort** and **binary_search**

The **sort** function requires random-access iterators. You can apply it to sort an array, vector, or deque, using one of these two versions:

*sort* (margin)

```
template<typename RandomAccessIterator>
void sort(RandomAccessIterator beg, RandomAccessIterator end)
```

```
template<typename RandomAccessIterator, typename relationalOperator>
void sort(RandomAccessIterator beg, RandomAccessIterator end,
    relationalOperator op)
```

The **binary_search** function searches a value in a sorted sequence, using one of the two versions:

*binary_search* (margin)

```
template<typename ForwardIterator, typename T>
bool binary_search(ForwardIterator beg,
    ForwardIterator end, const T &value)
```

```
template<typename ForwardIterator, typename T,
   typename strictWeakOrdering>
bool binary_search(ForwardIterator beg,
   ForwardIterator end, const T &value, strictWeakOrdering op)
```

**Note**

Some STL algorithms allow you to pass a function operator. It is actually a *function object* and pointer of the object is passed to invoke an STL function. There are three kinds of function objects: relational, logic, and arithmetic, as shown in Table 20.5. The **sort** and **binary_search** algorithms require the relational operator. To use function objects, include the **<functional>** header.

function object

**TABLE 20.5** Function Objects

| STL Function Object | Type | STL Function Object | Type |
|---|---|---|---|
| equal_to<T> | Relational | plus<T> | Arithmetic |
| not_equal_to<T> | Relational | minus<T> | Arithmetic |
| greater<T> | Relational | multiplies<T> | Arithmetic |
| greater_equal<T> | Relational | divides<T> | Arithmetic |
| less<T> | Relational | modulus<T> | Arithmetic |
| less_equal<T> | Relational | negate<T> | Arithmetic |
| logical_and<T> | Logical | | |
| logical_not<T> | Logical | | |
| logical_or<T> | Logical | | |

**Note**

Strict weak ordering operators are **less<T>** and **greater(T)**. The first version of the **binary_search** algorithm uses the **less<T>** operator for comparison, and the second specifies **less<T>** or **greater(T)**.

Strict weak ordering

Listing 20.12 demonstrates how to use the functions **sort** and **binary_search**.

## LISTING 20.12  SortDemo.cpp

```
 1 #include <iostream>
 2 #include <algorithm>
 3 #include <iterator>
 4 #include <functional>
 5 using namespace std;
 6
 7 int main()
 8 {
 9   int array1[] = {1, 7, 3, 4, 3, 3, 1, 2};
10
11   ostream_iterator<int> output(cout, " ");
12   cout << "Before sort, array1: ";
13   copy(array1, array1 + 8, output);
14
15   sort(array1, array1 + 8);
16
17   cout << "\nAfter sort, array1: ";
18   copy(array1, array1 + 8, output);
19
```

include algorithm

create an array

sort array

binary search

```
20    cout << (binary_search(array1, array1 + 8, 4) ?
21      "\n4 is in array1" : "\n4 is not in array1");
22
```

sort

```
23    sort(array1, array1 + 8, greater<int>());
24
25    cout << "\nAfter sort with function operator(>), array1: ";
26    copy(array1, array1 + 8, output);
27
```

binary search

```
28    cout << (binary_search(array1, array1 + 8, 4,
29      greater<int>()) ?
30      "\n4 is in array1" : "\n4 is not in array1");
31
32    return 0;
33 }
```

```
Before sort, array1: 1 7 3 4 3 3 1 2
After sort, array1: 1 1 2 3 3 3 4 7
4 is in array1
After sort with function operator(>), array1: 7 4 3 3 3 2 1 1
4 is in array1
```

The default function operator for **sort** and **binary_search** is `less_equal`<T>(). Invoking **sort(array1, array1 + 8, greater_equal<int>())** (line 23) sorts the array using the `greater_equal`<int>() function object. Since the elements are ordered in decreasing order, you invoke `binary_search(array1, array1 + 8, 4, greater_equal<int>())` (lines 28–29) to perform binary search to find element **4** in **array1**.

## 20.11  adjacent_find, merge, and inplace_merge

The `adjacent_find` function looks for first occurrence of adjacent elements of equal value or satisfying **boolFunction(element)**, using the following syntax:

**adjacent_find**

```
template<typename ForwardIterator>
ForwardIterator adjacent_find(ForwardIterator beg,
  ForwardIterator end)
```

```
template<typename ForwardIterator, typename boolFunction>
ForwardIterator adjacent_find(ForwardIterator beg,
  ForwardIterator end, boolFunction f)
```

The `adjacent_find` function returns the iterator that points to the first element in the matching sequence. If not found, it returns `end`.

The `merge` function merges two sorted sequences into a new sequence, using the following syntax:

**merge**

```
template<typename InputIterator1, typename InputIterator2,
  typename OutputIterator>
OutputIterator merge(InputIterator1 beg1,
  InputIterator1 end1, InputIterator2 beg2,
  InputIterator2 end2, OutputIterator targetPosition)
```

```
template<typename InputIterator1, typename InputIterator2,
  typename OutputIterator, typename relationalOperator>
OutputIterator merge(InputIterator1 beg1,
  InputIterator1 end1, InputIterator2 beg2,
  InputIterator2 end2, OutputIterator targetPosition,
  relationalOperator)
```

The `inplace_merge` function merges the first part of the sequence with the second part; assume that the two parts contain sorted consecutive elements. The syntax is

```
template<typename BidirectionalIterator>
void inplace_merge(BidirectionIterator beg,
  BidirectionIterator middle, BidirectionIterator end)

template<typename BidirectionalIterator, typename relationalOperator>
void inplace_merge(BidirectionalIterator beg,
  BidirectionalIterator middle, BidirectionalIterator end,
  relationalOperator)
```
*inplace_merge*

The function merges the sorted consecutive sequences `beg..middle-1` with `middle..end-1`, and the sorted sequence is stored in the original sequence. Thus, this is called *inplace merge*.

Listing 20.13 demonstrates how to use the functions `adjacent_find`, `merge`, and `inplace_merge`.

## LISTING 20.13 MergeDemo.cpp

```cpp
 1 #include <iostream>
 2 #include <algorithm>
 3 #include <list>
 4 #include <iterator>
 5 using namespace std;
 6
 7 int main()
 8 {
 9   int array1[] = {1, 7, 3, 4, 3, 3, 1, 2};
10   list<int> intList(8);
11
12   ostream_iterator<int> output(cout, " ");
13   cout << "array1: ";
14   copy(array1, array1 + 8, output);
15
16   sort(array1, array1 + 3);
17   sort(array1 + 3, array1 + 8);
18   cout << "\nafter sort partial arrays, array1: ";
19   copy(array1, array1 + 8, output);
20
21   merge(array1, array1 + 3, array1 + 3, array1 + 8, intList.begin());
22   cout << "\nafter merger, intList: ";
23   copy(intList.begin(), intList.end(), output);
24
25   inplace_merge(array1, array1 + 3, array1 + 8);
26   cout << "\nafter inplace merger, array1: ";
27   copy(array1, array1 + 8, output);
28
29   return 0;
30 }
```
*include algorithm*

*create an array*
*create a list*

*sort partial array*
*sort partial array*

*merge arrays*

*inplace merger*

```
array1: 1 7 3 4 3 3 1 2
after sort partial arrays, array1: 1 3 7 1 2 3 3 4
after merger, intList: 1 1 2 3 3 3 4 7
after inplace merger, array1: 1 1 2 3 3 3 4 7
```

The program creates an array and a list (lines 9–10). The contents of the array are

　　array1: {1, 7, 3, 4, 3, 3, 1, 2}

After sorting {1, 7, 3}, and {4, 3, 3, 1, 2} (lines 16–17), the array becomes:

　　array1: {1, 3, 7, 1, 2, 3, 3, 4}

After merging {1, 3, 7} and {1, 2, 3, 3, 4} into **intList** (line 21), **intList** becomes

　　intList: {1, 1, 2, 3, 3, 3, 4, 7}

After inplace merging {1, 3, 7} and {1, 2, 3, 3, 4} (line 25), **array1** becomes

　　intList: {1, 1, 2, 3, 3, 3, 4, 7}

## 20.12  reverse and reverse_copy

The **reverse** function reverses the elements in a sequence. The **reverse_copy** function copies the elements in one sequence to the other in reverse order. The **reverse_copy** function does not change the contents in the source container. The syntax of these functions is

reverse

```
template<typename BidirectionalIterator>
void reverse(BidirectionalIterator beg,
  BidirectionalIterator end)
```

reverse_copy

```
template<typename BidirectionalIterator, typename OutputIterator>
OutputIterator reverse_copy(BidirectionalIterator beg,
  BidirectionalIterator end, OutputIterator targetPosition)
```

Listing 20.14 demonstrates how to use the functions **reverse** and **reverse_copy**.

### LISTING 20.14  ReverseDemo.cpp

include algorithm

```cpp
 1 #include <iostream>
 2 #include <algorithm>
 3 #include <list>
 4 #include <iterator>
 5 using namespace std;
 6
 7 int main()
 8 {
 9   int array1[] = {1, 7, 3, 4, 3, 3, 1, 2};
10   list<int> intList(8);
11
12   ostream_iterator<int> output(cout, " ");
13   cout << "array1: ";
14   copy(array1, array1 + 8, output);
15
16   reverse(array1, array1 + 8);
17   cout << "\nafter reverse arrays, array1: ";
18   copy(array1, array1 + 8, output);
19
20   reverse_copy(array1, array1 + 8, intList.begin());
21   cout << "\nafter reverse_copy, array1: ";
22   copy(array1, array1 + 8, output);
23   cout << "\nafter reverse_copy, intList: ";
24   copy(intList.begin(), intList.end(), output);
25
26   return 0;
27 }
```

create an array
create a list

reverse array
reverse copy

```
array1: 1 7 3 4 3 3 1 2
after reverse arrays, array1: 2 1 3 3 4 3 7 1
after reverse_copy, array1: 2 1 3 3 4 3 7 1
after reverse_copy, intList: 1 7 3 4 3 3 1 2
```

## 20.13 **rotate** and **rotate_copy**

The **rotate** function rotates the elements in a sequence, using the syntax:

```
template<typename ForwardIterator>
void rotate(ForwardIterator beg, ForwardIterator newBeg,
   ForwardIterator end)
```

rotate

The element specified by **newBeg** becomes the first element in the sequence after the rotate.

The **rotate_copy** function is similar to **rotate**, except that it copies the result to a target sequence, using the syntax:

```
template<typename ForwardIterator, typename OutputIterator>
OutputIterator rotate_copy(ForwardIterator beg, ForwardIterator newBeg,
   ForwardIterator end, OutputIterator targetPosition)
```

rotate_copy

Listing 20.15 demonstrates how to use the functions **reverse** and **reverse_copy**.

### LISTING 20.15   RotateDemo.cpp

```
 1 #include <iostream>
 2 #include <algorithm>
 3 #include <list>
 4 #include <iterator>
 5 using namespace std;
 6
 7 int main()
 8 {
 9   int array1[] = {1, 2, 3, 4, 5, 6, 7, 8};
10   list<int> intList(8);
11
12   ostream_iterator<int> output(cout, " ");
13   cout << "array1: ";
14   copy(array1, array1 + 8, output);
15
16   rotate(array1, array1 + 3, array1 + 8);
17   cout << "\nafter rotate arrays, array1: ";
18   copy(array1, array1 + 8, output);
19
20   rotate_copy(array1, array1 + 1, array1 + 8, intList.begin());
21   cout << "\nafter rotate_copy, array1: ";
22   copy(array1, array1 + 8, output);
23   cout << "\nafter rotate_copy, intList: ";
24   copy(intList.begin(), intList.end(), output);
25
26   return 0;
27 }
```

include algorithm

create an array
create a list

rotate array

rotate copy

```
array1: 1 2 3 4 5 6 7 8
after rotate arrays, array1: 4 5 6 7 8 1 2 3
after rotate_copy, array1: 4 5 6 7 8 1 2 3
after rotate_copy, intList: 5 6 7 8 1 2 3 4
```

The program creates an array and a list (lines 9–10). The contents of the array are:

```
array1: {1, 2, 3, 4, 5, 6, 7, 8}
```

The pointer `array1 + 3` points to 4, so after invoking `rotate(array1, array1 + 3, array1 + 8)`, `array1` becomes

```
array1: {4, 5, 6, 7, 8, 1, 2, 3}
```

Now the pointer `array1 + 1` points to 5, so after invoking `rotate_copy(array1, array1 + 1, array1 + 8, intList.begin())`, `intList` becomes

```
intList: {5, 6, 7, 8, 1, 2, 3, 4}
```

## 20.14 `swap`, `iter_swap`, and `swap_ranges`

The functions `swap`, `iter_swap`, and `swap_range` are used to swap elements. They are defined as follows:

*swap*

```
template<typename T>
void swap(T &value1, T &value2)
```

*iter_swap*

```
template<typename ForwardIterator1, typename ForwardIterator2>
void iter_swap(ForwardIterator p1, ForwardIterator p2)
```

*swap_ranges*

```
template<typename ForwardIterator1, typename ForwardIterator2>
ForwardIterator swap_ranges(
    ForwardIterator1 beg1, ForwardIterator1 end1,
    ForwardIterator2 beg2)
```

The `swap` function swaps the values in two variables. The `iter_swap` function swaps the values pointed to by the iterators. The `swap_ranges` function swaps two sequences.

Listing 20.16 demonstrates how to use these three functions.

### LISTING 20.16 SwapDemo.cpp

*include algorithm*

*create an array*

*swap variables*

*swap via iterators*

*swap ranges*

```
 1 #include <iostream>
 2 #include <algorithm>
 3 #include <iterator>
 4 using namespace std;
 5
 6 int main()
 7 {
 8   int array1[] = {1, 2, 3, 4, 5, 6, 7, 8};
 9   ostream_iterator<int> output(cout, " ");
10   cout << "array1: ";
11   copy(array1, array1 + 8, output);
12
13   cout << "\nafter swap variables, array1: ";
14   swap(array1[0], array1[1]);
15   copy(array1, array1 + 8, output);
16
17   cout << "\nafter swap via pointers, array1: ";
18   iter_swap(array1 + 2, array1 + 3);
19   copy(array1, array1 + 8, output);
20
21   cout << "\nafter swap ranges, array1: ";
22   swap_ranges(array1, array1 + 4, array1 + 4);
23   copy(array1, array1 + 8, output);
```

```
24
25   return 0;
26 }
```

```
array1: 1 2 3 4 5 6 7 8
after swap variables, array1: 2 1 3 4 5 6 7 8
after swap via pointers, array1: 2 1 4 3 5 6 7 8
after swap ranges, array1: 5 6 7 8 2 1 4 3
```

Invoking `swap(array1[0], array1[1])` swaps `array1[0]` with `array1[1]` (line 14).

Invoking `iter_swap(array1 + 2, array1 + 3)` swaps the elements pointed by `array1 + 2` and `array1 + 3` (line 18).

Invoking `swap_ranges(array1, array1 + 4, array1 + 4)` swaps the elements in `array1..array1 + 3` with the elements in `array1 + 4..array1 + 7` (line 22).

## 20.15 **count** and **count_if**

The **count** function counts the occurrence of a given value in the sequence, using the following syntax:

```
template<typename InputIterator, typename T>
int count(InputIterator beg, InputIterator end, const T &value)
```
count

The **count_if** function counts the occurrence of the elements such that `boolFunction(element)` is true, using the following syntax:

```
template<typename InputIterator, typename boolFunction>
int count_if(InputIterator beg, InputIterator end, boolFunction f)
```
count_if

Listing 20.17 demonstrates how to use these functions.

## LISTING 20.17 CountDemo.cpp

```
1  #include <iostream>
2  #include <algorithm>                                    include algorithm
3  using namespace std;
4
5  bool greaterThan1(int value)
6  {
7    return value > 1;                                      create an array
8  }
9
10 int main()
11 {
12   int array1[] = {1, 2, 3, 4, 5, 6, 7, 8};               create an array
13
14   cout << "The number of 1's in array1: " <<
15     count(array1, array1 + 8, 1) << endl;                count
16
17   cout << "The number of elements > 1 in array1: " <<
18     count_if(array1, array1 + 8, greaterThan1) << endl;  count_if
19
20   return 0;
21 }
```

```
The number of 1's in array1: 1
The number of elements > 1 in array1: 7
```

## 20.16 `max_element` and `min_element`

You are already familiar with the `max` and `min` functions. You can use the `max_element` and `min_element` to obtain the maximum element and minimum element in a sequence. The functions are defined as follows:

max_element

```
template<typename ForwardIterator>
ForwardIterator max_element(ForwardIterator beg,
    ForwardIterator end)
```

min_element

```
template<typename ForwardIterator>
ForwardIterator min_element(ForwardIterator beg,
    ForwardIterator end)
```

Listing 20.18 gives an example of how to use these functions.

### LISTING 20.18   MaxMinDemo.cpp

```
 1 #include <iostream>
 2 #include <algorithm>
 3 using namespace std;
 4
 5 int main()
 6 {
 7   int array1[] = {1, 2, 3, 4, 5, 6, 7, 8};
 8
 9   cout << "The max element in array1: " <<
10     *max_element(array1, array1 + 8) << endl;
11
12   cout << "The min element in array1: " <<
13     *min_element(array1, array1 + 8) << endl;
14
15   return 0;
16 }
```

include algorithm — line 2
create an array — line 7
max element — line 10
min element — line 13

```
The max element in array1: 8
The min element in array1: 1
```

## 20.17 `random_shuffle`

The `random_shuffle` function randomly reorders the elements in a sequence, using the following syntax:

random_shuffle

```
template<typename RandomAccessIterator>
void random_shuffle(RandomAccessIterator beg,
    RandomAccessIterator end)
```

Listing 20.19 gives an example of how to use this function.

### LISTING 20.19   ShuffleDemo.cpp

```
 1 #include <iostream>
 2 #include <algorithm>
```

include algorithm

```
 3 #include <iterator>
 4 using namespace std;
 5
 6 int main()
 7 {
 8   int array1[] = {1, 2, 3, 4, 5, 6, 7, 8};
 9   random_shuffle(array1, array1 + 8);
10   cout << "After random shuffle, array1: ";
11   ostream_iterator<int> output(cout, " ");
12   copy(array1, array1 + 8, output);
13
14   return 0;
15 }
```

create an array
random shuffle

```
After random shuffle, array1: 2 6 4 3 7 5 1 8
```

## 20.18 **for_each** and **transform**

The **for_each** function is used to process each element in a sequence by applying a function, using the following syntax:

```
template<typename InputIterator, typename function>
void for_each(InputIterator beg, InputIterator end, function f)
```

**for_each**

You can use the **transform** function to apply a function on each element in the sequence and copy the result to a target sequence. The function is defined as follows:

```
template<typename InputIterator, typename OutputIterator,
  typename function>
OutputIteration transform(InputIterator beg,
  InputIterator end, OutputIterator targetPosition, function f)
```

**transform**

Listing 20.20 demonstrates how to use these functions.

### LISTING 20.20  ForEachDemo.cpp

```
 1 #include <iostream>
 2 #include <algorithm>
 3 #include <vector>
 4 #include <iterator>
 5 using namespace std;
 6
 7 void display(int &value)
 8 {
 9   cout << value << " ";
10 }
11
12 int square(int &value)
13 {
14   return value * value;
15 }
16
17 int main()
18 {
19   int array1[] = {1, 2, 3, 4, 5, 6, 7, 8};
20   cout << "array1: ";
21   for_each(array1, array1 + 8, display);
22
```

include algorithm

function display

function square

**for_each**

```
transform
                23    vector<int> intVector(8);
                24    transform(array1, array1 + 8, intVector.begin(), square);
                25    cout << "\nintVector: ";
for_each
                26    for_each(intVector.begin(), intVector.end(), display);
                27
                28    return 0;
                29 }
```

```
array1: 1 2 3 4 5 6 7 8
intVector: 1 4 9 16 25 36 49 64
```

The `display` function (lines 7–10) displays a number to the console. Invoking `for_each(array1, array1 + 8, display)` (line 21) applies the `display` function to each element in the sequence. Thus, all the elements in `array1` are displayed.

The `square` function (lines 12–15) returns the square of a number. Invoking `transform(array1, array1 + 8, intVector.begin(), square)` (line 24) applies the `square` function to each element in the sequence and copies the new sequence to `intVector`.

## 20.19 `includes`, `set_union`, `set_difference`, `set_intersection`, and `set_symmetric_difference`

The STL supports the set operations for testing subset, union, difference, intersect, and symmetric difference. All these functions require that the elements in the sequences already are sorted.

The `includes` function returns `true` if the elements in the first sequence contain the elements in the second sequence.

```
includes
        template<typename InputIterator1, typename InputIterator2>
        bool includes(InputIterator1 beg1, InputIterator1 end1,
          InputIterator2 beg2, InputIterator2 end2)
```

The `set_union` function obtains the elements that belong to either sequence.

```
set_union
        template<typename InputIterator1, typename InputIterator2,
          typename OutputIterator>
        OutputIterator set_union(InputIterator1 beg1, InputIterator1 end1,
          InputIterator2 beg2, InputIterator2 end2,
          OutputIterator targetPosition)
```

The `set_difference` function obtains the elements that belong to the first sequence, but not in the second sequence.

```
set_difference
        template<typename InputIterator1, typename InputIterator2,
          typename OutputIterator>
        OutputIterator set_difference(InputIterator beg1,
          InputIterator end1,
          InputIterator beg2, InputIterator end2,
          OutputIterator targetPosition)
```

The `set_intersection` function obtains the elements that appear in both sequences.

```
template<typename InputIterator1, typename InputIterator2,
  typename OutputIterator>
```

```
OutputIterator set_intersection(InputIterator beg1,
  InputIterator end1,
  InputIterator beg2, InputIterator end2,
  OutputIterator targetPosition)
```
set_intersection

The **set_symmetric_difference** function obtains the elements that appear in either sequence, but not in both.

```
template<typename InputIterator1, typename InputIterator2,
  typename OutputIterator>
OutputIterator set_symmetric_difference(InputIterator beg1,
  InputIterator end1,
  InputIterator beg2, InputIterator end2,
  OutputIterator targetPosition)
```
set_symmetric_
difference

Suppose **array1** and **array2** are given as follows:

| array1 | array2 |
|---|---|
| {1, 2, 3, 4, 5, 6, 7, 8} | {1, 3, 6, 9, 12} |

Their set operations are shown here:

| Operation | Result |
|---|---|
| array1 union array2 | {1, 2, 3, 4, 5, 6, 7, 8, 9, 12} |
| array1 difference array2 | {2, 4, 5, 7, 8} |
| array1 intersection array2 | {1, 3, 6} |
| array1 symmetric_diff array2 | {2, 4, 5, 7, 8, 9, 12} |

 **Note**

The set functions return an iterator that points to the position after the last element in the target.

return iterator

Listing 20.21 demonstrates how to use set functions.

## LISTING 20.21 SetOperationDemo.cpp

```
 1 #include <iostream>
 2 #include <algorithm>
 3 #include <vector>
 4 #include <iterator>
 5 using namespace std;
 6
 7 int main()
 8 {
 9   int array1[] = {1, 2, 3, 4, 5, 6, 7, 8};
10   int array2[] = {1, 3, 6, 9, 12};
11   vector<int> intVector(15);
12
13   ostream_iterator<int> output(cout, " ");
14   cout << "array1: ";
15   copy(array1, array1 + 8, output);
16   cout << "\narray2: ";
17   copy(array2, array2 + 5, output);
18
19   bool isContained =
20     includes(array1, array1 + 8, array2, array2 + 3);
21   cout << (isContained ? "\n{1, 3, 6} is a subset of array1" :
22     "\n{1, 3, 6} is not a subset of array1");
23
```

include algorithm

create **array1**
create **array2**
create **intVector**

includes

**set_union**

```
24    vector<int>::iterator last = set_union(array1, array1 + 8,
25      array2, array2 + 5, intVector.begin());
26    cout << "\nAfter union, intVector: ";
27    copy(intVector.begin(), last, output);
28
```

**set_difference**

```
29    last = set_difference(array1, array1 + 8,
30      array2, array2 + 5, intVector.begin());
31    cout << "\nAfter difference, intVector: ";
32    copy(intVector.begin(), last, output);
33
```

**set_intersection**

```
34    last = set_intersection(array1, array1 + 8,
35      array2, array2 + 5, intVector.begin());
36    cout << "\nAfter intersection, intVector: ";
37    copy(intVector.begin(), last, output);
38
```

**set_symmetric_ difference**

```
39    last = set_symmetric_difference(array1, array1 + 8,
40      array2, array2 + 5, intVector.begin());
41    cout << "\nAfter symmetric difference, intVector: ";
42    copy(intVector.begin(), last, output);
43
44    return 0;
45 }
```

```
array1: 1 2 3 4 5 6 7 8
array2: 1 3 6 9 12
{1, 3, 6} is a subset of array1
After union, intVector: 1 2 3 4 5 6 7 8 9 12
After difference, intVector: 2 4 5 7 8
After intersection, intVector: 1 3 6
After symmetric difference, intVector: 2 4 5 7 8 9 12
```

The program creates two arrays and a vector (lines 9–11).

```
array1: {1, 2, 3, 4, 5, 6, 7, 8}
array2: {1, 3, 6, 9, 12}
```

Invoking `includes(array1, array1 + 8, array2, array2 + 3)` (line 20) returns `true`, because {1, 3, 6} is a subset of `array1`.

Invoking `set_union(array1, array1 + 8, array2, array2 + 5, intVector.begin())` (lines 24–25) obtains the union of `array1` and `array2` in `intVector`. `intVector` becomes

```
intVector: {1, 2, 3, 4, 5, 6, 7, 8, 9, 12}
```

Invoking `set_difference(array1, array1 + 8, array2, array2 + 5, intVector.begin())` (lines 29–30) obtains the difference between `array1` and `array2` in `intVector`. `intVector` becomes

```
intVector: {2, 4, 5, 7, 8}
```

Invoking `set_intersection(array1, array1 + 8, array2, array2 + 5, intVector.begin())` (lines 34–35) obtains the intersection between `array1` and `array2` in `intVector`. `intVector` becomes

```
intVector: {1, 3, 6}
```

Invoking **set_symmetric_difference(array1, array1 + 8, array2, array2 + 5, intVector.begin())** (lines 39–40) obtains the symmetric difference between **array1** and **array2** in **intVector**. **intVector** becomes

intVector: {2, 4, 5, 7, 8, 9, 12}

**Note**

The set operations store the contents to a result container. The size of this result container must be large enough to hold the result. So, **intVector** is declared with 15 elements (line 11). More-over, the number of elements in **intVector** does not change in this program. The result ele-ments are between **intVector.begin()** and **intVector.end()**.

resulting container

## 20.20 **accumulate**, **adjacent_difference**, **inner_product**, and **partial_sum**

The STL supports the mathematical functions **accumulate**, **adjacent_difference**, **inner_product**, and **partial_sum**. They are defined in the **<numeric>** header.

The **accumulate** function has two versions.

```
template<typename InputIterator, typename T>
T accumulate(InputIterator beg, InputIterator end, T initValue)
```

**accumulate**

```
template<typename InputIterator, typename T,
  typename arithmeticOperator>
T accumulate(InputIterator beg, InputIterator end, T initValue,
  arithmeticOperator op)
```

The first version returns the sum of all the elements and the **initValue**. The second version applies the arithmetic operators (e.g., multiplication) on the **initValue** with all the elements and returns the result. For example,

| array1 | Result of accumulate(array1, array1 + 5, 0) |
|---|---|
| {1, 2, 3, 4, 5} | 15 |

| array1 | Result of accumulate(array1, array1 + 5, 1, multiplies<int>()) |
|---|---|
| {1, 2, 3, 4, 5} | 120 |

The **adjacent_difference** function has two versions.

```
template<typename InputIterator, typename T>
OutputIterator adjacent_difference(InputIterator beg,
  InputIterator end, OutputIterator targetPosition)
```

**adjacent_difference**

```
template<typename InputIterator, typename T,
  typename arithmeticOperator>
OutputIterator adjacent_difference(InputIterator beg,
  InputIterator end, OutputIterator targetPosition,
  arithmeticOperator op)
```

The first version creates a sequence of elements in which the first element is the same as the first element in the input sequence, and each subsequent element is the difference between the current element and the previous element. The second version is the same as the first version, except that the specified arithmetic operator is applied to replace the subtraction operator. For example,

| array1 | Result of `adjacent_difference(array1,` `array1 + 5, intVector.begin())` |
|---|---|
| {1, 2, 3, 4, 5} | {1, 1, 1, 1, 1} |

The **inner_product** function has two versions.

**inner_product**

```
template<typename InputIterator1, typename InputIterator2,
  typename T>
T inner_product(InputIterator1 beg1,
  InputIterator1 end1, InputIterator2 beg2, T initValue)
```

```
template<typename InputIterator1, typename InputIterator2,
  typename T, typename arithmeticOperator1,
  typename arithmeticOperator2>
T inner_product(InputIterator1 beg1,
  InputIterator1 end1, InputIterator2 beg2, T initValue,
  arithmeticOperator1 op1, arithmeticOperator2 op2)
```

The inner product of two sequences {a1, a2, ..., ai} and {b1, b2, ..., bi} is defined as

```
a1 * b1 + a2 * b2 + ... + ai * bi
```

The first version returns the sum of **initValue** and the inner product of the sequences. The second version is the same as the first, except that the default addition operator is replaced by **op1** and the multiplication operator is replaced by **op2**. For example,

| array1 | Result of `inner_product(array1, array1 + 5,` `array1, 0)` |
|---|---|
| {1, 2, 3, 4, 5} | 55 |

The **partial_sum** function has two versions.

**partial_sum**

```
template<typename InputIterator1, typename InputIterator2,
  typename OutputIterator>
OutputIterator partial_sum(InputIterator1 beg1,
  InputIterator1 end1, OutputIterator2 beg2)
```

```
template<typename InputIterator1, typename InputIterator2,
  typename OutputIterator, typename arithmeticOperator>
OutputIterator partial_sum(InputIterator beg1,
  InputIterator end1, OutputIterator targetPosition
  arithmeticOperator op)
```

The first version creates a sequence in which each element is the sum of all the preceding elements. The second version is the same as the first, except that the default addition operator is replaced by **op**. For example,

| array1 | Result of `partial_sum(array1, array1 + 5,` `intVector.begin())` |
|---|---|
| {1, 2, 3, 4, 5} | {1, 3, 6, 10, 15} |

Listing 20.22 demonstrates how to use the mathematical functions.

**LISTING 20.22**   MathOperationDemo.cpp

```cpp
 1 #include <iostream>
 2 #include <algorithm>
 3 #include <numeric>
 4 #include <vector>
 5 #include <iterator>
 6 #include <functional>
 7 using namespace std;
 8
 9 int main()
10 {
11     int array1[] = {1, 2, 3, 4, 5};
12     vector<int> intVector(5);
13
14     ostream_iterator<int> output(cout, " ");
15     cout << "array1: ";
16     copy(array1, array1 + 5, output);
17
18     cout << "\nSum of array1: " <<
19         accumulate(array1, array1 + 5, 0) << endl;
20
21     cout << "Product of array1: " <<
22         accumulate(array1, array1 + 5, 1, multiplies<int>()) << endl;
23
24     vector<int>::iterator last =
25         adjacent_difference(array1, array1 + 5, intVector.begin());
26     cout << "After adjacent difference, intVector: ";
27     copy(intVector.begin(), last, output);
28
29     cout << "\nInner product of array1 * array1 is " <<
30         inner_product(array1, array1 + 5, array1, 0);
31
32     last = partial_sum(array1, array1 + 5, intVector.begin());
33     cout << "\nAfter partial sum, intVector: ";
34     copy(intVector.begin(), last, output);
35
36     return 0;
37 }
```

*include algorithm*
*include numeric*

*include functional*

*create **array1***
*create **intVector***

**accumulate**

**accumulate**

**adjacent_difference**

**inner_product**

**partial_sum**

```
array1: 1 2 3 4 5
Sum of array1: 15
Product of array1: 120
After adjacent difference, intVector: 1 1 1 1 1
Inner product of array1 * array1 is 55
After partial sum, intVector: 1 3 6 10 15
```

The program creates an array and a vector (lines 10–11).

   array1: {1, 2, 3, 4, 5}

   Invoking `accumulate(array1, array1 + 5, 0)` (line 19) returns the sum of all the elements in `array1`.

   Invoking `accumulate(array1, array1 + 5, 1, multiplies<int>())` (line 22) returns the multiplication of all the elements in `array1`.

Invoking `adjacent_difference(array1, array1 + 5, intVector.begin())` (line 25) obtains a sequence for the adjacent difference of `array1` in `intVector`.

Invoking `inner_product(array1, array1 + 5, array1, 0)` (line 30) obtains the inner product of `array1` and `array1`.

Invoking `partial_sum(array1, array1 + 5, intVector.begin())` (line 32) obtains a sequence for the partial sum of `array1` in `intVector`.

## KEY TERMS

`accumulate` algorithm    609
`adjacent_find` algorithm    598
`binary_search` algorithm    596
`copy` algorithm    581
`count` algorithm    603
`count_if` algorithm    603
`fill` algorithm    583
`fill_in` algorithm    583
`find` algorithm    588
`find_end` algorithm    591
`find_first_of` algorithm    591
`find_if` algorithm    591
`for_each` algorithm    605
function object    597
`generate` algorithm    584
`generate_n` algorithm    584
heap algorithms    580
`includes` algorithm    606
`inner_product` algorithm    609
`inplace_merge` algorithm    598
`iter_swap` algorithm    602
`max_element` algorithm    604
`merge` algorithm    594
`min_element` algorithm    604
modifying STL algorithms    580
nonmodifying STL algorithms    580

numeric STL algorithms    580
`partial_sum` algorithm    609
`random_shuffle` algorithm    604
`remove` algorithm    585
`remove_copy` algorithm    585
`remove_copy_if` algorithm    585
`remove_if` algorithm    585
`replace` algorithm    588
`replace_copy` algorithm    588
`replace_copy_if` algorithm    588
`replace_if` algorithm    588
`reverse` algorithm    600
`reverse_copy` algorithm    600
`rotate` algorithm    601
`rotate_copy` algorithm    601
`search` algorithm    595
`search_n` algorithm    595
`sort` algorithm    596
`swap` algorithm    602
`swap_range` algorithm    602
`set_difference` algorithm    606
`set_intersection` algorithm    606
`set_symmetric_difference` algorithm    606
`set_union` algorithm    606
`transform` algorithm    605

## CHAPTER SUMMARY

- The STL separates the algorithms from the containers. This enables the algorithms to be applied generically to all containers through iterators. The STL makes the algorithms and containers easy to maintain.

- The STL provides approximately 80 algorithms. The algorithms can be classified into four groups: nonmodifying algorithms, modifying algorithms, numeric algorithms, and heap algorithms.

- All the algorithms operate through iterators. Many algorithms operate on a sequence of elements pointed to by two iterators. The first iterator points to the first element of the sequence, and the second points to the element after the last element of the sequence.

- The `copy` function can be used to copy elements in a sequence from one container to another.

- The functions `fill` and `fill_n` can be used to fill a container with a specified value.

- The functions `generate` and `generate_n` fill a container with a value returned from a function.

- The functions `remove` and `remove_if` remove the elements from a sequence that matches some criteria. The functions `remove_copy` and `remove_copy_if` are similar to `remove` and `remove_if` except that they copy the result to a target sequence.

- The functions `replace` and `replace_if` replace all occurrences of a given value with a new value in a sequence. The functions `replace_copy` and `replace_copy_if` are similar to replace and `replace_if` except that they copy the result to a target sequence.

- The functions `find`, `find_if`, `find_end`, and `find_first_of` can be used to find the elements in sequence.

- The functions `search` and `search_n` search for a subsequence.

- The `sort` function requires random-access iterators. You can apply it to sort an array, vector, or deque.

- The `adjacent_find` function looks for the first occurrence of adjacent elements of equal value or satisfying `boolFunction(element)`.

- The `merge` function merges two sorted sequences into a new sequence.

- The `inplace_merge` function merges the first part of the sequence with the second part; assume that the two parts contain sorted consecutive elements.

- The `reverse` function reverses the elements in a sequence. The `reverse_copy` function copies the elements in one sequence to the other in reverse order.

- The `rotate` function rotates the elements in a sequence. The `rotate_copy` function is similar to `rotate`, except that it copies the result to a target sequence.

- The `swap` function swaps the values in two variables. The `iter_swap` function swaps the values pointed to by the iterators. The `swap_range` function swaps two sequences.

- The `count` function counts the occurrence of a given value in the sequence. The `count_if` function counts the occurrence of the elements such that `boolFunction(element)` is true.

- The functions `max_element` and `min_element` obtain the maximum element and minimum element in a sequence.

- The `random_shuffle` function randomly reorders the elements in a sequence.

- The `for_each` function is used to process each element in a sequence by applying a function. The `transform` function is used to apply a function on each element in the sequence and copy the result to a target sequence.

- The STL supports the set operations `includes`, `set_union`, `set_difference`, `set_intersection`, and `set_symmetric_difference`. All these functions require that the elements in the sequences already are sorted.

- The STL supports the mathematical functions `accumulate`, `adjacent_difference`, `inner_product`, and `partial_sum`. They are defined in the `<numeric>` header.

## REVIEW QUESTIONS

### Sections 20.1–20.2

**20.1** Are the STL algorithms defined in a container class such as `vector`, `list`, or `set`? Which header file defines the STL algorithms?

**20.2** What are the four types of STL algorithms?

### Section 20.3 copy

**20.3** What is the `copy` algorithm for? What is the return value of the `copy` algorithm? Show the printout of the following code:

```cpp
int values[] = {1, 2, 3, 4, 5};
vector<int> intVector(5);

vector<int>::iterator last =
  copy(values, values + 3, intVector.begin());

ostream_iterator<int> output(cout, " ");
cout << "intVector: ";
copy(intVector.begin(), last, output);
```

**20.4** What is wrong in the following code?

```cpp
int values[] = {1, 2, 3, 4, 5, 6, 7};
vector<int> intVector(5);

vector<int>::iterator last =
  copy(values, values + 7, intVector.begin());
```

### Section 20.4 fill and fill_n

**20.5** What are the `fill` and `fill_n` algorithms for? Show the printout of the following code:

```cpp
int values[] = {1, 2, 3, 4, 5};
fill_n(values + 2, 2, 9);

ostream_iterator<int> output(cout, " ");
cout << "values: ";
copy(values, values + 5, output);
```

### Section 20.5 generate and generate_n

**20.6** What are the `generate` and `generate_n` algorithms for? Show the printout of the following code:

```cpp
int nextNum()
{
  static int n = 20;
  return n++;
}

int main()
{
  int values[] = {1, 2, 3, 4, 5};
  generate_n(values + 1, 2, nextNum);

  ostream_iterator<int> output(cout, " ");
  cout << "values: ";
```

```
        copy(values, values + 5, output);

        return 0;
    }
```

## Section 20.6 remove, remove_if, remove_copy, and remove_copy_if

**20.7**   What are the remove, remove_if, remove_copy, and remove_copy_if algorithms for? Show the printout of the following code:

```
bool greaterThan4(int value)
{
    return value > 4;
}

int main()
{
    int values[] = {1, 2, 3, 4, 5, 1, 1};
    remove_if(values, values + 7, greaterThan4);

    ostream_iterator<int> output(cout, " ");
    cout << "values: ";
    copy(values, values + 7, output);

    return 0;
}
```

## Section 20.7 replace, replace_if, replace_copy, and replace_copy_if

**20.8**   What are the replace, replace_if, replace_copy, and replace_copy_if algorithms for? Show the printout of the following code:

```
bool greaterThan4(int value)
{
    return value > 4;
}

int main()
{
    int values[] = {1, 2, 3, 4, 5, 1, 1};
    replace_if(values, values + 7, greaterThan4, 999);

    ostream_iterator<int> output(cout, " ");
    cout << "values: ";
    copy(values, values + 7, output);

    return 0;
}
```

## Section 20.8 find, find_if, find_end, and find_first_of

**20.9**   What are the find, find_if, find_end, and find_first_of algorithms for? Do these functions return a Boolean value?

## Section 20.9 search and search_n

**20.10**  What are the search and search_n algorithms for? What are the differences between search and find_end?

## Section 20.10 sort and binary_search

**20.11**  What are the return types for these two functions? What iterator types are needed for sort and binary search? Can you apply the sort algorithm on a list?

### Section 20.11 `adjacent_find`, `merge`, and `inplace_merge`

**20.12** What are the `adjacent_find`, `merge`, and `inplace_merge` algorithms for? Show the output of the following code:

```cpp
int values[] = {1, 2, 3, 4, 4, 5, 1, 1};
int *p = adjacent_find(values, values + 8);

ostream_iterator<int> output(cout, " ");
cout << "values: ";
copy(p, values + 8, output);
```

### Section 20.12 `reverse` and `reverse_copy`

**20.13** What are the `reverse` and `reverse_copy` algorithms for? Does the `reverse_copy` algorithm change the contents of the original sequence?

### Section 20.13 `rotate` and `rotate_copy`

**20.14** What are the `rotate` and `rotate_copy` algorithms for? Show the output of the following code:

```cpp
int values[] = {1, 2, 3, 4, 4, 5, 1, 1};
rotate(values, values + 5, values + 8);
ostream_iterator<int> output(cout, " ");
cout << "values: ";
copy(values, values + 8, output);
```

### Section 20.14 `swap`, `iter_swap`, and `swap_ranges`

**20.15** What are the `swap`, `iter_swap`, and `swap_ranges` algorithms for?

### Section 20.15 `count` and `count_if`

**20.16** What are the `count` and `count_if` algorithms for?

### Section 20.16 `max_element` and `min_element`

**20.17** What are the `max` and `max_element` algorithms for?

### Section 20.17 `random_shuffle`

**20.18** What is the `random_shuffle` algorithm for?

### Section 20.18 `for_each` and `transform`

**20.19** What are the `for_each` and `transform` algorithms for?

### Section 20.19 `includes`, `set_union`, `set_difference`, `set_intersection`, and `set_symmetric_difference`

**20.20** Suppose `array1` is $\{1, 2, 3, 4, 5\}$ and `array2` is $\{2, 4, 8, 9, 10\}$. Show the union, difference, intersection, and symmetric difference of these two arrays.

### Section 20.20 `accumulate`, `adjacent_difference`, `inner_product`, and `partial_sum`

**20.21** Suppose `array1` is $\{1, 2, 3, 4, 5\}$ and `array2` is $\{2, 4, 8, 9, 10\}$. Show the `accumulate`, `adjacent_difference`, and `partial_sum` for `array1`. What is the inner product of `array1` and `array2`?

## PROGRAMMING EXERCISES

**20.1** Create an array of double values with five numbers: 1.3, 2.4, 4.5, 6.7, 9.0. Use the `fill` function to fill the first three elements with 5.5. Use the `fill_n` function to fill the first four elements with 6.9.

**20.2** Create a `deque` with five numbers: 1.3, 2.4, 4.5, 6.7, 9.0. Use the `generate` function to fill random numbers in the deque. Use the `generate_n` function to fill random numbers in the deque.

**20.3** Create an `array` with these numbers: 1.3, 2.4, 4.5, 6.7, 4.5, 9.0. Use the `remove` function to remove all the elements with value 4.5. Use the `remove_if` function to remove all the elements that are less than 2.0. Use the `remove_copy` function to copy all the elements except 6.7 to a list. Use the `remove_copy_if` function to copy all the elements except those that are greater than 4.0 to a list.

**20.4** Create an `array` with these numbers: 2.4, 1.3, 2.4, 4.5, 6.7, 4.5, 9.0. Use the `replace` function to replace all the occurrences of 2.4 with 9.9. Use the `replace_if` function to replace all the elements that are less than 2.0 with 12.5. Use the `replace_copy` function to replace all occurrences of 6.7 with 9.7 and copy all the sequence to a vector. Use the `replace_copy_if` function to replace all the elements that are greater than or equal to 1.3 with 747 and copy the sequence to a multiset.

**20.5** Create an `array` with these numbers: 2.4, 1.3, 2.4, 4.5, 6.7, 4.5, 9.0. Use the `find` function to find the position of 4.5 in the array. Use the `find_if` function to find the position of the first element that is less than 2. Use the `find_end` function to find the position of the sequence {2.4, 4.5} in the array. Use the `find_first_of` function to find the position of the first common element in the array and the list {34, 55, 2.4, 4.5}.

**20.6** Create an `array` with these numbers: 2.4, 1.3, 2.4, 2.4, 4.5, 6.7, 4.5, 9.0. Use the `search` function to find the position of the sequence {2.4, 4.5} in the array. Use the `search_n` function to search for two consecutive elements with value 2.4.

**20.7** Create an `array` with these numbers: 2.4, 1.3, 2.4, 2.4, 4.5, 6.7, 4.5, 9.0. Use the `search` function to find the position of the sequence {2.4, 4.5} in the array. Use the `search_n` function to search for two consecutive elements with value 2.4.

**20.8** Implement the `fill` and `fill_n` functions.

```
template<typename ForwardIterator, typename T>
void fill(ForwardIterator beg, ForwardIterator end, const T
  &value)

template<typename ForwardIterator, typename size, typename T>
void fill_n(ForwardIterator beg, size n, const T &value)
```

**20.9** Implement the `generate` and `generate_n` functions.

```
template<typename ForwardIterator, typename function>
void generate(ForwardIterator beg, ForwardIterator end,
  function gen)

template<typename ForwardIterator, typename size, typename
  function>
void generate_n(ForwardIterator beg, size n, function gen)
```

**20.10** Implement the remove and remove_if functions.

```
template<typename ForwardIterator, typename T>
ForwardIterator remove(ForwardIterator beg,
    ForwardIterator end, const T &value)

template<typename ForwardIterator, typename boolFunction>
ForwardIterator remove_if(ForwardIterator beg,
    ForwardIterator end, boolFunction f)
```

**20.11** Implement the replace and replace_if functions.

```
template<typename ForwardIterator, typename T>
void replace(ForwardIterator beg, ForwardIterator end,
    const T &oldValue, const T &newValue)

template<typename ForwardIterator, typename boolFunction,
    typename T>
void replace_if(ForwardIterator beg, ForwardIterator end,
    boolFunction f, const T &newValue)
```

**20.12** Implement the find and find_if functions.

```
template<typename InputIterator, typename T>
InputIterator find(InputIterator beg, InputIterator end,
    T &value)

template<typename InputIterator, typename boolFunction>
InputIterator find_if(InputIterator beg, InputIterator end,
    boolFunction f)
```

# APPENDIXES

## Appendix A
C++ Keywords

## Appendix B
The ASCII Character Set

## Appendix C
Operator Precedence Chart

## Appendix D
Bit Operations

# C++ Keywords

The following keywords are reserved for use by the C++ language. They should not be used for anything other than their predefined purposes in C++.

| | | | | |
|---|---|---|---|---|
| asm | do | inline | return | typedef |
| auto | double | int | short | typeid |
| bool | dynamic_cast | log | signed | typename |
| break | else | long | sizeof | union |
| case | enum | mutable | static | unsigned |
| catch | explicit | namespace | static_cast | using |
| char | extern | new | struct | virtual |
| class | false | operator | switch | void |
| const | float | private | template | volatile |
| const_cast | for | protected | this | wchar_t |
| continue | friend | public | throw | while |
| default | goto | register | true | |
| delete | if | reinterpret_cast | try | |

# APPENDIX B

# The ASCII Character Set

Tables B.1 and B.2 show ASCII characters and their respective decimal and hexadecimal codes. The decimal or hexadecimal code of a character is a combination of its row index and column index. For example, in Table B.1, the letter A is at row 6 and column 5, so its decimal equivalent is 65; in Table B.2, letter A is at row 4 and column 1, so its hexadecimal equivalent is 41.

**TABLE B.1** ASCII Character Set in the Decimal Index

| | 0 | 1 | 2 | 3 | 4 | 5 | 6 | 7 | 8 | 9 |
|---|---|---|---|---|---|---|---|---|---|---|
| 0 | nul | soh | stx | etx | eot | enq | ack | bel | bs | ht |
| 1 | nl | vt | ff | cr | so | si | dle | dc1 | dc2 | dc3 |
| 2 | dc4 | nak | syn | etb | can | em | sub | esc | fs | gs |
| 3 | rs | us | sp | ! | " | # | $ | % | & | ' |
| 4 | ( | ) | * | + | , | - | . | / | 0 | 1 |
| 5 | 2 | 3 | 4 | 5 | 6 | 7 | 8 | 9 | : | ; |
| 6 | < | = | > | ? | @ | A | B | C | D | E |
| 7 | F | G | H | I | J | K | L | M | N | O |
| 8 | P | Q | R | S | T | U | V | W | X | Y |
| 9 | Z | [ | \ | ] | ^ | _ | ` | a | b | c |
| 10 | d | e | f | g | h | i | j | k | l | m |
| 11 | n | o | p | q | r | s | t | u | v | w |
| 12 | x | y | z | { | \| | } | ~ | del | | |

**TABLE B.2** ASCII Character Set in the Hexadecimal Index

| | 0 | 1 | 2 | 3 | 4 | 5 | 6 | 7 | 8 | 9 | A | B | C | D | E | F |
|---|---|---|---|---|---|---|---|---|---|---|---|---|---|---|---|---|
| 0 | nul | soh | stx | etx | eot | enq | ack | bel | bs | ht | nl | vt | ff | cr | so | si |
| 1 | dle | dc1 | dc2 | dc3 | dc4 | nak | syn | etb | can | em | sub | esc | fs | gs | rs | us |
| 2 | sp | ! | " | # | $ | % | & | ' | ( | ) | * | + | , | - | . | / |
| 3 | 0 | 1 | 2 | 3 | 4 | 5 | 6 | 7 | 8 | 9 | : | ; | < | = | > | ? |
| 4 | @ | A | B | C | D | E | F | G | H | I | J | K | L | M | N | O |
| 5 | P | Q | R | S | T | U | V | W | X | Y | Z | [ | \ | ] | ^ | _ |
| 6 | ` | a | b | c | d | e | f | g | h | i | j | k | l | m | n | o |
| 7 | p | q | r | s | t | u | v | w | x | y | z | { | \| | } | ~ | del |

# APPENDIX C

# Operator Precedence Chart

The operators are shown in decreasing order of precedence from top to bottom. Operators in the same group have the same precedence, and their associativity is shown in the table.

| Operator | Type | Associativity |
|---|---|---|
| :: | binary scope resolution | left to right |
| :: | unary scope resolution | |
| . | object member access via object | left to right |
| -> | object member access via pointer | |
| () | function call | |
| [] | array subscript | |
| ++ | postfix increment | |
| -- | postfix decrement | |
| typeid | runtime type information | |
| dynamic_cast | dynamic cast (runtime) | |
| static_cast | static cast (compile time) | |
| reinterpret_cast | cast for nonstandard conversion | |
| ++ | prefix increment | right to left |
| -- | prefix decrement | |
| + | unary plus | |
| - | unary minus | |
| ! | unary logical negation | |
| ~ | bitwise negation | |
| sizeof | size of a type | |
| & | address of a variable | |
| * | pointer of a variable | |
| new | dynamic memory allocation | |
| new[] | dynamic array allocation | |
| delete | dynamic memory deallocation | |
| delete[] | dynamic array deallocation | |
| (type) | C-Style cast | right to left |
| * | multiplication | left to right |
| / | division | |
| % | modulus | |

| Operator | Type | Associativity |
|---|---|---|
| + | addition | left to right |
| - | subtraction | |
| << | output or bitwise left shift | left to right |
| >> | input or bitwise right shift | |
| < | less than | left to right |
| <= | less than or equal to | |
| > | greater than | |
| >= | greater than or equal to | |
| == | equal | left to right |
| != | not equal | |
| & | bitwise AND | left to right |
| ^ | bitwise exclusive OR | left to right |
| \| | bitwise inclusive OR | left to right |
| && | Boolean AND | left to right |
| \|\| | Boolean OR | left to right |
| ?: | ternary operator | right to left |
| = | assignment | right to left |
| += | addition assignment | |
| -= | subtraction assignment | |
| *= | multiplication assignment | |
| /= | division assignment | |
| %= | modulus assignment | |
| &= | bitwise AND assignment | |
| ^= | bitwise exclusive OR assignment | |
| \|= | bitwise inclusive OR assignment | |
| <<= | bitwise left-shift assignment | |
| >>= | bitwise right-shift assignment | |

# APPENDIX D

## Bit Operations

To write programs at the machine-level, often you need to deal with binary numbers directly and perform operations at the bit-level. C++ provides the bitwise operators and shift operators defined in the following table.

| Operator | Name | Example | Description |
|---|---|---|---|
| & | bitwise AND | 10101110 & 10010010 yields 10000010 | The AND of two corresponding bits yields a 1 if both bits are 1. |
| \| | Bitwise inclusive OR | 10101110 \| 10010010 yields 10111110 | The OR of two corresponding bits yields a 1 if either bit is 1. |
| ^ | Bitwise exclusive OR | 10101110 ^ 10010010 yields 00111100 | The XOR of two corresponding bits yields a 1 only if two bits are different. |
| ~ | One's complement | ~10101110 yields 01010001 | The operator toggles each bit from 0 to 1 and from 1 to 0 |
| << | Left shift | 10101110 << 2 yields 10111000 | Shift bits in the first operand left by the number of the bits specified in the second operand, filling with 0s on the right. |
| >> | Right shift for unsigned integer | 1010111010101110 >> 4 yields 0000101011101010 | Shift bit in the first operand right by the number of the bits specified in the second operand, filling with zeros on the left. |
| >> | Right shift for signed integer | | The behavior depends on the platform. Therefore, you should avoid right shift signed integers. |

All the bitwise operators can form bitwise assignment operators such as ^=, |=, <<=, and >>=.

# INDEX